Winner of the Jules and Frances Landry Award for 2000

TO THE NORTH ANNA RIVER

To the North Anna River

Grant and Lee,
May 13–25, 1864

Gordon C. Rhea

Louisiana State University Press   *Baton Rouge*

MM

Typeface: Cochin, Times Roman
Typesetter: Crane Composition
Printer and binder: Thomson-Shore, Inc.

LIBRARY OF CONGRESS CATALOGING-IN-PUBLICATION DATA:

Rhea, Gordon C.
    To the North Anna River : Grant and Lee, May 13–25, 1864 / Gordon C. Rhea.
        p.   cm.
    Includes bibliographical references and index.
    ISBN 0-8071–2535-0 (alk. paper)
1. North Anna River (Va.), Battle of, 1864. 2. Grant, Ulysses S. (Ulysses Simpson), 1822–1885.
3. Lee, Robert E. (Robert Edward), 1807–1870. 4. Wilderness, Battle of the, Va., 1864.
5. Spotsylvania Court House, Battle of, Va., 1864. 6. Virginia—History—Civil War, 1861–1865—
Campaigns. 7. United States—History—Civil War, 1861–1865—Campaigns. I. Title.
    E476.52.R478 2000
    973.7'36—dc21
                                        99-050637

Contents

Illustrations

MAPS

Acknowledgments

SURPRISINGLY LITTLE HAS been written about the campaign between Grant and Lee from May 13 through May 25, 1864. Confederate sources are scarce. Union sources, while more plentiful, are frequently vague and contradictory. Many diarists who penned stirring accounts of the Wilderness, Laurel Hill, and the Mule Shoe were dead, wounded, or in prison. Those still living were too exhausted to scribble more than cursory jottings. After the war, when veterans wrote their reminiscences, the marching and fighting from the Bloody Angle to Cold Harbor had blurred into indistinct memories. Historians attempting to reconstruct those momentous days face a daunting task. Jedediah Hotchkiss, the Confederate 2nd Corps's cartographer, tried to make sense of existing accounts and found himself "wandering about in the entanglements of conflicting statements, at times well nigh lost and inclined to wash my hands of the whole matter, but am in for it and cannot escape." Time has not eased the undertaking.[1]

Few historians have explored this phase of Grant's and Lee's evolving generalship. I have been honored to know two brave souls who strode where others feared to tread. William D. Matter's *If It Takes All Summer: The Battle of Spotsylvania* (Chapel Hill, 1989), remains the best single recounting of Grant's and Lee's last days at Spotsylvania Court House. Mr. Matter and I have often walked Spotsylvania's fields together, and I was delighted when he reviewed my manuscript. By the same token, J. Michael Miller, author of *The North Anna Campaign: "Even to Hell Itself"* (Lynchburg, Va., 1989), is the foremost student of Grant's and Lee's maneuvers through Caroline County. Mr. Miller played an important part in establishing the North Anna Battlefield Park, preserving for posterity the spectacular left wing of Lee's inverted V formation. He, too, made time in his busy schedule to visit sites with me and to review my manuscript. This book would be considerably diminished without the help of those two exceptional scholars.

The most important sources for reconstructing the battles are the fields themselves. Much ground involved in the operations from May 13–20 lies within the Fredericksburg and Spotsylvania National Military Park. I am grateful to Robert K. Krick, chief historian of the park, and to the outstanding staff historians who work there, including Noel G. Harrison, John J. Hennessy, Gregory A. Mertz, Francis A. O'Reilly, Donald C. Pfanz, and Mac Wyckoff. They gave willingly of their time, exploring remote sites with me, guiding me to sources, and reviewing my manuscript. I am also indebted to the park's seasonal historian Eric J. Mink, now a full-time historian at the Richmond National Battlefield Park. The Ox Ford battlefield lies within the North Anna Battlefield Park. I thank Len Riedel and the Blue and Gray Education Society for supplying me copies of signs and maps the society installed at the park.

Many sites are privately owned. Owners graciously showed me their property and shared letters, newspaper clippings, and family stories. I am deeply indebted to Agnes V. McGee, who gave me free rein to wander the Harris farm; Raymond Bruce, Virginia Bruce, and their friend John Robert Davidson, who provided me coffee and a tour of the Catlett house and yard; Mrs. Vernon Lucy, who showed me the Motley house and let me sit on the porch where Grant singed Mr. Motley's furniture; Carroll Hayden, who showed me around Stirling Plantation, on Guinea Station Road; Michele Schiesser, for her hospitality at La Vista Plantation, on Guinea Station Road; Joyce Ackerman, of Roxbury Mills, who permitted me to explore the earthworks at Stanard's Mill; Cameron Wood, for permission to explore Henagan's redoubt; and Jeffrey McKinney, who turned me loose on the Jericho Mills battlefield site. Special thanks is due Ray S. Campbell Jr., clerk of Caroline County. Mr. Campbell, whose forebears rode in the 9th Virginia Cavalry, helped locate long-forgotten landmarks and supplied me with maps, surveys, and deeds.

Bryce A. Suderow, researcher extraordinary, assisted immeasurably in my quest for Civil War–era newspapers and gave insightful comments about my manuscript. Historians and buffs across the country guided me to obscure sources. Among those who helped were Tom Asselta, Edwin W. Besch, Daniel J. Beattie, Keith S. Bohannon, B. Conrad Bush, Mary Bandy Daughtry, David M. Guest, Theodore C. Mahr, Scott C. Patchen, Robert G. Poirier, Michael T. Russert, Robert J. Trout, Noah Andre Trudeau, Zack C. Waters, and Eric J. Wittenberg. I am also grateful to archivists and librarians for the institutions listed in the bibliography, and to Alfred C. Young, who helped me determine Confederate losses.

Robert E. L. Krick of the Richmond National Battlefield Park gave invaluable suggestions on the chapters covering cavalry operations. David D. Finney Jr., of Howell, Michigan, assisted with Michigan material and read much of the manuscript. Keith Poulter published modified versions of chapters II and VI as articles in *North & South* magazine and offered valuable editorial advice. I extend sincere thanks to Michael T. Snyder, of Pottstown, Pennsylvania, who gave my entire manuscript a careful reading, and to Patrick S. Brady of Seattle, Washington, who applied his red pen to the entire manuscript. Mr. Brady is completing a superb recounting of the Cold Harbor operations, and his comments were especially helpful.

George F. Skoch prepared maps for this volume, as he did for my previous two books, proving once again that a picture is worth a thousand words. Gerry Anders and Elizabeth Simon deftly wielded their editorial pens to my considerable advantage. I owe more than I can express to my wife Catherine, who patiently shared with me the trials attendant to a project of this magnitude, and to our two sons, Campbell and Carter. They have become eager participants in their parents' quest to understand the past and build a brighter future.

Abbreviations

AU	Auburn University Libraries, Special Collections
B&L	Buel, Clarence C., and Robert U. Johnson, eds. *Battles and Leaders of the Civil War.* 4 vols. New York, 1884–88.
BL	Bentley Historical Library, University of Michigan
CL	William L. Clements Library, University of Michigan
DU	William R. Perkins Library, Duke University
FSNMP	Fredericksburg and Spotsylvania National Military Park Library
GDAH	Georgia Department of Archives and History, Atlanta
HSP	Historical Society of Pennsylvania, Philadelphia
ISHL	Illinois State Historical Library, Springfield
LC	Manuscript Division, Library of Congress
MC	Eleanor S. Brockenbrough Library, Museum of the Confederacy, Richmond
MHS	Massachusetts Historical Society, Boston
MSU	Michigan State University Libraries
NA	National Archives, Washington, D.C.
NCDAH	North Carolina Department of Archives and History, Raleigh
NYSLA	New York State Library and Archives, Albany

OR   *The War of the Rebellion: A Compilation of Official Records of the Union and Confederate Armies.* 130 vols.Washington, D.C., 1890–1901. Unless otherwise stated, references are to Series I.

PMHSM   *Papers of the Military Historical Society of Massachusetts.* 14 vols. Boston, 1881–1918.

SHC   Southern Historical Collection, University of North Carolina

SHSP   *Southern Historical Society Papers.* 49 vols. Richmond, 1876–1944.

USAMHI   United States Army Military History Institute, Carlisle, Pennsylvania

UV   Alderman Library, University of Virginia

VHS   Virginia Historical Society, Richmond

VSL   Virginia State Library, Richmond

WRHS   Western Reserve Historical Society, Cleveland, Ohio

To the North Anna River

Introduction

WASHINGTON WAS ABUZZ with anticipation. It was the second week of May, 1864. No news had arrived from the front for days. Then a flurry of enthusiastic reports poured in. Lieutenant General Ulysses S. Grant stood poised to deliver the Confederacy a killing blow. "The city is pervaded with a feeling which can scarcely be called excitement," observed the newspaper correspondent Noah Brooks. "It is too intense—it is an absorbing eagerness which is more fervent than excited." Readers clutched newspaper "extras." Congress adjourned for three days because rumors from the front made it impossible to concentrate on anything else. Crowds pressed around anyone professing knowledge of the war's progress.[1]

At ten o'clock on the evening of May 11, a cheering throng jammed the White House lawn. President Abraham Lincoln strode onto the portico. Three years of war had etched deep lines in his face. Dramatic times were at hand, the tall, gaunt figure announced. Reading in his high, reedy voice, the president quoted from Grant's most recent dispatch. The general, unlike his predecessors, remained determined to stay the course. "I propose to fight it out on this line if it takes all summer," Grant had written. Precisely what he meant by "this line" was not entirely clear, but the resolve in his written words galvanized the listeners. "There was something like delirium in the air," Brooks reported. "Everybody seemed to think that the war was coming to the end right away."[2]

Newspapers trumpeted the heartening tidings. "We have abundant reason to believe that it will not 'take all summer,'" the *New York Tribune* asserted the next day. The Confederacy, the newspaper predicted, was "staggering to its fall from the crippling blows of Grant, and cannot survive the summer." Reports reached Washington that Grant had breached General Robert E. Lee's fortified bastion at Spotsylvania Court House. Enthusiasm burst forth anew. The rebels had been routed and were retreating, the northern press effused. "We believe Lee's army as an effective force has practically ceased to exist," the *Tribune* claimed.[3]

Grant's name was on everyone's lips. "The 'coming man' appears to have come at last, and Grant is the hero of the war," a newspaperman proclaimed. Only two months before, Lincoln had selected this champion of the war's western theater to command all the Union armies. The general had concentrated his talents toward defeating Lee and his Army of Northern Virginia, entrenched below the Rapidan River in central Virginia. The source of Washington's jubilation lay not in military victories, for there had been none. It came from Grant's determination. The North was accustomed to defeats, particularly in the Old Dominion. But a general who ignored setbacks and persevered toward ultimate victory was something new. The resolution that Grant proclaimed in his dispatches from the bloodstained fields above Spotsylvania Court House had brightened an otherwise dismal picture. Grant gave a pessimistic North cause to hope that its armies might yet prevail.[4]

The northern public, however, had yet to comprehend the terrible slaughter wrought by Grant's ten days of relentless campaigning in Virginia. Casualty returns were just appearing in local newspapers, and only a smattering of wounded soldiers had emerged from Dixie to tell their stories. On battlefields a scant sixty miles from the nation's capital, Grant had lost close to thirty-five thousand men.

Dr. William T. G. Morton, a pioneer in the use of ether, undertook the trip from Washington to Grant's army near Spotsylvania Court House the day after Lincoln had broadcast the new commander in chief's bellicose promise. His excursion resembled a descent into the darkest recesses of a medieval hell. Reality, Morton discovered, bore little resemblance to sugar-coated newspaper prattle.

Morton left Washington by steamer on the evening of May 12 and promptly fell asleep. The ship churned through forty miles of black Potomac water to a stream above Fredericksburg named Potomac Creek. Belle Plain, the nerve center of Grant's army, converged around a stubby, U-shaped wharf. The place had become a bottleneck where provisions, food, medicine, and reinforcements for Grant's war machine vied for dock space with wounded Federals and Confederate prisoners traveling north. From the port, wagons had to wind precariously over a steep ridge, traverse a rutted, nine-mile road to the Rappahannock River, and brave a rickety pontoon bridge into Fredericksburg. Confederate guerrillas added to the excitement. "The roads were rough, the vehicles crowded, and what we endured no imagina-

tion could depict or tongue declare," an injured soldier reported of the ordeal.[5]

Rattling from Belle Plain in the empty ambulance, Morton was appalled
by the desolation. Soldiers had denuded the formerly prosperous land.
Fences lay in shambles and weeds sprouted everywhere. "The place is inex-
pressibly wild," the doctor recorded in his journal, "and the only living beings visible were teamsters, wounded soldiers and mounted patrols." Four
riders, deceptively dressed in blue, materialized from the dreary landscape,
cut the reins and traces from the ambulance's lead horses, and disappeared
with the mounts. They were Confederates exploiting the opportunity presented by Morton's unguarded ambulance. Raids were commonplace, and
the small contingent of Federal soldiers posted at Belle Plain could do little to
deter them.[6]

Morton's conveyance at long last clattered over the pontoon bridge into
Fredericksburg. Nestled just below the Rappahannock River's fall line, the
town ranked among Virginia's queen cities. Battle-scarred mansions and
churches graced tree-lined streets reminiscent of the place's former glory.
Wounded men spilled from doorways onto sidewalks, and every serviceable
building doubled as a hospital. Invalids packed the Baptist church, where surgeons performed operations in the pastor's study and used the baptismal font
as a bathtub. The Freemason's hall reeked of filth and gangrene. A Union surgeon deemed Fredericksburg "one grand funeral." Another doctor, weary
from amputating limbs, pronounced the town a "scene of horror such as I
never saw."[7]

Devastation multiplied as Morton approached the front, eight terrible
miles southwest of town. Rain had transformed the road into a bottomless
quagmire. Broken-down ambulances and dead horses buried to saddle girths
in mud littered the roadside. Wagons crammed with wounded men foundered
in muck, and endless processions of mutilated souls plodded along on foot.
The macabre cavalcade had been wending its way to Fredericksburg, virtually unabated, for five days. Early on May 9, 325 wagons and 488 ambulances containing 7,000 Union soldiers had jostled into the town, emptied
their charges, and returned to the front for more. The next night, 2,294 invalids poured into Fredericksburg, and on May 11, some 2,500 more appeared. The troops that Morton encountered on May 13, another 3,200 rain-
chilled souls, were effluvia from a horrid fight at a place called the Bloody
Angle. Forms squatted by the roadside and dipped fetid water from mud pud-
dles to soothe inflamed wounds. "Some of the men [were] crying in their pain
for someone to kill them to put them out of their misery," a soldier recol-

lected. "Others patiently endured the pain in silent prayer to God for strength." [8]

Seven thousand sullen Confederate prisoners, no two dressed alike, shared the road with the injured Federals. Barefoot and hatless, few of the captives had coats, and nearly all carried blankets cut from carpets. They represented the sum total of Grant's captures since May 5. The sight of them confirmed one Yankee's fears. "They are the hardest two-legged things to see in America, by thunder—being just the color of the ground or one of their damned 'Johnny Cakes' of corn meal." The gaunt, expressionless figures struck another northern man as "the very creatures to be driven, unresistingly, into any wickedness, any vehemence of purposeless passion." On reaching Belle Plain, guards herded the rebels into a set of ravines called the Punch Bowl to await transport to northern prisons. Two artillery pieces were aimed into the mass of prisoners, and guards paced the perimeter at fifteen-yard intervals, their muskets loaded and half-cocked. [9]

Turning onto Gordon Road, Morton reached the Armstrong house, reportedly Grant's headquarters. The general, a sentry told him, had recently relinquished the building to the medical staff. The surgeon in charge invited Morton to administer anesthetics to wounded rebels, which he did. Morton watched the surgeon hack off injured limbs and pitch them into anonymous piles. The men appeared grateful, Morton thought, "for the kind treatment which they received." The doctor found Grant's headquarters at a nearby stand of woods. Grant, Major General George G. Meade, Assistant War Secretary Charles A. Dana, and several aides sat comfortably on chairs in front of a tent. They had propped up the fly like an awning to shelter them from the rain, which alternated between drizzle and downpour. Grant gave Morton a hearty welcome. The general's unassuming air impressed the physician. A stranger, Morton reflected, would never have imagined that the short, coarsely bearded figure headed the Union war effort. Grant seemed more tanned than Morton had remembered from an earlier meeting, but the general's straight mouth, clear eyes, and calm expression appeared as before. "Incessant, close and rapid thought is going on there, however quiet the external signs may be," Morton imagined. [10]

At Grant's suggestion, Morton visited the focal point of the most recent offensive. A mile and a half of muddy fields and trails led from headquarters to the site. Rain fell in torrents. The scene struck the doctor as "horrible enough to curdle the blood of the coldest." Wounded rebels lay heaped inside the earthworks—"men in the agonies of death groaning beside the dead bodies of their comrades," Morton noted. Corpses carpeted the ground on the Union side of the entrenchments, faces still contorted in their death throes.

"God forbid that I should ever gaze on such a sight again," he recorded in his journal.[11]

Intense personal dramas played across the bloody fields between the armies. Representative was the experience of Newton Kirk, of the 26th Michigan, who had been shot early on May 12. A slug of lead the size of a man's thumb tore through his chest, ruptured his right lung, and blew out a hole in his back where it exited, producing a sensation like an electric shock. Kirk lost consciousness, then awoke drenched with sweat and spitting wads of bloody froth. Panting for breath, he sprawled in the open, bullets striking all around. The year before, Kirk had asked his cousin Irving Snyder for a patent medicine called Radway's Ready Relief. The package had followed him in the mail from place to place and had finally reached him just as the spring campaign opened. It was in his haversack—a gift from Providence, Kirk reflected, meant for this very emergency. Pouring water from his canteen into a cup and mixing it with a slosh of Ready Relief, he swallowed the concoction. "It warmed me up nicely," he reflected. "It was worth its weight in gold." [12]

Kirk lay in excruciating pain as battle lines ebbed and flowed across the field. A wounded man stumbled by, crying for something to drink. "Damn you, I would rather shoot you than bring you water," a rebel answered. Kirk's canteen was almost dry, but the exchange gave him second thoughts about asking for water. Survival depended on lying still like a dead man, he concluded. "I lay on the field from early morn till sun down," he was to write, "with the wounded, the dying and the dead all around me; shot and shell of every kind, sort and description, passed over and around me, the cries and moans of the wounded could be heard in every direction. Heavy cannonading and awful volleys of musketry could be heard in the distance, while not far away, we could hear at times, the shrill yells of the rebels, mingled with the hoarser cheers of our own men." Near dark, Confederates took pity on Kirk and placed him under a tree near the abandoned home of the McCoull family. Another injured man—J. W. Bone, of the 31st North Carolina—lay near Kirk. "I was on wet ground, hungry, sleepy, weak, and bloody," Bone remembered. "I think it was the dreariest night I ever passed on earth," seconded Kirk, who sat in the mud propped against a tree, in unspeakable pain and shaking from cold. Artillery shells, accompanied by the whine of snipers' bullets, arched over the smoldering inferno. Rain pounded down in torrents, prompting a Confederate to accuse Heaven of "trying to wash up the blood as fast as the civilized barbarians were spilling it." [13]

The armies were locked in a campaign unlike any the war had seen. Previous battles had seldom lasted more than three days. Grant and Lee had been marching and fighting without pause three times that long, and no end was in sight. Soldiers stoically threw up elaborate earthworks as monuments to the emerging style of warfare in which shovels were as valued as muskets. "Spades are trumps," a North Carolina soldier wrote home. "We shovel dirt all night and fight all day. When the Yankees charge—and they have made and attempted to make many—they generally give a feeble huzza; which is answered by a loud and terrible yell from our men; and then the minnie balls, solid shot, shell and all manner of missiles, each playing a tune, keep up their infernal concert. I've been deaf, or nearly so, since this row commenced." A Mississippian similarly observed that from a soldier's point of view, "the country is made up of holes, each dug by hand." Glorious charges, he added, were relics of the past. "Fighting has become an everyday business," he concluded. "Now we have become hardened to it as our normal condition." [14]

Waging predominantly defensive battles, the Confederates had fought Grant to impasse in the campaign's opening battle in the Wilderness. In the campaign's next encounters, Grant had bludgeoned Lee's entrenchments in front of Spotsylvania Court House, but the Confederates had deftly parried his thrusts. It was clear to Grant that he would have to try another approach. Maneuver stepped to center stage. Henceforth, Grant resolved to beat Lee by striking unexpectedly at his vulnerable points. The coordination necessary for successful maneuver, however, would continue to elude Grant and his subordinates. Their challenge was to find a way to work together and make the Union army responsive to their designs.

Daunting challenges also faced Lee. Confronted by a powerful and determined foe that outnumbered him two-to-one, the resourceful Confederate could no longer employ the offensive tactics that had served him so well in the past. The question was whether Lee could anticipate Grant's maneuvers and shift quickly enough to repel them.

This book examines the phase of the campaign that opened on May 13, 1864, following the fight at the Bloody Angle, and that culminated with the stalemate at the North Anna River on May 25. Historians have generally ignored these thirteen days. For one thing, sources are scarce. For another, the interlude was bracketed by horrific battles that riveted the public's attention. But the period is important in its own right and demands close scrutiny. What made it particularly exciting was the complex game of guile and endurance between Grant and Lee. There was combat aplenty—cavalry duels at Meadow Bridge and infantry spats at Myers Hill, Harris Farm, Jericho Mills, Ox Ford, and Doswell Farm, to name but a few engagements. Grueling night marches, desperate attacks, and thundering cavalry charges became the order of the day. But the real story lay in Grant's and Lee's efforts to outwit each other. "Grant and Lee are both figuring their best," a soldier concluded in the midst of the campaign, "and the best figurer will come out ahead." For Grant the eventful days were to bring frustration and missed opportunities. For Lee they were to culminate in high tragedy. On the North Anna River, as had happened in the Wilderness and at Spotsylvania Court House, Lee once again misread Grant's intentions and neglected to fortify the very sector of line that Grant had targeted to attack. This time, the Federals breached the Confederate defenses with ease and girded to deliver a killing blow. But the southern chieftain rose to the crisis and devised a trap that cunningly exploited Grant's offensive mindset. And he watched Grant step blindly into his snare, only to have fate cruelly intervene before he could snap it shut.[15]

But let us not get ahead of the story.

I

MAY 13, 1864

Grant Lays New Plans

"No army in the world was ever in finer condition."

LIEUTENANT GENERAL ULYSSES S. GRANT rose early on May 13, 1864. All night, musketry and artillery had crackled from battle lines a mile to the south. The din subsided before sunrise. Rain dripped from trees and collected in rivulets, filling ruts cut by the wheels of the Union army's guns and wagons. Central Virginia's sky hung gray and heavy with clouds. Shadowy forms of aides and orderlies scurried about, walking stooped, like men aged beyond their years.

Grant breakfasted with Major General George G. Meade, the hawk-nosed, slightly disheveled Pennsylvanian commanding the Army of the Potomac. Meade's chief-of-staff, Major General Andrew A. Humphreys, pulled up a chair. Gruff, profane, and in the opinion of a fellow general, "given to flaming outbreaks in which all the vigor known or unknown to the English language burst forth like a bomb," Humphreys managed the army with a steel fist, much to Grant's approval. Joining them was Assistant War Secretary Charles A. Dana, who had arrived a few days earlier from Washington to ensure President Abraham Lincoln and his cabinet a steady flow of information from the front. Grant had commandeered the yard of a family named Armstrong for his headquarters. Tent tops peeked through a maze of telegraph wires, wagons, and sundry martial accouterments that spilled over the sodden yard.[1]

The Armstrongs were Unionists at heart, and their neighbors—most of whom had fathers and sons in the Confederate armies—regarded them with suspicion. Early in the war Mr. Armstrong had fled north, leaving his elderly wife to tend the property. This morning Mrs. Armstrong flitted around her distinguished guests, plying them with fresh bread, butter, and honey while apologizing profusely that she could not spread a more sumptuous table. Meade loved her butter, which she had seasoned with garlic. Grant scarcely noticed the fare. Matters more pressing than food preoccupied him. The campaign to destroy the Army of Northern Virginia was not going as he had expected.[2]

Early in March, President Lincoln had summoned the forty-six-year-old, plainspoken midwesterner to Washington to assume command of the Union war effort. Urgency impelled the appointment. The rebellion was three years old and showing few signs of ending. Delay worked to the Confederacy's advantage as the North tired of war. Draft riots had rocked New York during the previous summer, and the three-year terms of enlistment for volunteers who had entered the army in 1861 were fast expiring. A presidential election was approaching in November, and Lincoln needed military victories. Otherwise, a war-weary North might elect a candidate committed to peace, even if peace meant letting the errant South go its separate way. The *New York Herald* astutely observed that Lincoln's "political fortunes, not less than the great cause of the country, are in the hands of General Grant, and the failure of the General will be the overthrow of the President."[3]

In the western theater of war, Grant had masterminded a succession of victories—Fort Donelson, Shiloh, Vicksburg, and Chattanooga, to name a few— that filled northern breasts with hope. But the eastern theater had been a disaster. General Robert E. Lee and his Army of Northern Virginia had deflected every combination the Federals could marshal. While Meade's repulse of Lee at Gettysburg in July 1863 had raised prospects that the wily Virginian had met his match, Meade's hesitant maneuvers during the summer cruelly dashed those expectations. By early fall Lee had taken Meade's measure and expressed his contempt by dispatching a third of his army to help the beleaguered Confederates in the west. Then he embarked on a dazzling turning movement with his remaining troops that sent Meade scurrying back toward Washington. Shortly after Thanksgiving, Meade marched to attack Lee below the Rapidan River, but bristling rebel fortifications along Mine Run cowed him into retreat once again. Withdrawing above the Rapidan, Meade camped near Culpeper Court House. Lee entrenched opposite Meade along the river's southern bank near Orange Court House, and the armies spent the winter of 1863–1864 on a line remarkably similar to that of the previous year. Lincoln fretted that the war in Virginia might never end.

Lincoln brought Grant east to change all of this. In their first meeting on March 10, 1864, the president set the ground rules. Grant was to run the armies and secure victories, and Lincoln would ensure him the men and supplies that he needed. The president stressed that he did not want to know how

Grant intended to accomplish his feats, joking that he would only leak details to the press. Grant was delighted at the arrangement, as it gave him a free hand to conduct the war as he saw fit. A general could hope for no more.

Grant's recipe for victory embodied his straightforward approach to warring. The North boasted an overwhelming edge in men and supplies, which he intended to employ to smash the South's military capacity. No longer would Union armies wage uncoordinated battles. Forces east and west would attack in concert, denying the rebels opportunity to exploit their interior lines of communication. And no longer would Union armies try to capture and hold geographic areas. Instead, their objective would be the destruction of Confederate armies. Once engaged, they were to fight as never before. The days of short battles followed by lengthy respites were over. Grant expected his blue-clad hosts to pursue their Confederate foes and batter them into submission. The result would be a campaign such as the nation had never seen.

The day after receiving his commission, Grant journeyed to Culpeper Court House to meet Meade. Six years Grant's senior, the army commander was notorious for his explosive temper, and marriage to a well-heeled Philadelphia lady had only accentuated his overbearing tendencies. He could be impossibly closed-minded and condescending, and his demeanor aggravated matters. Large, owl-like bags drooped below his eyes, which peered back from either side of a prominent hooked nose. A snapping turtle, his aides called him, although the overall effect depended on the moment, as Meade could alternate between a sharp-beaked bird of prey and the vise-jawed amphibian of his staffers' nightmares. "He has none of the dash and brilliancy which is necessary to popularity," a soldier observed.[4]

To Grant's surprise, the temperamental Pennsylvanian offered to step aside so that he could appoint someone of his own choosing. In a magnanimous gesture that he would come to regret, Grant asked the older man to stay. Hoping to spur Meade into offensive operations and to avoid Washington and its intrigues, Grant decided to accompany the Potomac Army in the field. The arrangement was doomed from the start, as the generals differed fundamentally in personality and in their approach to warring. Grant, a westerner of relatively humble origin, eschewed pomp. "He is not so hard-looking a man as his photographs make him out to be," one of Meade's generals observed, "but stumpy, slouchy, and Western-looking; very ordinary in fact." The trappings of aristocracy came effortlessly to Meade. More to the point, Grant contemplated a blistering campaign of maneuvers and attacks. Meade preferred a more deliberate pace of combat. "General Meade was a nice sort of gentleman, who understood the art of war as taught by logarithms and abstruse engineering," was a wartime surgeon's assessment. "That sort of business

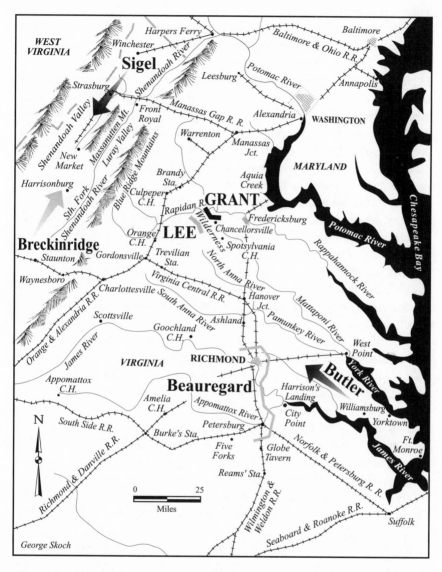

The eastern theater

may have answered the purpose some centuries ago, but a new era had dawned in the art of war."[5]

Grant firmed up his national strategy as spring unfolded. He intended to supervise the general conduct of the war and leave local commanders like Meade to develop their own tactics. His friend Major General William T. Sherman was to command the major Union force in the west, breaking up the Confederate Army of Tennessee under General Joseph E. Johnston, then getting "into the interior of the enemy's country as far as he could, inflicting all the damage he could against their war resources." After winding up a campaign in Louisiana, Major General Nathaniel P. Banks's Army of the Gulf was to capture Mobile, Alabama, then swing north to reinforce Sherman.[6]

In Virginia, Grant aimed to employ on a local scale the doctrine of concentration that underpinned his national scheme for victory. Converging armies were to focus irresistible force against the Army of Northern Virginia. Meade and his Army of the Potomac, swelled to 118,000 soldiers by the addition of Major General Ambrose E. Burnside's independent 9th Corps, were to cross the Rapidan River and immediately come to grips with the rebels. "Lee's army will be your objective point," Grant directed Meade in words that left no room for misinterpretation. "Wherever he goes, there will you go also." At the same time, Major General Benjamin F. Butler was to take the Army of the James, nearly 40,000 soldiers strong, from Fortress Monroe and swoop into Richmond from the rear, capturing the Confederate capital if possible, and otherwise swinging around the city to cooperate with Meade against Lee. Simultaneously, two Union forces—the larger one under Major General Franz Sigel numbering 15,000 troops, and a secondary contingent under Brigadier General George Crook—were to march into the Shenandoah Valley from two directions, cutting the Virginia and Tennessee Railway, closing the fertile valley to Lee's commissary, and denying the Confederate armies a favorite invasion route, all the while menacing Lee's left flank.[7]

The scheme looked good on paper, but time would disclose weaknesses. Sigel and Butler owed their positions to political clout and only superficially grasped military affairs. Whether they could hold up their end of the joint operation was anyone's guess. And the Army of the Potomac's imposing numbers concealed serious flaws in the force's capacity to fight with the steel and determination necessary to beat Lee's battle-wise veterans. Raw recruits, sprinkled liberally with "substitutes, bounty jumpers, thieves, and rogues," bloated the Union ranks, and the practice of placing new men into new regiments served to magnify their inexperience. Grant estimated that for every five men enlisted, "we don't get more than one effective soldier." In addition, the Union army's veterans had volunteered for three years. Their terms of service were due to expire, which understandably dulled their appetite for combat. After factoring in the elusive but important variable of morale—the Potomac Army had a tradition of defeat at the hands of Lee, particularly when fighting in Virginia—Grant's success was by no means assured.[8]

On the night of May 3–4, Grant started his armies in motion. Meade crossed the Rapidan east of Lee to turn him out of his formidable river line, Butler started by boat up the James River toward Richmond, and Sigel and Crook began converging on the Shenandoah Valley. Grant accompanied Meade and camped on the night of May 4–5 with the Army of the Potomac in a densely wooded tract known as the Wilderness of Spotsylvania. As Grant's thousands poured across the Rapidan, Lee reacted with accustomed audacity, thrusting two army corps into the Wilderness to pin the Federals in place while bringing up another corps to assault the Union flank. Sloppy reconnaissance by Meade's cavalry enabled Lee's Confederates to launch a surprise attack the next morning. For two days—May 5 and 6—the armies clawed viciously in the Wilderness. Hopes for a quick Union victory evaporated as the battle deteriorated into a slugging match. Grant watched in dismay as Lee's smaller force, half the size of his own, fought the Federal juggernaut to impasse.

Dismissing further assaults in the Wilderness as futile and costly in men, Grant on May 7 decided to loop south and interpose between Lee and Richmond in hopes of luring the Confederates onto ground more favorable to the Federals. That night Grant started the Potomac Army toward Spotsylvania Court House, a nondescript village at the heart of a strategic road network ten miles below the Wilderness. Once again, Grant's plan fell victim to faltering leadership. Subordinates misinterpreted orders, wagons and troops clogged the southbound arteries, and a single Confederate cavalry division slowed the march to a crawl. The southerners won the race to Spotsylvania Court House, and for five days Grant pounded Lee's fortified line above the tiny village. Flanking maneuvers and frontal assaults gained not an inch of ground. Union casualties soared, but Grant kept hammering in search of an opening. Finally he hit on an apparent weak point where Lee's entrenched line bulged forward in a protrusion half a mile deep and just as wide. Dubbed the Mule Shoe because of its shape, the bulge was difficult for the Confederates to defend against a determined frontal attack. On May 12 Grant launched a massive assault and pierced Lee's defensive formation. The Confederates counterattacked, and fighting centered around a shallow bend in the Mule Shoe called the Bloody Angle. The armies battled for twenty-two hours over a piece of real estate measuring but a few hundred yards across. In a fratricidal war memorable for bloodletting, the Bloody Angle ratcheted the stakes to a new extreme. Never had men maintained so ferocious a pitch of hand-to-hand killing for so long. A few hours before sunrise on May 13, the Confederates abandoned the Mule Shoe. Finding where they had gone became Grant's immediate concern.

The Army of the Potomac had endured grueling combat in past campaigns. Ten days of marching and fighting under Grant, however, had set a new standard. Thirty-three thousand Federals were dead, wounded, or captured, many of the army's best combat units were wrecked, and the survivors were exhausted. "I believe it is no exaggeration to say that the campaign of the last ten days in this state exceeds anything which has ever occurred in the annals of all modern warfare," a soldier wrote home. "Such terrible fighting, such slaughtering of human beings with war's tortures and deadly missiles, such tenacity and desperation of purpose on both sides to overcome and defeat each other, such displays of bravery, heroism and endurance, such an exhibition of scenes, incidents, and everything associated with the strife and carnage of battle, have few parallels in history." [9]

Dutifully sampling Mrs. Armstrong's breakfast fare, Grant reflected on the reasons for the campaign's failures. Slippage at the top was partially to blame. Grant could only wonder at how quickly his relationship with Meade had deteriorated. He had vowed to leave Meade in independent command of the Army of the Potomac "as far as possible," but the crusty general's cautious, deliberate style had driven Grant to distraction. The campaign was only two days old when an exasperated Grant broke his promise and began dictating the Potomac Army's tactical dispositions. The welter of assaults and maneuvers around Spotsylvania Court House was Grant's handiwork, not Meade's. Grant agonized over the indecision that had paralyzed Meade and his subordinates but decided to keep them on. Meade knew his army intimately, and his Gettysburg victory, ephemeral as it appeared from the trenches around Spotsylvania Court House, made him its logical head. Grant informally relegated the blustery army commander to the role of staff officer charged with seeing that the Potomac Army did Grant's bidding. For their part, Meade and his aides decried Grant's program of attacks, privately complaining that the impulsive midwesterner was wrecking the army and destroying its morale. Meade assured his wife that he would gladly resign if he could find a graceful way to do so. In the meantime, he endured the humiliation of his de facto demotion. [10]

Meade's infantry commanders were also responsible for the Union army's dismal showing. Major General Winfield S. Hancock, heading the Union 2nd Corps, had distinguished himself as the best of a mediocre lot. Tall, erect, and military in bearing—Hancock the Superb, his admirers called him—the general at forty-one years of age looked the part of a warrior and generally performed like one as well. Grant liked Hancock's uncomplaining readiness to follow orders and used the 2nd Corps for most of his offensive gambits. A Gettysburg wound, however, had undermined Hancock's endurance, and constant fighting had whittled the 2nd Corps to barely half its former size.

The commanders of the Potomac Army's other two corps were floundering badly. Major General Gouverneur K. Warren, heading the Union 5th Corps, was at thirty-four the army's youngest major general. He had made a good first impression on Grant, who had pegged him as Meade's logical successor. Ten days of combat had reversed Grant's assessment. Warren had proven intelligent, energetic, and brave, but glaring deficiencies canceled his strengths. The gangly New Yorker handled troops with excessive caution and habitually questioned orders rather than promptly executing them. A staff officer noted that Warren was "always ready to set up his own judgment against that of his superiors." Grant confided that Warren was not "as efficient as I had believed" and almost removed him on May 12 because of delays and "feeble" assaults. Meade's staffer Lieutenant Colonel Theodore Lyman noted simply, "Warren is not up to a corps command." The Union 6th Corps also labored under dubious leadership. On May 9 a Confederate sniper had killed the corps's popular commander, Major General John Sedgwick. Brigadier General Horatio G. Wright, a division commander, had succeeded Sedgwick and was elevated immediately to high command. The heavy-set, goateed general seemed overwhelmed by his new responsibilities and incapable of acting with decision. He also reputedly drank excessively. Time would show whether he, like Warren, had been promoted beyond his capabilities.[11]

The addition of Burnside's 9th Corps to the Union expeditionary force threw Grant's awkward command structure even farther out of kilter. Portly Burnside, boldly festooned with side-whiskers, had led the Army of the Potomac during its failed offensives around Fredericksburg in the bitter winter of 1862–1863, and his commission as major general had preceded Meade's. Grant's solution to this knotty issue of protocol was to let Burnside manage the 9th Corps as an independent command, with Grant serving as middleman. The arrangement was a catastrophe. Coordination proved impossible, and Grant's pace of warfare bewildered Burnside as completely as it exasperated Meade.

If Grant inclined toward introspection on Mrs. Armstrong's porch, he could not have turned a blind eye to mistakes on his own part. Perhaps he had expected too much of the Potomac Army. Rarely had a general demanded a military force to perform such complex feats of coordination and allowed so little time for preparation. Also, coming from the West, Grant had failed to

accommodate his rapid-fire style of warring to the eastern army's more deliberate tradition of waging combat. A young ordnance officer identified the
Potomac Army's weakness as a "lack of springy formation, and audacious,
self-reliant initiative" fostered by earlier commanders who had "dissipated
war's best elixir by training it into a life of caution." Caution did not figure in
Grant's program, but it loomed large in the thinking of Meade, Burnside, and
many subordinate commanders. Grant might have achieved more lasting battlefield success had he reconciled his impetuous instincts with the more con-
servative tendencies of his lieutenants. In the final analysis, Grant, Meade,
and Burnside made decidedly incompatible bedfellows.[12]

As sunlight pierced battle smoke on May 13, the fate of the campaign was
far from clear. The Army of the Potomac had bruised Lee's army, but the
Confederate force remained eminently capable of inflicting serious blows.
Attrition was depleting the Union army's numbers, Meade's cavalry had ridden off on a mission toward Richmond, and the soldiers who remained were
weary beyond anything in their experience. These subtractions left Grant an
effective force at Spotsylvania Court House approximating 73,000 soldiers—
on paper. In reality, the number of men physically and mentally capable of
shouldering muskets and resuming the previous pitch of combat was far
lower. If the trend continued—and so long as Lee continued fighting behind
earthworks, there was no reason to expect Union losses to diminish—the
prospects were daunting. Grant had to find a way to force Lee to fight outside
his entrenchments or face stalemate. Politically, stalemate meant Union defeat.

Compounding Grant's woes was the laggard performance of his supporting armies. Sigel's painstakingly deliberate advance through the Shenandoah
Valley had afforded Confederate Major General John C. Breckinridge—a
Kentuckian and former vice-president of the United States—time to scrape
together a force to oppose him. Battle north of Staunton, Virginia, seemed
imminent, and Sigel's inexperience made the outcome far from certain. On
the James River, Butler had started energetically enough but seemed more interested in feuding with subordinates than in fighting rebels. He, too, had frit-
tered away his initial advantage while the Confederates hurried reinforcements from the Carolinas to bolster the defenses around Richmond and the
vital rail center of Petersburg, twenty miles south of the capital. The next few
days would tell the fate of these auxiliary forces.

Grant and Meade exuded optimism. Reporting to his wife on the fight at
the Bloody Angle, Grant asserted that Lee had "found the last ditch," making
Union victory inevitable. "The enemy were really whipped yesterday but
their situation is desperate beyond anything heretofore known," he observed.

"To lose this battle they lose their cause. As bad as it is they have fought for it with a gallantry worthy of a better." Meade disingenuously proclaimed the operation of May 12 a "decided success" and issued a circular congratulating the Army of the Potomac. Lee, he assured his soldiers, had abandoned his "last intrenched position." The task ahead was clear. "Let us determine then to continue vigorously the work so well begun," he urged, "and, under God's blessing, in a short time the object of our labors will be accomplished." [13]

Spring had broken drearily over Virginia, mirroring the Confederacy's despondent mood. Rain lashed the countryside and hardship reached deep into southern homes as the rebellion entered its fourth year. Rampant inflation and scarcities in food and consumer goods were commonplace, weeds choked formerly prosperous farms, and civilians toiled to preserve a semblance of normal life. The South's military prospects appeared as bleak as the weather. Invaders had occupied Tennessee, seized the Mississippi River, and now roamed the Confederate heartland seemingly at will. In the East, General Robert E. Lee and his Army of Northern Virginia had served up dazzling victories, but success had eluded the Confederates there as well. In the spring of 1864, Federal armies, girding to bring the Confederacy to its knees, once again darkened Virginia's soil.

Thoughtful southerners had long ruled out the possibility of defeating the North by force of arms. "Conceding to our enemies the superiority claimed by them in numbers, resources, and all the means and appliances for carrying on the war, we have no right to look for exemptions from the vigorous use of these advantages," Lee had warned the Confederacy's President Jefferson Davis after Gettysburg. The "most effectual mode" for achieving southern independence, Lee had urged, was to give "all the encouragement we can, consistent with truth, to the rising peace party of the North." Lieutenant General James Longstreet, commanding the Army of Northern Virginia's 1st Corps, bluntly articulated the Confederacy's war aims for 1864. "If we can break up the enemy's arrangements early, and throw him back, he will not be able to recover his position nor his morale until the Presidential election is over, and we shall then have a new President to treat with," he predicted. Longstreet's recipe for victory was straightforward. "Do let us exert ourselves to the utmost of our resources to finish the war this year." [14]

Formidable Union armies advancing on all fronts imparted compelling urgency to Lee's and Longstreet's counsel. The season for elections was fast approaching, and manifestations of the North's flagging resolve encouraged southern leaders. If Confederate armies could hold the Yankees at bay, went the argument—better yet, if they could squeeze out a few victories—Lincoln faced defeat at the polls. "Every bullet we can send is the best ballot that can be deposited against [Lincoln's] election," a Georgia editor reminded his readers. "The battle-fields of 1864 will hold the polls of this momentous decision." [15]

The Army of Northern Virginia offered the South its best prospect for victories. By the end of April, Lee had amassed 65,000 soldiers, almost as many as he had taken to Pennsylvania and considerably more than he had wielded to impressive effect at Antietam and Chancellorsville. Most importantly, morale was high among Lee's combat-wise veterans. "We have more men here now than we have ever had before, and they are all in high spirits," a soldier announced, slightly exaggerating the numbers but not the optimistic frame of mind. "I don't have any fears but what we will give the Yanks the worst whipping they have got if they do attempt to take Richmond." [16]

Famed for aggressiveness and daring, Lee longed to take the initiative. But shortages in food and fodder, along with the possibility that portions of his army might be needed to relieve other threatened fronts, forced him to curb his combative instincts. Bowing to the necessity of a defensive campaign, he urged President Davis and his military adviser, General Braxton Bragg, to concentrate Confederate forces "wherever they are going to attack us." By mid-April, Grant's burgeoning force on the Rapidan's far bank had persuaded Lee that the blow was about to fall in his quarter, and he stepped up his petitions for reinforcements.

Competing demands in other sectors limited Davis's ability to honor Lee's request. On May 5—the same day that Grant and Lee locked horns in the Wilderness—Butler's transports began disembarking at Bermuda Hundred, midway between Richmond and Petersburg. Richmond was ill-prepared to protect itself, and Major General George E. Pickett, headquartered in Petersburg, was packing to rejoin Lee. Canceling his travel plans, Pickett did his best to paste together troops from several disparate commands and scrambled to fend off Butler. Pickett's flurry of activity, Butler's inertia, and a healthy measure of old-fashioned luck bought the southerners precious time. By May 10 fresh Confederate troops were pouring into Petersburg from the Carolinas, and General Pierre G. T. Beauregard had arrived to assume command of the growing force. [17]

Butler's threat raised profound implications for Lee. Until the capital was secure, he could expect no help from that quarter. Davis suggested to Lee that he pull reinforcements instead from the Shenandoah Valley, but Lee demurred. It was critical for Breckinridge to stop Sigel before the Federals reached the Virginia Central Railroad at Staunton and cut the Valley's communications with Richmond. Tension between Lee's need for troops and de-

mands from other theaters remained a central theme in the campaign unfolding. For the present, Lee could expect nothing more from Davis than moral
support.[18]

Lacking any realistic expectation of reinforcements, Lee formulated a defensive strategy. He would try to hold a line near the Rapidan and watch for
opportunities to lash out. At all costs, he would avoid retreating to Richmond.
Backed against the Confederate capital, he would lose his ability to maneuver, and the war would become a siege that the North must necessarily win. "If
I am forced to retire from this line," he warned Davis, "either by a flank movement of the enemy or the want of supplies, great injury will befall us." [19]

In the Wilderness and at Spotsylvania Court House, Lee had waged an impressive defense against determined Federal assaults. He viewed his accomplishments, however, with mixed emotions. His smaller army had fought the
Union monolith to impasse, but Grant had relentlessly persisted in his grind-
ing battles of attrition, which were exacting a debilitating toll on the
Confederates. Although Lee retained the capacity to deflect Grant's blows, he
no longer possessed the ability to initiate offensives of his own. By May 13
Grant had forced the Army of Northern Virginia fifteen miles below the
Rapidan. The catastrophe that Lee had predicted had not materialized. But
one more Union turning movement stood to advance the front so close to
Richmond that Lee would finally be locked in place. Lee's only salvation lay
in administering a stinging defeat to the Federal army. His manpower, however, had shrunk to critical proportions. Lee had lost 11,000 soldiers in the
Wilderness and as many more at Spotsylvania Court House. Three of his cavalry brigades were also absent, which left him about 40,000 Confederates to
fight Grant's 73,000 Federals. While the numerical strength of the opposing
forces remained in roughly the same proportions as at the campaign's outset,
the absolute number of troops available to Lee had become dangerously thin.
A Confederate officer aptly described the problem. "If it required the loss of
twenty thousand to rob us of six thousand, [Grant] was doing a wise thing for
we yield our loss from an irreplaceable penury, he from super-abundance,"
he observed, noting that "ultimately such bloody policy must win." The
Army of Northern Virginia's spirits remained high—"No army in the world
was ever in finer condition," Lee's artillery chief wrote home on May 13—
but its ability to foil Grant's onslaughts was questionable. Lee needed reinforcements, and he needed them quickly.[20]

The Wilderness and Spotsylvania battles had also seriously frayed the
Army of Northern Virginia's command structure. All three Confederate in-
fantry corps had been affected. The campaign was only two days old when
James Longstreet, commanding Lee's 1st Corps, was seriously wounded in

an accidental shooting. Lee found a replacement in Major General Richard H. Anderson, an affable, meerschaum-smoking South Carolinian and a natural choice to lead the Deep South outfit. Anderson had rewarded Lee's confidence by beating Grant to Spotsylvania Court House. His capacity for cooperative operations remained untested, although Lee took encouragement in the talented brace of subordinate officers—Brigadier General Joseph B. Kershaw of South Carolina and Major General Charles W. Field of Virginia—heading Anderson's two divisions.[21]

Two days after Longstreet's wounding, Lee had lost to illness the feisty commander of his 3rd Corps, Lieutenant General Ambrose P. Hill. To replace Hill, Lee had selected Major General Jubal A. Early, an acerbic, outspoken bachelor with a talent for aggressive warfare. Early had wielded with skill the 3rd Corps's three divisions under Major General Cadmus M. Wilcox, Major General Henry Heth, and Brigadier General William Mahone. On the rare occasions when Grant had dropped his guard—on May 10 at the Po River, and again on May 12 on Burnside's front—Lee had sent Early to exploit the opportunity, and the former prosecutor had done so with skill. Lee also used the reshuffling occasioned by Hill's disability to elevate Brigadier General John B. Gordon, a young Georgian with sterling leadership qualities, to command a 2nd Corps division. Hill, who shared Lee's frustration over his malady, insisted on accompanying his troops in an ambulance.

Lieutenant General Richard S. Ewell, the eccentric head of Lee's 2nd Corps, seemed dangerously close to collapse. Army wags blamed Ewell's decline on a wartime amputation and marriage at forty-six years of age to a domineering widow, once his childhood sweetheart. Lee's discretionary orders frustrated Ewell, who vacillated at Gettysburg and failed to exploit advantages in the Wilderness. His conduct on May 12 had bordered on the farcical as he hobbled among his routed men, cursing and whacking them with the flat of his sword. "General Ewell, you must restrain yourself," Lee had remonstrated. "How can you expect to control these men if you have lost control of yourself? If you cannot repress your excitement, you had better retire." A soldier noted that Lee calmly appealed to the men's dignity and manhood. "It is hardly necessary to say that Gen. Lee's course was by far the more effective of the two," the soldier observed. Lee later remarked that Ewell had become "too much overwhelmed to be efficient."[22]

Ten days of campaigning had decimated Ewell's corps, cutting its strength in half and costing it ten brigade commanders. Numerous smaller units were almost annihilated. After the Bloody Angle, a company in the 33rd Virginia contained only a captain and three privates, one of whom was a cavalryman who had lost his horse. Casualties in the army's lower command echelons read like a roster of Confederate heroes. Dead were Brigadier Generals Leroy A. Stafford, John M. Jones, Micah Jenkins, Abner Perrin, and Junius Daniel. Among the wounded were Brigadier Generals Harry T. Hays, Henry L. Benning, Samuel McGowan, Stephen D. Ramseur, Robert D. Johnston, James A. Walker, Henry H. Walker, Cullen A. Battle, and John Pegram. And captured were Major General Edward Johnson and Brigadier General George H. Steuart. The Army of Northern Virginia was fast becoming a ghost of its former self.[23]

The Bloody Angle had marked a watershed in Lee's management of his army. Riding to the battlefront, Lee had jettisoned his corps structure and personally selected outfits to send into the breach. Twice he attempted to lead troops into combat. His performance was a masterpiece of defensive fighting that underscored the dearth of dependable Confederate commanders at the corps level. In the past, Lee had pursued a style of leadership that delegated responsibility for tactical details to subordinates. He now saw no choice but to assume duties he had formerly relegated to others. Henceforth, he would oversee tactical details as well as broader campaign strategies.

Mounting burdens were exacting a toll on Lee. Now fifty-seven years old, he had shared his men's hardships for two years. His personal sacrifices and magnetism had forged a bond between the general and his soldiers that made them fearsome in battle, but spartan living was visibly undermining the gray-haired patriarch's health. "I am becoming more and more incapable of exertion," Lee had admitted after Gettysburg, "and am thus prevented from making the personal examinations and giving the personal supervision to the operations in the field which I feel to be necessary." On the eve of the spring campaign he complained of a "marked change in my strength," which he informed his son had rendered him "less competent for duty than ever." Yet throughout May 12 and into the morning of May 13, he supervised the Mule Shoe's defense and the construction of a new line across its base. Not until 3:00 A.M., when the new line was complete, did he withdraw his troops from the Mule Shoe. It is unlikely that he slept at all that terrible night.[24]

Dawn on May 13 saw Lee's army ensconced in an imposing set of entrenchments, masterfully sited to magnify its dwindling numbers. On the Confederate left, Anderson anchored Field's division of his 1st Corps on the Po River, near Block House Bridge. From there bristling earthworks stretched east along a shallow ridge known to the soldiers as Laurel Hill. Brushing the lower edge of Sarah Spindle's farm, the 1st Corps's entrenchments crossed Brock Road and continued under Kershaw's division another mile or so to a point near the Harrison farm. There the Confederate 2nd Corps manned a new line across the Mule Shoe's base. Major General Robert E.

Rodes's division held the left of Ewell's line as it traversed open fields, and John Gordon's division extended the formation another mile through woods to a junction with the 3rd Corps. The final segment of line—the 3rd Corps's battlements, commanded by Early with Hill watching from his ambulance—dropped south from Ewell's right flank, crossed Fredericksburg Road a quarter mile east of Spotsylvania Court House, and terminated a short distance below the road in a stand of woods. The 3rd Corps divisions of Heth, Wilcox, and Mahone ranged from north to south in that order. Confederate cavalry patrolled the country past each flank, with Brigadier General Thomas L. Rosser's mounted Virginia brigade watching Anderson's left, and more Virginia cavalrymen under Brigadier General John R. Chambliss Jr. exploring south and east of Spotsylvania Court House, below Early.

As finally arrayed, the Army of Northern Virginia formed a reclining L, the long leg extending west to east above Spotsylvania Court House, the short arm dangling south across the town's eastern approaches. The Confederates occupied interior lines that enabled them to shuttle troops as needed to fend off Union attacks. The Federal formation wrapped loosely along the outer perimeter of the Confederate position, mimicking its shape, with Warren and Wright facing Anderson, Hancock fronting Ewell, and Burnside opposing Early. "It was Gettysburg reversed," a newsman noted, "Lee having the inner circle." [25]

Lee's plans for May 13 involved strengthening his earthworks and resting his men. He saw no choice but to await Grant's next onslaught, much as remaining on the defensive galled his aggressive instincts. Writing to President Davis, he reiterated his need for reinforcements. A brigade of North Carolina troops commanded by Major General Robert F. Hoke had recently reached Petersburg. If the president could send them to him, Lee suggested, they "would be of great assistance." Otherwise, he feared that he might be overwhelmed. "We are outnumbered and constant labor is impairing the efficiency of the men," Lee warned. [26]

The president's reply offered little hope. Davis had intended to send Hoke to Lee, he wrote, and he had even brought Hoke's brigade to a depot for that purpose. Butler, however, had sallied from Bermuda Hundred and threatened Drewry's Bluff, the mainstay of Richmond's lower defensive line. With Federals advancing on Richmond, Davis had countermanded Hoke's instructions. The immediate danger to the Confederacy's capital was simply too great to permit the release of soldiers to Lee. "I anticipated your want of fresh troops, and have earnestly watched for an opportunity to send them," Davis assured Lee in closing, but "I dare not promise anything now." Unless the

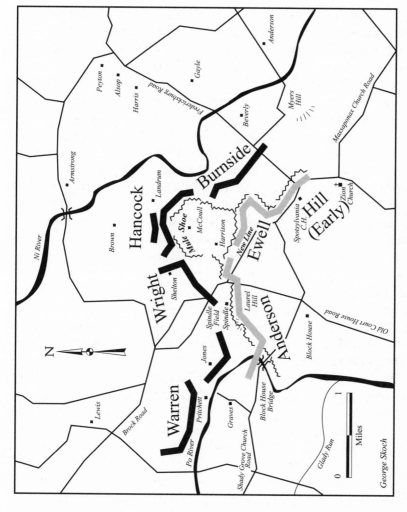

Grant and Lee at Spotsylvania Court House, May 13, 1864

George Skoch

strategic picture improved around Richmond or in the Shenandoah Valley, Lee would have to manage with the troops that he already had.[27]

"Found him in full force, rather stronger than the day before."

Grant's objective on May 13 was to determine the whereabouts of the Confederate army and to untangle his own units from the previous day's fighting. Rain, mud, rebel sharpshooters, and fatigue plagued both enterprises.

Morning's first light penetrated a thick haze of mist and rain to illuminate a ghastly scene. Even hardened veterans recoiled at the slaughter. "Not a blade of grass, twig, or shrub left standing," an observer whispered in awe. Corpses stained to nondescript dirty orange lay heaped to the top of the earthworks at the Bloody Angle. "Thick as you ever saw birds in a barnyard," reflected a New Yorker. Bodies floated in foul mixtures of rainwater, mud, and blood. "I saw several wounded men in the breastworks buried under their dead, just move a hand a little as it stuck up through the interstices above the dead bodies that buried the live ones otherwise completely from sight," a Federal reported. "Could anything in Hades be any worse?" he asked. "It seems like a horrible nightmare." A Wisconsin man reminisced: "The field was a horrible sight. We could there realize the havoc of war—the carnage was frightful." [28]

Troops from Wright's and Hancock's Union corps gingerly explored the abandoned Confederate works. A New Yorker thought that he and his companions resembled "pigs in dirt," they were so filthy and soaked to the bone. Colonel Horatio N. Warren of the 142nd Pennsylvania was lamenting the loss of his raincoat when he stumbled over a soldier covered with a rubber blanket. Assuming that the man was asleep, Warren gently lifted the blanket, only to discover that it cloaked a corpse. Was it right, he brooded, to rob a deceased comrade of covering? "After mature deliberation, I decided it was," the colonel admitted, "and took the blanket and made good use of it." Sergeant Wyman S. White of the 2nd United States Sharpshooters found a dead rebel officer astride a horse, which was also dead, a single shell having killed rider and mount. The Confederate's eyes stared wide open, and his face twisted angrily in a grimace capturing the excitement of his last charge. White needed a dry rag to clean his gun, so he sliced through the Confederate's clothing and snipped a piece of material from his undergarment. White's major laughed when White later told him about the Confederate. Other soldiers had rifled $300 and a gold watch from the dead officer, the major explained. White was nonplused. "I never allowed myself to take anything of value off a dead soldier's body excepting water and food and in one instance some tenting that I needed," he boasted.[29]

A Vermont man breathed a sigh of relief as he examined the Mule Shoe. The Confederates seemed to have left. "My prayer for Lee's withdrawal last night was granted," he scrawled in his diary, heartened at the prospect of a break in the incessant combat. He would soon be disappointed.[30]

A mile south, Ewell's Confederates sprawled in exhaustion behind their new entrenchments. Some wept, unabashedly rejoicing at having escaped the Mule Shoe alive. They splashed their hands and faces in pools of rainwater to wash away the gore and examined each other for injuries. Bill West of the 16th Mississippi provoked intense interest among his compatriots. He had gone into battle wearing a skullcap with a patent leather visor. Bullets had clipped the left and right sides of the headgear, shaping it into a triangular point, and a round had split the cap from front to back, giving West an unnatural part atop his head. Minié balls had severed one of West's earlobes, crisscrossed his blanket roll, and sliced his trousers in three places. A hole in his left breast pocket documented where a bullet had buried itself in a deck of cards that a comrade had urged West to chuck as he went into the fight. "No, my mother taught me how to play cards, and she is a good Christian and a member of the Episcopal Church," West had replied. "I have never gambled with this deck, and I am going to stand by my convictions." The decision saved his life. Camp rumor had it that the ball penetrated to the ace of spades, which West declared to be his lucky card.[31]

After roll call the southerners broke ranks and stretched out in the mud. Wagons brought up cornmeal and bacon, but the men were too tired to eat, and everyone's nerves were shot. A Texan precipitated a "terrible roll of musketry" along the entire line when he accidentally discharged his rifle. "For a few minutes the fusillade continued, before the half-awakened and startled men could be convinced that it was only a panic occasioned by their strained and nervous condition," an officer reminisced. The soldiers remained preoccupied with their close call with death in the Mule Shoe. "I don't suppose there is any man that can express the relief we felt after getting out of such a place," a Tar Heel wrote home. "There is not a man in this brigade who will ever forget it." Another Confederate admitted: "I am too worn out to write anything of interest. I am about half dead yet, as is every one else from the effects of the cannonading." A Georgian remembered the day for rain and mud. "We resembled more than anything else an aggregation of animated terra cotta models," he affirmed. Noted a Mississippian: "Got some rations, washed our powder stained faces, discharged and cleaned up our guns and slept."[32]

At 5:00 A.M. Hancock ordered a thorough reconnaissance of the abandoned

Confederate position. Skirmishers cautiously advanced into the gloom from Major General David B. Birney's division, which held the Mule Shoe's tip; from Brigadier General John Gibbon's division, which wrapped around the formation's eastern face; and from Brigadier General Francis C. Barlow's division, which connected on its left with Burnside's 9th Corps. Sharpshooters reconnoitered well into the former Confederate stronghold. They met no organized resistance. Nor did they uncover any indication of where Lee had gone. Had he retreated under cover of darkness or merely retired to a new line close by? Grant wanted to maintain the initiative and catch the Confederates before they could entrench. "I was afraid that Lee might be moving out," he later wrote, "and I did not want him to go without my knowing it." [33]

Union scouts were soon swarming over the abandoned Mule Shoe. Among them was the sharpshooter White, who warily approached the McCoull home, in the salient's interior. As he entered the clearing around the house, Confederates hidden in timber near the building opened fire. White picked his way to a corn barn and peeked through a crack. A rebel stood not six inches from his face. "I thought it was either him or me," White related, "so I quickly ran around the building, jumped inside, placed the muzzle of my rifle within a foot of the Johnny's head and said in a strong voice, 'Throw down that rifle!'" Dropping his gun, the rebel implored, "Don't fire Yank. I am sick. Don't murder me." White led the prisoner away at gunpoint, gave him food, and then took him to his division's provost guard. The Mule Shoe was crawling with rebels, White reported, but he had seen no organized enemy presence. He could not say how much of Lee's army remained or what had happened to the rest of it. [34]

Activity also picked up in Warren's sector. The 5th Corps's earthworks stretched from Brock Road to the Po River to form the Union force's western wing. Facing Warren was Field's division of Anderson's corps, steadfastly dug in along Laurel Hill. On May 12 Grant had dispatched two of Warren's three divisions to the Bloody Angle, leaving him only Brigadier General Samuel W. Crawford's division of Pennsylvania Reserves, the badly decimated Maryland Brigade, and two heavy artillery regiments under Colonel J. Howard Kitching. Concerned about the safety of his right flank, Warren had pushed elements from the 118th Pennsylvania and 1st Michigan into an extended skirmish line. The general and his staff had passed the night of May 12–13 in a "sea of mud," fearful that the rebels might attack. "There was not much sleep or rest," a soldier reported. A Michigan man christened the experience a "night of terrors." [35]

Early on May 13 Grant began returning to the 5th Corps the troops that he had borrowed the previous day. Brigadier General Lysander Cutler's division arrived first, and Warren posted the outfit east of Brock Road, on Crawford's left flank. Brigadier General Charles Griffin's division arrived soon afterward and slipped into earthworks immediately west of the roadway. Griffin formed Brigadier General Joseph J. Bartlett's brigade at a right angle to the 5th Corps's main line, connecting to the 6th Corps on its left. Around 7:00 A.M., inquisitive as to the strength of the Confederates on Laurel Hill, Bartlett directed the 83rd Pennsylvania to yell and discharge a few shots. The experiment provoked a fusillade of rebel musketry—delivered "with a great deal of animosity," according to a Pennsylvanian—that satisfied Bartlett's curiosity. "The enemy is still there with artillery in position enfilading my advance," Warren reported. Grant, who had learned to question the 5th Corps commander's judgment, reminded Warren that he was not to engage the enemy, but simply to determine the rebels' position and strength.[36]

Anxious to resolve once and for all what lay behind the Mule Shoe's smoldering wreckage, Hancock dispatched Brigadier General Joshua T. Owen's brigade on a reconnaissance in force. Owen's men were conveniently positioned for the operation, but Owen was unavailable, so Hancock directed Brigadier General Samuel S. Carroll to lead the brigade. "Brick" Carroll, distinctive for his red hair, reveled in combat. When Hancock's summons arrived, he was tending to his arm, which had been injured in the Wilderness. Ignoring his wound, he quickly set about executing his new assignment.[37]

At 8:00 A.M. Carroll's men vaulted over the Mule Shoe's eastern apex, scooped up a discarded Confederate flag, and pressed into the salient's interior. Rebel pickets offered stiff opposition. Carroll, riding high on horseback with his red hair flying like a battle flag, made an inviting target. A sharp-eyed rebel took deliberate aim at the plucky general—Carroll saw the raised musket in time to wonder where the bullet would strike—and shot him in his uninjured arm, shattering his elbow. Orderlies carried Carroll to the rear while his soldiers continued to the Mule Shoe's base. There the ground descended into a ravine. On the far side, a short distance behind the Harrison house, loomed Ewell's fresh earthworks. Concluding that the rebels were firmly entrenched, Carroll's party fell back to its starting position.[38]

Wreathed in cigar smoke on Mrs. Armstrong's porch, Grant pondered the meaning of the latest information from the front. Warren's reports made it clear that Confederates still held Laurel Hill, and Hancock's forays established that the rebels had left the Mule Shoe, apparently to assume a new position about a mile back. The strength of the new line was anyone's guess, but Grant suspected that Lee had lost severely during the previous day's melee. If so, he was most likely abandoning the town and had left behind a skeleton force to discourage pursuit. At 8:40 A.M. Grant committed his hunch to writing. "I do not infer the enemy are making a stand," he informed Meade, "but [are] simply covering a retreat, which must necessarily have been slow with such roads and so dark a night as they had last night." Enlarging on Grant's sentiments, a newspaperman at headquarters reported that Lee's "hungry and disorganized" army was streaming back "in disorder." Assistant War Secretary Dana remained skeptical. "Lee abandoned his old position during the night," he advised in a dispatch to Washington. "Whether to occupy a new one in the vicinity or to make a thorough retreat is not determined." As usual, the soldiers' instincts were more finely honed than those of their generals. "I heard the enemy was retreating but it cannot be unless he has left a large skirmish line," a man in the 126th Ohio wrote his wife.[39]

Lacking cavalry—the army's veteran horsemen had left on a raid toward Richmond—Grant turned to his infantry to gather intelligence. "Push with at least three good divisions to see beyond doubt what they are doing," he instructed Meade, who in turn directed each of his corps commanders to advance a division. The results were conclusive. On the Union right, Crawford eased into the Spindle field and stirred up another daunting burst of musketry. The 97th New York reported twelve men lost in the brief affair, prompting Warren to advise against further advance in his sector. "Found [Lee] in full force, rather stronger than the day before," noted one of Warren's aides. Wright, in the center of the Union formation, confirmed that Ewell's rebels had left the Mule Shoe. They seemed "pretty well entrenched" in their new line, he added, and predicted they would make their position "even stronger today." Hancock agreed. Two of his brigades—Owen's again, and Colonel H. Boyd McKeen's—retraced Carroll's earlier route, took a second look at Ewell's new line, and pronounced it impregnable.[40]

The new round of intelligence persuaded Dana to revise his assessment. "The impression that Lee had started on his retreat which prevailed at the date of my dispatch of this morning is not confirmed," he wrote Washington at noon. "Our skirmishers have found the rebels along the whole line, and the conclusion now is that their retrograde movement of last night was made to correct their position after the loss of the key-points taken from them yesterday, and that they are still before us in force."[41]

Newspapermen and politicians would put an optimistic face on the recent battles, but Grant and his soldiers felt discouraged. Lee stood firmly ensconced across the route to Richmond, unbowed and undefeated. Profound weariness of body and spirit gripped the sodden Union camps. Wright's 6th Corps, which had endured some of May 12's most severe fighting, settled into a line running from Warren's left to the Bloody Angle. On the 6th

Corps's left, Hancock's 2nd Corps resigned itself to a miserable day amidst corpses and rebel sharpshooters. Some units "reversed" the vacant Confederate earthworks while others constructed new barricades a short distance back. Burnside's 9th Corps continued the Union line southeast to Fredericksburg Road, facing Early's Confederates. In places Early's earthworks rose only a few hundred yards away, and "venomous little bullets" pelted the 9th Corps's position. "A feeling of dread uncertainty pervaded the troops," a Massachusetts man asserted.[42]

Letters home starkly mirrored the impact that constant exposure to death and inclement weather had wrought on the Potomac Army's morale. Whenever musketry slackened, troops buried corpses, hauled in wounded men, and picked off ticks, which seemed especially numerous. Burial details laid fallen comrades on blankets, threw more blankets on top of the corpses, and covered them with dirt. Cracker-box boards served as headstones, with names inscribed in large letters. "I am writing this seated in the mud covered with blood and dirt and powder," a Federal jotted home. "It was a dirty, despondent crowd of soldiers who gathered about the smoldering fires, made their coffee and recounted their experiences of the day," remembered another. "We are as dirty as possible," an aide wrote his sister. "I have not shaved since I left Washington, and only changed my shirt once." Hunger seemed universal and drove men to extreme acts. An officer in the 6th New Hampshire earnestly threatened to shoot his regiment's cooks unless they delivered coffee to the front three times a day. A soldier in the 45th Pennsylvania gauged the effect of scant rations by monitoring his belt notches. When the army started across the Rapidan, his belt had fit perfectly on the last notch. On reaching Spotsylvania, he had cinched the belt up one hole. Now he gave it another hitch. A military band wandering disconsolately behind Burnside's line mirrored the men's sinking spirits. A soldier thought the musicians resembled "wet fowls, in the rain and mud, their instruments bruised and clothing much the worse for the ten days south of the Rapidan."[43]

A Union artilleryman questioned whether his family could comprehend "the desolate country we are in—ten times worse than the Jersey pines." Another soldier reported "nothing here but water and mud." The troops, observed a colonel, were in a "deplorable condition of exhaustion" and could scarcely muster sufficient strength to dodge the constant flow of Confederate projectiles that winged through the drizzly gloom to explode randomly among them. "Here it is again," a New Yorker groused, "throwing up trenches under a hail of shells from the rebels." Burrowing into the mud, a Federal reflected that he was "alive and well, how or why God only knows." Every man was "anxious, weary, worn out," a New Yorker opined. Predicted a Pennsylvanian: "This thing cannot last much longer, for one side or the other must yield from sheer exhaustion."[44]

Newton Kirk, the wounded Michigan soldier, drifted in and out of consciousness all day. A Confederate surgeon offered him a swig from his canteen, which contained either brandy or whiskey. The field near the McCoull house where Kirk and hundreds of other wounded men lay had become a no-man's land between the hostile armies, home to snipers and skirmishers. Late in the day a Confederate ambulance picked up Kirk and carried him to a hospital behind Ewell's new line. He regained consciousness to find himself lying on a soggy patch of ground in a Confederate field hospital. Someone had stretched a tent cloth over a stick to shelter him from the rain. Severed arms and legs that surgeons had haphazardly pitched from an operating table lay strewn on the earth nearby. A list of the hospital's patients read like a roster of Ewell's 2nd Corps, which had defended the Mule Shoe. Colonel William Witcher had passed through, dazed from a blow to his temple, as had General Ramseur, wounded in the arm. Dr. Hunter McGuire had probed the limb of James Walker, commander of the famed Stonewall Brigade, who lay prostrate from shock, blood streaming from a shattered elbow. When Walker overheard a surgeon suggest amputation, he had pleaded, "Don't let them cut it off, McGuire. I'd rather die than lose my arm." McGuire called for Dr. Galt, of Baltimore, a skilled bone surgeon. Together they decided to saw out Walker's elbow joint, join the severed muscles and nerves, and stabilize the limb with wooden splints. Applying a dose of chloroform, they removed six to eight inches of bone. "I just wish I had you all at the front," the drugged general babbled. "I would put you where the bullets fly." The next morning, delirious and burning with fever, he was loaded on a wagon bound for his father's home in the Shenandoah Valley.[45]

Less fortunate was General Daniel, painfully shot in the abdomen. Doctors informed him that he would die before his wife could arrive. His last queries involved his men. Had they acquitted themselves well, he asked. How bad were the losses?[46]

"A movement by the left promised an opportunity."

The tapestry of rolling fields and woods between Washington and Richmond, bounded on the west by the Blue Ridge Mountains and on the east by Chesapeake Bay, framed the theater of operations for the Army of the Potomac and the Army of Northern Virginia. Virginia's rivers, railways, and roads provided paths for troops and supplies. Geography was to dominate Grant's and Lee's plans for the battles to come.

As rain transformed the countryside into bottomless pools of mud, Grant pondered his maps. How best could he get at Lee, who seemed more firmly entrenched than ever? Since crossing the Rapidan, Grant had striven to maintain the initiative by maneuvering and attacking. Should he probe once again for vulnerable points in the rebel defenses, or should he leave Spotsylvania Court House and seek battle elsewhere? Grant could not help noticing that in many respects his military posture on May 13 resembled the situation he had faced on May 7, following the Battle of the Wilderness. On that occasion, rather than blindly battering Lee's fortified line, he had swung south, gambling that Lee would follow to protect the Confederate capital. Lee had reacted as Grant had predicted, abandoning his earthworks and offering Grant a chance to engage him on ground favorable to the Federals. The episode confirmed a valuable point. If Grant nudged toward Richmond, Lee would follow. Perhaps, Grant reflected as he gathered his thoughts on Mrs. Armstrong's porch, the time had come to repeat the stratagem.

A look at the map clarified matters. At Spotsylvania Court House Grant was handsomely positioned to dart south. Telegraph Road, still lined with poles and wires that once buzzed with messages between Richmond and Washington, passed four miles east of town, in the Union army's rear. A few miles farther east, the Richmond, Fredericksburg, and Potomac Railroad provided a second path to the rebel capital. By starting his army in motion along these twin routes at night, Grant could advance well toward Richmond before Lee had time to react. But Grant also recognized that moving the battlefield south raised troubling prospects. When Lee learned of Grant's departure— the Confederate's network of scouts would see to it that he got immediate notice—the Army of Northern Virginia would most likely rush south along parallel roads. The Union army would be exceedingly vulnerable while in motion, offering the rebels a chance to close in like a pack of hungry wolves and attack the marching blue columns. Grant had no confidence that the Army of the Potomac, even with a head start, could beat Lee to the North Anna River, an imposing water barrier on the order of the Rapidan, twenty-five miles to the south. The Union army's record gave Grant sound cause for pessimism. Judging from the maneuver to Spotsylvania Court House, Lee would win the race to the North Anna. Grant had no desire to abandon his current line only to face the Confederates across another set of formidable works. Moreover, shifting the theater of operations south would serve to lengthen Grant's supply line and shorten Lee's. It would also put Lee near potential reinforcements from the Richmond defenses.

Balancing these factors, Grant decided to tarry at Spotsylvania Court House. He felt certain that the engagement of May 12 had seriously damaged the Army of Northern Virginia. Perhaps one more blow would finish the job. Rather than afford Lee time to regroup, he settled on renewing his attacks right away. If more pounding failed to crack Lee's defenses, Grant would still have the option of reconsidering a turning movement to the North Anna River.

Having determined a course of action—the Army of the Potomac would strike another massive blow before Lee could recover his equilibrium— Grant turned to the knotty problem of how best to get at Lee. Five days of battering had demonstrated the futility of frontal assaults. Perhaps maneuver held the answer. One option was to turn the Confederates out of their entrenchments by sending the Union army swarming across the Po past Lee's left, or northern, flank. Warren, who thrived on recommending strategies to his superiors, favored such a move. "It seems to me if General Burnside would intrench himself in a safe position, with his flanks on the Ni, that we could safely cross the Po and get a battle out of Lee in a fair field," the 5th Corps commander suggested. But Warren's plan neglected unpleasant realities. To get at Lee's left flank, the Union flanking force would have to cross the Po under fire. Even if the Federals survived that ordeal, Lee's army would stand between them and their supplies. Not only would the maneuver split the Union army and expose each portion to attack, but it would leave the route south open for Lee to escape. Meade's chief-of-staff Humphreys dismissed Warren's proposal on the ground that it would result "in Lee's abandoning his intrenchments at once and taking position behind the North Anna." Humphreys's objection carried the day, and Grant vetoed the idea of turning Lee's northern flank.[47]

Concentrating south toward Lee's right flank, on the other hand, posed intriguing possibilities. Fredericksburg Road entered Spotsylvania Court House from the northeast, and Massaponax Church Road approached the town from the east. The two routes reached the town less than half a mile apart. The lower end of Early's earthworks covered Fredericksburg Road, but Massaponax Church Road was only lightly defended. A resolute assault along both roads might succeed, particularly if simultaneous attacks against the rest of Lee's line prevented the Confederates from rushing reinforcements to Early. If the effort failed, Grant would still be favorably positioned to initiate his maneuver toward the North Anna, and his supply line to Fredericksburg would remain secure. Humphreys liked the idea. As he explained it, "a movement by the left promised an opportunity of attacking Lee's right before it could be reinforced from his left or his intrenchments extended [while] at the same time it would cover our hospitals and communication with our depots in Washington."[48]

Casting about for troops to execute the plan, Grant hit on an ingenious idea. After dark, Warren and Wright, constituting the Union army's right wing, would disengage and march behind Hancock and Burnside to become the army's left wing. Warren would form on Fredericksburg Road and Wright on Massaponax Church Road, on Warren's left. Hancock and Burnside would assume a "threatening attitude" to divert Lee's attention. The payoff would come on May 14 at 4:00 A.M., Grant's favorite time for launching attacks. At the commander in chief's signal, Warren and Wright would charge and overrun Early. As the lower end of Lee's line collapsed, Hancock and Burnside would jump in and administer the decisive blow. There was always the chance, of course, that Lee might discover Grant's redeployment and prepare to meet it by reinforcing Early. But it was equally possible that the stormy weather would work to Grant's advantage—as it had when Grant shifted large portions of his army in preparation for his attack on May 12—and conceal from Lee the fact that Grant had initiated a major troop movement.[49]

In Grant's book, the possibility of success justified the risk of discovery, and he directed Meade and Humphreys to prepare the orders necessary to set the troops in motion right away. Bold in conception, the scheme was vintage Grant. In his enthusiasm, however, the general afforded scant consideration to the fact that two days of rain had turned roads into quagmires, that ambulances and prisoners obstructed the thoroughfares, and that troops earmarked for the movement were tired, hungry, and without provisions. Grant also lacked concrete information about the configuration of Lee's lower flank and the strength of the units stationed there. The Union cavalry's expedition toward Richmond left Grant to initiate maneuvers on guesswork and hunches.

How was Grant's cavalry faring? Did its accomplishments justify its absence? The answer lay sixty miles south, on the outskirts of Richmond at a crossing of the Chickahominy River called Meadow Bridge.

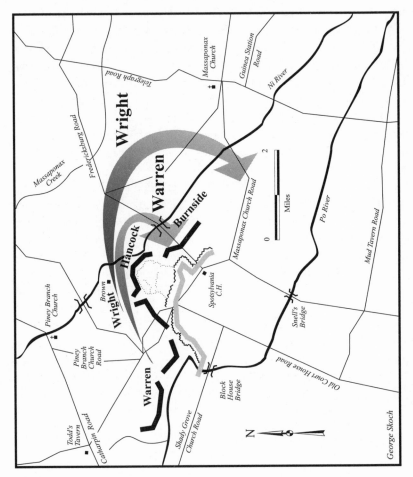

Grant's plan of attack for May 13–14

II

MAY 12–13

Sheridan Threatens Richmond and Escapes at Meadow Bridge

"You will find him big enough for the purpose."

MAJOR GENERAL PHILIP H. SHERIDAN, the Army of the Potomac's cavalry chief, had every reason to be pleased on the rainy evening of May 11, 1864. In three days he had substantially destroyed much of the Army of Northern Virginia's commissary, liberated several hundred Union prisoners, whipped the Confederate mounted arm, and mortally wounded the vaunted rebel cavalier Major General James Ewell Brown "Jeb" Stuart. Sheridan's horsemen stood at Richmond's gates, prepared to punch through the city's defenses and occupy the very seat of the Confederacy. What made the triumph especially sweet was the discomfort Sheridan knew his success was causing Meade. In the increasingly bitter feud between the two generals, the feisty son of an Irish immigrant was coming out on top.

The Army of the Potomac's cavalry corps had displayed heartening promise during 1863. Winter, however, had darkened its prospects. Brigadier General John Buford, the Union cavalry's illustrious star, died of typhoid fever; Brigadier General Judson Kilpatrick, the experienced and flamboyant division commander, went west in disgrace after a failed raid on Richmond; and Major General Alfred Pleasonton, the corps's head, had fallen out of favor. Shortly after taking charge of the Union war effort, Grant concluded that a shakeup was in order. Sheridan had impressed Grant with his aggressive performance at Missionary Ridge, and Grant offered him command of the cavalry corps. Lured by promises of promotion and fame, Sheridan took the job and the major general's stars that went with it.

Before assuming his new post, Sheridan met with President Lincoln. Only five feet five inches tall and disheveled, Sheridan worried that he might make an unfavorable impression, and he did just that. A "brown, chunky little chap,"

Lincoln later described him, "with a long body, short legs, not enough neck to hang him, and such long arms that if his ankles itch he can scratch them without stooping." The interview ended with a biting remark by the president. In the past the Army of the Potomac's cavalry had failed to accomplish "all that it might have done," he observed, and he repeated the popular gibe, "Who ever saw a dead cavalryman?" Sheridan privately vowed to change that perception.[1]

Sheridan was a curious choice for the cavalry job. His mounted combat experience was limited to a brief stint heading the 2nd Michigan Cavalry. Having fought only in the west, he knew little about Meade's army and operations in Virginia. Troopers resented serving under a general from a different arm of the service, and several senior officers were offended at having been passed over. Sheridan wisely retained most of the corps's staffers, easing his transition. According to one cavalryman, he made "everywhere a favorable impression," although his youth and short stature provoked disparaging remarks. The observation went around that he was "rather a little fellow" to handle the army's cavalry. "You will find him big enough for the purpose before we get through with him," Grant promised Lincoln.[2]

True to Grant's prediction, Sheridan rolled up his sleeves and went to work. Surprise visits to the army's stables disclosed broken-down horses, equipage in disrepair, and units shamefully unfit for battle. Sheridan blamed lax discipline, and he clamped down. He also faulted Meade's practice of using cavalry to man the sixty-mile picket line that encircled the army's encampments and requested an audience with Meade. The two men immediately disliked each other and clashed sharply over how cavalry should be used. Meade thought Sheridan's horsemen should shield infantry, protect wagons, and scout the enemy's positions. Sheridan wanted to act independently of infantry, massing his mounted arm to fight Lee's cavalry. Meade agreed to relieve Sheridan's troopers from outpost duty but would compromise no further. For the impending campaign he directed Sheridan to ride in the army's vanguard to conceal it from Lee.[3]

By mid-April Sheridan had selected his division commanders. Two had even less cavalry experience than he did. Brash Brigadier General James H. Wilson, one of Grant's former aides, was only twenty-seven years old and had never led troops in combat. He was smart and could cut through red tape, but nobody knew how he would do in battle. Brigadier General Alfred T. A. Torbert had never commanded cavalry either, but he at least was no stranger to warfare, having earned a distinguished record heading a brigade of New Jersey troops. The only professional cavalryman in Sheridan's top lineup was Brigadier General David McM. Gregg. Almost everyone liked the heavily bearded Pennsylvanian, who was singular for his modesty, a trait rare among the cavalry. Rumor had it that Gregg had angled to head the cavalry corps, but that his seemingly complacent demeanor had cost him the job, which went to Sheridan instead.

Sheridan embarked on the spring campaign with 12,424 cavalrymen "present for duty equipped." According to Wilson, the Federal mounted arm was as "nearly ready as volunteer cavalry ever is." Some regiments carried seven-shot carbines, which multiplied their firepower, and six batteries of horse artillery containing thirty-two cannon accompanied the mounted host.[4]

Opposing Sheridan was Jeb Stuart. Tall and athletic, with arresting blue eyes twinkling over a full beard and mustache, Stuart symbolized the brash, youthful spirit of the Army of Northern Virginia. He was also a daring and innovative leader of cavalry whose bold exploits had made him a legend. Stuart headed a force of about eight thousand troopers. Commanding his three divisions were Major General Fitzhugh Lee, General Robert E. Lee's nephew and a veteran of Indian campaigns; General Lee's son, Major General William H. F. "Rooney" Lee, recently released from confinement in Union prisons; and Major General Wade Hampton, a South Carolina planter with a natural aptitude for cavalry.

The critical question was whether Sheridan and his subordinates could continue the Union cavalry advancement that winter's setbacks had so cruelly curtailed. At first it seemed Federal horsemen could do nothing right. Wilson—Sheridan's least experienced combat officer, leading the smallest mounted division—botched his assignment of patrolling the countryside between the advancing Union army and the Confederates and enabled Lee to ambush Grant in the Wilderness. Then Sheridan failed to clear the way for the army's move to Spotsylvania Court House. The simmering feud between Meade and Sheridan boiled over on May 8 when the irate Irishman stormed into Meade's tent fuming that Meade was wrecking his cavalry by forcing it into disjointed operations. Meade retorted that Sheridan was responsible for the campaign's failures. After a heated round of expletives, Sheridan stamped off in a huff. When Meade informed Grant of Sheridan's boast that he could defeat Stuart if Meade would only let him, Grant perked up. After three days of watching Meade and his generals flounder, he found Sheridan's belligerence refreshing. "Did Sheridan say that?" Grant inquired. "Well, he generally knows what he is talking about. Let him start right out and do it."[5]

Freed from Meade, Sheridan planned to march his cavalry slowly toward Richmond. The plumed Confederate cavalry chief, he predicted, would take the bait and leave the protective umbrella of Lee's army. After defeating Stuart—an outcome that Sheridan never doubted—he planned to continue on to Haxall's Landing on the James River and rendezvous with Butler's Army of the James. Early on May 9 Sheridan swung his corps east of the armies, then headed south, intending to draw Stuart after him. His lead elements crossed the North Anna River and struck the Virginia Central Railroad at Beaver Dam Station, freeing several hundred captured Federals, burning boxcars of Confederate food and medical supplies, and destroying miles of track. Stuart reacted much as Sheridan had predicted, riding with Fitzhugh Lee's division to intercept Sheridan near Richmond and dispatching Brigadier General James B. Gordon's brigade to harass Sheridan's rear. On May 11 Fitzhugh Lee and Sheridan collided seven miles above the capital at Yellow Tavern. In a violent thunderstorm, Brigadier General George A. Custer's Michigan brigade overwhelmed the Confederates, and a Federal trooper gunned Stuart down. Aides led the mortally wounded general from the battlefield. "Go back! Go back!" Stuart exhorted his men. "I had rather die than be whipped." But whipped he was, having fatally underestimated the diminutive Yankee general from Ohio. As the sun dipped below the horizon, a somber procession accompanied the dying southern hero's ambulance on its roundabout way to Richmond.[6]

Fitzhugh Lee remained north of the battlefield near Half Sink, rallying the fragments of his broken command as they dribbled back from the fiasco. Even in this bleak hour, he began casting about for a way to avenge the humiliating loss at Yellow Tavern. Opportunity would come sooner than he imagined, and from an unexpected quarter. Sheridan's ambition was about to deliver the Union mounted force into Fitzhugh Lee's eager hands.

"I certainly don't expect to see the like again, and don't especially want to."

On the evening of May 11 Sheridan's troopers camped around Yellow Tavern, savoring victory. "I slept on the ground against a stump," a cavalryman recollected of his soggy bivouac. Confederates swarmed around, but the Federals, secure in their numbers, remained unconcerned. "All expressed confidence in the general being able to get us out," a Union man reminisced. The cocky troopers began styling themselves "Sheridan's Bold Men."[7]

Sheridan pondered his options. He had intended to circle east of Richmond and join Butler on the James River, but tantalizing opportunities beckoned. Richmond was less than seven miles away, defended by a few raw units of government clerks. From Yellow Tavern, Brook Pike ran due south, crossed a tributary of the Chickahominy River called Brook Run, then climbed a gentle slope to Richmond's outer defensive line. Only a token force of Confederates manned these fortifications, and some of Sheridan's advance

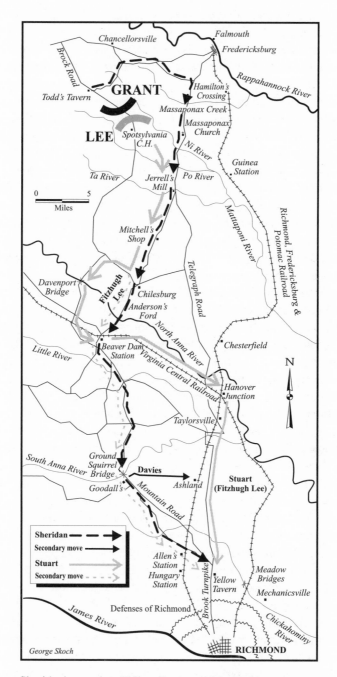

Sheridan's march to Yellow Tavern on May 9–11

units had already overrun them with ease. A second ring of earthworks, Richmond's intermediate defenses, loomed a mile and a half behind the first, and still farther back, star forts bristled along the city's outskirts. Sheridan expected no serious resistance, as veteran Confederate troops in the area were tied up confronting Butler.

Victory at Yellow Tavern had given the ambitious young general a name. Taking Richmond stood to make him the toast of the North. Never again would people inquire, "Who's Sheridan?" Tempted as Sheridan was to capture Richmond, however, sober reflection persuaded him that the venture's dangers outweighed its potential gains. The tactical advantages of entering the rebel capital were negligible. Even if Sheridan pierced Richmond's defenses, he could never hold the place, and he ran substantial risk that Confederates might trap him there.

It made better sense, Sheridan concluded, to proceed as initially planned, circumventing Richmond and hooking up with Butler on the James River. From Sheridan's bivouac at Yellow Tavern several roads offered a safe route to the east around Richmond. But the general's fighting blood was up, and he did not want to leave the impression that he was afraid of the capital's defenders. Before dark, Sheridan accompanied a reconnoitering party to Brook Church, which stood on Brook Pike a short distance inside Richmond's outer defensive line. A military road led east from the church, threading between the intermediate and outer works. Sheridan decided to bring his corps to Brook Church, then follow the military road to Fair Oaks Station, east of the capital. "If I could succeed in getting through by this road, not only would I have a shorter line of march to Haxall's landing, but there was also a possibility that I could help Butler somewhat by joining him so near Richmond," was the reason he later gave for his decision. Doubtless, he selected this route also because it afforded him a chance to tweak the Confederates in Richmond. His brazen decision was soon to cause some uneasy moments.[8]

Shortly after dark, Sheridan received news that further encouraged him in his plan. A major in the 6th New York Cavalry captured a rebel courier with a message from Braxton Bragg, military adviser to President Davis. The dispatch, directed to Stuart, cautioned that Richmond had no troops to spare. This intelligence reassured Sheridan that he had little to fear from the capital's defenders.[9]

At 11:00 P.M. on May 11, six short hours after the battle at Yellow Tavern, Sheridan started south along Brook Pike. The troopers sensed momentous events brewing, and some predicted that they would breakfast in Richmond. "The general impression was that we were going in," a cavalryman recalled. Wilson's division led, followed by Torbert's—commanded by Brigadier

General Wesley Merritt, filling in while Torbert convalesced from a spinal abscess—then by Gregg's. The broad highway, lined with hedgerows, presented a refreshing change after three days of rough Virginia roads. A mile below Yellow Tavern the pike descended to Brook Run, which the troopers crossed on a high arched bridge. Houses became frequent, and low clouds reflected the glow of lamps in Richmond. "The consciousness that we were moving straight upon the capital of the Southern Confederacy overcame the sense of fatigue and inspired everyone with a novel and ardent emotion," a Federal effused. Soldiers and horses, remarked another, shared a "magnetic unison of sentiment."[10]

Jubilation turned to concern as rain, mud, and darkness slowed the advance to a crawl. Musketry from stray rebel scouts crackled through the blackness. "Vivid flashes of lightning lit up the gloom," a Federal noted, "while peals of thunder rolled away in the distance, to be lost in fresh reverberations nearby, each one seeming to increase the fall of rain." Gaps opened in the line, accordionlike, setting Sheridan's officers scrambling to close the ranks. "I know of nothing which creates such an appalling sense of loneliness as the fact of being left behind in an enemy's country at night," an officer related of the march.[11]

The foremost troopers discovered that southern defenders had sewn the roadbed with land mines—torpedoes, in the vernacular—fashioned from live shells. Trip wires triggered some of the devices, Confederates hiding beside the road detonated others, and some were so sensitive that the concussion of horses' hoofs set them off. After losing several horses and men to the contraptions, Sheridan forced a squad of gray-clad prisoners to clear the way. Soon twenty-five Confederates, frightened out of their wits, were crawling on their knees in front of the mounted column, gingerly feeling for wires. "This kind of work required a delicate touch and was unpleasantly exciting," a captive later admitted. A soldier in the 6th Ohio discovered a thin line connected to several torpedoes and followed it to a rebel hiding in the woods. He returned with his captive and sliced the cord into short lengths as souvenirs.[12]

Slowed by torpedoes and rain, Sheridan took four hours to cover the three miles from Yellow Tavern to Brook Church. "We had the utmost confidence in our commander, and knew that he would take us safely through," a Massachusetts man affirmed. "Still it was discouraging to be hustled about in the dark, with the rain pouring down nearly all the time." Reminisced one of Merritt's aides: "It was thundering and lightning in the great style overhead, and the torpedoes blowing up under foot. Altogether, I certainly don't expect to see the like again, and don't especially want to."[13]

At 3:00 A.M. Wilson reached Brook Church and turned his division left onto the military road. Merritt's and Gregg's divisions halted as they reached the church and dismounted, waiting for daylight. They could hear Confederates filing into Richmond's intermediate fortifications, a mile and a half south.

Richmond was in a stir. Since May 5 Butler's Army of the James had been advancing slowly toward the capital from the southeast, riveting the city's attention. On May 10 rumors abounded that Butler had reached nearby Chester, and that fighting had erupted at Drewry's Bluff, five miles below the city on the James River. Yankees were too close for comfort, and the home guard assembled to the clanging of church bells. That evening, flames licked the horizon in the direction of Drewry's Bluff. Then reports arrived of Sheridan's expedition. Union cavalry, went the news, had burnt Beaver Dam Station and was descending from the north. Alarms sounded all night.

General Lee, who had delivered Richmond from Major General George B. McClellan in 1862, was miles away at Spotsylvania Court House, fighting Grant. This time, Richmond would have to fend for itself.

At 5:00 A.M. on May 11 Josiah Gorgas, the Confederacy's ordnance chief, visited War Secretary James A. Seddon, who expressed fear that Richmond's hours were "at length numbered." Sheridan was fast approaching, he cautioned, and might arrive before Stuart could intercept him. Virginia's governor posted a warning that Sheridan "may be expected at any hour with a view to [Richmond's] capture, its pillage, and its destruction." Able-bodied men were exhorted to assemble in Capitol Square. Soon the park overflowed with armed citizens, awaiting news. "Here anxiety was on the tiptoe," a reporter observed. The home militia congregated in the city's northern defenses, and Brigadier General Eppa Hunton's veteran brigade marched up from Chaffin's farm, a few miles away near the James River.[14]

Midmorning on May 11, President Davis received an enthusiastic dispatch from Stuart announcing his plan to intercept Sheridan at Yellow Tavern. Most likely, Richmond's gossips guessed, the Federals had veered off toward Dover Mills, in the direction of Goochland. The crowd breathed easier. Sheridan had apparently decided against taking Richmond and was instead making for the James River Canal. Consensus had it that he intended to cut the waterway, then swing counterclockwise below Richmond to join Butler.[15]

As Richmond's good citizens sat for supper on May 11, a reporter found them "relieved with the thought that the city was once more safe, and congratulating themselves that the Yankees had abandoned their advance on the city." At 8:00 P.M. news of Yankees on Brook Pike broke the calm. Two hours later, ambiguous reports of battle at Yellow Tavern reached Richmond. Stuart had been wounded in the hip, went the initial story, and Colonel Henry C. Pate of the 5th Virginia Cavalry killed, but otherwise the fighting had gone well. Sheridan, reports had it, was sandwiched between Richmond to his south and Stuart's horsemen to his north.[16]

To ensure that the sandwich's lower layer, Richmond's defensive line of forts, was sufficiently strong to contain Sheridan, more Confederates rushed to the city's northern suburbs. Brigadier General Seth M. Barton's brigade of Virginians, temporarily commanded by Colonel Birkett D. Fry, filed into the intermediate fortifications along Brook Pike, where Sheridan was likely to strike. A regiment of clerks—formally designated as the 3rd Virginia Battalion Defense Troops, and colloquially the Clerks and Citizens—shouldered muskets and deployed behind earthworks a mile east, across Meadow Bridge Road. To their right, near Mechanicsville Pike, a battalion of employees from Tredegar Iron Works—the 6th Virginia Battalion Local Defense Troops, known as the Tredegar Battalion—waited expectantly, muskets in hand. The civilians wanted Postmaster General John H. Reagan to command them, but President Davis insisted that he needed Reagan at cabinet meetings. At Reagan's urging, Colonel John McAnerney Jr., a northerner who had cast his lot with the South, assumed command of the home guard. Fires were forbidden, and troops remained under arms.[17]

While Richmond girded in anticipation of Sheridan's arrival, Fitzhugh Lee regrouped his shattered cavalry. Casting about to entrap the raiders, he hit on an ingenious plan. Richmond's authorities were confident that sufficient troops occupied the city's inner line of defenses to prevent Sheridan from continuing south. From Brook Church, where Sheridan was massing his command, no good roads led west. And to the north James Gordon's three North Carolina regiments were pestering Sheridan's rear and had firmly plugged Brook Pike. Three of Sheridan's four potential escape routes were closed, leaving him no choice but to angle east along the military road. As he did so, he would traverse a plateau bounded on the south by the Richmond defenses. To the north Brook Run and the Chickahominy joined to form a wide, marshy flood plain. Two causeways crossed this low-lying area. The western bridge carried Meadow Bridge Road, and the companion span supported the Virginia Central Railroad. East of the causeways Richmond's defensive line and the river slowly converged into a cul-de-sac at Mechanicsville Pike. Confederate siege guns dominated this dead end. Sheridan's only way out was to cross the twin causeways at Meadow Bridge. Rains, however, had flooded the lowland around the bridges waist deep. To reach the

Chickahominy's northern bank, the Federals would have to march in plain view over the spans. Fitzhugh Lee planned to be waiting on the northern bank to greet them.

Lee gathered his brigades under Brigadier Generals Williams C. Wickham and Lunsford L. Lomax at Half Sink, north of the Chickahominy. He started them toward Meadow Bridge before midnight, and men and horses stumbled along darkened byways through a drenching downpour. Near dawn they bivouacked on the Crenshaw farm, commanding Meadow Bridge. If things went according to plan, Lee would soon have Sheridan within his grasp.[18]

"All conspired to make things look gloomy."

Sheridan reacted precisely as Lee had anticipated. At 3:00 A.M. he began edging east along the military road, right into the open jaws of the Confederate trap. Wilson's division led, Colonel George H. Chapman's brigade in front, followed by the brigade of Colonel John B. McIntosh. They crossed Meadow Bridge Road and emerged onto the plateau near Mechanicsville Pike. The swollen Chickahominy flowed on their left, and Richmond's defenses loomed on their right. Farm roads branched out in several directions, confusing Wilson as to the proper route. As though answering Wilson's puzzlement, a man wearing a blue overcoat materialized from the blackness, held open a gate, and announced that Sheridan had sent him to show the way. Wilson followed the stranger, but the path became obscure, and Wilson sensed that he was veering toward the Confederate earthworks. Then the guide balked at accompanying Wilson farther, heightening the general's suspicion. He left the man with Colonel McIntosh and sent an officer to a nearby house to procure another guide. The officer returned with a farmer, who assured Wilson that he knew the country thoroughly. Wilson expressed concern that he had become wedged between the Chickahominy and the Richmond fortifications. "You're right, but you are also up against a battery of heavy guns not two hundred yards away completely sweeping the road on which you are standing as well as the country on both sides," the farmer responded. "It is impossible to pass between that battery and the river." [19]

Riding ahead with his headquarters entourage, Wilson emerged onto Mechanicsville Pike and directed his aide-de-camp, Captain Edward W. Whitaker, to find the fortified earthworks. It was still dark, and Wilson watched Whitaker's gray horse fade into the blackness. From Whitaker's direction, artillery exploded to life, and round shot whistled down the road, disemboweling some horses and severing the legs of others. Wilson and his staff sought cover in low ground, Chapman's brigade milled about in confusion near the pike, and McIntosh's brigade drew up in a freshly plowed field soft from the heavy rain. Musketry from nearby earthworks peppered the men as they waited, sabers drawn. "Shells were flying thick and fast around us," noted a Connecticut trooper, "but I did not see a man flinch." Studying the terrain in the gray dawn, Wilson realized that he was stymied. Rebel guns swept the plateau with deadly fire, barring his way out, and he immediately dispatched a courier to alert Sheridan. McIntosh had kept a close eye on the guide who led the column into the trap. Drawing his pistol, he blew out the man's brains.[20]

Sheridan recognized the dilemma. Wilson could go no farther. Merritt, coming behind Wilson, had halted near Meadow Bridge and was looking across the Chickahominy at Fitzhugh Lee's guns on the far bank. Gregg was still crowding onto the military road from Brook Pike, with Gordon's Confederates pressing hotly behind, intent on corking the trap's western end and sealing Sheridan's corps inside. A Federal observed that the "fortifications of the city behind us, and the cavalry of [Fitzhugh Lee] holding the strong and easily defended position at Meadow Bridge before us—this and the pelting rain and howling thunder all conspired to make things look gloomy."[21]

Sheridan identified Meadow Bridge as his way out of the trap. He gave Custer the daunting assignment of ousting Lee from the far bank. The flamboyant twenty-five-year-old general and his four Michigan regiments, nicknamed the Wolverines, were fast becoming Sheridan's favorites. They had given him his only bright spot in the Wilderness by routing a brigade of Confederate cavalry on May 6 and had broken Stuart's line at Yellow Tavern. Now Sheridan wanted them to repeat their feat at Meadow Bridge. Meanwhile the rest of Sheridan's force had to keep the southerners at bay by waging simultaneous battles on three fronts. On the western end of the Federal formation, near Brook Church, Gregg had to hold off Gordon. In the Union center, two of Merritt's brigades under Colonels Thomas C. Devin and Alfred Gibbs had to deflect sorties from the capital's fortifications. And on Sheridan's eastern flank, Wilson had to stave off assaults along Meadow Bridge Road and Mechanicsville Pike.

Sheridan's gamble was fraught with risks. Extricating the corps from its predicament required careful coordination by Sheridan and faultless performances by his subordinates. Failure on any front could spell disaster, and time was at a premium. Sheridan had no hope for reinforcements, and food, forage, and ammunition were low. He had to break out quickly because once he used up his supplies, he would be at the mercy of the Confederates. His men understood their predicament. One trooper proclaimed the situation the

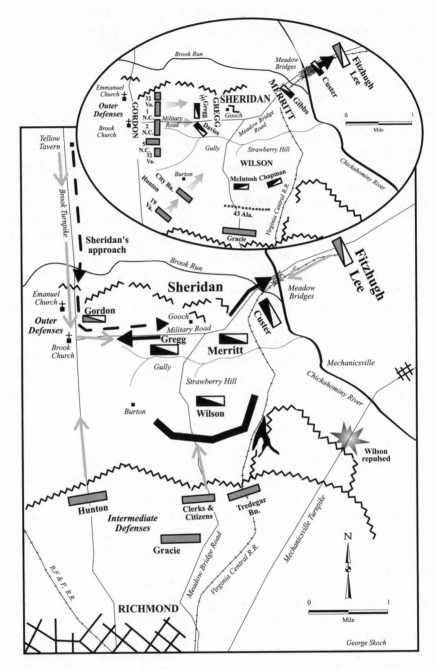

Battle of Meadow Bridge, May 12

"tightest place in which the corps ever found itself." Another called it simply the "most foreboding experience of my army life." May 12 would show whether victory over Stuart at Yellow Tavern had been a fluke or the dawn of a new day for the Union mounted arm.[22]

The battle opened in Wilson's sector. So far, the novice cavalryman had been a disappointment. Rebel horsemen had run circles around him in the Wilderness, and Sheridan had relegated him to a supporting role at Yellow Tavern. Now he had the critical assignment of fending off attacks from Meadow Bridge Road and Mechanicsville Pike long enough for Custer to find a way across the Chickahominy.

At first all was confusion. Musketry played along the rebel works, and projectiles screamed into Wilson's men. Outgunned, Chapman dismounted his brigade and sent his horses to the shelter of low ground near the Chickahominy. Then he marched his soldiers to the foot of a small rise called Strawberry Hill and formed them along the Virginia Central Railroad. McIntosh dismounted his brigade as well and extended it onto Chapman's right, occupying woods along the southern edge of the eminence. Lieutenant Charles L. Fitzhugh placed his horse artillery on Strawberry Hill and began dueling with Confederate siege guns five hundred yards away in the fortifications. It was an unequal match. "Our artillery began to play very lively but could not do much compared with the heavy artillery of the forts," a Federal conceded.[23]

Concerned about retreat, Lieutenant Fitzhugh began sending his caissons to the rear. "Hullo, Charlie," shouted Sheridan, who had ridden over to supervise the engagement. "What are you doing with your caissons?" The artillerist explained that he was hard pressed and wanted them out of the way. "Hard pressed!" Sheridan retorted. "Why, what do you suppose we have in front of us? A lot of department clerks from Richmond, who have been forced into the ranks. I'll stay here all day to show these fellows how much I care for them, and go when I get ready. Send for your caissons and take it easy." Inspired by the general's oration, Fitzhugh's gunners redoubled their efforts, making what one artillerist termed "lively music."[24]

As Sheridan predicted, clerks manning the Richmond defenses had no stomach for attacking Wilson's veterans. "Having made good our position," Wilson recounted, "there was nothing further to do but to hold on while Sheridan cleared the ground behind us, and repaired the bridge in rear of his center, and as soon as it became passable to withdraw by the flanks of divisions to the north side of the river." Wilson sent his other battery, under

Lieutenant Alexander C. M. Pennington, to assist Custer at Meadow Bridge.[25]

In the morning light, Sheridan's aide, Captain P. Lacy Goddard, rode up to Wilson and announced, "General Sheridan orders you to hold your position at all hazards while he arranges to withdraw the corps to the north side of the river." Wilson was amused, as he was already fiercely engaged and had no choice but to keep fighting. He jokingly suggested to Goddard that he assure Sheridan "our hair is badly entangled in [the enemy's] fingers and our nose firmly inserted in his mouth, and we shall, therefore, hold on here till something breaks!" [26]

At the western end of Sheridan's formation, David Gregg arrayed his division into a strong defensive line facing west, perpendicular to the military road, about a quarter mile east of Brook Church. Behind the thickly bearded Pennsylvanian's easygoing demeanor lurked a skillful tactician, and the general showed his soldierly talents to impressive advantage this day. Acting decisively, he extended Colonel J. Irvin Gregg's brigade north of the road and Brigadier General Henry E. Davies Jr.'s brigade below it. A small stream carved a deep, wooded gully a quarter mile to the south, near the Burton house. Davies anchored his left flank in the brush-filled depression and set his men to erecting shallow earthworks. Behind his line, on high ground dominating the military road, Gregg posted Lieutenant Rufus King Jr.'s battery.[27]

No sooner had Gregg arranged his men than Gordon's Confederates turned onto the military road and hove into view. Gordon's three mounted North Carolina regiments numbered among the Army of Northern Virginia's toughest cavalrymen, and they had recently proven their mettle by driving some of Gregg's best outfits—the 1st Maine and 10th New York Cavalry—in a running fight near a place called Goodall's Tavern. But the situation at Brook Church was different. Gregg's entire division—ten regiments in all—stood drawn up in an imposing battle line, supported by artillery and expecting Gordon to attack.

Canister from King's guns raked the head of Gordon's column as the Confederates turned east onto the military road. The majestically bearded Gordon was an aggressive fighter, but he instinctively recognized the importance of testing Gregg's position before charging ahead. He dismounted his 1st and 2nd North Carolina Cavalry and nudged them cautiously forward. Gordon's other regiment—the 5th North Carolina Cavalry—remained mounted in column immediately south of the road, ready to charge King's battery if the dismounted men made headway against Gregg's line.

The sheer size of Gregg's force gave Gordon pause. Federals extended well past his flanks. A determined attack might breach Gregg's line, but once the North Carolinians ruptured Gregg's center, Yankees would surround them and could crush their flanks. Bowing to the intimidating disparity in numbers, Gordon decided to seek reinforcements from Richmond. He dispatched his aide, Lieutenant Kerr Craige, to the capital bearing his recommendation that troops be sent to attack Gregg's southern flank. Artillery, he added, would also be welcome.[28]

Thus far, Sheridan's escape plan was unfolding precisely as the general had intended. Wilson and Gregg were holding the Confederates at bay. The time had come for Custer to free up the Meadow Bridge causeways. The flamboyant young cavalryman had his work cut out for him. Lee's Confederates had torn up the flooring of the highway bridge and were waiting confidently on the northern bank behind earthworks left over from McClellan's 1862 campaign. Union pioneers, as soldiers working as laborers were called, tried to repair the highway bridge, but Lee's marksmen and artillery kept them from their work.[29]

Custer decided that the railway bridge offered the best prospect of crossing the Chickahominy and dispensed picked troops close to the river, concealed behind the twenty-foot-high railway embankment. These Wolverines eased into the flooded lowland until only their heads showed, and waded to within fifty yards of the opposite bank. At Custer's signal these men, along with sharpshooters posted near the railway embankment, began picking off Lee's pickets on the northern bank, forcing the Confederates to keep down and preventing them from firing at the bridges. Dismounted daredevils from the 5th Michigan Cavalry mounted the railroad span and picked their way across, leaping single file from tie to tie, timing their steps to avoid projectiles from Lee's artillery screaming around them. "Creeping, crawling—any way to get across," a soldier described the impressive feat. In minutes the brave troopers were over. Fanning into underbrush along the river's northern bank, they drove back Lee's pickets and secured the bridgehead. Under their covering fire the rest of the 5th Michigan came across, followed by the 6th Michigan. Soon both regiments stood on Lee's side of the Chickahominy, safely ensconced in a bog. Shooting from behind trees and bushes with seven-shot carbines, they kept Lee's troopers occupied while Union pioneers labored to finish repairing the road span.[30]

Custer suffered remarkably few casualties. "It may have been a case of poor ammunition or poor marksmanship or both," speculated the 6th Michigan's Major James H. Kidd, who termed the exploit "one of the most desperate fights the regiment was ever engaged in." By any measure, Fitzhugh Lee had bungled his assignment. Excuses abounded. A Confederate in the 2nd Virginia claimed that he and his compatriots had confused the heads of Custer's riflemen in the flooded lowlands for turtles, and that their mistake had enabled the Federals to get close before being discovered. "Those damned rascals have played turtle on us," the southerner declared. "Let the damned rascals come out of the water like men." Still outraged, he added, "I'll fight them until hell freezes over, and then I'll fight them on the ice."[31]

Racket from Wilson's, Gregg's, and Custer's separate actions reverberated along the river. Discharges from heavy Confederate siege guns periodically drowned out the other firing. "It was here that I first heard the peculiar noise occasioned by pieces of railway iron being thrown from the guns," a New Yorker noted. Colonel Charles E. Phelps of the 7th Maryland, who had been tagging along ever since Sheridan's men liberated him at Beaver Dam Station, found the situation bewildering. "It was in fact a field of battle without a rear in the usual acceptation," he observed. "The rear if anywhere was in the middle, where trains were parked and hospitals established."[32]

Searching for a resting place, Phelps wandered down a lane. At the end stood an "old fashioned brick mansion," Phelps reminisced, "comfortably surrounded by the out buildings and appendages of an opulent country residence, and handsomely situated in a smooth and verdant lawn well shaded by locust, walnut, and oak." Union officers dozed under the trees. Looking inside, Phelps was greeted by Mrs. Gooch, a middle-aged lady who lived there with her aged mother and a handful of servants. Stragglers had looted the house and frightened the elderly Gooch nearly to death. Phelps tried to shoo the stragglers away, but as fast as one left, another entered. At Phelps's urging, one of Sheridan's aides assigned two orderlies to guard the place.

Mrs. Gooch's tribulations, however, were far from over. As the battle heated, Sheridan's surgeons commandeered the house as a field hospital. "The floors were slippery with blood and covered with men suffering from every variety of wound that could be inflicted by pistol, saber, carbine, shot or shell," observed Phelps. Then a squad of Confederate prisoners approached, each cradling a dark, round object and walking with extreme caution. Mrs. Gooch inquired what they were carrying. "Those are rebel torpedoes, madam," a doctor responded, obviously relishing the horrified look that spread over Mrs. Gooch's face. He elaborated that the devices had been found buried in the road in front of her house. "Where are you going to put them?" she asked. "In the cellar, I imagine," came the reply. Remonstrated Mrs. Gooch: "Not under my house. It is not possible that they are going to put such things under my house to blow us up."

"There is no occasion for alarm," the doctor assured her. "They are perfectly harmless when let alone."

Mrs. Gooch was not mollified. "Do they not go off by percussion?" she demanded.

"Yes," answered the doctor. "That is just the way in which two of them went off this morning when struck by horses hoofs."

Just then a loud thunderclap rattled the building. "Merciful Heavens!" Mrs. Gooch expostulated, glancing wide-eyed from her mother to the doctor. "Was that not thunder?" A surgeon assured her that lightning rods protected the house, but Mrs. Gooch became more agitated. Might not the rods attract lightning and increase the danger of the torpedoes blowing up, she asked? No sooner had the question left her lips than a blinding lightning flash illuminated the house, and thunder exploded overhead. Phelps and the doctors were so startled that they leapt to their feet. Mrs. Gooch shrieked and disappeared with her mother into an interior room, to be seen no more.[33]

"The rain poured in torrents and in sheets," observed Phelps. "Forked lightning flashed, and deafening claps of thunder burst with terrific energy from the dark fall of cloud that brooded low over the field of storm and battle."[34]

Sheridan was racing against time, and time was running out. The Confederate forces arrayed against Gregg and Wilson seemed to be growing stronger. Two of Custer's regiments had a firm grip on the Chickahominy's northern bank, but a forceful attack by Fitzhugh Lee might still drive them into the river. Bridge repairs were taking too long, Sheridan had no prospects of reinforcement, and provisions were seriously depleted. Wilson thought Sheridan appeared "much excited" over his "exceedingly dangerous position." A gunner in Captain Joseph W. Martin's battery confessed that he, too, was becoming "a little alarmed."[35]

Sheridan's concerns were well founded, as Confederate leaders in Richmond were doing their best to bag his entire force. Responding to Gordon's request for reinforcements, Bragg instructed Hunton to support Gordon in his attack against Gregg. He also ordered Brigadier General Archibald Gracie's Alabama brigade to march up Meadow Bridge Road to confront Wilson. Lee was to serve as the anvil against which Gordon, Hunton, and Gracie would crush Sheridan. For the scheme to work, Lee must keep Sheridan bottled up at Meadow Bridge.

At 9:00 A.M. Gordon received the artillery he had requested in the form of two shiny new guns and ordered them placed to the right oblique of the 5th

North Carolina. The guns opened, drawing the fire of King's Union battery. Union projectiles sprayed the Confederate pieces with dirt, sending the novice artillerists dodging for cover. Gordon cursed them as "Band Box Artillery." Recounted an officer in the 5th North Carolina: "We laughed at them, ridiculed them, and asked them to go back and man their guns. But they looked at us as if they thought we were surely crazy." Disgusted, Gordon rode away to look after his cavalry.[36]

A more experienced Confederate battery arrived and engaged King in a vigorous duel. Concealed in a depression, the Confederate guns gave Gregg's men some harrowing moments. Round shot crashed through the 10th New York's ranks and caused the regiment's horses to "fairly squat," as a Federal put it, "and with extended nostrils trembling crowd together awaiting the next visitation." A projectile partially severed a horse's foreleg, and the animal made pathetic efforts to place its missing foot. Gregg brought up the 1st Maine to support the battery, but the soldiers could only sit silently on their mounts, shells striking all around. Then another thunderstorm erupted, mingling "heaven's artillery," in the words of a soldier, with the brass and iron variety. King finally got the upper hand by borrowing a section of napoleons from Captain Martin's New York Battery and replying with solid shot, which forced back the rebel guns. "Taken from first to last, it was a brilliant artillery duel, in which the Yankees proved themselves the superior," a New Yorker claimed.[37]

Hunton's reinforcements began arriving around 10:00 A.M. with the appearance of Colonel Edward B. Montague's 32nd Virginia, which joined Gordon on the military road. Gordon placed a company from Montague's regiment on each flank of his cavalry line and ordered the combined force to attack Gregg. "Our boys raised the yell and were going in when the necessary support failed," a Tar Heel reported of the effort. Undeterred, Gordon ordered a second charge. "The only execution they did," a cavalryman complained of Montague's reinforcements, "was by firing into our dismounted men who were far in the advance, killing and wounding several." Gordon finally prodded his and Montague's men into concerted action but could make no headway against Gregg's superior force. Confederate losses mounted, with the 32nd Virginia losing about a third of its troops.[38]

Then the 25th Virginia Battalion, also called the City Battalion, came marching up Brook Pike from Richmond. Montague formed these newcomers below Gregg's southern flank, facing north. Davies's brigade, which manned this portion of Gregg's line, lay nestled in the bush-filled ravine near the Burton place with its left "refused," or bent back from Gregg's main line at right angles. To meet the threat posed by the City Battalion, Gregg pulled the 1st Maine from behind King's guns and shifted it onto Davies's left, reaching east toward Wilson. The City Battalion charged, only to run headlong into Davies's brigade and the Maine men. "Here the boys had fun," the 1st Maine's historian reported, firing from behind stumps and fences while their inexperienced opponents stood helplessly in line in a clearing, making excellent targets. The Maine soldiers agreed that it was "cruel to shoot at those brave fellows, to look at it now, but then the boys thought only of doing their duty, and really enjoyed selecting the men to shoot at." The one-sided fight ended when the 1st New Jersey launched a dismounted charge that cleared the home guards from Davies's front, leaving a single Confederate soldier and his Negro servant to stand their ground. The Federals freed the Negro and listened in amusement as his master, who had been on detached service from the regular Confederate army, "relieved his mind by very disrespectful observations on the character of the militia." [39]

North of the military road, Colonel Gregg's brigade—minus, of course, the 1st Maine—continued to hold Gordon at bay. "Not an inch of line was yielded," a New Yorker reported. "The rapid discharge of the seven-shooters in the woods to the right gave evidence of the hot work there." Gordon rode along the battle line, inspiring his troops by his presence. A soldier, concerned for Gordon's safety, urged him to dismount. "No, we must set the men an example of gallantry today," he replied. No sooner had he spoken than a bullet tore through his arm, exiting at the elbow. Gordon left the field in excruciating pain and passed command of his brigade to Colonel Clinton M. Andrews of the 2nd North Carolina Cavalry. [40]

Presently Colonel Henry Gantt arrived from Richmond with another of Hunton's regiments, the 19th Virginia. Andrews prepared his cavalry to attack along the military road while the 19th Virginia followed in the ill-fated City Battalion's footsteps and charged from the south. Raising the "usual yell," Gantt's men marched into a deadly trap. The 1st Vermont Cavalry—Wilson's rightmost unit—had extended westward, linking with the 1st Maine Cavalry on Davies's left. As the 19th Virginia advanced, the 1st Maine fired directly into it, and the Green Mountain men swung around and slammed into its right flank. Gantt's men broke and cascaded south to the Richmond fortifications. Andrews meanwhile shifted the 5th North Carolina Cavalry to the military road's north side and ordered another charge. The Tar Heels pressed ahead to a board fence perforated with bullet holes but could advance no farther. [41]

Gantt's abortive foray was the last effort by Hunton's brigade. Hunton attempted to blame others for his brigade's poor performance, asserting that Bragg had become "paralyzed with apprehension" that Sheridan would break through and had directed him to withdraw. Hunton claimed to have been "deeply mortified at being recalled," and later boasted that he could have "captured the whole party." In point of fact, Hunton handled his troops poorly, committing regiments one at a time and never effectively coordinating any of them with Gordon.[42]

A mile east of Hunton, Archibald Gracie was also busy. His brigade—the 41st, 43rd, 59th, and 60th Alabama, and the 23rd Battalion Alabama Sharpshooters—had clipped through Richmond to an enthusiastic welcome. Around 9:00 A.M. the Alabamians reached the fortified intermediate line and shifted left to Meadow Bridge Road, facing north toward Wilson. Fifteen miles of marching had left them tired and hungry. President Davis had meanwhile relented and permitted Postmaster Reagan to command the civilian troops near Meadow Bridge Road. While the Alabamians regrouped, Gracie and Reagan discussed measures to relieve the pressure mounting against Gordon and Lee. Gracie deployed his brigade in front of the earthworks, stationed artillery between the regiments, and pushed the 43rd Alabama forward as skirmishers. Reagan formed three hundred home guards behind Gracie to support the attack. Noticing Gracie's officers huddled in the rain, Reagan offered them a bottle of brandy. They quickly disposed of the gift, and a grateful Gracie promised to recommend Reagan for promotion after the battle.[43]

At 1:30 P.M.—approximately the same time that Andrews and Gantt were attacking Gregg—Gracie's soldiers started forward. Gracie rode among them "as cool as if directing farm operations," a spectator reported. The Alabamians first seemed headed toward Pennington's battery, which opened and temporarily checked their advance. Gracie re-formed his brigade under fire—"with as much regularity as on an old field muster," a witness related—altered its line of march forty-five degrees, and continued, this time aiming for McIntosh's brigade. Unnerved by Gracie's methodical approach, McIntosh asked Wilson for reinforcements, pleading that he was "too weak to repel the attack." Wilson was concerned that Gracie might turn to attack Chapman and told McIntosh to fend for himself. McIntosh began retiring, which uncovered Fitzhugh's battery on Strawberry Hill, but Fitzhugh elected to stand his ground and began firing his six three-inch guns over the tree line into the advancing Alabamians with deadly precision. Emboldened by Fitzhugh's success, Pennington turned his guns on the Confederates, as did Edward B. Williston, stationed to the right with four twelve-pound napoleons. A Federal smugly observed that the Yankees "had the advantage of the rebs for they had to advance through an open field, while we kept under cover of the timber."[44]

Gracie's attack never stood a chance. Gracie was slightly wounded and his horse was hit three times. Bloody rents opened in the Alabama line. Sheridan stood under a tree in the drenching downpour, puffing a cigar and monitoring his artillery's work. Noting that Wilson's gunners had expended most of their ammunition, he directed Merritt to send them more projectiles, then rode over to give them encouragement. "Boys, you see those fellows yonder?" Sheridan asked the artillerists, pointing to Gracie's men. "Well, we are going to knock hell out of them. They are green soldiers from Richmond. They are not veterans. You have fought them well today, but we have got to whip them. We can do it, and we will." A soldier marveled at the general's bravery. "Where the fighting was severest, the danger the greatest, there was Sheridan, encouraging his men by talking in his social, familiar manner." [45]

Buffeted by artillery and musketry, Gracie paused to fire a parting shot, then retired inside the fortifications. He had lost about seventy soldiers. He later tried to save face by claiming that Wilson had rejected his "proffer of battle," and Richmond newspapers followed his lead by characterizing Gracie's retreat as a ploy "to invite the enemy to battle and to draw him out of the woods." Reagan, who watched the maneuver, more accurately attributed Gracie's withdrawal to Wilson's "superior force." Wilson, of course, did not follow, and by 3:00 P.M. his front was clear of Confederates. [46]

Serenaded by the din of Gregg's and Wilson's escalating battles, Custer's troopers continued to perform yeoman work. Huddled in marshy ground along the river's northern bank, the 5th and 6th Michigan kept Fitzhugh Lee's men pinned in their earthworks and enabled Union pioneers to repair the road span at Meadow Bridge. Soldiers ripped boards from every fence, barn, and house in the vicinity and carried them to the bridge for flooring. The result was a rickety structure that one witness proclaimed "little better than a trap for mules and horses." At 4:00 P.M. Sheridan deemed the bridge fit for crossing and directed Merritt to reinforce Custer's bridgehead on the far bank. A severe rainstorm helped conceal the movement. Before the Confederates realized what was happening, Yankees were streaming over and deploying north of the river. [47]

The climax came as Colonel Gibbs—"a regular martinet," a cavalry chaplain described him—thundered over the bridge at the head of an imposing mounted column, four horses abreast, to administer the killing blow. "This was a fearful moment," a Pennsylvanian recounted, "for the road was but twelve feet wide, bordered on both sides by deep swamps, and nearly a mile long." Devin's 9th New York and 17th Pennsylvania executed a "rather neat flank movement," as a Federal described it, then charged into Lee's advanced rifle pits, "utterly routing him and capturing a number of prisoners in the works." More Federals swarmed into the breach and fired down the length of the Confederate trenches, forcing the rebels to lie low to avoid being shot. In short order, Lee's men fell back to a set of reserve entrenchments. "Boys, give them one volley before we leave," shouted Lieutenant Colonel Robert Randolph of the 4th Virginia, just before a bullet tore through his brain and killed him.[48]

The 1st New York Dragoons debouched into an open field facing Lee's reserve line of works. Gibbs asked a captured southerner whether infantry lay ahead. "Go to the front and you'll see," the Confederate answered. Gibbs cursed him and ordered his men to charge. "Fight on foot!" shouted the Dragoons' major as the soldiers rolled off their mounts and pressed on at a double quick, rapidly working their carbines. "It was one of the prettiest sights I saw while in the service, as well as one of the most exciting," recollected a New Yorker. The 2nd Virginia attempted to break Gibbs's momentum with a countercharge, but superior Union numbers prevailed. A trooper in the 9th New York summarized the fight in his diary. "[Merritt] went at them and cleaned them out, driving them out of strong breastworks and slaying many." Desperation helped explain the ferocity of the Union attack. "We had to fight or die," Michael Donlon of the 2nd United States Cavalry wrote his brother. A southerner concurred, admitting that the "enemy, brought to bay, fought like demons."[49]

Routed, Fitzhugh Lee retreated toward Mechanicsville, and Sheridan brought the rest of his corps over the river. Rumor had it that he lifted a bottle to his mouth with a flourish and declared, "Here's to you, Johnnies!" When a stray bullet shattered the bottle, he allegedly quipped, "That's damned unhandsome of you, Johnny." Merritt started in pursuit of Fitzhugh Lee while the rest of the troopers crossed, some swimming, some using the highway bridge, and still others waiting until the pioneers finished flooring the railway bridge. Three of McIntosh's regiments brought up the rear. The Confederates did not follow.[50]

"Richmond is again breathing freely for the moment."

Sheridan received a pleasant surprise while watching his corps pass safely onto the Chickahominy's northern bank. Two enterprising young newsboys, clad in military caps and gray jackets, circulated among the Union troops, selling copies of the *Richmond Examiner.* Soldiers rushed to purchase the newspaper. A lieutenant bought a copy and gave it to Sheridan, who read with amusement that Stuart had "repelled" him at Yellow Tavern and now had him cornered in front of Richmond. The newspaper also reported that at least two veteran Confederate infantry brigades had moved into the city's northern defenses, which confirmed Sheridan in his decision against trying to force his way in. The "sharp youngsters," as Sheridan referred to the newsboys, asked to go home after selling their papers. The general found them so "intelligent and observant" that he suspected they might be spies and ordered them detained until his corps had finished crossing the Chickahominy.[51]

Once his men were across, Sheridan set the Meadow Bridges on fire and resumed his march toward Haxall's Landing, intending to pass northeast to Mechanicsville, then easterly through Gaines's Mill and Cold Harbor. Once clear of Richmond's fortifications, he planned to drop south, cross back over the Chickahominy at Bottom's Bridge, and then continue on to the James River and Butler's gunboats. Fitzhugh Lee was not about to let Sheridan depart in peace. His division was in terrible shape—"out of forage, rations, and ammunition and command completely exhausted," he later reported—but he possessed the fighting spirit that had animated Stuart. Mistakenly assuming that Sheridan planned to join Grant, he shifted his frazzled troopers to Pole Green Church, which commanded the roads leading north.[52]

Around 7:00 P.M. Sheridan's column passed through Mechanicsville, where his medical director appropriated carriages to transport the wounded men. "Gradually accessions of fine barouches and landaus were made for the accommodation of staff officers, who seemed to enjoy the 'drives' very much, singing songs and smoking cigars," a trooper chuckled. A short distance past Mechanicsville, irregular musketry spattered from a side road. Lee had discovered Sheridan's line of march and had hurried a detachment to intercept him. Gibbs thrust his Regulars up the side road, and the Confederates halted and began stacking fence rails for cover. Dismounted elements from the 1st United States Cavalry broke through the improvised rebel barricade and opened the way for mounted troops to follow. Hard pressed, the Confederates fell back to a second barricade, where they re-formed, repulsed Gibbs's horsemen, and launched a counterattack of their own. "I had the run of my life to keep out of their way," a Federal confessed. "At one time I was in their rear and inside their line, but they were too busy with others to pick us up." Then Gibbs pumped the 1st New York Dragoons into the fray, breaking the Confederate counterattack and driving the rebels back to their second line of works.[53]

Sheridan's objective was to safeguard his advance, not to become embroiled in firefights with bands of Confederates, so he deployed Gibbs's brigade into a blue wall of troopers cordoning off the side road. Soon after dark, Merritt's lead elements reached Gaines's Mill and bivouacked near the Gaines house. The mounted column strung back several miles. Servants prepared a hot meal while officers lounged nearby, "ferocious as hungry bears," tantalized by the cooking and mystified over how Sheridan's commissary

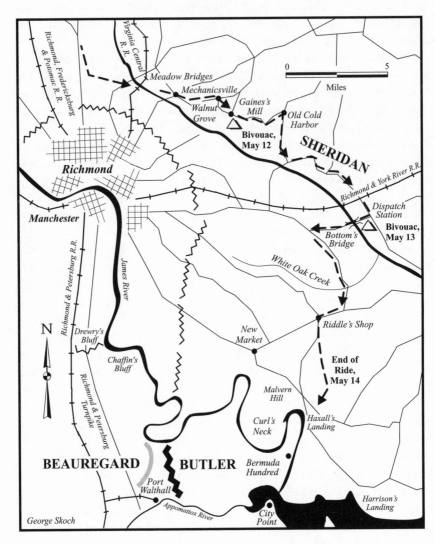

Sheridan's route to Haxall's Landing, May 12–14

wagon always managed to remain well stocked. Recollected a trooper: "Went into camp near Cold Harbor at 9:00 P.M., in a drenching rain, as wet, tired, and uncomfortable as it is permitted man to be." An infantryman who had been liberated by Sheridan's troopers scavenged some corn meal and knocked at a house looking for a stove to cook his loot. A "darkie woman," frightened nearly to death, answered the door and informed him that the white folk had "done gone to Richmond." On recognizing that the man was a Yankee, she mixed the corn meal with water, salt, and shortening. Within half an hour, he was feasting on an immense, steaming hoecake.[54]

Merritt had taken a gentleman named Algerine Storr from his home near Meadow Bridge and forced him to guide the Union column. Merritt suspected Storr of leading him into Lee's ambush and was preparing to shoot the unfortunate farmer when a local resident confirmed that Storr had taken the Federals over the only roads that existed. Persuaded that Storr had nothing to do with the attack, Merritt released him unharmed.[55]

A few miles north, at Pole Green Church, Fitzhugh Lee's troopers stretched out under the leaden Virginia sky. Theirs was a somber encampment. Men and mounts were exhausted, and two crushing defeats in as many days had demoralized everyone. With Sheridan veering away from Richmond, Lee called off the chase. He would rest his battered force until noon the next day, then return to Mechanicsville where he could draw supplies from Richmond. The rebel capital also settled in for a depressing night. The immediate threat was gone, but Butler and Sheridan might strike again soon, and the import of Stuart's mortal wounding was beginning to register. "The sullen roar of artillery at a distance, and the rattle of an army wagon over the stones, are the only sounds that break upon the ear," a newspaperman observed. "There is solemnity everywhere brooding over the town which far exceeds anything that has been witnessed since the beginning of the war." The storm that had blown across the battlefield had spawned tornadoes that uprooted trees and tore roofs off houses. One gust leveled a tower and spire on St. John's Episcopal Church, where Patrick Henry had made his famous speech against King George III. "If it be an omen, let us accept it," a dispirited citizen advised.[56]

Compared to the exciting events of May 12, the remainder of Sheridan's expedition proved relatively uneventful. Stragglers provided excitement early on May 13 by setting Gaines's Mill on fire. Sheridan organized a bucket brigade, doused the flames, and by 7:00 A.M. the Federals were under way, trailed by immense numbers of freed Negroes. "Some carried bundles, some had nothing but the rags that covered them, some were well mounted, others rode sorry jades, some drove ox carts, some buggies, and many were on foot," Phelps observed. "They only knew they were going away from slavery, and the prevalent sentiment among them was, as one of them expressed it, 'God bless the damn Yankees.'" In return for safe passage the former slaves agreed to destroy bridges and culverts in Sheridan's wake.[57]

The Federals reached Bottom's Bridge over the Chickahominy around noon. Confederate home guards had removed the bridge's planking, so Sheridan set his engineers to repairing the structure with boards from nearby buildings. He decided to camp there until morning, hoping, as he put it, to "demonstrate to the Cavalry Corps the impossibility of the enemy's destroying or capturing so large a body of mounted troops." Phelps was struck by the "hungry, hollow, jaded and squalid look" of troopers and mounts, and many riders had to lead their horses at a walk. "Out of rations," Wilson scratched in his journal. "Must get some and into a country where we can support ourselves, probably by the south side of the James." Sheridan discouraged looting, but, as a Federal noted, "gnawing stomachs disregarded the rules laid down." The Federals were treated to the unusual sight of civilians soliciting food. One proud lady visited the Union camp in search of bread. "To think that I, one of the first ladies of Virginia, should be obliged to beg, and that of a Federal soldier," she remarked.[58]

Setting off at a comfortable hour on the morning of May 14, Sheridan's column traversed White Oak Swamp and continued south. Bullet-scarred trees, rusty canteens, and shreds of rotten blankets from battles fought two years before lined the route. "Never were tired men and horses more delighted to leave the doubtful regions of the hated Chickahominy and reach terra firma," a Pennsylvanian maintained. Around noon, a party from the 1st Pennsylvania Cavalry mounted Malvern Hill near the James and began waving signal flags. A Union gunboat mistook the horsemen for Confederates and began shelling them. The projectiles, which Sheridan's troopers variously described as cast iron stoves or beer kegs, made whirring sounds as they tumbled through the air, hitting several men and horses before the gunners realized their mistake.[59]

Sheridan established headquarters at Dr. Haxall's elegant mansion. Bands played and soldiers splashed in the James River. Butler, whose stockpiled provisions were only a few miles away, sent food and fodder. Some troopers tried their luck fishing. A New Jersey man felt a tug and hauled in his line to discover that he had snagged a catfish and a torpedo. "No one could have dropped anything quicker," he reminisced.[60]

As the threat of invasion receded, Richmond's citizens expressed profound relief. Homes in Sheridan's path lay in shambles, and local newspapers reported numerous instances of "indiscriminate robbing and pillaging." Poor Mrs. Gooch's house was a complete mess, its contents plundered and its walls smeared with blood. Disappointment that the Federals had escaped tempered the celebrations. "Richmond is again breathing freely for the moment," observed Ordnance Chief Gorgas, although he expressed "much dissatisfaction" over the fact that "something might perhaps have been done more than was done." Complained the *Richmond Examiner:* "The Federal cavalry have escaped, when, by every principle of common sense, they should have been cut off to the last man." Had southern leaders exercised "bolder and wiser management," the newspaper suggested, they would have snagged the intruders, and Richmond "would never again have been troubled by raids." But even the critics in Richmond discerned silver linings. "So they have gotten off, by the same road they always go," carped the *Daily Examiner.* "The only consolation is that they have done even less injury than any raiders ever did, and that a large body of their cavalry has been put *hors de combat* for a long time by the fatigues, hardships, and losses of the campaign." [61]

Whether the Confederates could have corralled Sheridan is an intriguing question. Two sides of the rebel trap—the Richmond defenses and Gordon's mounted brigade—had held, although Sheridan had not seriously tested either of them. Surprisingly, the collapse came on Fitzhugh Lee's front, where terrain strongly favored the Confederates. One can only speculate whether the Federals would have found another escape route had Lee barred the way across Meadow Bridge. Sheridan might have located another Chickahominy crossing, he might have punched through Gordon to flee north along Brook Turnpike, or he might have made a concerted effort to overrun the forts protecting Richmond. All that can be said with confidence is that Lee's failure to hold Meadow Bridge deprived the Confederacy of an opportunity, however slim, to wreck the Army of the Potomac's cavalry arm.

Richmond spent the afternoon of May 13 mourning Stuart. At 5:00 P.M. pallbearers carried a metal casket with the fallen hero's remains up the center aisle of St. James's Church. An organ played a solemn dirge, and a choir sang. President Davis, General Bragg, and other notables mingled with the crowd. Following a prayer and more songs, the casket was taken to a waiting hearse, decorated with black plumes and drawn by four white horses. The procession slowly wound to Hollywood Cemetery, where the body was placed in a vault. "Thus has passed away, amid the exciting scenes of this revolution, one of the bravest and most dashing cavaliers that the 'Old Dominion' has ever given birth to," an onlooker reflected. [62]

General Lee, at Spotsylvania Court House, faced the painful and difficult task of selecting a replacement for Stuart. The problem was not an absence of worthy successors, but rather a surfeit of them. Stuart's senior division commander Hampton lacked formal military training but had proven himself an able leader and a hard fighter. Equally capable was Fitzhugh Lee. Sectional rivalries complicated the choice. Lee was a Virginian, while Hampton hailed from South Carolina. Not wanting to damage the army's morale, Lee decided to defer naming Stuart's successor. "Until further orders, the three divisions of cavalry serving with this army will constitute separate commands and will report directly to and receive orders from these headquarters of the army," he announced.[63]

Gordon's wound caused grave concern. "The country cannot afford to lose the services of such a gallant and successful officer in an active campaign," a Richmond editorial proclaimed. "May Heaven soon see fit to heal his wound and restore him to his devoted men." Gordon at first appeared to be improving, but he took a turn for the worse and died of complications on May 18 in the officers' hospital at Richmond.[64]

Sheridan and his men considered the raid an unqualified victory. "With regard to this expedition now at an end, it seemed upon all hands to be taken for granted that it was a brilliant and complete success," a participant reported. "Whenever in the course of conversation any allusion to it chanced to be made, it was referred to more as a matter which spoke for itself than as one requiring illustration or admitting discussion." The jubilant general wrote Meade that his command was in "fine spirits with its success" and gloated over the destruction of Confederate stores, rolling stock, bridges, and track. He emphasized that he had killed Stuart and roundly defeated the rebel cavalry. Although Sheridan had no way of comparing his own losses with those of the Confederates, he fared remarkably well. Union cavalry losses for the campaign approximated 625 men, as opposed to 800 Confederate casualties. Fitzhugh Lee's division was in shambles. Four of its seven colonels were lost. One in three of Lomax's men were casualties, as were one in five of Wickham's. Attrition in horses was extremely high, which left many uninjured cavalrymen without mounts. All told, Sheridan had cut Fitzhugh Lee's combat effectiveness in half.[65]

Serious criticism can be leveled against the broader features of Sheridan's campaign. By taking his cavalry from Spotsylvania Court House, Sheridan severely handicapped Grant in his battles against Lee. The Union army was deprived of its eyes and ears during a critical juncture in the campaign. And Sheridan's decision to advance boldly to the Richmond defenses smacked of unnecessary showboating that jeopardized his command. But his generalship in breaking out of the trap at Meadow Bridge was exemplary. He improvised a daring plan and supervised its execution in the best tradition of battlefield commanders. His subordinates performed reliably, although Wilson's faltering management of his division in the face of Gracie's attack raised eyebrows. Sheridan reputedly informed a Michigan colonel, "Custer is the ablest man in the cavalry corps," and few could take issue with his judgment.[66]

The Meadow Bridge fight advanced a style of warfare that was fast becoming the norm. The distinction between cavalry and infantry was blurring as cavalry evolved into a mobile infantry force that used horses to transport men to battlefields, where they fought on foot behind temporary barricades. Stirring charges still had their place—witness the mounted attack to overrun Stuart's line at Yellow Tavern, and the thundering Union foray across Meadow Bridge—but they now comprised only one of several tactics available to the mounted arm. Sheridan was emerging as an innovative master in a new school of combat.

Whether Sheridan could have captured Richmond—and whether there was any value in his doing so—remains an open question. On May 13 Sheridan assured Meade that it was "possible that I might have captured the city of Richmond by assault." He might have been correct, particularly if he had pushed south along Brook Pike during the night of May 11, before veteran Confederate reinforcements arrived. Union horsemen prancing on the Confederacy's capitol grounds would have seriously damaged southern morale, and rebel troops would have rushed to liberate the city, thereby diminishing the force opposing Butler. Even General Lee might have detached soldiers to recapture Richmond, easing Grant's task at Spotsylvania Court House. Sheridan resisted the temptation to enter Richmond, however, because he concluded that the venture would have "cost five hundred or six hundred lives and I could not have held the place." His men applauded his decision. An officer in the 1st Vermont summarized the prevailing sentiment. Occupying Richmond would have been "rash in the extreme," he wrote, and he acclaimed Sheridan's refusal "to hazard the safety of his command, or the success of the expedition, in a venture of such doubtful utility."[67]

The most enduring legacy of Sheridan's raid and the battle at Meadow Bridges was a big boost in Union cavalry morale. Hardship and adventure forged an iron bond between the outspoken midwesterner and his horsemen. "It was a pretty good introduction to active cavalry service for a green country boy," a cavalryman boasted of the exploit. "At any rate," he added, "Sheridan had made good." Another trooper thought that the satisfaction of throwing "rebeldom into a panic" amply compensated for his suffering. "The Old Soldier never saw anything like it," a veteran of the raid wrote with pride. "We averaged 18 hours in the saddle daily for over one week, many of the men sleeping in their saddles. We had one, two, and sometimes three close engagements per day, having to dismount and fight on foot—the fighting being in many cases furious hand-to-hand contests." He and his companions, he claimed, had seen "some of the closest cavalry fighting, and been the coolest under shells, ever known in cavalry warfare." [68]

Never again would Lincoln ask, "Who ever saw a dead cavalryman?"

III

May 14

Grant Forfeits an Opportunity

"Mud, rain, darkness, and misery."

RAW AGGRESSIVENESS PROPELLED by a restless urge to get on with things defined Grant's military temperament. The trait was both a blessing and a curse. The taciturn general had infused the Union war effort with a ruthless momentum that promised to crush the Confederacy. The danger was that he might exhaust his own armies first. Burial details had scarcely begun clearing the Mule Shoe of corpses when Grant announced his next offensive. On the afternoon of May 13—Ewell's tattered Confederates had fallen back to their new line only twelve hours before, and Sheridan's troopers were making camp sixty miles to the south at Bottom's Bridge—the Army of the Potomac began steeling for another grueling round of combat. If Grant had his way, the battles for Spotsylvania Court House would resume with a vengeance before daylight the next morning.

Grant concocted his latest scheme after a sober assessment of Lee's deployments and of the roads around Spotsylvania Court House. Roads had drawn the armies here in the first place, and they radiated from the town like spokes from the hub of a wheel. Brock Road spun off to the north, toward the Wilderness. Fredericksburg Road knifed northeast, toward the queen city of the Rappahannock. And Massaponax Church Road rambled east, in the direction of Telegraph Road. A fourth road—Lee's potential escape route if things went wrong for the Confederates—dropped south to the Po River and continued on to Traveler's Rest, where it connected with another road network extending south to Richmond, west to Gordonsville, and east to Mud Tavern, on Telegraph Road.

These roads had dictated the course of combat for the past five days. On

May 8 the armies had engaged on Brock Road. Battle lines had sprung up along Laurel Hill and to the east, at the Mule Shoe. Along this front Grant had concentrated his attacks on May 10 and May 12 in an effort to break though to Spotsylvania Court House. Sporadic fighting had also flared along Fredericksburg Road, haunt of Burnside's 9th Corps, but combat there had paled beside the slaughter to the north and west. Relegated to a supporting role, Burnside did little. Lee felt comfortable leaving only scattered elements to guard Fredericksburg Road. And Massaponax Church Road stood virtually undefended; a single Confederate cavalry brigade patrolled it.

On May 13 Grant lacked details about Lee's dispositions, but he possessed enough information to plan his next attack. The Confederate left flank at Laurel Hill, held by Anderson's 1st Corps, was too strong to assault. So too was the Confederate center along the Mule Shoe's base, occupied by Ewell's 2nd Corps. But Lee's right—manned by Hill's 3rd Corps, temporarily under Early—appeared vulnerable. A strong strike there might well overrun the southern end of Early's entrenchments and break into the Army of Northern Virginia's rear. Once Early collapsed, the Federals could exploit the breach by dashing into Spotsylvania Court House, routing the Army of Northern Virginia, and administering a coup de grace as the southerners fled in disarray. A Union newspaperman summarized the thinking at headquarters: "Taking advantage of the storm and darkness, we expected to surprise the enemy, at least such of him as remained about Spotsylvania Court House, and re-enact the brilliant affair of [May 12]."[1]

Lee knew his right flank was weak, but the Federals had shown little interest there. The only enemy force posted on Fredericksburg Road was Colonel Elisha G. Marshall's 9th Corps Provisional Brigade, and no Federals occupied Massaponax Church Road. During the afternoon Union artillery shelled Early's line, causing a "great deal of powder burned," a southerner noted, "but not many fatalities upon our side." Cannonading had become routine, and the Confederates took the shelling in stride. But Lee was cautious enough to send two brigades—Brigadier General Edward A. Perry's Floridians and Nathaniel H. Harris's Mississippians—to cover the Massaponax Church Road approaches. Near evening, Lee directed Early to reconnoiter Fredericksburg Road to ascertain whether Grant was concentrating troops there. Mounting his white pony, the grandly mustached division commander Cadmus Wilcox led Brigadier General Alfred M. Scales's North Carolina brigade along Fredericksburg Road toward Marshall's entrenchments. Firing from behind earthworks, Marshall's men easily pinned down the Confederates. The light volume of Union musketry and Marshall's failure to counterattack persuaded Wilcox that he had encountered only a small Federal force, and he hurried back to report his findings to Lee. The North Carolinians lay low under a torrent of musket balls until dark and withdrew.[2]

Wilcox's intelligence confirmed Lee in his belief that Grant was ignoring the remote southern reaches of the battlefield. With the approaches along Fredericksburg Road and Massaponax Church Road apparently safe, Lee saw no point in reinforcing the sector. Little did he suspect that Grant had targeted the area for a crushing offensive before first light on May 14. Two days before, on the night of May 11–12, Lee had misjudged Grant's intentions and had unwittingly withdrawn artillery from the Mule Shoe, the very point where Grant meant to attack. Lee made a comparable miscalculation, fraught with equally devastating consequences, on the night of May 13.

From Mrs. Armstrong's porch, the Union commander-in-chief mulled over how best to exploit the evident weakness on Lee's right. Burnside's corps was already in place on Fredericksburg Road, but Grant had no faith in its fighting ability. The outfit contained a surfeit of new recruits led by undistinguished commanders, and Burnside had proven woefully inept. Hancock's corps was Grant's favorite vanguard for offensives, but the corps had not yet recovered from its mauling at the Mule Shoe on May 12. This left Grant the 5th and 6th Corps, entrenched in the Brock Road sector. Using them entailed risk. Warren had no stomach for charging fortified positions, and Wright remained unproven as a corps head. The 5th Corps, however, had missed the worst of the slaughter on May 12 and remained relatively fresh. And while the 6th Corps had taken a terrible battering at the Bloody Angle, it had fared better than the 2nd Corps. At least one 6th Corps division—James Ricketts's— had emerged from the fracas largely intact.

Weighing these variables, Grant decided the 5th and 6th Corps would initiate his assault. Lee would never expect them to show up on his right flank, enhancing the element of surprise essential to the venture's success. The important thing was to shift Warren and Wright from right to left fast enough to catch Lee off guard. This required hard marching and flawless coordination, traits that had eluded the Army of the Potomac thus far in the campaign. Grant tried to keep the details simple. After dark, Warren was to leave his earthworks on the right of the Union line, swing behind the army, and emerge on the opposite end of the Federal formation on Fredericksburg Road. Wright's 6th Corps was to follow and form on Warren's left, facing west along Massaponax Church Road. By morning, if all went as planned, the Union army would hold a line running north to south. Hancock and Burnside would form the army's northern wing and keep their troops "well in hand to repel any attack, and to advance should success render it desirable." The maneuver would climax with a predawn assault by Warren and Wright, now constituting the army's southern wing. At 4:00 A.M. on May 14, "if practicable," their two Union corps were to charge along Fredericksburg Road and Massaponax Church Road, converge on Spotsylvania Court House, and pierce the Confederate line.[3]

That was a big "if." Assuming that Warren and Wright started at dark, they would have eight hours to march four and six miles, respectively, to their jumping-off points. Under favorable conditions troops could cover that distance in the allotted time with ease. But conditions were not favorable the night of May 13–14. Mud, rain, and darkness conspired against the operation. Grant had a bad habit of ordering movements without allowing enough time for preparation, and his spur-of-the-moment concentration against Lee's right was no exception. Grant settled on the idea around 4:00 P.M. on May 13. An hour later Warren knew nothing about his route except that headquarters promised to provide a guide. Wright's instructions were equally nebulous. He knew only that headquarters wanted him to move at the same time as Warren, but by a different route—"if roads can be found"—to avoid congestion. Warren's aide and future brother-in-law, Major Washington A. Roebling, anticipated serious problems. "We were expected to march all night," he griped, "get into position on the left of Burnside's in an unknown country, in the midst of an Egyptian darkness, up to our knees in the mud, and assault the enemy's position which we had never seen."[4]

Not until 8:00 P.M.—the hour Grant had set for the maneuver to begin— did Warren receive precise information about his line of march. To avoid detection by the Confederates, he was to swing behind Wright's entrenched line. After reaching Wright's headquarters at the Shelton place, he was to nudge east to the Landrum house, behind Hancock's earthworks, and from there follow a farm road to the Ni River, about a mile east of the Landrum farm through dense woods. Captain William H. Paine was to meet the 5th Corps at the river and guide it the remaining mile to Fredericksburg Road. If the Ni proved unfordable—the small stream was usually easy to wade, but rain had swollen Spotsylvania County's creeks into formidable obstacles— Warren was to turn south and follow Burnside's entrenchments until he struck Fredericksburg Road near the Beverly farm. To relieve congestion on these narrow, rain-drenched trails, Colonel Charles S. Wainwright, Warren's artillery chief, was to take his guns north to Gordon Road. From there Meade's chief engineer, Major James C. Duane, would lead the guns to Warren's infantry.

The 5th Corps's objective was the Beverly house. This fine homestead, on high ground along the eastern side of Fredericksburg Road a quarter mile south of the Ni, provided an excellent staging area. Broad fields extended from the house to the river, ensuring ample water for men and mounts. Troops could mass behind the ridge hidden from the Confederates. Griffin's division was to deploy near the Beverly house; Cutler's division was to form west of the road on Griffin's right, connecting with Burnside; and the rest of 5th Corps—Crawford, Kitching, and the Maryland Brigade—was to assemble in reserve. Grant questioned whether Wainwright could manhandle the 5th Corps's guns to the Beverly house in time for the attack and asked Burnside to make his artillery available to Warren. "Dispositions will be made immediately on arriving on the ground," Warren directed his subordinates. "Quiet will be preserved, and no fires built." Above all, the young general insisted, the 5th Corps had to reach the Beverly farm by 4:00 A.M. "Success depends upon it," he stressed, "and the saving of much loss of life." [5]

Warren knew all about the hazards of conducting night marches on short notice. His troops had led the army across the Rapidan on the night of May 3–4 and had spearheaded the shift to Spotsylvania Court House on the night of May 7–8. Now they were venturing once again into Virginia's inky blackness on a foray against Lee. Despite Warren's best efforts, rations arrived too late for issue to the soldiers, and wagons obstructed the 5th Corps's line of march. Rain had fallen for two days and held no promise of abating. "I am afraid we do not get notice of things in time," Warren protested. "I'll do the best I can, but very difficult things are being attempted on these night movements over such roads." [6]

Warren managed to prod Griffin into motion by 10:00 P.M., but he could not get his other two divisions—Cutler's and Crawford's—under way until midnight. By 1:00 A.M. Griffin, Cutler, and Crawford had passed behind Wright's 6th Corps earthworks. The Maryland Brigade and Kitching's brigade had yet to start, however, and the 5th Corps's artillery was stuck in traffic on the crowded roadways. Warren was hopelessly behind schedule. Worse still, Wright had no choice but to leave his men in their entrenchments until Warren had passed, a delay that threatened to consume several hours more. Meade's engineers searched for an alternate route for the 6th Corps but concluded that Warren's course was the only practicable way. "The column moves very slowly," Warren fretted. "It is one of the darkest nights at this hour I ever saw." [7]

The only good news to reach Union headquarters that rain-swept night was a report that Warren had slipped away undetected by the rebels. The bustle of Warren's departure and misleading remarks by Union pickets had persuaded Charles Field's Confederates on Laurel Hill that an attack was imminent.

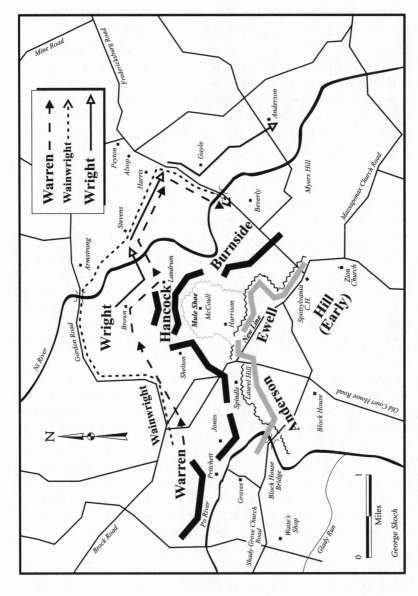

Warren's and Wright's march on the night of May 13–14

Field's gunners double-shotted their pieces with canister, and his men stood ready at their posts. When one o'clock passed, the Confederates began to relax. "Everything looked as it did the night before," a rebel observed of the camp-fires winking behind Warren's earthworks, little imagining that the blazes were the handiwork of Colonel James L. Bates, who had remained behind with his 12th Massachusetts and the 11th Pennsylvania to disguise Warren's departure. "I'm darned if I believe anybody's over there," a Georgian exclaimed. "I'm going to see!" Dashing across the field, he led a handful of Confederates to the Union earthworks. A fusillade from Bates convinced him that Warren was still in place.[8]

While Bates carried out his deception, Wright waited impatiently for Warren to pass so that he could start. Colonel Emory Upton, whose brigade was to lead the 6th Corps, posted an aide to alert him when the last of War-ren's column had dribbled past. Propped against a tree, the man watched the shadowy figures as they stumbled by, cursing the darkness. "I was feeling very blue, tired and worn out, sick of seeing dead and wounded," the sentinel ruminated. "The small fires on the road side threw a dim light on the passing soldiers, but enough for me to see how tired and haggard each man looked. It was a sad time to me."[9]

Slipping down a muddy hillside, Warren's strung-out column at long last came to the Ni. Water reached waist-high, but the men, already rain-soaked, waded across. All trace of road disappeared on the far bank, where Captain Paine was waiting as promised. It was pitch dark—"literally you could not see your hand held before you," Humphreys confirmed. Scouts had built fires to light Warren's way, but downpours put out the flames and dense clouds ob-scured the moon and stars. "A terrible piece of work, dirt up to our knees, rain from above," a Federal grumbled. "Many have their shoes stuck fast in the mud and march in stockings or barefoot." The column kept breaking, and staff officers darted about trying to reunite the pieces. Suddenly soldiers would jolt off again, a Pennsylvanian recounted, "cursing and floundering knee-deep in mud and mire that stuck with an unyielding persistency." George M. Barnard of the 18th Massachusetts saw troops "so utterly wretched that they threw themselves in the middle of the road wallowing in the mud under the horses' feet, howling and crying like mad men." He wrote home: "I never knew such a horrible night, all mud, rain, darkness and misery."[10]

Warren's foot soldiers trudged on in a daze, past signal fires flaring and hissing in the rain. Avery Harris of the 143rd Pennsylvanian collapsed within earshot of a group of skulkers. "Everything and everyone from old Abe Lin-coln down came in for their share of abuse," Harris reminisced. "Jeff Davis was as good as Lincoln," the skulkers chattered loudly. "They didn't come down there to fight for the damned Nigger, and they wasn't going to be driven out of their night's rest by any damned provosts." A handful of Massachusetts soldiers sat in the trail bemoaning their lot when a party of horsemen approached. Refusing to move, the malcontents cursed the riders. "Boys, I know you are tired, but I am General Warren and I must get through," a mounted figure announced. The men stopped swearing and made way for their commander.[11]

Around 3:00 A.M. the head of the 5th Corps' column emerged from the gloomy forest onto open farmland. Clement Harris lived here with his wife and three children, on a homestead named Bloomsbury. Harris's broad pastures extended to Fredericksburg Road, a short distance away. Roebling rode on to find Burnside and procure a guide. He located the 9th Corps commander at Susan Alsop's farm, adjacent to the Harris place. Burnside and his staff seemed unfamiliar with the country, a fact that surprised Roebling, as the 9th Corps had occupied the area for five days. Burnside sent for Colonel Marshall, whose Provisional Brigade still manned the earthworks on the Beverly farm that Warren was to occupy. Marshall offered to show Roebling the way, and soon Warren's lead element—Brigadier General Romeyn B. Ayres's brigade, of Griffin's division—was swinging along Fredericksburg Road toward the Beverly farm, about a mile away.[12]

Four o'clock arrived. Daylight was fast approaching. Only twelve hundred of Griffin's bleary-eyed soldiers had reached the Beverly place, where the 5th Corps was slated to launch its assault. Roebling looked the men over and pronounced them too "fagged-out" to attack. Warren rode up and concurred in his aide's assessment. "The head of my column came here a little while ago," he advised Meade by courier, "but in the night most of the men fell out of the ranks from weariness and the command became disjointed, and part lost their way." Warren estimated that he had barely enough men for a skirmish line. "Far and near stragglers were scattered in every degree of exhaustion," a Federal noted. At 6:30 A.M. Warren informed headquarters his soldiers were "gradually coming in, but a large portion will be all day, and are exhausted with fatigue." He doubted that he could fight "to advantage" and inquired what he should do next. "You will make your dispositions to attack and report as soon as ready," Meade curtly replied. Half an hour later, Meade and his staff visited Warren to assess the situation. Then they rode out to the Anderson farm, half a mile east of the Beverly house. The 6th Corps, Meade decided, would congregate at the Anderson place on its way to Massaponax Church Road. Meade selected the site as a convenient location for monitoring the deployment and set up his headquarters there.[13]

Grant read reports from the front in dismay. Shortly after 7:00 A.M. he dashed off a note to Washington. "The very heavy rains of the last forty-eight hours have made it almost impossible to move trains or artillery," he informed his chief-of-staff Major General Henry W. Halleck. "Two corps were moved last night, in the night, from our right to the left, with orders to attack at 4:00 A.M., but owing to the difficulties of the road have not fully got into position." He was not optimistic. "This," he concluded, "with the continued bad weather may prevent offensive operations to-day." [14]

At 7:30 Warren took another head count. Griffin now had 2,500 men up, and Cutler 1,300. Near the Beverly house, these troops had filed into earthworks formerly occupied by Colonel Marshall's brigade. Half an hour later Warren counted 5,000 men in hand, less than a third of his command. His signal officer climbed to the Beverly house's upper floor for a look at the Confederate fortifications. Six hundred yards away, Early's earthworks extended into woods on both sides of Fredericksburg Road. Rifle pits for sharpshooters dotted the fields in front of the entrenchments, and two lines of backup works rose ominously in the distance. The signal officer counted sixteen rebel artillery pieces, and he suspected correctly that Early had more. Spotsylvania Court House was visible a little over a mile away. A glance out the Beverly house's top window persuaded Warren's aide Roebling that the Confederates were "well entrenched along their whole front." At least one assumption underlying Grant's turning movement—that a Union corps could charge down Fredericksburg Road with little opposition—was plainly wrong. With the 5th Corps scattered and disorganized, and with the 6th Corps nowhere in sight, prospects for a successful assault were negligible. The frustrated commanders could only wait for more troops to arrive.[15]

The troops did not share their superiors' frustration. They were tired and welcomed the chance to rest. Besides, they had been fighting for days in a wooded, dreary countryside. Here tall pines, rolling fields, manor houses, and gardens delighted the eye. As though on cue, sunlight peeked through the clouds. A poetical Federal observed that the ray of sun imparted a "coloring o'er the scene it could not have commanded of itself alone." [16]

Finally, 5th Corps artillery rumbled up. Colonel Wainwright, commanding the ordnance, had started off at 10:00 P.M. with forty-six guns and 120 wagons and gotten onto Gordon Road as instructed. Prisoners, wounded soldiers, and wagons had clogged the way. "I had to exert the full force of my authority and constantly appeal to the spread eagle on my shoulders in order to get past these endless trains," Wainwright wrote of his travail. By the time he reached the Armstrong house, movement had become impossible. Fuming, Wainwright had paced back and forth, finding brief solace in a drink and cursing his superiors. "If it was General Meade's intention that I should move by this road, and I presume it was, as my guide is furnished here, he should have informed [the army's chief quartermaster] of it and held him responsible that the road was not blocked," he seethed. Finally a man had appeared who professed to know a shortcut, and Wainwright had jumped at the opportunity. Leaving Gordon Road, the artillery had plunged along a narrow track scarcely wide enough for gun carriages. Trees crowded from both sides, and the escort's white mount bobbed ahead in the darkness like a cork on the sea. Since the guns could not turn around, Wainwright and his staff stayed far enough back to give the guide leeway to find his path. After about a mile—a gunner recollected slogging "knee deep in mud, through forests, stumbling over tree stumps in the pitch dark, rain pouring"—the trail emptied into Warren's infantry route, and the guns slipped into a gap in the procession.[17]

Wainwright posted his guns as they arrived. Lieutenant Benjamin F. Rittenhouse's battery rolled onto high ground west of Fredericksburg Road. Captain James H. Cooper and Lieutenant George Breck unlimbered their batteries near the Beverly house to cover the 5th Corps's left flank. Before long the distinctive concussion of artillery punctuated the morning quiet. The Confederates had spotted Rittenhouse's Battery D, 5th United States Artillery, which faced a bulge in the Confederate line called Heth's Salient. Early's forty guns concentrated their fire on Rittenhouse's six pieces. While some Union artillerists threw up entrenchments, others returned fire until the guns were knocked out of action. On hearing a rumor that the battery had been destroyed, Warren and his division commander Griffin—a gruff former gunner who still considered himself an expert in artillery—rode over to investigate. Rittenhouse, it developed, had sustained severe losses but had managed to construct sufficiently strong works to hold his position. "They came to stay and they did stay," a Confederate admitted, citing Rittenhouse's stand as the "bravest act of the war." [18]

At long last—it was now 8:00 A.M.—the head of Wright's corps appeared. The soldiers had not left their assembly area at the Shelton house until nearly 3:00 A.M. and had struggled along in Warren's churned-up path. Five hours of "slipping and sliding in the mud," as an aide put it, left them in no condition to fight. Upton's brigade, leading the bedraggled procession, crossed over to the Anderson farm, east of the Beverly place, where Meade and his staff were waiting. The rest of the 6th Corps trailed behind.[19]

Grant and Meade saw no choice but to call off the assault, at least for now. "The elements seemed to oppose the plan," a soldier observed. "The entire region seemed soaked into one vast quagmire." Meade directed Warren to advance skirmishers and determine the enemy's strength. Wright was to collect his units at the Anderson place as they arrived. Later, if weather permitted, he could resume his march to the staging area at Massaponax Church Road, about a mile and a half away.[20]

Confederates spotted the massive Union concentration, and John Chambliss's cavalrymen monitored the buildup. At 8:00 A.M. Chambliss's superior, Rooney Lee, reported that Union troops were streaming into the Beverly farm. Hoping to keep the Federals bottled up along the Ni, Early's artillery began lobbing shells into Warren's infantry. Most of the projectiles passed harmlessly overhead, although one shell decapitated an orderly, and several exploded near Warren's headquarters at the Beverly house. The shelling threatened signalmen stringing telegraph wires from the Beverly house to the other corps's headquarters. "I recollect tossing up a cent with Ed Hall and George Henderson, once after a shell had broken the line, to decide who should go and tie up the break," telegrapher Samuel Edwards reminisced. "Before undertaking the serious work demanded, the one going out would say to the others, 'If my body stops a shell send my things home.'"[21]

The artillery demonstration further confirmed Grant and Meade in their resolve against attacking. The soldiers, becoming accustomed to Grant's insistent pace of warfare, expected the respite to be brief. "Everything betokens a heavy battle and I presume that today or tomorrow on this ground will be fought the fight that will close [the] cussed rebellion," a long-suffering Federal predicted.[22]

"He seems to be extending to our right."

While Warren's and Wright's troops straggled into place, Colonel Bates's two regiments continued their lively charade in the entrenchments that Warren and Wright had vacated during the night. Their job was to deceive the rebels into believing that the 5th and 6th Corps were still in the Brock Road sector. Two companies of the 1st Massachusetts Cavalry, under Captain Charles F. Adams Jr., were posted as vedettes off Bates's right flank. In support of the ruse, the Union 2nd Corps's artillery opened from near the Landrum House, and Francis Barlow's pickets feinted toward Ewell's new line across the base of the Mule Shoe. Ewell's pickets fired back from advance rifle pits, and sharp skirmishing broke out. The subterfuge, complete with noise and smoke, seemed to be working. Lee understood that Federals were concentrating near the Beverly and Anderson farms, but he did not know that Grant had evacuated the northern half of his position.[23]

Midmorning, as Confederate pickets in front of Laurel Hill intensified their probes, Bates began to question whether he could hold on. His two regiments and Adams's cavalry occupied four miles of earthworks. A tenacious

rebel attack was bound to break through. At 10:00 A.M. Meade concluded that
Lee must be onto his game and authorized Bates to leave. Hancock gave the assignment of extricating Bates to his aide-de-camp, Major William G. Mitchell.

Getting Bates out was a ticklish proposition. Once rebels discovered him
leaving, they were certain to overwhelm his small force. Mitchell decided to
withdraw Bates's force in stages, starting on the right. He began the maneuver
around 11:00 A.M., first pulling back Captain Adams's cavalry, then vacating
the works nearest the Po. Field's skirmishers spotted the Federals leaving and
dashed into the empty trenches, eager for loot. Then Kershaw's Confederates
sensed that Wright's corps was gone as well and crowded into breastworks the
6th Corps had abandoned. Fortunately for Bates the rebels failed to appreciate
that they faced only two regiments. By midafternoon Bates had disengaged
his entire force at the cost of only a few wounded men.[24]

Hancock now found himself hard pressed. His earthworks joined the left
end of Wright's empty line. With Wright gone and rebels taking his place,
Hancock's right flank was dangerously exposed. "The enemy's pickets followed [Bates's] line in and are now engaged with my skirmishers," Hancock
reported. To protect his right flank, Hancock ran a line of entrenchments
northward and anchored a stand of guns near the home of the Brown family.[25]

The Laurel Hill front fell silent. The Confederates were exhilarated. "We
felt like boys out of school," reminisced Brigadier General Edward P.
Alexander, who commanded the 1st Corps's artillery. "For a little while the
strain would be off. We could walk and sit outside the trenches, and shells
stopped coming around." The southerners merrily looted watches, rings,
money, and hats from corpses that dotted the fields. Lieutenant Colonel Frank
Huger, heading one of Alexander's battalions, took special interest in the fate
of a wounded Union soldier who had been trapped between the lines for several days. Occasionally the man would sit up, and once he tried to kill himself
by dropping a musket on his head. "It hardly seemed possible that a man
could really give himself a fatal blow in that way," Alexander thought. As
soon as the musketry ceased, Huger and Alexander ventured into the Spindle
field by Brock Road. The man was dead, and a Confederate had taken his
clothes, revealing eagles and flags tattooed across his arms and chest.
Alexander and Huger continued to Warren's abandoned line and studied the
empty artillery positions with interest. "We hurried our inspection," Alexander added, "for we anticipated orders at any moment to march."[26]

Shifting Warren and Wright from right to left had dramatically reoriented the
Federal line of battle. Only one infantry corps—Hancock's, which occupied

earthworks extending roughly from the Brown house to the Landrum house—faced south. Grant's three other infantry corps faced west in a line roughly perpendicular to Fredericksburg Road, which served as the Union army's axis and Grant's chief route for moving supplies and troops. The neglected region of the battlefield had become Grant's most important arena.

Four homes provided landmarks in the emerging battlefront. A mile and a half northeast of Spotsylvania Court House, on the eastern side of Fredericksburg Road, stood Josiah P. Gayle's graceful two-and-a-half-story mansion. The proprietor, a seventy-year-old Virginian, had two sons serving with the 9th Virginia Cavalry and harbored no sympathy for the invaders. He and his family had fled a few days earlier, taking what they could in light wagons and leaving the rest to the Yankees. Bracketed by two chimneys and surrounded by outbuildings, the Gayle house had served as Burnside's headquarters for several days, and wounded men still spilled across its fields. From the Gayle yard, Fredericksburg Road descended southwest sharply to the Ni, then rose to a plateau called Whig Hill. A sunken driveway ran three hundred yards east to Francis C. Beverly's handsome L-shaped house, which Warren had appropriated for his headquarters. Griffin's division camped along the Beverly driveway, and Cutler's division straddled Fredericksburg Road, reaching west to connect with Burnside. Warren's remaining troops bivouacked on the fields that sloped downhill gently from the Beverly house north to the Ni. Spotsylvania Court House's spires were plainly visible from the Beverly house's upper story, slightly over a mile away.[27]

On a companion elevation to Whig Hill three-quarters of a mile east of the Beverly farm stood the home of the Anderson family. The grounds were still well manicured and afforded fine views of the surrounding country. Lyman, who inspected the house with Meade, counted it among Virginia's grander dwellings and wrote glowingly about its "nest of out-houses in the Southern style." Large fields made the Anderson place a perfect assembly area for the 6th Corps. From the yard, a wagon trail wound along the Ni's upper bank to Massaponax Church Road, the 6th Corps's ultimate objective. Wright set up headquarters in the Anderson yard and was joined there during the morning by Meade, Grant, and their staffs.[28]

Another prominent knoll named Bleak Hill dominated the landscape. The hill and the farm around it belonged to the Myers family, who had purchased the property a few years earlier from the Gayles. The place was known locally as Myers Hill, and a tenant named Jett occupied the two-story house that perched strategically on the hilltop. Looming a mile southeast of the Beverly house and three-quarters of a mile southwest of the Anderson farm, Myers Hill afforded a bird's-eye view of the new Union dispositions and overlooked Wright's prospective route to Massaponax Church Road. Grant's attack was in trouble if Confederates controlled this high ground.

Peering through field glasses from the top floor of the Beverly house, Warren spotted gray-clad cavalrymen atop Myers Hill. The rebels had placed cannon there as well. Over at the Anderson farm Grant and Meade also saw the danger. Capturing Myers Hill became their primary objective for the morning. Reaching the distant piece of high ground, however, presented a challenge. The Ni flowed southeasterly between the Beverly and Anderson farms, then turned sharply south to carve out a V-shaped little valley with steep banks. Wright's corps had no convenient place to cross the stream and reach Myers Hill. Warren's corps, at the Beverly place, was on the same side of the river as Myers Hill, but a swamp and dense woods obstructed the way. The knoll must be taken, Meade insisted, and he gave the assignment to Warren, who had more troops on hand than Wright. Shortly after 7:00 A.M. Warren directed Lieutenant Colonel Elwell S. Otis of the 140th New York to seize Myers Hill with his own regiment and the 91st Pennsylvania.[29]

Warren was a "lean, yellow long-haired Indian looking sort of a man, high cheek bones, black eyes and hair," a young drummer remarked, "and also a black mustache which he twirls just before a fight." Doubtless he twirled his moustache now.[30]

Otis left the Beverly farm with three hundred men and headed across wooded and swampy low ground. Half an hour later—it was now about 8:00 A.M.—the sweaty band of Federals emerged onto a cleared portion of the Myers property. Their objective loomed ahead. Cooper's and Breck's batteries opened from the Beverly place to cover the attack, and projectiles arched across the intervening mile of greenery and exploded above the hilltop.[31]

At the Anderson farm Grant and Meade watched Otis's progress with interest. They were discussing Myers Hill with Wright when Emory Upton rode up. Recently recommended for promotion to brigadier general, the intense young man from upstate New York epitomized the aggressive field commander. He always seemed eager to fight and reveled in assaulting difficult positions. He had proven his mettle the previous fall by charging a Confederate bridgehead on the Rappahannock River, and more recently he had breached Lee's formidable earthworks at Spotsylvania Court House. Peering across at Myers Hill, Upton announced with customary enthusiasm, "I can take that hill with my brigade!" Meade hesitated. Upton had started the campaign with about sixteen hundred men, but severe fighting had seriously depleted his command. "I hope you will let me try it," Upton urged. "I'm certain I can take it." Meade asked Upton how many soldiers he had left. "About eight or nine hundred men," he replied. Satisfied that Upton had enough troops for the task, Meade directed him to move at once to support Otis's attack on Myers Hill.[32]

The Confederates belonged to Chambliss's cavalry brigade. One of Chambliss's three mounted regiments—the 9th Virginia Cavalry—had been recruited from this very region, and its men were intimately familiar with every trail and plantation road. The previous night, Chambliss's troopers and Captain William M. McGregor's four-gun battery had camped on Massaponax Church Road south of Myers Hill. Some of McGregor's guns and a detachment from the 9th Virginia Cavalry had ventured out a farm road and occupied the knoll. These were the guns and their supports that Warren had spied through his glass.[33]

While Upton painstakingly negotiated the steep and muddy slope from the Anderson house to the Ni, Otis's 5th Corps soldiers formed a battle line at the foot of Myers Hill. The rebels on top took cover in the Myers house and adjoining log slave quarters and opened fire. Charging into a "rain of bullets," the two Union regiments dislodged the Confederates by force of numbers. The tenant Jett fired at the Federals from the house with aggravating persistence and ran off with the rebels. To Otis's disappointment, McGregor hauled his guns to safety.

Reluctant to surrender Myers Hill without a fight, Chambliss hurried the rest of his brigade from Massaponax Church Road. The troopers dismounted in a stand of woods fringing the southwest edge of the Myers farm, and at Chambliss's signal they rushed the hill. It became Otis's turn to run. Retreating under a hail of gunfire, the Federals sought cover in the Myers dwelling, in the slave quarters, and in an orchard next to the house.[34]

Battle smoke wreathed Myers Hill. Warren's and Wright's soldiers strained to watch the spirited engagement from their box seats at the Beverly and Anderson farms. Otis's men fought for their lives, acutely aware of their precarious position far in front of the Union army. Upton had crossed the river, but he was still too far away to help. Warren understood Otis's predicament and directed Cooper and Breck to redouble their cannonading. Shells screamed into the Myers farm, forcing Chambliss's troopers to creep from tree to tree, inching toward Otis through a veritable blizzard of iron. "The fire was now terrible," a Virginian recounted, "and we found the trees no protection except for our bodies, our legs and arms being entirely exposed." In the nick of time, Upton's troops came scrambling up the hill's backside and fired two volleys into the southerners. Severely outnumbered, Chambliss ordered his men to fall back along the farm track toward Massaponax Church Road.[35]

After the southerners left, Otis regrouped his small command. Meade decided to let Upton's fresh troops hold Myers Hill and directed Otis to bring his men back to the Beverly place. The New Yorkers and Pennsylvanians returned to a round of congratulations from the 5th Corps. Upton began fortifying the hill, posting a lookout atop the house and constructing fence-rail breastworks across the farm track to Massaponax Church Road. The young colonel felt apprehensive, as Myers Farm was dangerously exposed and difficult to reinforce if attacked. Concerned that Confederates might return in force, Upton asked for support. Soon the 2nd and 10th New Jersey regiments were splashing over the Ni to join him on the Myers farm.[36]

While Upton oversaw the construction of his defensive perimeter, an aide strolled over to inspect the Myers house. Out of habit, he removed his footgear before entering. "This was the second time since the campaign opened that I took off my boots," he paused to reflect. "My feet were raw, my boots had become part of me."[37]

The final elements of Wright's and Warren's corps had straggled in by late morning and set to brewing coffee on the Beverly and Anderson farms. Myers Hill lay snugly in Union hands. Had Grant wished, he could have instructed Wright to complete his movement to Massaponax Church Road and proceeded with his delayed offensive against the southern end of Lee's line. The late arrival of Warren and Wright, it was true, had forfeited the advantage of surprise. But the other factors that had led Grant to try his luck here had not changed. The sector defined by Fredericksburg Road and Massaponax Church Road remained Lee's weakest point. Even after the appearance of massive numbers of blue-clad troops, Lee had shifted no soldiers to counter the Union buildup. Why did Grant, who personified aggressiveness, continue to hesitate?

Foul weather doubtless influenced Grant's thinking. "The whole country is a sea of mud," Wainwright scrawled in his journal. Rain disrupted the movement of troops and guns and made it difficult to bring supplies to the front. Sheridan's absence also played a part, as Grant lacked sufficient means to investigate Lee's troop dispositions. From the Beverly roof, the Confederate earthworks seemed more formidable than anyone had expected. Grant's low opinion of Warren, compounded by questions about Wright's ability, must also have entered into his thinking. Grant had hoped to compensate for these deficiencies by attacking at dawn, but his troops' late arrival had made that impossible. Two days after the Bloody Angle, Grant could ill afford another round of massive casualties with no discernible gains to show for his losses.

Grant's decision to cancel his attack reflected his heightened appreciation

of Lee's skills as a defensive fighter. He assumed that Lee had rushed reinforcements to the newly threatened portion of his line, which is what a general of Lee's skill ought to have done. Believing that Lee had countered his
movement, Grant withheld his blow. In fact, Lee had not moved a single soldier to counter Grant's deployment. In the psychological play between the
two generals, Grant's decision to cancel his attack on May 14 stands as compelling evidence that on that day at least, Lee had gained the upper hand.

Chambliss sent word to Lee that Federals had taken the Myers place. His
messenger, Lieutenant Robert J. Washington of the 9th Virginia Cavalry,
found the Confederate commander dozing on a plank at Zion Church, still
trying to recuperate from his sleepless night two days before. Staffers awak-
ened the general, and Washington briefed him on Chambliss's fight. Lee expressed concern that Grant be prevented from consolidating his lodgment
below the Ni. The interview closed on a sad note. Jeb Stuart was dead, Lee
informed the cavalryman. Lieutenant Washington rode back to Chambliss
with the sorrowful tidings. As word of the cavalry commander's death spread,
men bowed their heads in "bitterness and disappointment and grief." [38]

Washington's report gave Lee important intelligence. He now knew Grant
was concentrating toward the Confederate right. But why? Did Grant intend
to turn Lee's right? Did he mean to attack? Or was he simply undertaking a
diversion to disguise his real intentions? Lee needed more information before
he could respond. "The enemy is making movements here which are not yet
to be fully understood," Lee's aide Charles S. Venable wrote in a dispatch
that reflected the Confederate commander's uncertainty. "He seems to be extending to our right," Venable went on, "having occupied the position at the
Beverly house, and the [Myers house], on this side of the river." [39]

Surprisingly, Lee did not reinforce his right. Anderson and Ewell were securely entrenched and had troops to spare. Borrowing men from them to buttress the defenses facing Grant's new point of concentration made eminent
tactical sense. But Lee ignored the danger. The record suggests no reasons for
his neglect. Most likely, he did not understand the extent of Grant's buildup
in the Fredericksburg Road sector.

But Lee, true to his aggressive nature, remained determined to disrupt
Grant's plans. His first step was to recapture Myers Hill. The eminence stood
in front of Jubal Early's section of line, and Lee told Early to take it. The
crusty former prosecutor from Franklin County, Virginia, selected two brigades from Mahone's division, placing chief responsibility on Brigadier
General Ambrose R. Wright's Georgians, that day commanded by Lieutenant
Colonel Matthew R. Hall of the 48th Georgia. The outfit had escaped the
worst of the fighting around Spotsylvania Court House and was relatively

fresh. To support the Georgians, Early picked Nathaniel Harris's Mississippians. This battle-scarred brigade had recently proven its tenacity with a grueling twenty-hour stand at the Bloody Angle. The outfit had been seriously mauled, but its effectiveness in combat remained beyond question. Screened by Chambliss's riders, Early led his two brigades east along Massaponax Church Road, veered left at the rutted wagon trail to the Myers farm, and deployed troops into the woods. Quietly they formed a battle line, Mississippians left of the trail and Georgians to the right. A quarter of a mile away, across the open fields of the Myers farm, the Confederates could make out Upton's line of fence rails piled with dirt. Men in blue uniforms could be seen milling about, oblivious to the gray-clad figures deploying under cover of the forest.[40]

"Upton's Run."

The situation along the northern wing of Grant's line—Hancock's and Burnside's sector—was degenerating into a version of trench warfare, portending bitter days to come. Musketry and artillery scored the contending earthworks. Shell-shocked soldiers wandered a smoldering no-man's land between the lines. One "curious specimen of humanity" strolled into the 9th Corps's fortifications. Mud-caked and clothed in mixed Yankee and Confederate garb, he had long, stringy hair and gaunt looks that stamped him a rebel. He claimed to belong to a Michigan regiment but was unable to name his superiors and recalled nothing of his own background. Convinced that the man was a spy, soldiers brought him to headquarters for questioning. His inquisitors had no success. "He was either daft, or very successful in the imitation thereof," a witness concluded. Exasperated, they took him to his outfit to see if anyone recognized him. "The boys in the Michigan regiment received us with a great shout," a soldier related, "and their officers vouched for our prisoner as OK." [41]

Grant had planned no immediate action for his army's northern wing, affording Hancock's and Burnside's soldiers time to rest and write letters. Some of Hancock's men amused themselves trying to extricate two Confederate twelve-pound guns that stood marooned between the lines. Under cover of a friendly artillery bombardment, Union gunners and volunteers from the 61st New York ran to the pieces, hitched ropes to them, and hauled the trophies into the Union works. The guns, like pieces captured the previous day, were too shot up to be serviceable. Burnside's soldiers whiled away the lull improving their earthworks, hanging clothing to dry, and keeping up the "threatening" posture Grant had prescribed. Near noon, General Potter, com-

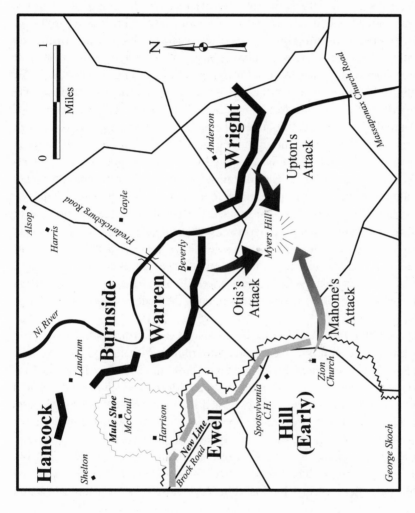

Operations at Myers Hill on May 14

manding the 9th Corps's northernmost division, directed Brigadier General Simon G. Griffin to advance his brigade into the no-man's land between the armies to determine whether Confederates still occupied the opposing earthworks. "Terrific fire" from Early's guns raked Griffin's men and drove them back. A soldier grumbled that the operation was "not attended with any especial results." Elements from Cutler's division, which bridged the gap between Burnside's left and the 5th Corps's main body on Fredericksburg Road, also ventured toward Hill's line. They succeeded only in stirring up Confederate artillery and went running back. "The enemy is in plain view not a mile from us and busy as bees fortifying," a soldier in Colonel William W. Robinson's Iron Brigade proclaimed. "They have a strong position and one that will cost many lives to get if we are compelled to advance upon it." [42]

Upton's position was still quite vulnerable. His closest support—Warren's corps—lay a mile away through intractable forest at the Beverly house. A steep-banked stretch of the Ni separated him from Wright. If the rebels attacked, he would have to fend for himself. Anticipating the worst, he spent the afternoon buttressing his defenses. The 95th Pennsylvania, 96th Pennsylvania, and 121st New York constructed fence-rail barricades at the base of Myers Hill, commanding the farm track that threaded over to Massaponax Church Road. Upton's fortifications looked across six hundred yards of cleared ground to a tree line bordered by a fence. It was from these woods, Upton surmised, that the Confederates were likely to attack. Lighting fires in anticipation of cooking their afternoon meal, the Federals watched the forest closely. [43]

Around 4:00 P.M. Upton's lookout sounded the alarm. Confederates were approaching. Upton directed Lieutenant Colonel William H. Lessig to take his 96th Pennsylvania and two companies from the 2nd New Jersey and investigate. Just as Lessig was preparing to go, Meade and Wright rode up, and Upton invited them to watch. Lessig led his men over the earthworks and started across the field toward the line of woods. A skirmisher, Henry Keiser of the 96th Pennsylvania, spotted a felt hat lying near the far tree line. "There is a Rebel hat, and the Reb is not far off," he shouted and went closer to look. Sure enough, a Confederate—an officer from a Georgia regiment who had crept to the field to get a look at Upton's deployments—was crouched in a ditch, and Keiser called on him to surrender. "For God's sake, don't shoot," the rebel cried as he stood and raised his hands. Lieutenant Van Hollern of the 96th Pennsylvania took the prisoner's pistols and sword—the captive was a major—and began interrogating him. Were other Confederates nearby? he demanded. The major swore that he was alone. Van Hollern did not believe him and led him to the rear for more questioning. [44]

Lessig decided to send a scout into the woods before committing his entire command. Anxious to prove himself, a thirteen-year-old boy from the regiment's mess begged Lessig to let him go. Lessig assented and gave the young man a horse. The "bright little fellow," as a Federal later described him, galloped to the edge of the forest, stopped, and peered inside. A flurry of shots whizzed past his head. Waving his cap, he spurred his mount back to Lessig's wide-eyed troops. "Lots of them in the woods," he screamed as he sped past.[45]

Close behind the boy came Ambrose Wright's Georgians, led by Colonel Hall. Into the clearing they marched, muskets leveled. The 3rd Georgia, on the brigade's right, pushed somewhat ahead and began firing into Lessig's command, which stood in a line midway across the field. Outnumbered by the Georgia brigade, Lessig retired a short distance, and the 95th Pennsylvania and 10th New Jersey rushed into the clearing to reinforce him. The rest of Upton's men began shooting from behind their barricade at the Confederates over the heads of Lessig's troops. The 3rd Georgia came under concentrated musketry that "quickly thinned its ranks," according to a rebel. Captain D. B. Langston, heading the regiment, fell severely wounded, and command devolved on Captain L. F. Luckie, who halted the regiment in the field. "Some imaginary command, or misunderstood order, brought about this destructive move," a witness surmised. "In full view, in good range of the enemy's guns," he added, "the gallant old Regiment stood for a moment a target." Luckie decided that it was safer to advance than to retreat and urged his soldiers to continue the charge. "The men didn't seem at all anxious to do so," a Confederate related. They remained still, uncertain of what to do.[46]

Spurred to action by the sight of his companions falling around him, Lieutenant R. G. Hyman of Company F grasped the Georgia regiment's flag and dashed forward. "Rally on your colors, 3rd Georgia!" he shouted. Hyman's example was electrifying. With a piercing yell, the 3rd Georgia charged into Lessig's detachment, routed it, and marched resolutely toward Upton's earthworks. The rest of the brigade pitched in and sprang "tiger-like" over the Union barricade. The 2nd Georgia Battalion planted its colors on the works, followed closely by the 22nd Georgia, the 48th Georgia, and the 10th Georgia Battalion, which had recently joined the brigade. "No nobler bearing on the battle field could have been exhibited than they displayed," a witness testified. "Their alignment was perfect, their steps regular and unwavering. When cannon shots or bullets made gaps in their line, they were promptly filled up. And when a color-bearer was shot down, another man at once seized the flag."

Then Early sprang his trap. He had deployed Chambliss's horsemen and

McGregor's gunners in woods below Upton's line. When the Georgians charged, McGregor's pieces opened with full force into Upton's southern flank, taking the Federals by surprise. As the Union line wavered in confusion, Early sent Chambliss's dismounted troopers screaming into its exposed left flank. To complete the rout, Harris's Mississippians charged around the northern end of Upton's formation, wrapping the Federals in a double envelopment. "The rebs had flanked us on both sides," a soldier in the 96th Pennsylvania admitted of the debacle.[47]

Upton's only avenue of escape lay to the rear across the Ni. His men streamed back toward the river, seeking the protection of the 6th Corps's guns on the far bank. "It was really a ludicrous and laughable retreat," confessed a soldier in the 5th Maine, whose regiment managed to escape without loss. "Some tall running was done to prevent being captured," added a man in the 121st New York. Soldiers jumped into the river only to be fished out by their companions, who proclaimed them "wetter and wiser men." Keiser of the 96th Pennsylvania conceded, "We were not slow in getting back, each one for himself." Keiser crossed the Ni on a submerged log, ignoring the Confederates who were running close behind him and shouting, "Halt, you Yankee son of a bitch!" A Federal jumped into the water next to Keiser and went straight to the bottom. In the confusion Keiser's prisoner, the Confederate major, escaped. "Here we had another run for sweet life," a surgeon admitted of the affair. "Plenty of grape and canister, minnie balls and shot help[ed] us over the ground." The engagement was easy to name. "From the fact that we ran so well and after the command to advance, it is henceforth to be known as 'Upton's Run,'" the surgeon proclaimed.[48]

The aide Thomas Hyde found himself bolting back with the wreckage of Upton's brigade. He was startled to hear a voice talking loudly in a thicket, as though lecturing. Stopping to investigate, Hyde found a sergeant sitting on the ground. His legs were both broken and blood gushed from a grisly head wound. The man rattled on deliriously at the top of his lungs as though preaching to an imaginary congregation. Reminisced Hyde: "The pathetic mournfulness of it all followed me long."[49]

Meade and Wright were watching the engagement from near the left of Upton's line with Major Nathaniel Michler, the army's chief topographical engineer, when Chambliss's men broke from the woods. The generals bolted for the rear, inspiring one of Upton's aides to wish that he could be a major general and leave with them. Michler was familiar with the terrain and guided Meade and Wright to a ford lower down the Ni. A major from the 13th Virginia Cavalry materialized from the woods and tried to snatch Meade. Soldiers from Meade's headquarters guard rescued the general and caught the major.

After a hair-raising ride that cost Meade his spectacles, the distinguished party emerged on the far bank. "Quite an excitement was caused at headquarters by the incident," a reporter noted, "and it was rumored that an advance of the enemy at this part of the line was being made for the purpose of turning our left flank." [50]

Early congratulated his men for a foray "handsomely made" and set them to consolidating their position at Myers Hill. Some Confederates took the opportunity to rob fallen Yankees, who were plentiful. They had "terribly cut up" the New Jersey regiments, shot both of the 10th New Jersey's color-bearers, and scooped up a regimental flag. Wright's Georgians captured two hundred Federals, mostly from the 10th New Jersey, and seized three stands of colors, two by the 48th Georgia and one by the 3rd Georgia. Upton's aide Francis W. Morse reported the Union brigade "very much shattered." [51]

A Union soldier had been sitting on a rocking chair on the porch of the Myers house when the Confederates attacked. He had begun shooting at the rebels without getting up. A ball had killed him where he sat, and his corpse slumped awkwardly in the chair. The ruckus had also brought out the family dog, who ran into the yard barking. Bullets had cut the animal down, and its body lay in front of the porch in the company of dead and wounded Federals. [52]

Lee received Early's report of the engagement with satisfaction. At little loss to his own force, Early had cleared the Federals from Myers Hill. On the heels of Early's tidings came news from Anderson that shed light on why the Federals seemed so interested in the place. "The enemy have disappeared from off our extreme left," Lee's 1st Corps commander advised. "Their pickets and sharpshooters have just retired, and there are no troops in the breastworks." Anderson could not determine the extent of the Union movement, but he was "inclined to believe that it includes the entire right of the enemy line." Lee now had concrete evidence that the forces collecting opposite Early were those that had previously opposed Anderson. [53]

The intelligence galvanized Lee into action. Grant was reorienting his army. Perhaps he would leave an opening the Confederates could exploit. Lee immediately advised Ewell of Anderson's discovery. "Can you find out anything on your front?" he asked the one-legged commander of his 2nd Corps. "Should you find that the enemy is changing his line be prepared to draw out to follow him." [54]

With Warren and Wright shifting to the opposite end of the Union formation, Lee saw no reason to detain his entire 1st Corps at Laurel Hill, to face only empty trenches. Grant's concentration along Fredericksburg Road clearly

heralded a major Union offensive. Alerted at last to the necessity of reinforcing Early, Lee directed Anderson to withdraw Field's division from Laurel
Hill and rush it to the Confederate right flank. In short order, Field's soldiers—sons of the Deep South from Texas, Arkansas, South Carolina,
Alabama, and Georgia—filed onto Brock Road and marched to Zion Church,
Lee's headquarters at the head of Massaponax Church Road. By nightfall
they were constructing entrenchments that prolonged Early's earthworks
south, toward Snell's Bridge on the Po River. Massaponax Church Road now
lay securely in Confederate hands. The back door to Spotsylvania Court
House that had stood ajar all day was firmly closed.[55]

Lee also ordered a reconnaissance of the country north of Grant's lines to
determine whether the Federals harbored aggressive designs in that quarter.
Wade Hampton's division of cavalry was handily situated along Shady Grove
Church Road, and Hampton selected Rosser's brigade of veteran Virginians
for the mission. Around 5:00 P.M. Rosser's horsemen splashed across the Po
and pursued a network of trails to the Alsop farm, at the junction of Brock
Road and Gordon Road. Turning east on Gordon Road, Rosser set off in the
direction of the Armstrong farm, Grant's former headquarters. From there, he
intended to skirt above Grant's flank and strike Fredericksburg Road well
north of the Union Army.

Two miles east of the Alsop farm, Rosser's riders came on a wooden two-
story house named Laurel Hill. Sixty-four-year-old Elizabeth Couse presided
over the gambrel-roofed estate. Her family hailed from New York, and her
son Peter's outspoken Union sympathies had landed him in a Confederate jail
in 1862. He now lived in Alexandria and had left the house in the care of his
mother and three sisters. In recent days the Couse home had become a gathering place for distinguished Yankees, including the battlefield artist Edwin
Forbes, of *Leslie's Illustrated.* Mrs. Couse had also opened her dwelling to
her less fortunate neighbors. One guest was Mrs. Brown, whose farm
Hancock had selected for the northern terminus of his line. She, her three
children, a black family, and a dog lived in Mrs. Couse's small upstairs room.
The crowded conditions, along with Mrs. Couse's brazenly Union sympathies, had made Mrs. Brown irritable. She became especially miffed when
her hostess asked to borrow some "boughten starch" to powder her face so as
to look fresh for her northern guests.[56]

Warren and Hancock had commandeered Mrs. Couse's yard as a field hospital. More than six hundred injured men spread across the grounds. Mrs.
Brown complained that the "tortures of the lost could not be any more awful
to witness than the shrieks and groans of those wounded and dying men."
Mrs. Couse and her daughters were carrying supper to a wounded officer

when Rosser's men rode up—"a very unwelcome sight to me," remarked the youngest daughter, Katherine H. Couse. The troopers stole "everything they could lay hands on," the young Couse complained in a letter to a friend. They also took several Union medical attendants and eighty wounded Confederates who could walk. A Virginian boasted that he procured six days rations, five pounds of sugar, coffee, and some "very important cooking and eating utensils." When Hancock got wind of the raid, he dispatched the 12th New Jersey to the Couse place. By the time the regiment arrived, Rosser had departed in the direction of Fredericksburg with his loot. In the waning twilight, a Union sergeant mistook Surgeon Thomas Jones of the 8th Pennsylvania Reserves for a rebel and shot him dead. The New Jersey men loaded 270 wounded Federals into wagons and ambulances and took them back to the Union lines. The more seriously wounded men were left to their fate in Mrs. Couse's yard.[57]

On the other end of the Union formation, Meade was firming plans to recapture Myers Hill. He instructed Wright to attack from the Anderson place with two divisions under Brigadier Generals Thomas H. Neill and James B. Ricketts. "It was a grand sight to see six lines of battle stretching across the hills and through the vales," a Federal recorded as Wright formed his troops. At the same time, Ayres's 5th Corps brigade prepared to initiate a companion assault from the Beverly farm.[58]

At 6:30 P.M. Meade launched his offensive. Fire from guns at the Beverly and Anderson places converged on Myers Hill, Wright's two divisions waded smartly into the Ni where Upton had earlier crossed, and Ayres started south along the route blazed by Otis. Ayres reached the Myers farm first, and his men stacked their knapsacks in preparation for a concerted rush. "When all was ready the bugle sounded the charge and we broke from cover like quarter horses," a Federal recounted, "and with a volley of cheers mounted the hill." Ayres's dramatic dash to the crest proved anticlimactic. From Myers Hill, Early's detachment had watched the imposing Federal forces approach from two directions. The southerners were hopelessly outnumbered and too distant from the main Confederate line to expect reinforcements. And with the 1st Corps shuttling over from Laurel Hill and extending Lee's formation below Massaponax Church Road, the Myers farm no longer held strategic importance for the rebels. Rather than sacrifice men to no purpose, Early decided to relinquish the high ground without a fight.[59]

Ayres reached the top to find it vacant. A Federal later boasted that the brigade's cheering had persuaded the southerners that a "mighty host was coming and they ran like the devil." In the dusk, Breck's and Cooper's gunners mistook the distant figures swarming over the hilltop for Confederates and began shooting their own troops. "We had to get behind the hill to get out of our own fire," a northerner related. "Several men were killed before we could let them know their mistake." Union corpses, stripped naked by the Confederates, sprawled across the yard. One body was that of Lieutenant Colonel Charles Weibecke of the 2nd New Jersey, killed earlier in the day. "We passed a man sitting upon a stone, presenting a horrible appearance," a Union chaplain recalled. "His arms had been torn off, and his whole face was hanging in a bloody mass before him." The Federals got their revenge by ferreting out six rebels hiding in the Myers house cellar.[60]

While Ayres's soldiers scoured Myers Hill for Confederates, Wright's troops, unaware the hill had been taken, splashed over the Ni in water up to their armpits. A Marylander drowned during the crossing, and several men lost their muskets. The dripping Federals dressed their ranks on the Ni's western bank and girded to attack. "The sight was grand and terrific," an onlooker observed as he contemplated the prospect of storming the ridge. "We expected to taste the soldier's dish of grape ere completing the undertaking."[61]

As the 6th Corps's battle line jolted forward, a messenger from Ayres spurred up with welcome tidings. Myers Hill was in Union hands. Wright's men broke into smiles, and Warren gleefully telegraphed headquarters the news and asked that Ayres's brigade be rewarded with "complete rest tonight." Meade was delighted. Something was finally going right. "I thank you and Ayres for taking the hill," he gushed in a note to Warren. "It was handsomely done." Grant, who had censured Warren a few days earlier, expressed relief over the young general's prompt and successful movement. He liked Warren and hoped that his success at Myers Hill meant that he was improving.[62]

Union earthworks soon enclosed the Myers farm and arched back on both sides of the hill to the Ni. Two hundred men from the 110th Ohio, stationed five to ten paces apart, picketed toward Massaponax Church Road. "Very unpleasant," an Ohio man pronounced the assignment, which he detailed in a letter home as "cold, wet, hungry; scolding, shivering, sleepy, and withal watchful." The rest of the soldiers settled behind freshly dug entrenchments, and a few paused to admire the Myers home. Snowball bushes in the yard conjured visions of Virginia's better days. "It occasioned more than a sigh of regret to see the beautiful enclosures trodden by the marching columns, torn by the spades of the fortifying squads, desolated by the axes of the pioneers," a Bay Stater reminisced. "As beautiful a plantation as I ever saw," commented a Vermonter. "It seems a pity to spoil such finely laid out grounds, but such is war." [63]

Grant ventured forth on his horse Jeff Davis to get a feel for the situation. Splattered with mud, he stopped at the Gayle house to write dispatches. Walking past several wounded men lying on the porch and in the hallway, he searched for a dry room in the back of the house. Opening a door and peering in, he saw a Confederate corporal upright in a chair. The man had been shot under his right eye, and the ball had come out near his left ear, leaving a ghastly wound. On noticing Grant, the man rose and offered the general his chair. "Ah, you need that chair much more than I," Grant told him. "Keep your seat." The injured rebel smiled. "If you folks let me go back to my lines, I think I ought to be able to get a leave to go home and see my girl," he replied, then added with a sigh: "But I reckon she wouldn't know me now." Grant instructed a surgeon to tend to the Confederate's injuries and found another room for writing dispatches.[64]

Grant's subordinates were uncomfortable with the new deployments. Meade protested that Grant had divided the Army of the Potomac by shifting Warren and Wright to the lower end of the Union line, leaving Hancock at the formation's northern extreme, above Burnside. Meade wanted his army united. "I would like to get the Army of the Potomac together," was how he put it, "and Burnside would have the right flank." Grant had no objection to Meade's proposal but did not want to leave Burnside protecting the army's northern flank by himself. He agreed to let Hancock shift his corps in the morning to the Harris Farm, where it could both backstop Burnside and cooperate with Meade's other corps. He insisted, however, that Hancock leave a division with Burnside.[65]

For the night, Hancock was to remain on the Union army's northern flank. He felt exceedingly vulnerable with Rosser prowling about on Gordon Road and with Kershaw's Confederates probing insistently at his line, so he shifted a brigade to Mrs. Brown's house to strengthen his flank and telegraphed Meade for guidance. The day's bungled operations had left the army commander wrathful. "You must look out for your right," Meade curtly wired back, stating the obvious. Meade also lost patience with Wright, who fretted endlessly that rebels might cut off his two divisions at Myers Hill. The appearance of Field's Confederates below Massaponax Church Road set Warren to whining that Lee might assail the Union left flank, and a hint of panic crept into his dispatches to headquarters. Even Wright seemed to have lost his nerve. "If my suppositions as to the enemy's movements are correct, this force [at Myers Hill] should be brought back beyond the Ni River tonight," the 6th Corps's commander urged. "The depth of the stream generally is above the waists of the men, and the country exceedingly broken and tangled." Headquarters, however, elected to leave Wright's troops where they stood. "You had better have roads open to your rear from your advance position, also toward the Fifth Corps," Meade suggested. Withdrawing was not an option in Grant's program. "Nothing done here today," Meade wrote in frustration. "Men too tired." [66]

Near dark, Grant and Meade pitched their headquarters tents on Fredericksburg Road, near the Harris farm. Grant's aide Horace Porter noted that the general was a "mass of mud from head to foot, his uniform being scarcely recognizable." Before retiring, Grant washed in a barrel that had been cut in half to fashion a bathtub. "Campaign life is not a good school for the cultivation of squeamishness," Porter reflected.[67]

Warren, Wainwright, and their staffs spread their blankets in the Beverly house after evicting a handful of Michigan men who had curled up under the porch. The roof leaked where shells had smacked the chimney, and an inch of mud covered the floor, which was stained red from the blood of wounded soldiers. Wainwright considered the place "such a pig sty one would hesitate to enter at home—certainly without thick-soled boots and turning up one's pants," although he welcomed the chance to get out of the rain. His subordinates were less fortunate. An officer in Company H, 4th New York Heavy Artillery, which had recently joined the 5th Corps, spent the night "burrowing in the mud and sleeping under sheets of water." A 6th Corps staffer at the Anderson house proclaimed the day "one of the most fatiguing we have had." [68]

Across the waterlogged no-man's land, Lee's Confederates also settled down for an anxious night. "Tho the shells are bursting all around us and the minie bullets are cheeping just over our heads, we have dug ourselves deep enough into the ground to be tolerably protected," Eugene Blackford of the 5th Alabama wrote his sister. In Mahone's sector of line, a soldier in the 61st Virginia climbed a tree to study the enemy position. A Federal sharpshooter spotted him and fired, missing the climber but mortally wounding Marshall O. Creekmore, who was sleeping in his tent. Creekmore's friend Isaiah Hodges rushed to the stricken man and was shot in the head. The lookout in the tree scampered down unharmed. "It was an appalling tragedy," an onlooker recalled, "occurring while we were lying around in the shade of the trees." Death, men reminded one another, could come any time without warning.[69]

The Confederates were still taking the measure of the new Union commander. "Grant is the most obstinate fighter we have ever met," Blackford grudgingly admitted. "He has resolved to lose every man rather than retreat, which he knows is equivalent to our independence." Sergeant Marion Hill Fitzpatrick of the 45th Georgia seconded Blackford's assessment, although he saw no reason for concern. "Old Grant is a tough customer but Lee is an overmatch for him," he declared. "The prisoners say that Grant says he is going to [either] Richmond or Hell before he quits," Fitzpatrick claimed, "and has no idea of recrossing the river as long as he has a man left." G. W. Grimes of the 16th Georgia asserted emphatically that the "general opinion [is] that Old Grant is waiting for reinforcements and as soon as he gets them that we will have another big fight." Grimes and his companions harbored no doubts about the outcome. "We shall be able to give him a good whipping," the Georgian promised in a letter home.[70]

Lee, too, was optimistic, although he remained deeply concerned over the shortage of troops. President Davis continued to urge him to borrow soldiers from Breckinridge, but Lee recognized the Shenandoah Valley's importance and was reluctant to weaken the Confederate force there. "Breckinridge is calling for reinforcements to defend Valley," he reminded the president. "If withdrawn there will be no opposition to Sigel." Lee made sure, however, that Breckinridge knew to send him any men that might become available. "If you can drive back the different expeditions threatening the Valley," he telegraphed the Kentuckian, "it would be very desirable for you to join me with your whole force."[71]

The Army of Northern Virginia's commander would doubtless have slept soundly had he known that Breckinridge's reinforcements, and more, would soon be on their way.

May 14 was remarkable in the annals of the campaign, not for what Grant and Lee did, but for what they failed to do. The Union commander had begun the day with an ambitious march designed to strike Lee's thinly defended right flank. His maneuver had caught the southerner unaware. The Confederate artillerist Alexander later noted that Grant had "devised an attack which would have had a very fair chance of taking us quite by surprise, had he been able to make it." Alexander thanked "darkness and mud" for delivering the Confederates. Uncharacteristic caution on Grant's part, however, had actually saved the Confederates. Darkness and mud, it is true, had delayed the Union march and had forced Grant to postpone his attack. But by 10:00 A.M. Grant had achieved the very advantage that he had hoped to attain at daybreak. Warren and Wright were up in force, and Lee had done nothing to strengthen his position across from them. Yet Grant hesitated. He could not imagine that Lee had left the southern portion of his line vulnerable. But even though Lee had learned of Grant's concentration shortly after daylight and had received confirming reports throughout the day, he took no serious countermeasures until late afternoon. Only at nightfall, when Field's division reached Massaponax Church Road, did Lee secure his right.[72]

The day closed with Grant pondering how best to protect his flanks. He had nothing to show for his efforts except a knoll that had cost him dearly. The dearth of tangible results after eleven days of constant fighting fed the growing sense of dissatisfaction among Federal soldiers. "I cannot perceive that our army has in reality made any advance since leaving the Wilderness," the 5th Corps artillerist George Breck groused. "Were it not for the handsome success of last Thursday gained by Hancock, in the capture of several thousand prisoners and eighteen pieces of artillery, there would be no very great substantial advantages to recount in our favor." In a typical soldier's letter, an Ohioan pointedly questioned Grant's fitness for command. "One fact is clearly established in everyone's mind," he asserted. "Grant as a general is no match for Lee. We have men enough, and good men too, to 'eat up' the Johnnies. But with such a leader as Grant, we would indubitably be routed or completely broken up as an army by Lee if our forces were anything like evenly matched numerically." A soldier from Maine complained that Grant's failure to make significant headway had worked a "most pernicious effect on morale." [73]

The Confederates realized they had narrowly escaped disaster and were thankful that their losses had been light. The Georgians who had led the attack against Myers Hill had lost only 200 men, and Harris's and Chambliss's subtractions had been negligible. That evening a Georgian visited his brigade's field hospital. A young boy, severely wounded, was crying pitifully for his mother. "No mother was near to soothe him," the visitor wrote. "The next morning he was dead, eased of his suffering, without mother near." The dying boy's cries continued to haunt the Georgian over the years. He regretted that he had not asked the boy his name or inquired after his mother's address. "But it was all confusion and in the night, and I expect a thousand [were] there wounded," he offered by way of explanation. "I was wounded and suffering myself." [74]

IV

MAY 15–16

Grant Settles on a New Offensive

"Colt's was not generally used in that church."

MAY 15, A SABBATH, dawned wet and dismal. Blue and Gray stared sullenly across the no-man's land from waterlogged bivouacs reeking of wood smoke and mildew, bracing for the next big fight. "Everything quiet on the lines," a Confederate recorded in his diary. A Federal expressed like sentiment. "By a 'quiet day,'" he penned, "I mean comparatively so, for skirmishing is going on incessantly, and more or less wounded constantly coming in from the front, but there has been no attack on either side." A Connecticut man asked his family to imagine lying "for forty-eight hours behind a ridge of earth in front about twenty rods another like ridge back of which the enemy is in force continually popping away." A Georgian grumbled that he had never been "as tired of a thing in my life" and was "pretty well worn out from fatigue and loss of sleep." He concluded that the "Yanks are about as fond of shooting as we." A New Yorker articulated the consensus of soldiers of both armies. "We are in mud up to our ass," he wrote his wife. His sole wish was to "fight and come home or die damned quick, for this is no fun in these mud holes of Virginia." Everyone knew that the lull was deceptive. The relative quiet was the calm that precedes a storm.[1]

Grant wanted to resume operations, but foul weather ruled that out. "The very heavy rains of the past three days have rendered the roads so impassable that but little will be done until there is a change of weather, unless the enemy should attack, which they have exhibited little inclination to do for the last week," he informed his chief of staff, Halleck, in Washington. Until the deluge stopped and the ground dried, military operations were necessarily limited to probes and forays designed to determine the position and strength of opposing lines.[2]

Grant employed the unwelcome respite to tend to mundane tasks. First was the matter of supplies. The road between Fredericksburg and Belle Plain was difficult and vulnerable to guerrilla attacks. And the wharfs—a second pontoon dock had been constructed a few days after the first—were too small to accommodate the army's needs. The previous year, during the Fredericksburg campaign, the Army of the Potomac had drawn supplies from Aquia Creek, a landing on the Potomac River six miles northwest of Belle Plain. The harbor there was ample, and a railroad ran to Falmouth, across the Rappahannock from Fredericksburg. Confederates had torn up the tracks, but with the armies stymied in front of Spotsylvania Court House, Grant concluded that the rail line might become useful. Mindful that his engineers would need at least a week to repair the tracks, he ordered them to begin right away.

On May 10, as casualties mounted, Grant had urged Halleck to send every infantryman to Virginia that he could "rake and scrape." Grant's army was firmly positioned between the Army of Northern Virginia and Washington, and the general felt safe culling troops from the capital's defenses. The next day, he reminded Halleck that the "arrival of reinforcements here will be very encouraging to the men and I hope they will be sent as fast as possible and in great numbers." On May 12, at the height of the attack against the Mule Shoe, Grant directed Halleck to have Major General Christopher C. Augur, commanding the Department of Washington, forward "ten thousand of the best Infantry" from the capital's garrisons.[3]

Grant's persistence produced results. "We have already got underway at Belle Plain, in the river and on the road, not less than 10,000 men," Halleck wrote on May 13, "and I hope to add 3,000 or 4,000 more within the next two days." Brigadier General Robert O. Tyler would be heading the new troops. A veteran campaigner, Tyler had commanded the Potomac Army's artillery reserve at Chancellorsville and Gettysburg and was manifestly a good choice. To manage the Belle Plain depot, Halleck appointed Brigadier General John J. Abercrombie, a sixty-six-year-old professional military man with a knack for administration. Abercrombie, Halleck assured Grant, had been enjoined to "push forward the troops and stores with all possible dispatch." Later that day, Halleck revised his forecast upward. He now promised that 27,500 soldiers would embark for Belle Plain within the next forty-eight hours, 3,000 of them earmarked for Butler and the rest for the Army of the Potomac. "I shall not fall much short of this," Halleck assured Grant but added that it was "about as much as I can do."[4]

On May 15 Grant articulated his thoughts on how best to employ the fresh troops. "On reflection," he wrote Halleck, "I believe it will be better to strengthen the corps here with all reinforcements coming than to have them formed into separate commands." The first reinforcements arrived that morning. The 2nd New York Mounted Rifles (dismounted)—a thousand men strong—swung onto Fredericksburg Road and was assigned to Colonel Marshall's 9th Corps Provisional Brigade. Not long afterward came the 1st Vermont Heavy Artillery and two companies of conscripts—another 1,750 soldiers—commanded by Colonel James M. Warner. These newcomers joined Colonel Lewis A. Grant's combat-worn Vermont brigade. The veterans welcomed their fellow Vermonters with a round of cheers, gleefully commenting that the new outfit contained more soldiers than remained in all five of the brigade's veteran regiments combined. "It was finely equipped, ably officered, and in all respects a splendid body of soldiers," a veteran noted of Warner's regiment. Its arrival "more than made good in numbers the losses of the brigade in the campaign, and put new heart into the survivors." [5]

Grant also monitored developments on other fronts. Sherman was on the move. He had flanked Johnston's Confederates out of Dalton, Georgia, and driven them back in battle at Resaca. Banks had advanced well up the Red River in Louisiana. And in Virginia, Butler finally seemed to be taking the initiative. Reports had him moving on Richmond. His infantry faced the Confederates at Drewry's Bluff, and his cavalry under Brigadier General August V. Kautz had sortied forth to cut the Danville Railroad and the James River Canal, two vital supply lines to the Confederate capital. Even Sigel seemed energized. When last heard from, he had reached Woodstock and was girding to engage Breckinridge's small Confederate force between there and Staunton. The pieces on Grant's strategic chessboard seemed to be clicking into place.

Grant's chief concern, however, was finding a way to pry Lee from his earthworks. The Union line ran generally north to south, with Hancock holding the Landrum farm, Burnside extending south, Warren arrayed along the Beverly property, and Wright anchoring the formation's lower end at Myers Hill. Federal soldiers were most strongly concentrated in the southern portion of the line, near Fredericksburg Road. Conversely, Lee's line was weakest toward its southern end, where Fredericksburg Road and Massaponax Church Road angled into Spotsylvania Court House. Moving Field's division from Laurel Hill did little to offset Grant's preponderance in the sector. Grant decided to stick with the general plan he had formulated on May 13 to attack the southern portion of Lee's line, but to change two important features. The Confederates had tightened their grip on Fredericksburg Road, so he chose to aim farther south and funnel the weight of his assault along Massaponax Church Road. He also questioned whether the defensive-minded Warren

would attack when ordered and wanted Hancock—cool, professional, and
dependable—to lead the assault. So Grant relegated Warren's 5th Corps to a
supporting role and gave Hancock chief responsibility for the venture. "My
opinion now is that our next attack should be from Wright's position [and] be
supported by Hancock," was Grant's explanation of this latest wrinkle to
Meade. Hancock and Wright would attack while Warren and Burnside remained in their entrenchments "ready to advance from where they are, if any
strong impression is made by our attack."[6]

Having worked out the details of the offensive, Grant considered how best
to move his troops into position. His revised plan required Hancock to attack
from the battlefield's southern sector. Hancock, however, presently occupied
the northern end of the Union formation, fully six miles from Massaponax
Church Road. By coincidence, the previous evening Grant had authorized
Hancock to withdraw most of his corps to the Harris farm, leaving a division
at the Landrum place to support Burnside and to anchor the army's northern
flank. The maneuver fit Grant's new scheme perfectly. Shifting Hancock to
the Harris farm, Grant reasoned, would place the 2nd Corps within an easy
march to its jumping-off point at Massaponax Church Road and would also
deceive Lee as to his real intentions. And leaving a 2nd Corps division in the
earthworks formerly occupied by Hancock's troops would further mislead
the rebels.

Early on May 15 Hancock began withdrawing from entrenchments he had
occupied since May 13. Barlow's and Gibbon's divisions slipped quietly
away and toiled toward the Harris farm along the rutted farm trail that Warren
and Wright had followed twenty-four hours before. Birney's division, left behind by Hancock, extended to fill the vacated lines. Ewell's and Kershaw's
vedettes quickly discovered the movement, and Confederates pressed insistently against the portion of Hancock's entrenchments curving north toward
the Brown house. Disengaging under the eyes of a vigilant foe was a dangerous undertaking in the best of circumstances, particularly for the last troops
to leave. Brigadier General Gershom R. Mott's brigade of Birney's division
was especially hard pressed. In the wake of faltering performances in the
Wilderness and at the Mule Shoe, Hancock had dissolved Mott's division—
he deemed the outfit "of no service under its present commanders, who seem
not to control their men"—and had placed its two brigades under Birney.
Now the brigade that remained under Mott's personal command dangled at
the far end of Birney's right flank, near Mrs. Brown's house. Kershaw's infantry, supported by Hampton's cavalry and horse artillery, pinned Mott's
soldiers in their earthworks under a deadly fire.[7]

Concluding that he lacked sufficient soldiers to hold the full length of

Hancock's old entrenchments, Birney contracted his lines, bringing his four brigades closer together, accordionlike. First he withdrew Mott from the Brown place south to Landrum ridge. Then he deployed Colonel John S. Crocker's brigade onto Mott's left and extended it south to connect with Burnside's right, filling the interval formerly occupied by Barlow's division. A violent thunderstorm helped conceal Crocker's movement, but the shift brought the brigade within range of Ewell's artillery, posted near the Harrison house. When the rain let up, Ewell's guns opened and elements from John Gordon's division—"rebellious subjects of Uncle Sam bent upon homicidal intent," a Federal pronounced them—stormed Crocker's new position.[8]

Birney found himself in a tight spot. Ewell's gunners were lobbing shells into his line with disconcerting accuracy, Kershaw's Confederates were pressing hard from the west, and Gordon's implacable warriors were boiling up from the south. Birney was used to scrapes and tight places—he had grown up in Alabama the son of an abolitionist and had clawed his way to the top of Philadelphia's legal world—but the rearguard assignment taxed the full measure of his considerable talent.

Deadly little fights sparked along Birney's line as Confederates probed insistently for weak points. Things got especially hot when a battery of Hampton's horse artillery rolled onto the Brown farm and began dropping shells into Birney's position from the northwest. Burnside, who bore ultimate responsibility for the sector, grew anxious. He ordered Birney to hold the Landrum farm "if possible," then alerted Grant to the situation. A Confederate battery had moved to the Brown house, he warned, and had rendered the Landrum farm untenable. Birney might have to abandon the high ground at the Landrum site, he went on, and the consequences would be dire, as the Confederates could enfilade the 9th Corps's line from there.[9]

Grant reviewed Burnside's dispatch with dismay. Why, he wondered, did these eastern generals think only in terms of retreat? Why did they not silence the Confederate guns instead of running away? Burnside's missive epitomized the defensive mindset that Grant found so upsetting. Unable to suppress his contempt, he penned a characteristically bellicose response across the bottom of the note. "Would it not be well for General Birney to drive the enemy from the Brown house," he queried, "and hold the place until something is decided upon?"[10]

While the generals debated their next step, Mott's soldiers huddled for dear life along the Landrum ridge. Projectiles from Hampton's and Ewell's guns rained down from two directions with pinpoint accuracy. Mott termed the fire "very destructive," and portions of the 6th New Jersey and 26th

Pennsylvania of his brigade panicked and stampeded to the rear. Skirmishers temporarily plugged the breach until Mott could rally the frightened soldiers and persuade them to return. During the bombardment, Lieutenant Joseph C. Baldwin of the 11th New Jersey started a letter to his sister. Lieutenant Colonel John Shoonover and Colonel Robert McAllister sat crouched in the mud nearby, looking on. "The rebs keep throwing shells, but they are well spent, and from my position I can't see that they do any harm," Baldwin scrawled. The words were to be his last. With a deafening whine, a projectile burst through the works, crushed Baldwin's head, and bounced to a stop next to Shoonover and McAllister. The two men held their breaths and grimaced, expecting an explosion. To their relief, the missile lay quietly on the ground.[11]

Barlow and Gibbon camped their divisions on the Harris farm's broad fields, within hearing of Birney's vigorous rearguard action. The soldiers were delighted to be beyond range of the Confederate guns. "I hope that we will lay still," a man in the 1st Delaware wrote home. "I thank God that I am safe." Hancock, Gibbon, and Barlow lunched with Meade and his staff. Barlow was in an expansive mood. "Headquarters are a good place," he announced. "You can get victuals and stationery there!" After dashing off a letter to his wife, he regaled the assemblage with anecdotes about the Bloody Angle. He had whacked a soldier with a saber for hiding in a hole, he proudly announced, and he had forced two officers to resign, endorsing on their papers that they were cowards.[12]

Shelling tapered off toward noon, and Birney breathed easier. His line had held. Mott's brigade now occupied the Landrum place, Crocker's brigade bridged the gap to Burnside, and the brigades of Colonels Thomas W. Egan and William R. Brewster stood in reserve, supporting Crocker. To link up with the rest of Hancock's corps, Birney spun a line of skirmishers east toward the Harris farm. As a precaution, he directed Mott to thrust pickets toward the Brown house to sound the alarm if the Confederates attacked from that quarter. The rebels, however, seemed content to scavenge supplies from the battlefield. They were especially excited to recover thirteen caissons, which they viewed as partial compensation for the guns the Federals had taken from them on May 12. "All is quiet in my front," Birney reported at 12:45.[13]

From Grant's perspective, Hancock's redeployment had been a success. Most of the 2nd Corps was now resting at the Harris farm, positioned to march to Massaponax Church Road during the night. Birney's division, firmly entrenched on the Landrum farm, anchored the northern end of the

Union formation. Barring surprises, Grant's grand assault could proceed the next morning as planned.

Lee was unsure what to make of all the activity in Hancock's sector. Where was the Union 2nd Corps going? Would the morrow bring a Federal retirement in the direction of Fredericksburg, an advance toward Richmond, or an assault against some portion of the Confederate formation? A southern newspaper correspondent surmised that Grant might be shoring up his supply route to Fredericksburg in preparation for swinging east around the Mattaponi River, then dashing south to join Butler. "If such be his plans," the reporter opined, "it is plain that he has had enough of General Lee and does not desire to cross swords with him again, at least without material reinforcements." [14]

During the morning, Lee received heartening assurances from Davis. The president was drawing cavalry and infantry from South Carolina, Georgia, and parts of Florida to report to Richmond. And Beauregard, Davis assured Lee, was completing plans to attack Butler at Drewry's Bluff. The president expected Beauregard to separate Butler from his base at Bermuda Hundred and to defeat him "so as to prevent any further trouble from that source." Once Butler was out of the picture, Davis promised, "we can then reinforce you, and enable you to close your brilliant campaign with a complete victory." Davis reported that he was also trying to "get out" reserves in Virginia and North Carolina to guard rail lines and depots, which would free Breckinridge's force and other veteran outfits to join Lee. The president closed on a personal note. "I have been pained to hear of your exposure of your person in various conflicts," he wrote. "The country could not bear the loss of you, and, my dear friend, though you are prone to forget yourself, you will not, I trust, again forget the public interest dependent on your life." [15]

Lee now knew that reinforcements—if any were to be had—were several days away. As long as Grant persisted in attacking the Army of Northern Virginia's earthworks, Lee was confident that he could hold on. The danger was that Grant might maneuver and strike from an unexpected quarter. To ensure accurate intelligence about Grant's deployments, Lee ordered cavalry reconnaissances around both Union flanks. Once again, Tom Rosser was to probe the byways north of the Union army and ferret out evidence of Grant's intentions. And on the southern flank, Chambliss was to scout aggressively along Massaponax Church Road, swinging far behind the enemy lines and advancing north on Telegraph Road, toward Fredericksburg.

Confederate horsemen had Grant's cavalry at a decided disadvantage.

When Sheridan rode off on May 9, he took with him almost the whole cavalry corps of the Army of the Potomac, leaving behind only the 5th New York Cavalry under Colonel John Hammond. That superb combat outfit had been severely mauled in the Wilderness and was in no shape for strenuous duty. Aside from the fought-out New Yorkers and the mounted units assigned to Meade's headquarters guard—the 3rd Pennsylvania Cavalry and two companies of the 1st Massachusetts Cavalry—the only other horsemen available to Grant at Spotsylvania Court House were four regiments attached to the 9th Corps. Two of the 9th Corps regiments—the 13th Pennsylvania Cavalry and the 2nd Ohio Cavalry—contained a respectable number of veterans. The other two—the 22nd New York Cavalry and the 3rd New Jersey Cavalry— were painfully inexperienced. The 22nd New York Cavalry had behaved so poorly that Meade's aide Lyman had suggested its commander "ought to have been shot." The 3rd New Jersey had served for a time in the Washington defenses but had no experience in the field. Dubbed the "Butterflies" for their gaudy uniforms, the New Jersey troopers struck one onlooker as a "glittering, gorgeous spectacle of gold braid and trimmings." They made a stirring sight on the parade ground but would be of questionable utility against seasoned Confederate cavalrymen.[16]

On May 15 Meade assigned the novice 3rd New Jersey and 22nd New York to guard wagons, escort prisoners, and watch the Rapidan crossings. The veteran 5th New York and 13th Pennsylvania were to patrol the roads branching off from Grant's lower flank, and to spar with Chambliss's riders as necessary. The 2nd Ohio was to picket the roads skirting the northern end of Grant's infantry line, where Rosser's troopers were skulking about.

The morning started peacefully for the 2nd Ohio. Commanded this day by Major A. Bayard Nettleton, the regiment lolled in camp near Piney Branch Church on Catharpin Road, a major thoroughfare that ran a few miles above Gordon Road. The encampment occupied high ground overlooking the Ni. Troopers washed their clothes in the river and cooked breakfast, little suspecting that Rosser's Confederates were approaching.[17]

Rosser's horsemen had spent the night at Todd's Tavern, at the junction of Catharpin and Brock roads, two miles west of Nettleton's bivouac. A native Virginian and former resident of Texas, twenty-seven-year-old Tom Rosser headed the famed Laurel Brigade, touted by some as the Army of Northern Virginia's elite mounted unit. Assigned to probe the battlefield's northern reaches, Rosser decided to divide his brigade. His main body of riders was to head east along Catharpin Road, wind past Piney Branch Church, and continue on to the Alrich farm, at the intersection of Orange Plank Road. Grant had used the Alrich fields and nearby clearings at Chancellorsville as staging areas early in the campaign, and his wagon train was supposedly still there. At the same time, a small Confederate contingent was to retrace the brigade's route of May 14 along Gordon Road to Mrs. Couse's residence.

The smaller party quickly accomplished its mission. By the time it reached Mrs. Couse's house, the 12th New Jersey had long departed, leaving the Couse family and guests, a handful of doctors, and several hundred seriously injured soldiers to fend for themselves. The Confederates searched the house and yard, satisfied themselves that the Federals were gone, then rode north along farm roads to join their compatriots on Catharpin Road. Their visit did nothing to improve humors in the Couse household. "I feel so tired and disagreeable, everything is so disgustingly dirty," Katherine Couse complained in a letter.[18]

Rosser's main body of horsemen meanwhile rode toward Piney Branch Church. As they approached the structure, they spied Nettleton's camp. The last thing the Ohioans expected was a fight. They had ridden hard during the past week, and now they were resting. Their horses grazed unsaddled. One soldier, Rogers Hanneford, had dismantled his carbine, greased the pieces, and spread them on a blanket to dry. "Every person felt nearly as secure as though at church at home," Hanneford recollected.[19]

A shot rang out, followed by a drum roll of discharges. Piercing rebel yells rent the morning air. Rosser's horsemen thundered up the road, firing their pistols and riding straight toward the Union encampment. "If the fool Johnnies had only kept their throats closed, they would have bagged the regiment almost entire," Hanneford speculated. Caught completely by surprise—apparently Nettleton had posted no pickets—the Ohioans sprang to their feet, and officers darted about, shouting conflicting orders. Confederates seemed to be everywhere as horsemen in gray rushed by, firing and yelling. Several rebels headed east along Catharpin Road in an attempt to break past the Ohioans and close off their avenue of retreat across the Ni. Stumbling to his feet, Hanneford scattered the pieces of his disassembled carbine and scorched his coat tails in his campfire. By the time he had mounted, Confederates had cut off his retreat. A field north of the road provided the only way out. Bodies of disorganized Ohioans streamed across the clearing, then reentered the roadway east of the Confederates.[20]

Nettleton regrouped his scattered command and hurried it east along Catharpin Road, hoping to reach the Alrich farm and reinforcements. Virginians came screaming close behind. The way twisted and turned through a dense stand of woods, and Nettleton left a rear guard at each curve. "As the rebs would come around the next corner, we would empty our seven shooters, then fall back," a trooper reported of the wild flight. "When they got to the next corner, another volley awaited them." Hanneford could hear

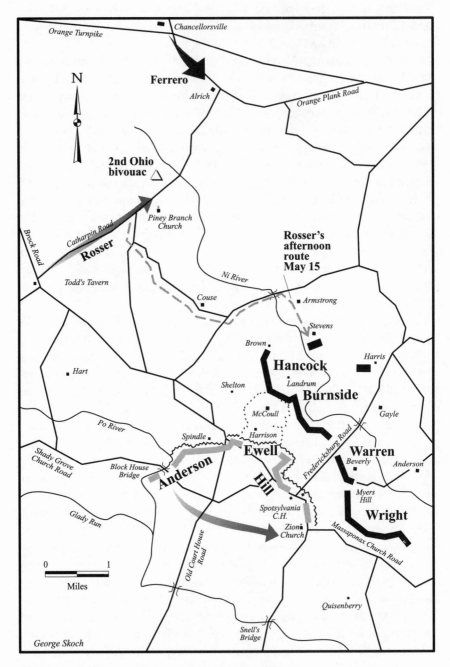

Cavalry operations north of the armies on May 15–16

rebel horses clattering behind him and imagined the burn of bullets across his back. The Virginians relished the chase, although their foremost regiment, the 11th Virginia Cavalry, lost several men, including its adjutant. "Some of the boys said [Rosser] only took the brigade down to hold the usual Sunday morning's service, as the General had recently joined the Episcopal Church," a captain in the 35th Virginia Cavalry quipped. "Others remarked that he made a mistake in the prayer book, as Colt's was not generally used in that church." [21]

Correctly estimating that Rosser outnumbered him better than two to one, Nettleton sent a courier for help. The man spurred his lathered horse to the Alrich farm and veered left toward Chancellorsville, where Brigadier General Edward Ferrero's 9th Corps division was stationed to guard the Union army's wagon train. Ferrero was a former dance instructor who had proven his mettle in several engagements, including a brave charge under fire at Antietam. Ferrero's outfit represented an experiment. It was made up of black soldiers, many of them former slaves. The division was a political hot potato, and Grant had kept it from combat out of concern that the southerners might massacre the black soldiers. Until now, he had relegated Ferrero's command to protecting wagons. Rosser's surprise foray was about to change all of that.

Nettleton's breathless courier explained the 2nd Ohio's predicament to Ferrero. The regiment was outnumbered and on the run, with Confederates in hot pursuit. Ferrero's division was the only Union force sufficiently close to assist. Ferrero immediately directed the 23rd United States Colored Troops (USCT) to double-quick to the Alrich farm. As the regiment set off along Orange Plank Road, Ferrero hurried to marshal more of his troops in support. [22]

The 23rd USCT numbered about a thousand men, few of whom had fired a musket in anger. Marching quickly, they reached the Catharpin Road intersection at the Alrich property to find that Rosser had driven the 2nd Ohio Cavalry across Orange Plank Road and into the adjacent fields. Company B, on the 23rd USCT's left flank, deployed as skirmishers. Captain Free S. Bowley, of the 30th USCT, came up with his regiment's color guard and was also ordered into the skirmish line. The soldiers, spaced five or six paces apart, started marching the final few yards to the intersection. "Now just imagine you are hunting for coons, and keep your eyes open!" shouted Major Leake, who directed the movement. "Skirmishers, forward, guide left— March!" A soldier shouted back: "'Pears like there was the coons doing the huntin' this time." [23]

Major Leake's skirmishers reached Catharpin Road in the nick of time. Rosser's men had stopped short of Orange Plank Road and had dismounted to deploy in woods. "They were well covered and invisible to us," an Ohioan observed of the rebels, "while we were in an open field and just far enough to be a pretty shot." Without fanfare, the 23rd USCT faced to the right and charged toward Rosser. The Confederates had fixed their attention on the Ohioans and were taken by surprise. Bowley raised his Enfield and aimed at a mounted figure. Conscious that he was about to fire his first shot for the Union, he squeezed the trigger. The Enfield "kicked spitefully," he reminisced, but he missed.[24]

Arrival of the 23rd USCT had shifted the balance. Now Union troops substantially outnumbered Confederates. "I saw General Ferrero and staff rapidly approaching, bearing the division flag and followed by his darkies on the double quick," an Ohio man related. "It did us good to see the long line of glittering bayonets approach, although those who bore them were Blacks, and as they came nearer they were greeted by loud cheers." Confronting an infantry force of unknown strength, Rosser fell back. More of Ferrero's troops came up and secured the intersection. Bent on revenge and emboldened by the infantry support, the 2nd Ohio Cavalry set off after Rosser, "hastening the laggards by a few shots," according to a Federal. Rosser fled in "perfect rout," Ferrero gloated. "Rebs didn't wait to say goodbye, but got a move on them," an Ohio trooper added. Rosser reported only that he met a "small force of infantry at Mr. Alrich's" and disengaged. No Federals were killed, although four were injured, along with some twenty horses. Several Confederates lay dead in the roadway.[25]

The 2nd Ohio Cavalry pursued Rosser west across the Ni and back through the site of its encampment, still strewn with clothing, knapsacks, weapons, and tents abandoned in haste a short hour before. Rain was falling in torrents by the time the antagonists reached Piney Branch Church. Nettleton called off the pursuit and led his men back to their bivouac, where they salvaged their gear. Each side claimed victory in the spirited little action. Rosser boasted that he had routed the 2nd Ohio Cavalry and had gained valuable intelligence about Grant's dispositions. The Ohio horsemen relished turning the tables on Rosser and chasing him away. Rosser paid the Union regiment an unintentional tribute twenty years later when he claimed to have encountered a "brigade of cavalry" at Piney Branch Church that had retired only after "spirited resistance." But the real winners were Ferrero's men. For the first time, black soldiers had come up against the vaunted Army of Northern Virginia, and they had acquitted themselves well.[26]

Rosser sped his findings to Lee. The 9th Corps, he reported, was posted near the Alrich farm on Grant's northern flank, and the Federal army's wagon trains and cattle had moved on to Fredericksburg. He was wrong on both scores. Only one of Burnside's divisions, Ferrero's, was at the Alrich place. The rest of the 9th Corps—three divisions under Potter, Major General Thomas L. Crittenden, and Brigadier General Orlando B. Willcox—was entrenched several miles south with Birney on the right wing of Grant's fortified line. And the Union army's wagons and cattle were not at Fredericksburg. They were still encamped along Orange Turnpike from Chancellorsville to Salem Church, where they had been since the campaign opened. Rosser attributed his information to prisoners, and they had clearly misled him. His report created the erroneous impression that Grant's combat strength extended north considerably farther than it actually did.

While Rosser's Virginians and Nettleton's Ohioans skirmished along Catharpin Road, Chambliss's Virginians and Hammond's New Yorkers locked horns on the byways below the armies. Chambliss's three regiments were stretched thin, and their responsibilities were staggering. Their theater of operations extended from Spotsylvania Court House east to Guinea Station on the Richmond, Fredericksburg, and Potomac Railroad, a front of more than fifteen miles. Well over a hundred miles of roads, lanes, and farm tracks threaded through the region. Chambliss's duties included guarding the railhead at Guinea Station, where supplies for Lee's army arrived from Richmond, and protecting the wagon route from the station through Mud Tavern to Spotsylvania Court House. He was also charged with probing north along Telegraph Road to investigate Union troop dispositions; with manning fortifications at Smith's Mill and Stanard's Mill, where Telegraph Road crossed the Ni and the Po; and with keeping Lee apprised of developments in his sector. These assignments overtaxed a force numbering no more than a thousand men. Chambliss was to be stretched to his limit on May 15.

Seizing Telegraph Road as far south as Massaponax Church—and even farther south, if the Union cavalrymen could do it—had become increasingly important to Grant as he matured his plans to attack along the Massaponax Church Road corridor. His projections called for Hancock to mass his corps during the night at Anderson's Mill, near where the Ni crossed Massaponax Church Road. Once Hancock bivouacked at Anderson's Mill, Telegraph Road would become an important supply route for his 2nd Corps. Chambliss was in Grant's way, and clearing him from the area became a Union priority.

All morning, squads of Chambliss's horsemen clashed along Telegraph Road with elements of the 13th Pennsylvania Cavalry. Neither side achieved the upper hand. After lunch, Meade decided to shift the 5th New York Cavalry to Telegraph Road as well. The regiment, some three hundred strong, was to proceed south from its camp near the Harris farm, cut cross-country to

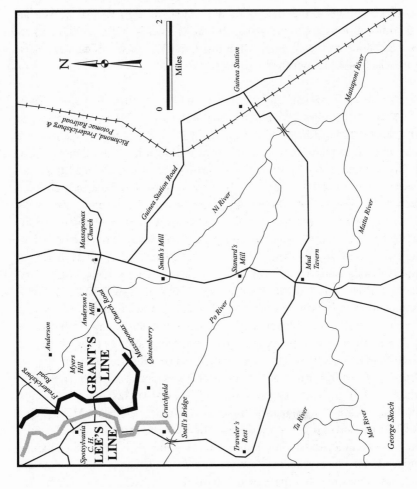

Field of cavalry operations south of the armies on May 15–16

Massaponax Church Road, and, according to Meade's instructions, probe the terrain in front of Wright's corps and "endeavor to obtain some information about roads and the grounds on which to predicate an offensive move in that direction." Meade also directed Wright to hold an infantry brigade in readiness to assist the New Yorkers if they requested help.[27]

Colonel Hammond started by riding over to the Beverly farm, where his men confiscated corn and wheat for their horses and killed the few sheep and chickens that Warren's soldiers had overlooked. At 3:30 P.M. Hammond reported to Wright at the Anderson house. By this time, the military picture had changed. Some of Chambliss's troopers had moved onto Massaponax Church Road and were congregating near Anderson's Mill, the site of Hancock's prospective deployment. Before Hammond went scouting, Meade wanted him to clear Massaponax Church Road of rebels.[28]

Hammond responded with enthusiasm. Leading his command onto Massaponax Church Road by way of the wagon track from the Anderson place, he routed a small force of Confederate horsemen and drove them east to Telegraph Road. "Our boys," a New Yorker wrote, "had a little skirmish with rebel cavalry which fled beyond Massaponax Court House." Hammond hooked up with the 13th Pennsylvania Cavalry at Massaponax Church, and the two regiments rode south together along Telegraph Road, herding Chambliss's Confederates in front of them. About a mile and a half south, the road descended a gentle slope to Smith's Mill, on the Ni. Hammond halted. He was wary of straying too far from the Union army, and he risked being cut off if he tried to cross the river. Leaving a handful of pickets at Smith's Mill to sound the alarm if rebels returned, he withdrew his cavalry to Massaponax Church and made camp.

Massaponax Church, in the northwest quadrant of the junction of Telegraph Road and Massaponax Church Road, had been founded in 1788. The congregation had outgrown the original wooden church. A new brick structure, five years old, now dominated the intersection. One of Hammond's men noticed an inscription on the building: "Massaponax Church, July 4th, 1859." "I could not but think, truly these people have forgotten the memorable 4th with its history and association," the cavalryman mused. He learned to his disappointment that the current pastor hailed from Philadelphia but had become "strong 'Secesh.' "[29]

"Shall this harvest of death never cease?"

Hammond was well placed at Massaponax Church to screen Grant's southern flank and rear against enemy cavalry probes. The northern end of the Union line, however, remained vulnerable to Rosser, who was prowling about, eager to continue his forays. His band of Virginia horsemen would soon have the satisfaction of putting a scare into the entire Union army.

After posting a small force on Catharpin Road to keep an eye on Nettleton, Rosser set off along a farm road that paralleled the western bank of the Ni and struck Gordon Road at the Couse place. He continued east along Gordon Road, crossed the Ni, and paid a brief visit to the Armstrong house. Verifying that the Yankees had left, Rosser turned southeast along the narrow wagon trail that Colonel Wainwright had used to move his guns on the night of May 13–14. The riders threaded through a macabre landscape of abandoned wagons and decomposed corpses crawling with worms, left over from the fighting on May 12. Troopers from the 7th Virginia Cavalry recoiled in shock when they stumbled on a corn crib stuffed with dead or dying Confederates. The men were prisoners so severely injured that the Federals had left them to perish rather than attempt to carry them to Fredericksburg. Most were dead and the rest nearly so. "Great God, heavenly father, shall this harvest of death never cease?" a Virginian wrote after witnessing the scene.[30]

A mile along the trail, Rosser reached the ruins of the Stevens house. The home had burned—how and when is not known—and only its two chimneys and a wall remained. Referred to by Federals as the Deserted House, the Stevens place occupied a high knoll with an open view across the Ni. Birney had established a picket outpost at the ruins, and the pickets were understandably surprised to see Confederates emerging from the dark forest. Rosser's recent brush with Ferrero at the Alrich farm had made the rebel cavalryman cautious about rushing into a fight until he knew the odds. He halted north of the Stevens place and dispatched his forward elements to probe Birney's pickets and find out what was behind them.[31]

Rosser's appearance at the Stevens house sent shock waves through the Union high command. Birney's pickets could not be sure whether the rebels streaming in from Gordon Road were cavalry or infantry. There was no doubt, however, that there were plenty of them. The implications were serious. If the Confederates managed to capture the Stevens knoll, they could play havoc behind Union lines. Not only would they cut off Birney from the rest of the 2nd Corps at the Harris farm, but they also could take the 9th Corps from its northern flank and rear. A short march east would bring them into Barlow's and Gibbon's unsuspectingly divisions. They might even threaten the supply trains on Fredericksburg Road. Impressed with the need for urgency, the outpost's commander dispatched a courier east to Mrs. Alsop's house, where Burnside had his headquarters. Burnside forwarded the alarming report to Grant. "Our pickets on the right report a strong column of the enemy moving to my right," he advised in a 2:40 P.M. dispatch. "It is yet impossible to say in what strength or with what object." Grant, who was camped nearby on Fredericksburg Road, took the news calmly. Burnside's formation was below the Ni, he pointed out in reply, and Birney ought to have sufficient strength to hold the river. Burnside agreed, but suggested that Grant send a brigade and a battery from the 2nd Corps to shore up the pickets.[32]

Short on cavalry, Federal commanders had no way to ferret out Lee's troop dispositions. The foggy, drizzly atmosphere set the mood for confusion and alarm. There was no telling what the rebels were up to behind that brooding curtain of forest. Thus far in the campaign, Grant had kept Lee busy with remorseless combinations of assaults and maneuvers. But rain had ended Grant's offensive operations, and Lee had used his cavalry superiority to draw an impenetrable screen across his army. Grant had received no reliable intelligence about Lee's doings for over twenty hours. "It is almost impossible to discover the exact position of the enemy," a Federal observed, "as they keep in and behind the woods, their pickets only being observable by us." Now Confederates were swarming above Grant's northern flank, emerging first at the Alrich farm, then at the Stevens place. Grant knew Lee's penchant for flanking maneuvers and for delivering unexpected blows with stunning success. One of the campaign's most trying moments had come on the evening of May 6, when Confederates commanded by John Gordon had slammed unexpectedly into the northern flank of Grant's formation in the Wilderness. The appearance of Confederates at the Stevens grounds raised the alarming prospect that Lee was about to repeat that performance. Lee seemed to have targeted with disconcerting accuracy the very sector Grant had weakened when he withdrew Warren, Wright, and Hancock. Edgy Federals began imagining a mighty rebel host descending from Gordon Road and enveloping the northern end of the Union line.[33]

Anxious minutes passed, rumors flew, and more panic appeared in Burnside's dispatches. Confederates in brigade strength were heading for the Stevens place, he told Grant at 3:30. With no Federal cavalrymen available to scout along Gordon Road, who could say how many Confederates were coming his way? Grant must send reinforcements "as soon as possible" to hold the Stevens grounds, Burnside insisted.[34]

Grant could not ignore Burnside's alarms, although he suspected the 9th Corps commander was overreacting. Shortly after receiving Burnside's latest dispatch, he put his thoughts in a note to Meade. Burnside, Grant explained, "just now informs me that the enemy are moving on his right in considerable force, but he does not know yet in what force or for what object." Grant had alerted Ferrero to watch for rebel incursions and he had put the commander in Fredericksburg on notice. "We now have a large force between here and Fredericksburg," he observed, "which, if it does its duty, can prevent any serious disaster to our trains." [35]

Grant decided to bide his time. He had deployed his army for a major assault in the morning. He wanted to retain the initiative, and changing his troop dispositions to buttress Burnside would undermine his ability to attack. Grant had a talent for turning adverse developments to his advantage, and he discerned opportunity in the reports of rebels emerging on his northern flank. Lee, he reasoned, could not launch a turning movement in force without drawing troops from his line. If Lee really meant to attack, he had necessarily created a weak spot somewhere in his defenses. Grant wanted to find that vulnerable point. Convinced, as always, that offensive action constituted the best defense, Grant toyed with immediately attacking. Federal troops storming the rebel earthworks would nullify Lee's flank attack and might even uncover that elusive weak spot. By moving boldly, Grant reasoned, he might yet secure victory.[36]

Keeping with his aggressive designs, Grant issued firm instructions to Meade. If Confederates attacked Burnside, "the best possible relief will be to move the whole Army of the Potomac forward from Wright's and Warren's front," he advised. Meade promptly directed his subordinates to hold their troops "ready at short notice to advance against the enemy." Warren characteristically proffered a suggestion. "Would it not be better for me to reinforce [Burnside] so as to meet the enemy without cover, than to attack his intrenchments which are in my front?" he asked. The query infuriated Grant, who was fed up with Warren's quibbling and second-guessing. Warren's suggestion seemed the very embodiment of the defensive mindset of the Army of the Potomac. During the crisis caused by the Confederate flank attack on May 6, Grant had enjoined his staffers, "Think what we are going to do ourselves, instead of what Lee is going to do." He considered the advice especially appropriate now, as he wanted to wrest the initiative from Lee, not to react defensively to Lee's moves. "Dispatch containing suggestions received," Meade curtly responded to Warren. "Your orders will be sent to you when Burnside is attacked. In the meantime they are unchanged." [37]

As a precaution, Meade directed Gibbon to shift from the Harris farm to the Stevens house to support Birney's pickets. Birney meanwhile began digging rifle pits from the Landrum house toward the Stevens grounds to strengthen his connection with Gibbon.

Grant's hunch that Burnside was exaggerating soon proved correct. The rebels menacing the Stevens place were only Rosser's horsemen, and they had no intention of tangling with Birney's and Gibbon's infantrymen. After capturing some of Birney's skirmishers, Rosser backtracked to Gordon Road and forwarded his findings to Lee. This time he got the facts straight. The Union 2nd Corps had encamped behind the Stevens place, he reported, and its right rested near the Brown house. On their way back to Todd's Tavern, the Confederate horsemen paid poor Mrs. Couse another visit. They rummaged through her yard and took "everything they can lay hands on," she confided to a neighbor. Later in the evening, Rosser posted guards at the Couse place, and a doctor from the 11th Virginia Cavalry came by to tend the injured Federals.[38]

The Union high command remained concerned, however, that Rosser's foray might presage an assault. Wright's and Warren's soldiers stood at the alert, ready to counterattack. So far as the tired men could tell, the call to arms was a pointless aggravation, and they grumbled openly at having to leave their tents and wait idly in the rain. Meade's aide Lyman rode from headquarters to supervise the 5th and 6th Corps's deployment. He found Warren in the Beverly house, caked with mud and surrounded by officers. The 5th Corps commander complained bitterly that his provisions were depleted—all he had left was sugar and hardtack—and seemed preoccupied with rounding up stragglers. Warren and Wright had been bickering over troop dispositions all afternoon but appeared to have ironed out their differences. To cement the link between their corps, Warren was having his pioneers cut two roads through the woods to the Myers place. Lyman located Wright at the Anderson farm, busily repositioning his troops to attack. Wright had formed Russell's and Ricketts's divisions in battle lines at Myers Hill and had placed Neill's division in reserve along the crest in front of the Anderson house. Upton's brigade reached south along the western bank of the Ni toward Massaponax Church Road, where Grant still hoped to deploy Hancock when this latest crisis eased. Colonel Grant's Vermont brigade anchored the 6th Corps's left flank at Anderson's Mill, near Massaponax Church Road.[39]

Lyman met Neill on the ridge overlooking the Ni and asked him to point out the 6th Corps's deployments. The division commander—"Beau," his friends called him—was in a gregarious mood and responded with a dramatic wave of his left hand toward the near ridgeline. "Ah! Yes! My division, in position," he explicated. Pointing farther on with his right hand, he gestured broadly and pronounced, "Skirmishers." Then, gazing over the green treetops toward Spotsylvania Court House, he declared, "Enemy!" A tremulous flourish of both hands mimicked the rough earthen mounds marking the Confederate line, barely visible in the hazy distance. His skirmishers, Neill noted, were out about six hundred yards, facing Lee's vedettes. Everything, however, seemed quiet. The only firing Neill had heard came from the 5th New York Cavalry's skirmishers in the direction of Telegraph Road.[40]

A cluster of Pennsylvanians in Neill's division lying quietly behind log fortifications received the order, "Don't cheer." Shortly Grant appeared, riding his bay horse slowly along as he inspected the 6th Corps's earthworks. At the commander in chief's appearance, soldiers began tossing their hats and pantomiming cheers. The 61st Pennsylvania ignored the admonition to remain silent and voiced several full-throated yells. Rebel batteries immediately opened, and shells burst close to the general, showering debris over him and his mount. "General Grant gave no evidence that he heard the cheering or the firing," an onlooker reminisced. "The incident ended, the men liking the general better for not 'making a fuss about nothing.' "[41]

At 8:00 P.M. Grant concluded that Rosser's flurry of activity represented nothing more than a probe and issued orders for the soldiers to stand down. The grand assault that he had been planning all day along the Fredericksburg Road–Massaponax Church Road axis had to be postponed. Hancock's corps, which was to lead the attack, was spread over a front of several miles, with Birney's division on the Landrum farm, Gibbon's division at the Stevens place, and Barlow's division on Mrs. Harris's property. Inclement weather made it unlikely that Hancock could gather his forces and march them to their jumping-off point at Anderson's Mill before daylight. Bowing to the inevitable, Grant called off the attack.

Years later, many Federals considered May 15 the campaign's low point. "The enemy's works were close to ours and in full view," one of Burnside's men recollected, "with their battle flags flying defiantly in our faces, their bands playing, and the singing of good old Methodist hymns was plainly heard." The sight of orderlies carrying the popular Lieutenant Colonel Weibecke's body from Myers Hill for burial incited a spontaneous outburst of emotion. Troops vented their anger by burning the Myers house and its outbuildings. "The owner was a rebel and upon our evacuating yesterday, fired into our 'demoralized' ranks," a surgeon offered by way of explanation. "It was a good building," he added, "and its destruction helped to pay for that shot." Another Federal exulted that when the traitorous owners returned, they would find "more desolation than they ever dreamed of." Constant marching and fighting had discouraged the army, and the leaden, overcast sky did nothing to brighten spirits. It seemed to the bleary troops that whenever they managed to fashion sticks and tarps into primitive shelters and to coax smoking bundles of kindling into flame, orders would come to pack and move. "The brigade changed position frequently, without any apparent object except to obey orders," was one officer's description of the incessant shuffling. "We were always against [the Confederates] and under fire, always ready to attack or repel attack," recollected Major Ellis Spear of the 20th Maine. The men "felt that they were doomed to slaughter," a soldier remembered.[42]

Grousing over the afternoon's false alarm, disgruntled soldiers returned to their camps for another night of cold and rain. Hungry from unaccustomed exertion, Colonel Warner's newly arrived 1st Vermont Heavies stacked arms and went in search of water and firewood. Veterans snatched the Green Mountain men's gum rubber blankets and traded their old muskets for new ones. On discovering what had happened, Warner marched to Neill's tent and announced, "General, many of your men have taken our guns, blankets, and other equipment." Neill drew to his full height. "Impossible, colonel," he answered gravely. "My men have no use for your guns or other property." Warner would not drop the matter. Pointing to a group of haggard veterans, he protested, "There is a man with one of our guns, and there is another, and beyond I see some of our new blankets." Neill had a ready answer. "Oh, no, you are mistaken," he insisted. "When you stacked arms you put a guard over them; you are too good a soldier to leave your property unguarded. Besides, if you need any guns you can pick up on this battlefield ten for every one you have lost." Understanding the futility of further protest, Warner returned empty-handed to his men. They fell asleep, wetter but wiser for the experience.[43]

Rosser's and Chambliss's forays had provided Lee valuable information. The withdrawal of Warren, Wright, and now Hancock from the northern sector of the battlefield seemed to confirm Lee's hunch that Grant was shifting south. Hancock's move to the Harris farm made it possible for Lee to pull Kershaw's division from its trenches and reunite it with Field—the rest of Anderson's corps—on the army's southern flank. Kershaw received marching orders at 10:00 P.M. Under a cloud-covered moon, his soldiers filed onto Brock Road and marched south. Alexander's artillery followed. Laurel Hill, which the Confederate 1st Corps had defended against determined Federal attacks since May 8, lay vacant in the night.

Of great interest to Lee was a Yankee dispatch that one of Chambliss's vigilant scouts intercepted. Purportedly from Meade, the dispatch ordered two days' rations for the Union soldiers. Clearly a major movement was brewing, although Lee could still not say with certainty what it would be. Lee meant to be ready for anything. "The enemy may make a night attack as before, or commence at early dawn, or may push on and endeavor to pass us,"

Lee's aide Venable noted. Lee instructed his lieutenants to remain alert. They were to awaken their men by 3:00 A.M., prepared to fight or march as circumstances dictated.[44]

Colonel Clement A. Evans, commanding a brigade of Georgians in Ewell's corps, jotted an optimistic letter home. "Grant appears to be exhausted and the hope is that the fight is ended," he began. "But that is only a hope, for he is yet in our front and we may still fight another great battle." Late that night, Lee's aide-de-camp Taylor committed his thoughts to paper. The campaign, he reported, had been "severe," and, except for the debacle at the Mule Shoe on May 12, "eminently successful." The soldiers, he added, remained "in good heart and condition—our confidence, certainly mine, unimpaired." Grant, he concluded, was "beating his head against a wall." The day's intelligence suggested that more fighting was imminent. "He is moving tonight," Taylor closed on a grim note. "We expect a renewal of the battle tomorrow." [45]

Another message sped to Richmond that night. Breckinridge had whipped Sigel. "Two miles above New Market, my command met the enemy, under General Sigel, and defeated him with heavy loss," read the Kentuckian's dispatch. The victory halted the Union threat to the Shenandoah Valley and brightened Lee's prospects for reinforcements.[46]

Berry Benson, a Confederate sharpshooter from the 1st South Carolina, examined the Bloody Angle, which the Federals had now abandoned. His compatriots had fought at the angle on May 12, and many of his friends had died there. Corpses swollen twice the size of living men covered the ground, and the air hung foul from decaying flesh. Water black as ink filled rifle pits. Muskets, cartridge boxes, belts, knapsacks, canteens, and blankets lay strewn about. "If a man wants to see hell upon earth, let him come and look into this black, bloody hole—upon this horrid confusion, these wet muddy graves—this reeking mass of corruption of rotting corpses, that fill the air with this intolerable stench," Benson contemplated. "How a man can look upon such a scene and still take pleasure in war seems past belief." [47]

"The elements alone have suspended hostilities."

May 16 brought more wet and gloom. Rain had lashed the armies through the night, completing the battleground's transformation into viscous mire. "The mud was so deep that any offensive operation, however successful, could not be followed up," Assistant War Secretary Dana concluded as he studied the downpour through his tent flaps. "There was nothing to do but lie still and wait for better weather and drier roads." [48]

In no mood to wait, the Union commander in chief paced his headquarters tent in agitation. "Grant seems to be nonplused and to have got to the end of his tether," a colonel observed; "Things remain just as they were yesterday." At 8:00 A.M., Grant conceded that the elements had gotten the best of him. "We have had almost constant rain without any prospect yet of its clearing up," he informed Halleck in his morning dispatch to Washington. "The roads have now become so impassable that ambulances with wounded can no longer run between here and Fredericksburg." This meant that "all offensive operations necessarily cease until we can have twenty-four hours of dry weather." Grant insisted that his men remained in good spirits and shared his confidence in the campaign's outcome. "You can assure the President and Secretary of War that the elements alone have suspended hostilities," he stressed, lest his inaction be misunderstood. "It is in no manner due to weakness or exhaustion on our part."[49]

A lively stream of visitors relieved the tedium. The staffer Lyman was especially intrigued by a touring surgeon from the British Fusileer Guard—"a perky John Bull, one Baker," Lyman described him—who dropped by to inquire about medical matters. "He walked on the tips of his toes," Lyman noted, "with his knees bent, was dressed in full uniform, and had a smirk on his face." Meade pawned the Englishman off on the Potomac Army's medical director, surgeon Thomas A. McParlin, whom he quickly bored. McParlin finally rid himself of Baker by persuading him to examine a field hospital. Lyman later checked on Baker and was horrified to see him gleefully wielding a large medical instrument. "I hope they don't let him do much to the wounded," Lyman wrote home.[50]

Governor William Sprague of Rhode Island and Senator John Sherman of Ohio also came to visit. Lyman eyed the exalted guests with interest. Sprague struck him as a "small-headed, black-eyed, sparrow little man, who rode fearlessly about in a straw hat." Sherman, who was General Sherman's brother, was exceedingly tall and thin—"so flat," Lyman observed, "you wonder where his lungs and other vitals may be placed"—and he wore a linen duster that accentuated his spare frame. "Why anyone who could stay away should come down is not plain," Lyman wondered, but he found the company enjoyable. The politicians complimented Meade and assured him that Washington gave him credit for the battlefield victories. Meade corrected them. At first he had maneuvered the army, he related, but Grant had gradually taken control. It would be impossible, he explained, for the army to have two heads. As for the division of labor among the various generals, Meade observed that a recent magazine article described the relationships correctly. The army, the article claimed, was "directed by Grant, commanded by

Meade, and led by Hancock, [Wright], and Warren." Meade considered this a "quite good distinction, and about hits the nail on the head." [51]

The lull let Union field commanders complete their casualty returns. After breakfast, Grant, Meade, and Dana sat down to review the tally. The results were appalling. Since May 5 the 2nd Corps reported 11,553 lost; the 5th Corps, 10,686; the 6th Corps, 9,492; and the 9th Corps, 5,021. Another 120 casualties from the artillery arm made the grand total 36,872 men. This did not include Sheridan's casualties, which were not available. Grant expressed regret that so many soldiers were dead, wounded, and missing. Meade, who nursed growing resentment over Grant's aggressive tactics, saw an opportunity for a jibe. "Well, General, we can't do these little tricks without losses," he interjected. [52]

Replacing losses remained a top priority. And with terms of service fast ending, keeping the army's current soldiers seemed as important as acquiring new ones. Thus far, expiring terms of service had caused marginal subtractions, but the floodgates were about to swing open. Ten regiments comprising Samuel Crawford's Pennsylvania Reserves were due to go home soon. Rather than watch idly as the division dwindled to nothing, Meade struck a bargain. All of the regiments would remain until May 31, which represented their average discharge date. On May 15, the 8th Pennsylvania Reserves, which contained only seventy-five men, reached the end of its enlistment. Meade reminded the soldiers of the compromise, but they demanded to go home. Rather than provoke a protest, Meade authorized Warren to release the regiment so long as the Pennsylvania Reserves's nine remaining regiments agreed to stay until May 31. With thousands of heavy artillerymen expected to arrive momentarily, the loss of seventy-five soldiers seemed inconsequential. [53]

Mindful of his eroding numbers and anxious to augment his strength for the coming offensive, Grant kept pressing for reinforcements. To his satisfaction, General Abercrombie, who had taken over management of the supply depot on Potomac Creek, reported Tyler's arrival at the port, along with some 6,700 soldiers "fully equipped and armed." Unaccustomed to doing things Grant's way, Abercrombie promised to start Tyler from Belle Plain the next afternoon. Grant was not one for delay, and he fired off a letter to Abercrombie. "Direct General Tyler to forward such of his troops as have reached Belle Plain immediately, and forward all others arriving as fast as they land," he urged the general. "Small bodies get along more comfortably than large ones," he added, "and then, too, we get the benefit of reinforcements from day to day." He also wrote Tyler, insisting, "I want and must have the whole of your command here by tomorrow night at farthest." Time was of the essence. "If your troops have not yet all arrived at Belle Plain," Grant admonished Tyler, "you must bring forward by that time without fail such as have arrived, leaving the remainder to follow as fast as they land." [54]

On May 16 Colonel Mathew Murphy reported with his Irish Legion—four New York regiments, two thousand men in all. Resplendent in fresh uniforms and carrying newly issued firearms, the Legion joined Gibbon's 2nd Corps division. Many Irishmen, the story goes, showed up drunk, but they still received a hearty welcome from Gibbon's veterans. Halleck warned of "considerable dissatisfaction" in the cavalry and artillery units being forwarded as infantry and suggested that they be incorporated into veteran outfits. "One successful fight will remove all dissatisfaction," he predicted, "and, if not, dissatisfaction will do no harm there." [55]

Grant also used the days of forced inactivity to reorganize his artillery. At the start of the campaign each infantry corps had been assigned an artillery brigade, with an artillery reserve for the entire army. "The Wilderness and Spotsylvania battles convinced me that we had more artillery than could ever be brought into action at any one time," Grant complained. "It occupied much of the road in marching, and taxed the trains in bringing up forage." The reserve had proven unwieldy in central Virginia's difficult terrain. Meade had converted Colonel Kitching's artillery brigade into infantry and had attached it to various infantry corps, but the Potomac Army's two reserve artillery brigades—twelve batteries in all—had simply tagged along behind the army, seeing little service. Grant considered the reserve guns hindrances and directed Meade to get rid of them. Burnside, who had his own artillery reserve of six batteries, was to send back his guns as well.[56]

Brigadier General Henry J. Hunt, the Potomac Army's artillery chief, had created Meade's artillery reserve and was especially fond of his brainchild. He opposed sending all the reserve guns back and proposed instead distributing the reserve's batteries among the infantry corps, assigning twelve four-gun batteries to each corps to replace the eight six-gun batteries they presently had. Hunt's plan had an appealing logic. Each corps would retain forty-eight guns, and the corps heads could use the reorganization to send away damaged guns and worn out teams and replace them with fitter units from the reserve. "The change has at least the advantage of enabling us to put the remaining guns in complete order," Wainwright remarked in approving Hunt's proposal. Grant endorsed Hunt's idea. Within a day, the artillery had been reorganized and the excess guns were on their way to the rear. The results, Grant hoped, would be a leaner and more effective artillery force.[57]

Grant received news of developments in the war's other theaters. Sherman, Halleck reported, had defeated Johnston at Resaca and had crossed the

Oostanaula River with part of his force. Banks, whom Grant had intended to cooperate with Sherman, was faring poorly. His Red River venture had bogged down entirely, and Grant had received complaints about his performance. One letter implored Grant to "do justice to the Mothers and Sisters of those brave men, who have been most cruelly, most shamefully sacrificed, and slaughtered, to atone for the gross mismanagement of Major General Banks, in his late battles." Grant recommended Banks's immediate removal.[58]

Developments closer to home seemed to be going well. Butler, the day's reports stated, had carried the outer works at Drewry's Bluff. Word had also arrived from Sheridan. Grant gleefully noted that his protégé had "cut both railroads leading from Richmond; had whipped Stuart's cavalry; and had carried the outer works at Richmond, besides whipping the infantry sent out to drive him away: thinks he could have gone into the city, but not knowing our operations, nor those of Butler, did not know that he could stay; therefore went on in pursuance of his orders." Crook, who was cooperating with Sigel, had cut the New River Bridge, destroyed rebel stores in Dublin, and was well on his way to Lynchburg. Grant had no news from Sigel—the general had not yet informed Washington of his defeat—but he presumed that all was fine with him as well. So far as Grant could tell, his subsidiary armies were accomplishing something despite the rain.[59]

Dana forwarded a report to Washington at 7:00 A.M. "No change has been made in the situation of this army since my dispatch of yesterday morning," he wrote, "except that Birney's division, of Hancock's corps, which was left behind in the night when the mass of that corps was moved into the rear of our center, has also been withdrawn, leaving Burnside's corps alone to hold the right." Prospects for action seemed remote. "The rain had continued at intervals," Dana observed, "and the mud is as bad as ever." [60]

The Union army now ranged along the valley of the Ni. Burnside's corps held the line's northern extreme, extending from the eastern face of the Mule Shoe south to a point near Fredericksburg Road. Warren's corps continued the line across the Beverly grounds. Wright's corps maintained its forward position at the Myers house, reaching south along the river to Anderson's Mill, on Massaponax Church Road. And Hancock's corps, with Gibbon at the Stevens place and Birney and Barlow at the Harris farm, served as a reserve. Fredericksburg Road was the army's main artery for moving troops and supplies. The Confederates had responded by shifting the mass of their army southward, roughly corresponding to Grant's new alignments. Ewell remained in his entrenchments across the base of the Mule Shoe. Early faced

Burnside, Warren, and Wright. Anderson stretched southward, buttressing the lower end of Early's line and anchoring the Confederate formation on the Po.

Viewed from the roof of the Gayle house, the distant Confederate earthworks looked like ragged scars across the fresh spring landscape. Rebel sharpshooters crouched in pits in front of the line, and the entrenchments bristled with artillery. "It is evident why the enemy do not attack us," a northern newspaperman reflected as he took in the scene. "A position could hardly be more secure, and behind these defenses it is evidently [Lee's] plan to remain until he is drawn out of it by strategic maneuvering or beaten out by overwhelming attack." Around noon, Meade directed Warren and Wright to advance a force to determine whether Lee's army was really behind the far heaps of red dirt. Meade cautioned that the probe was "not designed to bring on a general engagement with the enemy in his works." [61]

Warren, and Grant's aide Cyrus Comstock, were scanning the rebel line through field glasses when Meade's order arrived. Warren was flabbergasted. He could plainly see that the distant works were crawling with Confederates. Not only was it suicidal to send troops against those fortifications—Warren's aide Roebling also foresaw "great loss"—but the venture would stir up the rebel batteries, which lay blessedly dormant. Besides, the 5th Corps's ration wagons had finally arrived, making it a bad time to arouse Early's gunners. After petitioning Meade for permission to move the wagons, Warren dutifully directed Griffin to advance his pickets as close to the Confederate works as possible. "What the intentions are I can't say," a soldier wrote in his diary, "but if we are to charge across the plain in front exposed for more than a mile to grape and canister from 24 guns, to say nothing of the small arms, then I never expect to tell the tale, for it would sweep us into eternity in no time." Comstock was also dumbfounded by Meade's directive and went to headquarters to voice his objection. An advance was unnecessary, he urged, as he had seen for himself that Confederates manned the earthworks in force. To everyone's relief, Meade rescinded his order. [62]

Burnside was feeling unusually aggressive and volunteered to probe Early's entrenchments with small attacking columns. The 9th Corps's forward field headquarters stood in a copse of hemlocks and pines within shelling distance of the Confederate batteries. "With our glasses we can see [the rebels] strongly intrenched, with artillery in position," a newspaperman observed, but Burnside still meant to proceed. At 4:00 P.M. two sections of Lieutenant John W. Roder's battery opened from the right of the 9th Corps's line, and elements from Potter's and Crittenden's divisions darted toward the northern segment of Early's works. Spearheading the attack, the 11th New Hampshire reeled under scathing fire from Georgians and North Carolinians and quickly tumbled back. At the cost of fifteen casualties, the regiment had confirmed what everyone already knew. "There was a large rebel force in our front, strongly entrenched, and ready to offer us battle," a soldier noted bitterly.[63]

Meade used the break in fighting to finish evacuating wounded soldiers from Mrs. Couse's yard. Concerned that Rosser might make another visit, he directed Gibbon to bring the injured men back. Around 2:30 P.M. Gibbon started off with his entire division, Captain Frederick M. Edgell's battery, two hundred ambulances, and several wagons. Despite his expedition's formidable size, Gibbon remained on edge. Mrs. Couse's home was more than a mile from the Union army. Rosser's men were reputedly nearby, and Confederate infantry could be prowling about as well.[64]

Mrs. Couse had just finished her laundry when Gibbon appeared. The general posted skirmishers on high ground around the house to watch for Confederates while his soldiers filled the ambulances with wounded. "Never were a set of men more rejoiced than were these poor sufferers on seeing our men come to rescue them," a correspondent reported. Gibbon's staff whiled away the time sipping tea with Mrs. Couse in her parlor. Gibbon had become so nervous over the prospect that Confederates might interrupt the operation that he refused to come inside. He sipped coffee instead by the window. "Everything was hurry and all excitement," Katherine Couse reminisced. Near dark, Gibbon and his men departed, leaving the Couses a supply of sugar, coffee, and meat. Gibbon's commissary promised to send a calico dress.[65]

For the first time in days, silence settled over the Couse property. "They left us weeping, sad and lonely," Katherine Couse confided to a friend. The place lay in shambles. Clothes and military accouterments littered the yard, and freshly turned earth marked grave sites. "It seems as if some great funeral procession had lately passed through," the younger Couse observed. "These great armies leave ruin, desolation in their track," she added: "The whole country has a laid waste look." Mrs. Brown, to everyone's relief, finally went home. She found that Federals had used her parlor for a hospital. Blood and gore smeared the walls and stained the carpet. Some of Birney's pickets were milling about, and one of them shot at her husband, whom the Federals had locked in the basement during the battle. The bullet intended for Mr. Brown ricocheted off a brass door hinge. Another Federal fired at Mrs. Brown's twelve-year-old son but hit a chair instead.[66]

Grant's foot soldiers remembered May 16 as the day when mail arrived. Fingers accustomed to ripping open cartridges fumbled with envelopes containing letters penned by familiar hands. Rain dominated everyone's existence. The downpour was no longer just an inconvenience. It had become an ever-present burden that complicated the simplest tasks. "An ordinary rain, lasting for a day or two, does not embarrass troops," Grant's aide Porter observed. "But when the storm continues for a week it becomes one of the most serious obstacles in a campaign. The men can secure no proper shelter and no comfortable rest; their clothing has no chance to dry; and a tramp of a few miles through tenacious mud requires as much exertion as an ordinary day's march. Tents become saturated and weighted with water, and draft animals have increased loads, and heavier roads over which to haul them. Dry wood cannot be found; cooking becomes difficult; the men's spirits are affected by the gloom, and even the most buoyant natures become disheartened." [67]

Rain also brought out Virginia's insects. "I'm so tired and lousy," Major Lemuel A. Abbott of the 10th Vermont scrawled in his diary, "I do wish we could stay somewhere long enough to boil our underclothing." Abbott noted that the pests held no regard for rank and had infested his superiors. "I hope this won't shock anyone when they read it when I have passed along," he wrote. "It's a part of the history of the civil war though, and should be recorded." Wainwright bathed and changed clothes, "luxury no one can imagine who has not been living as we have since Culpeper." He could "not imagine how the line officers of infantry manage, for they have no means of carrying ought with them beyond what they have on their backs. They must simply go dirty; a fortnight without a change is simply something awful to contemplate." [68]

A soldier from the 126th Ohio strolled up Myers Hill in search of a quiet place to rest. He thumbed his Bible, trying to read, but visions of combat kept intruding. "My mind pictured before me the fiery furnaces," he remembered of his vigil, "the Red Sea waters coming together, and the inhuman struggles of men killing men I had so lately passed through." [69]

Lee's men were just as miserable as Grant's. "Human gore and Virginia red clay do not make a pleasant mixture to have on one's clothes," a Mississippian observed, "but we had to stand it and did not grumble." Rations of sour bacon and corn bread "gave heartburn of the most distressing character," according to one rebel, "to say nothing of diarrhea, which we considered as a matter of course." A squad of Georgians discovered eggs, flour, and two guinea fowls in an abandoned house. Using gunpowder as seasoning, they prepared a feast that one diner recalled as the "one square meal we got during the campaign of 1864." Soldiers from the 21st Virginia stumbled on four baby rabbits and spent the day building elaborate shelters for the orphaned animals. "I do not know that I ever saw men more solicitous for the welfare of anything than were those grizzly warriors for those little bunnies," a Confederate reminisced.[70]

Anderson's 1st Corps put the finishing touches on its new line. Brigadier General John Gregg's Texas and Arkansas brigade overlapped Early's right flank near Zion Church to block Massaponax Church Road. Field's division manned the entrenchments that extended from Zion Church to the Po. Colonel John Bratton's South Carolinians hooked onto Gregg's right, and Colonel Dudley M. DuBose's Georgians, Brigadier General George T. "Tige" Anderson's Georgians, and Brigadier General Evander McI. Law's Alabamians strung south to the river. Lieutenant Colonel William W. Parker's battery anchored the 1st Corps's right flank on high ground at the Crutchfield place, overlooking Snell's Bridge. The Crutchfield house served as the corps's headquarters, and Kershaw's division bivouacked in reserve nearby. Frank Huger's artillery battalion commanded Massaponax Church Road, Major John C. Haskell's battalion controlled the approaches from the south, and Colonel Henry C. Cabell's battalion waited in reserve.[71]

The 1st Corps's line was a masterpiece of military engineering. Situated along a ridge, it looked across a mile of relatively open ground toward the Federals. Converging waves of musketry and artillery fire dominated the approaches. A Confederate boasted that the fortifications were so strong that he regretted he could not carry them with him when the army moved on. "The only trouble was that we made these lines too good," Alexander reminisced in mock regret. "So good that the enemy never attacked them."[72]

May 16 brought Lee encouragement. Late in the morning the general received a letter from Secretary of War Seddon. Attached was Breckinridge's dispatch announcing his victory over Sigel. And Seddon had still more heady news. Beauregard had at last attacked Butler, he advised, and battle was raging south of the James. Lee dashed off a telegram to Breckinridge congratulating him on his victory. "Press [Sigel] down the valley," Lee urged, "and if practicable follow him into Maryland." The telegram had scarcely left Lee's hands before he sent another. "If you can follow Sigel into Maryland, you will do more good than by joining us. If you cannot, and your command is not otherwise needed in the valley or in your department, I desire you to prepare to join me."[73]

While Lee's foot soldiers rested, Chambliss drove his cavalry hard. All day, the 5th New York and 13th Pennsylvania probed Chambliss's cavalry screen, which stretched from Guinea Station to Stanard's Mill, where Telegraph Road crossed the Po. Federal scouts ventured within two miles of Guinea Station but retired without attacking the Confederate supply depot. A squadron of Hammond's horsemen reconnoitered south along Telegraph

Road, drove off Chambliss's pickets at Smith's Mill, and pushed on toward Stanard's Mill. Soldiers from the 1st Confederate Engineers worked feverishly to prepare a reception for the interlopers at the Po, where high bluffs along the river's southern bank provided ideal defensive positions. While engineers dug rifle pits, Chambliss posted two of McGregor's three-inch guns on high ground commanding the roadway.

To lure Hammond into his trap, Chambliss positioned troopers along Telegraph Road north of the Po as bait. Hammond's troopers saw the decoys and gave chase, little suspecting they were being drawn into an ambush. The Confederates splashed across the Po with Hammond's men in hot pursuit. When the Federals reached the river, Chambliss's artillery and muskets roared into action from the bluffs. Confronted by a well-fortified foe, the Federals called off the chase and withdrew to Smith's Mill. Chambliss's troopers followed and camped for the night, facing the Union horsemen across the Ni. Rooney Lee discounted the Union cavalry probes. "I do not look upon [the Federals] picketing Smith's Mill bridge as anything more than a security to their pickets at Massaponax Church," he reported.[74]

General Lee was unsure what Grant meant to do. "The enemy has made no movement against our position today," he informed Davis in his daily dispatch. "He has retired his right [Hancock] and extended his left [Wright] toward Massaponax Church, occupying the line of the Ni River, his main force being apparently east of the stream." That evening Lee informed Ewell that aside from the Union cavalry probe toward Stanard's Mill, "everything appears perfectly quiet." He advised Ewell to watch the country off his left flank, although he felt "no apprehension" for Ewell's safety "if the men do their duty."[75]

Lee saw no choice but to remain on the defensive. Unless reinforced, he lacked the means to maneuver or attack. Confident in the strength of his position, he believed another Union assault would deliver another victory to southern arms. Privately, Lee mourned Stuart. The cavalry commander had been like a son to Lee, and he had depended on him to ferret out the enemy's intentions. "Ah, major," Lee remarked to an officer, "if my poor friend Stuart were here I should know all about what those people are doing."[76]

V

May 17–18

Grant Launches His Grand Assault

"Tomorrow we shall begin fighting again."

RAIN SPATTERED FITFULLY a bit after dawn on the morning of May 17, then stopped. Sunlight spread across central Virginia, clear and bright, lifting the damp chill. Soldiers peered from waterlogged tarps to behold spring at its most glorious. Basking in warmth, the Blue and the Gray spread their clothes and blankets to dry, like hobos after a rain. "The two armies confront each other in plain sight," observed the artillerist George Breck, "both being in strong positions and both, apparently, waiting for the other to attack first." [1]

"Weather is splendid," Dana noted, "and roads rapidly becoming dry, even where mud was worst." Grant was ebullient. He had been striving to resume the offensive, and the elements at last seemed willing to cooperate. The strategic picture, however, had altered dramatically. Lee had reacted to the Federal maneuvers by shifting his 1st Corps south of Spotsylvania Court House and now confronted Grant along a line extending to the Po River. In spite of Lee's countermoves, Grant still considered Massaponax Church Road the Confederate line's most vulnerable point. To overcome Lee's strengthened defenses there, he set about increasing the size of his attacking force. [2]

Early on May 17 a courier galloped into Lee's camp with news every bit as cheering as the weather. Beauregard had launched his offensive against Butler at Drewry's Bluff on May 16. Mistakes had plagued both sides, but by the end of the day, Beauregard had declared victory. Butler's Army of the James was falling back to Bermuda Hundred in the angle formed by the James and Appomattox Rivers. Once there, the Federals would be locked into a bottle of land whose neck was only four miles wide. A small force could seal Butler's army in place, leaving it, Grant later observed, "as completely shut off from further operations directly against Richmond as if it had been in a bottle strongly corked." Lee was quick to note that keeping Butler confined at Bermuda Hundred required considerably fewer troops than it took to fight him. Perhaps infantry formerly engaged defending Richmond could now join the Army of Northern Virginia. Lee's men received word of Beauregard's victory "with joy." [3]

Lee realized that reinforcements from Beauregard would take time to materialize. Prospects that Breckinridge might join him soon, however, were improving. Another dispatch informed Lee that General Crook, whose column had been moving toward Lynchburg in support of Sigel, was now retiring. "If you can organize a guard for valley and be spared from it, proceed with infantry to Hanover Junction by railroad," Lee hastily telegraphed Breckinridge. "Cavalry, if available, can march." [4]

The respite forced by the weather had given Grant time to refine his plans. His last major assault—against the Mule Shoe on May 12—had failed because he had not massed reserves to exploit Hancock's initial breakthrough. Grant was determined not to repeat that mistake. This time, he made sure to have adequate reserves. He planned to attack with his two best infantry corps, the 2nd and the 6th, in unison, Hancock along Massaponax Church Road and Wright on Hancock's right flank. Burnside would wait close by, poised to exploit the breach, while Warren provided covering fire. The Union army would concentrate its considerable strength against the southern wing of Lee's army. Grant was enamored of the scheme—it faithfully embodied his ideas of concentration—and Dana also endorsed it. "Had there been such a column to support Hancock on Thursday last," he wrote his superiors in Washington, "there is no doubt that Lee must have been routed." [5]

Grant began preparations for the offensive during the morning. He and Meade left their headquarters on Fredericksburg Road around 9:30 A.M. and took up new quarters near the Anderson house, where they could more easily communicate with Hancock's, Wright's, and Burnside's staging areas. Mr. Anderson, a short, fifty-year-old man, had seen his fill of Yankees and made his displeasure known. Lyman noted that he acted "as sullen as he dared, and all the family was in the same order." [6]

To maintain secrecy, Grant decided to postpone the deployments until after dark. At nightfall, Burnside was to withdraw to the Anderson house and take a reserve position. Warren was to extend his 5th Corps to occupy the 9th Corps's entrenchments as Burnside's men moved out. Hancock was to remain at the Harris farm until dark, when his lead division under Barlow was to follow the Ni south to Anderson's Mill, near Massaponax Church Road, and form to charge west along the roadway. Birney and Gibbon were to fan out on Barlow's right, reaching toward Myers Hill to connect with Wright. Once the maneuvers were complete, the 5th Corps would comprise the Union formation's northern end, stretching Warren thin. He was to advance Griffin's left and post some of Cutler's men across the Ni, toward Ewell, to give advance warning if the Confederates tried to attack his right flank.[7]

As the sun meandered across a cloudless sky, word arrived that Tyler would reach the front with five regiments of heavy artillery in time to participate in the assault the next morning. Early in the day, Colonel Elisha S. Kellogg's 2nd Connecticut Heavy Artillery arrived and was assigned to Upton's brigade. The regiment contained 1,900 soldiers, more than double the number of men in the battle-weary brigade it was joining. The addition, an aide observed, made the brigade "very respectable." [8]

General Wright was uneasy about Grant's new scheme. The more he studied the distant Confederate earthworks, the stronger they looked. Midafternoon, he sent the 10th Massachusetts and 3rd Vermont for a close look. The two regiments strode onto Massaponax Church Road, drove off some stray rebel pickets, and felt their way through overgrown fields above the roadway toward Spotsylvania Court House. Early's southerners greeted the reconnoitering force with a burst of fire from their earthworks, and the Union soldiers scurried back with disheartening news. Heavy brush obstructed much of the country that the Union assault columns would have to traverse. Even worse, the Confederates were entrenched in strength, buttressed with artillery and eagerly awaiting Grant's attack.[9]

This grim report confirmed Wright in his conclusion that charging across a mile or so of difficult ground into the teeth of Confederate armament was a bad idea. The 6th Corps commander strolled over to headquarters and discussed his misgivings with Meade's chief of staff, Humphreys. The staffer, a first-rate combat commander, had also begun questioning the wisdom of assaulting along Massaponax Church Road and was not surprised to learn that Lee had firmed his defenses there. His talk with Wright simply confirmed Humphreys's hunch that Lee's former weak point was now the strongest part of his line. Assaulting as Grant now intended, even with the combined might of the 2nd and 6th Corps, risked slaughter on the scale of the bloodbath of May 12.

Where, then, was Lee vulnerable? For several days, Grant had drawn troops from the battlefield's northern sector, and Lee had mirrored his moves. This suggested that Lee must now be weakest in the northern portion of the field, along Ewell's line. Perhaps the Federals should abandon the Massaponax Church Road corridor, where Lee expected the blow to fall, and instead strike Ewell's line, where Lee least expected to see Federals. The fighting on

May 12 had shattered Ewell's corps. Of all Lee's combat units, it was probably least able to withstand another bout of Grant's hammering. The more
Humphreys and Wright discussed the idea, the better it sounded. Ewell's
earthworks must be Lee's vulnerable point, they concluded, and the Federals
should assault there in force.[10]

Humphreys and Wright explained their thinking to Grant, who immediately saw things their way. Wright's reconnaissance, he agreed, had demonstrated that the ground around Massaponax Church Road was "entirely impracticable to pass troops over." He also agreed that a powerful assault aimed
at Ewell might catch the Confederates off balance. Without hesitation, he
once again revised his plans. He still wanted Hancock and Wright to deliver
the attack. But now they were to strike Ewell, on the northern end of the battlefield, instead of Early and Anderson, at the southern end.[11]

Turning to his maps, Grant was relieved to see that his new scheme did not
overly complicate the logistics of moving troops into position. He would not
have to postpone the assault. Hancock was at the Harris farm and could easily return before daylight to his former post at the Landrum place. Wright had
time to withdraw from Myers Hill, march north to the Harris farm, then continue past the Stevens ruins to old entrenchments at the apex of the Mule
Shoe. By 4:00 A.M. on May 18 the two army corps could be aligned in a fearsome assault formation, Wright on the right and Hancock on the left, across
the top of the abandoned Mule Shoe. Charging south through the battleground of May 12—"Hell's Half Acre," the troops had christened that bloodstained soil—they would emerge in front of Ewell's new line. Burnside and
Warren would meanwhile engage Early and Anderson, preventing them from
assisting Ewell, then join the assault when Ewell's line collapsed.[12]

Grant was not able to put the finishing touches on this new plan until
nearly 7:00 P.M. By then, Hancock, ignorant of Grant's latest revisions, had
already sent most of his artillery to Anderson's Mill, his staging area under
Grant's earlier plan. Grant decided not to interrupt the artillery deployment,
reasoning that the sight of guns moving south might deceive Lee as to his real
intentions. In any event, he could easily recall the pieces after dark.

Despite Grant's secrecy, the troops sensed that something was brewing.
Word spread that the army would soon initiate a "decisive movement."
Reporter D. A. Hendrick predicted a "great and severe battle." The army was
"very quiet," an officer in the 10th Vermont wrote in his diary. "Things look
suspicious tonight; mistrust something's afoot." Colonel Wainwright agreed.
"A big move is on foot for the night," he wrote. He hoped for "great things,"
but feared that Grant would not "find Lee asleep." Even Meade saw cause for
optimism. "Tomorrow we shall begin fighting again," he wrote home, "with,

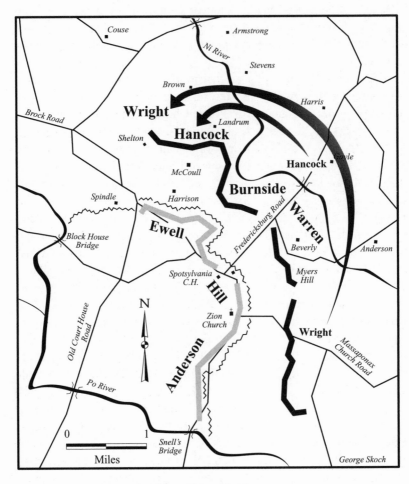

Grant's deployment on the night of May 17–18

I trust, some decided result, for it is hardly natural to expect men to maintain without limit the exhaustion of such a protracted struggle as we have been carrying on." The past few days, Meade observed, had "given our men rest, and the arrival of reinforcements has put them in good spirits." He sensed "determination on all sides to fight it out, and have an end put to the war." [13]

Around noon, Lee informed Richmond that Grant had "made no demonstration against our position today." The inaction puzzled him. It was unlike Grant to suspend offensive operations. "For some reason there seems to be a pause in [Grant's] movements," he wrote, but he refrained from speculating as to the cause. Lee's soldiers also remarked on the unaccustomed quiet. "Since Sunday, with the exception of an occasional boom of a heavy gun, it has been almost as quiet on the lines and in the camps near by as if the army was in winter quarters," a Confederate observed.[14]

Lee was prepared for the assault that he believed the morning would bring. The lull in hostilities had afforded Hill and Anderson ample time to complete their dispositions. Siting their earthworks along high ground, they had cleared fields of fire, dotted with rifle pits and extending at least three hundred yards toward the Federals. As for Ewell, Lee had no misgivings about the peppery Virginian's ability to hold his line. Ewell's left, manned by Robert Rodes's division, was fronted by heavily wooded terrain that dropped off into a deep ravine. Ewell's right wing, from the Harrison house to the Mule Shoe's eastern leg, was the province of John Gordon's division. From the Harrison house, cleared land afforded the Confederates an unobstructed view to the McCoull place, half a mile north. If the Federals staged an assault from the abandoned tip of the Mule Shoe—precisely the operation that Grant intended to try—they would have to cross the open field, descend sharply into a ravine, traverse a marshy stretch of bottom land, and mount a long slope, all under fire from Ewell's artillery and musketry.

The crowning feature of Ewell's line was his earthworks, later appraised as "lethal" by Meade's aide Lyman. High dirt barricades ran along the ridge line. Logs, elevated with sticks to create narrow slits, permitted the defenders to shoot while fully protected. Trenches gave them safe places to load, and every ten to twelve feet traverses jutted back at right angles from the main structure to guard against enfilading fire. A second earthen wall, behind and parallel to the barricade, connected the traverses and made the structures resemble rows of square pens when viewed from above. Elevated towers with loopholes—"I never saw any like them," Lyman declared—afforded convenient perches for sharpshooters, and in front lay row on row of felled trees, sharpened branches facing north, to form an impenetrable barrier. Both armies had used abatis, as the slashings were called, to break up charges. But never had they employed them so extensively.[15]

Brigadier General Armistead L. Long, commanding the Confederate 2nd Corps's artillery, had massed twenty-nine guns with care, taking special precaution to defend the approaches from the north. Seven artillery pieces stood behind the Harrison house, where they could play on the Federals as they moved across the open ground, and several more pieces were posted to the left to control the ravine in front of Ewell's bastion. A gunner in the 3rd Richmond Howitzer Battalion, stationed near the Harrison house, examined the open approaches, the ravine, the abatis, and the earthen fortifications with the cool eye of a veteran. "No infantry the world ever saw," he announced, could survive an attack against Ewell's line.[16]

Toward the end of the day, Lee ordered infantry probes of each end of Grant's entrenched formation. At 4:00 P.M. Ambrose Wright—commanding the Georgia brigade that had helped take Myers Hill three days before— led two regiments east along Massaponax Church Road to examine the lower end of the Union line. He ran afoul of Federal pickets and retired after a few minutes of skirmishing. General Hill, still too ill to resume command of the 3rd Corps, witnessed Wright's repulse from his ambulance. The hot-tempered Virginian was furious at Wright's failure to press his attack and threatened to convene a court of inquiry to investigate Wright's conduct. "General Wright is not a soldier; he's a lawyer," Lee gently reminded Hill, adding that patience was the key to managing this citizen army. "You understand all this," Lee told Hill, "but if you humiliated General Wright, the people of Georgia would not understand. Besides, whom would you put in his place? You'll have to do what I do: When a man makes a mistake, I call him to my tent, talk to him, and use the authority of my position to make him do the right thing the next time."[17]

Engrossed in his examination of the 3rd Corps's entrenchments, Lee nearly became a casualty himself. Lieutenant Colonel William T. Poague, commanding a 3rd Corps battalion, was proudly showing Lee his gun emplacements when Union artillery opened on them. A gunner offered Lee shelter, but the general declined to dismount, apparently forgetting President Davis's admonition to take care for his safety. A shell exploded nearby, and the gunner grabbed Lee and dragged him into the pit. "These little incidents will serve to show how General Lee's boys value him and love him," Poague wrote his father of the incident.[18]

Lee also directed Ewell to investigate Federal dispositions in his sector. At 6:00 P.M. Stephen Ramseur's North Carolina brigade slipped from the Confederate 2nd Corps's line and followed the western leg of the Mule Shoe northward. Pickets from Thomas Egan's brigade of Birney's division stationed along the Mule Shoe's blunt tip observed the Confederates coming. Hastening to their brigade's bivouac on the Landrum farm, they alerted Egan, who filed his men into nearby entrenchments and directed them to lie in wait for the rebels. The Tar Heels marched unsuspectingly into the trap. "We held our fire until they came close up and then sent them howling back with a single volley," a soldier in the 141st New York recounted. Several Confederates were killed or wounded, and three were captured. Ramseur concluded that the enemy were too strongly entrenched for his brigade to dislodge and deemed it "prudent to retire." The 20th Indiana and 99th Pennsylvania followed Ramseur as he fell back, occupying portions of the Mule Shoe's tip that Gibbon had evacuated on May 15.[19]

Ramseur reported the situation in the northern sector unchanged. This confirmed Lee in his conviction that the Federals were planning to attack his southern flank. In point of fact, Grant was preparing to move against the northern Confederate flank with his two best infantry corps. Fully half of the Federal army would strike where Lee least expected. Grant's deception was complete.[20]

The thrusts and parries that began with the march on May 13–14 were escalating to a violent climax. In a few hours Hancock and Wright would return to the Mule Shoe's tip to deliver what Grant hoped would be the knockout punch. This time Grant would catch Lee by surprise. No rain-soaked roads and wayward wagon trains would stand in his way. Fate was giving the Federals another chance to attack in overwhelming numbers an unsuspecting portion of Lee's line. May 18 would tell, once and for all, whether frontal attacks could break Lee's fortifications at Spotsylvania Court House.

"It was almost sure death."

Grant began positioning his infantry after dark like chess pieces on a game board. Burnside and Warren stood fast, facing Early in an entrenched line stretching from the lower edge of the Mule Shoe to the Beverly farm. Hancock's men hefted rifles and packs and retraced their steps to the Landrum fields, taking up positions eerily similar to those they had occupied during the grand assault on May 12. And Wright's soldiers left their encampments at Myers Hill and the Anderson farm and began trudging north to join Hancock at the Mule Shoe's tip. The exercise had become painfully familiar. The long-suffering troops found it difficult to summon enthusiasm for another night march followed by a rush against Lee's frowning battlements.

Hancock's first step was to bring back his artillery. He had forwarded his guns to Anderson's Mill, on the army's southern flank, in furtherance of Grant's earlier scheme to attack along Massaponax Church Road. At 11:00 P.M. the 2nd Corps's artillery chief, Colonel John C. Tidball, began shuttling guns to the deserted Stevens place, which was to serve as Grant's and Meade's command center during the attack, and west to the Landrum ridge. The batteries of Captain T. Frederick Brown, Lieutenant John W. Roder, Captain Nelson Ames, and Captain R. Bruce Ricketts continued on to the Landrum house where they could better support the infantry.[21]

Hancock began deploying his foot soldiers near the Mule Shoe's broad top. Birney's division, which was to serve as a reserve during the attack, remained massed near the Landrum house. Gibbon's division tramped to the apex of the Mule Shoe and formed in two lines, one behind the other, their right flanks resting near the Bloody Angle. Gibbon's first line consisted of Colonel McKeen's brigade and Colonel Murphy's newly arrived Irish Legion. In the second line, Joshua Owen's brigade formed behind McKeen, and Thomas Smyth's brigade—previously commanded by Samuel Carroll— backstopped the Irishmen. Barlow arrayed his division in two lines on Gibbon's left, near the sharp bend in the Mule Shoe's apex known as the East Angle. In front was Colonel Clinton D. MacDougall's brigade of New York regiments—adjoining Murphy's Irishmen on its right—with Colonel Richard C. Byrnes's brigade on MacDougall's left. The brigades of Colonels Nelson A. Miles and John R. Brooke comprised Barlow's second line.[22]

Shortly after midnight, true to Tyler's promise, the lead elements of his new division came swinging down Fredericksburg Road. The force consisted of the 1st Maine, 1st Massachusetts, and 2nd, 7th, and 8th New York Heavy Artillery regiments, approximately 8,800 soldiers in all. The greenhorns had started from Belle Plain early on May 17, paused briefly at Falmouth for dinner, and then pushed through Fredericksburg to the battlefront. By 3:00 A.M. Heavies had reached the Harris farm, although, as Hancock observed, "in rather broken order." Some regiments approximated 1,800 soldiers, making them larger than many of Hancock's existing brigades. "What regiment is that?" a veteran inquired of the soldiers marching by, resplendent in clean outfits. "First Massachusetts Heavy Artillery," came the reply. After watching an interminable line of troops tramp past, the veteran repeated his question. To his astonishment, he received the same answer.[23]

The Heavies were still in shock, having only three days before left their comfortable Washington quarters. "Grant will have you fellows down to fighting weight before many days," maimed veterans had taunted them at Fredericksburg. A young lady had given an officer flowers with the observation, "You are too good looking a Yankee to become food for powder." And later in the day, a cavalryman had huffed prophetically to a greenhorn in the 1st Massachusetts, "First Heavies, eh? Well, you will catch hell before this time tomorrow." [24]

Hancock concluded that Tyler's raw regiments were in no condition to participate in the assault. As the footsore troops trudged up—"It was a muggy, muddy morning," a newcomer remembered—Hancock directed them behind a line of earthworks running from the Mule Shoe's east angle to the Landrum place. This was their first exposure to combat. "The fields were strewn with clothing, knapsacks, canteens, muskets, dead horses and broken artillery caissons, and the trees were riddled with bullet, shot and shell," a wide-eyed drummer boy in the 2nd New York Heavy Artillery noted. "One time as we came to a halt I was horrified to see a human hand protruding from the earth near my foot." [25]

While Hancock's corps spread across the apex of the Mule Shoe, Wright's corps trudged along darkened byways to Fredericksburg Road. The men had left Myers Hill shortly after dark. "We marched all night, and accomplished scarcely half a dozen miles," a soldier complained, adding that he had often covered "twenty easier." Reaching the Harris farm after midnight, Wright's soldiers wound past the Stevens house, emerged into the Landrum clearing, then continued west along the Landrum farm road to deploy on Hancock's right, near the Bloody Angle. The 6th Corps's guns parked on Fredericksburg Road near the Harris farm, ready to rush to the Landrum place if needed. [26]

Wright planned to use two divisions—Neill's and Ricketts's—in the attack, and to hold his third division under Russell in reserve. Neill's division moved up first, and Wright directed it into line on Hancock's right. Next came Russell's men. Wright sent them over to the Shelton house, site of his former headquarters, where they anchored the western end of the assault formation. Ricketts's soldiers had fallen behind, but Wright left a space open for them between Neill's right and Russell's left. The 6th Corps occupied chillingly familiar ground. Neill's left rested near the apex of the Bloody Angle, where his soldiers had fought bitterly six days before. The remainder of his division extended west along an earthen embankment constructed on May 13. Burial parties had not completed their work, and the stench was overpowering. Corpses lay in rotting heaps. Soldiers stuffed leaves into their nostrils to mask the smell and tried to snatch a few minutes of rest. [27]

Neill waited impatiently for Ricketts, who was to deploy on his right. As four o'clock approached and Ricketts was nowhere to be seen, Neill went ahead and completed his preparations. He arranged his division into a formation of four lines facing south, toward Ewell. Brigadier General Frank Wheaton's brigade, drawn from Pennsylvania and New York, constituted

Neill's first line. Behind Wheaton stood Colonel Oliver Edwards's brigade from Massachusetts and Rhode Island; followed by Colonel Daniel D. Bidwell's brigade from Maine, New York, and Pennsylvania; and finally by Lewis Grant's six Vermont regiments, the veteran Green Mountain regiments in front and the large 1st Vermont Heavy Artillery behind. As finally aligned, the entire assault force—minus Ricketts, whose division was still on the road—resembled a huge sledgehammer resting across the Mule Shoe's apex, ready to smash its way south. Gibbon and Barlow, extended in two lines, formed the handle, and Neill's compact formation made up the head. On the Landrum ridge, behind this mass of nearly twelve thousand soldiers, stood the 2nd Corps's artillery.[28]

During the night Grant decided to assign Burnside an active role in the assault. Terrain influenced his decision. Ewell's right flank rested on the Mule Shoe's eastern leg, forming a junction with Early's entrenchments. The sharp bend in the rebel works at the intersection of Ewell's and Early's corps offered Burnside an opportunity to enfilade the eastern end of Ewell's line. If the 9th Corps thrust forward in tandem with Hancock and Wright, the Federals could pound Ewell simultaneously from north and east. A dual attack, Grant concluded, would increase the chances of breaching the Confederate formation, and he directed Burnside to make ready to charge.

Burnside focused his attack along the northern sector of his line, where he could enfilade Ewell. Robert Potter—Burnside's ablest division commander and a "grave, pleasant-looking man, known for his coolness and courage"— held this important position. Fortune had also placed Brigadier General Simon Griffin, Potter's ace brigade commander, on the division's northern wing. Griffin had earned promotion for attacking over this very ground on May 12, and he and his men knew every tree and hollow.[29]

Selecting another 9th Corps brigade to support Griffin was difficult. Potter's other brigade, under Colonel John I. Curtin, had been roughly handled in earlier bouts. And the division stationed on Potter's left was badly demoralized, having changed leaders three times in two weeks. Its current head, Thomas Crittenden, had arrived recently from the western theater. He was long on political clout and short on military prowess, and nothing about him inspired confidence. Lyman mercilessly lampooned him as the "queerest looking party you ever saw, with a thin, staring face, and hair hanging to his coat collar—a very wild-appearing major general." Crittenden's largest brigade, a mix of Massachusetts and regular United States regiments, exemplified the deleterious effect of attrition on the army's combat units. The outfit began the campaign under Colonel Sumner Carruth, who became "sun-struck" and was succeeded by Colonel Jacob P. Gould of the 59th Massachusetts, who became

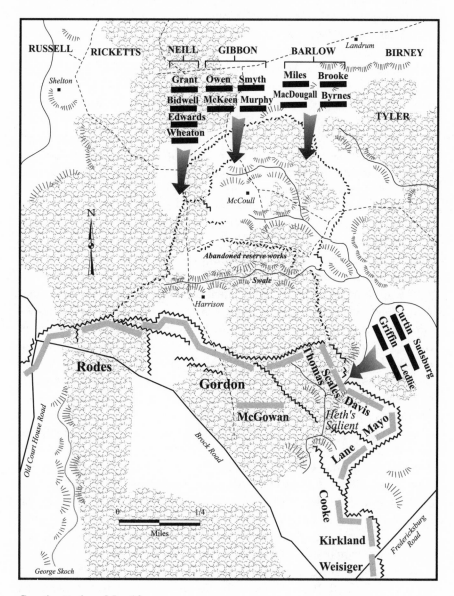

Grant's attack on May 18

"sun-struck" as well. Colonel Stephen M. Weld Jr., of the 56th Massachusetts, ably managed the brigade during the bitter fighting on May 12, but two days later, Weld was replaced with a political appointee, Brigadier General James H. Ledlie. Ledlie had no appreciable combat experience, drank excessively, and would quickly prove himself bereft of common sense.[30]

For reasons known only to himself, Burnside decided to take a chance with Ledlie. The 9th Corps's attack, he ordered, was to be made on a two-brigade front, Griffin on the right and Ledlie on the left. Curtin's brigade and Crittenden's other brigade—a small outfit of three regiments under Colonel Joseph M. Sudsburg—were to form behind Griffin and Ledlie and support the assault as needed. Burnside concentrated most of his artillery toward the southern end of his line, where it could drive off Early's Confederates if they counterattacked. Fortunately Ledlie recognized his limitations—this may have been the only time that he did so—and he chose combat-hardened Colonel Weld to command his brigade. Weld was to lead the brigade's assault with his own veteran regiment—the 56th Massachusetts—and with the 35th Massachusetts, which had just arrived from a detail guarding wagons.[31]

The 5th Corps comprised Grant's final combat element. During the night Warren had extended his line to fill the gap created by the 6th Corps's departure. The Maryland Brigade and part of Kitching's brigade moved to Myers Hill. To buttress the left end of the formation, four batteries under Captain Patrick Hart, Captain John Bigelow, Lieutenant Lester I. Richardson, and Lieutenant Aaron F. Walcott massed on the Anderson farm. Sixteen 12-pounders, Wainwright noted with satisfaction, occupied a "beautiful position completely protecting our left and rear." Warren's aide Roebling located another "capital" position for guns on a ridge left of Fredericksburg Road. Wainwright was duly impressed with the site and stationed Cooper's, Breck's, and Captain Charles A. Phillips's three batteries on the rise, giving them clear oblique fire into Spotsylvania Court House. Captain Albert S. Sheldon's and Rittenhouse's batteries occupied an advanced set of works on Fredericksburg Road only fourteen hundred yards from town. Before morning, they were joined by Captain Elijah D. Taft's battery of six 20-pound Parrott guns, temporarily attached to the 5th Corps.[32]

At 3:30 A.M. 9th Corps aides began rousing Griffin's and Weld's men. Soldiers of the 56th Massachusetts fell into line, and the 35th Massachusetts formed behind them. Officers whispered orders. The 56th regiment was to "feel" the enemy, the 35th to provide support. Griffin's men stared vacantly at the shadowy outline of Early's works rising ominously a few hundred yards away. Reaching their objective would require crossing a field carpeted with bloated bodies from May 12th's fight, fording a stream, and scaling an imposing embankment, all in full view of southern marksmen. "We felt that it was almost sure death to go down into and across the field before us and up the slope on the opposite side," a 6th New Hampshire man remembered.[33]

"The charge was a very noble effort, but absolutely hopeless."

The stage was set. At 4:00 A.M. sharp, Union artillery was to unleash a fearsome barrage, pinning the Confederates fast in their trenches. From the north, three divisions—and a fourth, if Ricketts arrived in time—were to charge south against Ewell's fortifications. At the same time, two of Burnside's brigades were to attack from the east. If Ewell's line collapsed—an event that Grant considered likely—then the rest of the 9th Corps and all of the 5th Corps would close for the kill. Once again, Grant had devised a plan that concentrated tremendous might against a short stretch of the rebel line.

Promptly at 4:00 A.M. Union guns sprang to life. The 5th Corps's artillery—fifty pieces in all—roared into action, and the 9th Corps's ordnance on their right—forty-eight pieces more—chimed in as well. The Confederate 3rd Corps's armament responded in kind, and a "sharp" artillery duel, as Wainwright styled the battle, sounded across the woods and fields, "the practice being excellent on both sides, and the range short." Among the victims of the Union artillery was Major Joseph McGraw, second in command of Lieutenant Colonel William J. Pegram's battalion. An exploding shell severed his hand and shattered his arm.[34]

The bone-jarring salvo announced that Grant's assault was on. Under cover of a thick fog, Griffin's and Ledlie's 9th Corps brigades groped gingerly forward. A brigade of Georgians under Brigadier General Edward L. Thomas occupied the works directly across from Griffin, and Confederate pickets patrolled the intervening ground. Sergeant Marion H. Fitzpatrick of the 45th Georgia was on picket duty when Griffin's soldiers emerged ghostlike from the fog not twenty feet away. Discovering that they faced an entire Union brigade, Fitzpatrick and his compatriots backed toward their earthworks, firing "hot and heavy" to delay the onslaught.[35]

Alerted to Griffin's approach, Thomas's main body of troops took its post and sighted into the mist ahead. Gunners of Poague's battalion, stationed near the Georgians, likewise squinted expectantly into the fog. On the field's far side Griffin's troops pressed forward under harassing skirmish fire, stepping around swollen corpses of soldiers and horses killed during the combat on May 12. By the time the Federals had reached midfield, the Confederates could make out the dark shape of the approaching battle line. Poague's guns leapt to life. Flashes from rebel muskets sparked along the top of the earthworks. Shells exploded among the corpses, splattering Griffin's horrified soldiers with fragments of decomposed flesh.[36]

Griffin's ordeal was only beginning. As shells whined into the Union ranks, Griffin's lead element—the 6th New Hampshire—moved at the double-quick across the clearing, splashed through the stream, and began clawing up the embankment toward the Confederates. The regiment's pluck provoked the Georgians to "renewed energy," a Federal reported. Poague's gunners shifted to canister and blasted huge gaps in the 6th New Hampshire's line. "There was heavy ordnance in front of the brigade," a Federal recollected, "and it did sad havoc as its deadly missiles came tearing through." The 9th New Hampshire dashed up only to recoil under a blaze of musketry. Captain Andrew J. Stone, leading the regiment, fell mortally wounded, and canister and shells scoured its ranks. Raked from the right, the New Hampshire regiments drifted left and slipped behind the 32nd Maine. The Granite State men faced a deadly dilemma. They could not fire without hitting the Maine soldiers in front of them. Their right flank was dangerously exposed, and Poague's guns were shredding them with canister at short range, "cutting the men down like grass before the mower's scythe." Then Confederates—Thomas's Georgians, and perhaps North Carolinians from Alfred Scales's brigade—leaped over the works and attacked Griffin's vulnerable northern flank. The Maine regiment tried to change front under fire, but the maneuver proved impossible. Running for their lives, soldiers from the 32nd Maine stampeded rearward through the two New Hampshire regiments. "As the men rushed back, with the screeching 'Johnnies' pouring volley after volley into them, some of our boys rose up to retreat," a 6th New Hampshire soldier related. "But the officers all [cried] out, 'Steady, men! Hold your ground!' Not one gave way, but all poured a volley into the rebels, checking them, and compelling them to retire within their works."[37]

While the antagonists regrouped, a messenger zigzagged back across the clearing to Griffin, who had remained near his brigade's jumping-off point at the Union earthworks. The front line was in peril, the courier rasped. Hoping to consolidate his meager gains, Griffin ordered his troops to hold their ground. They stacked logs and dug "like beavers." The 6th New Hampshire huddled within fifty yards of the Confederate works, and the 11th New Hampshire entrenched close behind, grumbling about their "perilous position." Bullets whizzed overhead, and cannonballs knocked down trees.[38]

Ledlie's brigade, temporarily commanded by Colonel Weld, had stepped promptly off in "admirable style" on Griffin's left. The men of the 56th Massachusetts, in advance, had no inkling they were walking into a trap. On their left the Confederate line jutted forward to form the finger of earthworks called Heth's Salient. As Weld advanced west, on the north side of the salient, Confederates in the salient enjoyed a clear line of fire down the length of his line. The rebels manning this sector of earthworks—Mississippians and North Carolinians under Brigadier General Joseph R. Davis, a Mississippi lawyer and nephew of President Davis—could scarcely believe their good fortune. They cocked their muskets and waited for Weld's men to drift unsuspectingly into range.[39]

Weld fixed his attention on the Confederate earthworks to his front, dimly visible in the fog. He was oblivious to Heth's Salient on his left. Suddenly his men stumbled into a dense tangle of felled bushes and logs that he took for abatis, and he ordered the 56th Massachusetts to charge. At the same moment, Davis unleashed a deadly fusillade into Weld's flank, and Confederates in the main works opened fire. Caught in a deadly crossfire, Weld's soldiers scrambled for cover behind rocks and dips in the ground. "I could not blame them much," Weld admitted, "for the limbs, and even trees, were cut down like grass, and the place was most decidedly uncomfortable." The brigade's remaining regiments—the 57th Massachusetts, and the 4th and 10th United States Regulars—came up to add their weight to the attack. Shortly they, too, lay pinned down by crossfire.[40]

Weld's attack, like Griffin's on its right, was stymied. Rebels fired into Weld's formation from two directions, forcing his soldiers to the ground. Weld dispatched an officer for instructions, but the man could not find Ledlie and returned empty-handed. Weld concluded that continuing the attack offered the best chance for survival and instructed his soldiers to charge. The 56th Massachusetts, in the brigade's front, angrily protested, as it would bear the brunt of the assault. Before Weld could repeat his order, Confederates redoubled their volleys, and a Bay State soldier took it on himself to decide the issue. "Retreat!" the man screamed and bolted toward the safety of the Union earthworks. Word rippled through the ranks that Weld had ordered a retreat. "The troops went back in a decidedly hasty manner," recounted a soldier in the 35th Massachusetts, "the first line running over our men, who—thinking it was an overwhelming counter attack and that the order to fall back was by authority—went to the rear with equal celerity." Weld tried to stem the rout, but its momentum was impossible to stop.[41]

A nattily dressed officer greeted Weld's battle-grimed warriors as they clambered over their earthworks. "Fall in, Thirty-fifth! Steady, Thirty-fifth!" he admonished with a flourish and began excitedly babbling orders. The winded troops at first decided that the man must be a greenhorn lieutenant. "Don't trouble yourself," a soldier called out in a bemused voice. "You attend to your business and we'll attend to ours!" The officer made no reply, acting

as though he had not heard the remark. Weld's men were shocked to learn
that the comical figure was none other than General Ledlie, their new commander.[42]

While Griffin and Ledlie tallied their losses, their companion brigades—
those of Curtin and Sudsburg—edged left in search of an opening. Curtin advanced his 7th Rhode Island and 51st New York to silence a rebel battery, but
the Confederates swung their guns around and broke the attack with canister
and solid shot. Caught in a predicament like that which had already befallen
Griffin and Ledlie, Curtin's men began digging trenches. "The very earth
trembled at times from the thunders of shell and artillery," a Rhode Islander
remembered. Soldiers hugged the ground closely, "for none could stand long
and live." Lying low did not guarantee survival either, as the 7th Rhode
Island's color sergeant discovered. Feeling the powerful thud of a shell, he
glanced over. A twelve-pound solid shot had hit the man next to him, ripping
off his left arm and gouging out his bowels. May 18 was a "severe, sad day,"
one of Curtin's troops lamented. The brigade lay "more exposed than at
Fredericksburg," he related, and the terrain afforded the luckless soldiers
"barely chance to return a single shot."[43]

Burnside also experienced the wrath of Early's artillery. To better supervise the assault, the general had moved his headquarters to a knoll directly
behind Roemer's battery. A shell exploded above Burnside's tent, wounding
an aide and showering several staffers with fragments. Then a spherical case
shot landed among the headquarters staffers and badly burned another aide.
Concluding that the Confederates had found his range, Burnside moved to
the back side of a neighboring ridge.[44]

While the 9th Corps waged an unequal contest against Early's veterans, the
2nd and 6th Corps waited in their entrenchments along the Mule Shoe's apex.
Gibbon and Barlow stood ready to charge, as did Neill. The problem was
Ricketts, whose 6th Corps division was not yet in place. Meade decided to
delay Hancock's and Wright's attack "a little" to give Ricketts's laggard
troops time to deploy. The soldiers waited to the rumble of Burnside's, Warren's, and Early's guns to the south. "In the damp morning air, the hum of the
shot was very distinct, though distant," Lyman noted.[45]

Half past four came. Ricketts was still not in place. The sky was beginning
to gray, and Meade felt he could wait no longer. The attack had to begin.
Otherwise, the Federals risked losing the advantage of surprise. At 4:35 A.M.
Hancock barked the order for his men to advance. Gunners manning 2nd
Corps artillery at the Landrum place jerked their lanyards. Powerful concus-
sions rocked the ground, and projectiles screamed over the waiting soldiers.

Three of the Army of the Potomac's best combat divisions—Gibbon's, Barlow's, and Neill's—rose from the chill Virginia ground, scampered over the earthworks, and started south through a dense morning fog. "It was a memorable scene," a Federal reminisced. "From right to left, for miles, the artillery crashed and roared. The woods and fields all about were filled with howling shot and bursting shell." Many soldiers anticipated disaster. "The first glimmer of morning was ushered in by the booming of big guns," a northerner reported, "and the men said another butchery has begun." [46]

Pickets from Company A, 9th Louisiana, had edged into the woods near the apex of the Mule Shoe, where they joined pickets from Colonel John S. Hoffman's brigade on their right. They could hear troops milling about, and the unmistakable accent of Union officers. "Forward! March! Halt! Right dress," northern voices half whispered. Then came the sound of soldiers counting off. "Right face! As skirmishers, deploy!" someone hissed. Pressed by skirmishers leading the attack columns, Ewell's pickets offered token resistance, then dropped slowly back. Scouts quickly informed Ewell that a Federal battle line was approaching, and the Confederate earthworks came alive with bustle and commotion. Infantrymen loaded muskets and stacked ammunition, artillerymen readied their pieces, and staff officers rode about, making sure that all was ready. "Oppressiveness seemed weighing on one's breast," a Confederate recollected of the wait. "The result of anything would be a relief—the painful anxious anticipation being such a burden." [47]

The suspense broke as a blue wave spilled from the mist. The last of the Confederate pickets—sharpshooters from the 21st Virginia—vaulted into the works. Ewell's men gaped in disbelief at the Yankees headed their way. "All were astonished at this and could not believe a serious attempt would be made to assail such a line as Ewell had, in open day, over such a distance," recounted Major Wilfred E. Cutshaw, whose artillery stood trained on the approaching northerners. Ewell's men broke into smiles. The Yankee formation was tightly packed. Every shot would find its mark. Hancock and Wright had hurt Ewell badly on May 12. Now was Ewell's chance for revenge. The rebels looked forward to the opportunity, Cutshaw recollected, "to pay off old scores." [48]

The Union battle line—the divisions of Neill, Gibbon, and Barlow extending west to east in that order—struggled through a stretch of woods below the Mule Shoe's apex. Hancock's aide William Mitchell, who marched with Gibbon's division near the center of the line, had seen his share of carnage, but the sights here appalled him. "The stench which rose from [unburied corpses] was so sickening and terrible that many of the men and officers became deathly sick from it," he related. "The appearance of the dead who had been exposed to the sun so long, was horrible in the extreme as we marched past and over them—a sight never to be forgotten by those who witnessed it." [49]

Gibbon's division broke into the clearing around the McCoull house and paused to dress its lines. The right half of Gibbon's formation—McKeen's and Owen's brigades—was now clearly visible to Ewell's gunners. Hancock's artillery had been lobbing shells at the Confederate earthworks from the distant Landrum and Stevens farms. The Federal pieces were causing no appreciable damage—Hancock's artillerists could not see their targets through the trees and battle smoke—and Armistead Long, commanding the Confederate 2nd Corps artillery, had ignored them. Instead he hoarded his ammunition for use against the Union infantrymen, whose closely massed lines made irresistible targets.

The view from Hancock's headquarters near the Landrum place was stirring. "The troops moved forward in fine style on a double-quick," an engineer with Hancock later wrote. "On they went over the rising ground up towards the long line of yellow fresh earth on the summit. Our batteries in their rear played vigorously over their heads in order to keep the enemy down." [50]

"Fire!" Long shouted, and twenty-nine cannon barked. Thick smoke billowed up. Solid shot tore gaps in Gibbon's ranks. Troops shifted to close up, then continued steadily ahead, flags flying proudly. The Confederate artillerist Cutshaw could not help admiring the mighty host. It made a "most magnificent and thrilling sight," he later wrote, "covering Ewell's front as far as could be seen." As the Federals neared, Long shifted from solid shot to case shot and shell, showering the assault troops with deadly shrapnel. "The rebels allowed our column to advance within point blank range, and then let out their death volleys," a Federal recalled. "Heads, arms and legs were blown off like leaves in a storm." Noted a Confederate: "Our artillery played sad havoc with their columns as they advanced." [51]

Gibbon's soldiers, in the center of the Union formation, were badly bloodied but kept on, accelerating to the double-quick. Like a skilled craftsman selecting a tool for the task at hand, Long adjudged Gibbon to have reached canister range. Combined volleys of shrapnel and canister shredded the Union ranks. McKeen's brigade continued ahead despite the deadly fire until it reached the remnants of a fortified line that Ewell had dug several days before. Now abandoned, the entrenchments marked the Confederate 2nd Corps's former reserve line. Sited along the northern edge of the ravine fronting Ewell's current earthworks, the dirt ridge afforded the Federals the only available shelter. McKeen's men "reversed" the former reserve line and lay close against it. Owen's brigade came up in a "zig-zag direction," according to a soldier, and also found refuge behind the reserve entrenchments. Owen quickly realized that the low embankment provided scant protection from artillery. Worse, it held the Federals in place and afforded Long's gunners stationary targets. Owen declared the site too exposed and ordered his men back across the field. Gibbon, who had instructed Owen to support McKeen, later preferred charges against Owen for disobeying orders.[52]

Slaughter escalated. Murphy's Irish Legion, advancing on McKeen's right, slanted into the clearing. "A battery of four brass pieces played on our men incessantly, as they advanced on the double quickstep," a survivor reported. The Irish Legion became separated into two fragments. An officer on Gibbon's staff took charge of the 155th and 164th New York regiments, and Murphy stayed with the 69th New York National Guard and the 170th New York. Murphy's contingent descended into the ditch beyond Ewell's former reserve line where McKeen was ensconced and started up the rise toward Ewell's abatis. Musketry and artillery fire became so intense that the men dropped flat against the ground, seeking protection from the natural curvature of the slope. Rebel sharpshooters posted in trees picked off anyone who raised his head. Murphy tried to run back and bring up his other two regiments, but he was shot in his arm. Seriously wounded, Murphy passed command of the brigade to Colonel James P. McIvor. Smyth's brigade, crowding urgently behind Murphy, also took a terrible licking. Crammed against the reserve works, Smyth's troops began digging to reverse the stubby barricades and make them defensible from the north. Ewell's gunners, a soldier in the 8th Ohio noted, kept up "sharp and effective cannonading." A hot-blooded Irishman leaned on top of the parapet, waving his regiment's flag. "Come on boys," he hollered, "and I will show you how to fight!" Jumping from the battlement, he ran toward the Confederate position, followed by a handful of men. The charge was doomed, and a bullet through the Irishman's knee brought him down.[53]

Barlow's division, advancing on Gibbon's left, bushwhacked through a densely wooded region of the Mule Shoe that wrecked its alignment. Most of Barlow's troops reached the reserve entrenchments, but pressing farther under Ewell's punishing artillery fire was impossible. The attacking line's leftmost component, under Colonel Byrnes, managed to reach the slashings in front of Gordon's Confederates, where some of Byrnes's soldiers climbed on top of the obstacles to get at the rebels. A sergeant in the 116th Pennsylvania penetrated ten feet into the tangle but could go no farther. Blue-clad corpses hung limply in the branches around him. Corporal Dick McClean, who had achieved fleeting glory a few days earlier by capturing the Confederate brigadier general George "Maryland" Steuart, lost his arm. A shell smacked into Franz Poffenberger of the 116th Pennsylvania, splintering his bones and driving the shards through his flesh. Another shell tore the wig from Robert Glendenning's head. His compatriots presumed he was dead and were relieved to see him stand up with his bald head still firmly on his shoulders. "The charge was a very noble effort, but absolutely hopeless," a survivor related.[54]

On the far right wing of the attacking line, Neill's 6th Corps division marched into a slaughter pen every bit as nasty as that encountered by Gibbon and Barlow. Neill had the affectations of a dandy; an associate described him as a "man of fine personal presence, very cultivated in his tastes and manners." But the thirty-eight-year-old Philadelphian ranked high among the Union army's battle-wise commanders. He had fought Mexicans, Indians, and Confederates, and he had won a brevet for conspicuous gallantry at Malvern Hill. Grant's attack on May 18 was to demand more than even Neill's considerable skills were capable of delivering.[55]

Frank Wheaton's brigade, Neill's first line, stepped off in tandem with Gibbon on its left and immediately stumbled into corpses that had been laid out several days before for burial. Wheaton's skirmishers stepped among the bodies, but the ranks coming behind tramped blindly on the bloated forms. "Such a presentation of death, on the moment when death faced the living, was such an experience that had not confronted the [men] before," a soldier observed.[56]

Deadlier obstacles lay ahead. Continuing south, Wheaton's brigade guided along the abandoned Confederate earthworks that made up the Mule Shoe's western leg, two regiments on the right side of the entrenchments, and two on the left. Split in half by the dirt mound, Wheaton's formation lost its alignment. The regiments west of the works floundered into dense woods, while those to the east marched through the open fields of the McCoull farm. Wheaton's leftmost regiments—the 102nd and 93rd Pennsylvania—came under galling fire from Ewell's artillery, quickened their step, and outpaced the 2nd Corps troops on their left. General Wright had initially planned for Ricketts's division to shield Wheaton's right flank, but since Ricketts was not yet in place, the cover did not materialize. Ewell's sharpshooters, posted in trees, viciously exploited the opportunity. The brigade's cohesion evaporated when the 102nd Pennsylvania climbed to the western side of the entrenchments to escape the open field. Deeming it "unsafe" to continue, Wheaton halted the scattered fragments of his brigade several hundred yards short of the abandoned rebel reserve line. A Federal remembered that he and his compatriots "hugged the ground closely."[57]

Wheaton's unexpected halt jumbled the rest of Neill's brigades coming behind him. Oliver Edwards's brigade, next in order, passed through Wheaton's stationary troops, obliqued left, and wound up jammed against Gibbon at the former Confederate reserve line. Ewell's gunners "saluted our approach with spherical case, canister, and rifle balls, in no stinted measure," a soldier in the 10th Massachusetts observed wryly. The feisty Edwards ordered his brigade to continue into the ravine and seek cover in the dead space where Confederate musketry could not reach them. His men complied, only to come under fire from the right, where Ewell had posted guns to command the ravine. "Clinging tenaciously to what they had gained," a soldier in the 37th Massachusetts reminisced, "the dauntless fellows waited in terrible suspense for the cooperating lines to make a corresponding advance and relieve them from the furious cross fire." [58]

Help, such as it was, came in the form of Daniel Bidwell's brigade. This veteran unit had passed through Wheaton's stalled troops and forged ahead, seemingly oblivious to the death raining on it. Bidwell's soldiers climbed over the Confederate reserve works and marched into the ravine to join Edwards's men huddled against the slope. They could do nothing other than quail under a "heavy fire of all sort of missiles," as a New Yorker described their predicament. Captain John Chauncy of the 7th Maine blamed the brigade's misfortune on a brass gun shooting down the length of the ravine. He could see the piece and when it was about to fire alerted his companions to duck by hollering, "Look out boys, here it comes!" He failed to heed his own advice, and an exploding projectile sliced a deep gash above his right eye. Blood streaming over his face, Chauncy shook his fist at the rebel gunners. "I have fought you a good many times and I'll fight you again," he shouted in defiance. "Here it comes," he screamed once again as the cannon's muzzle flared. Then he turned and hobbled for the rear. Edwards acknowledged that Bidwell had "ably supported" him, although the effort only produced more Union corpses.[59]

The last brigade in Neill's lineup—Colonel Grant's Green Mountain boys—pressed into the confused muddle of 6th Corps troops accumulating behind the former Confederate reserve line and huddling against the hillside immediately before it. "We soon overtook the front line and were kindly permitted to take the front," a soldier in the 4th Vermont recalled. Grant stopped at the entrenchments and traded fire with rebels on the far ridge. Confederate gunners had Grant's range down perfectly and left the colonel no choice but to order his men to lie behind the works. This was the 1st Vermont Heavy Artillery's baptism of fire. "We had but a short time to observe the effect of the shells upon the trees and speculate upon our own chances of life and limb when we were ordered into an open field," a soldier recalled. "The sharp ring of the bursting shell and the rattling musketry seemed to fill every element with their terror and confusion." Colonel Warner, commanding the heavy artillerists, fell seriously wounded from a sharpshooter's bullet, but his men held to their posts. "What we accomplished I do not know," a Vermont man reflected.[60]

Neill's situation was hopeless. "Their artillery cut our men down in heaps," wrote Elisha Hunt Rhodes of the 2nd Rhode Island. Rhodes began sending a few men at a time to the relative safety of nearby woods. Darting to the trees himself, Rhodes met Wheaton's assistant adjutant, Major George Clendennin. The major had his servant with him and invited Rhodes to join him for breakfast. Producing hot bread and broiled shad caught earlier from a stream, the servant set a rustic table, and the two men feasted, temporarily oblivious to the tempest swirling around them. "Notwithstanding the rebel shells I enjoyed my breakfast," Rhodes later jotted in his diary.[61]

The sight of Confederates edging around their right flank persuaded the men of the 10th Massachusetts that it was time to leave. Soon Edwards's entire brigade was streaming back. Dodging rearward across the McCoull fields, the soldiers experienced the full force of Ewell's firepower. "Steady, Thirty-seventh," Lieutenant Colonel Franklin P. Harlow of the 37th Massachusetts admonished his men. One soldier retained a vivid image of the stern Harlow putting his soldiers through their paces as though on a drill field. "With the firmness of review the regiment face[d] to the rear and move[d] back through the tempest of fire to the sheltering earthworks from which it had come." [62]

Wright's staff tried to accommodate Neill's withdrawal. Ricketts had finally moved his division to its jump-off point, but his troops were cowering under vigorous shelling. Rebel sharpshooters had infiltrated the woods near Ricketts's right flank and were picking off soldiers as they huddled in their trenches. Union scouts caught a few sharpshooters and gave them to an Indian from the 9th Corps. He left with the captives and returned shortly to announce, "I kill them." [63]

Wright equivocated over whether to advance Ricketts, who would become vulnerable as soon as he moved out. Uncertain what to do, he instructed Ricketts to proceed "if practicable," provoking a strong protest from Ricketts. Rebel sharpshooters were harassing his right flank, he stressed, and sending the division ahead risked severe casualties. Wright's aides visited the front and saw for themselves that throwing Ricketts into the fray would only afford the rebels more targets. Wheaton, who watched in frustration as the Confederates methodically blasted his brigade to pieces, fumed that the belated visit by Wright's aides was the first attempt by staff officers to learn the state of affairs. Wright finally decided to leave Ricketts where he was. So far as the Union field commanders were concerned, the assault was over. Flesh and blood could do no more against Ewell's artillery, and Wright did not want to sacrifice more men in an ill-fated operation.[64]

The situation on Burnside's front was no better than that on Hancock's and Wright's. Griffin's men lay trapped behind their makeshift log and dirt entrenchments across from Thomas's Georgians. Somehow Griffin managed to extend his rightmost regiment north to connect with Barlow's left flank, cementing the junction between the 2nd and 9th Corps, but neither he nor Barlow was in any shape to attack. At 5:00 A.M.—Neill, Gibbon, and Barlow were stymied in front of Ewell, and Wright was pondering whether to thrust Ricketts into the melee—Ledlie tried to renew his assault. The 56th Massachusetts edged once again past Griffin's left into the clearing fronting Early's earthworks. Predictably, musketry and artillery scoured the field, forcing the Bay Staters to the ground. Shortly the rest of Ledlie's brigade came up, the 57th Massachusetts on the left, the 35th Massachusetts on the right, and the 4th and 10th Regulars farther to the right. Advancing across the clearing was impossible, so the soldiers followed the 56th Massachusetts's example and fell prone. A northerner justified the brigade's response by observing that its assignment was "'to feel the enemy,' and as it was plain they were ready to receive us, no final assault was ordered." [65]

Ledlie's Federals, flat on their bellies near the field's eastern boundary, were surprised to see a stranger in staff officer's garb strolling among them. Hefting a cannonball in one hand, the figure inquired about the location of a certain battery. Then he walked through the gawking soldiers, stepped into the clearing, pulled out a white handkerchief, and darted across to the rebel earthworks. The soldiers debated the man's identity. Styling him the "mysterious stranger," they speculated variously that he was a spy, a deserter, or perhaps even a Confederate officer who had become marooned behind Burnside's lines.[66]

At 6:10 A.M. Potter informed Burnside that the steam had gone out of his attack. Early's Confederates had pinned Griffin and Ledlie under a plunging fire, and to the north, Ewell had stopped Barlow cold. Until Barlow received further orders, Potter continued, it made no sense to advance Griffin by himself. Besides, Potter added, Barlow's line partially overlapped Griffin. The troops risked being killed by friendly fire if they tried to advance.[67]

While Burnside pondered his next move, Ledlie endured a devastating artillery bombardment. Rebel sharpshooters picked off anyone reckless enough to expose himself. Griffin's men, who had held their advanced position for about an hour, exchanged potshots with rebel marksmen. It was a risky game. A. F. Drew of Company H, 6th New Hampshire, peeked over his makeshift log barricade. A bullet whizzed in, and Drew tumbled back with a hole neatly through his forehead. Irishman John Garrity took Drew's place and asked his captain to raise a hat above the works on a ramrod. The captain complied. Smoke puffed from the far woods and a ball clipped through the hat. Garrity fired at the smoke, and a figure in gray threw up its arms and fell backward. "Take that, you mother's son of a varmint!" he shouted. "My name is John Garrity." [68]

Ledlie finally ordered his brigade to retire. The 56th and 35th Massachusetts maintained covering fire while the rest of the regiments crawled back. The venture had achieved nothing except to reduce the brigade by another hundred men. "Fruitless," wrote Major Charles J. Mills, at division headquarters, of the affair. "The result," noted an officer in the 6th New Hampshire, "proved that no advantage commensurate with the sacrifice incurred could be secured by such operations."[69]

At 5:40 A.M.—the Union 2nd and 6th Corps had been slugging it out with Ewell for an hour—Hancock informed Humphreys that the situation looked bleak. Gibbon had occupied the old rebel reserve works but had lost his connection with Neill. Barlow was also up, but abatis barred his way. "Doubtful if our men can penetrate it," Hancock reported. His prognosis was glum, but he offered to keep trying until headquarters directed him to stop. "I have no option but to order them to continue, unless I hear from you to the contrary," he wrote Meade.[70]

Messages between headquarters and the front bristled with urgency. The attack was stalled, and Ewell's cannoneers were pounding Meade's prime divisions. At 6:15 Humphreys beseeched Hancock to inquire of Wright "if he had found a practicable point of attack, so as to move in that direction, should he find one." Humphreys left it to the 2nd Corps's commander to decide for himself whether continuing the assault was feasible. Wright endorsed on the communication that he had found no "practicable point of attack as yet." Half an hour later, Wright pronounced Ewell's abatis the "most dense" he had ever encountered. Hancock reported that Gibbon and Barlow "think that the point is impracticable for attack from their fronts" and recommended against pursuing the offensive. Wright added his voice to the chorus. Neill had "tried all and found no weak point," he advised, and closed on a pessimistic note. "I do not believe there is any point of the enemy's front on my line that can be attacked with any reasonable prospect of success, and therefore advise that the attack be no further prosecuted."[71]

Grant rode from his Anderson farm headquarters to monitor the offensive. Approaching the Stevens ruins—a doctor proclaimed the spot, which doubled as army headquarters and the 2nd Corps's hospital, "one of the most desolate places I ever saw"—Grant passed rows of wounded soldiers sprawled beside the trail. He looked down to meet the eyes of a young man near death, blood frothing from his mouth and a ragged hole in his breast. Just then a staff officer galloped past, callously splashing mud in the dying man's face. Visibly affected, Grant reined in his horse and began to dismount. Horace Porter, who was riding with Grant, perceived the general's intentions and jumped down, wiping the man's face with his handkerchief. Grant glared angrily after the careless staffer, who had long disappeared. "There was a painfully sad look upon the general's face, and he did not speak for some time," Porter related. "While always keenly sensitive to the sufferings of the wounded, this pitiful sight seemed to affect him more than usual." [72]

Joining Meade, Grant was briefed on developments. Meade informed him that the attacking force lay trapped under a murderous fire. The two generals sat under a tree and watched the distant woods, where a line of smoke marked the battle front. Grant nursed a cigar in his mouth, artillery booming all around him. "His face was immovable and expressionless," a man working one of Hancock's guns observed. "He sat quietly and watched the scene as though he was an uninterested spectator." Meade, by contrast, continually stroked his face, betraying "great anxiety." It was clear to everyone, the gunner noted, that the assault had failed, and that the massive Union artillery bombardment could never blast an opening through the Confederate earthworks. "The fire resulted in emptying our limber chests, and in the remarkable discovery that three-inch percussion shells could not be relied upon to perform the work of a steam shovel," he sarcastically observed. [73]

For another hour Gibbon and Barlow struggled to maintain their grip on the Confederate reserve works. Sheets of lead from Ewell's fortifications made it dangerous for men to peer over the low rampart. Charging was out of the question, and soldiers huddled to find shelter wherever they could. The 9th Corps had abandoned its offensive, freeing Early's gunners to concentrate their fire northward, toward Barlow. A bad situation for the Federals worsened. "The whole morning's work was a deed of blood," a soldier proclaimed. "That strip of land was more costly than any in the vicinity of Wall Street." [74]

Throughout the ordeal Tyler's heavy artillery regiments waited near the Landrum place, where projectiles clipped the trees around them. "It's an awful sight, but we are getting used to it," a Massachusetts man remarked as wounded soldiers streamed from the front. "Probably there is no more trying situation for troops to be placed in than to be held as a reserve during a battle," another greenhorn concluded. "The tension on one's nerves is something awful. If one is going to be shot, it is something of a satisfaction to be able to return the compliment."[75]

At 8:45 Meade directed Hancock and Wright to call off their offensives. Grant issued companion instructions to Burnside at 9:00. Barlow's, Gibbon's, and Neill's soldiers stumbled back under a hail of bullets, demoralized but relieved that their ordeal had ended. Ewell's guns unleashed a parting salvo, then fell silent. Hancock's pieces at the Landrum and Stevens farms continued firing blindly, but Ewell saw no point wasting ammunition. His men scampered onto their earthworks and chided the Federals to return. "They had no notion of coming again," a Louisiana man crowed. Ewell's skirmishers pursued the Federals to the McCoull house, tarrying to scoop up prisoners and loot. The carnage wrought by the artillery shocked even these combat-hardened veterans. "They said they never saw such terrible sights, that men were torn all to pieces with cannon balls," a southerner recorded in his diary. "Terrible execution," another Confederate pronounced. One of Armistead Long's gunners studied the ground in front of his cannon to better gauge the effectiveness of his fire. "Horrible, horrible," he muttered as he examined his handiwork. "Few men were simply wounded," he observed with a calculating eye. "Nearly all were dead, and literally torn into atoms; some shot through and through by cannon balls, some with arms and legs knocked off, and some with their heads crushed in by the fatal fragments of exploded shells."[76]

Retreating Federals regrouped near the Landrum house, and Hancock posted the 116th Pennsylvania and 69th New York as pickets along the Mule Shoe. "The whole ground stunk horribly with dead men and horses of previous fight," noted the aide Oliver Wendell Holmes Jr., who had the unenviable job of carrying dispatches between Wright and his combat units as they retired. Meade's staff took pity on Holmes. Inviting him to their headquarters, they plied him with brandy, hardtack, and guava. The luxuries "greatly revived me," Holmes admitted.[77]

Ewell's veterans celebrated their victory. They had broken Grant's attack with negligible losses. One of the few Confederate casualties was Lieutenant C. B. Coiner, of the 52nd Virginia, who had been shot by a Yankee sniper through both cheeks, losing some teeth and a wad of chewing tobacco. A few Federals had reached the abatis, but not one had reached the Confederate line. In places, the Yankees had not approached close enough for Ewell's riflemen to shoot at them. "Very little musketry was used in this engagement, for the reason that the enemy did not come near enough to our lines," reported the Richmond newspapers. "This attack fairly illustrates the immense power of artillery well handled," Long preened. "A fairly select force of 10,000 to 12,000 infantry was broken and driven from the field in less than thirty minutes by twenty-nine pieces of artillery alone." [78]

Confederate gunners reveled in praise from their infantry counterparts. On May 12 most of Ewell's guns had been absent, enabling Hancock to overrun the Confederate line. This time the pieces had been in place, and they had dictated the battle's outcome. William S. White of the Richmond Howitzers felt his heart beat with the "proudest throb of emotion" as soldiers congregated around his smoking napoleon, patting its breech and muzzle with affection and discussing its accuracy and effectiveness, as one might dote over a beloved pet. A soldier recognized the piece from an earlier incident. "Look, here, Jim, here's our gun!" he exclaimed. "This is the gun we pulled out'n the mud that 'ar night." [79]

Responsibility for the botched Union assault lay squarely on Grant. Once again, he had initiated an operation on the spur of the moment without reconnoitering the enemy position. And once again, despite the preceding week's brutal lessons, he had sent troops across open fields into the teeth of Lee's fortified line. Acting on hunches rather than hard evidence, he had fatally misjudged the strength of Lee's earthworks and the readiness of the rebel army. "So far from being surprised," Lyman wrote after the attack, "the rebels had spent the last days in strengthening their front and had rendered it impregnable." Grant should have known this before sending thousands of men to be killed or wounded.[80]

Grant's decision to stay at Spotsylvania Court House had cost time and lives. The general had nothing to show for his losses, and ceaseless marching and attacking to no evident advantage had eroded his army's morale. The offensive on May 18 marked the end of his failed policy—for a few weeks, at least—of assaulting Lee's army in its entrenched line. It was unfortunate that he did not reach that conclusion earlier.

"Ill news from all sides."

For Grant the day's bad news seemed endless. At 8:00 A.M. a courier spurred up with dispatches bearing tidings of twin disasters. Breckinridge, Grant read, had defeated Sigel at New Market and was driving him down the valley in full retreat. "If you expect anything from [Sigel], you will be mistaken," Halleck warned. "He will do nothing but run. He never did anything else." And Beauregard had repulsed Butler at Drewry's Bluff. Prospects that the political general from Massachusetts would take the Confederate capital and move to join Grant had disappeared. Grant immediately drafted orders removing Sigel. Butler's political capital saved him his job.[81]

These setbacks, following on the heels of General Banks's failure in Louisiana, left Grant in a sour mood. "All this news was very discouraging," he admitted. "All of it must have been known by the enemy before it was by me. In fact, the good news (for the enemy) must have been known to him at the moment I thought he was in despair." Grant understood the implications. With the subsidiary Union armies stymied or defeated, Lee no longer faced threats to his flank and rear. He could concentrate on fighting the Army of the Potomac. And Confederate forces that had defeated Sigel and Butler could now forward reinforcements to Lee. "I am prepared to see Lee's forces in our front materially strengthened," Grant predicted to his aide Porter. The campaign that had started with so much promise seemed to be unraveling. If the trend continued, there would be but two significant forces in the East— Grant's and Lee's—and the fate of the war in Virginia would be decided solely between the two.[82]

"It was a depressing day," Lyman confided to his journal. "Ill news from all sides, and the enemy securely on guard, despite our success of the 12th." The staffer wandered to a 2nd Corps hospital to console a friend hit by a piece of spherical case. "He exhibited great stoicism under the terrible trial of seeing most of his brother officers shot down within these few days, but plainly was deeply depressed by it," Lyman observed. Most of the wounded men, Lyman noted, had been injured by artillery. The army's medical director, McParlin, likewise reported an unusually high number of patients that day with severe shell and canister wounds.[83]

Union losses for May 18 were high for the short time that the troops were engaged. Hancock's aide, Francis Walker, placed Union 2nd Corps casualties at 650. Commentators attributed 250 casualties to Gibbon and 400 to Barlow. Some units suffered disproportionately. A soldier asserted that the Corcoran Legion was "blown to atoms." Neill's division was also hit hard and lost about 600 men. Total Union casualties, including those of the 9th Corps, exceeded 1,500 men. Confederate losses were negligible.[84]

The Union 2nd Corps, already seriously weakened in earlier battles, felt its losses acutely. "It was perhaps supposed that the corps could be urged to greater efforts to repeat its previous achievements on the same ground," Hancock's chief of staff, Major Charles H. Morgan, commented. "But such was not the fact. All the circumstances were such as to dishearten the men rather than to encourage them." Even the usually upbeat Barlow complained.

"We have been at it now 15 days," he wrote home, "and it has become rather tedious." Later that day Hancock ducked into Lyman's tent to sleep. "Tired as he was," Lyman recorded, "he could not rest until he had smoked a short pipe and poured out a volume of energetic conversation." Then Hancock rested his head on his arm, and, in Lyman's words, "went off like a babe." [85]

The experience of May 18 confirmed the Federals in their aversion against assaulting earthworks. The day's debacle afforded dramatic proof that Lee could not be budged. A soldier grumbled that the army had "gone in on the 18th, lost some twelve hundred men, and accomplished nothing." Another soldier complained that "this constant hammering was very severe work for the army, with no advantage gained to compensate for the terrible slaughter experienced in these useless and aimless attacks without adequate preparation." Writing his mother, a cavalryman assigned to headquarters cautioned against rumors that the Confederates were whipped. "If you were to ride out to the front rifle pits you would not think so," he advised. "The rebs fought very obstinately, and we also, but they are still before us, patiently awaiting our attack upon their very strong position." Meade smugly informed his wife that "Grant thought it useless to knock our heads against a brick wall, and directed a suspension of the attack." [86]

Grant was loath to admit that Lee had thwarted him, but circumstances allowed no other conclusion. It had become "impracticable," he conceded, "to make any further attack upon the enemy at Spotsylvania Court House." [87]

Resilience was Grant's strength, and action his favorite antidote to bad news. "This was no time for repining," the wiry general later asserted. Lee was now so firmly burrowed in that no attack could succeed. It was time, Grant concluded, to seek more promising fields. "The experience of the two weeks we spent before the lines of Spotsylvania brought the conviction that that position could not be carried save by an expenditure of blood out of all proportion to the results of any possible victory that could be achieved there," a reporter for the *New York Times* wrote. "Day by day the commanding general continued to throw out toward the left, with the hope of overlapping and breaking in the rebel right wing. But just in proportion as we stretched to the left, Lee extended his right to conform to our line, and intrenched himself, till finally he came to have a front practically impregnable." [88]

Grant had been weighing his options. He had vetoed a turning movement around Lee's northern flank, which would only force Lee west toward Gordonsville, where wooded, broken country would work to the rebels' advantage, and where the Union supply line would be stretched to the breaking point. Advancing south, however, presented intriguing possibilities. "Simply massing on the left of our front we could so threaten Lee's communications as to compel him to evacuate his fortified line," a reporter noted. "In other words, we would effect a turning movement on the rebel right flank." By seizing the North Anna River, Grant would force Lee either to come out and fight, or to abandon Richmond.[89]

The Union commander had been seriously eyeing the North Anna River as a strategic objective for several days. The river's banks rose sharply into bluffs and steep, brush-covered inclines. Crossings, particularly this rainy spring, were confined to bridges and fords, making the river a magnificent defensive position. And a short distance below the river was Hanover Junction, where the Richmond, Fredericksburg, and Potomac Railroad crossed the Virginia Central Railroad, coming from Staunton and the Shenandoah Valley.

Grant's analysis took into account the terrain that the armies would have to cross. Telegraph Road offered Grant his most direct path south but required him to cross the Ni, Po, and Matta rivers, risking opposition at each stream. A few carefully positioned Confederates could delay his progress while Lee's army pursued parallel roads and beat him to the North Anna. Grant, however, had devised a way to use the river system to his advantage. A few miles east of Telegraph Road, the Ni, Po, and Matta merged to form the Mattaponi, which flowed due south. By swinging east from Spotsylvania Court House and remaining north of the Ni, Grant could move past the bothersome streams, then descend along the Mattaponi's far side. He would have only open terrain to traverse, and the river network would work in his favor, shielding him from attack. In the inevitable race south, Lee, not Grant, would have to cross the irksome tributaries.

Grant, however, wanted to do more than simply beat Lee to the North Anna River. He also wanted to lure Lee into the open. He decided to start by sending a single corps south. Once the rebels began moving, the rest of the Union army could attack and crush them. Grant had no difficulty deciding which corps to dangle as the decoy. Hancock had spearheaded most of his operations, and he saw no reason to change his practice. Although the 2nd Corps had sustained terrible losses since crossing the Rapidan, Grant counted on Tyler's division to offset those subtractions, in numbers if not in experience. Under Grant's emerging scheme, the Union 2nd Corps was to step boldly out to become the anvil against which the rest of the Union army would hammer Lee. Hancock's route was critical. He had to advance sufficiently far from the main Union force to tempt Lee, but remain close enough for Grant to rescue him. Dispatching Hancock along Telegraph Road toward Richmond was certain to provoke Lee but also ran a substantial risk of leaving Hancock too vulnerable. Hancock's survival would hinge on how quickly Warren, Wright, and Burnside could march to his assistance, and their past performances afforded scant comfort. Grant could not risk the loss of his 2nd Corps.

Grant decided to hedge his bets. He would send Hancock east to Guinea Station, then dispatch him south along roads passing through Bowling Green and Milford Station, on the Richmond, Fredericksburg, and Potomac Railroad. This would place Hancock about twenty miles from the Union lines, where he was certain to attract Lee's attention. Hancock's danger would be slight, since the Federal army would be closer to him than would the Confederates. If Lee took the bait and attacked Hancock, Grant would have time to descend Telegraph Road and ambush the Confederates. If Lee ignored the bait, Hancock could continue to the North Anna River as the vanguard of an armywide movement south.

Dispatching Hancock toward Bowling Green and Milford Station advanced another of Grant's objectives. As the Union army moved south, it would need a new supply line. Port Royal, several miles below Fredericksburg on the Rappahannock River, was the next logical depot. Ships could reach the town from Chesapeake Bay, and a good road connected the river port to Bowling Green, capital of Caroline County. From there, roads radiated to Grant's potential routes.

Wounded men were still hobbling back from the morning's abortive attack when Grant began issuing orders to put his new plan in motion. Wright was to retrace his steps as soon as possible, Grant directed, and deploy in his former line running from Anderson's farm to Massaponax Church Road. After dark, Burnside was to form on Wright's left and extend the Union line south. Hancock was also to march after nightfall and bivouac at Anderson's Mill, on Massaponax Church Road, to create the impression that he was supporting Wright and Burnside. By morning on May 19 Grant expected to have Warren, Wright, and Burnside arrayed in a line running roughly north to south from the Ni to a point below Massaponax Church Road, with Hancock massed in their rear. As a diversion Wright and Burnside were to "force their way as close to the enemy as they can get without a general engagement, or with a general engagement if the enemy will come out of their works to fight." On the night of May 19 Hancock was to set off on the march that Grant hoped would lure Lee from his earthworks. As Grant put it, he wanted Hancock to swing southeast, taking "all his force and as much cavalry as can

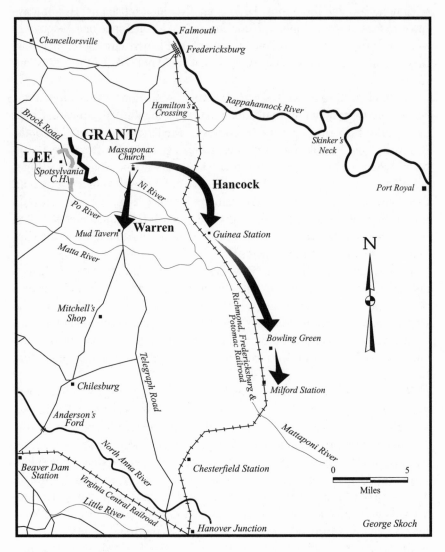

Grant's new plan of maneuver

be given to him, to get as far toward Richmond on the line of the Fredericksburg railroad as he can make, fighting the enemy in whatever force he may
find him." Grant expected Lee to pursue. "If the enemy make a general move
to meet this," he wrote, "they will be followed by the other three corps of the
army, and attacked if possible before time is given to intrench." [90]

With this directive, Grant ended his attempts to defeat Lee at Spotsylvania
Court House. Lee had fought him to tactical impasse, but he remained true to
his strategic goal. Lee's army was Grant's objective. Rather than persist in futile attacks, Grant once again resorted to maneuver to break the stalemate.
Grant saw the war in terms of campaigns, not individual battles. The move
south seemed the next logical step to bring this bloody chapter to a close.

At 11:00 A.M.—Grant had canceled the offensive against Ewell's entrenched line only two hours before—Wright's battle-worn corps started
back toward the Myers farm, accompanied by Tyler's heavy artillery division. They marched behind Burnside's and Warren's lines and reached Myers
Hill at 2:00 P.M. Wright again set up headquarters at the Anderson house,
leaving Russell and Ricketts at the Myers farm, and deploying Neill so as to
continue the 6th Corps's line to Anderson's Mill. The soldiers, an officer
commented, appeared "ready to lie down anywhere and sleep." Holmes revived his spirits with a bath and dinner. "I was nearly dead beat and am now
quite well," he recorded. [91]

During the afternoon Warren's batteries traded shots with Early's guns,
but neither side dared attack. Roebling considered the artillery practice
"nothing more than an immense waste of ammunition." Under cover of
smoke from the artillery, twenty-five soldiers from the Bucktails regiment—
the 13th Pennsylvania Reserves, nicknamed after their distinctive headgear—crawled into an advanced position in front of Roebling's "capital"
knoll and hacked impromptu rifle pits with their bayonets. Their post gave
them clear shots at a Confederate battery a short distance away. Rebels ensconced in nearby rifle pits kept the Pennsylvanians from exploiting their position by firing every time a Federal raised his head. The opposing pickets
quickly reached a mutual understanding. "Git down thar, Yanks," the southerners would holler before unleashing a volley. In short order the men were
trading newspapers, coffee, and tobacco. General Charles Griffin, of the 5th
Corps, rode up during one of these informal truces, lost his temper, and ordered a battery to fire on the Confederates. "I thought it was a barbarous thing
to do under the circumstances," a Union officer related, "and it was not sur-
prising that the enemy got square on a later and similar occasion." [92]

After dark, musketry erupted in front of Crawford, on Warren's left, sig-

naling a Confederate probe. The Bucktails retired from their advanced position, and the 83rd New York, which had just relieved the 97th New York on
the main skirmish line, fell back to Crawford's works. Colonel Richard
Coulter, whose brigade was posted along this sector, hastened to supervise
the withdrawal. A ball struck the colonel in his left breast, deflected off a rib,
and coursed around his body under the skin before exiting through his back.
Coulter was carried off the field in a stretcher, and command of the brigade
devolved on Colonel Bates of the 12th Massachusetts. The attack ended almost as quickly as it had started, with Confederates occupying the works dug
by the Bucktails.[93]

All night, Grant continued to rearrange his forces. Gibbon, followed by
Barlow, started for Anderson's Mill promptly at 9:00 P.M. Then Birney withdrew, as did Potter on Burnside's right, followed in turn by Crittenden and
Willcox. As morning approached, the pieces of Grant's giant puzzle fell into
place. Warren's corps, which had occupied the southern end of the Union line
on May 18, now formed its northern end. Wright's corps picked up on
Warren's left and carried the line in front of Myers Hill and across Massaponax Church Road. Burnside's corps formed the line's lower terminus, pro-
longing the line south, then doubling back to anchor on Massaponax Church
Road. Hancock's corps—minus Tyler's division, which camped on the
Anderson farm—lay in bivouac at Anderson's Mill.[94]

The no-man's land between the armies crawled with Confederates searching for plunder. Thomas's Georgians felt cheated because Griffin's Federals
had carried their dead and wounded back with them. The rebel picket
Fitzpatrick could find only one freshly killed Yankee, and someone had already taken his watch. "We can see where they drug off their dead, and blood
in profusion through the woods," Fitzpatrick wrote his wife.[95]

Inside the Mule Shoe, Corporal Harger of the 10th Massachusetts lay with
a shattered hip. "For God's sake, give me a little water!" he cried. A Confederate stopped, his face distorted with anger. "Give you water, you damned
Yankee?" he growled. "You killed my brother here yesterday." Discarding
his canteens, he lunged at Harger with his musket, then drew back. "I am not
going to kill you yet," he announced in a playful tone. "I am going to torture
you," and he jabbed the bayonet toward Harger once again. The corporal
squeezed his eyes shut and braced for the blow, which did not come. He
opened his eyes, and the rebel lunged at him again, stopping the blade inches
from Harger's face, then pulled the weapon back and lunged a third time.
Harger grimaced, keeping his eyes closed. Harger peered through fluttering
lids to find that he was still alive. The rebel's face had changed. Anguish had

replaced anger. "For God's sake, what am I thinking of?" the Confederate muttered, addressing no one in particular. "I may be where you are tomorrow." Kneeling down, he gave Harger a drink and bathed the injured man's brow. Then he stabbed a pine branch into the ground to shelter the corporal. "I will send an ambulance for you when I get into camp," he promised, and disappeared into the darkness.[96]

Union field hospitals were busy that night. In a 2nd Corps camp near the Mule Shoe, surgeons labored over Captain John Kelliher of the 20th Massachusetts, hit by an artillery round during the morning's attack. A doctor had discovered the mangled captain when investigating a pair of boots protruding from under a bush. So many of Kelliher's bones had been shattered that no one thought he would live. To relieve his suffering, the surgeons decided to remove the shards, clean his wounds, and stitch them closed. They took out his shattered lower jawbone and cut away his arm, including the shoulder blade, collarbone, and upper two ribs, which stuck through his flesh and exposed his lungs. When the doctors had finished, sutures ran from Kelliher's ear to within an inch or two of his pelvis. The next day, they loaded Kelliher and other seriously wounded men into a wagon lined with straw to begin the journey to Belle Plain. Kelliher was nursed back to health and later rejoined the 20th Massachusetts, remaining in active service with his regiment until the end of the war.[97]

The easy victory had left Lee's men feeling cocky. "It is the general opinion that Old Grant is waiting for reinforcements and as soon as he gets them that we will have another big fight and we all feel confident that if we do that we shall be able to give him a good whipping," a Georgian wrote home. "Grant is twice as badly whipped now as was Burnside and Hooker but he is so determined he will not acknowledge it," another Confederate observed. "But I think before he gets through with Lee he will have to own up."[98]

Lee expected Grant to attack at dawn along Massaponax Church Road. He instructed his chief engineer, Major General Martin L. Smith, to inspect the lines in front of Zion Church, and General Pendleton, his chief of artillery, to supervise placement of guns along this critical terrain. Pendleton positioned Lieutenant Colonel Charles Richardson's 3rd Corps battalion by the roadway and an additional battery in reserve.[99]

Lee received important news from other quarters. Breckinridge was on his way! "I have organized guard for Valley and will move as rapidly as possible," the Kentuckian wrote, adding that he had no cavalry to send to Lee. Breckinridge's force was small, numbering only 2,500 men, but it was a start.

If only President Davis could pry loose a few brigades from Richmond, the Army of Northern Virginia might have sufficient numbers to wage war on its own terms.[100]

A second dispatch raised new concerns. Sheridan was on the move. Fitzhugh Lee's scouts monitoring Union cavalry camps around Haxall's Landing and Malvern Hill had observed ominous stirrings on May 17. That evening, Sheridan had started north. "Hanover Junction is threatened by Sheridan and is unsafe," President Davis advised Lee. "The supplies there will be brought here if it can be done by morning." With Breckinridge on his way to Hanover Junction, Lee was not overly concerned about the place's safety. He wanted to keep an eye on Sheridan, however, and alerted Fitzhugh Lee to "collect all the cavalry and watch his course," enjoining his nephew to inform him of Sheridan's route and to protect the railways and depots.[101]

At 7:00 P.M. Lee reported the day's highlights to Richmond. "The enemy opened his batteries at sunrise on a portion of Ewell's lines, attempted an assault, but failed," he related, noting that the Federals had been "easily repulsed." Confederate casualties, Lee added, were "very few." Later in the evening Lee penned another dispatch to Davis. Grant, he began, was too strongly entrenched for him to attack "with any prospect of success without great loss of men." Lee, however, believed that the recent battles had hurt Grant. "I shall continue to strike him whenever opportunity presents itself," Lee promised, "but nothing at present indicates any purpose on his part to advance." Unfortunately, Lee pointed out, "neither the strength of our army nor the condition of our animals will admit, of any extensive movement with a view to draw the enemy from his position." Stated plainly, the Army of Northern Virginia lacked the strength to do anything other than await Grant's next onslaught.[102]

Lee had learned that Grant was receiving reinforcements. Heavy artillery and other units had already arrived, Lee reported, and calls had been issued in the North for volunteers. Rumors abounded that Federal forces no longer needed in Louisiana were on their way to Virginia, and that Grant was contemplating bringing Butler above the James as well. "The recent success of General Beauregard may induce the fulfillment of this report," Lee observed with a tinge of irony. Above all, stressed Lee, "The importance of this campaign to the administration of Mr. Lincoln and to General Grant leaves no doubt that every effort and every sacrifice will be made to secure its success." The war, he emphasized, had reached a crisis. "From all these sources," he stressed, "General Grant can, and if permitted will repair the losses of the late battles, and be as strong as when he began operation." [103]

"The question is whether we shall fight the battle here or around Richmond," Lee reminded the president. The Army of Northern Virginia, he stressed, had to receive reinforcements to counter Grant's infusion of troops. Otherwise, Lee feared that he might "be forced back." The prospect that the campaign might end in siege—the very eventuality that Lee had sought to avoid since the armies first grappled in the Wilderness—seemed dangerously near.[104]

VI

MAY 19–20

Ewell Strikes at Harris Farm

"Band Box Soldiers."

MAY 19 OPENED CLEAR and hot. The Federals were exhausted from marching all night to their new positions. The Confederates were weary as well, having remained alert at their posts in anticipation of an attack. Mutual exhaustion, concluded D. A. Hendrick of the *New York Herald,* guaranteed a "particularly quiet day," and he took advantage of the calm to ride along the length of the Union line. Any other time, he reflected, the venture "would have been attended with too much peril to make the excitement compensate for the personal risk it involved." Starting at the northern end of Grant's line on the Ni, the reporter tracked Warren's entrenchments southeastward across Fredericksburg Road, visited Wright's men at Myers Hill, and continued across Massaponax Church Road to examine Burnside's new earthworks. Everywhere soldiers lounged about, eating, playing cards, writing letters, and chatting. Union and Confederate pickets, Hendrick noted, seemed like old friends. "By a sort of tacit agreement, there had been no firing among them," he jotted in his notebook. "They have met and interchanged remarks and congratulations as if they never had been and never expected to be engaged in murderous strife." The Confederates bartered tobacco for Yankee coffee and sugar. Newspapers were especially popular commodities.[1]

Thursdays always brought fighting. May's first Thursday had witnessed the collision of the armies in the Wilderness. A week later came the slaughter at the Bloody Angle. It was Thursday again. The soldiers welcomed the lull, but few expected it to last long.

After the overnight troop movements were finished, the Union commanders discovered a gap in their defenses. Fredericksburg Road was the Army of the Potomac's lifeline. Wagons rumbled down the route carting provisions and ammunition from Belle Plain and returned to the docks with wounded men and prisoners. Cutler's 5th Corps division anchored the formation's northern end on the Ni. About a mile and a half north of Cutler, Gordon Road entered Fredericksburg Road from the west. The stretch of Fredericksburg Road between the Ni and Gordon Road stood undefended. The danger was acute, as Ewell's troops were entrenched only two miles away. Now that Hancock and Burnside had shifted to the Massaponax Church Road sector, no Federals remained between the Confederate 2nd Corps and Fredericksburg Road. Grant's oversight offered Lee an enticing opportunity to sever the Federal army from its base.

Warren selected Colonel Kitching's brigade, posted near the Anderson house, to fill the void. Kitching's outfit was an anomaly. At the beginning of the campaign the brigade consisted of only the 6th and 15th New York Heavy Artillery. These men had signed on as artillerists, not as infantrymen, but Meade had ignored the distinction and thrust them as foot soldiers into the vortex of combat in the Wilderness. After serving briefly with various corps, they were finally attached to the 5th Corps, where they saw brutal service in the trenches at Spotsylvania Court House. On May 18 the 2nd Battalion, 4th New York Heavy Artillery, joined Kitching's brigade. These troops had been manning forts around Washington and had led relatively sheltered existences, enlivened occasionally by horse races and concerts. Combat was a thing they read about in newspapers, and the only rebels they encountered were surly civilians caught smuggling contraband across the Potomac.

Spring of 1864 had turned the world of the 4th New York Heavy Artillerymen upside down. As part of Grant's program to augment his field armies, the regiment was transferred to the Army of the Potomac. Marching, drilling, and sleeping on hard ground became the daily regimen. Meade's soldiers regarded the Heavies, as the artillerists were called, with contempt. "Abe's Pets," "Paper Collars," and "Band Box Soldiers," the veterans chided the greenhorns. To the New Yorkers' dismay, their regiment's three battalions were assigned to different infantry corps. Most of the 2nd Battalion— Companies D, H, and K, about 440 men strong—was sent to the 5th Corps, and on May 18 it was incorporated into Kitching's brigade. "I shall never cease to condemn in the strongest terms the action of the Government in enlisting us for one branch of service and then, without our consent, transferring us to another," railed Captain Augustus C. Brown of the 2nd Battalion, Company H. "It cannot be sustained even as a military necessity. It is a wanton violation of good faith, an outrage upon fair dealing, and an imposition upon a patriotic soldier that would hardly be practiced upon a senseless beast." [2]

Before sunrise on May 19, Kitching received orders to pack. Warren had designated him to plug the gap along Fredericksburg Road by establishing a picket line west of the road and parallel to it, facing in the direction of the Confederates. The 6th New York was to anchor its left on the Ni, directly across from Cutler's right flank. The 15th New York was to continue the formation north through choppy, wooded terrain to Clement Harris's farm, site of Hancock's recent encampment. The brigade's newcomers—the 4th New York Heavy Artillerists—were to extend the line north across Susan Alsop's farm—home to a twenty-five-year-old widow and her four-year-old child—and secure the extreme right of the line on the Peyton farm, near Gordon Road. The obscure homesteads of the Harris, Alsop, and Peyton families would soon become all too familiar to Kitching's men.[3]

The 4th New York began establishing picket outposts along a little tributary of the Ni. The creek originated as a marsh on the western margin of the Peyton farm and flowed south through the Alsop and Harris properties, cutting a deep depression about a half-mile west of Fredericksburg Road. The tributary was an important tactical feature, since the Confederates would have to cross it if they tried to attack the road. Half of Company K of the 4th New York, commanded by Captain Seward F. Gould, deployed west of the swampy ground. Gould commandeered an abandoned two-story log house on the Alsop place for his headquarters and established five-man posts every five or six rods reaching south to the Harris farm. The 4th New York's Company D, led by Captain D. K. Smith Jones, continued the picket line north onto the Peyton farm, and then angled east toward Fredericksburg Road to protect the formation's upper flank. Company H, under Captain Augustus C. Brown, and the other half of Company K, under Lieutenant Michael J. Lee, set up camp in Mrs. Alsop's yard. At an early hour, three hundred horsemen commanded by Major George A. Forsyth of the 8th Illinois Cavalry clattered past the New Yorkers and fanned west along Gordon Road to watch for rebels. Near noon, four 3-inch guns of Company C, 1st New York Artillery, under Captain Almont Barnes, deployed on a knoll near the Harris house, to the left of the 4th New York's line. When everyone was in place, the arrangement resembled an upside-down L. Artillery anchored the formation's southern end at the Harris house, and pickets carried the long leg north across the Alsop place to the Peyton property, where the short leg veered east to Fredericksburg Road.[4]

All morning small bands of rebels kept materializing from woods to the west, but Kitching was not overly concerned. At ten o'clock Federals spotted two rebel flags waving over earthworks recently vacated by Burnside. Later, soldiers in Company K were settling down for a card game when a handful of

Confederate cavalrymen stormed from the woods and almost trampled the players. Both sides were equally surprised and began firing wildly. After emptying their pistols into the New Yorkers, the Confederates wheeled and galloped away. Around 11:00 A.M. more rebels emerged from trees in front of Company D and initiated a lively firefight, shooting a New Yorker in the hand. At 11:30 Warren informed headquarters that Kitching had seen "a little skirmishing" north of the Ni, but that the spats involved only stray groups of rebels. Nothing suggested that a major attack might be brewing. Warren expressed concern, however, that Kitching's line might be stretched thin. Meade reminded Warren that Tyler's heavy artillery division was encamped at the Anderson farm, less than two miles away. If the 5th Corps's far-flung outfits got in trouble, Warren was to summon Tyler immediately.[5]

A few miles south, at the Confederate command center at Zion Church, Lee had been sifting through reports. It was plain to him that Grant was once again contracting his northern flank and extending his line south. It was not clear, however, which Federal units were involved in the move. Nor was it clear what Grant's latest flurry of activity meant. Was he girding to attack, or was he massing to dash toward Richmond? Lee needed more information, and to get it he decided to order a reconnaissance in force of the Union line's northern end. It occurred to Lee that Grant might have weakened his right by shifting the weight of his army south. Possibly the Federals had neglected to safeguard Fredericksburg Road. By sliding a force north of the Union army—the very interval that Kitching, unknown to Lee, had been sent to fill—the Confederates might separate Grant from his base and play havoc with his plans, whatever they might be. In Grant's and Lee's fast-paced game, opportunities vanished quickly. Lee suspected that Grant had left an opening, and he moved right away to exploit it.

Ewell's 2nd Corps was in the right spot for the mission. Now that Hancock and Wright had moved to Massaponax Church Road, Ewell was unopposed and free to maneuver. His position on the northern end of the Confederate line situated him perfectly for the excursion that Lee had in mind. Unfortunately, the 2nd Corps had been decimated during the campaign, many of its best field commanders were gone, and Ewell seemed disturbingly excitable under stress. The outfit fought brilliantly when behind earthworks, but its offensive capability at this stage of the campaign was open to question. The 2nd Corps would be more than two miles from the Army of Northern Virginia. Danger attended the operation, and a misstep could prove fatal.

Lee must have had misgivings, but rather than lose this fleeting opportunity to catch Grant napping, he decided to go ahead with Ewell. According to Lee's aide Taylor, the Confederate commander directed Ewell to "demonstrate against the enemy in his front as he believed that Grant was about to move to our right and he wished to force his hand and ascertain his purpose." Ewell demurred, arguing that a frontal attack was unwise. He urged instead that he simply "feel out" the Union right and threaten Grant's communications by cutting Fredericksburg Road. Lee emphasized concern over Grant's southward "drift" and repeated his instruction that Ewell was to "find Grant's right" and "develop his purpose." Ewell went back to his troops with the understanding that he was to "demonstrate" against the Federals in his front to ascertain whether Grant was moving south.[6]

Ewell prepared to take his entire corps, accompanied by cavalry and artillery, across the Ni to strike Fredericksburg Road near the Harris and Alsop farms. Although Ewell had considerable artillery at his disposal, he elected to bring only Lieutenant Colonel Carter M. Braxton's six-gun battery, leaving the rest of his ordnance in case the Federals attacked while he was gone. Rosser's cavalry and Captain James W. Thomson's battery of horse artillery were to escort the expedition. Lee arranged for Kershaw's division to march from its reserve post below Spotsylvania Court House and temporarily occupy Ewell's fortifications during the 2nd Corps's absence.[7]

Marching orders came as a surprise to Ewell's soldiers. They had passed the morning "quiet in the ditch," as they called their mud-caked entrenchments. "Have been fighting more or less every day," Colonel Bryan Grimes, commanding a brigade in Rodes's division, wrote to his wife. "If [the Federals] would retire beyond the river and give us a breathing spell, it would be decidedly advantageous. Nearly all fagged out and need rest." [8]

But rest played no part in Lee's program. At 2:00 P.M. Ewell started his corps on its way, Rodes leading and Gordon marching behind. The line of ragged gray-clad troops filed across the Spindle farm, which was crisscrossed with rows of corpses from earlier fighting. Gravediggers had thrown dirt over the bodies, but recent rains had left heads and feet protruding from the ground. "It was an awful sight and the stench was horrible," a Confederate recollected. A chaplain accompanying the expedition complained that a "dense sea of corrupted atmosphere" filled the hollows. Walking quickly and holding his nose, he prayed "never again [to] experience such sensations or witness such scenes." [9]

Turning east onto Gordon Road the Confederates trod past Mrs. Couse's home and continued across the Ni. The column extended nearly three miles to the rear. At Mrs. Armstrong's house, Ewell decided to split his force. Rosser was to continue east on Gordon Road with Thomson's horse artillery while Ewell took his infantry and Braxton's guns along the wagon track to the Stevens ruins, then east to Fredericksburg Road. The trail to the Stevens

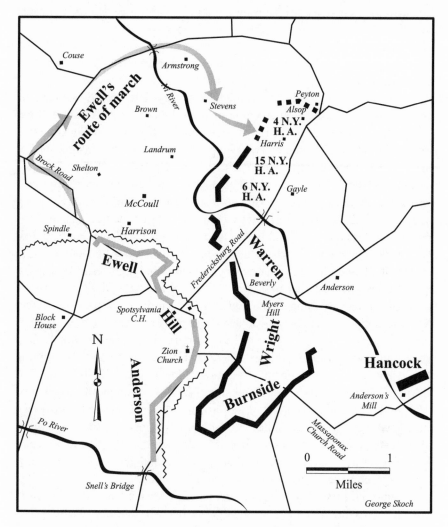

Union and Confederate deployments and Ewell's route on May 19

place was thickly mired, and Braxton voiced concern that his guns might become stuck. Rather than risk losing the pieces, Ewell decided to send them back.[10]

"The memory of some horrid dream."

As far as Grant could tell, the Confederates were dormant. Most likely, he conjectured, they were strengthening their earthworks in anticipation of another attack. Oblivious to the threat posed by Ewell, Grant continued preparations for Hancock's southward swing. "I shall make a flank movement early in the morning, and try to reach Bowling Green and Milford Station," he wrote Halleck. "If successful, Port Royal will be more convenient as a depot than Fredericksburg. I wish you would stir up the navy and see if they cannot reach there." Halleck promised to send ships up the Rappahannock as far as Fredericksburg if Grant would take steps to keep Confederate guerrillas off the southern bank, where they could fire down on the boats.[11]

Meade alerted Hancock that he was to march that night at 2:00 A.M., escorted by cavalry. Passing by way of Guinea Station, the 2nd Corps was to proceed through Bowling Green and entrench on the Mattaponi River near Milford Station. If Hancock encountered Confederates, he was to "attack vigorously" and immediately inform headquarters. The order provoked Hancock's aide Morgan into a tirade. "There is an old adage that it is the willing horse that is worked to death," he railed, lamenting the status of the 2nd Corps as Grant's workhorse. "And now," Morgan announced indignantly, "on the third consecutive night, it [is] proposed to send [the 2nd Corps] on a flank march over twenty miles, to 'attack vigorously in the morning.'" Hancock calmed his staffer and wrote Meade asking permission to start earlier, as he wanted to clear Guinea Station before daylight to avoid detection. "Start at such hour as you deem best," Meade replied.[12]

Around 3:00 P.M. disturbing reports reached Meade's headquarters from Kitching's sector. Confederate probes were intensifying. Six rebel cavalrymen rode into a 4th New York outpost shouting, "Surrender! Get up and don't fire your gun!" A Federal fired anyway, alerting the rest of the pickets, who escaped. Meade sensed trouble and ordered Tyler to start his heavy artillery division from the Anderson farm to reinforce Kitching. Two regiments—the 1st Massachusetts and 2nd New York Heavy Artillery—were closest to Kitching, and Tyler dispatched an orderly to begin them on their way immediately. The rest of the division was to make ready to move, but not to march until receiving further orders.[13]

Tyler's orderly spurred his horse to Colonel Thomas R. Tannatt of the 1st

Massachusetts Heavy Artillery and handed him a message. A trumpet sounded, and men sprang into formation. Nearby, the 2nd New York Heavy Artillery, commanded by Colonel Joseph N. G. Whistler, was going through a similar drill. The Massachusetts men started first and filed north onto Fredericksburg Road. Veering left at the Harris farm, they massed near the house, not far from Barnes's guns. Colonel Tannatt ordered Companies D and F to deploy as skirmishers and probe west toward the woods at the farm's far edge, by the creek. Then he began extending the rest of his regiment into a line of battle, posting the 1st Battalion, under Major Frank A. Rolfe, on the regiment's left, by the Harris house; Major Nathaniel Shatswell's 2nd Battalion in the center, reaching north; and Major Horace Holt's 3rd Battalion on the right, reaching toward the left flank of the 4th New York.[14]

A little after 4:00, Tannatt's Companies D and F shouldered their rifles and headed across the cornfield on a reconnaissance toward the tributary. A short hike brought the Massachusetts men to the 4th New York's picket line. The pickets—this was the sector of Captain Gould's Company K—exchanged jokes with the Bay Staters. To the north the 4th New York's other two companies were preparing to rotate, with Captain Brown's Company H relieving Captain Jones's Company D on the picket line near the Peyton farm. Jones's men retired to Susan Alsop's house and began cooking dinner while Brown's troops slipped into the entrenchments recently vacated by Jones. Brown placed Lieutenant William C. Edmonston in charge of the left of his line, next to Company K; Lieutenant Henry L. Carpenter in charge of the center; and First Sergeant T. A. Theben in charge of the far right, near Fredericksburg Road. The afternoon sun burned hot, and the sky darkened as clouds accumulated in the northwest. Thunder rumbled along the valley of the Ni. Rain began falling, lightly at first, then in torrents.[15]

Ramseur's North Carolina brigade, leading Rodes's division at the head of Ewell's column, reached the tributary just as the skies opened. There Tar Heel skirmishers ran headlong into the forward pickets of Gould's Company K, 4th New York. Musketry sputtered through the woods. Then the foremost Massachusetts companies pitched in, supporting Gould. "The firing began to increase in intensity," a Federal recollected. "The bullets hummed over our heads and we began to think there was a skirmish in earnest." [16]

Warren Works of Company K had just entered the deserted two-story house serving as Gould's headquarters when the shooting started. "There they come!" someone shouted, and Works glanced out the window to see rebel skirmishers streaming from the woods. Works and the handful of men in the house began firing through the upstairs window and through chinks in the wall. They could see more soldiers in butternut, battle colors unfurled, be-

hind the skirmishers. A substantial body of Confederates was advancing toward Fredericksburg Road, and the only troops available to stop them were
the novice Heavies. While Gould looked on from the upstairs window, the
Tar Heels splayed into two lines of battle. Making the best of a bad situation,
Gould began rallying his men near the abandoned house.[17]

Captain Brown was busy getting Company H into position on Gould's
right when the Confederates appeared. The sound of shooting brought him
running to investigate. The pageantry of Ramseur's veterans striding across
the field transfixed him. "It was a magnificent sight," Brown recollected
years later, "for the lines moved as steady as if on parade, and if ever I longed
for a battery of artillery with guns shotted with grape and canister, and my
own men behind those guns, it was then and there." The Confederate battle
line extended out of sight into the woods north of Brown, troubling the captain. His formation resembled a fishhook, the barbed end resting near
Fredericksburg Road, and he feared that rebels might lap past the end of his
line and get into his rear. "I determined to withdraw the center of my line
slowly, firing as we fell back," he explained, "keeping in touch with
Company K, and straightening out my fish hook as far to my right as I could,
all in the hope that we might hold the 'Johnnies' until troops attracted by the
noise we made should come to our assistance." [18]

While Brown braced for the onslaught, Captain Gould gathered his pickets toward the log house. "The balls came through as if the building were
paper, and several men were struck," Gould recounted. His soldiers posted in
the house felt as though they were fighting the entire Confederate army. "It
seemed to me that [rebel volleys] tore away the whole side of the building,"
Private Works remembered. A soldier standing next to Works clasped his
hands to his chest, gasped, and fell dead. Another man fired steadily from a
kneeling position through a crack in a fragment of wall that remained standing. "Works, I'm killed," a companion shouted as a bullet struck his chest. It
turned out that the round was spent, and the man bolted for the rear in a manner that persuaded Works of the "liveliness of that particular corpse beyond a
shadow of doubt." When a bullet ripped off the heel of his shoe, Works decided that it was time for him to leave. He sprinted from the house only to become mired in the swamp. "The flags and cattails were cut about my head in
a way that was anything but pleasant," he related. Tossing aside his blanket
and frying pan, Works clambered from the bog and joined his compatriots
east of the swamp, where Gould was rallying remnants of Company K behind a rail fence. Ramseur's Confederates swarmed around Gould's deserted
headquarters and continued into the bog. When the southerners came within

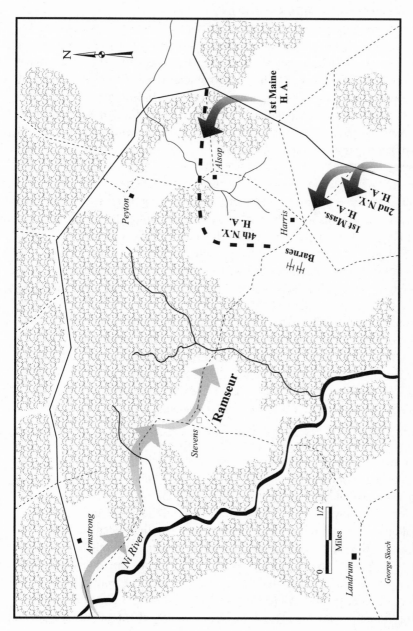

Battle of Harris Farm, first stage

George Skoch

range, Gould's men shouted a loud "Hurrah!" and fired. "Their line staggered," Gould noted with satisfaction.[19]

When the ruckus started, Captain Jones's Company D was at the Alsop house drawing rations. Jones ordered his soldiers to double-quick to Gould's assistance, as did Lieutenant Michael Lee, who was still at the Alsop place with his half of Company K. The reinforcements deployed along the edge of a pine forest near Gould's men, who were single-handedly fending off Ramseur's brigade from behind their rail fence. A handful of soldiers from Company D under Corporal A. Eugene Cooley ducked into a swale and began banging away at the Confederates in the old house. Cooley shot a man standing in the doorway, and another Federal dispatched a Confederate on the roof. "We got a shower of lead in return that would have annihilated us if it had been correctly aimed," related Cooley, who jumped out of the ditch with his companions and began running back. A bullet slammed into Frederick Knapp's leg, and Cooley and another man hefted the injured soldier between them. Another volley sounded, and several bullets hit Knapp. "He went limp in our hands as a wet rag," remembered Cooley. "I observed the wadding in front of his dress coat sticking out in shreds, made apparently by two or three balls passing through him."[20]

Companies D and K blazed away from the edge of their pinewoods, a few hundred greenhorns pitted against an elite Confederate brigade. The bog gave the New Yorkers defensible ground, but the numbers were decidedly lopsided, and Ramseur's battle line extended past both ends of the 4th New York's formation. "My gun got so hot in the rapid firing that I had to hold it by the strap in loading," Cooley related. "The enemy's fire was simply terrible," he remembered. "The ground, which was brown and bare when we formed the line, was soon covered with a carpet of green leaves and foliage, cut from the limbs of the young pine trees." A drummer boy snatched a musket and began shooting at Confederates. "Their bulldog fighting, together with advantage of ground—as there was a swampy spot, which made it difficult for the enemy to cross in their front—was all that saved the plucky little battalion from entire destruction," he later wrote of the heated combat.[21]

Colonel Kitching set a stirring example by strolling leisurely along the 4th New York's line. "No ducking!" he called to anyone dodging the bullets, which were whizzing all around. "Stand up!" he urged. A soldier thought that the colonel's demeanor would have "made heroes of the meanest cowards." Never did he display his martial qualities to better effect, admiring soldiers later claimed.[22]

On Kitching's right, Captain Brown of Company H directed Carpenter and Edmonston to straighten their line and withdraw stubbornly if pressed.

Then he returned to the left, where Companies D and K were heavily engaged. "I found the enemy struggling through the swamp and our boys peppering them as fast as they could load and fire, some lying down and some firing from stumps or from any other point offering the slightest protection," he recorded. As more Tar Heels slogged onto the New Yorker's side of the bog, the Federals retired into the pine forest, fighting from tree to tree. A yellow bulldog that belonged to a man in Company D tried to catch bullets in his teeth as they zipped past. Ears and tail raised high, the animal jumped and snapped excitedly at the humming minié balls. The show ended when a ball clipped off the end of his tail. Captain Brown last saw him running for the rear "like a yellow streak." [23]

A few hundred yards south, on Gould's left, the 1st Massachusetts Heavy Artillery was experiencing a wrenching baptism of fire. As Confederate skirmishers emerged from the woods west of the tributary, Major Rolfe, whose 1st Battalion formed the left of the Massachusetts line, hollered "Forward!" As if on parade, Rolfe's 360 Bay Staters marched elbow to elbow across the cornfield and into the swale. The rebels retired into trees on the far side of the creek, enticing Rolfe's battalion to follow. "Instantly every man seemed to know by the look in his face that there was serious work ahead for the regiment," recollected a Federal.[24]

Rolfe was walking into a trap. The right wing of Ramseur's battle line had deployed in the woods in preparation for charging into Mr. Harris's farm. When the Tar Heels saw Rolfe coming, they crouched low to the ground, concealed in underbrush. After the Federals had advanced fifty yards into the thickets, the Confederates stood—a northerner described them as rising "up out of the earth"—and fired in unison. The first volley was "like a stroke of lightning from clear skies," a northerner asserted. "In an instant the scene was transformed from peace and quiet to one of pain and horror." Rising high in his saddle, Rolfe exhorted his men to hold their ground. His mounted figure made a conspicuous target, and a second volley riddled him with eleven bullets, killing him. Some of Rolfe's soldiers knelt and fired toward the smoke billowing from Ramseur's formation. "Words cannot describe the feelings of the men who still remained standing in line," a survivor reminisced. "About them lay about a third of their comrades dead, dying, or wounded; the cries of pain, the noise of musketry, the hiss of the rifle ball, the dull thud as the leaden messenger of death finds lodgment in the body of some beloved comrade, remain with us today like the memory of some horrid dream." [25]

Unleashing a third volley, the southerners charged into Rolfe's fractured line, stepping over bodies and shooting anyone who resisted. The remnants of the battalion—"broken and disorganized, with almost every officer gone," a participant recollected—ran back toward the Harris house. A Federal who had watched the battalion charge gaped in disbelief as it stampeded across the field. "The throng increased rapidly," he observed, "and soon the whole column that fifteen minutes previously had marched orderly and gallantly in, came tumbling out, some dropping as they came, some covered with blood, staggering on, some supported by their comrades; riderless horses, officers and men all in confusion, a struggling, retreating mass, in the midst of a hail of bullets." [26]

Rolfe's survivors re-formed at the Harris house to receive the Confederates, who were now marching up the hillside from the creek. "The demon thirst for revenge took possession," a Federal remembered. Major Shatswell's 2nd Battalion, on the 1st Battalion's right, braced for the shock of Ramseur's attack. As the rebels came into range, the Massachusetts men loosed a volley, and Barnes's artillery spewed a "most effective dose of canister." At this critical moment Colonel Whistler's 2nd New York Heavy Artillery reached the Harris house, having come at the double-quick over from Fredericksburg Road in the wake of the Massachusetts men. A New Yorker paused to admire his regiment's faultless alignment. "It was thrilling, inspiring, and to have been there was to have the scene fixed in one's memory forever," he effused.

"Steady men, don't shoot too high," Whistler called out, and his regiment delivered a volley. Several shots were misdirected—a Bay Stater claimed that the 2nd New York fired its volley "into us instead of the enemy, " and that Barnes's artillery shells killed two Federal soldiers—but the concentration of lead produced the desired effect and stopped Ramseur's Confederates cold. Cheering loudly, the remnants of Rolfe's battalion spontaneously launched a countercharge. With his right flank exposed and a large Federal force in his front, Ramseur ordered his men back to the cover of the woods. [27]

Regrouping on the western side of the creek, Ramseur decided to wait for the rest of the 2nd Corps before resuming his attack. East of the creek, the 4th New York, 1st Massachusetts, and 2nd New York, arrayed north to south in that order, dressed their lines in anticipation of another Confederate attack. For a short while the shooting stopped. The only sound was the cries of wounded men.

Shortly Rodes's remaining brigades appeared on the trail and joined Ramseur. Colonel Bryan Grimes, commanding the North Carolina brigade formerly under Junius Daniel, deployed on Ramseur's left. Brigadier General Cullen A. Battle's Alabama Brigade formed on Ramseur's right, and the decimated Georgia brigade under Brigadier General George Doles moved up in reserve. Gordon's division emerged on high ground between the Alsop and Peyton homes, on Rodes's left, and staked out a defensive line along the gentle ridge. Gordon advanced two brigades—Louisianians under Colonel Zebulon York, and a mixed force of Virginians culled from the remains of "Allegheny" Johnson's division, which had been severely mauled on May 12—toward Fredericksburg Road. These Confederates passed north of the 4th New York's line and fortuitously emerged onto Fredericksburg Road in time to intercept a wagon train groaning with provisions from Belle Plain. Hungry Confederates broke ranks and swarmed toward the wagons.[28]

Captain Brown of Company H, 4th New York, was worried. The right end of his fishhook dangled near Fredericksburg Road, where Gordon's rebels were looting the wagons. Teamsters had cut their traces, and horses were darting everywhere. The battle had reached a moment of crisis. If the rebels turned Brown out of his position—and there was nothing to stop them from doing so—the Harris and Alsop farms would become untenable for the Federals.[29]

At their headquarters on the Anderson farm, Grant and Meade had just sat down to dinner when musketry broke out to the north. The sound was coming, a diner observed, from "behind us in just the last position at which we should have expected it." Calling for horses and orderlies, the generals listened with concern. Grant's aide Porter had been dozing when his servant woke him with disturbing reports that Lee's army had popped up in the Union rear. Peering from his tent, Porter saw Grant and a cluster of staffers deep in conversation. Porter directed his servant to fetch his mount and hurried to the knot of men. Grant hailed him as he approached. "The enemy is detaching a large force to turn our right," he told the aide. "I wish you would ride to the point of attack, and keep me posted as to the movement, and urge upon the commanders of the troops in that vicinity not only to check the advance of the enemy, but to take the offensive and destroy them if possible." As Porter turned to go, Grant called out by way of reminder: "You can say that Warren's corps will be ordered to cooperate promptly."[30]

Tyler's three remaining heavy artillery regiments—the 1st Maine, 7th New York, and 8th New York—were waiting on the Anderson farm, sizing up the gunfire to the north. A staff officer dashed up to Tyler, who sent couriers scurrying to his regimental commanders. "Fall in, 1st Maine!" announced Colonel Daniel Chaplin. "Fall in, 7th New York!" cried Colonel Lewis O. Morris. "Fall in, 8th New York!" echoed Colonel Peter A. Porter, and the soldiers shuffled into place, eager to prove their worth to the veterans whose jibes still rang in their ears. "We did not know why they should sneer and scoff and insult us," a Maine man reflected. "But they did so, and it only made us the more anxious to 'go in' and show them that we could fight." Reminisced a soldier: "We got ready in less time than it takes to tell the story and were off on the double quick."[31]

Tyler's regiments—Chaplin's, Morris's, and Porter's, in that order—clipped north along Fredericksburg Road. At the far edge of the Alsop clearing, they approached the exposed end of Captain Brown's fishhook, with Gordon's Confederates plundering wagons a short distance away. Novice officers barked out contradictory orders. Chaplin drew his sword and rode conspicuously to the head of his regiment. A boy named Johnny Welch sat down, rested his gun on his knee, and began firing at distant figures in gray. The colonel gently suggested to Welch that he was starting the battle a little too soon, and the boy returned to his place in the ranks.[32]

Chaplin's 1st Maine pressed past Captain Brown's dangling flank and on toward the wagons, where rebels were breaking open barrels of pork. Greed cost the Confederates dearly, enabling Chaplin to close the gap on Brown's flank and deploy to attack. Realizing their peril, the southerners abandoned their loot and melted into a stand of woods west of the road. Chaplin dispatched part of his regiment to guard the wagons. The larger portion of his command formed on the road, as did Morris's 7th New York, and the two regiments started west along the face of Brown's line. Elements of the 7th New York became jumbled with Chaplin's Maine soldiers. Brown later termed the affair "the noisiest kind of a mix-up."[33]

Chaplin's regiment, Morris's men lockstep on their left, slashed through a stretch of dense evergreens and emerged onto the Peyton fields. Ahead was the tributary—it was little more than a spring-fed swamp here, lined with trees—and beyond rose Gordon's battle line. Without missing a beat, Chaplin advanced into the depression worn by the stream. Gordon's veterans had stacked logs and branches for cover, but the 1st Maine Heavies stood erect, "just as you see them in pictures," a soldier recalled. The Confederates opened fire with devastating results. Private Ervin Chamberlin of Company E, 1st Maine, was shot seven times and saw men fall on both sides of him and to the rear. Major Charles J. House, who was near Chamberlin, counted marks on his own clothing from nine bullets. Mechanically repeating their drills, the Federals pursued a misguided policy of firing, then methodically clearing smoke from their muskets "by half cocking, throwing off the old cap and blowing into the muzzle, always giving the guns due time to cool before reloading."[34]

Morris's 7th New York meanwhile advanced on Chaplin's left through a cedar thicket to a relatively high piece of ground on the Alsop farm, where it hooked onto the 4th New York's right. The march had thrown the 7th New York's line into shambles, and a Confederate volley into the right portion of the regiment stampeded some green troops. "Don't let news of this break go back to Albany," Morris admonished. An unbroken line of heavy artillery regiments now extended across the Harris, Alsop, and Peyton farms. The 2nd New York, 1st Massachusetts, and 4th New York made up the Union left wing, facing Rodes. Then came the 7th New York, which faced a gap in the Confederate line. On the 7th New York's right, the 1st Maine Heavy Artillery stood locked in mortal combat with Gordon's rebels.[35]

Ewell faced a critical juncture. He had located the upper extremity of Grant's line. But Lee also expected him to "disrupt" Grant's operations by "demonstrating" against the Federals. In this he had been less successful, having only briefly gained a lodgment on Fredericksburg Road. Perhaps hoping to bolster his standing in Lee's eyes, Ewell decided to escalate his offensive. He was encouraged in that the enemy opposing him consisted of raw units. Counting on his veterans to shatter the heavy artillery regiments before experienced reinforcements could come to their assistance, Ewell ordered an attack across his entire front. It was a decision that nearly proved to be his undoing.

On Ewell's right wing, Rodes set his sights on the sector of the Harris farm held by Tannatt's 1st Massachusetts. Orderly lines and unsoiled uniforms marked the regiment as greenhorns. "Your men did not know how to protect themselves by taking advantage of the inequalities of the ground which they defended," Sergeant Cyrus B. Watson of the 45th North Carolina told a gathering of Massachusetts survivors after the war. "You marched as if on dress parade." [36]

At the command, "Forward, charge!" Rodes's division broke from the woods. "I shall never forget my sensation as we made that charge," a Confederate recollected. Advancing uphill, Rodes's men were slammed back by a barrage of musketry. "To escape in the midst of such a fire as we were exposed to seemed almost miraculous," a Confederate marveled. On the right of Rodes's line, Grimes's brigade came under intense fire from Tannatt's muskets and Barnes's artillery. Colonel Samuel H. Boyd of the 45th North Carolina fell mortally wounded before reaching the brook. Confederates described the opposition as "stiff" and "murderous." A Tar Heel asserted that his regiment "did as hard fighting as we did in the war for the length of time engaged." [37]

Rodes's troops swarmed out of the swale in waves, only to be driven back, re-form, and charge again. A Massachusetts soldier counted three distinct

Confederate attacks. Others thought there were more. "Charges and counter-charges swayed the action back and forth," a northern witness reported, "deflecting the line, bending it back here and pushing it forward there, but never breaking it, and scarcely changing the mean position." Major Shatswell was shot in the neck, and surgeons ordered him to the rear. No sooner had orderlies bandaged his wound than he returned to the firing line, inspiring his men by example. "Tall and grand, with a voice like the roar of a lion, hatless, blood trickling from beneath the bandage down his cheek until his coat was saturated with it," a witness recalled the major. Blue-clad soldiers fell where they stood, but the formation held. "The crash of musketry had turned into a roar like thunder," a Federal recalled, "and it seemed as if we must be swept from the field by the superior force of the Confederate veterans." Harris and his family huddled in their cellar.[38]

As the battle seesawed back and forth across the creek, a handful of Tannatt's troops advanced into the far woods only to find themselves surrounded. "Halt! Throw down that gun!" Charles Lewis of Company B heard a southerner drawl. He looked into the muzzles of several rifles leveled at him and stood motionless, expecting to be killed. A rebel snatched his musket. "Why didn't you throw down that gun?" the southerner asked. "You came near getting shot." Confederates hurried past Lewis toward the front. An officer stopped and demanded of him, "How many men you got out there?" Lewis answered, "Go out and see, if you want to know." [39]

At the peak of the attacks, the aide Porter located Tyler overseeing his division. The two men were friends from before the war. "Tyler, you are in luck today," Porter called out. "It isn't everyone who has a chance to make such a debut on joining an army. You are certain to knock a brevet out of this day's fight." Tyler shouted back with a smile. "As you see, my men are raw hands at this sort of work, but they are behaving like veterans." [40]

"They fought confounded plucky."

The battle was less than an hour old when Union reinforcements began streaming to the front. First to appear was a provisional battalion comprised of the 1st Maryland and 87th Pennsylvania, returning from a stint of guard duty at Belle Plain. The sound of musketry greeted the outfit as it neared the Alsop farm. Colonel Nathan T. Dushane, commanding the battalion, advanced his troops westward into dense thickets on a course calculated to bring them onto the right flank of the 1st Maine. A detachment of Gordon's Confederates reached the thickets at the same time as Dushane and drove the battalion back to Fredericksburg Road. But a twist of fortune brought Tyler's

final regiment—Colonel Porter's 8th New York Heavy Artillery—marching
up the roadway just as Dushane's situation seemed hopeless. Forming on
Dushane's left, Porter's regiment advanced into the thickets in tandem with
Dushane, repulsed the rebels, and pushed onto the Alsop clearing. The 8th
New York settled behind the 1st Maine Heavy Artillery, and Dushane's battalion shifted to high ground near the Peyton house, opposite Gordon's northern flank. Sharpshooters from the 21st Virginia shot Dushane's horse from
under him and made life miserable for his men until a handful of Maryland
soldiers under Sergeant Jesse Childs drove them away.[41]

Now fully alert to Ewell's threat, Meade directed Warren and Hancock to
hustle troops to the Harris farm. By 6:00 P.M. Federal reinforcements were
hurrying toward the battle zone in earnest. Warren ordered the Maryland
Brigade—minus, of course, the 1st Maryland, which was with Dushane—
into the fray, along with Crawford's entire division of Pennsylvania
Reserves. On the other end of the Union formation, Hancock started Birney's
division north toward the Harris farm, readying Barlow and Gibbon to follow
if needed. Birney's soldiers, who had been washing their clothes, gamely
donned their dripping garments, shouldered their muskets, and filed onto
Fredericksburg Road next to the Maryland Brigade. One of Birney's men
recollected that the two columns marched side by side and "quickened their
pace to a run" as they neared the fight.[42]

Colonel Richard N. Bowerman, commanding the Maryland Brigade, had
something to prove. On May 8 the Marylanders had failed to capture an important Confederate position. Warren had faulted them and placed them
under his personal command as punishment. Bowerman's men resented the
slight and were anxious for vindication. Pushing past Birney's troops to
elbow through a "great stampede of trains, camp followers, and other rub-
bish," they tumbled toward the sound of combat. Warren's aide Roebling was
waiting and directed the Maryland troops into an interval between the 1st
Maine and Dushane's battalion, where they became "heavily engaged at
once." Then Birney pulled up. Roebling, who found himself informally supervising the deployments, shunted Crocker's brigade behind the 1st Maine,
Egan's brigade in support of Bowerman's Marylanders, and Mott's brigade in
reserve along Fredericksburg Road. Crawford's division arrived next, and
Roebling dispatched the Pennsylvania Reserves onto Birney's left to backstop the 4th New York. Next came Captain Patrick Hart's 15th New York
Independent Battery, which joined Barnes's pieces.[43]

The concentration of Union troops caused inevitable confusion. One of
Crocker's men stared in bewilderment at the sight of the heavy artillerymen
standing neatly in line, surrounded by corpses. "Being novices in the art of

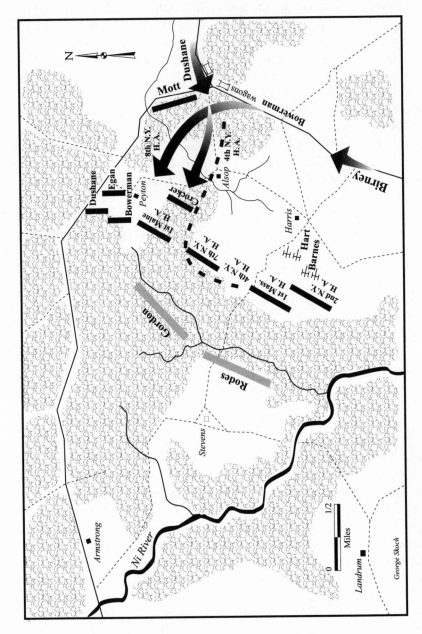

Battle of Harris Farm, second stage

war, they thought it cowardly to lie down, so the Johnnies were mowing them flat," he reported. "Being simple and cowardly enough to lie down and take advantage of the situation, we lost but two men in the time the other regiment had lost over 200." Colonel Wainwright recorded a quartermaster's tongue-in-cheek rendition of the fight. "First there was Kitching's brigade, firing at the enemy; then Tyler's men fired into his; up came Birney's division and fired into Tyler's; while the artillery fired at the whole d——d lot." [44]

As more and more Federals confronted him, Ewell realized that he was in trouble. Fredericksburg Road was manifestly beyond his reach. The trick now was finding a way to disengage before Federals overwhelmed him. Curtailing his assaults, Ewell set about strengthening his defensive line. Evening was approaching. If he could fend off the northerners a few hours more, he could withdraw under cover of darkness.

In the waning daylight, the Confederate 2nd Corps waged a desperate battle for survival. Several times, disaster seemed imminent. On Ewell's left, Crocker's brigade passed through the Maine Heavies and slammed into Gordon's front while Bowerman's and Egan's brigades on the Peyton farm enfiladed Gordon's left flank. The bastard Confederate brigade concocted from Johnson's fragmented Virginia regiments broke, exposing the end of Gordon's line. Gordon had posted Colonel Hoffman's veteran Virginia brigade for just such an emergency. Fixing their bayonets, Hoffman's troops pushed through the retreating soldiers, who were "running like dogs and the Yankees right behind," a southerner reported. "Firing and yelling and making all the noise we could," Hoffman's brigade broke the Union attack and deployed in the Peyton outbuildings. The disgraced Virginians returned and took position on Hoffman's right. A bitter fight swirled around weathered sheds and pens. "Although the Yanks made several attempts to dislodge them," a Confederate observed of Hoffman's unyielding troops, "they stood their ground and repelled every attack." Ewell, who rode up to supervise Hoffman's deployment, was nearly killed when his horse was shot. The injured animal pitched him unceremoniously to the ground and collapsed on top of him. Hoffman's soldiers rolled the horse off the general, helped him onto another mount, and led him to the rear.[45]

On Ewell's southern wing, Rodes faced only novice Heavies who seemed satisfied to stay on their side of the creek. Confederates here suffered severely from artillery fire but were spared the welter of charges that racked Gordon's sector. Ramseur's brigade, which had initiated the battle, tenaciously defended its position. Several Tar Heels climbed into treetops and methodically picked off Massachusetts soldiers arrayed in orderly lines on the eastern bank. A man in the 14th North Carolina accurately noted that

"[Ramseur's] brigade aided by [Hoffman's] brigade fought gallantly and saved the rest of our corps from becoming entangled and perhaps routed."[46]

From his headquarters at Zion Church, Lee monitored Ewell's predicament with apprehension. Realizing that his 2nd Corps was in trouble, he directed Early to close the gap between Ewell and the Army of Northern Virginia. Early selected Wilcox's northernmost brigades, under Thomas and Scales, for the assignment. Those splendid outfits worked their way through dense woods to a point across from Cutler's 5th Corps division, punched in Cutler's pickets, and seized the advanced Union rifle pits. Sharpshooters from Thomas's left flank reached leftward and effected a junction with Ewell. "The whole scene was a perfect picture of gloom, destruction and death—a very Golgotha of horrors," a Georgian recounted of the scene. McGowan's South Carolina brigade—commanded by Colonel Joseph N. Brown since McGowan's wounding on May 12—added its muscle and pressed on to Cutler's main entrenchments. "Charge! You charge!" the Federals called out defiantly. Brown, however, judged the Federal works too strong to assault. "The 'charge' was not 'charged,'" a South Carolinian reported.[47]

Late in the evening Rosser's cavalry belatedly reached the battlefront. After leaving Ewell at the Armstrong house, Rosser had headed northeast along farm roads until halted by his old foe, Nettleton's 2nd Ohio Cavalry, backstopped by the 3rd New Jersey Cavalry. After a short and relatively bloodless skirmish that also pulled in elements from Ferrero's 9th Corps division, Rosser disengaged. Apparently Ewell contemplated sending Rosser against the Federal flank at the Peyton farm, but nothing came of the venture. Around 8:00 P.M. Thomson's horse artillery opened fire "to cool the ardor of the Yankee infantry and to acquaint them of the fact that we had something around there a little heavier than a common musket," a gunner later explained. After a tepid demonstration Rosser fell back along Gordon Road, leaving Ewell to fend for himself.[48]

Near dark, the Federals opposing Gordon formed for another attack. "Forward! Remember Fort Pillow!" Union officers shouted, invoking a recent western battle in which Confederates had massacred black troops. But the Federals had no stomach for the darkening woods and desisted after a few tentative lunges. "Perhaps they feared the fate of their Fort Pillow comrades and obeyed the order to 'remember' it," a Confederate retorted. In a botched offensive against the center of Ewell's line, the 2nd New York angled in front of the 7th New York, which mistook its fellow regiment for rebels and fired into it. "The woods were so dense and full of smoke that it was hard to discern a body of troops a short distance away," a participant explained.[49]

Ewell's soldiers lay behind their log and dirt breastworks in the dripping woods, expecting a night attack. In some places the combatants waited within speaking distance, separated only by the tributary and a dense pall of smoke. Musketry crackled sporadically, but neither side dared assault. Occasionally the Yankees cheered, and the Confederates replied with rebel yells. Finally Ramseur could bear the suspense no longer. "Come on, Yankees," he shouted, but no one came. "We lay there about half the night, in the mud and water, behind our little mound of earth thrown up with our bayonets and hands," a Tar Heel later informed his family.[50]

Darkness ended the Battle of Harris Farm, as the engagement came to be called. Grant still hoped to salvage the maneuver toward Bowling Green that he had planned for the evening. But the 2nd Corps, which was to start shortly after dark, was now widely dispersed, with Gibbon and Barlow at Anderson's Mill and Birney and Tyler spread across the Harris, Alsop, and Peyton farms. Grant considered asking Crawford to relieve Birney and Tyler, but Warren protested, citing reports that Early and Ewell had occupied entrenchments in front of him formerly held by Burnside. He strongly recommended keeping Birney and Tyler in place until morning. Otherwise, cautioned the 5th Corps's commander, Confederates might "drive in our right and get all our train at Fredericksburg."[51]

Grant had heard so many of Warren's alarms that he had stopped taking them seriously. Reports that Early had advanced to support Ewell, however, rang true, and he agreed to postpone his maneuver a day to clear Confederates from his northern flank. "The enemy came out on our right late this afternoon and attacked, but were driven back until some time since dark," he reported to Washington. "Not knowing their exact position, and the danger our trains at Fredericksburg will be in if we move, I shall not make the move designated for tonight until their designs are fully developed."[52]

Warren made only halfhearted efforts to cut off Ewell's retreat. Near dark, he directed Crawford to turn Ewell's right flank and interpose between the Confederates and the Ni. Colonel Martin D. Hardin's brigade of Pennsylvania Reserves advanced to the river and threw the Bucktail regiment across as skirmishers. The soldiers pushed north along the watercourse, capturing a Confederate captain and several of his men. It had grown too dark, however, for Hardin to block the Confederate escape route.[53]

At 10:00 P.M. Ewell began the delicate task of withdrawing. Orderlies rousted his exhausted soldiers with instructions to creep away "rapidly and noiselessly, one man at a time." The retreat degenerated as bands of Confederates sought shortcuts and became hopelessly lost. Many southerners tried to retrace their route. "Soldiers were riding and walking up all night long," the younger Couse recollected, "rapping at the doors to inquire the way back to their breastworks." Brigadier General Robert D. Johnston's brigade—temporarily commanded by Colonel Thomas F. Toon, who was filling in following Johnston's wounding on May 12—served as rear guard. McGowan's brigade, which had retired after dark to the Mule Shoe, greeted clusters of Ewell's dispirited men as they trod past. "These last came in scatteringly" one of McGowan's soldiers recorded, "giving every one his own account of the doings." Ramseur's chief of staff scribbled in his diary: "We quietly retired under cover of an Egyptian darkness, regaining our original lines, wet and exhausted, about midnight, when we threw ourselves on the cold, damp ground and slept until morning."[54]

On discovering that Ewell had left, soldiers from the 4th New York Heavy Artillery ventured across the creek. Stragglers, "completely worn out with the fatigue of their long march," were all that remained of the Confederate force. "Likely their want of success was one cause of their dejection," a Federal surmised. The Heavies slept where they had fought. "Get up!" an enraged staff officer demanded on encountering a row of men stretched out on the ground. "What do you mean by going to sleep at such a time as this?" Closer inspection disclosed that the forms were corpses, lying in rank where they had fought. Major House of the Maine regiment looked on as moonlight struggled fitfully through gaps in the clouds to illuminate the lifeless faces of his comrades smeared with battle grime. "It was a solemn moment as I gazed on the scene at that midnight hour, my first look upon a deserted battle field," House reflected. "How forcibly those rows of dead men reminded me of the gavels of reaped grain among which I had worked on my native hills, but here the reaper was the angel of death."[55]

Birney's veterans began relieving the heavy artillery regiments. They were appalled at the slaughter. Standing erect on the crest of their ridge, the greenhorns had furnished "admirable targets for the Confederates who fought, as usual, in the woods and from behind trees, fences, and boulders." Birney's old hands instructed the novices in the practicalities of combat, putting out a picket line and using plates, eating utensils, and bayonets to construct rough earthworks. Two drummers in the 86th New York discovered that many Heavies were new recruits and had gone into battle carrying bounty money. The youths rifled the corpses until their pockets and caps overflowed with money, watches, rings, and other valuables. "This to me was the most uncivilized act that I saw during my four years army experience," a soldier remarked.[56]

For the Confederates the battle's fleeting gains scarcely justified the casualties. Catapulting Ewell's depleted corps miles from the Confederate army had put the troops at significant peril. A southerner rightly proclaimed the exercise a "useless and unnecessary sacrifice of valuable lives." Had Hoffman's brigade "not stopped the Yankees, all of Ewell's corps would have been captured and the war ended right then," he speculated. The only accomplishment was to postpone Grant's maneuver toward the North Anna River one day. Ewell estimated his loss at 900 soldiers, more than 10 percent of those engaged. A Tar Heel counted a "heap of men killed and wounded but not so many killed as wounded." A Confederate correspondent concluded that "we certainly accomplished very little, whilst we lost some good men." [57]

Fault lay at many levels of the Confederate command structure. Lee had used poor judgment in ordering the exercise in the first place. Cavalry could have acquired the information that he sought. If Lee meant to provoke a fight, he should have sent a stronger force and arranged for reinforcements. He had set Ewell an impossible task. But Ewell deserved criticism as well. Rushing Ramseur ahead was a mistake that afforded the Federals opportunity to respond, and Ewell neglected to use Rosser to advantage. Critics later faulted Ewell for sending back his guns, but here he probably acted wisely, since the pieces might have been captured. May 18 had demonstrated that the Confederate 2nd Corps could hold an entrenched position, but May 19 hinted that its days of daring maneuvers were over. The outfit had lost too many good men too quickly, and Ewell's currency as a leader was seriously debased. Fairly or not, the soldiers blamed Ewell, and his reputation became a major casualty of the debacle. The high-strung general had missed a superb opportunity in the Wilderness on May 6 and had faltered under stress on May 12. May 19 presented yet more evidence that he lacked the judgment necessary to command a corps. A soldier in Hoffman's brigade claimed to have overheard Ewell boast that "Jackson had a stonewall brigade but I have one of cast iron." Observed the soldier: "I think it was a great pity that he did not take better care of it." One of McGowan's men said it best. "Only one thing was plain, and that was dreadfully plain—the flank movement had failed." Lee continued to monitor the failings of his eccentric subordinate with deepening apprehension. [58]

The Federals considered the battle a victory. They had repulsed Ewell and retained possession of the field. "Altogether, the result of this attack by Ewell is eminently encouraging to the army," wrote Sylvanus Cadwallader of the *New York Daily Tribune*, who witnessed the engagement. "It is accepted as a fit offset to our failure on nearly the same ground [on May 18]." If this was a victory, it was an expensive one. The 4th New York's 2nd Battalion suffered 76 casualties, almost 20 percent. The 1st Massachusetts went into the fight with 1,617 men and amassed 394 casualties, including Major Rolfe, com-

manding its 1st Battalion. The 1st Maine, which went into the fight 1,800 soldiers strong, sustained a staggering 524 casualties, nearly one man in three.
The 7th New York reported 98 casualties, and the 8th New York fewer than
40. Hancock reported 1,013 men killed, captured, and wounded. His 2nd
Corps's hospital received 636 wounded during the night, and the 5th Corps's
hospital 406. Many men had been accidentally shot by their comrades. Union
losses for the day approximated 1,500 men.[59]

Grant suspected Meade and his subordinates might have accomplished
more had they acted with greater daring. Ewell's detached corps had presented a unique opportunity. This was the first time in the campaign that a
substantial Confederate infantry force had ventured unsupported outside its
earthworks. On learning of Ewell's attack, Grant had hoped not just to check
the Confederates but, as he told Porter, to "destroy them if possible." In hind-
sight, the Federals had a fair chance to do just that. Tyler's brigade alone had
more troops than did Ewell's entire corps. Warren could have blocked
Ewell's route of retreat had he advanced Cutler and other 5th Corps elements
in tandem with Hardin. The Union army had moved too slowly to exploit a
fleeting but substantial opportunity.

Grant's regrets aside, the soldiers of the heavy artillery regiments had reason to be proud. They had held their own against the Army of Northern
Virginia's vaunted 2nd Corps and had won the respect of foes and friends
alike. "You had the courage, the discipline and the soldierly qualities that
meant a stubborn fight for us," a southerner admitted to a gathering of heavy
artillerymen after the war. "Well, you can fight if you did come out of the defenses," a veteran assured a Maine man after the battle. Another veteran told
a reporter, "After a few minutes they got a little mixed, and didn't fight very
tactically, but they fought confounded plucky—just as well as I ever saw the
Old Second [Corps]." Roebling thought that "the whole affair reflected great
credit upon the Heavy Artillery, and the honors belong exclusively to them
and the Maryland Brigade." The next day, Meade expressed his gratitude.
Kitching's and Tyler's men had "met and checked the persistent attacks of a
corps of the enemy led by one of the ablest generals," he wrote in a special
commendation. They had earned the respect reserved for heroes. "After
Spotsylvania," a soldier affirmed, "I never heard a word spoken against the
heavy-artillery men."[60]

"A good judge of horses as well as a good general."

At 3:00 A.M. on May 20, Birney's Federals pushed across the creek and into
the woods recently vacated by Ewell. Only gray-clad stragglers remained,

"footsore, tired, and well nigh exhausted," a Union man reported. Marching cautiously along the trail to the Stevens place, the Federals captured Confederates in droves. A soldier in the 63rd Pennsylvania found it amusing when several rebels mistook his regiment's skirmish line for Ewell's rear guard. On discovering their error, the southerners surrendered with "good grace." During the morning, Birney and Tyler turned 412 prisoners over to the provost marshal.[61]

The dribble of Confederates past Mrs. Couse's house slowly tapered off, much to the family's relief. "After being in Fed lines I can scarcely tolerate the sight of the graybacks," Katherine Couse remarked. "I hate their old rusty uniforms. I am disgusted with the sight of them. Every hour some of them ride or walk up [and] rummage the whole place. We do not ask them to come in, have as little to do with them as possible." [62]

While Union ambulances collected corpses from the battlefield, Federal pioneers dug a trench two feet deep, six feet wide, and three hundred feet long near the Alsop house. A gray, overcast sky provided a somber setting. Burial details laid the bodies, still clad in new uniforms, in the ditch, covered the forms with blankets, and shoveled dirt over them. "I never saw such a line of dead men lying side by side in one grave before or since," a soldier in the 86th New York reminisced. "The sight was the most horrifying I had yet seen in our three years at the front." Major House of the 1st Maine was heartbroken. "Until now we had actually known nothing of the anguish we were to experience when we gave to our own comrades the rude burial in the long trench upon the battlefield," he wrote later. "We could only cover their faces tenderly and faithfully mark, as best we could, their names, regiment, and company at their heads." [63]

At 7:00 A.M. Gibbon's troops assembled to witness an execution, the army's first during an active campaign. Gibbon had a compulsive need for orderliness—"he is quite a fancy fellow and everything around him must be nice and clean," an aide observed—and deserters and stragglers set his teeth on edge. He tackled this "growing evil," as he called it, by recommending that patrols round up stragglers and shoot them without court-martial. First, one straggler in a hundred would be shot. If that was not enough, he urged that the percentage be increased. Meade rejected Gibbon's draconian proposal but encouraged his generals to bring deserters to trial immediately "that no time may be lost in inflicting summary punishment for this disgraceful crime." Gibbon philosophically accepted Meade's measure as "better than nothing" and two days later issued his own stern injunction. He would try stragglers before shooting them. It would suffice for conviction that a man was escorted back under guard after battle and could show no authority for his absence. Trials were to be "of the most summary character," he added, and no record of testimony need be preserved. Most important, courts were to impose "in every clear case the penalty of death, in order to save life and maintain the efficiency of the army." [64]

Gibbon made an example of young John D. Starbird of the 19th Massachusetts. Starbird's transgressions were flagrant. After enlisting, he had deserted and signed up with another regiment to collect a bounty. He had been apprehended and convicted, but his mother had saved him by appealing to President Lincoln and obtaining a pardon. Starbird, however, proved incorrigible. He had deserted under fire on May 7 in the Wilderness, had managed to talk his superiors into giving him yet another chance, then had run away once more on May 10 at Spotsylvania Court House, when his brigade was going into action. He was tried and convicted on May 19 and scheduled for execution the next day.[65]

Early on May 20 the adjutant of the 19th Massachusetts solicited officers to head the firing squad. He collared Captain John G. B. Adams, but Adams talked his way out of the assignment and persuaded a Captain Mumford to take his place. At 7:00 A.M. Mumford assembled a detail of eight men. According to custom, he loaded seven weapons with live ammunition and put a blank shot in the eighth. Starbird walked to the edge of a grave and sat blindfolded on his coffin. A witness thought that his calm behavior while facing death belied his conviction for cowardice. "Fire!" Mumford shouted. "Oh, my poor mother," Starbird cried as six bullets struck near his heart, and one hit his leg. He toppled backward into the grave, killed instantly. An onlooker expressed relief that the execution had involved none of the hitches "which are usual in those terrible affairs." Most soldiers took the incident in stride. "It is a solemn scene but cannot have much pity for him," a witness decided. Another considered the punishment "severe, but just." The regimental historian reported that the shooting miraculously improved morale. "Men who had straggled and kept out of battle now were in the ranks, and the result to our corps alone was as good as if we had been re-enforced by a full regiment." [66]

Grant usually rose early, but he made an exception on May 20 and slept until the sun was up. "Bill! Ho, Bill! What time is it?" he called to his servant, an escaped slave who had served as his orderly since early in the war. Within minutes the general appeared fully attired at his mess table, prompting the aide Porter to remark that he could dress "as quick as a lightning-change actor in a variety theater." Smoking in front of his tent after breakfast, Grant took interest in a passing group of men and horses from Battery A, 1st Rhode Island Light Artillery. An accomplished horseman, Grant strolled over to inspect the animals. Why, he asked, did some of them seem so fit? A lieutenant tilted his head toward the artillerist Thomas Aldrich and explained, "He gets punished more than any other man in the battery for stealing grain for them." Grant smiled, gave a nod that Aldrich took as a signal of approval, and remarked that Aldrich had the finest horses he had seen in the army. Aldrich returned to his post convinced that Grant was "a good judge of horses as well as a good general." [67]

Grant's objective on May 20 was to resume the operation that Ewell had disrupted. After confirming that Ewell had left, he began moving his jumbled units into position. Midmorning, Birney and Tyler started for Anderson's Mill to join the rest of Hancock's corps for its march southeast. Passing where the 1st Maine Heavy Artillery had fought, the veterans stopped to scavenge uniforms from corpses. To fill the gap created by Birney's and Tyler's withdrawal, Meade shifted Russell's division and Wheaton's brigade, both of the 6th Corps, to the Harris farm. Warren shuttled the Maryland Brigade to the Beverly house, leaving Crawford and Kitching to hold the 5th Corps's works next to Russell. Cutler and Griffin occupied the rest of the 5th Corps's line, Wright's corps manned the works to Massaponax Church Road, and Burnside's corps continued the formation south. By noon Grant had completed his deployments.[68]

The sight of soldiers opening letters and luxuriating under the spring sky reminded a Federal of "an out-of-door reading expanse, rather than a vast army under fire from a vigilant foe, though the latter also appeared to be quite good natured, and the bands of both armies made the air resound with music." Warren's soldiers picked the Harris and Alsop fields clean. "One man's loss is another's gain," a soldier philosophically observed. "I realized what stepping into dead men's shoes really meant when I found a pair to replace my own, which were nearly worn out, giving the despoiled wearer a burial in exchange." Ruminated a New Yorker: "Is there a greater anomaly in the world than this matter of fighting between man and man?" A soldier from Michigan voiced the prevailing sentiment. "I am tired and sick of this inhuman butchery," he announced. "The minds of the people [at home] cannot begin to draw the scenes that we have to look at every day. I have looked at pictures in magazines and thought it was horrid but when you come to look at the reality the artist's pencil fails." This was a hard campaign, concluded Colonel McAllister, "putting in the shade all others." [69]

Grant worked to establish a new supply line to facilitate his shift toward the North Anna River. The Belle Plain route had never functioned adequately, as evidenced by wounded soldiers and prisoners spilling into the streets of Fredericksburg. Work was under way on the rail spur from Aquia Creek, but the line's completion was still a few days off. As soon as the armies started south, the existing supply system would become obsolete. Grant had settled on Port Royal, fifteen miles south of Fredericksburg on the Rappahannock River, as his new supply center. To expedite the shift, he directed Halleck to occupy the river from Chesapeake Bay to Fredericksburg. By evening on May 20, Union gunboats controlled the Rappahannock, and instructions went out to General Abercrombie to evacuate Fredericksburg when Hancock reached the Richmond, Fredericksburg, and Potomac Railroad on his maneuver around Lee.[70]

Tension at Union headquarters heightened toward evening. Soon, Hancock would begin a daring march to entice Lee from his earthworks. After dark, Barlow, followed by Gibbon, was to proceed east from Anderson's Mill along Massaponax Church Road. Tyler was to shift from the army's right flank and march cross-country by way of a farm road, spilling onto Massaponax Church Road behind Gibbon, and Birney was to bring up the 2nd Corps's rear. Ambulances and wagons carrying ten extra rounds of ammunition per man and entrenching tools were to trail each division. "It is of the first importance that the command be kept compact and in hand," Hancock cautioned his generals. "All stragglers will be likely to fall into the hands of the enemy."[71]

Two miles into its march, the 2nd Corps would reach Massaponax Church and pick up a cavalry force headed by Alfred Torbert. Recently returned from sick leave, Torbert had been put in charge of some 1,900 horsemen drawn from the 5th New York, the 1st, 13th, and 16th Pennsylvania, and the 1st Massachusetts cavalry regiments, accompanied by four guns from Lieutenant Frank S. French's 1st United States, Batteries E and G. For a day, at least, Hancock and Torbert would be on their own, following the Mattaponi's northern bank. Hancock initially intended to destroy bridges along the way to discourage pursuit, but Meade advised him to leave the spans intact, as wrecking them would disrupt his communication with the rest of the army.[72]

Late in the day, Meade sent Warren his marching orders. If all went well, the 5th Corps was to proceed to Massaponax Church at 10:00 A.M. on May 21, then turn south along Telegraph Road. If Lee sent a force against Hancock, Warren was to attack. If Lee ignored the bait, Warren was to secure Telegraph Road for a general advance toward the North Anna River. Once Hancock and Warren were under way, Wright's corps would constitute the right wing of the force left behind, and Burnside's the left. To bolster this shortened formation, Wright was to retire a quarter mile east, and Burnside was to extend south to the Quesenberry farm, a mile above the Po. Both generals were to press close to the Confederate earthworks and look for indications that the rebels were responding to Hancock's and Warren's departure.[73]

Although Grant kept the details of the maneuver to himself and his generals, soldiers could tell that a movement was imminent. After dinner, Private Frank Wilkeson of the 11th New York Light Artillery strolled over to a nearby infantry regiment. Most of the men were sleeping. A few, however, were earnestly studying a map of Virginia, and Wilkeson sat and scrutinized it with them in an attempt to divine the army's likely route. They correctly concluded that Grant meant to maneuver Hancock around Lee's right flank. "Not a man in the group I was with believed that the movement would be successful," Wilkeson remembered. "But whether the movement would be successful or not, it was the only thing to be done, unless it were to return to the camps north of the Rapidan." The soldiers were unanimous on one point. "Every intelligent enlisted man in the Army of the Potomac knew that we could not wrest the Confederate intrenchments at Spotsylvania from Lee's veteran infantry."[74]

"Everything quiet," the Confederate mapmaker Jedediah Hotchkiss assured his diary on May 20. "Not a cannon fired and nary a musket." For Lee the day had involved a high-stakes juggling act where a single misstep threatened disaster. It was clear that Grant was girding for a major offensive, although precisely where and how was still not evident. And Sheridan was moving again, apparently toward Hanover Junction. Lee could spare no troops to protect the vital rail intersection. Fitzhugh Lee, however, was hurrying toward the junction, as was Breckinridge, and Beauregard had finally relinquished four brigades from Richmond. Lee's task on May 20 was to coordinate these far-flung military elements to deflect Sheridan while at the same time retaining flexibility to react to Grant's potential moves.[75]

For several days, Beauregard had been advocating a strategy starkly at odds with Lee's ideas. Lee's overriding concern was to keep Grant from pinning him against Richmond, where he feared he would forfeit his ability to maneuver. Beauregard, on the other hand, wanted to mass his and Lee's forces near the Confederate capital. "Without such concentration nothing can be effected, and the picture presented is one of ultimate starvation," the Louisianian stressed. On May 14—two days before the Drewry's Bluff battle—Beauregard argued that Lee should retire to the Chickahominy River and reinforce Beauregard, who would defeat Butler, and then join Lee against Grant. On May 18, after bottling Butler at Bermuda Hundred, Beauregard reiterated his concern that the armies were "too far apart to secure success."

Again he urged that Lee retire to the Chickahominy, drawing Grant after him. This time, with Butler quiescent, Beauregard suggested that he and Lee first cooperate to defeat Grant, then destroy Butler at their leisure.[76]

Beauregard was rightly concerned that the Confederates were squandering their advantage of interior lines. Rather than waging disparate holding actions against separate Union armies, the southerners would do better to combine their forces and defeat the Federal armies piecemeal. But Beauregard's suggestion fell on deaf ears. Bringing Lee back to Richmond, President Davis's military adviser Bragg objected, would require abandoning the Virginia Central Railroad and the Shenandoah Valley, dangerously exposing the Army of Northern Virginia as it retreated. Davis deferred to Lee's judgment. "How far the morale of your army would be affected by a retrograde movement no one can judge as well as yourself," he assured the general. "It would certainly encourage the enemy," he continued, and promised to "leave the matter to your decision."[77]

Reassured by the president's confidence, Lee hewed to his goal of keeping Grant as far as possible from Richmond. Grant's intentions, however, still eluded him. "The enemy has continued quiet today," Lee advised the Confederate war secretary on May 20, observing that Grant was "taking ground toward our right and intrenching, but whether for attack or defense is not apparent." By evening, Lee had settled on a working hypothesis. Scouts reported three Union gunboats at Port Royal, suggesting that Grant meant to relocate his supply depot there. And Torbert's horsemen seemed unusually determined to clear Chambliss from Telegraph Road below Massaponax Church. Late on May 18, Torbert had sent Major Forsyth's cavalry on a raid to Guinea Station. The raiders had burned the station and cut the rail line. This, along with the southward shift of Grant's forces, seemed to signal a Union movement along Telegraph Road.[78]

Lee identified Stanard's Mill as the ideal place to block Grant's progress. The 1st Confederate Engineers and Chambliss's troopers had already fortified bluffs overlooking the Po, and the road from Traveler's Rest to Mud Tavern afforded the Army of Northern Virginia ready access to the position. By Lee's reckoning, an entrenched line at Stanard's Mill would be even stronger than the current one at Spotsylvania Court House. Stanard's Mill seemed the logical place for the next big battle, and Lee set about preparing to fight there.

Circumstances dictated the details of Lee's deployment. Grant's army faced Anderson and Early, but Ewell's front was clear, freeing his 2nd Corps to lead the shift south to block Grant's anticipated movement. Ewell, Lee directed, was to start south at daybreak on May 21, pass behind Hill and Anderson, cross the Po, and deploy on the right of the Confederate army, reaching east to Mud Tavern. The 2nd Corps would control the high ridge between the Po and Matta rivers, firmly athwart Telegraph Road and Grant's prospective path. If Grant tried to drive south—the eventuality that Lee considered likely—he would run directly into Ewell, entrenched and ready to receive him at Mud Tavern. If Grant then pulled troops from Spotsylvania Court House and fed them into the fight against Ewell, the Confederates could counter by drawing troops from Spotsylvania Court House as well. Lee recognized that Grant might take a different route, or that he might beat Ewell to Mud Tavern, so he hedged his bets. His contingency plan was to fall back to the North Anna River, or even farther back to the South Anna. That evening, he summoned his chief engineer, Martin Smith, to prepare for that eventuality. "Lee thinks of retiring behind South Anna," the engineer wrote in his diary after the conference, "and wishes routes for columns to move on designated and lines of battle indicated on way." [79]

Sheridan complicated Lee's plans. On May 17 Grant had directed the Army of the Potomac's cavalry to return "as soon as possible." That night, Sheridan had started back. Fitzhugh Lee had discovered the movement right away, but his command was too small to engage Sheridan in battle. Sheridan posed a serious threat. If he captured Hanover Junction, he could cut off the Army of Northern Virginia's supplies and block its avenue of retreat. Lee instructed his nephew to stay between Sheridan and the railroads, "falling back if necessary and strengthening the threatened section." [80]

Sheridan's path ran east of Richmond, then curved north. His first obstacle was the Chickahominy River. He intended to cross at Jones's Bridge—sometimes called Forge Bridge—but Confederates had destroyed the span. Guarded by the 1st Maine Cavalry, Sheridan's engineers managed to construct a serviceable bridge by sunrise on May 18, in time for Sheridan's lead troops to cross. Mud slowed Sheridan's progress. By evening, his lead division under Gregg had advanced only five miles past Jones's Bridge to Baltimore Cross Roads. Wilson, bringing up the column's rear, did not catch up until May 19. Then Sheridan's scouts discovered that rain had swollen the Pamunkey River, barring the way north. Fitzhugh Lee moved parallel to Sheridan several miles to the west, keeping pace with Sheridan's advance. The evening of May 18 saw the Confederate cavalry camped near Mechanicsville. The next day, as Sheridan concentrated around Baltimore Cross Roads, Lee inched north along the Virginia Central Railroad to Atlee's Station, stopping that night at Timberlake's Store, skirmishers prowling east toward Old Church and Old Cold Harbor. Sheridan, Lee surmised, would probably continue his advance "up the Pamunkey and strike in about Hanover Court House, or [Hanover] Junction." [81]

Sheridan impatiently waited for the Pamunkey to subside, fearful that the Confederates might trap him below the river. As a diversion, he decided to split his force into three parts. Early on May 20, he would ride with Gibbs's and Devin's brigades of Merritt's division to White House, the Pamunkey's highest navigable point and coincidentally the site of Rooney Lee's home, where they could obtain provisions from Fortress Monroe and arrange for a way to cross. Gregg meanwhile was to lead his and Wilson's divisions west to Old Cold Harbor and "engage the attention of the enemy, or attack him, if in your judgment it can be done to advantage." A third force, under Custer, was to ride northwest to Hanover Court House and damage the Virginia Central Railway as severely as possible. [82]

Early on May 20 Gregg and Wilson proceeded to Old Cold Harbor, where they encountered Fitzhugh Lee's skirmishers. The 8th and 16th Pennsylvania Cavalry pushed the Confederates to Gaines's Mill but halted when the rebels threw up fence rail barricades. Lee pumped reinforcements into the fray, and both sides settled down to a lively sparring match. Understanding that he was to avoid a major battle, Gregg left the fighting to skirmishers, encamping the main body of his division at Cold Harbor while Wilson drew up at the nearby Tyler farm. The young general lounged at the Tyler place, nibbling strawberries and cream and catching up on his reading. His men "vigorously and successfully" plundered nearby plantations. [83]

While Gregg and Wilson kept Fitzhugh Lee occupied, Custer pressed northwest along the Pamunkey's southern bank to Hanover Court House. There his men burned two trestles over Hanover Creek, tore up a mile of Virginia Central track, and raided a station. Near dark, Fitzhugh Lee learned of Custer's foray. Leaving his three North Carolina regiments to stave off Gregg and Wilson at Gaines's Mill, he started after Custer with the remainder of his command. He had eight miles to cover and did not reach the smoldering trestles until dark. Halting Lomax's brigade at Peake's Station, south of Hanover Court House, he continued on with Wickham's brigade. Uncertain of the size of the approaching Confederate force, Custer declined battle and withdrew downriver to Hanovertown. Fitzhugh Lee correctly interpreted Gregg's and Custer's twin attacks as diversions to occupy him while Sheridan's main body crossed the Pamunkey farther east. He was powerless to take on Sheridan, but he saw an opportunity to catch Custer. Leaving Lomax at Peake's Station, he posted Wickham near Hanover Court House, poised to sweep into Custer's rear if he returned to complete his destructive work. That evening Lee received reinforcements. Colonel John Dunovant's 5th South Carolina Cavalry, the first of several regiments commanded by Brigadier General Matthew C. Butler, rode into Peake's Station.[84]

At Spotsylvania Court House, General Lee could breathe easier. Sheridan was passing east of Hanover Junction, Fitzhugh Lee had Custer well in hand, and reinforcements were on the way. Pausing only a day after defeating Sigel at New Market, Breckinridge had marched to Staunton and loaded his little army onto flatcars pulled by the engine "General Stuart." Chugging east on the Virginia Central, the train reached Hanover Junction on May 20. Breckinridge incorporated into his command Colonel Bradley T. Johnson's 2nd Maryland, which had been holding the junction since May 5. Lee could consider Hanover Junction safe.[85]

Lee was also cheered to learn that four brigades were on their way from Richmond. Robert Hoke's brigade, commanded by Lieutenant Colonel William G. Lewis; Brigadier General Seth M. Barton's brigade; and part of James L. Kemper's brigade, commanded by Colonel William R. Terry, were already in transit. According to Davis's count, they numbered 3,377 men. More troops—the rest of Kemper's brigade and part of Brigadier General Montgomery D. Corse's brigade, another 1,600 men—were slated to leave Richmond that evening. Still more soldiers, Davis assured Lee, were expected from the south, and he would send them as soon as they arrived.[86]

By noon on May 20 Hoke's and Barton's brigades were jolting north on the Richmond, Fredericksburg, and Potomac Railroad. Since Torbert's cavalry had burned Guinea Station on May 18, Milford Station was the depot most convenient to the Army of Northern Virginia. The troops disembarked there and started a twenty-mile march to Spotsylvania Court House. "The men were all in very low spirits" at leaving the relative safety of the capital, a soldier recorded, and did not "want to go to Lee's army." Not so with Kemper's brigade. Virginians all, Kemper's men had returned home from North Carolina in time to fight at Drewry's Bluff. Commanded by Colonel Terry while Kemper recuperated from a Gettysburg wound, the soldiers strutted through Richmond proudly displaying captured battle flags, and then assembled below the equestrian statue of George Washington at Capitol Square to be regaled by dignitaries. "I have no doubt that if Washington was there in sprit, he looked on approvingly," a soldier commented. The 1st Virginia, which had been recruited from Richmond, quietly dissolved as soldiers took informal leaves to visit their families.[87]

Around 2:00 P.M. the 1st Virginia, now down to about 50 men, boarded a train with Companies A, B, C, E, and K of the 11th Virginia, most of the 7th Virginia, and an artillery company from Georgia. Altogether the force numbered between 450 and 500 men and was placed under the senior officer on the train, the 1st Virginia's Major George F. Norton. Corse's brigade and the rest of Kemper's brigade—the 24th Virginia and the remaining portions of the 1st and 11th Virginia—waited for a train later in the day. Chugging north, Norton's train crossed the North Anna River, steamed through Chesterfield and Penola Stations, and finally—seven hours after the journey began—arrived at Milford Station, a rundown aggregation containing a depot, an engine house, and a handful of dwellings and outbuildings. Norton's soldiers scampered off the flatcars, marched over the nearby Mattaponi River, and camped for the night. "After our strenuous ordeal for several weeks, we gladly dropped on the ground and were soon fast asleep, hardly caring what the morning might bring," recollected Marion Seay of the 11th Virginia.[88]

Twenty-five miles north, Hancock's thousands filed from their camps at Anderson's Mill to start a long swing around Lee's army. Fate had placed Norton's men directly in their path.

Warren's 5th Corps headquarters at the Beverly house, May 19, 1864

Library of Congress

The twin docks at Belle Plain on Potomac Creek, Grant's supply depot
Library of Congress

Soldiers from the 1st Massachusetts Heavy Artillery preparing to bury a dead
Confederate at Mrs. Alsop's house on May 20, 1864

Library of Congress

One of Ewell's soldiers killed during the fighting at Harris Farm, near the Alsop
house on May 20, 1864
Library of Congress

Wounded soldiers from the Union 6th Corps at Fredericksburg, May 20, 1864
Library of Congress

Captured Confederates from Lee's army in the Punch Bowl at Belle Plain, May 16 or 17, 1864
Library of Congress

Grant and Meade pausing at Massaponax Church on May 21, 1864. Grant is sitting in front of two large trees with his legs crossed; Assistant Secretary of War Dana is in civilian clothes on Grant's left; Grant's aide Brigadier General John A. Rawlins is reading a newspaper next to Dana; and Meade is sitting on an adjacent pew to Grant's right, wearing a turned-down slouch hat.

Library of Congress

Union engineers preparing the crossing for the Union 5th Corps at Jericho Mills on the afternoon of May 23, 1864
Library of Congress

Chesterfield Bridge photographed on May 25, 1864, from the North Anna's south bank, with Henagan's redoubt visible in the distance at the center of the image
Library of Congress

View from near Henagan's redoubt looking south on May 25, after Hancock's men had captured the fort and "reversed" the earthworks
Library of Congress

Smoldering ruins of the Richmond, Fredericksburg, and Potomac Railroad bridge over the North Anna on May 25, 1864
Library of Congress

Union pioneers constructing two pontoon bridges across the North Anna near the destroyed railroad bridge on May 24, 1864; drawing by Alfred R. Waugh

Library of Congress

Union soldiers bathing in the North Anna during a lull in the fighting
Library of Congress

VII

MAY 21

Grant Swings South and Lee Counters

"The enemy is apparently again changing his base."

HANCOCK'S 2ND CORPS, 20,000 strong, began its march around Lee at ten o'clock on the night of May 20, an hour ahead of schedule. The race for the North Anna River was on, and the Federals had a comfortable head start. If the movement progressed as Grant expected, Lee would set off after Hancock during the morning with all or part of his army. Grant intended to respond by hurling Warren south on Telegraph Road to catch Lee's assault column in motion. The plan was vastly more complicated than anything the Army of the Potomac had attempted thus far in the campaign, and it was fraught with risks. There was a serious possibility that Confederates might cut Hancock off and attack him before Grant could bring up reinforcements. Grant, however, was impatient to maintain the initiative and attack Lee outside his entrenchments. A few harrowing hours seemed a tolerable price to pay for a chance to fight Lee in the open.

The 148th Pennsylvania of Colonel Brooke's brigade, Barlow's division, led the procession from the 2nd Corps's campsite at Anderson's Mill. The troops vigorously debated their destination. Some thought they were marching to Port Royal to set up a supply depot. Others were certain they were on their way to join Butler. A few optimistic souls concluded that the campaign was over and that they were returning to Fredericksburg. "The men understood an important point was to be sought, and they were full of good cheer," a soldier noted as he and his compatriots trod east along Massaponax Church Road. "Never did they march with so little complaining and so little straggling." Another man, however, remembered that troops around him "growled and marched, and grumbled and enjoyed life right savagely." Fifty rounds of ammunition and five days' rations weighed more than some soldiers were willing to carry. They stuffed their cartridge boxes full of ammunition and discarded the excess rounds, reasoning that they could scavenge bullets from dead men.[1]

A three-mile march from Anderson's Mill brought Barlow to Massaponax Church, where he was to rendezvous with Torbert's makeshift cavalry brigade, some two thousand troopers cobbled together from the mounted regiments around Spotsylvania Court House. It was 12:30 A.M. To Hancock's consternation, Torbert's horsemen had not yet saddled their mounts and were lounging about waiting for rations. Since the 2nd Corps could not move until Torbert was ready, Hancock halted at the church and marked time by massing his divisions as they arrived. Precious minutes ticked by as Gibbon's division pulled up, then Tyler's, then Birney's. The movement was falling dangerously behind schedule, and Hancock was getting worried. He wanted to cover as much ground as possible before daylight, when the Confederates were certain to discover his departure from the Spotsylvania line.[2]

Not until 2:00 A.M. did Torbert's troopers start south, the 2nd Corps marching behind. Striking out on Guinea Station Road, the procession jostled left. The country byway hugged the backbone of a ridge slanting gently southward to the Ni. "It was a beautiful moonlit night," a soldier recollected, "and the tedium of a night march when sleep was much needed was somewhat relieved as we reflected that during the day the heat and dust would have been almost intolerable." Officers had instructed their men to march quietly and remain alert for Confederate scouts. Woods pressed close along the roadside, creating the illusion that the Union column was gliding through a moonlit tunnel of trees. A novice in Tyler's division made the heartening discovery that he could doze while walking. "Ask any old soldier," he later explained. "One would hardly get into a nice nap before there would be a halt away up at the head of the column and several thousand men would go bumping into each other." At one juncture, a pack mule broke loose and clattered along the file, kettles and equipage banging on its back. Another time, shots rang out near the column. "Lie down! Lie down!" an insistent voice whispered. The soldiers complied, and skirmishers scurried into the woods to investigate. "It was an impressive sight that I saw above me," Private Wilkeson noticed as he crouched beside the road, peering into the shadows. "Two lines of veteran infantry, with rifles almost aimed, with set faces and blazing eyes, gazing intently into the darkness of a dense forest in search of an unseen enemy whom we thought was lurking there." The quiet was so complete that soldiers could hear their hearts beat. After an interminable wait, the scouting party returned. "There is nothing there. Don't fire! Don't fire! We are coming back!" skirmishers shouted as they emerged from the thickets. It had been a false alarm.[3]

At 4:00 A.M. Torbert's horsemen approached Guinea Station. The charred ruins of the railway depot occupied a strategic intersection in the broad valley where the Ni and Po Rivers merged. Approaching from the west along high ground above the Ni was the route from Massaponax Church, now packed with Torbert's and Hancock's men. Another major road meandered southwest from Guinea Station, crossed the Mattaponi half a mile away at Guinea Bridge, climbed a ridge to Hugh Catlett's farm, and continued on to Telegraph Road at Mud Tavern, two miles west of the Catlett place and three and a half miles below Massaponax Church. Another road forked south from the Catlett farm past Samuel Schooler's fine brick mansion and Edgehill Academy, crossed the Matta River on a rickety bridge, and entered a main east-west road at the Welch farm, by a country store called Madison's Ordinary. The route from Welch's ran east to New Bethel Church and Bowling Green, and west to Telegraph Road, which it struck at Nancy Wright's Corner, almost three miles below Mud Tavern. The road network at Guinea Station also reached north toward Fredericksburg and southeast toward Bowling Green. The latter town, eight miles southeast of the station, was Hancock's immediate goal.[4]

Two bridges were especially important to Hancock. Guinea Bridge, a rough-hewn wooden span over the Mattaponi, lay along the direct route from Guinea Station to Telegraph Road via the Catlett farm. Two miles downriver from Guinea Bridge was Downer's Bridge, the next crossing of the Mattaponi. Here a road hooked south to New Bethel Church, intersecting the road from Nancy Wright's Corner to Bowling Green. Confederates attacking across either bridge could maul Hancock's column as it followed the railroad and ancillary roadways toward Bowling Green. And both bridges were to serve as Hancock's potential link with Warren, who was slated to advance down Telegraph Road during the morning. Torbert's instructions were to secure the crossings in advance of Hancock's infantry and to hold them.

The Confederates also recognized the importance of the two bridges. Hugh Catlett's farm, Laurel Springs, occupied the crest of a ridge overlooking the Mattaponi River and Guinea Bridge. The rebels had built a signal station there, and a contingent from the 9th Virginia Cavalry under Lieutenant John T. Stewart was posted in bottomland near Guinea Bridge, supported by a mock cannon fashioned from a stovepipe and a pair of cart wheels. More cavalrymen under Lieutenant George W. Beale, also from the 9th Virginia Cavalry, were bivouacked near Guinea Station, horses saddled and ready for action. Beale had scattered pickets at intervals along the road to Massaponax Church to fire warning shots if Federals approached.[5]

Toward dawn one of Beale's pickets discharged a warning shot. Beale ordered his men into their saddles and hurried them west on the road to Massaponax Church, hoping to ambush the enemy at a small creek. The Confederates were prying up boards from a bridge over the creek when clanking sabers announced Torbert's approach. Beale's soldiers hid behind trees as shadowy forms of Union horsemen bobbed up the road. When the Federals paused to inspect the damaged bridge, Beale signaled his soldiers to open fire. Muzzle flashes lit the woods, men shouted, horses whinnied, and bullets spattered through the trees. In the darkness, no Federals were hit, and Torbert's officers quickly restored order. Beale's men mounted and rode frantically back toward Guinea Station, stopping at a hedgerow that offered a promising place for another ambush. They dismounted and again deployed along the roadside.[6]

Sobered by the ambush at the milldam, Torbert's lead regiment—Hammond's 5th New York Cavalry—spread flankers along both sides of the road in advance of the column. Beale's scouts discovered Hammond's flanking force in time to warn the main body, and Beale ordered his men to fall back once again. They retired through Guinea Station and continued south to Downer's Bridge, where they slipped into hiding west of the Mattaponi, waiting for the Federals to pass.

Lieutenant Stewart's small Confederate force looked on from its fastness west of Guinea Bridge as Torbert's horsemen cantered into Guinea Station. The first blush of dawn was appearing in the east.

Premonitions of death were commonplace, and the dire predictions of Sergeant Samuel W. Sortore of Company E, 5th New York Cavalry, had aroused no undue attention. In December 1863, Sortore had asked to be transferred from his assignment with the ambulance corps because he considered it cowardly for an able-bodied man not to fight. "I know I shall be killed," a friend recalled him saying, "but I am going back to my company." On May 21, before leaving Massaponax Church, Sortore told a messmate that he expected to die that morning and gave the man his valuables. As the head of the mounted column passed into Guinea Station, an officer called out, "Send a platoon to charge the bridge." Sortore turned to Captain F. S. Dickinson and said, "That means me. I am first on the detail. I shall be killed, but I'll go." Boldly riding toward Guinea Bridge at the head of his men, Sortore was shot from his horse, becoming the first casualty of the operation. Uncertain of the strength of the opposing Confederates, Torbert decided against risking a pitched battle and ordered Hammond to halt at the bridge.

Stewart's Confederates watched the New Yorkers bury Sortore under a swamp willow. After a few brief remarks and a prayer, Hammond led his troopers back to the station. A southerner rejoiced that the Federals had been "handsomely repulsed."[7]

Hancock's column filed into the fields around Guinea Station. "When light came, from our position on the hills overlooking the river, Guinea's, and the country beyond, dense columns of bluecoats could be seen passing down the road to Bowling Green," a Confederate noted. Hancock ratified Torbert's decision to leave Guinea Bridge to the rebels and instructed his division commanders to post guards on the road to the bridge until their commands had passed. His mission was to reach Bowling Green, not to scrabble over the Mattaponi River crossings. During the brief halt, Hancock's soldiers investigated the Chandler family's plantation adjacent to the depot. Word passed through the ranks that Stonewall Jackson had died there a year ago. "Everybody seemed to agree that we were having an easier time because Jackson was dead," an officer from Maine remembered.[8]

Torbert followed the rail line south. After half an hour—the sun was now fully up—he reached Downer's Bridge. Beale's men had removed planks from the span and were waiting on the far bank of the Mattaponi. Elements from the 5th New York Cavalry advanced dismounted, but Confederate musketry drove them back in "spirited skirmishing." Realizing that he could not dislodge Beale by frontal assault, Hammond dispatched a party to cross upriver. Beale failed to discover Hammond's stratagem until Union soldiers materialized in his rear. "There was some lively running to get to our horses," Beale admitted. His men sped off at a gallop, dodging a volley from Hammond's flankers, who almost cut off their retreat route. Miraculously, Beale's sole casualty was a horse.[9]

Leaving Companies A and B at Downer's Bridge under Captain Theodore A. Boyce to protect the flank of Hancock's column, Hammond led his regiment back to the main road. Bowling Green lay but a few miles ahead.[10]

Confederates learned of Hancock's departure not long after the 2nd Corps had left Anderson's Mill. Sometime around 1:00 A.M. on May 21—Hancock had reached Massaponax Church and was waiting impatiently for Torbert to get under way—Lee received word that Union troops were streaming east. His response was immediate. Anticipating that Grant might attempt to shift south along Telegraph Road, he had already instructed Ewell to prepare to rush the Confederate 2nd Corps to Mud Tavern to block that route. It seemed to Lee that Hancock was initiating the expected movement, and he directed Ewell to begin his march right away. By 4:00 A.M. the Confederate 2nd Corps had left its trenches and was marching south behind Early's and Anderson's earthworks. Its route led across the Po River at Snell's Bridge, continued on to Traveler's Rest, and then cut east to Mud Tavern.[11]

Union pickets detected Ewell's deployment. At 1:30 A.M. an outpost of Griffin's 5th Corps division heard Confederate drums beating reveille. Half an hour later 6th Corps pickets heard bugles. At 3:00 A.M. rebel drums started up again, and pickets in front of Ricketts's division detected sounds of artillery, wagons, and cattle moving south. Meade did nothing to investigate the commotion until dawn. By then, activity behind Lee's lines had set pulses racing at Union headquarters. "Reports that the enemy also is in motion," Lyman scrawled in his notebook. Shortly after 5:00 A.M. Meade directed Warren and Wright to advance pickets to determine whether Confederates still occupied the earthworks in front of Spotsylvania Court House. Neither general favored the exercise, as they could see the works brimming with rebels. At 6:00 A.M. a signal officer informed headquarters that the air appeared "very smoky," presumably from Confederate cooking fires, and that he saw no change in the enemy's guns or troops. Griffin bridled at sacrificing pickets to confirm an obvious point. "The enemy is in force in my front, his artillery in plain sight," he wrote caustically to Warren. "Before I advance my pickets, I desire this fact to be known." Lest Warren miss the point, Griffin added: "A stronger force than my picket line is visible." Warren forwarded Griffin's observation to headquarters, and the note persuaded Meade to modify his order. "The object of advancing your pickets is to ascertain as far as such an operation will admit the force and position of the enemy," the army commander lectured Warren. "If you are satisfied the enemy is in as full force as he was yesterday, and are positive of this without advancing your pickets, they need not be advanced, although no objection is seen to their being pushed out even under the above condition." Warren and Wright left their pickets in place, instructing them to "fire away occasionally at the enemy's, and ascertain all they can and report." [12]

The movements behind Lee's lines troubled Grant. The southerners were reacting quicker than he had expected. If the Confederates advanced beyond Telegraph Road before Warren could get under way, Hancock might find himself facing more rebels than he could handle, and Union reinforcements would be too far away to help him. Grant found comfort in Warren's and Wright's assurances that the Army of Northern Virginia was still dug in at Spotsylvania Court House. Reports from Hancock also lent encouragement. At 7:30 A.M. a dispatch, written at 4:30 A.M., arrived from the Union 2nd Corps's commander. His column had advanced a mile and a half beyond Guinea Station. A sprinkling of rebel skirmishers—Beale's men—had fired on his troops, but otherwise the march had been uneventful.[13]

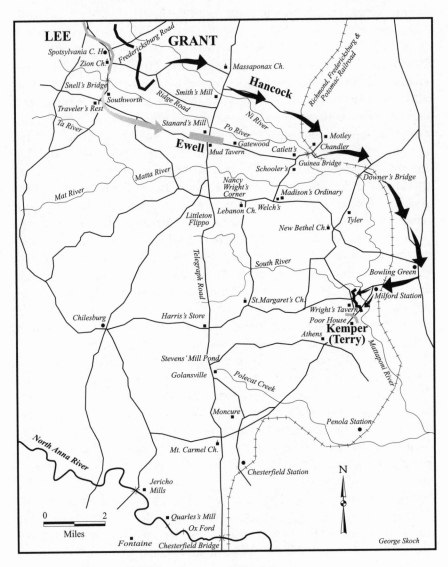

Hancock's and Ewell's deployment early on May 21

Grant, persuaded that Hancock was well away from the Confederates, decided to continue with the maneuver as planned. His next step was to set Warren in motion. In a few hours Warren was scheduled to follow Telegraph Road to the Po and deploy near Mud Tavern, maintaining communication with Burnside to his northwest and opening contact with Hancock to his east. "Everything is quiet here just now," headquarters advised Hancock. "The enemy is still in force in front of General Warren, although there are indications that he made a considerable movement to his right last night." [14]

Tension at Grant's headquarters grew as the morning advanced. With each passing moment, Hancock was moving farther from the Union army. Confederate scouts swarmed behind his column, making it difficult for couriers to get through. If Hancock got into trouble, it would take at least three hours for word to reach Grant and another five hours for Grant to send him help. Grant was certain that Lee knew about Hancock's departure, but how the Confederate leader intended to respond was a mystery. Chambliss's diligent cavalrymen had drawn an impenetrable curtain across the countryside below the Po. For all Grant could tell, Confederates might already be passing through Mud Tavern and be well on their way toward gobbling up the Union 2nd Corps. Grant smoked cigars and waited for information. He must have cursed the day that he had permitted Sheridan to ride off with most of the Union army's experienced cavalry. Jeb Stuart's absence at Gettysburg in 1863 had left Lee groping blindly until he stumbled unsuspectingly upon the enemy. Grant doubtless experienced similar frustration as he tried to gauge Lee's movements in response to Hancock's maneuver. If Warren started south too soon, he would close Grant's trap before Lee stepped into it. If he waited too long, the quarry would have passed by, and Hancock would be in serious trouble.

Watches at Union headquarters read 8:30 A.M. when another courier thundered up, reached into his pouch, and drew out a second message from Hancock. Like the earlier letter, this one was also three hours old. Confederates held Guinea Bridge, Hancock reported, referring to Stewart's men. They were too strongly entrenched for Torbert to dislodge them, so he had ordered his division commanders to block the road from the bridge until the wagons at the rear of his column had safely passed. Any Union force coming behind Hancock faced the threat of a Confederate attack across Guinea Bridge and would have to fend for itself. [15]

Hancock's latest communication gave Grant pause. It suggested that rebels were accumulating between Hancock and the Union army in numbers greater than he had expected. Perhaps Lee was on the move. Grant decided that the time had come to spring his trap. At 9:30 A.M. orders went out to Warren to prepare to march, taking care to avoid open fields around the Anderson house where Confederates might spot him. A reminder also went out to Wright. After Warren had withdrawn from the Spotsylvania line, the 6th Corps was to retire several hundred yards east to a new set of entrenchments prepared during the night. Burnside was to remain in place until further orders. By evening, if the movement transpired as planned, Wright was to march to Guinea Station, following Hancock, and Burnside was to trail Warren down Telegraph Road.[16]

Lee, unlike Grant, was receiving an uninterrupted flow of reliable information about his adversary's activities. Henry H. Sturgis of the 44th Alabama crept close enough to Hancock's troops to hear them chanting, "On to Richmond, boys, we'll be there in three days," then hurried back and reported what he thought was the movement of Grant's entire army. The Confederate signal station at the Catlett farm flashed messages every fifteen minutes. Both armies used a common system of flag signals developed before the war, enabling Hancock's signal officers to decode the rebel messages and forward them to Grant. Ironically, the commanders of both armies relied in part on the same source to monitor Hancock's progress.[17]

At 8:40 A.M. Lee summarized developments for the War Department in Richmond. Three Union gunboats had visited Port Royal two days before. Most important, Federal infantry had marched past Guinea Station during the past few hours, and cavalry was reported at Downer's Bridge. "The enemy is apparently again changing his base," Lee asserted with confidence. "He is apparently placing the Mattaponi between us, and will probably open communication with Port Royal. I am extending on the Telegraph Road, and will regulate my movements by the information of his route." [18]

Riding out to examine his line, Lee stopped by a battery and scrutinized the Federal earthworks through his field glasses. "Open your guns on the enemy's position," Lee ordered the battery's commander, hoping to determine whether Grant's men were still there. The rebel battery fired a shot, and several Union pieces fired back. Lee sat calmly astride Traveller, field glasses to his eyes. Alabama troops stationed near the battery looked on, apprehensive that the general might be killed. Finally a soldier jumped up and shouted, "Won't someone take that damn fool away from there?" Lee looked over at the man, put up his glasses, and rode away.[19]

Midmorning saw the Confederate 2nd Corps filing into formidable works along the south bank of the Po at Stanard's Mill and Mud Tavern. Ewell established headquarters at the Stanard house, north of the river and adjacent to

Telegraph Road, then shifted to the nearby Beasley house. Union scouts watched Ewell's infantrymen stride onto the ridge and reported their appearance to Grant.[20]

Lee's bold deployment of Ewell to Mud Tavern spelled the end of Grant's ambitious plan for May 21. Lee had now closed Telegraph Road to the Federals. Grant's bait—Hancock—was in place, but Ewell's strong position made it impossible for Grant to waylay whatever force Lee might send against Hancock. Ewell was handily situated to march via the Catlett farm to Guinea Station. Not only had he made it impossible for Warren to support Hancock, but he had severed Hancock from the rest of the Union army.

Flexibility was one of Grant's strengths, and that trait never served him better than on May 21. Battling Lee resembled playing chess against a master. By shoving Ewell forward to Mud Tavern, Lee had checked Grant's ability to exploit Telegraph Road. Grant was learning to expect surprises, and he reconsidered his overall scheme. He could still proceed with his initial plan, advancing Warren south along Telegraph Road and engaging Ewell in battle at the Po. In this scenario, Hancock could menace Ewell's eastern flank while Warren hit him head-on. But if Lee sent the rest of his army to Ewell's support, Mud Tavern might become another Spotsylvania Court House. Entrenched above the river, the Army of Northern Virginia could thwart the Federals once again. Grant recognized that the time had arrived to change course.

A more palatable option for Grant was to dispatch Warren to Guinea Station along the same route that Hancock had taken. This cautious approach offered clear-cut advantages. It was the most direct way to get reinforcements to Hancock, and it placed Hancock and Warren—fully half of Grant's infantry strength—well ahead of Lee on the way to the North Anna River. If Lee concentrated at Mud Tavern, he would find himself wedged between Burnside and Wright to the north and Warren and Hancock to the east. A Union turning movement might be a realistic possibility. If all else failed, Grant could still beat Lee to the North Anna and fight him there.

At 9:45 A.M., fifteen minutes before Warren was scheduled to begin his march, Grant made up his mind. Rather than aggressively taking the offensive as he had initially intended, he decided to pursue the safer alternative. Caution, born of exhaustion, scant information about the enemy's movements, and Grant's growing respect for Lee's generalship, would govern Union deployments for the rest of the day. Instead of sending Warren down Telegraph Road to face an uncertain fight against Ewell, Grant directed the 5th Corps commander to follow Hancock. "You will proceed to Guinea's

Bridge by way of Massaponax Church and Guinea's Station, instead of taking the Telegraph road from Massaponax Church," read Grant's revised order to Warren. "Report your arrival there and what you meet." Also at 9:45 A.M., headquarters alerted Hancock to the change in plans. "Hold Guinea's Bridge until the arrival of the head of Warren's column," the message advised. "He moves at 10 o'clock, and the head of his column may be there by 2 or 3 o'clock this afternoon."[21]

The directive took five hours to reach Hancock. By then the Union 2nd Corps had left Guinea Station far behind, and Confederates held Guinea Bridge. A nerve-wracking day lay ahead for the Federals.

"We started down the Telegraph Road as hard as we could."

Several miles east, ignorant of Ewell's counterthrust, Torbert and Hancock were advancing boldly toward Bowling Green, alternately along the Richmond, Fredericksburg, and Potomac Railroad and along roads parallel to the tracks. A land of plenty, very different from the bleak tableau of earthworks and corpses around Spotsylvania Court House, greeted the invaders. "The day was a warm and pleasant one, and our march, through a country as fresh and bright as any we had seen since our march into Pennsylvania the year before, was more like a picnic excursion than a trial of speed with our enemy," a Federal recollected. "Corn looked very well—some nearly a foot high," marveled Sergeant John L. Ryno of the 126th New York. Wheat fields blossomed, and prosperous houses beckoned. "It was like a garden blooming in the midst of desert places," a Federal effused. "An earthly paradise," affirmed another battle-grimed warrior. Men sang as they marched, admiring the bounty around them.[22]

Caroline County's fine houses—"stately mansions surrounded by the mud-chinked cabins of the Negroes," a northerner described the dwellings—whipped Hancock's soldiers into a frenzy of pilfering. "Our army, operating in hostile territory, was like a swarm of locusts," a Federal admitted. "Hens, geese, chickens, ducks, and turkeys made a joyful sound, which found gleeful echoes in the neglected stomachs of tired soldiers." Private Wilkeson took pity on a bedraggled woman whose children clung to her skirts while she begged the Federals not to take all of her family's food. Moved by her pleas, he paid her two dollars for a piece of sweet bacon.[23]

Slaves poured from fields, anxious to view their liberators. "It was a pleasing spectacle," a northern correspondent recollected, "and co-mingled with not a little pathos, to hear the benedictions which the aged and infirm

Negroes poured out upon our soldiers as they marched by." A gray-haired slave, his eyesight nearly gone, cried out, "I've been waiting for you. I've been waiting for you gentlemen for some time. I knew you were coming, because I heard massa and misses often talking about you." He chuckled loudly, the correspondent reported.[24]

Around 7:00 A.M. Torbert's horsemen clattered into the sleepy village of Bowling Green. This was the first real town they had seen since leaving Culpeper Court House almost three weeks before. The place had an illustrious history. A prosperous settler in 1665 had laid out a plantation and named it after his ancestral home of Bowling Green, England. His descendants had donated land for a courthouse in 1803, and the county seat that grew up around the structure took its name from the plantation. Bowling Green had been the gem of Caroline County. Tree-lined streets wound past graceful southern homes to a town center lined with stores and two hotels.

Word that Federals were coming had already reached the townspeople. Except for blacks congregating along the main street to gape at the intruders, the place seemed deserted. Torbert and his staff ate breakfast at the Bowling Green Hotel while the men rested and poked around for fresh food. As a precaution, Torbert dispatched a detachment from the 13th Pennsylvania Cavalry under Major George F. McCabe west to New Bethel Church, hoping to hook up with Captain Boyce's detachment of 5th New Yorkers at Downer's Bridge and clear the neighboring roads of rebel scouts. After an hour the main mounted column started off again, pursuing the road to Milford Station, three miles southwest on the Richmond, Fredericksburg, and Potomac Railroad.[25]

Toward 9:00 A.M.—Warren had not yet left his trenches in front of Spotsylvania Court House, twenty miles away—the van of Hancock's corps reached Bowling Green. The Yankees entered with a flourish, regimental bands blaring. Blacks lined the streets. They still refused to believe that Federal troops had arrived. "If you are Yankees, where are your horns," one of them asked. A Federal pointed to the national flag at the head of the column. "The rebs don't carry that kind of a flag," one black exclaimed. "No," agreed another. "They used to have that kind, but they don't have it any more." A soldier broke the ice by handing out scraps of clothing, and soon the blacks were scrambling for discarded wares. One "sable female," a New Jersey man recollected, pranced beside the marchers, burdened down with coats, shirts, and boots. Soldiers shouted encouragement, egged on by her infectious grin. Before long, related a Union man, Bowling Green's main street was "crowded with joyous darkies, who hailed us with delight."[26]

A Rhode Island man proclaimed Bowling Green a "quaint-looking old Virginia town [that] contained some of the sauciest rebels I had ever met." Stores were closed, and no able-bodied white men were to be seen. "Great destitution was apparent everywhere," a Michigander noted, "and the inhabitants, composed almost entirely of women and children, were poorly and thinly clad, and hungry." A Massachusetts soldier sneered at the "Secesh loafers, gray as to hair, beard and clothing, sitting on the piazza of the village hotel with their feet on the rail, expressing the hatred they felt for us." Studying the drawn faces peering back from windows and porches, a correspondent recognized that "it was no difficult matter to see that we had arrived among foes." Women ventured forth clad in mourning clothes and bragged to the intruders in unequivocal language that they were "bitterly disloyal," a New Jersey soldier recollected. "Many were the prophecies of evil bestowed upon us," another Federal confirmed. "You'll be coming back over these roads faster than you are going now!" a woman shouted. Another queried, "Are you going 'on to Richmond'?" then supplied the answer in a withering voice. "You'll all lay your bones in the ground before you get a sight of it."[27]

The Federals considered looting an acceptable way to teach Virginia's rebellious population a lesson while filling their own haversacks. Soldiers broke into stores for tobacco, "which they needed," an officer reflected, "and some other things which they did not need." When an apothecary shop proprietor hid his well bucket to prevent Federals from drawing water, the troops retaliated by gutting his store. Lieutenant Colonel Charles B. Merrill of the 17th Maine reprimanded a soldier for pilfering medicine. "I proceeded to make some very pointed remarks concerning a couple of ducks that the colonel's cook was at that very moment preparing for his palate," the soldier rejoined. Later the soldier observed philosophically: "I see no great difference between the sins of stealing medicines or ducks, but Colonel Merrill is a lawyer, and he doubtless can discriminate." Soldiers also freed two inmates from the local jail—"a gentleman of color and a representative of the poor white trash element," a Federal reported—and a handful of slaves from a slave pen. Vermonters of Company F, 1st United States Sharp Shooters, liberated several blacks whom the white inhabitants had corralled in hope of transporting them south in advance of the armies.[28]

Private Wilkeson studied the scornful stares of Bowling Green's women as they watched the hated Yankees saunter by on their way to do battle with the town's menfolk, most of whom had joined Lee's army. A girl in a calico gown caught Wilkeson's eye, and he opened her gate and asked if he could drink from her well. "She calmly looked through me and over me, and never by the slightest sign acknowledged my presence," Wilkeson reminisced.

Nonplused, he filled his canteen and drank to her health. Remarked Wilkeson: "I liked her spirit." [29]

Rebel scouts falling back before Torbert's advance streamed into Milford Station. Major Norton and the five hundred or so soldiers from Kemper's brigade who had ridden from Richmond the night before on flatcars were still there, breaking camp and preparing to march to Spotsylvania Court House and join Lee. Norton at first thought that the Yankees approaching from Bowling Green were a few cavalrymen on a raid. Unconcerned, he let his men finish their breakfasts, then deployed to meet the raiders. He posted the 1st Virginia along the track, where it took cover in depot buildings and nearby houses. Sergeant Charles T. Loehr of the 1st sequestered his company in a blacksmith shop east of the depot that gave him an unobstructed view of the Bowling Green Road. Norton kept the rest of his force—the 11th and 7th Virginia—west of the Mattaponi.[30]

Loehr climbed onto a roof for a better view of the Bowling Green Road, which wound into town along the edge of a ridge. Blue-clad horsemen were racing in his direction. Loehr had just braced his foot on a shutter to climb down when he heard a woman call from inside, "Be careful, or you will damage my shutters!" Loehr shouted back that she had better leave, as Yankees were coming. Then he jumped down and watched the Union riders stop in a grove to reconnoiter the town. Loehr took careful aim and fired, signaling his compatriots to join in. The Federals retired under a blaze of musketry and disappeared behind the hill. Shortly a squadron of horsemen appeared in their place and charged toward the depot, shooting as they came. The men of the 1st Virginia opened fire from the cover of their buildings and broke the assault. Twice more the northerners attacked, and twice more the Virginians' steady musketry kept them at bay.

More troopers from the 5th New York Cavalry and 16th Pennsylvania Cavalry pulled up, and Torbert fanned them into a semicircular formation extending beyond both sides of the road, ends thrust forward. At his command the Union line began advancing relentlessly toward the depot. Fearing that the enemy would envelop the station, Norton summoned the 11th Virginia, commanded by Captain Thomas B. Horton. By the time the outfit reached the depot, wounded Confederates lay sprawled on the platform.[31]

Pointing toward the center of Torbert's formation on a rise a half mile away, Major Norton called on the 11th Virginia to "charge the hill, and hold it at all hazards." Captain Horton formed most of his regiment around the depot buildings and dashed toward the hill at the head of companies C and E. "We were soon in the midst of a hail of bullets, but no one fell out of ranks," recalled Marion Seay, who participated in the attack. Loehr watched from the blacksmith shop as Horton's men overran Torbert's skirmishers "like a lot of grass-hoppers." In short order the Confederates had secured an ideal defensive position. The hilltop gave them an unobstructed view southwest to the station and the bridge. To the east the hill dropped off to a wooded slope. Beyond ran the Bowling Green road, teeming with Torbert's horsemen. Near the crest, at the site of a former icehouse, was a pit, and a gully four feet deep extended from the pit to form a trench facing the enemy. Horton sheltered some of his men in this natural fortification. "We felt very comfortable and as if we could whip all the cavalry in the Federal army," a Confederate remembered.[32]

Torbert gave the assignment of prying the southerners from the hilltop to Captain F. W. Hess of the 3rd Pennsylvania Cavalry, commanding a hundred-man detachment from the 1st and 16th Pennsylvania Cavalry. Advancing from the road, Hess's men opened on Horton's troops with repeating rifles, and Lieutenant French's horse artillery shelled Horton's hilltop. The Confederates hunkered low in their earthen declivity. "They kept up an incessant fire, having ammunition to spare," a Virginian recollected, "while we simply waited for targets among them, and we made nearly every shot count."[33]

As the contest heated, it finally dawned on Major Norton that he was not facing a mere detachment of cavalry raiders as he had assumed. A full brigade of mounted Federals, two thousand strong, was deploying in his front, and Hancock's entire corps was tramping up a short distance behind them. "We lay watching their squadrons advancing and dismounting, expecting every moment to see them come thundering down upon us," a soldier in the 1st Virginia wrote. Realizing that he was powerless to stop the force arrayed against him, Norton decided to withdraw west across the Mattaponi and regroup on the far side of the river. Sending a courier to alert Horton of his change in plan, Norton directed the soldiers around the depot to drop back. A contingent from the 7th Virginia maintained covering fire by the bridge while Loehr's Virginians evacuated the hamlet, some swimming across the river and others sprinting single file over the span. Two men from the 7th Virginia guarded the bridge until most of the Confederates were safely across. Then they ripped planks from the bridge floor and tossed the boards into the river to discourage pursuit.[34]

Major Norton's courier never reached Captain Horton's hilltop. Ignorant of the order to withdraw, Horton fought on until a soldier ran to him screaming, "Where is the bridge?" Glancing over his shoulder, Horton saw that his supporting elements had abandoned Milford Station and torn up the bridge. "It then dawned upon us that we had been sacrificed to save the troops across the river," a dispirited rebel realized. "Good generalship, I suppose," he sighed in resignation, "but 'tough on the frogs.'"[35]

Horton resolved to hold his isolated position. "The [Federals] had a double column reaching to the river, forming a horseshoe, and we were 'it,'" a Confederate wrote of the predicament. "Boys, you see our position," Horton candidly informed his soldiers. "There is no escape," he continued. "We will probably all be killed. But we will make them pay a big price for our lives. Be careful with your cartridges and make every shot count. If they charge us, it will soon all be over." Someone suggested trying to cut their way out, but the men protested that they would be killed as they ran across the bottom. Horton reminded his troops that their orders were to take and hold the hill. "We have taken it and will hold it as long as possible," he insisted. "It will give the brigade that much more time to save themselves."[36]

The fighting had left Horton's command scattered around the hilltop. A Confederate recalled his compatriots "among the trees, embracing about an acre in area, without any regard to lines, fighting on the Indian style, some protecting themselves behind trees, some lying down, while most of them stood out in the open, watching for and shooting at every Yankee who showed himself within range." Before long, Horton's ammunition ran out. "Boys, we had as well end it," the captain announced. "The balance of the brigade are probably safe by this time." No one could find a white handkerchief, but a soldier rummaged through his bedroll and came up with a light-colored towel, which soon fluttered from a ramrod. As Hess's troopers approached to accept Horton's surrender, someone discharged a musket, killing a Federal. No one was certain which side had fired the shot, but angry northerners accused Horton's soldiers of violating their surrender. The Confederates were at the mercy of the Union men, and a slaughter seemed imminent. "I thought sure we would now be butchered," a Confederate reminisced, "but their officer interfered and we were spared."[37]

The Pennsylvanians led the survivors of Horton's little band—variously estimated at between sixty-six and seventy-five men—from the hilltop. They treated the captives with respect, giving them tobacco and rations. Torbert sent an enthusiastic message informing Hancock that he had driven Kemper's brigade across the Mattaponi at Milford Station and was holding the bridge. He doubted that he had enough men to force a passage and planned to wait for the 2nd Corps. At 10:30 A.M. Hancock forwarded Torbert's report to Meade, but the messenger could not get through.[38]

At the Anderson farm, Grant and Meade busily supervised Warren's evacuation of the northern sector of the Union earthworks. A Pennsylvanian could

not help reflecting on the irony of the withdrawal. For two weeks Union soldiers had spilt their life's blood to secure this very ground. Now they were
"leaving behind as useless what before had been fought for so tenaciously." [39]

Abandoning an entrenched position in the face of a watchful foe was always a delicate undertaking, and Warren's retirement from Spotsylvania
Court House was no exception. Union and Confederate picket lines stood so
close that the only way soldiers could leave was to crawl. "Pretty bold thing
to withdraw in broad daylight from the enemy's front," a soldier reckoned.
Warren pulled his men back in stages. Crawford and Kitching left first, provoking Early's Confederates into a fierce attack against Cutler and Griffin,
who remained in their earthworks to shield the retirement. After an hour of
brisk skirmishing Griffin slipped away, then Cutler. "They packed up as soon
as we did and followed our skirmishers right in," a Federal reported. Confederates nipped at Warren's heels until the 5th Corps had crossed the Ni and
moved behind Wright's entrenchments. Falling back in tandem with Warren,
Wright slid east to a line that his engineers had laid out during the night. Once
the movement was complete, Wright's pickets, who had remained in advance
fortifications to keep the rebels back, broke into a "dead run amid flying bullets to the rear." Wright now held the right wing of the entrenched Union line,
and Burnside the left.[40]

Satisfied that Warren's withdrawal was progressing smoothly, Grant and
Meade rode onto Massaponax Church Road and trotted ahead of the 5th
Corps's column. By 11:00 A.M. they had established headquarters at Massaponax Church. Orderlies removed pews from the church and set them by the
roadside. Grant puffed an ever-present cigar, examined maps, read and sent
dispatches, and talked over plans with his aides and Meade. The photogra-
pher Timothy O'Sullivan posted a camera in the church's upper story and
recorded the scene. His images caught the generals and their staffers against
the backdrop of 5th Corps troops and wagons moving along Massaponax
Church Road. Soldiers from the 114th Pennsylvania of Meade's headquarters
guard passed the time inscribing their names inside the building.[41]

Grant remained frustrated over the dearth of news from Hancock. He had
heard nothing from the 2nd Corps since the 5:30 A.M. dispatch. Under Grant's
timetable, Hancock should have occupied Bowling Green and been well on
his way to Milford Station. Grant, however, could not be certain that either of
these things had happened. During most of the hot and dusty afternoon, he
had to lay his plans in ignorance of developments in Hancock's quarter.

Lee also was busy making important decisions. He was now certain that
Grant had set much of his army in motion. It was also clear to him that Grant
was initiating a broad swing around the far side of the Mattaponi rather than

taking the direct route to Richmond down Telegraph Road as he had expected. Grant's purpose was evident to Lee. The Federal general, he concluded, meant to march along the far side of the Mattaponi and cross the Pamunkey to the east. The maneuver, Lee wrote Richmond, might well "secure [Grant] from attack till he crosses the Pamunkey." Lee's aide Walter Taylor explained matters succinctly in a letter home. "With several rivers between us," he wrote, "[Grant] could move to Bowling Green and below without any danger of our intercepting him." [42]

The Confederate commander recognized that staying at Spotsylvania Court House was tantamount to giving Grant the keys to Richmond. He selected Hanover Junction as the best point to concentrate the Army of Northern Virginia to counter Grant's likely deployments. If Grant headed back to Telegraph Road or followed the rail line south, the Army of Northern Virginia would stand directly in his path. If Grant pursued a wider arc to the east, Lee could slide east below the Pamunkey River to oppose him, keeping the Army of Northern Virginia between the enemy and Richmond. The disadvantage of Hanover Junction was its proximity to the Confederate capital. Lee would stand a scant twenty-five miles from Richmond. The Confederate artillery chief Pendleton explained Lee's dilemma in a letter to his wife. "If [Lee] attempted to head Grant off at some point more distant from Richmond than [Hanover Junction] he might not be in time, and the force which might slip by could possibly surprise them in Richmond on the north side, while Beauregard is attending to Butler on the south side." [43]

Although Lee was anxious to start south to deflect Grant's turning movement, he did not feel that he could initiate his maneuver just yet. Grant had kept two army corps—his 6th and 9th—in front of Spotsylvania Court House. Lee was concerned that by withdrawing, he would expose the rear of his army to attack. Until Grant evacuated more troops from Spotsylvania Court House, reasoned Lee, he would have to leave a substantial force in the earthworks to oppose the Federals. Lee could rest easy, however, about the safety of Hanover Junction. Breckinridge was now entrenched at the rail junction, Pickett's four brigades were nearby, and Fitzhugh Lee's cavalry was only a short distance away at Hanover Court House. Lee issued orders for any additional troops arriving from Richmond to halt at Hanover Junction and changed his supply depot from Milford Station to the junction. "Enemy reported moving toward Richmond," Lee warned Breckinridge. "One column by the Bowling Green Road, another by Downer's Bridge from Guinea toward Milford." The Kentuckian's assignment was clear. "Remain at Junction," Lee tersely instructed. "Defend the position. Get up your transportation and be prepared to move." [44]

Hanover Junction was indeed in good hands. Breckinridge had advanced a substantial force along the North Anna and had stationed the 30th Virginia Battalion at Chesterfield Bridge, where Telegraph Road crossed the river. And Fitzhugh Lee was doing a superb job keeping Sheridan at bay. Anticipating that Custer would return to Hanover Court House, Fitzhugh Lee had deployed his brigades under Wickham and Lomax near the town. Midmorning, the Wolverines rode into Hanover Court House, just as Lee had expected. Leaving the 6th and 7th Michigan to hold the town, Custer dispatched the 1st and 5th Michigan to scout for Confederate cavalry and continue the previous day's work of destroying the rail line. Michiganders probed south along the railroad and ran into Lomax's men. Then they discovered that a "heavy column" of Confederates—elements from Breckinridge's force, advancing from Hanover Junction and joined by Wickham—was closing from the west. Correctly surmising that he was outnumbered, Custer relinquished Hanover Court House and retired several miles down the Pamunkey, in the direction of Sheridan's main force. Before leaving, he visited Rosser's home and left a note for the Confederate cavalryman, whom he had known before the war. In the note, he expressed hope that Rosser had recovered from the "thrashing" the Wolverines had administered at Todd's Tavern on May 7. He had subsequently beaten Lomax, Custer added, and he was ready to "serve" Rosser up again.[45]

Sheridan meanwhile busied himself supervising the repair of a bridge over the Pamunkey at White House. Anxious to return to the Army of the Potomac, he remained oblivious to his opportunity to harass the rebel army's supply line. His cavalry outnumbered the Confederate force at the junction, and a determined cavalry raid in that quarter could have caused Lee considerable concern. But Sheridan was in no mood to prolong his expedition. His men and horses were exhausted and he had no ready means for communicating with Grant. Rather than risk his entire command, he ordered his far-flung elements, including Custer, to join him at White House. The threat of a cavalry raid against Lee's supply line was over.

Lee meanwhile firmed his plans to evacuate Spotsylvania Court House. At noon, once he became certain that Warren was following Hancock toward Guinea Station, he directed Ewell to start the 2nd Corps south along Telegraph Road, leaving a small contingent of cavalry and engineers at Stanard's Mill. "Some of us think we are falling back upon Richmond," a Confederate speculated. "Others think we are going to reinforce the right wing of the army." A soldier admitted that "the men don't like much the idea of going backwards but can trust to Bob Lee."[46]

Lee placed the rest of his army on alert and waited to see what Grant would do. He directed Anderson to make ready "at a moment's notice" to take his 1st Corps to Traveler's Rest, cross to Mud Tavern, and proceed down Telegraph Road behind Ewell. Hill was also to prepare to move. Since Anderson and Ewell would fill Telegraph Road, the 3rd Corps was to take an ancillary route a few miles to the west, passing through Chilesburg and crossing the North Anna at Island Ford. The army's wagons were to follow the 3rd Corps. Lee's scenario risked stringing Ewell and Anderson along Telegraph Road, where they would be vulnerable to attack by Hancock. To counter the threat posed by Hancock, Lee ordered Hampton to rush cross-country with his cavalry division, find Hancock, and block his access to Telegraph Road.[47]

In the midst of these delicate operations, Hill announced that he was sufficiently recovered to resume command of the 3rd Corps. For the third time in the campaign, Lee had to revamp his army's command structure while conducting active maneuvers. Jubal Early, who had led the 3rd Corps with skill during Hill's incapacity, and John Gordon, who had managed Early's division in the interim, had performed superbly, and Lee wanted to keep them in elevated posts. His solution was to organize Ewell's 2nd Corps, which had been operating with two divisions since the Mule Shoe debacle, into three divisions. Early's division would consist of Hoffman's Virginia brigade and Robert Johnston's North Carolina brigade under Colonel Thomas Toon. Gordon would head a division containing his former brigade, now commanded by Clement Evans, a Louisiana brigade (containing all the army's Louisiana troops) under Colonel Zebulon York, and a Virginia brigade under Brigadier General William Terry consisting of the various Virginia troops that had survived the Mule Shoe. Robert Rodes would continue at the head of his own division, giving Ewell three strong subordinates.[48]

After orderlies had departed with Lee's orders, the rebel commander shifted his headquarters below the Po to the Southworth house, where he could better supervise the evacuation of his Spotsylvania line. Servants began dismantling the general's tent and packing his gear. "Come, gentleman," Lee announced gravely as he mounted Traveller and started along the road leading south.[49]

"A shame and disgrace."

At 1:40 P.M.—roughly the same time that Lee rode from Spotsylvania Court House—Grant and Meade left Massaponax Church and turned onto the road to Guinea Station. The distinguished cavalcade passed in front of the 5th Corps column and pressed on alone. Warren's soldiers trudged in a daze through heat and dust. "In trying to recall the scenes of this period, there are some that seem like fragments of a half-forgotten dream, distinct in themselves, but without any definite connection to time or place," a Pennsylvanian reflected in later years. Everyone agreed that the scenery had improved greatly since the Wilderness. A Federal paid Caroline County his highest compliment. "It looks like New England!" he exclaimed.[50]

Enterprising 5th Corps soldiers who stopped to loot discovered that Hancock's men had already appropriated the choicest items. Outrages against civilians deeply offended the artillerist George Breck. "Pillaging and marauding," he wrote his wife, had become "more characteristic of this campaign than any other I ever participated in." Troops ransacked houses, destroyed libraries, and thoroughly vandalized the countryside. "A shame and disgrace is all this to our army and cause," Breck lamented, "doing us no good, but working us great evil." Brigadier General Marsena R. Patrick, the army's provost marshal, blamed Grant. "I learned that his staff, were, themselves, engaged in sheep stealing, fowl stealing and the like," Patrick noted, and he decried Grant's "notions of discipline." Meade's aide Lyman also regarded Grant's "rather Western ideas on foraging" with dismay. He watched in amusement while Grant's staffer Rawlins issued a forage order to a "purveyor" who interpreted the directive "as a privilege to steal every eatable he could see." General Russell caught the man flagrante delicto and gave him a sound caning to the "huge amusement of the bystanders."[51]

The headquarters cavalcade crossed the Richmond, Fredericksburg, and Potomac Railroad around 2:30 P.M. Half an hour later, the generals halted in front of a grand brick house on a hill overlooking the broad meadowland around Guinea Station. The estate was well tended and stocked with fruit trees, flowering roses, and the largest strawberries Lyman had seen. The owner, George Motley, struck Lyman as an "elderly man of a certain sour dignity, a bitter rebel plainly." Grant and Meade decided to stop for the day and instructed orderlies to set up headquarters on the edge of pine woods behind Mr. Motley's house.[52]

Rest, however, was not on the agenda. The quartermaster of the headquarters train spotted Confederates—Stewart's men of the 9th Virginia Cavalry—massed at Guinea Bridge and flew into a "deuce of a stew" at the prospect that rebels might charge across the flatland after his wagons. Hancock was long gone and Warren was not expected for an hour, leaving Grant and Meade exceedingly vulnerable. Their only armed escort was Meade's headquarters guard and a detachment of engineers. An aide recommended to the generals that they retrace their steps and join Warren's column. "I think, instead of going back, we had better hurry Warren forward," Grant proposed

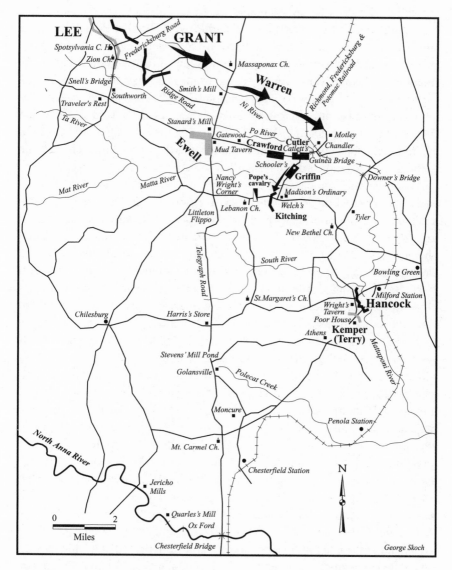

Warren's deployments on the morning and early afternoon of May 21

with accustomed belligerence. His aide Porter noted that "suggestions to the general to turn back fell as usual upon deaf ears." [53]

Acting on Grant's cue, Meade ordered Provost Marshal Patrick to "go in and force the bridge." Patrick jumped at the opportunity to do something more exciting than transporting prisoners and ordered Major James W. Walsh's 3rd Pennsylvania Cavalry to the front. The horsemen were delighted at the prospect of action. Trotting past staff officers and orderlies, they deployed in skirmish order across the road leading to Guinea Bridge. Grant and Meade stayed to watch the show. Dismounting, they lit cigars and sat on a white paling fence around Guinea Station that had somehow survived the burning of the station a few days earlier.[54]

Under Patrick's guidance, the 3rd Pennsylvania cavalrymen rode deliberately toward the bridge, pushing back a handful of gray-clad pickets. The main body of rebels, it developed, was waiting on the far bank and seemed full of fight. One company of the 9th Virginia Cavalry formed in column on the brow of the hill west of the river, sabers drawn and ready to charge, and another company took up defensive positions along the Mattaponi's west bank. Several Confederates nonchalantly strolled to the bridge and began setting fire to the structure. Faced with a brazen show of force, the 3rd Pennsylvania Cavalry eased back toward the station.[55]

Patrick in the meantime arrayed the rest of the headquarters guard to attack. Soldiers of the 114th Pennsylvania, a Zouave outfit commanded by Colonel Charles H. T. Collis, spread into fields left of the road, making a colorful spectacle in their scarlet pants, blue jackets, and tasseled fezzes. Lieutenant Colonel Robert E. Winslow's 68th Pennsylvania, less gaudy in regulation blue, marched into line north of the road. Captain Adams placed elements from the 1st Massachusetts Cavalry in front. To swell the force to a more imposing size, Lyman directed Captain Charles N. Turnbull to advance his contingent of engineers. "I have no officers!" Turnbull protested, but Lyman remained unmoved. He ordered them into service anyway, with Company C acting as skirmishers and Company D held in reserve.[56]

Colonel Collis, the senior field officer with combat experience, assumed command of the makeshift force. Collis was a flamboyant Philadelphian with an inflated view of his own prowess. Performing in front of Grant and Meade was especially to his liking, and he rode grandly in front of his troops, theatrically pointing the way toward Guinea Bridge. "Colonel Collis now had a fine opportunity to show himself off," an officer sarcastically noted. But to the surprise of Collis's detractors, the colonel's impromptu performance went off without a hitch. Dividing his command, Collis sent troopers splashing breast-deep across the river above and below the bridge and routed the rebels on the far bank. While Collis's main body pressed on, soldiers doused the burning bridge, saving most of the structure. As the 3rd Pennsylvania Cavalry disappeared in a cloud of dust toward the Catlett farm, Collis paused to pen a dramatic message to Meade. "I have met the enemy and he is mine," he announced with great flourish but little originality.[57]

At 3:45 P.M., as Collis's little battle was reaching its climax, Warren and his staff trotted up to Guinea Station. Crawford's division followed closely behind, exhausted and caked with dust. Colonel Hardin, whose brigade was in the fore, immediately charged into the melee. The 6th and 13th Pennsylvania Reserves ran across the bridge and joined Collis's men on the Mattaponi's west bank. "Go in, Bucktails, and give 'em fits," Collis's troops called to their fellow Pennsylvanians.[58]

Warren generally handled his corps with maddening caution, but he was reckless when it came to his own safety. Spotting a dozen rebel cavalrymen on a knoll near the road, the lanky young general spurred his horse ahead of his staffers and charged up the rise. The Confederates recoiled in surprise, leaving Warren to strike a bellicose pose on the knoll while winded foot soldiers struggled to catch up with him.[59]

Colonel Hardin regrouped west of the river and started his brigade toward the Catlett farm. The 9th Virginia Cavalry and a flock of chickens that had been swept up in the charge fled ahead of them. It just so happened that an escaped slave with the Bucktails had belonged to the owner of a house along the route. Blessing the fates that had brought him to the site of his former servitude, he knocked on the door. His past mistress answered, and the sight of her former slave in the company of armed Yankee escorts impressed her deeply. He asked for milk, eggs, and chickens, which she gave without protest. Forging ahead to the crest, Hardin secured the critical road junction at the Catlett farm. While the Catlett slaves ran to greet the Federals, Hugh Catlett and his wife quailed in the cellar, fearful that the Yankees might suspect that rebel cavalrymen were holed up with them and burn the house. Warren commandeered the home for his headquarters and settled down for dinner. Stewed chicken figured prominently in the menu.[60]

With Guinea Station safely in Union hands, Grant repaired to the Motley house, where he sat on the porch and lit a cigar. Deep in thought, he forgot about the embers and burned the arm of the bench. Mr. Motley stormed through the door and scolded the Union commander. "What are you trying to do," he thundered, uncowed by the Federals who had occupied his property. "Burn my house down?" Duly chastised, Grant strolled over to the Chandler house north of the station and sat on the porch with his aide Porter. Presently a lady came to the door. Grant stood up, took off his hat, and introduced himself. Soon he and Mrs. Chandler were chattering away like old friends. "This house has witnessed some sad scenes," she remarked, referring to Stonewall Jackson's death the previous year. Grant interjected that he and Jackson had been contemporaries at West Point for a year, and that they had together served in Mexico. "Then you must have known how good and great he was," she asked. "Oh, yes," Grant answered. "He was a gallant soldier and a Christian gentleman, and I can understand fully the admiration your people have for him." Mrs. Chandler became "very affected," Porter observed, in describing the events surrounding Jackson's death. After promising to place a guard to protect her property, Grant and his aide took their leave.[61]

Besides tending to the immediate task of fighting Lee, Grant had to make critical decisions about the war's other theaters. Especially nettlesome was Butler, who had withdrawn turtlelike into an entrenched position near City Point. Grant's recipe for victory called for throwing every available soldier against the rebels, and he was not happy about Butler's tying down thirty thousand men. If Butler could not occupy a Confederate force at least equal to the size of his own army, then Grant wanted his troops for the campaign against Lee. "I fear there is some difficulty with the forces at City Point which prevents their effective use," Grant wrote Halleck and directed him to send a competent officer right away to investigate. "The fault may be with the commander, and it might be with his subordinates," he added.[62]

Then there was Hancock. Grant had heard nothing from the imposing Pennsylvanian since his 5:30 A.M. message. Late in the afternoon Meade's assistant adjutant, Seth Williams, dashed off a note to Hancock that reflected Grant's concern. "The commanding general considers that with the cavalry force placed at your disposal, you should have kept open communication with him during the day, and he wishes you to use this cavalry force in keeping up frequent communication with these headquarters, and also with General Warren, who is near Guinea Bridge." A detachment from the 3rd Pennsylvania Cavalry rode off to Milford Station to deliver the dispatch.[63]

Grant and Meade need not have worried about Hancock. The 2nd Corps had occupied Bowling Green for about an hour—long enough for Colonel Merrill "to dispose of his ducks and his scruples," the soldier from the apothecary store remarked—then headed for Milford Station to support Torbert. Along the way the corps passed Holly Hill, the home of Thomas T. Fauntleroy, who had been a colonel of the 1st United States Dragoons at the outbreak of the war. Torn between loyalties to his country and to Virginia, he had decided to sit out the conflict. Several of Hancock's generals knew him and stopped to pay their respects.[64]

The day turned blistering hot. "I remember seeing some of our soldiers on their hands and knees crawling on the ground under the thick brush, suffering with sunstroke," an officer recounted. Realizing that Confederate guerrillas would snatch up stragglers, Hancock assigned guards to follow the column and prod anyone who lagged behind. A young lieutenant became so sick that he could not catch up with his command until night. There he collapsed under a wagon and was found dead the next morning.[65]

Barlow's division, still leading Hancock's advance, reached Milford Station shortly before noon. Torbert's force had drawn up between the station and the Mattaponi and was exchanging pot shots with Norton's Confederate skirmishers on the far bank. Milford occupied the highest navigable point on the Mattaponi and during its heyday had been a shipment point for tobacco. Signs of prosperity were still evident, although the recent fighting had taken a toll. "One railroad station, a commodious hotel, a few tumble-down out houses, with a large whiskey distillery, and you have an idea of the village of Milford," was the impression of a soldier in the 50th New York Engineers. Torbert's men had intercepted a train carrying mail to Lee's army and had scattered letters along the tracks. Hancock's soldiers found several packages of clothing and delicacies that Richmond's ladies had forwarded to Lee's army the previous day. "Some of the boys requested your correspondent to thank the benevolent ladies of Richmond through the widely circulating columns of the *Herald* for their generous donation," a correspondent for a New York newspaper wrote, "and assure them that similar favors will always be thankfully received." The depot buildings lay in ashes, having been set afire by Torbert's men, and the only visible white inhabitants were women frantically trying to protect their chickens from Yankee predators.[66]

The 2nd Corps crossed the railroad and deployed along the Mattaponi. Barlow's soldiers waded through waist-deep water near the partially disman- tled bridge, holding their ammunition, haversacks, and muskets overhead. The 148th Pennsylvania captured a small Confederate camp near the ford and took the abandoned equipage while the rest of the division spread along flat bottomland west of the river. Tyler and Gibbon came over next, leaving Birney on the east bank as a reserve. The 148th Pennsylvania scouted west along a winding country road, driving back small parties of rebels and dodg- ing occasional shots from the rest of Barlow's division following behind. None of the Pennsylvanians was injured, and their colonel, Beaver, described the expedition as a "most pleasant trip." [67]

Hancock, however, was deeply concerned. He had not expected to en- counter any appreciable number of rebels on his march. Norton's determined stand at Milford Station had persuaded Torbert that Kemper's entire brigade was close by. Perhaps the rest of Pickett's division was in the vicinity as well. Finding himself several miles from the rest of the Union army and confronting an enemy force of uncertain strength, Hancock immediately began searching for a strong position where he could entrench.

A mile west of the river, the route—descriptively named Devil's Three Jumps Road—ascended a low range of sharp little hills. Norton had hoped to establish a defensive position for his Confederates there, but the Federals swarming his way persuaded him to retire west of the hills. He deployed his thin force from Wright's Tavern on the north to Caroline County's poorhouse on the south, blocking the routes leading from Hancock's position to Telegraph Road. Hancock arrayed his corps along the ridgeline and set his men to throwing up earthworks as they arrived. A heavy artillerist proclaimed the day's march "the longest and most trying of all we made." Noted a New Yorker: "The ceaseless marching by day, and sometimes by night, the digging and the fighting were telling upon our men, in some cases almost as seriously as wounds." Even Hancock's chief aide, Walker, was heard to complain. He and his fellow staffers had not changed clothes for seventeen days.[68]

Norton received welcome reinforcements during the afternoon. Around 3:00 P.M. Corse's brigade, along with the portion of Kemper's brigade that had missed the train from Richmond the previous day, arrived at Penola Station, the stop immediately before Milford Station. On learning that Federals had taken Milford Station and were picketing the tracks ahead, Corse sent the train back to ensure its safety. Then he received reports that Union troops were marching toward Chesterfield Station, a few miles back down the tracks in the direction of Richmond. Having passed through Chesterfield Station an hour or so before, Corse knew that the depot contained large quantities of stores destined for Lee's army. Leaving his 30th and 32nd Virginia regiments at Penola Station, Corse backtracked with the rest of his force and took a stand squarely athwart Hancock's direct route to Chesterfield Station, throwing out skirmishers and awaiting Hancock's approach. He was only a few miles from Norton, but neither knew of the other's proximity, and each acted independently.[69]

Toward dark, Hampton arrived at the poorhouse with his cavalry. Rosser's brigade, riding in Hampton's advance, overran Barlow's pickets near the poorhouse and drove them back to Hancock's main line. Hampton's horse artillery shelled the Federals until Hancock's guns responded and silenced them. Hearing the fighting, Corse prepared to attack. Hampton, however, found Corse and explained to him that he faced an entire Union infantry corps.

Lee's army was on the move, Hampton added, and he invited Corse to help block Hancock's access to Telegraph Road. One of Corse's soldiers recorded the men's relief when they learned that they would be defending a position rather than attacking. "We would have played thunder with a brigade and a half fighting the whole Yankee army," he wrote home. For the rest of the evening, Confederate horsemen probed Hancock's formation for weak points. By nightfall Corse had reached north to link with Hampton, and Colonel Terry, commanding Kemper's brigade, had reunited the two halves of his outfit. Confederates now stood firmly across the roads leading from Hancock's position toward Telegraph Road. For a while, at least, Lee could set his mind at ease about Hancock disrupting his march to the North Anna.[70]

That evening Hampton optimistically informed Breckinridge that he, Corse, and Terry had trapped Hancock west of the Mattaponi. With assistance, Hampton believed he could cut off Hancock's troops and defeat them. "I am sure that I could burn the bridge behind them, and an attack in front would destroy them," he assured Breckinridge. "Could you send any more troops up to effect this? I know this country thoroughly," Hampton insisted, "and I think that a good blow might be struck." Breckinridge, however, had no troops to spare, and Lee was fully occupied shifting from Spotsylvania Court House to the North Anna. The opportunity to attack Hancock's isolated force went unexploited.[71]

Hancock watched the Confederate buildup with concern. For all he could tell, Pickett's division was massing in his front and Lee's entire army was coming his way as well. Captives did their best to feed his fears. Tom Yowell of the 7th Virginia assured Hancock during an interrogation that Confederates were pouring in from all directions. The inventive southerner went so far as to point out a distant house where he claimed that Lee had set up his headquarters.[72]

Meade's orders authorized Hancock to continue toward Telegraph Road and Hanover Junction. The 2nd Corps's commander, however, was loath to leave his strong natural position. His men were tired, reinforcements were far away, he had yet to establish communication with Meade, and he faced a Confederate force that seemed to be growing by the minute. He decided to stay put and ordered his men to keep digging in. Barlow formed the right of the 2nd Corps's line, Gibbon the center, and Tyler the left, covering the road that Corse had blockaded. Birney moved up from Milford Station and camped in reserve, and Torbert sent feelers out adjacent roads. Trenches and barricades crisscrossed the countryside, artillery lunettes plugged every ravine, and pickets patrolled the crest. Soon, a soldier observed, the 2nd Corps was tucked behind "tremendous field works, constructed with so much skill and labor." [73]

Hancock's troops had no sooner pitched their tents than they sent out foraging parties. The occupants of one estate professed to be Union sympathizers and requested a guard. Hancock obliged them, but the guard was powerless to keep fences and livestock from disappearing. Asked why he did not shoot looters, the guard replied that he was reluctant to kill Union soldiers, as Grant had none to spare. Two notorious members of the 4th New York Heavy Artillery, known as Black Jack and Irish Mike, donned Confederate uniforms and frightened soldiers into giving them their loot. Hancock punished sheep stealers by confiscating their booty and forcing them to watch other soldiers cook and eat the animals they had caught. A Federal became the talk of his company when an elderly southern lady hit him squarely in the forehead with a mud ball when he tried to steal her rooster. Hoots from onlookers incited the lady's daughter to pipe up. "Laugh, you cowardly Yanks," she shouted. "You will meet old Bob Lee pretty soon, and then you will laugh out the other side of your mouths." [74]

"There was none of the usual joking or chaffing."

General Lee was indeed interested in meeting Hancock's Federals. First, however, he wanted to determine the size of the force that Grant had left in front of Spotsylvania Court House. Did Hancock's corps constitute nothing more than an enormous raiding party? Or had Grant launched most of his army on a wide sweep toward Richmond? The answer would govern Lee's next move. If the force at Milford Station represented only a feint, Lee would continue to hold Spotsylvania Court House with Anderson and Hill. But if Grant had put his entire army in motion, Lee intended to start for Hanover Junction at once. Every minute lost magnified the Army of Northern Virginia's peril.

At 3:00 P.M. Hill and Anderson sent detachments into the no-man's land between the armies to probe Wright's and Burnside's positions. An hour later, they reported their findings to Lee. The Union 2nd and 5th Corps were gone, but the 6th and 9th Corps were still in place, holding a contracted line. Lee concluded that he could not withdraw any more soldiers. "Unless we can drive these people out, or find out where they are all gone," Lee wrote Anderson in frustration, "we are detained here to our disadvantage." [75]

Lee was not the only worried general that afternoon. Grant, at his headquarters in Mr. Motley's yard, began having serious reservations about his troop dispositions. The plan that had looked so promising in the morning now seemed fraught with danger. Union combat elements lay scattered across a twenty-mile front. Wright and Burnside were at Spotsylvania Court House, Warren was at Guinea Station, and Hancock's precise location was anyone's guess, as none of his messages had reached headquarters. Judging from surviving communications, Grant learned late in the day that Hancock had encountered part of Pickett's division at Milford Station, but he knew no details of the engagement until the next morning. Not only were the discrete pockets of Union troops at Spotsylvania Court House, Guinea Station, and Milford Station too far apart to assist one another, but also the appearance of Confederates from Richmond had dramatically altered the strategic picture. The southerners had stymied Hancock without drawing a single infantryman from Lee. And at Spotsylvania Court House, three Confederate corps now faced two Union corps.

Years later, when Grant penned his memoirs, he made pointed reference to his quandary on the afternoon of May 21. "Lee now had a superb opportunity to take the initiative either by attacking Wright and Burnside alone, or by following the Telegraph Road and striking Hancock's and Warren's corps, or even Hancock's alone, before reinforcements could come up," he explained. In Grant's judgment, Lee "never again had such an opportunity of dealing a heavy blow." [76]

Grant's frustration must have run deep. He had begun the day intending to catch part of Lee's army. Now it seemed to him that the tables had turned. It was possible, of course, that Lee might not notice the Union army's precarious situation, but Grant was not willing to take that risk. Exhaustion, inability to establish communication with Hancock, and the lack of reliable intelligence about Lee's deployments magnified his concern.

Assuming that Lee was capable of discovering the scattered condition of his army and had the wherewithal to exploit the Union disadvantage, Grant abandoned any thought of offensive operations. He immediately scrambled to concentrate his far-flung elements before Lee could attack them piecemeal. At 4:00 P.M. he issued a new round of orders reflecting his defensive mindset. After posting the Maryland Brigade at the Motley house to protect headquarters, Warren was to concentrate the rest of his corps between Guinea Station and the Catlett farm, sending a cavalry detachment to Downer's Bridge to guard against a surprise attack from that quarter and an infantry brigade to guard the bridge over the Matta. This, Grant reasoned, ought to cover the possible Confederate approaches to Guinea Station and Bowling Green. The next step was to evacuate the Spotsylvania line. Burnside was to leave his earthworks "as soon as practicable" and march via Telegraph Road to Mud Tavern. If Ewell still held the Po crossing at Stanard's Mill in force, Burnside was to backtrack and take the route to Guinea Station that Hancock and Warren had used. Wright was to follow the 9th Corps. By these deployments, Grant hoped to achieve a more compact, and hence more defensible, formation.[77]

Warren began dispersing the 5th Corps around Guinea Station as Grant had instructed. He posted Cutler at the critical road junction by Mr. Catlett's farm, placed Griffin at the Schooler property, overlooking the Matta, and advanced Crawford west along the road toward Mud Tavern. Crawford bivouacked midway between the Catlett place and Telegraph Road and sent skirmishers to within a mile of Telegraph Road. They encountered Chambliss's troopers, skirmished briefly, then fell back and entrenched. Warren also advanced a mounted detachment along the road that forked southwest from the Catlett place past Mr. Schooler's home. Taking two companies of the 8th New York Cavalry, Lieutenant Colonel Edmund M. Pope crossed the Matta, traversed the river's swampy floodplain, and continued onto high ground at Welch's. He met only token resistance from scattered Confederate horsemen. Establishing headquarters at Madison's Ordinary, Pope sent a squad of horseman looping northeast to Downer's Bridge and another squad west toward Nancy Wright's Corner. The latter contingent stopped short of Telegraph Road at Lebanon Church.[78]

Although Grant had deployed Warren with defensive objectives in mind, he had unwittingly positioned the 5th Corps superbly for offensive operations. Ewell was marching south along Telegraph Road, and Anderson was soon to follow. The Confederate column would necessarily pass through Mud Tavern and Nancy Wright's Corner. Warren now controlled the roads feeding into both places and was handsomely situated to catch the rebels on the march. He was situated to deliver a devastating two-pronged attack against their left flank. Grant, however, remained blind to the opportunity. He lacked the cavalry to reconnoiter Lee's movements, and he was preoccupied with concentrating his own army to fend off an imagined attack by Lee.

Fatigue was taking a toll on the high command of both armies. Thinking defensively, both Grant and Lee missed superb offensive opportunities. Lee remained concerned with evacuating Spotsylvania Court House and never seriously considered attacking Grant's scattered combat elements. Grant, also anxious to evacuate Spotsylvania Court House, focused on concentrating his force into a more defensible formation and neglected to exploit the vulnerable rebel column moving down Telegraph Road. May 21 represented

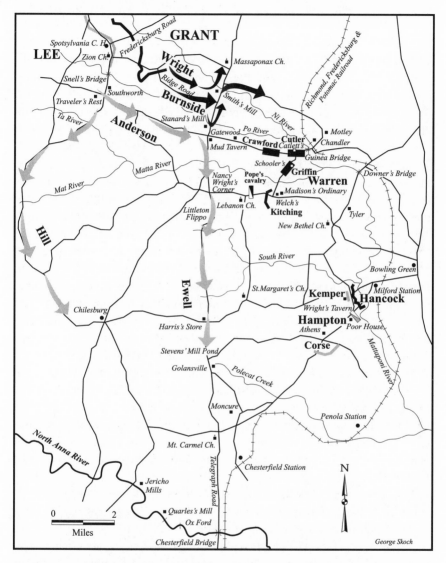

Grant's and Lee's evacuation of Spotsylvania on the evening and night of May 21–22

a low point in the campaign for both generals. Each seemed governed by concern over what the other might do, and each missed chances to strike telling blows.

Grant's four-o'clock directive had instructed Burnside to evacuate his entrenched line and march south along Telegraph Road. To cover his withdrawal, Burnside deployed Ledlie's brigade as skirmishers and sent it forward to clear the rebels from their advanced rifle pits. Ledlie executed the diversion, a correspondent observed, in a "most dashing manner, and with very slight loss." Burnside also dispatched Curtin's brigade of Potter's division, supported by the 11th Massachusetts battery, to ascertain the status of the Po River crossing at Stanard's Mill. Curtin slipped from his earthworks and headed east along a wagon trail—Federal reports called it the ridge road—threading along high ground between the Ni and the Po. He struck Telegraph Road a short distance below Smith's Mill, on the Ni, and turned south. A detachment of Chambliss's cavalrymen blocked Curtin's path, but he brushed aside the small mounted force and pressed on to Stanard's Mill. Imposing earthworks on the Po's far bank gave him pause. Rather than trying to cross, Curtin spread his brigade into thick pinewoods lining the road and awaited reinforcements. He had no idea that Stanard's Mill was practically his for the asking. Ewell had departed, leaving only the detachment of Chambliss's horsemen and a few engineers to guard the vital river crossing.[79]

Soon Simon Griffin's brigade and the 19th New York Battery pulled up at Stanard's Mill. McGregor's guns, still attached to Chambliss, opened a lively fire that disguised the sparseness of Confederate numbers and pinned down the Federals. Impressed by the strength of the Confederate position, the division commander Potter sent scouts along the river to find a crossing. The banks were steep, night was approaching, and the reconnaissance was not fruitful.[80]

Ignorant of the stalemate at Stanard's Mill, Burnside started the rest of his corps in Potter's footsteps. Wright also began disengaging by sending Ricketts's division along with the 9th Corps.

No sooner had the last of Burnside's troops left—it was now about 6:30 P.M.—than Lee launched a reconnaissance in force to determine once and for all the strength of the Union force at Spotsylvania Court House. Hill shifted two North Carolina brigades under James Lane and Alfred Scales onto Massaponax Church Road near Zion Church. Lane spread the 33rd, 28th, and 27th North Carolina above the roadway, Scales deployed his brigade below the road on Lane's right, and Lane's 7th and 18th regiments formed in reserve. Marching through dense undergrowth on both sides of the road, the Tar Heels emerged in front of entrenchments held by Neill's division of Wright's corps. "I'll bet five dollars there isn't a Yankee in those works," drawled Lieutenant John P. Rainey of the 13th North Carolina. Rainey had scarcely spoken when double lines of Federals—250 men from the 1st Vermont Heavy Artillery—rose and delivered a scathing volley. The Vermonters were novices at warring, and their shots flew high. Confederate artillery near Zion Church replied, and Lane's and Scales's men sprinted toward the enemy works.[81]

The Vermont men had been at the front less than a week. Their disastrous attack against Ewell on May 18 had left them shaken, and the sight of rebels materializing from the woods completely unnerved them. Vastly outnumbered, they tumbled back to Wright's main set of earthworks. Adding to the confusion, a violent windstorm blew in, felling trees and putting a momentary halt to combat. This gave Colonel Thomas O. Seaver time to form his 3rd Vermont in support of the 1st Vermont Heavy Artillery. As the tempest calmed, two 6th Corps batteries—the 5th Maine Battery and the 3rd New York Battery—shelled the advancing Tar Heels. A Confederate planted his regiment's colors on the Union works, and southerners pressed forward. Captain A. F. Walker of the 1st Vermont Heavy Artillery managed to halt the rebel advance until Colonel Seaver could bring his regiment into play. The rebels were checked where Federal guns "swept them down like grass," a Union man reported.[82]

After holding their lodgment for a respectable interval, the southerners retired to their own earthworks. Hill estimated his casualties at a hundred soldiers. A surgeon with Upton's brigade waxed ecstatic over the little victory. "For once in their lives," he crowed, the rebels had "got a belly so full as to cause puking and purging at the same time—a perfect emeto-cathartic!" Another Federal gloated that the Confederates "took to their heels and left quicker than they had come."[83]

Musketry from Hill's attack alerted Burnside that Wright was in trouble. He quickly sent back Ricketts's 6th Corps division and his own division under Willcox. The fighting was over by the time the reinforcements arrived, so they turned around and joined the 9th Corps at the Po. By then Burnside had reached the river. He did not like what he saw. Night had fallen, and flashes from muskets and artillery lit up the rebel earthworks along the far bank. Burnside had no reliable intelligence about the size of the Confederate force opposing him and was in no mood to risk a contested river crossing in the dark. Grant had given him discretion to take an alternative route if Confederates held the Po River crossing "in such force as to prevent you using it," and the burly general concluded that he faced precisely that situation. He ordered his corps to turn around and march north to the Guinea Station Road.

Burnside's timidity at Stanard's Mill ended any prospect of coordinated assaults against Lee by the 5th and 9th Corps. Gone also was any chance of catching Lee before he reached the North Anna River. Six months later, when Burnside prepared his official report, he claimed that carrying Stanard's Mill by assault "would have resulted in a very great loss even if it should be successful." In truth, Burnside could have overwhelmed the small Confederate force with little effort. It would be unfair, however, to fault him for failing to press across the Po. Burnside had no way of knowing the strength of the Confederate force confronting him, and he had heard nothing from headquarters for hours. Grant was miles away at Guinea Station, providing virtually no guidance while his scattered corps drifted aimlessly across Spotsylvania and Caroline Counties. Left to his own devices and ignorant of Grant's overall plan, Burnside understandably took the more cautious course open to him.[84]

Leaving Curtin's brigade at Stanard's Mill to guard his rear, Burnside started the rest of his command north. Reversing direction was more easily ordered than done. The night was dark, and troops and wagons packed the roadway. An unexpected obstacle arose as Griffin's brigade neared the Ni. Griffin was approaching from the south, which is where Confederates customarily came from, and no one had alerted the 13th Pennsylvania Cavalry, which was picketing the Ni. The vigilant Pennsylvanians dutifully shot at everyone who appeared on the southern bank, including staffers sent to inform them of Burnside's approach.[85]

Griffin directed Sergeant Franklin J. Burnham of the 9th New Hampshire to deliver a note to the pickets. Burnham strolled up Telegraph Road to the Ni, saw no one, and crossed on a partially destroyed bridge. The northern bank also appeared deserted—the Pennsylvanians were watching from behind trees—so Burnham crossed back over. As soon as he stepped from the bridge pickets began shooting at him from the far side with repeating rifles. "It was one of the liveliest serenades of that sort that I have ever experienced," Burnham was to write, "and there was no doubt about who it was intended for either." Burnham jumped into a ditch with Griffin's adjutant, who had come to monitor his progress. When the musketry subsided, the two men crawled to safety and hurried back to Griffin. "Why, those are the very chaps you want," the general informed Burnham on hearing his tale. "You must get that dispatch to them," he added. "The whole column is waiting for you." Burnham started back without the adjutant, who felt that he had experienced sufficient excitement for one day. "Hurry up!" Griffin called insistently.[86]

By the time Burnham reached the river, the pickets had learned that Burnside needed to pass and were repairing the bridge. The span was in service by 10:00 P.M., and the 9th Corps, wagons and all, went rumbling north. The 6th Corps, which had left its entrenchments two hours before, marked time on the ridge road while Burnside's men filed past. A few 6th Corps units jostled onto Telegraph Road to become hopelessly entangled with the 9th Corps's men. The pace, a frustrated general recalled, seemed "very slow and tedious." Curtin's soldiers settled down for the night at Stanard's Mill, harassed by rebel artillery firing at them from the far bank. "The screeching shells were not conducive to sound sleep," a soldier in the 45th Pennsylvania observed, "but we managed to get some rest, having become partially used to that sort of thing." [87]

The last hours of May 21 saw the Union army in disarray. Guidance from the high command was nonexistent. Burnside and Wright toiled north on Telegraph Road, away from the Confederates, going in precisely the opposite direction than Grant had originally intended. Warren meanwhile completed his deployment of the 5th Corps, assuming erroneously that Burnside was on his way to occupying Mud Tavern and accordingly shifting the weight of his corps from the Catlett farm toward Telegraph Road. Roebling accompanied Kitching's brigade along the route Pope's cavalry had pursued earlier, crossing the Matta and continuing on to Welch's farm and Madison's Ordinary. At 9:00 P.M. Kitching's heavy artillerists began digging in at the Welch farm, facing Telegraph Road. Pope posted his cavalry a short distance west at Lebanon Church. Kitching's men were "thoroughly tired out and hungry as bears," Captain Brown of the 4th New York Heavy Artillery complained, "having had nothing to eat on the long march of twenty-five miles." Roebling speculated that "so much Dutch cursing will never be heard again in the valley of the [Matta]." [88]

Kitching held strategic high ground extending to Telegraph Road. Roebling wondered whether Confederates occupied the neighboring stretch of Telegraph Road at Nancy Wright's Corner but apparently did nothing to find out. Kitching initiated no reconnaissance either, as he was busy devising a way to defend his camp. The flat, open terrain afforded no natural protection, and Warren had neglected to provide entrenching tools, so the resourceful commander set his men to constructing barriers from fence rails. He remained uneasy and wrote Warren that his force was "quite insufficient to hold the position against a determined attack." [89]

Warren took Kitching's concerns seriously. The brigade was only a mile from Nancy Wright's Corner. Telegraph Road, for all the Federal leaders knew, might be swarming with Confederates. By contrast, the closest Union reinforcements—Griffin's division, camped at the Schooler place—was over two miles from Kitching. Cutler, at the Catlett farm, was three miles away, and Crawford faced a five-mile march from his bivouac on the Mud Tavern road to reach Kitching. Any reinforcements would have to brave a "rickety truss" over the Matta that was patently unfit for artillery.[90]

At 9:30 P.M. Warren asked permission to advance Cutler to the Welch farm to bolster Kitching. By now, headquarters had learned that Burnside and Wright had changed their route. Instead of marching down Telegraph Road as initially intended, they had backtracked and were cutting over to Guinea Station along the road previously taken by Hancock and Warren, leaving Telegraph Road below the Po in Confederate hands. Not only were Burnside and Wright now unable to assist Warren, but Warren's position was precarious, as Confederates might attack at any moment from Mud Tavern, from Nancy Wright's Corner, or from both places at once. Humphreys alerted Warren to concentrate toward Guinea Station, where Burnside and Wright were expected to arrive later that night. "Under the present circumstances Cutler's division had better remain where it is," Humphreys insisted. "Withdraw Kitching, leaving the cavalry at the [Matta River] bridge and take up as strong a position as you can find, with your whole force in the vicinity of Catlett's, withdrawing Crawford as far back as necessary for that purpose, but leaving some mounted men or infantry where he is."[91]

Warren decided to let Kitching and Crawford rest before bringing them back to the Catlett farm. It was nearly midnight, and he doubted that the Confederates would attack before morning. "The command will be prepared to move at 4:00 A.M. tomorrow," he instructed his division heads, "the object being to take up at that time a defensive position in this vicinity to receive an attack of the enemy should he advance in this direction." The Federal commanders had abandoned any pretense of going on the offensive.[92]

Scales's and Lane's late-afternoon reconnaissance in force gave Lee the information he sought. Hancock, Warren, and Burnside were definitely gone. Only Wright remained as a rear guard. Lee could now assume with confidence that Grant was withdrawing his entire force from Spotsylvania Court House. The Confederates were free to participate in the race to the North Anna River.

At 7:00 P.M. Lee issued orders activating the plan that he had devised earlier in the day. Lamkin's Virginia battery, bringing up the rear of Ewell's Corps, had already left Mud Tavern and was marching south along Telegraph Road with the rest of the Confederate 2nd Corps. The 1st Engineers slipped into place behind Lamkin, leaving only some of Chambliss's horsemen and McGregor's guns to hold the Po River crossing at Stanard's Mill. An engineer described the march as "half-walking, half-running thro mud, rain, creeks, etc. for nearly ten miles without a halt." At Jerrell's Mill, where Telegraph Road crossed the Matta, Hoke's brigade from Richmond joined Ewell. The newcomers were tired, having marched since five o'clock that morning. Ewell sat on a rock and greeted them as they trudged up. Soldiers from the 43rd North Carolina crowded around the one-legged general and listened to him outline the campaign's progress. Ewell concluded with an appeal for hard fighting, and the men cheered. After a brief rest, Hoke's men filed into place behind Ewell's column.[93]

Not all of the marchers were impressed with Ewell. St. George Tucker Bryan of the Richmond Howitzers was trying to get his gun teams moving after letting them stop to drink. He had just climbed onto a horse to adjust its bridle reins when Ewell stormed up, crutches strapped to his saddle and a cane in his hand. The general angrily accused Bryan of having held up the entire column. Bryan replied that he was a gunner, not a driver, and that he would gladly turn the horses over to someone else. "If you get off that horse I'll have you shot," Ewell snapped. "Drive on!" In later years Bryan recollected that "the dear old fellow could hardly refrain from punching me with his stick which he brandished."[94]

In response to Lee's request for guides, a detail of local men from the 9th Virginia Cavalry rode into the Southworth house headquarters. Lee was conferring with Hill, Early, Anderson, and his son Rooney. Anderson, he instructed, was to withdraw the 1st Corps from its entrenchments right away and follow in Ewell's path. Hill was to pull out as soon as the 6th Corps left, but certainly no later than 9:00 P.M. Early suggested sending part of the Confederate army along the Mattaponi, but Lee rejected the idea on the grounds that Hancock was fortifying west of the river. The meeting ended, and the Confederate chieftains returned to their various commands with guides to help them find their way. Lee prepared to ride with the van of Anderson's corps.[95]

As the distinguished party mounted to go, one of the guides, Private Eustis C. Moncure, asked Lee's aide Taylor where he should ride. Lee overheard Moncure and called out, "You and your comrade come here and ride by my side."[96]

Anderson's soldiers filed out of their trenches and hurried into the fading daylight to catch up with Ewell. At 8:00 P.M. the last of Anderson's outfits—John Bratton's brigade of South Carolinians—fell into line in the rear of the 1st Corps. Anderson's men seemed uncharacteristically silent. "There was none of the usual joking and chaffing among the men though all were in good humor," the artillerist Alexander observed. Everyone appeared "serious and created the impression of being on serious business." Bratton described the march as "severe and weary."[97]

Around 10:00 P.M. Lee reached Mud Tavern. Moncure, still at Lee's side, had ridden across the surrounding countryside earlier in the evening and was familiar with Warren's troop dispositions. He pointed out the road toward the Catlett farm and informed Lee that Federals—Crawford's men—were encamped a mile east. Lee instructed Anderson to send a regiment down the road to protect the column as it passed. The party then crossed the Matta at Jerrell's Mill. Telegraph Road was choked with troops, and Lee came upon teamsters cursing as they labored to clear broken wagons from the roadway. Moncure watched as Lee "spoke very kindly to some of the infuriated men and officers, who by intuition seemed to recognize him, and the road in a few minutes was clear and all hands moving along."[98]

The headquarters party plodded on to Nancy Wright's Corner, where the road from Madison's Ordinary entered Telegraph Road. Moncure alerted Lee that he also had seen Federals (in this case, Kitching's brigade) along this road, and once again Lee asked Anderson to send a regiment out the side road to protect the column. Then the entourage continued south past clusters of weary men. Once, the general stopped to warn soldiers lying by the roadside to move on, as they risked being captured. What gave him the right to speak to them that way, they demanded. After all, he had a horse and all the rations he could eat. Then a man recognized the mounted figure. "Marse Robert," he cried, and the soldiers sprang to their feet. "Yes, Marse Robert," they reverently promised. "We will move on and go anywhere you say, even to hell itself!"[99]

At 10:00 P.M.—the same time that Lee reached Mud Tavern—the head of Ewell's corps arrived at Golansville, a tiny settlement on Telegraph Road eight miles west of Milford Station. The troops had marched twenty hot and dusty miles and were "completely broken down." A mere nine miles remained to the North Anna River. Fields on both sides of the road made inviting campsites, and nearby Polecat Creek provided ample water. Ewell ordered a halt for the night. The closest Federals were Hancock's men on their ridge near Milford Station, and Hampton, Corse, and Terry had the approaches from there well protected. Ewell's men settled down to a peaceful rest for the first time in weeks.[100]

After dark the last of the Confederate army, Hill's 3rd Corps, left the Spotsylvania Court House earthworks, crossed the Po, and headed toward Chilesburg, followed by most of the wagons. Mahone's division, bringing up the 3rd Corps's rear, did not start until midnight. Soldiers proclaimed the march "most fatiguing," but none voiced disappointment at leaving Spotsylvania Court House. "The night was pleasant, all nature seemed in repose and in joyous expectancy of spring now past the meridian," a chronicler reminisced. "Only the shuffling of the marching feet as they moved over the road, an order or an imprecation would be heard." A soldier broke into song, voices joined in, and music engulfed the marching column. "As far in front and rear as the ear could hear came welling up the stanzas of that old song of the long ago, 'When I Was Seeing Sweet Nellie Home,' " a soldier remembered years later. Never, he swore, had mortal man heard "such music as Lee's old veterans improvised on that midnight march from Spotsylvania Court House to North Anna." [101]

At 2:00 A.M. on May 22, a weary General Lee reached the residence of Dr. Joseph A. Flippo. He dismounted, exchanged brief courtesies with the doctor, whom he had known for years, then mounted and rode on. Within the hour he was at Golansville, site of Ewell's encampment. Orderlies pitched two tents at Stevens' Mill Pond, one for the general and another as a clerk's tent and dining room. Before retiring, Lee invited Moncure and his companion to share his rations and take feed for their horses. They ate hungrily—"a couple of very bad biscuits and a cup of very inferior coffee without sugar" was Moncure's description of the fare—then curled up under a cedar. Lee stretched out on his cot for a brief night's sleep. [102]

The hostile armies were widely scattered. Grant's host was dispersed across a broad front of twenty miles. Burnside was inching toward Guinea Station, Wright was marking time on Telegraph Road, Warren was centered west of Guinea Station, and Hancock was tucked behind fortifications west of Milford Station. West of the Union force, the Army of Northern Virginia was marching south in two parallel columns stretching fifteen miles to the rear. On Telegraph Road, Ewell had bivouacked at Golansville, nine miles above the North Anna, and Anderson was coming up behind. Farther west, Hill and the Confederate wagon trains were laboring toward Chilesburg. Lee expected both prongs of his army to reach the North Anna at midmorning on May 22.

May 21 had yielded mixed results for the Federals. Grant had succeeded in his primary goal of ousting Lee from Spotsylvania Court House. But he had also hoped to engage Lee in battle outside of his entrenchments, and in that he had failed. Rather than jump at Grant's bait, Lee had seized Telegraph Road and secured an unobstructed path south. In retrospect, Grant's plan of operation was flawed. "Had Grant originally started his movement as a race for the North Anna, having the initiative, he might easily have won it," the

Confederate artillerist Alexander later remarked. "But Hancock's delay, while acting as bait, enabled Gen. Lee to seize the advantage, which he was quick to do." Meade's chief of staff, Humphreys, voiced a similar complaint. "The chief object of Hancock's circuitous movement was not accomplished," he conceded after the war. "There would probably have been more chance of success had Hancock moved by the Telegraph Road on the night of the 20th, followed by Warren," Humphreys thought, since Grant then might have "brought on a collision before Lee could intrench on new ground." [103]

The normally aggressive Grant had missed a rare opportunity. During the night of May 21–22, fully two-thirds of Lee's infantry passed south along Telegraph Road. Warren stood poised near Mud Tavern and Nancy Wright's Corner, only a mile from the vulnerable Confederate column. Never had Grant held a more favorable tactical advantage. By launching Warren into Lee's flank, he could have severed the Confederate column and opened the way for Burnside and Wright to cross the Po. Ewell and Anderson, caught outside their earthworks, were ripe for plucking. This was the chance that Grant had been seeking throughout the campaign, and it had slipped through his fingers.

Several factors combined to rob Grant of his windfall. Sheridan had not returned from his raid toward Richmond, and the absence of experienced cavalry hindered Grant in determining Lee's precise whereabouts. Warren's soldiers, who could hear the Confederate army marching along Telegraph Road, never reported the movement to their superiors. Perhaps the most glaring failing was the absence of firm leadership from army headquarters. Grant and Meade remained preoccupied concentrating their forces to deflect imagined attacks by Lee. After nightfall they made no attempt to coordinate the movements of their corps and seemed content to leave decisions in the hands of local commanders. The Union army floundered like a force without a head for several critical hours. Later in the war General John B. Hood, commanding the Confederate Army of Tennessee, was roundly criticized for dropping his guard and permitting his opponent to march unmolested past his encampment at Spring Hill, Tennessee. Grant and Meade made a comparable mistake, every bit as egregious as Hood's, during the night of May 21–22. Fortunately for Grant, his popularity and the glare of the momentous events that soon followed relegated the oversight to the status of a minor incident.

Lee, too, was not his usual self this day. He astutely interpreted Hancock's maneuver as a prelude to a Union shift toward Richmond and placed Ewell across Telegraph Road, thwarting Grant's scheme and preserving the direct route south for the Army of Northern Virginia. And his selection of Hanover Junction as the focal point for concentrating his forces represented a thoughtful assessment of Grant's likely moves. But Lee's decision to evacuate Ewell and Anderson along Telegraph Road was ill conceived. Telegraph Road was his most direct route to the North Anna, but it passed dangerously near Grant's army and seriously exposed the Confederates. Why Lee persisted in using Telegraph Road with Warren posted so close remains unclear. Most likely Lee mistakenly presumed that the 5th Corps had continued toward Bowling Green, in Hancock's wake. Had Grant acted with his usual decisiveness, the oversight would have cost Lee severely. And like Grant, Lee forfeited excellent chances to deliver blows of his own. Grant's aide Adam Badeau later claimed that "if Lee ever meant to assume the offensive, this was the moment, with Grant on the arc of the circle of which he held the chord; one national corps at Milford, another at Guinea, and two at Spotsylvania, and all in motion by different roads with which they were unacquainted, while the rebels knew every plantation path and every ford, and every inhabitant was a friendly guide for them and a spy on Grant." A Confederate cavalryman aptly quipped, "Old Ewell says [Grant] puts him in mind of a measuring worm, and the time to strike him is when he has just lengthened out his line." May 21 was just such a time, but Lee hesitated. The specter of Grant's beating him to the North Anna blinded him to the offensive opportunities that Grant had left open.[104]

Although aggressiveness and daring usually distinguished the duel between Grant and Lee, the generals on May 21 acted conservatively. Fatigue dulled their judgments, and each overestimated the other's prowess. Grant worried that Lee would exploit the scattered Union dispositions, when in fact Lee had no offensive gambits in mind. And Lee tarried at Spotsylvania Court House out of concern that Wright and Burnside might attack his rear, when in reality they were only covering the Union withdrawal. Both generals questioned the competence of their subordinates, dampening their enthusiasm for complicated maneuvers. Grant considered Meade cautious, Warren rebellious, Wright unproven, and Burnside bereft of any aptitude whatever for combat. Only Hancock followed orders and exercised discretion consistent with Grant's plans, but he was twenty miles away at Milford Station and unavailable to fight Lee. Lee had similar reservations about his own lieutenants. The disaster at Harris Farm had lowered his opinion of Ewell, Hill was recuperating from two weeks of illness, and Anderson was still learning the business of commanding a corps.

The last Confederate outfit to leave Spotsylvania Court House was a scouting party under Lieutenant Samuel Grubb of Colonel Elijah V. White's battalion, Rosser's brigade. Returning from outpost duty after Hill's men had left, the cavalrymen captured several Union stragglers, frisked them for valuables, and released them on parole. Their haul included a dozen brass watches that failed to keep time, a hundred pocketbooks containing a total of two dollars, and a handful of useless sutler tickets. "Hundreds of dead men lay still unburied," an officer in the unit recollected, "and the squadron was obliged to pass directly over them, when, as the hoof of the horses would strike the corpses, the flesh would strip from the bones, leaving them glistening in the phosphorescent light that played around them." He thought that the "weird, ghostly influence of the scene affected the men, in the silence and gloom of that early morning, more than the presence of any number of live Yankees could have done." [105]

The battles for Spotsylvania Court House were over.

VIII

MAY 22

Lee Wins the Race to the River

"Never was the want of cavalry more painfully felt."

HILL'S SOLDIERS MARCHED through the evening of May 21. A footsore
Virginian likened each step to "treading on nails." Occasionally the column
halted to allow stragglers to catch up. The story of one gaunt, bedraggled
warrior enlivened postwar gatherings. Stopping near the Guilford Grays,
27th North Carolina, a threadbare soldier propped wearily against his musket
and began recounting his ordeals. Tales of hairbreadth escapes and heroic
survival spilled from his lips. An incredulous Tar Heel remarked in jest that
the storyteller ought to keep a diary for future historians. Mistaking "diary"
for "dia-ree"—the soldiers' term for diarrhea—the man leaned forward as
though divulging a great confidence. "Lord, stranger!" he announced. "That's
what ails me now. I have had it nigh on to four months." [1]

Near midnight, hungry and fatigued, Hill's men labored into Chilesburg
and halted for a brief rest. A Confederate affirmed that "most of us were too
weary to spend much time in spreading down blankets, but lay down and
slept without cooking." To the east, Ewell's dust-caked soldiers dozed at
Golansville, and Anderson's corps followed in Ewell's footsteps, wending
through Mud Tavern and south along Telegraph Road. Huddled behind
fence-rail barricades on the Welch farm, Kitching's Federals listened intently,
as did Crawford's men in their entrenchments near Mud Tavern. Clanking
canteens and groaning wagons told them that Confederates were marching
past. No one, however, troubled to inform headquarters. [2]

Grant remained ignorant of Lee's proximity. Even if Warren had alerted
him to the gray-clad column tramping along Telegraph Road, his combat elements remained so scattered that he probably could not have exploited the
opportunity. Warren's corps slumbered in camps guarding the roads radiating

from the Catlett farm. Hancock's troops lay behind earthworks fifteen miles away, near Milford Station. And the balance of the Federal army—Burnside's and Wright's outfits—toiled slowly toward Guinea Station on one of those interminable night marches that had become the bane of the Union soldiers' existence. "Rode up and down the road crowded with wagons, artillery, and troops until I had enough of it," a 6th Corps aide scratched in his notebook. "Since the fourteenth we've done nothing but march and countermarch and change about," a Vermont man complained. Contemplating the week's events, a northerner proclaimed it a "great mystery what Grant is doing or what he is going to do." [3]

At midnight an exasperated General Wright reported that his corps had "hardly got out of the intrenchments, and is now halted, the road being blocked ahead by General Burnside's column." Troops moved with their "usual snail-like rapidity," a Vermonter joked. As Wright neared Massaponax Church and the turnoff to Guinea Station, he heard shots and directed his aides Thomas W. Hyde and Ranald S. MacKenzie to make sure that the way was clear. Hyde set a detachment of dismounted troopers to peppering the dark forest with their repeating rifles. Satisfied that the woods were clear of rebels, Hyde ordered the troopers to stop firing. They ignored his pleas and blazed away until their ammunition gave out. Wright presumed from the racket that Hyde was heavily engaged and rushed an infantry brigade and artillery to his assistance. Hyde's companions chided him unmercifully. "It was some time before I heard the last of the 'Battle of Massaponax Church,'" the aide admitted, "but it was quite a lesson on the improper use of rapid-firing arms." [4]

Grant hunched over maps into the wee hours of morning. His anxiety over a possible Confederate attack had abated, and he was thinking offensively again. He remained undecided, however, about what to do. Burnside and Wright were not up, Hancock's situation was unclear, and information about Lee's location remained sketchy. At this juncture, Grant concluded that he could do nothing more than direct Meade to prepare to advance as soon as circumstances permitted.

At 2:00 A.M. on May 22, in keeping with the more aggressive mood at headquarters, Meade revised his instructions to Warren. He had earlier ordered the 5th Corps's commander to concentrate his widespread units toward the Catlett farm. Now he wanted Warren to prepare to advance to Telegraph Road, taking either the road to Mud Tavern, held by Crawford, or the road to Nancy Wright's Corner, held by Kitching. Warren, however, was unclear about what Meade wanted him to do. He responded that Crawford was already "well out" toward Mud Tavern, adding that he had received no reports from the Pennsylvanian but hoped to obtain "definite information" soon. As for Kitching, Warren wrote that he had already ordered the heavy artillerist to withdraw, but he promised to countermand the directive. "Orders changed three times during the night," the flustered corps commander jotted in his journal. "Kept me up all the time." [5]

Crawford's Pennsylvania Reserves had camped between the Catlett farm and Mud Tavern. At Warren's instruction, 125 soldiers under Captain Joseph B. Pattee left Crawford's bivouac and advanced west. A half-mile march brought them to the Gatewood house, where they encountered Chambliss's skirmishers. Driving the Confederates away, they continued another half mile to a fence-rail barricade. There they met a substantial body of southern-ers—probably the regiment that Lee had instructed Anderson to post to safe-guard the column passing on Telegraph Road—and found themselves in a brisk firefight. Unable to dislodge the rebels, Pattee retired to the Gatewood property and awaited reinforcements. Help came in the form of Coulter's brigade, commanded since Coulter's wounding on May 18 by Colonel James Bates of the 12th Massachusetts. Forming in column along the road, Bates spread skirmishers in front, threw out flankers, and began pressing his com-mand cautiously along the ridgeline toward Mud Tavern, driving Confed-erates. Near daylight Bates reached the tavern. A resident—Mr. Pound by name—informed him that Ewell and Anderson had "marched down the Telegraph Road all last night, and are gone south." Discarded items con-firmed Pound's report. Bates sent a handful of prisoners to headquarters and reported that the Confederates had left.[6]

At the same time he was setting Crawford in motion, Warren directed Cutler to reinforce Kitching at the Welch farm with his "best" brigade. "Do not stop to make coffee," he stressed. Cutler selected the remnants of Colonel Robinson's famed Iron Brigade for the mission, and at 5:00 A.M. Roebling started south with the veteran outfit. Approaching Madison's Ordinary, Roebling directed Robinson to advance west along the ridgeline in the direc-tion of Telegraph Road, keeping the Matta River on his right. Roebling then continued alone to the Welch farm, where he found Kitching. The colonel was relieved at the prospect of reinforcements and mentioned offhandedly that his men had heard Confederates marching south on Telegraph Road all night. Roebling was dumbstruck. Spurring his horse, he trotted a quarter mile west to Lebanon Church, where Lieutenant Colonel Edmund Pope's cavalry vedette was posted. There Roebling listened in amazement as the cavalryman repeated Kitching's description of wagons rumbling by all night. Why had this intelligence not been reported to headquarters, Roebling queried? Completely flustered, the aide rode on to assess the situation. Half a mile west of Lebanon Church, he climbed onto a gentle ridge. Nancy Wright's Corner was visible in the distance. "I could see a wagon train and ambulances moving rapidly to the south," he observed in astonishment. "No troops were seen accompanying it, or between us or them." He watched in fascination for half an hour as the end of Anderson's column passed.[7]

Robinson's troops soon arrived and joined Roebling. "We were in plain view of the Telegraph Road," a Wisconsin officer confirmed. "I had a line of skirmishers out and I lay on the ground a long time on the skirmish line and watched this moving column of the enemy." Roebling hurried back and conferred with Pope. From Lebanon Church a road slanted southwest to strike Telegraph Road at Littleton Flippo's farm, a mile and a half below Nancy Wright's Corner. By taking that road, Pope stood a good chance of intercepting the rebel wagon train and inflicting considerable damage. Roebling urged Pope to attack, but the cavalryman demurred. His command, he insisted, was too small to take on a Confederate force of unknown strength.[8]

At 6:00 A.M. Roebling fired off a dispatch to headquarters. "I have just returned from the road leading to Nancy Wright's, on the Telegraph Road, and was at a point half a mile from the Telegraph Road," he began. "A rebel wagon train was passing south on the Telegraph Road and had been passing since daylight," he went on. "Our cavalry under Lieutenant Colonel Pope are out there," he continued, "and can capture it, I think, if they try." Roebling's frustration remained palpable months later. "Here was the chance to capture the whole of Lee's wagon train," he fumed in his report. "Never was the want of cavalry more painfully felt. Such opportunities are only presented once in a campaign and should not be lost." [9]

By 6:30 A.M., with reports in hand from Bates and Roebling, Grant began to comprehend what had happened. Lee had escaped and was now well on his way to the North Anna River. The Federals had no realistic possibility of catching him. Hancock, it was true, was sufficiently far south to intercept the rebel column, but it would be foolhardy for him to leave the safety of his entrenchments until Grant could send reinforcements. By then the Confederates would be long gone. Once again the Army of the Potomac had held victory in its hands but had failed to recognize its advantage. Lee had gotten away clean. Meade was despondent. "I am afraid the rebellion cannot be crushed this summer," he grumped to Lyman over breakfast.[10]

Grant was not one to dwell on lost opportunities. He sat on Mr. Motley's porch, doubtless more careful this time about the placement of his cigar, and pondered his next move. Two courses of action seemed promising: pushing straight south to the North Anna or sweeping southeast to the Pamunkey. Sending the rest of the army along Hancock's trajectory to the Pamunkey had much to recommend it. Sheridan was already at White House, where he could rejoin Meade, and the Pamunkey afforded a superb avenue for reinforcements and supplies. Once across the Pamunkey, the Federals would find themselves on McClellan's former battlefields of 1862, where the country was well known to the Union army's veterans and where Butler's proximity would facilitate joint operations between the Army of the Potomac and the Army of the James. Lee would doubtless try to intercept the Federals at the Chickahominy, Grant reasoned, but this, too, might operate to the Union army's advantage. Backed against the Confederate capital, Lee would forfeit his ability to maneuver.

The merits of Grant's second option—following Lee to the North Anna River—were not immediately evident. If Grant marched toward Lee, the Confederates would unquestionably entrench below the river to protect Hanover Junction. Once again, Grant would confront the Army of Northern Virginia behind a heavily fortified position. Grant would also have difficulty supplying the Union host, as the depot at Port Royal would be thirty miles away. Butler, too, would be too distant to assist. Even if Grant defeated Lee at the North Anna, the Confederates could retire to a series of fortified lines closer to Richmond. All told, advancing to the North Anna offered Grant none of the advantages of sidestepping to the Pamunkey and raised daunting obstacles as well.

Meade urged Grant not to move against Lee at the North Anna. The Pennsylvanian needed no more slaughter to persuade him of the futility of assaulting the Army of Northern Virginia behind earthworks. Meade thought that the North Anna offered Lee his strongest position between Spotsylvania Court House and Richmond. Tangling with the Confederates on ground of their choosing struck him as senseless. The better approach, Meade urged, was to initiate another turning movement and swing around Lee's right flank to the Pamunkey, crossing at Hanovertown or White House. "I suppose now we will have to repeat this turning operation," Meade wrote his wife, "and continue to do so, until Lee gets into Richmond." [11]

Grant's and Meade's relationship had deteriorated sharply. Since the Wilderness, Grant had kept major battlefield decisions for himself, leaving Meade to administer the army and handle matters ordinarily relegated to staff officers. Meade's letters home bristled with anger. "If there was any honorable way of retiring from my present false position, I should undoubtedly adopt it," he wrote his wife on May 19, "but there is none and all I can do is patiently submit and bear with resignation the humiliation." Taking a cue from their boss, Meade's aides were especially venomous. The staffer Major James C. Biddle derided Grant as a "rough, unpolished man" of only "average ability, whom fortune has favored." Meade, he assured his wife, was "as a general as far superior to Grant as day is to night." Rawlins he loathed. "One of the roughest, most uncouth men I ever saw," Biddle called Grant's close friend and chief aide, whom he accused of knowing "no more of military affairs than an old cat." [12]

In a decision that could only widen the rift, Grant, over Meade's strong objection, chose to follow Lee to the North Anna River. "Meade was opposed to our crossing the North Anna, but Grant ordered it, over his head," Provost Marshal Patrick recorded. The decision underscored the difference between Grant's aggressive approach to warring and Meade's more cautious style. Grant was determined to adhere to the objective he had voiced at the beginning of the campaign. "Lee's army will be your objective point," he had instructed Meade. "Wherever Lee goes, there you will go also." Lee had gone to the North Anna River, and Grant would go there, too. Grant also questioned whether Lee still had the capacity to fight, as Lee had let a favorable opportunity pass on May 21 when he failed to attack Grant's scattered forces. Now was the time to strike, Grant concluded, and the surest way to retain the initiative was to push on to the North Anna. [13]

Concern that the campaign was taking a disturbing turn might also have influenced Grant to move directly against Lee. Breckinridge had broken Sigel's offensive in the valley, Beauregard had neutralized Butler, and Lee had withstood everything Grant had thrown at him. Grant had whittled down Lee's numbers, but Confederate reinforcements from the Shenandoah Valley and from Richmond were nullifying Grant's gain. In a day or so, Grant faced the prospect of fighting a reinvigorated Army of Northern Virginia ensconced behind a formidable river line. Compounding these woes were Banks's defeat in Louisiana and Sherman's inability to strike a decisive blow against Johnston. It was important to attack Lee as soon as possible, Grant concluded, before reinforcements could reach him.

Grant also understood the importance of public perceptions. Lincoln did not have to remind him that November was drawing close, and with it the election. Grant needed a victory. Embarking on a wide swing to the Pamunkey would take Grant away from the enemy, not toward him, and would give Lee time to receive reinforcements. And when Grant reached the Pamunkey, he would doubtless find Lee waiting for him there. The better course, Grant concluded, was to attack Lee at the North Anna.

President Lincoln had promised Grant a free hand in the management of the war. Thus far, Lincoln had remained true to his commitment, leaving Grant to make military decisions without interference. Talking privately with his secretary, John Hay, the president remarked that if "any other general had been at the head of that army it would have now been on this side of the Rapidan." It was Grant's "dogged persistency," Lincoln stressed, that was winning victories. Unfortunately, there had been no significant victories since May 12. Wounded men were jamming Washington's hospitals, and casualty lists dominated newspapers across the North. The staggering cost of war on Grant's terms was becoming painfully evident. The defeats of Banks, Sigel, and Butler, following one after the other, hit the president hard. He took to pacing the floor at night, eyes sunken, brushing the hair back from his temples. "My God! My God!" a visitor heard him remark as he contemplated the campaign's bloody toll. "I cannot bear it! I cannot bear it!" [14]

The public's mood had changed. People had expected too much from Grant's accomplishments in the Wilderness and at the Mule Shoe. Now they were taken aback to find Lee's army alive and well. Navy Secretary Gideon Welles observed that the "painful suspense in military operations" was causing "intense anxiety" that "almost unfits the mind for mental activity." Newsman Noah Brooks pressed his finger to Washington's political pulse and discerned that "our people, who have been unduly elated at the success of Grant, are unduly downcast at the temporary check which has attended the National arms." Public feeling, he sensed, was "decidedly blue, everybody forgetting, apparently, that reverses, great and small, must form a part of every campaign." George Templeton Strong described the mood in New York as "despondent and bad." The citizens had formed "an exaggerated view of Grant's hard-won success in opening the campaign," Strong related, "and now, finding the 'backbone of the rebellion' is not 'broken at last' into a handful of incoherent vertebrae, and that Lee still shows fight 'on the Po' and elsewhere, they are disappointed, disgusted, and ready to believe any rumor of disaster that the wicked ingenuity of speculators can devise and inculcate." Brooks likened the fickle public to a "spoiled child" who "refuses to be comforted, because Richmond is not taken forthwith, and because we do not meet with an unbroken success at every point." The answer, Brooks cautioned, was patience. "We must learn," he insisted, "possibly by greater reverses, that as there can be but *one issue* in this war, it is not of the first importance how each individual fight terminates." [15]

Conceding that Lee had won the race to the North Anna, Grant used May 22 to concentrate and rest his army. Warren, he directed, was to advance to Harris's Store, where Telegraph Road intersected the road running between Milford Station and Chilesburg. Burnside was to camp at New Bethel Church, on the road between Madison's Ordinary and Bowling Green. Wright was to cross the Mattaponi at Guinea Bridge and follow Warren's column at least as far as Madison's Ordinary. And Hancock was to remain at Milford Station, opening communication during the day with Warren to his west and Burnside to his north. By evening Grant expected to see his army arrayed in a horseshoe. Warren at Harris's Store and Hancock at Milford Station would comprise the southernmost elements, forming the horseshoe's two lower prongs. Wright at Madison Ordinary and Burnside at New Bethel Church would constitute the horseshoe's curved head. The compact formation would enable the corps to support one another, effectively guarding against a surprise attack from Lee. Most important, the army would be poised to make an easy march the next morning to the North Anna.[16]

Lee awoke at his bivouac near Dickinson's Mill after less than two hours sleep. Ewell's campfires winked in the darkness. Anderson's lead elements lay bedded down close behind. Five miles west, near Chilesburg, Hill's corps, after a two-hour rest, was preparing to resume its trek south. Lee's objective was to unite his army below the North Anna River by noon.[17]

At 5:00 A.M., before setting off, Lee penned a letter to President Davis outlining the military situation. Hoke's and Barton's brigades, the general began, had joined him. Corse and Kemper were near Milford Station, and he hoped to see them before day's end. Grant, he went on, had started toward Bowling Green the night of May 20–21. "The movement was not discovered until after daylight, and in a wooded country like that in which we have been operating, where nothing is known beyond what can be ascertained by feeling, a day's march can always be gained." Moreover, Lee continued, "the enemy left in his trenches the usual amount of force generally visible, and the reports of his movement were so vague and conflicting that it required some time to sift the truth." Lee believed Grant was "endeavoring to place the Mattapony River between him and our army, which secured his flank, and by rapid movements to join his cavalry under Sheridan to attack Richmond." Lee's inclination was to fight—"I should have preferred contesting the enemy's approach inch by inch," he insisted. But out of "solicitude" for Richmond, he was instead moving to Hanover Junction, where he could intercept Grant and stay within supporting distance of the Confederate capital.[18]

Lee confessed uncertainty about Grant's intentions. He thought that the entire Union force—except perhaps part of the 9th Corps—had left Spotsylvania Court House. So far as he could gauge, Bowling Green and Milford Station marked the farthest point of the Federal advance. While Lee presumed that Grant was shifting his supply depot to Port Royal, intelligence was ambiguous on that score as well. Federal engineers were repairing the rail connection from Aquia Creek to Fredericksburg, an effort that would be

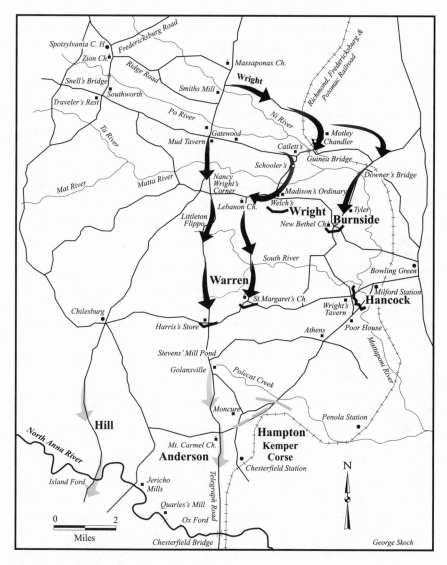

Grant's concentration on May 22

unnecessary if Grant intended to change his base. "As soon as I can get more positive information concerning the movements of the enemy, I will forward it to you," Lee promised. After giving his guide Moncure a message instructing Hampton to continue holding Hancock in check, Lee mounted Traveller and resumed his journey south.[19]

A hot sun rose over Ewell's ragged column as it tramped along Telegraph Road, stirring up dust clouds visible to Hancock's men eight miles to the east. Morning warmed as the Confederate 2nd Corps's veterans marched past Mt. Carmel Church. Two miles farther on the parched soldiers reached Long Creek, filled their canteens in the stream, and pressed ahead. The terrain began dropping toward the North Anna. Immediately beyond a small earthen fort constructed the previous year, Telegraph Road descended abruptly. A quarter mile in the distance, at the foot of the slope, a well-defined line of trees wound through the fields below. Sunlight glinted through leafy spring foliage, marking the course of the river. The Army of Northern Virginia had reached the North Anna.

At 8:30 A.M. Traveller's hooves clattered over the planks of Chesterfield Bridge, carrying Lee up the far bank and onto the farm of the Fox family. A mile and a half south at Hanover Junction, Bradley Johnson's Maryland troops scrutinized dust billowing on the horizon. Soldiers by the thousand were approaching from the north. "Who are they and what does it mean?" wondered John W. F. Hatton, of Captain William F. Dement's 1st Maryland Battery. The distant forms slowly emerged into view. Clad in uniforms stained dirty orange from weeks of use, haggard soldiers strode with distinctive, swaggering gaits. The Marylanders cheered. Jubal Early rode in front of the butternut column, at the head of his division. Behind marched the rest of the Confederate 2nd Corps.[20]

Johnson's Marylanders had recently vacated the musty settlement of log cabins they had occupied during the winter and moved into an extravagant tent city, resplendent with flags. Earlier in the month, anticipating an active campaign, Lee had promulgated orders strictly limiting tents and baggage. Johnson had ignored Lee's stricture, reasoning that his outfit was detached from the main army. Riding up, Early looked across the sprawling sea of canvas and fluttering banners. "What army corps headquarters is this?" he inquired facetiously. "General Lee will be along presently," Early cautioned, "and he will be very apt to say something about his order as to sending tents and baggage to the rear." Taking Early's warning to heart, Johnson and his aides fell to dismantling their excess tents and packing their gear.[21]

The Maryland colonel and his staff, spotlessly attired in fresh uniforms, contrasted sharply with the bedraggled veterans marching past. "Go home, you nice soldiers: we are here now," Ewell's soldiers called out. "Go home, boys, and tell mammy Marse Bob's boys are right down here, and they won't let you get hurt, son."[22]

Shouts rang from afar. A bearded horseman, looking "much worn and troubled," bobbed above the column of unkempt troops. "It is Robert E. Lee!" Hatton cried. "Boys, we know now that the front has come to us!" A soldier exclaimed, "There's a spectacle for the Gods!" Stopping at Colonel Johnson's headquarters—now only a solitary tent bereft of flags and baggage— Lee inquired after Early. George Booth, of Johnson's staff, was shocked at Lee's condition. "The terrible responsibilities that had been forced upon him, and the strain to which he had been subjected for the three or four weeks past," Booth was to write, "were telling on his endurance, and added to this, he was really a sick man." Booth summoned Early, who had been in the tent with Johnson, and the general came out to talk with Lee. Early must begin forming his division in a defensive line, Lee ordered. Early protested that his men were exhausted and needed rest. "General Early," Lee insisted, "you must not tell me these things, but when I give an order, see that it is executed." Lee rode on, and Early turned to walk back into the tent. "General Lee is much troubled and not well," Booth heard him mutter.[23]

Lee telegraphed Davis at 9:30 A.M. that he had reached Hanover Junction with the head of Ewell's corps. Anderson's men, he added, were close behind. Grant's deployments, however, remained a mystery to the Confederate commander, although he suspected that the greater portion of the Union army was still east of the Mattaponi. "I have learned as yet nothing of the movements of the enemy," Lee informed the president. "Nothing certain known," a Marylander echoed in his diary, "but all confident that all is right and Lee knows what he is about."[24]

Lee established his headquarters at the home of the Miller family, a short distance north of Hanover Junction. He remained perplexed over Grant's intentions, making it difficult for him to formulate his next move. If Grant meant to advance along the axis of Telegraph Road and the Richmond, Fredericksburg, and Potomac Railroad, Lee had chosen the right spot to intercept him. But if Grant intended to follow a more easterly route, as Lee suspected, the Confederates needed to be prepared to quickly shift east.

Evidence available to Lee suggested that Grant intended to march to the Pamunkey. Hancock and Warren had erected an infantry screen barring the Confederates access to the Mattaponi, apparently to conceal Grant's activities on the river's far side. The implication was that Burnside and Wright meant to press on to the Pamunkey, hidden from Lee's view by Hancock and Warren. Once they had cleared Guinea Station, Warren would likely follow, and Hancock would bring up the rear. Grant's interest in Port Royal lent further credence to Lee's view that Grant was aiming for the Pamunkey. Grant had earmarked Rooney Lee's homestead on the Pamunkey as the next link in his chain of supply depots as he moved south, and Sheridan was safeguarding White House until Grant arrived with his infantry. Finally, the pattern of Grant's generalship during the campaign pointed toward a Union movement to the Pamunkey. Grant had initiated the campaign by swinging east of Lee in an attempt to turn the Army of Northern Virginia out of its entrenched Rapidan line. Grant's answer to stalemate in the Wilderness had been another turning movement past Lee's east flank to Spotsylvania Court House. And after conceding deadlock there, the Federals were apparently once again sidling east to get between Lee and Richmond. "I think it probable [Grant] will make still another move to the right and land somewhere near [White House]," Lee's aide Taylor wrote, echoing his boss's thinking.[25]

Lee's reading of Grant's likely route was based on verifiable intelligence, but the stakes were too high to risk everything on a hunch, however well founded. Lee decided to let his men rest until he could garner more information. If he guessed wrong and Grant came his way, Lee reasoned, he would have ample time to set his men to digging. If he proved correct, then rest would render his troops all the more fit for the hard march east. As a precaution, Lee consulted Jedediah Hotchkiss, the 2nd Corps's talented mapmaker, on where to locate a defensive line, should one become necessary. Hotchkiss recommended against fortifying the river. In places the North Anna's north bank was higher than its south bank. Hotchkiss suggested that Lee entrench along the Virginia Central Railroad, which hugged the high watershed between the North Anna River and Little River to the south. Lee agreed with Hotchkiss's suggestion, in part because it permitted him to establish a relatively straight line. Referring to the experience of May 12, Lee cautioned, "We do not want any more salients." [26]

Lee had always taken pride in his ability to divine his opponent's intentions. Grant, however, was hard to read. On May 7 Lee had underestimated the scope of Grant's movement to Spotsylvania Court House. On May 11 he had misread Grant's deployment to attack the Mule Shoe and had removed artillery from the very point that Grant was preparing to strike. On May 14 Lee had missed Grant's concentration near the weak Confederate right flank until Federal dispositions were complete. And on May 21 Lee had unwittingly marched two infantry corps across Grant's front. May 22 was another such day. Concluding that Grant was making a turning movement to the east, Lee elected to rest his troops in anticipation of a hard march to the Pamunkey. He made virtually no preparations to fight Grant at the North Anna, once again leaving undefended the very sector that Grant had targeted. In the past, hard fighting and good luck had saved Lee from predicaments created when he misunderstood Grant's designs. It remained to be seen whether his luck would hold once again.

By noon, the entire Army of Northern Virginia had crossed to the North Anna's southern bank. The 2nd Corps filed into camp near Hanover Junction. The 1st Corps arrived close behind and pitched tents along the Virginia Central Railroad, extending west from the junction. Hill's corps passed through Chilesburg, crossed the river at Island Ford, and continued to Hewlett Station on the Virginia Central Railroad, eight miles west of Hanover Junction. "Under one of General Breckinridge's staff tents I have, through the kind hospitality of two or three of his officers, enjoyed a refreshing lunch and delightful nap," the artillery commander Pendleton wrote his wife. "Now I am sitting on the ground, in the shade, at [his son Sandie Pendleton's] tent, with my back against a pine stump, and writing this on my knee." Lee's aide Taylor proclaimed May 22 the first day in the campaign that he had been "spared the sight of the miserable Yankees." Confederate supply wagons did not arrive until late, and provisions were scant. "We drew some meal and in a mess tin made something we call mush," a Confederate recollected. Another soldier—George Cary Eggleston of Lamkin's battery—had not eaten for thirty-six hours. "If I had a million dollars I would give it all for a piece of meat as big as two fingers," he announced to his brother, who obligingly pulled a piece of grimy, bruised bacon fat from his pants pocket. Eggleston refused the meat until his brother goaded him into taking it by threatening to toss it over a fence. Years later, Eggleston described the morsel as "the most luxurious food" he ever ate.[27]

Before leaving Dickinson's Mill, Lee had dispatched Moncure with instructions for Hampton to "hold [Hancock] in check, falling back gradually." Hampton selected a strong position along Polecat Creek, two miles west of the poorhouse. Hampton's cavalrymen, along with Kemper's and Corse's infantry brigades, entrenched along a five-mile arc running roughly north to south from Wright's Tavern to Penola Station, blocking Hancock's access to Telegraph Road. Hampton sent scouts to probe Hancock's line, but they were unable to pierce the Union infantry screen and discover anything about Grant's activities behind the Mattaponi.[28]

"If sheep attack you, you are obliged to fight."

Union forces on May 22 moved with a plodding, slow-motion quality. For three interminable hours Grant watched Burnside's troops dribble past Guinea

Station. Not until 9:00 had the 9th Corps cleared the depot and made way for Wright's men coming behind. Then Burnside started his short march to New Bethel Church. His men were ravenous, and Caroline County offered ample opportunity for scavenging. "This is the best part of Virginia," a Federal concluded. "Good houses and fruitful fields hereabouts." By noon the 9th Corps was filing into camp around the church. Soldiers boiling coffee were interrupted by an elderly rebel who berated them with a "volley of maledictions" from his window. They laughed at the old man's agitation and wolfed down their rations.[29]

Wright's troops were in terrible condition by the time they reached Guinea Station. They had been awake for thirty hours and were "mad enough to kill," a New Yorker claimed. Many soldiers had only coffee and corn to assuage their hunger. Wright's tardy arrival—caused, in fairness to the 6th Corps, by Burnside's lackadaisical progress—threw the Union timetable badly off schedule. Grant had wanted Warren to start for Harris's Store as soon as Wright reached Guinea Station, and for Wright to follow Warren. Humphreys took one look at the blown troops and realized they could never maintain the pace that headquarters had envisioned. "Wright's men have been up all night, and want rest," Humphreys concluded and recommended that the 6th Corps halt for the day at Madison's Ordinary. Warren, who was responsible for coordinating the 6th Corps's advance with his own, agreed.[30]

Warren found himself embroiled in a logistical nightmare created by the Union army's inaccurate campaign maps. This was the first time that Federal troops had visited Caroline County. The maps, prepared during the winter, were extremely unreliable, particularly this deep in the Old Dominion. They depicted roads that did not exist and pictured distances that bore no relation to reality. Warren dispatched his own reconnoitering parties and identified two routes leading from Madison's Ordinary to the 5th Corps's objective at Harris's Store. One option was to proceed to Nancy Wright's Corner, then follow Telegraph Road past Littleton Flippo's farm, through the tiny hamlet of Cedon, and on to Harris's Store. A second possibility was to veer south at Lebanon Church and follow a road that ran parallel to Telegraph Road and two miles east of it. This subsidiary route came out at St. Margaret's Church— sometimes called Bull Church—a mile east of Harris's Store on the crossroad from Milford Station to Chilesburg. To make up for lost time—the 5th Corps had been waiting nearly four hours for Wright to arrive—Warren elected to use both routes. Griffin's division, followed by Crawford's, was to proceed via Madison's Ordinary to Nancy Wright's Corner, then descend Telegraph Road to Harris's Store, a nine-mile march. Cutler's division was to take a slightly shorter course by turning off at Lebanon Church and pursuing the auxiliary road to St. Margaret's Church.[31]

By 11:00 A.M. the 5th Corps was threading south. The morning felt "soft and balmy," a soldier recorded, "and nature all about us seemed to invite rest and pleasure rather than obedience to the stern and relentless call of war." Roebling rode in Griffin's advance with Bartlett's brigade. Bartlett was sick, and his brigade was being led by Colonel Joshua L. Chamberlain of the 20th Maine. It was noon before the head of the column reached Nancy Wright's Corner. Roebling estimated that the rear of Lee's army was about three hours ahead. "As we had no cavalry," the staffer noted in frustration, "we had no expectation of catching up." Bartlett's advance guard hurried on, picking up Confederates who had straggled and a few broken-down wagons and ambulances. After lunch the weather turned scorching hot, and troops labored along in choking swirls of dust.[32]

Wright's soldiers were in no condition to begin the last leg of their march until well after noon. Dust-caked and exhausted, they pried themselves from fields around Guinea Station and started a toilsome three-hour tramp. At long last Madison's Ordinary came into view. The troops occupied the entrenchments erected by Kitching the night before. Many fell asleep without waiting to cook dinner. The 126th Ohio camped in Mr. Welch's yard—"a splendid house and a grand yard, flower garden," a soldier noted. Mr. Welch had departed with his horses but had left behind a considerable number of slaves to the Yankees. "It hasn't been a very profitable Sabbath to me, nor kept as the Sabbath should be," a Michigan man noted, although he took heart from the fact that no one had shot at him all day.[33]

Hancock spent an uneasy morning watching dust raised by Ewell's and Anderson's Confederates. An early-morning probe by Hampton's riders and horse artillery spooked some of Tyler's men, who fired wildly and ran away, abandoning their equipment to the rebels. "We got awfully scared but not much hurt," a soldier in the 8th New York Heavy Artillery observed. The greenhorns complained that breastworks were virtually useless against artillery. "Well, tell them to take it comfortably," Hancock suggested. "The Rebs have a way of throwing shells and I am sure I can't stop them!"[34]

To forestall surprise attacks, Hancock dispatched Torbert's horsemen along roads leading toward the Confederates. Most of the mounted force rode northwest toward New Bethel Church to cement the 2nd Corps's link with Burnside. Hancock also instructed Birney to send a regiment west along Devil's Three Jumps Road to "ascertain what is immediately in your front." Birney selected the 1st United States Sharpshooters for the assignment. They found food but no rebels. This was a "red letter day for the men who had been confined to such rations as they could carry on their persons," a sharpshooter recollected years later. Advancing to the county poorhouse, they found it well stocked with chickens, mutton, milk, and eggs. "If these are Virginia poor house rations," the Federals laughed as they stuffed their haversacks, "the poor of Virginia are greatly to be envied." Continuing to Polecat Creek, the scouting party came on Hampton's new line and turned back to report its findings.[35]

Around 10:30 A.M. Hancock received alarming news that unidentified troops were moving in his direction. In fact, these were Birney's men returning from their scouting mission. Nervous 2nd Corps officers had mistaken them for Confederates deploying to attack. At Hancock's urging, Barlow sent two reconnoitering parties to investigate. The first—consisting of a substantial portion of Colonel Smyth's brigade—marched west to Wright's Tavern, where it found only a few Confederate cavalrymen. Colonel James Beaver's 148th Pennsylvania meanwhile scouted northwest toward New Bethel Church, following the road Torbert had taken a few hours earlier. "We went some five miles out," Colonel Beaver later wrote, "met the enemy's cavalry in front and were fired into by our own cavalry in rear, but fortunately lost none." These probes persuaded Hancock that he was safe. "I don't believe at present that there is any enemy immediately in my front except videttes, which we fire at occasionally," he wrote headquarters at 12:45 P.M. Hancock's report caused considerable merriment when Meade received it several hours later. "There came news that a line of battle was advancing against Hancock, which turned out to be Birney's division, of his own men!" Lyman chortled.[36]

Early in the afternoon, Birney advanced a short distance to the Coleman family property and erected an elaborate line of earthworks. Colonel Egan of Birney's division meanwhile undertook a reconnaissance in force to determine Hampton's strength once and for all. His secondary objective was to capture rebel cavalrymen reportedly holding Penola Station. Egan dispatched the 3rd Maine, 40th New York, and 99th Pennsylvania on the mission. The detachment reached the railway station and found a single dismounted Confederate cavalryman. Taking the lone prisoner to Birney, Egan announced: "We captured the enemy's outposts and main body—horse, foot, and dragoons. Not a man escaped—and here he is!"[37]

Around 1:00 P.M.—Burnside's corps was pouring into New Bethel Church, Wright's fatigued warriors were steeling to march from Guinea Station, and Hancock was investigating phantom Confederates in his front—the head of

Warren's 5th Corps column emerged onto the broad expanse of Littleton Flippo's farm. Here Telegraph Road descended sharply to a small tributary of the Motto River—not to be confused with the Matta, to the north—then climbed a partially wooded hillside to the tiny settlement of Cedon. At the edge of the farm, small groups of Confederate horsemen sparred with Bartlett's advance elements—commanded by Chamberlain, of the 20th Maine— firing from behind trees and fences, then disappeared into the surrounding woods. "We have picked up stragglers since crossing the [Matta] from both Ewell and [Anderson]," Warren wrote headquarters. "They began passing here yesterday at 3:00 P.M., and the rear of the main party an hour after sunrise. I think we shall have trouble in crossing the [Motto]," he predicted. "A colored man who came up the road says [Anderson] is resting about 2 miles ahead of where we are." [38]

As Chamberlain's command splashed across the stream, a projectile from a rifled cannon winged overhead and landed among the Federals, killing a soldier in the 118th Pennsylvania and another in the 44th New York. Smoke floated above a wooded crest to the right of the road, near Mr. Flippo's home, revealing the Confederate position. Chamberlain ordered his men to halt along the wooded stream bank and hurriedly conferred with Griffin. [39]

By chance, Chamberlain had encountered Chambliss's brigade. During the morning the resourceful Confederate cavalryman, assisted by Rooney Lee, had assembled his three regiments, McGregor's battery, and the brigade's ambulances and wagons in Mr. Flippo's fields. Chambliss was preparing to start south in Anderson's rear when he spied Chamberlain's Federals approaching from the north. Concerned for the safety of his wagons and artillery, he had arrayed part of his force to delay the Federals. Two pieces unlimbered near Flippo's house, where they had clear shots at the roadway. The 10th Virginia Cavalry and two companies from the 9th Virginia Cavalry dismounted and hid in woods along Telegraph Road. The rest of the 9th Virginia Cavalry massed near the pieces in the Flippo yard, sabers drawn and ready to charge. The 13th Virginia Cavalry rode west to safety along a farm road with the outfit's wagons and McGregor's other guns. [40]

Chambliss watched in satisfaction as blue-clad forms scurried for cover. A rebel cavalryman glanced at McGregor expecting to see "very deep concern for the escape of his guns." To his surprise, McGregor sat "composedly on his horse with one leg across the boot of his saddle and reading an open volume with an intentness that the roar of his guns did not seem to disturb with the smallest degree." The artillerist had been in tight scrapes before, and he was confident that he could hold off the Federals long enough for his battery to get away. [41]

Joshua Chamberlain was a citizen soldier of the first order. At Gettysburg he had proven his ability to act decisively, and he hoped to win new laurels at Mr. Flippo's farm. Aiming to silence McGregor and capture a few Confederate guns to boot, he thrust the 16th Michigan and 83rd Pennsylvania straight up the road in echelon. Simultaneously the 44th New York, 20th Maine, and 118th Pennsylvania began circling around the edge of the field under cover of woods. Chamberlain's objective was to fix Chambliss's attention on the road while the flanking force cut off the artillery and killed the horses before the Confederates could haul the pieces away.[42]

Chamberlain led his three rightmost regiments along the tree line until they reached a fence and a creek. "Take the fence along with you, my men," he shouted. "Throw it in, and yourselves after it!" Soon a jumble of boards spanned the stream, providing footing for the Federals to cross.[43]

Company E of the 118th Pennsylvania crept through the trees at the head of the flanking force. In a patch of woods across from the rebel guns, Captain Walters, leading the company, came on a Confederate major. The rebel was sitting erect on a gray horse, hand cupped to his ear, intently following the battle. Walters, the story goes, circled the southerner like a hunter stalks a deer. Chamberlain, who saw Walters's game, signaled the approaching troops to be quiet. Tiptoeing around the major, Walters snatched the Confederate's reins with his left hand and pointed a pistol at him with his right. "I demand your immediate and unconditional surrender," Walters shouted. "Not so," answered the major with a start as he reached for his carbine. "You are my prisoner!" Walters belted. "Touch that and you die!" The Confederate was so humiliated when the Federals requested his sword that he angrily drew the blade from his scabbard, stabbed it into the ground, and broke it off at the hilt. "The major was rather a [testy] fellow," a witness observed, "and an inspection of his saddle disclosed a brand new uniform coat, evidently intended to be worn on distinguished official or high social occasions."[44]

The Confederates discovered Chamberlain's turning movement, and McGregor's men "whirled their battery about, and gave us canister, inflicting quite a loss on us," a Pennsylvanian recounted. The 10th Virginia Cavalry fought doggedly to buy time to save the guns. Under a brisk covering fire, McGregor withdrew his last two pieces to safety along the farm trail. Unlimbering the guns on the plateau overlooking the Flippo farm, he fired a parting shot. "A wide gap was made in the column," a Confederate observed, "and a good many of the enemy ran in confusion." Griffin, who had a special fondness for artillery, directed Rittenhouse's Battery D, 5th United States Artillery, into position. "Give them hell!" the general shouted. Rittenhouse's pieces fired with such precision that a Federal claimed the rebels "made off and were not heard from again that day." A Confederate maintained that by the time Rittenhouse opened, Chambliss had moved out of range, and the Union shells "fell fast and furious, but harmless, behind us." Rooney Lee and Chambliss led their troops and artillery along country byways to safety.[45]

Ellis Spear, commanding the 20th Maine, decried the missed opportunity to bag the southerners; the Confederates "ran as soon as we appeared through the bushes, and apparently they were there only for the purpose of compelling us to go into line, and to lose a little time to their advantage," he seethed. "We ought to have smashed right on with only a skirmish line ahead." The rebels agreed that the brush at Flippo's place had been a close call. "We soon were nearly surrounded by Yankee infantry but managed to keep them off us," one of Chambliss's men recorded in his diary.[46]

With Telegraph Road clear again, Warren resumed his march. Flanking columns kept well out on both sides of his force, and details searched every house and barn, taking care to avoid another ambush. "The country now became more open, and our route lay through a rich section of Virginia, but little frequented by either army, and highly cultivated," a Massachusetts soldier noted. "There was a decided tendency to renew once more our acquaintance with the bountiful products of this fertile, smiling country." Officers winked at the looting. When Major O'Neill of the 118th Pennsylvania discovered a soldier had broken rank to seize a goose, he had the man brought to him. "Don't you know the orders?" the long-suffering major admonished. The soldier replied loudly over the goose, which was violently hissing from its perch under his arm. "Sure, sir," he said. "The only orders I know is not to leave anything behind me, and ain't I obeying them, sir?" The major had a ready response. "Well, if it's prisoners you mean you'll not leave behind you, you may turn him over to me." Taking the goose and handing it to his orderly, the major announced with a wink, "Put the dirty rebel in the guard house."[47]

The two 5th Corps columns—Griffin and Crawford descending Telegraph Road, and Cutler on the ancillary road to the east—captured several hundred Confederates who had fallen behind. Major Abner R. Small of the 16th Maine spotted a gray-clad drummer boy sitting on a log and eased beside the forlorn youth. "Couldn't keep up," the boy volunteered, and added, "I'm hungry." Small extracted a morsel from his knapsack, which the youth devoured. After a few minutes of banter, the boy stood up. "I reckon I must go now," he said, but it was apparent to Small that he had no particular destination in mind. Before either could speak, a bugle sounded, and the Federal column moved on. The image of the forlorn boy standing by the dusty roadside remained vivid to Small years later. "When we bivouacked and built our fires near [St. Margaret's] Church that night, I wondered what had become of him," Small reminisced. "I never knew." [48]

At 5:00 P.M. Griffin reached Harris's Store and stopped for the evening. Crawford camped in Griffin's rear. Cutler, who had pursued the companion route from Lebanon Church, halted a mile east at St. Margaret's Church. Warren and his staff established headquarters at the residence of Lee's friend, Dr. Flippo—a "most delightful place to camp," a Federal observed—and nearly captured fifty Confederate wagons that had delayed in getting off. The doctor's fence rails made excellent cooking fires, his tobacco barn afforded soldiers a welcome smoke, and his sheep assured the invaders a "very acceptable temporary change of diet." Bartlett, who was fast recovering from his malady, wryly remarked to a group of soldiers feasting on Dr. Flippo's livestock, "If sheep attack you, you are obliged to fight." A private in the 44th New York wisecracked back, "It was the most decisive victory since the beginning of the campaign." The fare at St. Margaret's Church was spartan, although Cutler's men made good use of an ice house near the church. A sergeant from Massachusetts rationalized sleeping in a cornfield as "a new way to starve the Rebs by treading down their corn." [49]

As Warren, Wright, and Burnside completed their deployments, Hancock's isolation came to an end. At 4:00 P.M. Meade sent Hancock a message—it reached the 2nd Corps's commander an hour later—advising that Burnside had settled in at New Bethel Church and was prepared to assist Hancock if summoned. At 5:30 P.M. Warren dispatched Pope to report the 5th Corps's appearance at Harris's Store and St. Margaret's Church. [50]

The mood in Union camps was upbeat. "Chickens and turkeys are found quite abundantly," a Pennsylvanian announced, "but they will not last long." Everyone was relieved to be moving toward Richmond. "Here things are jolly," a New Yorker noted with satisfaction. "The troops felt good and were in fine condition," seconded a man from Wisconsin. "This night and day marching is tough on our men," concluded a surgeon in Upton's brigade. "We begin to feel used up, but full of faith that we are using some one up! I hope it is the rebels." [51]

As Theodore Gerrish of the 20th Maine dozed off, it occurred to him that the ground might be cooperating with the Confederates. "I shall always believe that the soil of Virginia is at least several degrees harder than that of any other State in the Union," Gerrish reflected. "We always found, when we camped for the night, that the ground would not adapt itself to our wants. There was always a hummock where we wanted a hollow, and a hollow where it was desirable to have a hummock, and no matter how frequently we changed positions, the result was always the same. I never knew whether this strange phenomenon was due to the geologic formation of the country, or to the fact that the sacred soil itself was so hostile to the Yankees who were desecrating it, that it was determined to add to our misery." [52]

Details of maneuvering south and rearranging the army's supply network kept Grant and Meade busy all day. Early in the morning, Meade alerted his chief quartermaster, Rufus Ingalls, to move the wagons and ambulances to Bowling Green. The Potomac Army had started the campaign with some 4,300 wagons and 835 ambulances. During the advance from Spotsylvania Court House, 15 wagons had been assigned to follow each division and pick up soldiers too exhausted to continue. A few supply wagons also accompanied the marching columns. Most conveyances, however, stayed with the main train, as did a large herd of cattle nicknamed the "Bull Corps," escorted by Ferrero's 9th Corps division of black troops. Near dark, Ferrero and his charges marched into Bowling Green. Someone had set the courthouse on fire—accounts do not make clear who started the blaze—and the sight of five thousand black soldiers striding through town singing "John Brown's Body" struck terror into the citizens. [53]

At 8:30 A.M. Grant notified Halleck that Milford Station was in Federal hands and directed him to shift the supply network from the Fredericksburg–Belle Plain complex to Port Royal and Bowling Green. Halleck alerted the Engineer, Quartermaster, Commissary, Medical, and Railroad Departments. The task was enormous. Halleck wanted all war material evacuated from Fredericksburg and Belle Plain, leaving nothing for the Confederates. Empty wagons were to be loaded and driven to Bowling Green, and the remaining supplies and the garrisons guarding them were to proceed by boat to Port Royal. The only Federals who would remain behind were those necessary to tend the wounded and to oversee the evacuation. [54]

Brigadier General Abercrombie, who was responsible for the Fredericksburg–Belle Plain supply line, bombarded headquarters with inquiries. What was he to do with the six reserve artillery batteries that Grant had sent him on May 18? Should the Belle Plain garrison take the direct overland route to Port Royal or pass by way of Fredericksburg? What should he do about the railway to Aquia, which was almost repaired? Did Grant want the thousand feet of bridging stored at Belle Plain sent back to Washington, or did he want it forwarded to Port Royal? The details were important, and they were endless. Grant and Rawlins grappled with them all day. [55]

Moving the wounded men proved particularly difficult. Working at peak capacity, Abercrombie had transferred an average of 1,500 patients a day

from Belle Plain to hospitals in Washington. By the evening of May 18, surgeon R. O. Abbott, medical director for the Department of Washington, had
received 14,878 injured soldiers along with 600 malingerers who had fina-
gled transport to the capital using "bloody bandages and judicious limping."
A wave of injured men from Ewell's attack on May 19 hit Fredericksburg just
before Grant began south. According to the Federal army's medical director,
many wounds were "so blackened with powder as to prove that the injury
was self-inflicted either by design or accident." Inexperienced heavy artillerymen unwittingly aggravated their injuries by applying tourniquets too
tightly. Abercrombie decided to keep the most serious cases in Fredericksburg on the assumption that transporting them over rough roads to
Belle Plain might prove fatal. The bottleneck caused by bad roads disappeared on May 20 when Union gunboats made the Rappahannock safe for
Union ships to navigate. The remaining invalids were loaded onto barges
towed by two light-draft steamers and ferried past Port Royal to Tappa-
hannock. There they transferred to hospital transports fitted with beds and
kitchens. Late on May 22 Abercrombie pronounced the railroad to Aquia
Creek in running order and began evacuating seriously injured men that way
as well. The evacuation was not finished until May 28. The final tally of
wounded and sick men forwarded to Washington from Fredericksburg and
Belle Plain totaled 26,191.[56]

A story made the rounds during the day that Butler had been thoroughly
defeated. "Rumors with us had not at this time much weight," Major Spear of
the 20th Maine observed. "But in this particular case of Butler being driven
back, the report had distressing earmarks of truth, and tallied with the probability, as if one should report that a man fell out of a tree, this being in accord
with the law of gravitation." The rumor was true. Hunkered in entrenchments
at Bermuda Hundred, between the James and Appomattox Rivers, the corpu-
lent Bay State general was tying up thirty thousand Federal troops, apparently to no purpose. As Lyman put it, "Butler has just bottled himself up in
Bermuda Hundred and has indeed made a nice mess of it!" According to
Grant's intelligence, Pickett's division had left Richmond to join Lee, as had
Breckinridge's army from the Shenandoah Valley, which meant that the
Army of Northern Virginia was fast repairing its losses. Grant had ordered
Halleck to send an envoy to investigate the reasons for Butler's failure and to
recommend whether Butler's troops should join Grant. News of reinforcements streaming to Lee's army so irritated Grant that he decided not to wait
for the envoy's report. He had put up with Butler's incompetence long
enough. "The force under Butler is not detaining 10,000 men in Richmond,
and is not even keeping the roads south of the city cut," he complained to

Halleck. "Under these circumstances I think it advisable to have all of it here except enough to keep a foothold at City Point." Butler's troops were to start north immediately to join Grant.[57]

Around noon, Grant, Meade, and their entourages left the secessionist Motley's yard and took a roundabout route to New Bethel Church. They crossed Guinea Bridge, stopped briefly at the Catlett home—Lyman noted that the place was "full of cross women"—and continued on to Madison's Ordinary. Lyman tried the door on the store and found it locked. Peeking inside, he saw that the building was empty. Orders for goods from surrounding plantations littered the yard. Patent medicine comprised the most frequently requested item, followed by molasses, hymn books, and blue cotton.[58]

The distinguished party turned left at Madison's Ordinary and continued through a luxuriant oak forest to New Bethel Church. They reached the structure around 4:00 P.M. Burnside and his aides were inside and reminded Lyman of a "comfortable abbott, in one of the pews, surrounded by his buckish staff whose appearance is the reverse of clerical." The sight of urban New Yorkers in spanking new military garb skulking about rural Virginia struck him as especially amusing. Outside, troops were slouching past, and entire companies were sitting down to rest. Burnside's unconcern over the unmilitary appearance of his command provoked Rawlins into issuing a firm reprimand to institute "strong and efficient" rear guards and to "summarily punish" stragglers.[59]

North of the church, on the road to Downer's Bridge, was the Tyler plantation. A stately home called "Blenheim," made of bricks brought from England in colonial times, rose above a clover field. A cavalryman in Meade's headquarters guard warned Lyman to be wary of the owner, reputedly a "rank secesher." Undaunted, the staffer went to the door to see for himself. He knocked and was greeted by the elderly Mrs. Tyler and her visibly pregnant daughter-in-law. The sight of a Union officer at first sent the younger Tyler into tears, but soon she settled down and chatted amiably with Lyman. The older woman—a "simple and narrow person," Lyman described her—had lost a son at Antietam, and she was ill disposed toward Yankees. She recognized the advantage of having Union brass camping on her lawn, however, since her home would be safe from looting. Lyman returned to New Bethel Church with eggs, milk, fresh vegetables, and hot cornbread.[60]

Around 5:00 P.M. Lyman came back to Mrs. Tyler's yard with Grant, Meade, and their staffs. The Tyler ladies were waiting in the doorway. "With your permission, I will spend a few hours here," Grant announced. The younger Tyler answered, "Certainly sir," but the older lady wanted to make sure that the general would provide protection. "I do hope you will not let your soldiers ruin our place and carry away our property," she ventured. "I will order a guard to keep the men out of your place," Grant obligingly responded, "and see that you are amply protected."[61]

While Grant gave the necessary orders, the elderly woman leaned over and whispered in Horace Porter's ear. With whom, she asked the aide, had she been speaking? "General Grant," Porter answered, and she excitedly informed her daughter-in-law. The younger woman immediately became animated. Her husband, it developed, was a colonel serving with General Johnston in the west. Did Grant have news from that quarter, she wondered? Grant answered that Sherman was advancing on Rome, Georgia, and had probably taken the town. "General Sherman will never capture that place," the younger Mrs. Tyler huffed. "I know all about that country, and you haven't an army that will ever take it. We all know very well that Sherman is making no headway against General Johnston's army." Grant politely responded that his news was to the contrary, which only aggravated the ladies. The elderly woman assumed a "bantering tone," recounted Porter, and the younger woman became "excited and defiant," insisting that Rome would never fall to the Yankees. As though on cue, a courier rode up with a telegram from Sherman announcing his capture of Rome. The news upset both women terribly, and the distraught wife burst into tears. "I came from Richmond not long ago," the older lady finally spit out, "and I had the satisfaction of looking down every day on the Yankee prisoners. I saw thousands and thousands of them, and before this campaign is over I want to see the whole of the Yankee army in southern prisons."[62]

In the midst of this tirade, Burnside rode up, strode onto the porch, removed his hat with a flourish, and bowed low to the ladies. Lyman thought the 9th Corps commander, decked out in a short military jacket and a bell-crowned felt hat with its brim turned down, presented "an odd figure, the fat man!" Gazing across the lawn sprinkled with blue uniforms, the portly general asked Mrs. Tyler, "I don't suppose, madam, that you ever saw so many Yankee soldiers before?" Her response was immediate. "Not at liberty, sir." Everyone, Porter recalled, was "greatly amused, and General Grant joined heartily in the laugh that followed at Burnside's expense."[63]

Grant seldom moved into houses that he selected for his headquarters. He invariably commandeered porches, and he did so this sticky Virginia evening, after the ruckus with the Tyler ladies had subsided. Torbert rode up, having established a picket line from Hancock's entrenchments to Bethel Church. Formerly fastidious about his appearance, Torbert was wearing a sailor's shirt that made Lyman suspicious that he had "grown rough" since joining the cavalry. Dana, who had returned from a quick visit to Washington—"some regard him as a sort of spy on Grant," Lyman observed—also sat down to catch up on gossip. "Our talk that night was that in all probability we should meet the enemy on the North Anna, a day's march to the south of our position," Dana recorded. Major Charles J. Mills, of Crittenden's 9th Corps staff, passed the time with "two or three very pretty and quite pleasant though of course 'secesh' young ladies." They treated him to ice, milk, and hoecake. "Altogether," Mills wrote his mother, the interlude provided a "most romantic experience of campaigning." [64]

Grant's soldiers were painfully aware that the attempt to catch the Army of Northern Virginia away from its entrenchments had failed. "The strangest move ever made is on the board now," one of Burnside's men remarked. "Lee is marching on parallel roads and has the inside track," an officer in the 3rd Pennsylvania Cavalry tersely observed. "Just now there appears to be an obstacle in the way of our marching any further," a soldier wrote home in playful reference to Lee's army, "but how long 'Old Useless,' as the boys mischievously call the Lieutenant General, will allow it to hinder his onward progress, remains to be seen." Grant came in for the lion's share of blame. "I fear that Grant has made a botch of this move also, for Lee is certainly ahead of us now," Colonel Wainwright stewed. "If the demonstrations on his part which kept the whole army idle through most of today were intended to hold us until [Lee] had got sufficient force at Hanover to keep the place, they have probably succeeded." [65]

At 10:00 P.M. Grant issued orders calculated to bring on a battle the next day. At 5:00 A.M. each corps was to send out "cavalry and infantry on all roads to their front leading south, and ascertain, if possible, where the enemy is." If Lee was on the other side of the North Anna—where Grant believed him to be—then the army was to follow. The 2nd Corps was to proceed to a place identified on Union maps as Chesterfield Ford, near the Richmond, Fredericksburg, and Potomac Railroad bridge; the 9th Corps was to cross upriver at a place marked Jericho Bridge; and the 5th Corps and 6th Corps were to cross farther upriver. "The map only shows two roads for the four corps to march upon," Grant noted, "but no doubt by the use of plantation roads and pressing in guides, others can be found to give one for each corps." Headquarters, Grant added, would follow the 9th Corps, and supply trains would proceed to Milford Station.[66]

The battles for the North Anna River were about to begin.

IX

MAY 23

Grant Attacks at the North Anna

"This is nothing but a feint."

MORNING OF MAY 23 saw the roads and byways of Caroline County alive with blue-clad columns on the march. Warren started south along Telegraph Road from Harris's Store, driving straight toward the North Anna River. A few miles behind Warren, Wright broke camp at the Welch farm, headed for Nancy Wright's Corner, then turned onto Telegraph Road behind the 5th Corps. Several miles east, Hancock left his hillside encampment near Milford Station and stepped onto roads leading through Athens and on to Mt. Carmel Church, on Telegraph Road. And at New Bethel Church, Burnside began threading south toward Wright's Tavern, where he was slated to slip into place behind Hancock. The two Union columns—Warren and Wright descending Telegraph Road, and Hancock and Burnside pursuing roads to the southwest—were to converge at Mt. Carmel Church. By evening, if Grant's plan unfolded according to schedule, the entire Federal force would be united along the North Anna.

Hoping to start early, Warren thrust Lieutenant Colonel Pope's cavalry down Telegraph Road at 4:30 A.M. Carbines sputtered as the horsemen sparred with scattered detachments from Chambliss's indefatigable Virginians. Griffin was upset to learn that Jacob Sweitzer, commanding one of his brigades, was still eating breakfast. The general cursed loudly until he noticed the 118th Pennsylvania's chaplain standing nearby. "Beg pardon parson, I did not know you were here," he offered contritely. "I cannot help swearing sometimes, but I am ashamed of it." At St. Margaret's Church, Cutler's soldiers broke into a smokehouse that belonged to two elderly ladies who had treated the Federals kindly. The sight of looters swaggering along with stolen meat skewered on their bayonets rankled their companions, who reported them to the provost.

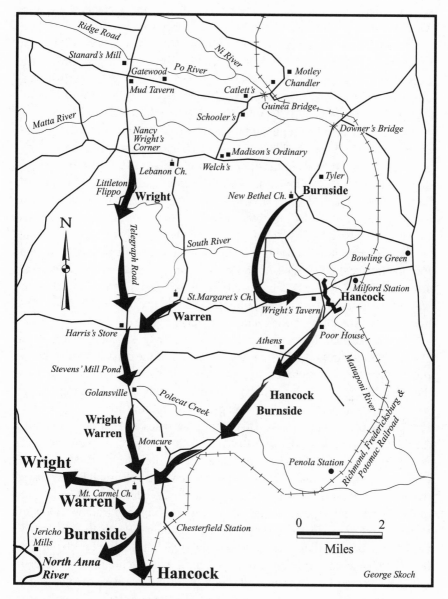

Union routes to the North Anna River on May 23

"All the boys would justify anyone for taking anything from the Rebs," a sergeant observed, "but after kindness was shown by them, and they had done what they could to help us, [the theft] was not approved by anyone." [1]

The 5th Corps was under way by 5:00 A.M. Cutler cut across to Telegraph Road from St. Margaret's Church to lead the procession, and Griffin and Crawford fell in behind. Kitching's brigade kept watch over the corps's wagons, and the Maryland Brigade brought up the rear. "No incident of note occurred until we reached Mt. Carmel Church," Roebling observed. [2]

Torbert's cavalry had rejoined the 2nd Corps during the night. Soon after daylight Torbert dispatched troopers along Hancock's prospective route, extending feelers out roads in the direction of the rebels. By 5:30 A.M. Birney's division had started, followed by Tyler, Gibbon, and Barlow. Two artillery batteries accompanied each division, and wagons carrying pontoons for bridging the North Anna lumbered behind. A former slave stood along the roadside, swinging his hat. "Come on!" he called by way of encouragement. "I am a free man now!" Farther on, at a tumbledown settlement consisting of four log huts and a few sheds, two ladies joyfully greeted the invaders "with arms akimbo." The day became swelteringly hot, and the farmland along the way afforded scant shade. "Perspiration ran down my face and into my eyes, burning my eyeballs as if with acid," a marcher reported. [3]

Warren reached Mt. Carmel Church—an easy six-mile march from Harris's Store—around 10:00. "It was evidently of the class described by the Italian cab drivers as a church for religion, not for show," observed Spear of the 20th Maine. Cutler's division continued south along Telegraph Road while Warren stopped to study his maps. The scribbling bore no apparent resemblance to the actual roads. Dismissing the maps as "utterly erroneous," the 5th Corps's commander sent Roebling to try and piece together an accurate picture of the network of roads and trails fanning from Mt. Carmel Church. The structure stood at the intersection where Telegraph Road crossed the east-west thoroughfare from Milford Station to Chilesburg. A mile south of the church Telegraph Road forked, the rightmost branch leading southwest toward Ox Ford, and the leftmost prong continuing south to Chesterfield Bridge. Roebling explored the branch to the right but was kept from the river by Confederate cavalry. Then he looped back and ventured down the main left fork, crossed Long Creek, and rode toward the North Anna. The staffer caught sight of Confederates on the far bank, "flags flying and bands playing." As Grant had expected, Lee was waiting below the river. [4]

Roebling returned to Mt. Carmel Church at 11:00 A.M. to find Warren, Torbert, and several of Hancock's staffers talking things over. The 2nd Corps had made excellent time. Hampton's Confederate cavalry and their supporting infantry brigades had abandoned their defensive line along Polecat Creek with scarcely a fight. All morning they filtered over to Telegraph Road along farm tracks. Hancock crossed Polecat Creek virtually unopposed and pressed on to Old Chesterfield, a mile and a half from Telegraph Road. He halted his column there and sent aides ahead to make contact with Warren and coordinate the advance of their two corps.[5]

Coordination was definitely needed. From Captain William D. W. Miller, Hancock's aide-de-camp, Warren discovered that Cutler was marching on the road that Hancock was supposed to take. The confusion arose from erroneous designations on Union maps. Hancock had been directed to proceed to Chesterfield Ford, but there was no Chesterfield Ford. Grant and Meade were several miles away, and no staffers from headquarters were on hand to make decisions. The absence of firm leadership was curious, as Grant had expected to encounter Lee at the river. Yet he and Meade remained in the army's rear, and neither general delegated a field commander to coordinate the corps and deal with emergencies as they arose. The absence of decisive leadership at the tactical level that had dulled the Union army's movements on May 21 and 22 persisted on May 23.

Lacking guidance from headquarters, Warren and Captain Miller devised a solution. The Chesterfield reference, they agreed, must mean Chesterfield Bridge, and they selected the bridge as the 2nd Corps's proper objective. The orders left the 5th Corps's objective ambiguous, but Warren and Miller decided that Grant intended for Warren to cross somewhere upriver from Hancock. Jericho Bridge was mentioned, but inquiry revealed that no such bridge existed. There was, however, a ford upriver at a place called Jericho Mills, and Warren and his staff decided that Jericho Mills must be their intended objective. Finding the crossing, however, promised to be an adventure. The only guide Warren could rustle up was an elderly black man who had last visited the ford fifty years before. Seeing no better alternative, Warren decided to commit his corps to crossing at this "indefinite locality on the river," as Roebling termed it.[6]

At 11:30 Warren forwarded a dispatch to Hancock detailing the state of affairs. "The map is so erroneous that it is difficult to tell which way to go, by anything named on it," he warned, and went on to lay out Roebling's findings. Telegraph Road's main trunk went to the river, as depicted. The map was also correct in its location of the Richmond, Fredericksburg, and Potomac Railroad, which turned south at Chesterfield Station and paralleled Telegraph Road to the river, striking it about half a mile below the road bridge. Warren doubted, however, the existence of ancillary roads the chart showed running between Telegraph Road and the railway. Torbert, he advised, was following Telegraph Road toward the river. To make way for Hancock, he had ordered Cutler to return to Mt. Carmel Church and had halted the rest of his corps for lunch on the roadside. "I will not be in the way," he promised.[7]

While Warren and Hancock ironed out their routes—Hancock would move directly down Telegraph Road to Chesterfield Bridge, and Warren would shift a few miles west to Jericho Mills—the rest of the Union army labored toward Mt. Carmel Church. Wright had started from Mr. Welch's farm on schedule, Neill's division leading, followed by Russell and Ricketts. Meade had assigned Major Forsyth's Illinois cavalrymen to assist Wright, and the 6th Corps's commander set the horsemen to patrolling side roads and watching his rear. Food was a major problem. The corps's supply wagons had not arrived, and the troops were ravenous. "Straggling and marauding have become a great evil—families are robbed and houses burned constantly by ruffians," the aide Holmes noted. The men of the 10th Massachusetts, who served as Wright's advance guard, were elated at their assignment. "To be sure there is always the prospect of coming upon the enemy or being met by a volley of their bullets," a soldier observed, but he considered the risk more than offset by the opportunity to arrive "first upon the houses before all the chickens are carried off." Near noon, Wright caught up with the tail of Warren's column about a mile past Dr. Flippo's house. The corps's supply wagons miraculously appeared, and Wright stopped to feed his men. "I am doubling up and issuing," he informed Humphreys, "and as fast as issues are made will move on." Soldiers threw down their knapsacks and sprawled about the good doctor's fields. "Oh, how hot it is!" a marcher wrote during the halt. "I am seated by the roadside under a fence rail and covered with the dust of the wagons and artillery with the hot rays of the sun pressing upon me, and the sweat and dust rolling down my face."[8]

The 9th Corps also got off to a timely start and followed behind Hancock, taking shortcuts along plantation roads. Still smarting under Rawlins's upbraiding, Burnside issued a circular denouncing the "disgraceful laxity" of his officers and warning against pillaging. Rear guards, he directed, were to "use their bayonets freely, and if necessary, shoot any straggler." Provost Marshal Patrick, who followed Burnside, remained unimpressed, proclaiming the 9th Corps "in very bad discipline and its staff departments worthless." A few miles past Wright's Tavern, Burnside caught up with Hancock's rear elements. Major James St. Claire Morton, the 9th Corps's engineer, peeled off a regiment to see if a side road provided access to Telegraph Road. Burnside hoped to use the alternative route to avoid entanglement with Hancock's men.[9]

At 7:45 A.M., with the army in motion, Grant, Meade, and their staffs left the clover fields of the Tyler house, "to our grief," Lyman recorded, "and to that of the women, who counted on our protection." After stopping briefly at the home of the Campbell family, the mounted generals made their way through the mass of marching 9th Corps troops. "Grant went nimbly ahead on his black Mississippi pony, which piqued Meade," Lyman reported, "who pushed on with his big trotter, beating Grant very soon, and followed by staff and orderlies as best they might." Describing the wild ride a few days later, Lyman added that Meade's rapid pace raised a cloud of dust "and left the Lieutenant General far behind; whereat George G. was much pleased." [10]

A few miles short of Telegraph Road, the headquarters entourage came on Major Morton, who had discovered that his side road offered the alternative route Burnside sought. Meade's portion of the distinguished cavalcade took the detour, riding with Willcox's division in the 9th Corps's fore. Grant stayed on the main road with Hancock's column. The priggish Lyman recorded with displeasure that many soldiers pled sickness and were riding on caissons—"probably lazy!" he concluded. At Polecat Creek—"a clear brook with a stony bottom, and overhanging elders"—the party paused, affording the staffers opportunity to bathe. Learning that four women lived alone in a nearby house, Meade dispatched a guard to protect them from stragglers. Farther on, the detour looped back to the main road. Telegraph Road was but a short distance west. It was now 1:40 P.M., and Meade decided to set up headquarters at the Moncure home, near the junction of the detour and the main road. Soon Grant rode up and established his command center there as well. [11]

The dwelling the generals had chosen for their headquarters—an estate called Ellerslie—was home to the parents of Lee's guide, Eustis Moncure. Lyman had no use for Mrs. Moncure, whom he considered a "vulgar, railing old woman." Mrs. Moncure had no use for the Federals, either. "Ah," she exclaimed, "We shall soon see you coming back on the double quick." Making the best of a distasteful situation, she agreed to sell the invaders her sheep after "a haggling worthy of a New Englander." Payment, she insisted, had to be in gold. [12]

The Confederate high command began May 23 convinced that Grant intended to swing east. Lee made no preparations to receive the Federals at the North Anna. Early in the morning, Lee's aide Taylor wrote his fiancée that Grant was moving through Bowling Green and predicted that the Federals would emerge near White House. "This," he added, "would of course neces-

sitate our moving between that point and Richmond." The Army of Northern
Virginia, Taylor continued, remained "in excellent condition—as good as it
was when we met Grant, two weeks since for the first time." Grant, he went
on, was "such a brute, he does not pretend to bury his dead, leaves his
wounded without proper attendance, and seems entirely reckless as regards
the lives of his men. This and his remarkable pertinacity are the only qualifi-
cations he has exhibited, which differ in any way from those of his predecessors." But Taylor could not conceal a hint of admiration for his opponent.
"He certainly holds on longer than any of them," he admitted. "He alone of
all would have remained this side of the Rappahannock after the battle of the
Wilderness. This may be attributable to his nature, or it may be because he
knew full well that to relinquish his designs on Richmond even temporarily,
would forever ruin him and bring about peace." Concluded Taylor: "This is, I
think, surely the *last* campaign. God Grant us his assistance to bring it to a
speedy and successful issue. Of late He has certainly favored us most sig-
nally." [13]

Lee spent the morning catching up on correspondence. "At present, all my
information indicates that the movement of General Grant's army is in the direction of Milford Station," he wrote President Davis. Hampton, he added,
believed that Grant intended to follow the Richmond, Fredericksburg, and
Potomac Railroad to Hanover Junction, an interpretation that Federal repairs
on the line from Aquia Creek to Fredericksburg tended to support. For the
time, however, Grant seemed to be lingering behind the Mattaponi, "very
much shaken" by recent battles. Whichever route Grant took—south along
the railroad toward Hanover Junction, as Hampton suspected, or southeast
toward the Pamunkey, as Lee thought more likely—Lee was positioned "to
move against him, and shall endeavor to engage him while in motion." Lee
observed that his army was now within cooperating distance of Beauregard
and urged Davis to take the offensive. "General Grant's army will be in the
field, strengthened by all available troops from the North, and it seems to me
our best policy to unite upon it and endeavor to crush it," counseled Lee. "I
should be very glad to have the aid of General Beauregard in such a blow," he
added, "and if possible to combine, I think it will succeed." As for the Army
of Northern Virginia, Lee thought its sprits were high, and he feared "no injury to [morale] from any retrograde movement that may be dictated by
sound military policy." Most important, cautioned Lee, Grant must not be
permitted to cross the Chickahominy. "I think it would be a great disadvantage to us to uncover our railroads to the west,"Lee warned, "and injurious to
open to him more country than we can avoid." Lee wrote his wife in a simi-

lar vein, informing her that Grant had "become tired of forcing his passage through us" at Spotsylvania Court House and had shifted toward Bowling Green, "placing the Mattaponi River between us." Lee had countered by moving to Hanover Junction "so as to be within striking distance of Richmond and be able to intercept him." The weather had warmed, the general noted in closing, and he wanted cotton drawers and socks sent to him.[14]

May 23 promised Lee's soldiers another day of rest. A rebel in the 45th Georgia caught the prevailing sentiment. "I think I am nearer worn out, dirtier, and more in want of rest than I have been since I can recollect," he wrote home. "Last night was the first night in three weeks that I have been able to pull off my boots and shoes to sleep." He reported that he and his companions "all look very much like a horse after a week's hard driving on the shortest kind of rations." The Confederates remained, however, in excellent spirits. "I believe this campaign to be the decisive one," the Georgian concluded, "and know we are going to whip the detestable enemy." An ordnance sergeant in the 7th North Carolina was equally optimistic. "Grant was badly whipped at the Wilderness and Spotsylvania Court House," he wrote home, "and if he still desires to fight, he can be accommodated; and, I think, with the same results as before." [15]

Lee's troops remained south of the river in the camps they had prepared on May 22. Ewell was near Hanover Junction, extending east; Anderson remained west of the junction along the Virginia Central Railroad; and Breckinridge and Colonel Johnson's Marylanders stood in reserve on Telegraph Road, toward Taylorsville. Early in the morning, Hill left Hewlett's Station and marched east to Anderson's Tavern, where the Virginia Central Railroad crossed an old stage road from Richmond to Fredericksburg. This placed Hill on the army's left flank, four miles west of Hanover Junction. The 14th South Carolina of McGowan's brigade remained behind at Noel's Station, a mile south of Jericho Mills, to picket the army's extreme left flank and watch the ford there. Elements from Chambliss's cavalry patrolled the river. Later in the morning Hill developed second thoughts about the security of the ford at Jericho Mills and ordered the rest of McGowan's brigade to return to Noel's Station and join the 14th South Carolina.[16]

Lane's 3rd Corps brigade settled into oak woods near Anderson's Tavern. A soldier spied a flock of sheep and persuaded William H. McLaurin, adjutant of the 18th North Carolina, to loan him a pistol. McLaurin became suspicious when he heard a flurry of pistol shots. An elderly farmer huffed up to report that soldiers had shot his sheep. A search was conducted, but nothing turned up until a luckless soldier from the 37th North Carolina sauntered past headquarters carrying a leg of mutton. Lane punished the man by requiring him to walk in a circle carrying the mutton on his shoulder. After his initial anger had passed, the farmer beseeched Lane to pardon the man and offered the remainder of his flock to the soldiers. The incident was to provoke pointed jibes later that day.[17]

West of Telegraph Road, on a bluff north of the river, stood a small earthen redoubt built the previous year to protect Chesterfield Bridge against Union marauders. The three-sided fort faced north toward Long Creek, a quarter of a mile away. Short walls extended back on both sides of the redoubt, and the rear was open. Anderson had left Kershaw's South Carolina brigade, commanded by Colonel John Henagan since Kershaw's elevation to division command, in the redoubt to guard the bridge. These were the only Confederate infantrymen north of the river. To strengthen the redoubt, Henagan's men had dug an eight-foot-wide trench along its face, confronting prospective attackers with a ten-foot-high wall. The 2nd South Carolina occupied the redoubt, the 7th South Carolina held an entrenched line west of the fort, the 3rd South Carolina Battalion reached east from the fort to Telegraph Road, and the 3rd South Carolina manned entrenchments east of the road toward the railroad bridge. Anyone charging the position would have to cross a six-hundred-yard field. Henagan's brigade was too small to repulse a determined attack, but no one expected the Army of the Potomac to appear on Telegraph Road.[18]

Around 11:00 A.M. Henagan's South Carolinians waded into the North Anna to bathe. They expected to receive instructions any moment to withdraw and burn the bridge behind them. "Everything was quiet," a soldier recalled. Suddenly Hampton's horsemen, retreating in front of Hancock's advancing column, splashed across Long Creek and rode into the field above the redoubt. Union cavalry—Torbert's soldiers—came behind them in pursuit, backed by French's horse artillery. Whether the Federals represented only part of the Union army or Grant's entire force was far from clear to the startled southerners.[19]

A lively cavalry brawl erupted in view of the South Carolinians. Thomson's battery of Confederate horse artillery clattered across Chesterfield Bridge, unlimbered on high ground along the southern bank, and began firing back across the river into Torbert's troopers. A Confederate in the 7th Virginia Cavalry called the engagement a "very spirited little fight." Lacking reinforcements, Torbert retired to Long Creek, counting himself fortunate to have lost only one man killed and five wounded. Captain French's Union horse artillery dueled vigorously with Thomson's pieces on the far side of the North Anna, then scampered rearward for cover. A rebel deserter shouted encouragement to the Yankees. "Go on," he urged. "You've got them on the run now!" [20]

Thomson's pieces settled into a steady fire at the distant Federals, who had found cover in low ground beside Long Creek. A carriage pulled up to one of Thomson's smoking guns, and Lee stepped out. The general customarily supervised his lines on horseback. Today, however, he felt weak, and rather than expend his limited energy on riding, he had taken a carriage. Leaning against a pine tree, the general pulled out field glasses and studied the far line of Federals north of the river. Cavalry was plainly visible, and infantry seemed to be arriving as well. "Orderly, go back and tell General A. P. Hill to leave his men in camp," Lee announced. "This is nothing but a feint, the enemy is preparing to cross below." Satisfied that Grant's main force was still miles away behind the Mattaponi, and probably heading toward the Pamunkey, Lee returned his field glasses to their case, climbed into his carriage, and resumed his tour of the army. "When the enemy arrived on the north side of the North Anna," a correspondent wrote, "the impression prevailed in certain official and private circles that his demonstration on our left was merely a feint to cover an intended movement further down the river, perhaps to the Peninsula." [21]

"I do not believe the enemy intends holding the North Anna."

Lee was dangerously mistaken. Grant's juggernaut was feeling its way toward the North Anna. The two lead Union corps—the 2nd and the 5th—were nearing the river's northern bank directly across from the Confederates. The situation had the makings of a disaster for the Army of Northern Virginia. Only Henagan's small force and some of Hampton's cavalry stood between the Federals and the river. The rest of Lee's soldiers were resting complacently in camps along the Virginia Central Railroad, south of the river.

At noon Warren started west along the road from Mt. Carmel Church. Griffin was now in the 5th Corps's fore, followed by Crawford, then by Cutler, who had returned from his unscheduled detour toward Chesterfield Bridge. The elderly escort led the way. A trek of two and a half miles brought the troops to an old farm road. The aged guide pointed to the dirt path and announced that he thought it led to Jericho Mills. Warren started his command along the road, unruffled by shrieks from a homeowner trying to keep Union marauders from stealing his potatoes. The trail descended sharply to the North Anna. Half a dozen mounted home guards were the only Confederates in sight, and they melted into the woods as the Federal column approached. "It was determined to cross at once while there was a chance," Roebling reported. At 1:30 P.M. Warren dispatched a courier to Meade. "The enemy made no show of resistance at this point," he reported. "I do not believe the enemy intends holding the North Anna." [22]

Hancock meanwhile pushed on from Old Chesterfield to Mt. Carmel Church, where he turned left onto Telegraph Road. He estimated that his lead elements were three-quarters of a mile from the river. There was a bridge— not a ford—in his front, he informed headquarters, and he was throwing out infantry to seize it. "I don't think the Confederates have any force," he advised. "They have some little artillery, but appearances indicate that they are not strong." [23]

Warren's report from Jericho Mills reached Mrs. Moncure's house, site of Grant and Meade's headquarters, around 2:00 P.M. "It appears from the withal that Warren had crossed the river," Meade jotted across the bottom of the message before forwarding it to Grant. "Should he go on or only hold the crossing? What should Wright do; cross after Warren or go to some point higher up?" Hancock, Grant wrote back, was to secure Chesterfield Bridge and the railroad span to the east "if possible." Burnside was to move to the 2nd Corps's right flank and seize Ox Ford, midway between Chesterfield Bridge and Jericho Mills. And Warren was to "occupy the bank of the river"—presumably the southern bank—to "cover and hold Jericho Ford." Wright, Grant suggested, should continue upriver from the 5th Corps and seize any crossings he might find in that direction. By day's end Grant hoped to see the army arrayed in a line stretching five miles along the river, from the railroad bridge to a point upstream from Jericho Mills, with as many troops across as possible. [24]

Meade sped a directive to Warren. "Pass your whole corps across the river and intrench yourself," he instructed. Warren was already doing exactly that. Without waiting for orders, he had resolved to ford the North Anna and establish a bridgehead on the southern bank. Warren was having a good day. He had displayed commendable initiative at Mt. Carmel Church when faced with inaccurate maps. And now, without prodding from his superiors, he was preparing to gain a lodgment on the Confederate side of the river. Warren seemed to be maturing as a general and had come to understand the importance of seizing opportunity when it beckoned. [25]

The ford at Jericho Mills posed a challenge for Warren's engineers. Banks rose sharply a hundred feet on both sides of the North Anna, and the road winding up the far escarpment was little more than a progression of rocky steps gouged into the steep slope. A milldam spanned the river, and a rowboat that apparently doubled as a ferry rested on the shore above the dam. The river was 150 feet across, the bottom was firm, and the water ran four feet deep at most. Warren decided that his initial wave of troops could wade over. He supervised the operation, closely studying the high ground across the river through field glasses for signs of Confederates. A soldier thought Warren appeared "exceedingly anxious." Griffin and Wainwright posted Rittenhouse's battery on the north bank immediately left of the road and moved Breck's battery downstream about a quarter of a mile, giving the gunners a clear view of the plain on the far side.[26]

The Confederate cavalrymen Warren had surprised at Jericho Mills were Rooney Lee's men. They spurred their horses back to Noel's Station where McGowan's troops were encamped. McGowan had been wounded during the brigade's engagement at the Bloody Angle on May 12, and Colonel Brown of the 14th South Carolina was commanding the brigade. Uncertain of the strength of the Federal force at the ford, Brown ordered Orr's Rifles—the brigade's largest regiment—to advance toward the river while he posted the rest of the soldiers along the rail line.[27]

Warren's crossing proceeded smoothly. Sweitzer's brigade, Colonel William S. Tilton's 22nd Massachusetts leading, splashed into the North Anna. The current swept a few men off their feet, and everyone emerged soaked to the armpits. Once across, Tilton's soldiers climbed a steep bank choked with undergrowth and emerged onto a cleared, relatively flat plateau. They checked their weapons for moisture and began falling into line, oblivious to the fresh garden plot they had blundered into. An elderly woman strolled onto the porch of a nearby farmhouse and began scolding the water-logged soldiers. "Gentlemen, why have you come?" she inquired. "Mr. Lee is not here. You are spoiling my garden." A Federal admitted that he felt "gratified by her information regarding 'Mr. Lee,' as we were not disposed to interview him with the small delegation present." The Massachusetts men, understandably preoccupied with forming their lines and drying their weapons, ignored the woman's admonitions to stay off her plants. Finally Tilton intervened on her behalf. "Boys, keep between the rows," the colonel ordered.[28]

Reduced in size by hard fighting, Tilton's Bay State regiment had frequently served as skirmishers during the campaign, winning a reputation, its historian reported, "for gallantry, and reliability under fire, in the most trying circumstances, second to none in the Army of the Potomac." A few hundred yards west of the ford, the road turned sharply south, traversed several hundred yards of field, then disappeared into a forest in the direction of the Virginia Central Railroad. Tilton could see gray-clad forms milling among the distant trees. Sending back to Sweitzer to hurry up the rest of the brigade, Tilton wheeled his men south toward the woods. Captain Frederick K. Field commanded the formation's left wing, and Major Mason W. Burt the right.[29]

Sweitzer rushed the rest of his brigade across the river to support Tilton. Lieutenant Colonel Patrick T. Hanley, commanding the 9th Massachusetts, noticed his regiment's shortest soldier—nicknamed Napoleon—standing beside the road. "What's the matter, Napoleon?" Hanley inquired. "The water is too deep for me and I can't swim," Napoleon replied, provoking an outburst of humorous suggestions from the passing men. As the rear of the regiment descended into the water, the colonel ordered a strapping soldier to lift Napoleon onto his horse. The little man rode across in style behind the colonel, "proud as a peacock."[30]

Tilton deployed the 22nd Massachusetts along a fence separating the field's southern edge from the woods and waited for reinforcements. Major Burt called for a scout to probe the forest, and Private Charles F. Alger volunteered. As Alger stepped into the trees, he spotted Confederates lying in ambush. Making himself small behind a trunk, Alger took careful aim and fired. The rebels answered with a volley—a Bay Stater estimated that he heard fifty Confederate muskets—and the 22nd Massachusetts shot back, followed by a volley from the 9th Massachusetts, which had just pulled up behind Tilton.[31]

The rebels—skirmishers from Orr's Rifles, commanded by Captain J. S. Cothran—melted into the woods. Tilton started after them. Encountering only light opposition, the northerners pressed through the trees in skirmish order and emerged into a field. They could see the Virginia Central Railroad half a mile ahead. Confederates—McGowan's entire brigade—were waiting on the other side of the railway embankment. Having outdistanced his supports, Tilton decided against continuing further. He set soldiers to felling trees and erecting makeshift earthworks. Sweitzer arrayed the rest of his brigade as it arrived from the river along the wood line where Alger had first stirred up the rebels, buttressing the right end of Tilton's skirmish line with fifty soldiers from the 32nd Massachusetts. When an officer asked Alger why he had risked his life shooting at the Confederates in the woods, the plucky private answered that he had fired "a shot for luck, and held his ground without looking back, because he knew the boys would stay." Noted the officer: "I do not believe the regiment ever had a more sincere compliment paid it."[32]

News of Warren's crossing prompted Hill to dispatch the remainder of Wilcox's division from Anderson's Tavern to Noel's Station with orders to "attack [the enemy] at once." Shouldering muskets, Wilcox's men started the three-mile trek west along the railway and the road paralleling the tracks.

They made an impressive, if insufficient, force. Remnants of the Light Division, these veteran troops had delivered stunning victories under General Hill in the war's earlier years. In addition to McGowan's South Carolina brigade, the division consisted of two North Carolina brigades—those of James Lane and Alfred Scales, commanded this day by Colonel William L. J. Lowrance of the 34th North Carolina—and Edward Thomas's Georgians. William Pegram's battalion, sixteen guns strong, brought up the formidable column's tail.[33]

Griffin's division finished fording the river while pioneers from Company D, 50th New York Engineers, erected a pontoon bridge. Soldiers halted briefly at the river's edge to remove their shoes and socks and hang them on bayonets before wading over. A small battle nearly erupted when a pioneer accidentally cut a soldier on the nose with his axe. "An axe is a good weapon in a contest at close quarters, but a musket with bayonet fixed is a better one, so I declined to take up the gantlet he had so promptly thrown down," the pioneer later related. Officers on the southern bank rushed the troops along, as Griffin wanted his division formed in case the rebels counterattacked. "So hastily was this movement made that in some cases the men were not given time to put on their shoes, and the march through the woods and across the stubble of the fields in bare feet elicited many grunts from those in this unfortunate predicament," the 146th New York's historian recorded. Ayres formed his brigade on Sweitzer's left, facing south along the wood line. Bartlett assumed a reserve position several hundred yards back. During the crossing, Warren received two letters from his wife, Emily. "Twice I had to crush them in my pocket to attend to the emergency of battle," he later wrote her.[34]

Crawford's Pennsylvania Reserves forded next, deployed in line on the high ground, and pushed forward, keeping the river on their left. Reaching a point opposite Griffin's left, they stacked arms and began digging near the house of the Fontaine family. "Time was when the first thing to be done after a halt was to make coffee, in whose grateful fumes all weariness was forgotten," a Federal observed. "Now the first thing the men do is entrench." Crawford's soldiers entertained themselves recounting the adventures of a teacher-turned-warrior named Moreland. During the crossing the rotund soldier had lost his footing and was pulled feet-first from the river by his comrades. They joked that he had been "making a critical examination of the bottom of the stream." [35]

Warren fired a note to Meade at 3:30, advising him of developments. Griffin had crossed the river, tangled with South Carolina infantry, and thrust skirmishers within sight of the Virginia Central Railroad. According to a captured rebel, Wilcox's entire division was lying in wait behind the railroad grade. "I am still of the opinion they are only trying to delay us," Warren informed headquarters. "They gain time everywhere perhaps by the slowness of my crossing." Forty-five minutes later Warren reported that Crawford was over and the pontoon bridge was nearly complete. Scouts had located a ford two and a half miles upstream from Jericho Mills, and Warren suggested that Wright seize the crossing for the army's trains. Meade, however, wanted to ensure that Warren had sufficient support and directed Wright to post his corps on the northern bank at Jericho Mills.[36]

Warren's pontoon bridge was finished by 5:00 P.M. Stretching 160 feet across the river, it was strong enough to bear artillery. Wainwright immediately sent his twenty-four napoleons across. He placed Hart's and Stewart's batteries behind Crawford's right, on high ground protected by abandoned rebel earthworks. Mink's battery rolled west along the farm road and halted near the sharp turn south, supporting Griffin. Matthewson's, Walcott's, and Bigelow's batteries remained near the lip of the plateau where the trail wound up from the river. Warren's final division under Cutler marched across the pontoon bridge, climbed the steep bank, and stopped to rest. Adjutant William Wright of the 150th Pennsylvania recollected that the men "were bent with fatigue, and some who had never before complained now declared they could go no farther." Cutler's soldiers gathered fence rails for firewood and prepared to camp—"probably in pursuance of an order originating in the brain of some very tired man," Adjutant Wright observed.[37]

Warren now had his entire corps across the river, facing south toward the Confederates, and he felt secure. The North Anna carved a pronounced loop, about a mile and a half across at its base, protruding north. Jericho Mills was at the apex. The 5th Corps formed a line across the bottom of the loop with both ends anchored on the river. Crawford held the left wing of the formation, near the Fontaine house, and Griffin the center along the farm road leading toward Noel's Station. Before dark, Cutler was slated to move onto Griffin's right and extend the line to the river on the right. As Wainwright put it, Cutler's maneuver would "complete the chord across the bend in the river." Skirmish fire crackled sporadically through the woods, but Warren did not expect trouble. "We lay about carelessly," lighting fires in anticipation of eating, a soldier recollected. The woods were filled with pigs, which brightened the prospects for dinner.[38]

The 2nd Corps meanwhile pushed vigorously south from Mt. Carmel Church. At 2:00 P.M. Birney reached Long Creek and sent soldiers from Colonel Thomas Egan's brigade across. Ahead, barring the way to Chesterfield Bridge,

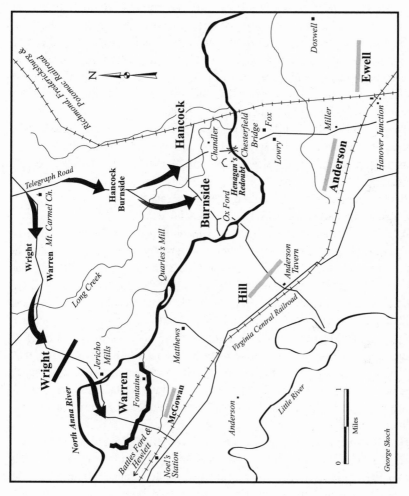

Union deployment along the North Anna River on May 23

stood the small redoubt held by Henagan's Confederates. "We could hear the whistles of the locomotives on the Virginia Central Railroad," a man in the 19th Maine wrote, "and some of the boys suggested that we might capture the train and start for Maine."[39]

Long Creek did not appear on Union war maps. Hancock at first believed that Birney had reached the North Anna River, and that the redoubt was on the southern bank. At 2:35 he erroneously informed headquarters that skirmishers had crossed the North Anna and were establishing a bridgehead on the far side. He was extending troops left toward the railroad bridge, he added, and was picketing upriver to his right in the direction of Ox Ford. Confederates occupied high ground in the distance. "In position the enemy appear to have some advantage over me," Hancock advised. "Shall I force a crossing?" Meade studied the message and inscribed a note to Grant. "I have ordered Warren to cross his whole corps and intrench. Wright, I think, had better take position on this side, to support Warren. Shall Hancock force a crossing?"[40]

"By all means," Grant replied, delighted at the ease with which the Potomac Army had breached Lee's North Anna defenses.[41]

At 3:15 Hancock reported that his leftmost elements had reached the railroad, and that his right flank extended toward Ox Ford. In his center, he added, he had pushed three regiments across the river—in fact they had crossed only Long Creek—and he was waiting for his artillery to catch up before pressing on. Meade interpreted Hancock's uncontested crossing as confirmation that the Confederates had abandoned the North Anna. "I think, from present indications, Lee is going to hold the Pamunkey and South Anna," he wrote Grant. "Shall Hancock cross his whole force, if practicable?" Grant's answer was predictable. "If Hancock can secure a crossing, he should do so," he wrote back. "If, however, the bulk of the enemy appears to be to the left of him, our cavalry should picket well down, to see that no detachment of the enemy gets in on our left."[42]

Hancock began to suspect the stream Birney had crossed was really not the North Anna River. After all, there was no bridge, and the creek was only twelve feet wide and scarcely a foot deep, with a sandy bottom. At 3:30 Birney clarified matters. Egan's men had crossed Long Creek, he reported. The river lay five hundred yards farther on. The redoubt blocking his way stood on the North Anna's northern bank, between Long Creek and the river. "I think the earthworks can be taken between the creek and the river," Hancock assured headquarters. He already had a brigade across the creek, he added, and was only waiting for his artillery to find suitable positions before attacking.[43]

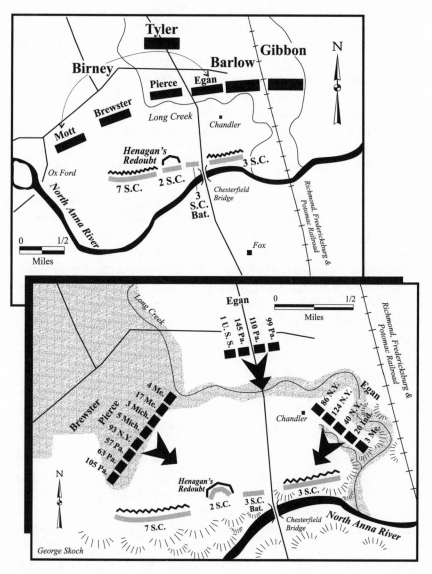

Hancock's attack at Henagan's Redoubt

Hancock interrogated a slave who had escaped from the southern side of the river. The Army of Northern Virginia, the man claimed, lay in camps between Chesterfield Bridge and Hanover Junction. The river was easy to ford, he added, and the bridge was intact. At 4:35 Hancock informed headquarters that the situation was very different than he had initially believed. "No crossing of the river can be forced here at present, as all accounts agree that the enemy are in force, and there is a creek between us and the river, with obstacles," he wrote. "I have a brigade across the creek, and am endeavoring to get my artillery to open to enable them to take the works, but the country is so wooded and unknown, as well as little favorable for artillery, that it takes time." Addressing Grant's suggestion that he send cavalry downriver, Hancock reported that he had not seen Torbert for two hours.[44]

Hancock fanned his corps into a line across Telegraph Road and the Richmond, Fredericksburg, and Potomac Railroad. Birney's division held the roadway and the terrain to the right, with Mott's brigade reaching upriver toward Ox Ford. Tyler's division remained in reserve behind Long Creek, backstopping Birney. Barlow, forming the line's center, reached from Telegraph Road east to the railway. And Gibbon, on the 2nd Corps's left, deployed on a high ridge overlooking the river east of the tracks. Colonel Tidball, heading the 2nd Corps's artillery, arrayed his guns to command the southern bank. On the corps's far right, supporting Mott, stood the batteries of Roder, Ames, Sleeper, Edgell, and Brown. Dow was positioned beside Telegraph Road, where he could fire directly at the redoubt. Two more batteries—those of Arnold and Gilliss—held high ground left of the road. Five more batteries under Ricketts, Burton, Brown, McKnight, and Clark commanded the railroad bridge, with most of the artillery posted on high ground east of the span.[45]

Tidball's guns opened in unison with a deafening roar at 5:30, and the Confederates responded. Anderson, whose corps was nearest Telegraph Road, advanced Kershaw along the heights south of Chesterfield Bridge and dispatched Field downriver toward the railroad bridge. Alexander ran Parker's battery onto a knoll next to the Lowry house, adjacent to Telegraph Road. Advancing another battery to support Parker, Alexander started eight guns from Huger's battalion west of Telegraph Road and sped four pieces from Cabell's battalion east to cover the railroad bridge. Braxton's Confederate 2nd Corps battalion, commanded by Major M. N. Moorman, rolled onto high ground near the Doswell house, north of Hanover Junction, and engaged in a "sharp little duel" with Hancock's pieces across the river.[46]

Parker's battery, temporarily commanded by J. Wilcox Brown, became a prime target for Tidball's gunners. Union shells slammed into the Lowry farmhouse, and the family "swarmed out like bees and fled as fast as they could run—man, wife, and daughters," recounted Alexander, who had been trying to persuade the owner to sell him chickens. "I say, won't you sell me those chickens now," Alexander shouted. The man called back, "Yes, pay me next time you see me." [47]

On the Union right the men of Sleeper's battery of the 2nd Corps studied a line of red dirt that marked the position of Lieutenant Colonel David G. McIntosh's 3rd Corps battalion, near Ox Ford. Rebel sharpshooters fired at Sleeper's gunners, who in turn shelled McIntosh. Fire, smoke, and fragments spewed skyward from the Confederate position. Sleeper had hit a limber chest in Valentine J. Clutter's battery. The explosion killed Lieutenant Pierce, commanding the battery, but miraculously spared McIntosh, who was standing nearby. "For a few minutes silence reigned in that locality," a Federal recalled, "and it was rather amusing to see the fugitives from the spot returning, first a head, then the body attached to it, cautiously reappearing from the bushes." Shifting to a less exposed position, Clutter's men resumed the duel.[48]

On the eastern end of the Union line, near the railroad bridge, Law's Alabamians and Bratton's South Carolinians began digging earthworks to prevent the Federals—Gibbon's troops on the opposite bank—from crossing. Alexander posted two howitzers behind heavy dirt fortifications built the previous year and began trading rounds with Brown's, McKnight's, and Clark's guns. "It was rather a one-sided fight, and the inequality was calculated to make the service of the howitzers rather slow," noted Union gunner Frank Wilkeson, who had watched shells burst over the tiny fortification at the rate of two every three seconds. "We had got the range to an inch," Wilkeson recollected. "The plain beyond the work was furrowed and torn with shell. The works must have quivered with the steady and heavy shocks. I can imagine no hotter place than that little fort was." When a Confederate officer rode toward the guns, Wilkeson watched in fascination through his binoculars, certain that the man would be killed. Trotting to the fort, the officer passed a paper inside, saluted, then rode deliberately toward the safety of a nearby line of woods. "Dust rose above him," Wilkeson remembered. "Tiny clouds of smoke almost hid him from view. Shot struck the ground and skipped past him, but he did not urge his horse out of a walk. He rode as though lost in meditation and deaf to the uproar that raged around him." To Wilkeson's relief, the figure disappeared into the trees. "Thank God that that brave man was not killed," he thought.[49]

Parson Thomas H. Fox's two-story brick house, Ellington, occupied a conspicuous point on Telegraph Road a quarter mile south of the river. When the artillery barrage opened, Lee was sitting on the porch drinking buttermilk. Suddenly a round shot whizzed within feet of Lee and lodged in the doorframe. The Confederate commander finished his glass, gave thanks to Parson Fox, and rode away. Soon after Lee left, Anderson made the Fox house his headquarters and was joined there by Alexander, who rested against the sill of a basement window. Couriers lounged nearby, holding the generals' horses. Without warning, a shell tore through a chimney. Anticipating a shower of bricks, Alexander leapt onto the sill and flattened his back against the closed window, where the recess shielded him from debris cascading down. Broken bricks lay piled on the ground and sloped against the wall to Alexander's ankles, which were badly bruised. Two couriers were caught in the avalanche, and one of them was killed. After the war, Alexander remembered the Fox house as the place where he was almost killed by bricks.[50]

Henagan's men were growing anxious. Tidball's artillery was keeping them pinned in their earthworks, and they could see Birney massing for an assault. The 7th South Carolina, holding an extended line upstream from the redoubt, was especially apprehensive. "We were promised the cooperation of the artillery just on the other side of the river," recounted Henagan's adjutant. A scout in the redoubt armed with a Whitworth rifle and globe sight passed the time picking off distant Yankees, including an officer on a horse.[51]

Exploiting the cover of Tidball's artillery barrage and the undulating terrain's dips and rises, Birney edged his men close to the redoubt. To initiate the attack, he selected a hard-fighting brigade led by Colonel Egan, the talented head of the 40th New York. Egan posted the 1st United States Sharpshooters on the right of his formation, the 141st Pennsylvania in the center, and the 99th Pennsylvania on the left, and nudged them down Telegraph Road toward the redoubt. Advancing into the clearing, the three regiments came under blistering fire from the South Carolinians and from Alexander's artillery south of the river. The 1st United States Sharpshooters scampered into woods on the right, and the 99th Pennsylvania slid obliquely left and edged forward under cover of a hillock. The 141st Pennsylvania found protection in a drainage ditch. Better shelter—a gentle hollow behind a rise—lay several hundred feet ahead, and the men of the 141st resolved to reach it. "Forward!" came the command, and they leapt from the ditch and darted into the depression. Here they were joined by the 110th Pennsylvania, which Egan had dispatched to reinforce them. A few marksmen fired at Confederates peeking over the redoubt. "Brushing the fly off Johnny's Cap," they called the sport.[52]

Birney next worked troops toward the sides of the redoubt, like pincers on a crab. On the left, the remainder of Egan's brigade—the 20th Indiana, 3rd Maine, and the 40th, 86th, and 124th New York—crept forward, the 86th New York's right touching Telegraph Road. Concealed by woods, these troops slid past their sister regiments and deployed facing the 3rd South Carolina Battalion. On the right the other pincer—a brigade of hardened veterans under Colonel Byron R. Pierce of the 3rd Michigan—pressed close to the 7th South Carolina under cover of woods and a ridge. Behind Pierce were two regiments from Colonel William R. Brewster's Excelsior Brigade. Egan's center contingent engaged the Confederates' attention while the arms of Birney's pincer moved into position. "These flats were being literally plowed by missiles of every description," an onlooker wrote. "The two brigades mentioned were quietly advancing from opposite directions, each under shelter of a favoring crest, until they got within springing distance of the object of their attack."[53]

Birney attacked at 6:30. Supported by Dow's guns, Pierce's and Egan's pincers—three thousand men strong—rose and sprang toward the Confederate line. "As much as I like to be, or would like to be a hero, I would not stand again with the same before me to go through for the whole world," the 86th New York's color-bearer Stephen P. Chase later reminisced. "The Confederate pickets fired, then ran to their fortifications, which instantly began to smoke in jets and puffs and curls as an immense pudding" a Federal described the scene, "and men in the blue-coated line fell headlong, or backward, or sank into little heaps." Volleys from the redoubt shredded the Union ranks in "one of the most savage fires of shell and bullets I had ever experienced," a Federal asserted. Alexander's guns across the river redoubled their cannonading, and the right of Pierce's battle line, consisting of the 63rd and 105th Pennsylvania, came under punishing enfilading fire. A shell fragment hit the flagstaff of the 124th New York, spinning the color-bearer several times, and the 124th and 86th New York regiments, which had been temporarily consolidated, began to stampede to the rear. Deciding that it was safer to advance than to run back across the open field, color-bearer Chase whirled his flag and shouted, "Come on boys!" Emboldened by Chase's example, the sister New York regiments rallied and pressed on.[54]

Birney slammed Henagan's formation from three directions. "All moved forward in solid mass with a cheer," recollected a man in the 3rd Michigan. The 7th South Carolina immediately collapsed. "Look out, boys! Look to the left!" a southerner in the redoubt shouted. Glancing over, James A. Milling saw that the 7th South Carolina had abandoned its entrenchments and was running for the river. Union colors were streaming through the breach.[55]

Egan's soldiers reached the redoubt and jumped into the ditch only to discover that the walls were steeper than they had expected. "Mount my shoulders!" Sergeant William T. Lobb of the 141st Pennsylvania called as he braced his hands and head against the embankment. Using Lobb as a ladder, the regiment's Sergeant J. T. R. Seagraves climbed onto the rampart, followed by a crowd of men. "How many went up that ladder I do not recollect," Lobb was to write, "but I do recollect the colors of the One Hundred Forty-First were soon up." Sergeant James Anderson, of the 72nd New York, Company F, scaled a ladder that troops constructed by thrusting bayonets into the face of the fort, then bracing the gun butts on their shoulders. Other soldiers catapulted their companions onto the battlements. A sergeant in the 86th New York dropped into the works and was shot in the head. Color-bearer Chase climbed over the sergeant's body, and the rest of the regiment piled in behind him.[56]

On the south side of the river a Confederate in Parker's battery watched the Federals charge through the ferocious shelling. "Some general officer attended by a numerous staff galloped around the left of his line," recounted the gunner, "seized a regimental flag, and holding it aloft, with its brightest stripe gracefully swinging to the breeze, galloped straight up to the earthwork, and upon the embankment, and there drove the staff down into the sand." The Union officer's bravery transfixed the gunner. "We stopped firing," he reminisced, "took off our hats, waved them and cheered him until he and his men were over and into the fortifications."[57]

The avalanche of Federals overwhelmed the Confederate defenders. "Every man for himself!" shouted Major R. C. Maffett of the 3rd South Carolina. "It was but a few seconds' work to cause a radical change in the enemy's position," a Federal chuckled. "We were soon studying the pattern of their coat tails and we went in hot pursuit under a pitiless storm of shot, shell, and we know what not." Many of the redoubt's garrison fell prisoner, and the remainder tumbled toward the river in "wild confusion," bolting across Chesterfield Bridge or leaping into the water. "Before I got half way, the bullets were splashing around me," related a southerner who elected the latter course. Elated northerners gave chase, and blue-coated forms dove into the river after the rebels. "I struck out for the bridge, and it was a close race between me and the Yankees," recollected James W. Reagan, of the 3rd South Carolina. "As I ran onto the bridge the Yankees were on top of the hill limbering up some cannon preparatory to shelling the road, but I got over anyway." Hilliard Sheely of the same regiment ran up the far bank, looked back, and was shot in the face with a minié ball. "The shells would strike into the hills and explode," Reagan recounted, "and blow out a hole large enough to bury a mule in." Survivors related with amusement the story of a Confederate officer painfully wounded in the stampede across the river. "Oh! That I had been a good man," the injured warrior repented. "Oh! That I had listened to my mother." [58]

The 4th Maine dashed across the bridge under a rain of artillery fire and captured a small breastwork the rebels had erected on their side of the river. Finding the place too hot to hold, the Maine men retired to the north bank. The rest of Birney's division formed along high ground north of the river and blazed away at the Confederate side until dark. Union troops had the redoubt firmly in hand and were assisted by a battery of brass napoleons that Tidball placed there to command the bridge.[59]

On the left of Hancock's line, near the railway bridge, Union artillery engaged in a lively exchange with Confederate pieces firing Hotchkiss shells. The projectiles, perforated near the base and wound with a metal band that released during flight, made a "terrific cutting and slashing scream" that frightened new men and veterans alike. Gibbon's soldiers dubbed the Confederate battery firing these shells the "Great Demoralizer." Near dark, Gibbon cleared the last pocket of rebels from the north side of the river, opening the way to charge across the railroad bridge. Anticipating just such a move, the Palmetto Sharpshooters of Bratton's brigade set the railroad bridge on fire. Flames lit up the river for more than an hour.[60]

Hancock counted 285 casualties for the day, mostly from the 3rd and 5th Michigan, 86th and 124th New York, 17th Maine, and 99th Pennsylvania of Birney's division. Colonel Moses Lakeman of the Third Maine and Lieutenant Colonel Jacob H. Lansing of the 86th New York were wounded. Hancock considered this a small price to pay for firm control of the river crossings from Telegraph Road to the railway. Most Confederate casualties were from Henagan's brigade, which had been badly mauled. A Union source reported 110 Confederate prisoners, mostly South Carolinians. Confederate sources listed close to 100 casualties and 55 men captured.[61]

"Now was the time to show what artillery could do."

At Noel's Station, Colonel Brown, commanding McGowan's brigade, received reports that Warren's Federals were pouring across the ford at Jericho Mills. Concerned about his brigade's safety, Brown at 5:00 P.M. decided to abandon Noel's Station and march east toward Anderson's Tavern and the rest of the 3rd Corps. He had just started when Wilcox appeared with the remainder of the Light Division. Then Rooney Lee rode up. The interlopers south of the river at Jericho Mills, the cavalryman assured Wilcox, constituted only two cavalry brigades. They had camped on the south bank, Lee added, and were preparing to cook dinner. He promised Wilcox that "to rout them would be no great work for a division of infantry." [62]

In fact, the force that Rooney Lee had spotted was the entire Union 5th Corps. Crawford's division, its left anchored on the river a mile downstream from the ford, made up Warren's eastern wing. Supporting Crawford were Stewart's and Hart's batteries, posted on high ground on the Fontaine property, and Rittenhouse's, Breck's, and Cooper's batteries on the river's north bank. Griffin's division picked up on Crawford's right, with Ayres's brigade on the left of Griffin's line, abutting Crawford; Sweitzer's brigade reaching west across the farm road where Tilton had encountered the South Carolina skirmishers a few hours before; and Bartlett bivouacking in reserve, near the lip of the plateau. Warren intended for Cutler's division, resting in the field behind Griffin, to hook onto Griffin's right flank and continue the 5th Corps's line a mile upriver from Jericho Mills. Around 6:00—Wilcox was just preparing to attack—Cutler directed his men to march into place on Griffin's right. Robinson's Iron Brigade led off and slipped into line next to Sweitzer. Cutler's remaining brigades, under Colonel Edward S. Bragg and Colonel J. William Hofmann, started west across the field. Colonel Peter Lyle's brigade remained near the trail head at the ford.

Colonel Tilton, whose 22nd Massachusetts still manned the picket line toward the Virginia Central Railroad, was relieved to learn that Cutler was closing the gap on Griffin's right. "I had feared [a turning movement] all the afternoon," Tilton was to write, "and impressed upon many staff officers who came to the front from brigade, division, and corps headquarters the necessity of covering it." Now, with Cutler on the way, Tilton could breathe easier.[63]

Misled as to the size of the enemy force, Wilcox prepared to attack before nightfall. His plan was to form his division facing north and send it across the railway, through the woods, and into the enemy enclave south of the river at Jericho Mills. Lane's Tar Heels made up the right of Wilcox's line, McGowan's South Carolinians the center, and Thomas's Georgians the left. Wilcox posted the Georgians well west toward Noel Station so that they could turn the Union line and envelop it when they advanced. To assist Thomas in this turning movement, Wilcox placed Scales's North Carolina brigade, now under Colonel Lowrance, behind him and to his left. "If it was found that the right of the enemy did not extend beyond Thomas' left," Wilcox later explained, "[Lowrance] was to move around the enemy's flank and strike him in rear and flank." Pegram's artillery rolled into position on the right of Wilcox's line, where rising ground concealed the guns from the unsuspecting Federals. By 6:00 P.M. Wilcox had his troops formed for attack and ordered

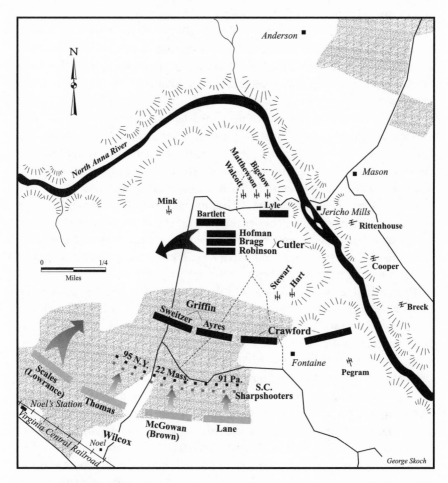

Battle of Jericho Mills, first stage

them to advance immediately. Captain William H. Brunson's sharpshooters probed forward, feeling for the Federal picket line.[64]

A dust cloud in the direction of the railway caught Tilton's attention. Southern flankers came into view, gliding through the fields along the railroad. "Soon the flankers halted, faced toward us, and advanced" a Bay State soldier recollected. "Then came their line of battle, and soon A. P. Hill's Corps was bearing down on us."[65]

At the Fontaine house, Crawford's men had stacked muskets and were stoking campfires to life. One wit joked that the name "Jericho Mills" reminded him of the Bible story about a man who had gone to the town of Jericho and fallen among thieves. Sergeant Austin C. Stearns of Company K, 13th Massachusetts, was anticipating a restful evening and paid little notice to the crackle of distant musketry. "They are shooting pigs," one of Stearns's messmates ventured. Suddenly rebel yells sounded across the fields, and musketry swelled to a roar. Crawford's soldiers gulped their coffee and fell into line. Bummers, cooks, and sundry civilians accompanying the troops darted toward the river for protection.[66]

Pegram's sixteen guns rolled onto the ridge south of the Fontaine house and opened on Crawford. "The air seemed filled with the shrieking shells and whizzing fragments," a Federal recounted. "The men could do no more than lie down and let the storm rage." Blue-clad figures ran for shelter along the river, and horses broke free from their tethers. "Soldiers who had been through all the battles of the Potomac army, affirmed that they never experienced such a noisy onset, except at Gettysburg," a northerner asserted. Crawford and his staff clapped spurs to their horses and, according to a witness, rode off "without a parting adieu; not an order was left for the action of our division." A shell fragment struck Colonel Hardin, commanding a brigade. The colonel was carrying a large pocketbook in the side pocket of his coat that absorbed most of the fragment's force, leaving him severely bruised but otherwise uninjured.[67]

Stewart's and Hart's batteries replied, as did the three Union batteries north of the river, twenty guns in all. "Now the tumult was doubled," a soldier from the Keystone State observed as he huddled under the arc of projectiles flying overhead from two directions. "The earth seemed to shake." To one impressionable Federal, it seemed that "at least a hundred canon were belching their howling shot upon those storm-swept hills." Noted he: "The missiles screamed, shrieked, fluttered, whistled, and spitefully plunged with terrific force all around, over, before, behind, and everywhere else among the crouching soldiers; no place appeared to be secure from their devilish course, except the insignificant spots where the soldiers lay." Pack mules burdened with pots, kettles, and blankets leaped from the bluffs into the river. Miraculously, few Federals were injured in the fray, and the greater weight of Union artillery soon drove Pegram to seek protection behind his hill. The battalion, a Confederate reported, sustained "severe loss." [68]

Preceded by sharpshooters, Wilcox's battle line crossed the railroad and slammed into Tilton's men. The rebels tore through the Union pickets, according to a southerner, "like an Alpine avalanche," dispersing them and capturing several prisoners. Federal accounts agreed that the retreat was "not dilatory." Tumbling precipitously back, the 22nd Massachusetts became wedged between Wilcox's Confederates and Sweitzer's main body, which was firing back without regard for its pickets. Under fire from front and rear, Tilton's men clambered to safety over Sweitzer's low earthworks. The 9th Massachusetts held Sweitzer's line on the right of the farm road, and the 32nd Massachusetts stood on the left of the road. Winded men from the 22nd Massachusetts intermingled with both regiments.[69]

Hogs, cattle, and chickens spilled from the woods as Wilcox pressed north. Ayres's brigade, on the left of Griffin's line, watched Lane's Tar Heels emerge into a field directly in front of them. Readying their arms, Ayres's Federals knelt close to the ground and trained their sights on the rebels. Soldiers who had been clearing brush in front of Ayres's line darted back "with amusing rapidity," a New Yorker recounted, "and in came our skirmishers pell-mell." Waiting until Lane's Confederates were halfway across the clearing, Ayres's soldiers fired. The volley jarred the rebels, who paused to close gaps in their ranks, then kept coming. "Give 'em hell, boys! Give 'em hell!" Captain James G. Grindlay, commanding the 146th New York, shouted above the din. In previous battles Ayres's troops had suffered severely when attacking well-entrenched Confederates. They were delighted that the customary roles were reversed. "We were now on the defensive behind breastworks," the 146th New York's historian reported, "and we responded to [Captain Grindlay's] injunctions with right good will, pumping charge after charge into the advancing Confederates." [70]

A finger of dense woods fronted the portion of Ayres's line manned by the 155th Pennsylvania. While the Federals could not see the Confederates, they could hear them yelling and fired toward the noise. Lane's men fired back, but sloping terrain made their shots go high. "Not a man with us wavered—some stood, some kneeled and some lay down," a Federal attested. "Boys, as long as you keep up such a fire as that was, no troops in the world can charge up to you!" Major John Ewing of the 155th Pennsylvania shouted. Lane refused to budge. "Our first volley halted them," a soldier in the 12th United States Regulars recalled, "but they stood their ground manfully for some minutes and give and take was the order of the day." Then Union guns from across the river found the range. "The sharp buzz of rifle balls around us, that bursting shell crashing of trees, and wild yells of the rebs went to make up a very devil of a row," a Regular reported.[71]

McGowan's brigade, on Lane's left, had fallen behind and lost contact with the Tar Heels. Concerned that his brigade might be isolated, Lane sent back for instructions. Wilcox assured him that the South Carolina troops were on his left and ordered him to "push on." But the 37th North Carolina, near Lane's center, broke under the pounding and tumbled rearward, endangering the brigade. Recalling the incident earlier that morning involving the farmer and his sheep, Lane's men began making animal noises to shame the 37th into returning. "It was ludicrous in the extreme," a soldier in the 18th North Carolina recalled, "fighting for all we were worth and bleating like sheep." [72]

Sensing that the Tar Heels were wavering, Ayres's soldiers sprang to their feet and fired another volley. Troubled about the gap left by the 37th North Carolina's collapse, Lane fell back into the woods to re-form. Griffin meanwhile pulled Ayres back, connecting his line more evenly with Sweitzer on his right. The respite was short-lived. Once more Lane pressed close to Ayres, and the battle resumed. The 37th North Carolina, however, was finished for the day and broke again. The rest of the Confederate brigade stood its ground and "fought very gallantly," Lane reported.[73]

On Ayres's right, Sweitzer held McGowan's men at bay. Griffin loved a good brawl, and his fighting blood was up. Riding back and forth along the line, he exhorted Ayres's and Sweitzer's soldiers to greater effort. "Sock it into them, boys!" he laughed. "Give them regular hell!" Invoking recent fights where his troops had gotten the worst of it, he added, "Pay them up for the 5th and 12th!" [74]

Cutler's division proved to be the weak link in Warren's line. When the attack hit, Robinson's Iron Brigade had just moved into place on Sweitzer's right. The 6th Wisconsin held the Iron Brigade's left and connected with Sweitzer's 9th Massachusetts. To the right of the 6th Wisconsin stood the 7th Wisconsin, 2nd Wisconsin, 24th Michigan, and the 7th and 19th Indiana. Cutler's remaining brigades under Hofmann and Bragg were marching behind Robinson, intending to hook onto Robinson's right and extend the line to the river. Lyle's brigade remained in reserve near the ford.[75]

Thomas's Georgians pitched into Robinson with tremendous force, striking the western end of his formation and lapping east, toward Sweitzer. Cattle ran back and forth between the contending forces, bellowing loudly. Then Lowrance's North Carolinians, extending well past Robinson's exposed flank as Wilcox had intended, came pouring in from the west, threatening to cut off Robinson's command. The Iron Brigade was having a rough campaign. In the Wilderness, Gordon's Confederates had overrun the outfit, and it had lost severely at Spotsylvania Court House. Now it was in a tight spot again. Colonel Rufus R. Dawes of the 6th Wisconsin directed his men to fire right oblique to the west, where rebels seemed thickest. Noticing that Union musketry was declining in volume, Dawes sent his adjutant, Edward P. Brooks, to find out why. Brooks reported that the regiments on the right end of the line were falling back. Bullets flying from the right confirmed his report.[76]

The Iron Brigade broke as Georgians attacked from straight ahead and Tar Heels poured in from the west, rolling up the Union line from right to left. Dawes swung his line clockwise and bent back his right flank, placing his regiment perpendicular to Sweitzer's line and facing Lowrance's flanking force. Now the Wisconsin regiment was vulnerable to Thomas's Confederates, who enfiladed its left. Dawes rallied his soldiers around the regimental colors and retired with a semblance of order. His withdrawal, however, uncovered Sweitzer's right. Sweitzer's 4th Michigan broke, as did part of the 9th Massachusetts, which streamed rearward "in great disorder," intermingling with Dawes's men.[77]

Wilcox was encouraged. The western wing of Warren's line was collapsing and his men were advancing in "good order." He sent a courier to Hill with news that he was driving the enemy "handsomely." The engagement was "going on well," he added, and he predicted that the "enemy would be whipped."[78]

When Thomas and Lowrance struck, Cutler and Captain Charles E. Mink had been looking for a place to position Mink's Battery H, 1st New York Light Artillery. Cutler directed Mink to post his pieces on a ridge several hundred yards behind the Iron Brigade and to its right, west of the sharp turn in the road from the ford. The ridge overlooked a deep, tree-filled gully extending west toward the North Anna. To reach the artillery Confederates would have to descend into the swale and climb up the far side, all the while exposed to Mink's guns. Deeming the situation "very ticklish," Wainwright dispatched an aide to summon Matthewson's and Walcott's batteries to assist Mink. "Our whole right was open, and unless the enemy could be stopped they would seize our bridge, and make sure work of Griffin and Crawford, for we had no troops in reserve on the plain except my batteries," Wainwright later wrote. "I felt that now was the time to show what artillery could do."[79]

A mob of Federals—the Iron Brigade and elements from the right of Sweitzer's brigade—tumbled toward Mink's little ridge. On the way they ran into Bragg's Bucktail Brigade of Cutler's division, which was marching in fours along a trajectory slated to take them where Robinson had posted his right flank minutes before. Bragg's men had not expected fighting and were accompanied by cooks, musicians, and packhorses. Suddenly Thomas's and Lowrance's rebels came screaming from south and west. The combination of Confederates tearing into Bragg's exposed right flank and the infectious panic of Robinson's men proved too much for the Bucktails. Bragg attempted to extricate his outfit by sliding left, but he moved too late. "They flanked us on the right and such running you never saw," an officer reported. Recounted another: "Our line for a few moments became almost panic-stricken and went back towards the river at as lively a pace as I had ever seen them move." The 150th Pennsylvania made a brief stand until rebels charging past both sides of the outfit rendered its position untenable. Bragg abandoned any pretense of making a stand. Ordering his troops to save themselves, he spurred his horse and "seemed to fly like the wind." Noted a soldier: "We followed, though at a slower pace." On reaching Mink's guns, Major George W. Jones of the 150th Pennsylvania planted his colors and announced that he had come to stay. Fifteen or twenty troops from the 121st Pennsylvania and elements from the Iron Brigade joined him. The remainder of Bragg's men rallied near the river, where servants, musicians, and mules splashed wildly to get across. Discarded packs covered the banks, and corpses of drowned animals floated in the water.[80]

Of Cutler's brigades only Hofmann's stood firm. Expecting to deploy along the extreme right of the 5th Corps's line, Hofmann's collection of New York and Pennsylvania regiments had been marching west across the field. When shooting started, the outfit was near Mink's ridge. Hofmann swung his line clockwise, pivoting on his left, to form a new line at a forty-five-degree angle from his former position. The snappy maneuver afforded Mink an unobstructed field of fire. As debris from Robinson's and Bragg's broken commands streamed past, Union guns showered double-shotted canister into Confederates approaching across the swale. "We unlimbered while the bullets were flying about our ears," Lieutenant David F. Ritchie of the battery wrote, "and as soon as our front was clear of our own troops we opened on the yelling and howling rebels."[81]

Matthewson's Battery D,1st New York Light Artillery, and Walcott's Battery C, Massachusetts Light Artillery, came up at a trot. Wainwright posted them on Mink's right at intervals of fifty yards, covering the ridge to the river, and ordered them to "hold on at all hazards." Robinson's and Bragg's soldiers careered past the guns "much disorganized and in all shapes upon the double-quick," a gunner recollected. "We urged them to stay by the battery, assuring them if they would do so we would stop the enemy." Wainwright rode over to Bigelow's 9th Massachusetts Light Artillery, posted south of the river near the ford. Warren was there—he looked a "good deal scared," the artillerist recorded—and had ordered Bigelow to fire blindly into the distant woods. "Elevate your guns," Wainwright shouted, apprehensive that projectiles were falling into Griffin's line. "You are firing into our own men." Bigelow's gunners adjusted their pieces and kept firing as rapidly as possible. Stray musket balls occasionally winged into their position.[82]

Wilcox was encouraged by Thomas's and Lowrance's success. Lane, it was true, remained stymied in front of Ayres, and the three regiments on the right of McGowan's line—the 13th and 14th South Carolina, and Orr's Rifles—lay pinned in front of Sweitzer. However, McGowan's leftmost regiments—the 1st and 12th South Carolina—had drifted left into the gap created by the Iron Brigade's collapse. Now they and Thomas's Georgians pressed into the swale fronting Mink's, Matthewson's, and Walcott's batteries. On the far Confederate left, Lowrance pressed forward as well. All that stood between the left half of Wilcox's line and the river were three Union batteries. Matthewson fired canister and case shot timed to explode with half-, three-fourths-, and one-second fuses. Mink relied chiefly on canister, inflicting severe carnage. But gun crews were falling fast. Captain Henry W. Davis, Wainwright's inspector, received a mortal wound in his neck and shoulder while trying to rally the mob of Federal fugitives collecting behind the guns. Matthewson received a flesh wound in his leg and relinquished command to Lieutenant Lester I. Richardson. Lieutenant Thomas M. Cargill of Walcott's battery fell seriously injured. Lieutenant Ritchie of Mink's battery perceived that the "fate of the division and perhaps the whole corps depended on us—on me." Drawing his saber, he cheered the men on. "Once I had to ride forward in the face of the bullets," he wrote the next day. "I set my teeth hard together, threw out my chest, and actually rode up to the guns with a feeling of defiant exultation such as I never felt before in a battle."[83]

Grant and his staff were several miles east at the Moncure house when guns roared into action on Hancock's and Warren's fronts. A soldier with the signal corps described the din as a "continuous roar, the like of which I had not heard in my two years of constant service in the Army of the Potomac." A broad yard spread grandly in front of the house. Orderlies had hitched their horses to a fence, and officers sprawled under stately elms. Grant rested his hands on the upper fence rail and listened intently. Then he walked leisurely over to his staff. Grant's self-control impressed the soldier. "He had the gift of keeping a calm exterior when the interior was boiling with the fierceness of the warrior," he later wrote.[84]

The battle had reached its moment of crisis. If Confederates overran the artillery, they could swing right and cut off Warren's avenue of retreat. Federals stationed north of the river could see the field and "trembled for the result of the issue as they saw our troops breaking and hurriedly falling back toward the steep banks of the river." The 5th Corps's predicament reminded onlookers of the Federal disaster at Ball's Bluff earlier in the war, when Confederates had driven a Union force into the Potomac River. Mink, Walcott, and Richardson made ready to spike their guns and roll them into the North Anna if the rebels broke through. "The battery was ready then to fight to the last minute and go with their guns," Richardson recalled.[85]

Griffin's remaining brigade, Bartlett's, had bivouacked in the field behind Sweitzer and Ayres. When the Iron Brigade broke, taking with it the right of Sweitzer's line, Griffin summoned Bartlett to buttress the shattered formation. Bartlett had recovered from his earlier illness and was in fighting form. He divided his brigade, sending the 20th Maine, 18th Massachusetts, 44th New York, and 118th Pennsylvania straight ahead to support Sweitzer, and ordering the 83rd Pennsylvania and the 1st and 16th Michigan toward the gap created by the Iron Brigade's collapse. Spear of the 20th Maine was felled by a shell fragment to the groin.[86]

Accompanied by a color-bearer, Sweitzer galloped to meet Bartlett's reinforcements. "Fiery as a comet," an officer in the 83rd Pennsylvania described him. Sweitzer screamed to Bartlett above the roar of combat. Rebels—McGowan's two leftmost regiments—were attacking his flank, and he needed support. The 83rd Pennsylvania and Bartlett's two Michigan regiments swung sharply west across the eastern neck of the swale. The right end of the Confederate battle line, the 1st and 12th South Carolina, was straight ahead. The 83rd Pennsylvania's Colonel DeWitt C. McCoy—a hero of Little Round Top at Gettysburg—seized the opportunity and ordered his regiment to charge. His men and the Michigan soldiers poured "stunning volleys" directly into the rebel flank, then ran toward the startled southerners, who turned to meet them. The opposing forces collided head-on, a Pennsylvanian recollected, like "two rams." [87]

The two South Carolina regiments, about three hundred strong, never had a chance. During the advance, Thomas's Georgians had drifted left and lost contact with the Palmetto State troops. The commanders of the 1st and 12th South Carolina were both shot, and Colonel Brown, who was leading the South Carolina brigade, was captured while trying to bring up reinforcements from his troops in front of Sweitzer. Wainwright's guns north of the river shifted their fire toward the swale as well. "Grape and canister from the smooth-bores, and conical bolts from the rifles went through the rebel ranks," a correspondent wrote. "I have seen patent mince-meat cutters with knives

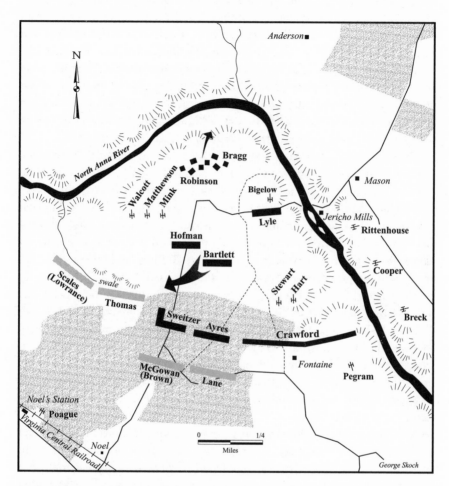

Battle of Jericho Mills, second stage

turning in all directions, but this double-angled line of fire exceeded them all. The check was instantaneous." Slammed by artillery fire converging from two directions and by McCoy's unexpected counterattack, the two isolated Palmetto regiments broke. The southerners panicked, a Federal claimed, and "fled without firing over a dozen shots." The Confederate brigade historian agreed that the two regiments suffered severely but insisted that they retired under orders. "The infantry of the enemy enfiladed them for some space," a southerner reported, "and when they were out of that, the canister of the artillery poured into them with greater fury than ever." [88]

The retreat of the Palmetto State soldiers uncovered Thomas's right flank. The Georgians reeled under canister in front and Bartlett's musketry from the right. Thomas fell back, a Georgian wrote, expecting support from Lowrance, who had been on Thomas's left. The Tar Heels, however, had drifted farther left, breaking their connection with Thomas. "To move forward without support was folly," a Georgian explained. Another Confederate called it "the tightest place I was ever in." Colonel Bolling H. Holt of the 35th Georgia urged his men to advance, but they refused. With both flanks bare and no support behind, Thomas fell back to the rail line, in the process exposing Lowrance, who fell back as well. During the retreat the 16th North Carolina became separated from the rest of Lowrance's troops. The soldiers followed the swale downhill to the river, then took a roundabout course west along the river until reaching the railway. For a time Wilcox thought that his division and the opposing Federals were both retreating. "The singular spectacle was exhibited of two opposing lines giving way at the same time," he wrote in his report.[89]

As Wilcox's left folded, 5th Corps elements drove forward in pursuit, and Warren hurried fresh elements into the fight. Hofmann pressed south from near Mink's guns, cleared the last of the rebels from the swale, and continued toward the railroad, joined by the 83rd Pennsylvania and its companion Michigan regiments. Warren shifted Colonel Bates's brigade from the Fontaine house and sent the fresh troops to different portions of his line, holding the 12th Massachusetts in reserve. Lyle moved in front of the 9th Massachusetts Battery, which kept firing canister at the retreating rebels. One of Lyle's men remembered Cutler riding about, admonishing his aides, "Don't hurry! Don't hurry!" [90]

Driving back Wilcox's left, victorious Federals slipped past Lane's brigade and the portion of McGowan's brigade still fighting Sweitzer. Realizing that the Union counattercharge had rendered his position untenable, Lane ordered his men back to the Virginia Central Railroad. Captain E. Price, commanding Company E of the 33rd North Carolina, took his men out "with arms shouldered as though it were on a drill." Wilcox hoped to regain the initiative by sending Lowrance into the fray, but his plans were dashed when he discovered Lowrance falling back in disorder.[91]

Cannon and musketry from Jericho Mills finally galvanized Hill into action. He directed Heth to support Wilcox, and Mahone to deploy along the railway west of Anderson's Tavern where he could join the fight if needed. Rushing west, Heth received "pretty smart shelling" from Wainwright's artillery posted on the northern bank. Heth intended to advance north from the railroad to support Wilcox, but Wilcox feared that Warren might turn his right flank and wanted strong support along the railway. Without consulting Heth, Wilcox ordered Heth's men to shift to the right, which they did, much to Heth's surprise. Afterward, when Heth learned the reason for Wilcox's action, he agreed that Wilcox had acted appropriately "under existing circumstances."[92]

Warren's guns terribly overmatched Pegram's lone battalion, huddled against the backside of its knoll. Heth had brought Lieutenant Colonel William Poague's battalion to help correct the artillery imbalance. As Poague passed behind Pegram, he dispatched six guns under Major George Ward to assist Pegram. Ward, a popular Mississippian and Poague's close friend, pushed his pieces onto the knoll. Union counterbattery fire instantly killed him, and his men hauled the guns back behind the knoll with Pegram. Poague continued with the remainder of his artillery to Noel's Station, where he found things in "bad shape." Thomas's men were "somewhat demoralized" over their repulse and expected Warren to counterattack. Poague pushed five guns onto high ground north of the station to receive the expected assault. Confederate leadership had collapsed. "There was no general officer present," Poague noted, "and the subordinate officer seemed doubtful about staying there, as we were some distance from the main body of our army and he thought the force which he had failed to dislodge were then aiming to cut us off."[93]

Hill sped a courier east to find to Lee. The situation at Jericho Mills seemed to be spinning out of control. Federals had crossed the river on the Confederate left in considerable numbers, and Hill needed reinforcements. Unable to find Lee, the courier gave the message to Martin Smith, Lee's chief engineer, who suggested that Ewell might be able to help. Ewell, however, had ridden to oversee the defense of the Richmond, Fredericksburg, and Potomac Railroad bridge, and the courier could not find him until after dark. By then the battle was over, and Hill had no need for reinforcements.[94]

Warren decided against pressing his advantage. Grant and Meade were too far away for him to consult, and he had no idea how many Confederates he faced. Calling off the chase, he resumed fortifying his position south of the river according to his initial plan. Both 5th Corps flanks rested on the North Anna, with Cutler on the right, Griffin in the center, and Crawford on the left. Wainwright maintained a steady fire, and Confederate sharpshooters shot back from the woods, harassing the Federals as they threw up earthworks. Colonel Tilton stumbled across a rebel while inspecting his picket line, and the two men rolled on the ground in a fistfight. Mistaking a cluster of Tilton's soldiers for Confederates, the southerner called out, "Shoot this Yank!" Instantly, the Bay Staters pressed their bayonets against the rebel's throat. "You'uns would do the same," their prisoner pled. "Don't kill me for that." Tilton intervened and spared the man's life.[95]

Throughout the night, Warren's pickets rounded up stray rebels. Major George Hooper, of the 1st Michigan, was waiting for his coffee to boil when his messmates grabbed their muskets, dashed behind a tree, and emerged with a Confederate in tow. "Come in Johnny, come in," Hooper welcomed the captive. "The 1st Michigan has got to have one prisoner." The southerner had lost his way when his regiment retreated. Hooper and his companions shared supper with him. "By the time the provost guards had come to take him away he was pretty well filled up," Hooper reminisced. "They assured him that he would get plenty to eat at Elmira [Prison] and they knew he would enjoy it." On another part of the battlefield, seventeen-year-old Natt Nixon lay seriously wounded. Nixon's friend M. H. Freeman found the boy by calling out for him. "Natt, I'm coming after you," Freeman shouted as he set down his gun. "I am coming unarmed, and any man who shoots me is a damned coward." No one fired at Freeman, and he carried the injured boy back to his regiment, the 28th North Carolina. Nixon died before daylight.[96]

Union soldiers were encouraged by the day's successes. "We have been now for four weeks constantly on the go, with very few luxuries in food or dress," a gunner wrote in his diary, "and begin to think that comfortable quarters in Richmond, with plenty of sherry cobblers, would come in well." A New Yorker reveled that "Old Lee is out-maneuvered and all his fortifications from Gordonsville to Fredericksburg to Spotsylvania have been for nothing and we stand only 21 miles from Richmond and soon we will be still nearer to it."[97]

Congratulations flowed freely in Union camps. Hancock had secured Chesterfield Bridge and the railway bridge. In an excess of exuberance, fostered perhaps by the dearth of Union successes in recent days, he proclaimed Birney's capture of Henagan's redoubt among the "most brilliant assaults of the war." The Federal attackers had performed well, it was true, but the preponderance of Union might never left the outcome in doubt. For a relatively trifling loss Hancock had gained a critical lodgment on the North Anna.[98]

Hancock's bombast notwithstanding, Jericho Mills was the day's major victory. Fighting had lasted an hour and had been extremely intense, but Union casualties were relatively light. Griffin reported 99 lost, Cutler 223, and Crawford only a handful of men. Wainwright counted only 16 casualties among his artillerists. Meade commended Warren and his "gallant corps for the manner in which you repulsed the enemy's attack." Some commentators wondered how Warren had permitted his troops to be caught with their backs to a river, but criticism seemed out of place. Warren considered his victory a coup that would bolster his sagging reputation. He had, after all, outperformed Hancock! "General Meade sent me a congratulatory note last night, on my success for the day," he preened in a letter to his wife, Emily. "The enemy kept General Hancock from getting over the river at all. In that, we have all the honors of the day, I think." Warren was especially elated at having bested Hill. Before the war Hill had courted Warren's future wife, and Warren relished his fights against Hill. After beating the Virginian at Bristoe Station in 1863, he had sent Hill a note crowing, "I have not only whipped you, but married your old sweetheart." Now he had defeated Hill again. "It was your old beau Hill (A.P.) that I fought with yesterday—same as it was at Bristoe," he informed Emily. "I think he must begin to feel unkindly toward me."[99]

Most of Warren's subordinates had reason to be proud. "There can be no doubt but that Sweitzer's gallantry saved the corps from a disgraceful rout; nor can there be any doubt but that the Eighty-third [Pennsylvania] and the Sixteenth [Michigan] saved Sweitzer," the historian of the 83rd Pennsylvania wrote. Praise was also due Hofmann's brigade, which had resolutely held its ground and had spearheaded the counterattack. Everyone acknowledged that Wainwright and his guns had performed yeoman's work. "Never was the strength and efficiency of the artillery arm of the service more marked than on this occasion," the gunner Breck effused. "It saved the day, in all probability, saved the 5th Corps, or changed what was likely to prove a terrible disaster for our army into a victory."[100]

But some reputations suffered. Crawford had unaccountably left his troops to fend for themselves under Pegram's shelling. And Robinson's Iron Brigade had "damaged their good name by breaking and running back in confusion," a reporter judged. Wainwright viewed the brigade's "bad behavior" as a "strong instance of how panic at times seizes a whole command." Half of the soldiers, Wainwright observed, had run "clear across the river, and two-thirds of the other half were brought back with difficulty by their of-

ficers to support the batteries." Cutler also seemed to lack the fire that had
distinguished his earlier service. "The old man has not been at any time during this campaign what he was last year," Wainwright grumbled. "He is evidently very much broken and lost his head when his men behaved so badly."
The criticism was not altogether fair, as the Iron Brigade had faltered under
circumstances that would have challenged any outfit, and Cutler's rallying of
his forces after the breach had been exemplary.[101]

Warren had indeed won a noteworthy victory. In retrospect, however, his
success might have been even greater. Had he pressed his advantage, he
could have seriously damaged Wilcox's division and threatened the rest of
Hill's corps, which was strung along the Virginia Central Railroad. But
Warren required Wright's support and headquarters' approval before he could
launch such an ambitious undertaking. Grant and Meade were miles away,
and no headquarters staff officer was present to authorize the movement. The
opportunity to turn a tactical victory into a strategic triumph passed unexploited.

That night a roaring fire of fence rails illuminated Warren's headquarters.
Captain William Howard, a Georgian and adjutant to General Thomas, had
lost his brother during the battle, and Federal soldiers caught him wandering
the field. They brought him to the 5th Corps's camp, where Griffin and his
staff quizzed him. Howard refused to answer questions, even after Griffin assured him that he was only trying to help Howard find his brother. "The fool
was so taken with his own consequence that he would hardly say anything,"
noted Wainwright, "even when told that we knew from other prisoners exactly what troops they had engaged." The Federals gave him tobacco and
whiskey and amused themselves with his "absurd airs and obstinacy," Wainwright recorded. Warren asked a few short questions, received no answers,
then offered to send Howard under guard to look for his brother. Howard refused, and Warren ordered him to the rear, remarking offhandedly that the
man was a fool. "I heard that you were a good general, but no gentleman,"
Howard retorted. "If they only think me a good general, I don't care to be
considered a gentlemen," Warren muttered as he walked away.[102]

There were no congratulations on the Confederate side. "The movement
was a failure," the historian of McGowan's brigade admitted. "We fell far
short of our usual success, and infinitely below the anticipations with which
we entered the battle. The truth is General Lee's scouts have been miserably
deceived. Instead of two brigades of cavalry, resting and cooking, there were
two corps of infantry between us and the river, perfectly prepared for us."
Wilcox reported 642 casualties. The actual number was 730. A recent count
shows that Lane lost about 120, Thomas 150, McGowan 218, and Scales 239.

According to Wilcox, Lowrance left 200 men sleeping on the railway after the battle, and they were captured early the next morning. The 35th Georgia alone reported 59 casualties, among them some of Lee's most experienced combat veterans. The Army of Northern Virginia could ill afford more debacles such as occurred at Jericho Mills.[103]

Mistakes had occurred at every level of Confederate command. Lee had misinterpreted Grant's design. Assuming the main Federal body would strike east, toward the Pamunkey, he had left Henagan exposed and had neglected to safeguard the North Anna crossings. Rooney Lee had fatally underestimated the strength of the Union force at Jericho Mills, precipitating a train of misadventures. Without consulting Lee, Hill had sent only Wilcox's division to repulse Warren's Federals; Wilcox had moved boldly forward to discover that there were far more Federals than he had expected; and by the time Hill could bring up reinforcements, the situation was past redeeming. Warren had a firm foothold on the southern bank and Wright was close behind. While fingers could be pointed at nearly all the Confederate commanders involved in the bungled affair, ultimate responsibility lay with Lee, who had failed to comprehend that Grant meant to fight on the North Anna River.

"Everything looks exceedingly favorable to us."

Fighting was over at dark, and Grant's combat elements had reached their assigned positions for the night by 9:00 P.M. Warren's troops settled behind entrenchments at Jericho Mills, on the North Anna's southern bank. Wright's corps camped across the river from Warren, within supporting distance of the 5th Corps. Two miles east, at Ox Ford, Burnside's men slipped off their knapsacks after a long day's march. Willcox's division held Ox Ford, with pickets extended downriver to Hancock. Crittenden bivouacked behind Willcox, and Potter closed up the rear. Hancock comprised the Federal left, with Birney occupying a line from Chesterfield Bridge to the railway and the remainder of the 2nd Corps encamped east of the tracks. "The wounded were brought in and cared for," a correspondent observed, "the dead were buried where they fell, the living slumbered on the ground, and the generals consulted about the work to be done on the morrow."[104]

During the evening Grant sorted through reports from his corps commanders. The ease of Warren's crossing at Jericho Mills suggested that Lee did not intend to fight along the North Anna. Escaped slaves reported that the Confederates were shifting south, probably to defend the South Anna. "Everything looks exceedingly favorable to us," Grant concluded in his report to Washington. In the morning he would put the rest of his army across the river and try to catch the rebels before they could fortify a new position farther south.[105]

Grant was uncertain, however, about the details of his advance. Warren was already across the river, and Wright was posted to cross at Jericho Mills and follow the 5th Corps. Burnside at Ox Ford and Hancock at Chesterfield Bridge, however, faced formidable obstacles. High bluffs confronted Burnside, and Confederate artillery on high ground south of the river barred Hancock's path. The 2nd Corps's commander assured headquarters that he could carry the crossing at Chesterfield that night if necessary, although he believed the feat would be "difficult." Hancock suggested instead that he hold firm while the rest of the army crossed at Jericho Mills. "It is desirable you should cross [at Chesterfield Bridge], but the attempt should not be made unless, in your judgment, there is a reasonable degree of probability of success," Meade wrote back. "The matter is, therefore, left to your discretion." [106]

Grant decided to wait until morning to complete his plans. By then, he reasoned, the Confederates might have loosened their grip on Ox Ford and Chesterfield Bridge. If not, Hancock and Burnside could slip west to Jericho Mills and cross behind Wright. The mood in northern camps was upbeat. "Everybody felt in good spirits and confident of a victory on the coming day," a correspondent noted. "The result of today's operations is that we secured the passage of the North Anna River and inflicted a defeat upon the enemy wherever we encountered him." The Confederates, he thought, "meant merely to delay our passage in order to gain time to place their whole army in position on the South Anna, along which it is known a defensive line has been prepared for some time with a view to the possibility of the compulsory retreat of Lee before Grant." [107]

At dusk, Lee held a conference near his headquarters at the Miller house. The general, his staff, and some of his subordinate generals assembled in a forty-acre field, under a large oak. Troops were going into bivouac for the night, mules were braying, and cooks were lighting fires. "The air was still," remembered the artillerist Alexander, "and it was one of those evenings when all sounds are distinct and far-reaching." The growl of guns could be heard from the north, by Chesterfield Bridge, and from northwest toward Jericho Mills. A root doubled as Lee's stool. Anderson was there, as was Ewell, along with their staffs and various subordinates and engineers. The meeting numbered among Lee's most important conferences.[108]

Lee listened to reports from his lieutenants. Ewell, whose 2nd Corps formed the right wing of the Confederate line, was camped east of Hanover Junction. Federals were pressing hard against the railway bridge, Ewell advised, and they extended a considerable distance downriver. From Anderson, Lee learned that Union troops had overrun Henagan's redoubt and controlled Chesterfield Bridge. News from Hill's quarter was especially disturbing. Warren had crossed at Jericho Mills and had foiled Hill's attempt to drive him back. The entire Union corps was entrenching, and more of Grant's army was moving up in support. Grant had secured a lodgment below the river that he could exploit to turn Lee's left flank.

Lee asked his subordinates for their views. Was it still possible to defend Hanover Junction? Was retreat the only recourse? Where was the next defensible line? Was it the South Anna River, or must the army retire to the Chickahominy?

Lee looked to his chief engineer, Martin Smith, for advice. A northerner by birth and a graduate of West Point, Smith had married a southerner. When war came, he resigned his commission and joined the Confederate army. A talented engineer, he oversaw the construction of Confederate defenses in Florida, at New Orleans, and at Vicksburg. When Vicksburg fell in July 1863, Smith was captured. He was exchanged and shortly before the spring campaign joined the Army of Northern Virginia, where he played a pivotal role in the evolution of earthworks in the eastern theater. Lee recognized Smith's skill in fortifying defensive positions and relied on him extensively in the Wilderness and at Spotsylvania Court House. "I seem to have acquired the confidence of General Lee to the extent of his being willing to place his troops on the lines of my selection and stake the issue of a battle," Smith wrote his wife with pride. "More than this is hardly to be expected." [109]

Smith had closely examined the terrain south of the North Anna River. Early in the morning he rode from Hanover Junction to Chesterfield Bridge and explored downriver for sites to position guns. In the afternoon he rode upriver to Ox Ford and then followed the old stage road southwest to Anderson's Tavern and Little River, where Hill had his camps. From there he returned along the Virginia Central Railroad to Hanover Junction. During the fight at Henagan's redoubt he had visited the Fox and Lowry properties. [110]

As the conference progressed, everyone agreed that Hanover Junction had to be defended at all costs. Abandoning the vital rail link would permit Grant to sever Richmond and Lee's army from the Shenandoah Valley. And where else was Lee to take his army? The South Anna offered fairly strong ground for drawing a defensive line, but retreating there would back the Confederates perilously close to the capital. The discussion kept returning to the same point. A way must be found to cover Hanover Junction. Jedediah Hotchkiss, the 2nd Corps's cartographer, argued in favor of fortifying the grade of the Virginia Central Railroad. Running east to west along high ground, the rail line offered a good line of defense against an attack from the north. But Warren's appearance below Jericho Mills, Lee pointed out, had changed all of this. If the Army of Northern Virginia dug in behind the rail line, Warren could easily turn its left flank.[111]

Smith, whose day-long excursion had given him a firm grasp of the terrain, proposed an ingenious solution. The old stage road from Richmond intersected the Virginia Central Railroad at Anderson's Tavern and followed a ridge northeast to Ox Ford. Here was ideal ground for resisting a Federal attack from the direction of Jericho Mills. A strong formation could be drawn with its left anchored on Little River, a quarter of a mile south of Anderson's Tavern, and its right terminating on high bluffs overlooking Ox Ford. Running on high ground along the old stage road, the line would be all but impregnable.

Terrain favored defense downriver from Ox Ford as well. From Ox Ford, bluffs hugged the river for half a mile. Then the defensible high ground angled southeast toward Hanover Junction. If the Confederates entrenched along the land's natural contours, they would have to abandon Chesterfield Bridge and the railroad bridge. But as Smith viewed the situation, the Confederates would profit from the trade, since they would control an extremely strong position. Swampy land northeast of Hanover Junction could anchor the formation's right flank. The generals liked Smith's idea, although they disagreed over whether the line should pass in front of the morass or behind it. Lee decided to thread the line behind the swamp, then bend back his right flank to foreclose a hostile movement from the east.

As finally drawn, the proposed line described an inverted V, its left leg anchored on Little River, its apex at Ox Ford, and its right behind the swamp near Hanover Junction. The previous day Lee had denounced salients. Now he was planning to place his entire army in a giant salient. This wedge-shaped formation, however, had none of the drawbacks of the Mule Shoe that had brought Lee to grief at Spotsylvania Court House. The Mule Shoe's wide, blunt apex had fronted an open field, inviting attack. The tip of the North Anna formation was to rest on precipitous bluffs and was unassailable. In addition, with the Virginia Central Railroad connecting the two feet of the inverted V, Lee could shift troops from one side to the other across the base as needed.

It dawned on Lee that chance had presented him a marvelous opportunity. He recognized that when he pulled his forces back from the river to construct the wings of the V, it would appear to Grant that the Confederates had retreated, leaving only a token force at the V's apex, Ox Ford. Grant was aggressive, and judging from his behavior thus far in the campaign, he would doubtless throw his army across the river in pursuit of the Confederates.

Proceeding southeast from Jericho Mills, Warren and Wright would encounter the left wing of the Confederate wedge. Burnside, at Ox Ford, would confront the strong tip and be locked in place on the northern bank. And Hancock, crossing at Chesterfield Bridge and along the railway, would advance alone until he struck the Confederate formation's right wing. At this juncture the Union army would be separated into three parts—Warren and Wright to the west, below the river; Burnside north of the river; and Hancock to the east, below the river. Neither Union wing could reinforce the other. For Warren to assist Hancock, the 5th Corps would have to backtrack to Jericho Mills, cross to the northern bank, march by a circuitous route to Chesterfield Bridge, then cross the river once again.

Lee, on the other hand, would hold a tremendous advantage. If Grant attacked either leg of the inverted V, Lee could quickly shift troops from the other leg to defend. And for the first time in the campaign, the Army of Northern Virginia would be positioned to take the offensive. Lee could leave a skeleton force in the western leg to fend off Warren and Wright, concentrate the mass of his army along the eastern leg, and attack Hancock with overwhelming strength. "Our holding a half mile of river made the Federal line very bad," observed Alexander. "To go from one of their flanks to the other, one must cross the river twice. We had the interior lines." [112]

Toward the end of the conference, a teamster began berating his mule. "Get around there you damned infernal long-eared son of a jackass!" he hollered, giving the animal a resounding whack. Lee hated seeing animals mistreated and gave a distinctive shake of his head that his staffers recognized as a sign of agitation. "Snapping his ear," they called the movement. As the contest between mule and teamster escalated, Lee could remain quiet no longer. "What are you beating that mule for?" he shouted. Assuming that someone was joking with him, the teamster modulated his voice into a whine and called back, "Is this any of you-r-r mule?" The generals around Lee fell silent, biting their lips to keep from smiling. Lee snapped his ear twice, then returned to planning his trap for Grant. [113]

The meeting broke up shortly after dark, and couriers rode off carrying instructions. Hill was to form the 3rd Corps into the left wing of the inverted V by anchoring Heth at Little River, extending Wilcox along the stage road past Anderson's Tavern and completing the line to Ox Ford with Mahone. Anderson was to join his 1st Corps onto Mahone's right and angle his line southwest toward Telegraph Road, Kershaw on the left and Field on the right. Near the Miller farm, Ewell's 2nd Corps line—the divisions of Gordon, Rodes, and Early, left to right in that order—was to run east to the swamp and then curve south, securing the right end of the line past Hanover Junction.

Breckinridge's and Pickett's men, along with some of Ewell's, would form a reserve near Hanover Junction, poised to shift to either wing of the formation as needed.[114]

Work progressed to the sound of sniper and artillery fire. On the western flank Hill ordered Wilcox back to Anderson's Tavern at 8:00 P.M. Heth remained behind the rail embankment east of Noel's Station, expecting Warren to assault any moment. "The situation was uncomfortable," recollected Poague, who stayed behind with his artillery. "There were no signs of the enemy in our front, although the infantry pickets several times reported them as advancing. On account of the dense woods nothing could be seen thirty yards away." Near ten o'clock Hill ordered Heth to withdraw, followed by Mahone. All night, Hill's men moved into position to form the western leg of the inverted V. "It is useless to talk about how tired and sore I am," a Georgian wrote home. "I have not changed clothes or shaved since the fighting commenced."[115]

East of Ox Ford, Anderson began pulling the 1st Corps back from the river to construct the inverted V's eastern leg. Toward midnight, Kershaw directed Colonel A. J. McBride of the 10th Georgia to burn Chesterfield Bridge. To elude Federal pickets stationed on high ground north of the bridge, McBride and a handpicked detachment crept to the span under cover of bushes. They set fire to the timbers, and a few Confederates scurried up the steep slope toward Henagan's redoubt, now filled with Federals. The 20th Indiana counterattacked, drove the southerners away, and extinguished the flames in time to save the bridge. The 7th New York Heavy Artillery settled into the earthworks for the night, and Captain Ames's 1st New York Light Artillery, Battery G, reversed the works to afford the guns unobstructed fire south. The 1st Maine Heavy Artillery covered Birney's line from the redoubt east to Telegraph Road.[116]

"I was out the entire night," Lee's artillery chief Pendleton wrote his wife, "aiding in choosing our line and adjusting positions."[117]

X

MAY 24

Grant Marches into Lee's Trap

"The enemy have fallen back from North Anna."

THE SUN ROSE on May 24 "like a disc of molten brass," a soldier recalled, "presaging a day of terrible heat." Lee woke early as usual and conferred with his chief engineer, Martin Smith, and the colonel of the 1st Engineers. All night the Army of Northern Virginia had been filing into a wedge-shaped formation. "Troops busy building breastworks along the entire line," a signal officer recorded. "Everybody seems satisfied with the position General Lee has selected." In a few hours the fortifications would be complete. Lee was hopeful that Grant would split his army across the apex of the V at Ox Ford and afford the Confederates the opportunity to take the offensive. "If I can get one more pull at [Grant]," Lee predicted, "I will defeat him." [1]

Lee took breakfast at Hanover Junction with Ewell, Anderson, and several aides. He was ill from dysentery but concealed his discomfort to avoid alarming his subordinates. Work on the eastern leg of the formation was progressing smoothly. Anderson had anchored his left on bluffs at the river and pivoted the rest of his line southeast to construct the wedge's eastern leg, extending from the river to a point near Telegraph Road south of the Lowry House. Ewell's corps picked up on Anderson's right, sliced east across the railway, then bent south to cover the eastern approaches to Hanover Junction. Lee held Pickett's division, Breckinridge's little army, and parts of Ewell's corps in reserve near the junction, ready to support either wing. Anderson's and Ewell's pickets occupied rifle pits along high ground south of the river. Their job was to delay Hancock until the Confederate fortifications were complete.[2]

Satisfied with Anderson's and Ewell's preparations, the ailing Lee rode in a buggy to Anderson's Tavern and visited the western leg of the inverted V held by Hill. Lee was concerned about Hill's sector. Warren was south of the river and Wright was close behind. Hill would have to fend off both corps and perhaps a third if Burnside shifted to Jericho Mills.

Lee met with Hill for the first time since the debacle at Jericho Mills. Fatigue and illness made Lee cantankerous—a doctor observed that the general had not slept two consecutive hours since May 5 and was "cross as an old bear." Lee could not conceal frustration over Hill's failure to repel Warren. "General Hill, why did you let those people cross here?" he snapped in a biting rebuke. "Why didn't you throw your whole force on them and drive them back as Jackson would have done?" Hotchkiss, who witnessed the outburst, reflected that Lee was "evidently of the opinion that Hill had been caught napping and addressed him rather savagely." Lee's reproach must have cut deeply. Hill was often quick to anger, but he held his tongue.[3]

Suspecting that Grant intended to attack east along the Virginia Central Railway from Noel's Station, Lee shifted Pickett's division and portions of Ewell's corps under Gordon and Early to Anderson's Tavern and placed them at Hill's disposal. Hill hurried artillery into line, posting Poague's battalion on his left at Little River, in support of Heth; Pegram's battalion along the face of the leg, supporting Wilcox; and McIntosh's battalion at Ox Ford, backing Mahone. Colonel Allen S. Cutts's battalion, under Major John Lane, dug in atop bluffs downriver from Ox Ford, where it controlled the ford and had an unobstructed range downstream to Chesterfield Bridge. Richardson's battalion and Braxton's guns, brought over from the 2nd Corps, formed a second tier behind Anderson's Tavern in anticipation of an assault along the railway.[4]

Grant began the day convinced that Lee was retreating. "The general opinion of every prominent officer in the army on the morning of the 24th," Dana remembered, "was that the enemy had fallen back, either to take up a position beyond the South Anna or to go to Richmond." Grant's goal was to catch the Confederates on the move. At daylight the entire Union army—the left under Hancock at Chesterfield Bridge, the center under Burnside at Ox Ford, and the right under Warren and Wright at Jericho Mills—made ready to push south.[5]

Warren's soldiers were hungry. Provision wagons had been delayed threading through Wright's camps north of the river and negotiating the steep banks at Jericho Mills. Warren presumed that Hill's Confederates had fled across Little River. Keeping most of his corps in bivouac until food arrived, he sent skirmishers south toward the Virginia Central Railroad. Confederates hiding behind trees retarded their progress.

Wright began crossing at Jericho Mills. By 6:00 A.M. two 6th Corps divisions were on the south bank in support of Warren. Union skirmishers pressed

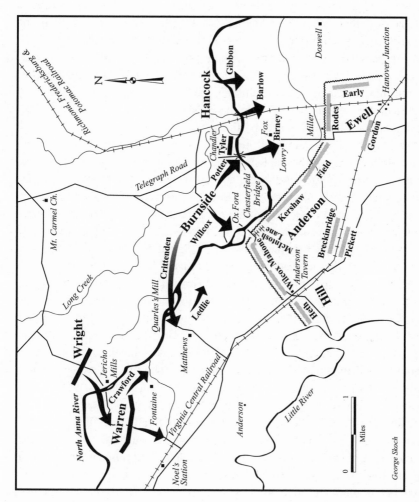

Union lines of advance on May 24

south through woods and fields toward the Virginia Central Railroad, scooping up prisoners and fighting heated actions with rebel sharpshooters. "Had one bullet pass through my coffee kettle, which was tied on top of my knapsack," a Michigan man reported, "and one ball passed through the bottom of my haversack, spoiling quite a bit of paper and envelopes." When rebels in a barn held up the veteran 20th Maine, Colonel Chamberlain asked his friend Captain Charles A. Phillips of the 5th Massachusetts Battery for assistance. Firing percussion shells, Phillips blew the barn "skyward, in flames," Chamberlain reported with satisfaction. Warren's dogged skirmishers soon reached the rail line. So far as Warren could tell, the way was clear to Little River. "I shall keep feeling out till I develop the enemy's position, if he is about," the general advised headquarters at 6:00 A.M.[6]

Warren's soldiers examined the previous afternoon's battlefield. "Trees were rent and torn by shot and shell, the ground up to the felled trees in our front was strewn with guns, belts, and all sorts of trash, together with the dead bodies of many Greybacks," a Regular observed. "They carried off all their wounded and I passed over the ground to the railroad in different directions and could everywhere see pools of blood, shreds of bloody clothing, and so." Rebel corpses seemed "miserably clad and dirty, resembling skeletons," a New Yorker noticed, more like "lumps of flesh than human beings." Everything suggested that the Army of Northern Virginia was retreating. "Large numbers of the enemy kept coming in, and they appear, for the most part, very glad to reach a point where food is possible" a Federal reported. "Totally demoralized," another northerner remarked of the captives. In earlier years, reflected Colonel Dawes of the 6th Wisconsin, the southerners would have driven the 5th Corps into the river. Now they showed substantially less "vigor in attack," persuading Dawes that "General Hill's corps could be defeated on an open field by half their number of resolute men."[7]

Warren sent the 1st Pennsylvania Reserves of Crawford's division downriver to clear the rebels from Ox Ford, where Burnside was to cross. Lieutenant Colonel W. Warren Stewart marched the regiment single file in the shadow of the high south bank, hoping to conceal the movement. Confederate scouts discovered the maneuver, however, and alerted Mahone, whose division was entrenched at Ox Ford. During the winter Mahone had organized an elite battalion of sharpshooters, specially trained and armed with Enfield rifles. Mahone dispatched this picked force west to intercept the Pennsylvanians.[8]

Halfway between Jericho Mills and Ox Ford, a farm road crossed the North Anna at a shallow place called Quarles's Mill. The 1st Pennsylvania had just reached the steep, rocky ford when Mahone's sharpshooters attacked. "We advanced, firing as we did so," a sharpshooter recalled, "taking advantage of such protection from the trees as we could." Pinned in place, the Pennsylvanians formed along a farm road leading to the ford. More Confederates from Colonel John C. C. Sanders's Alabama brigade arrived in support of the sharpshooters, and the engagement heated as soldiers on both sides stacked fence rails and dug in. Stewart became concerned when Confederates slipped west and interposed between his regiment and the rest of the 5th Corps, cutting off his escape route. Isolated at Quarles's Mill, Stewart sent word of his predicament to Burnside's scouts on the north bank.[9]

Wright meanwhile brought the rest of his corps across the pontoon bridge at Jericho Mills. Musketry rattled from south and east, but Wright's men were unconcerned. Their assignment was to support Warren, and for the time that meant waiting in the fields around the Fontaine house. Soldiers took the opportunity to bathe in the North Anna. "The whole army seemingly has been in swimming," a Vermonter wrote. "At any rate I never saw so many in bathing at once before or those who seemed to enjoy it more." A group of fortunate New Yorkers found tobacco and a pig hidden in a barn. "The pig made us a good breakfast," a soldier reminisced.[10]

Several miles downstream at Chesterfield Bridge, Hancock debated whether to try and force his way across the North Anna or shift upriver to Jericho Mills and follow Wright and Warren. Confederate sharpshooters lined high ground south of Chesterfield Bridge, and Major Lane's rebel artillery near Ox Ford fired straight up the river, shelling the bridge. Hancock dispatched scouts to find a sheltered crossing and directed Birney to fortify the southern end of the bridge in case he decided to cross there.[11]

Shortly after 6:00 A.M.—Warren was skirmishing toward the Virginia Central Railroad, Wright was marching over pontoons at Jericho Mills, and Hancock was debating where to cross—Grant and Meade left Mrs. Moncure's yard and rode to Mt. Carmel Church. "If you want a horrible hole for a halt," Lyman reflected, "just pick out a Virginia Church, at a Virginia crossroads, after the bulk of an army has passed by, on a hot, dusty Virginia day!" Staffers laid boards across pews as desks and settled to work. The scene reminded Lyman of a town hall peopled by men in dusty uniforms. "General Meade is of a perverse nature," the aide noted. "When he gets in a disagreeable place, he is apt to stay there." [12]

But before settling down at Mt. Carmel Church, Meade wanted to inspect his lines. Riding south on Telegraph Road, he met Hancock at the Chandler house, near Henagan's redoubt. Meade shared his latest intelligence with the 2nd Corps's head. Everything suggested that the rebels were retreating. Warren's skirmishers had reached the Virginia Central Railroad, and prisoners confirmed that Hill had fallen back during the night. While Meade and Hancock were talking, soldiers brought in two slaves who had escaped across the North Anna on a log. Gordon's Confederates, they told Meade, had left during the night. One slave had overheard Gordon tell Major Doswell, who lived east of the railway, that "the Union army would cross today, and that [Gordon] was going to march to Richmond at once." Meade forwarded this information to Grant, adding that only a few rebel guns remained active in front of Burnside and Hancock. He felt certain that the Confederates had "fallen back beyond the South Anna." [13]

At 8:00 A.M. Grant wrote his morning dispatch to Washington. "The enemy have fallen back from North Anna," he assured Halleck. "We are in pursuit." Reports about Lee's destination varied, but if the slaves who had brought Meade information were correct, the Confederate army was retreating to Richmond. "If this is the case," Grant observed, "Butler's forces will all be wanted where they are." Halleck was to instruct Butler to hold the 18th Corps, under Major General William F. Smith, ready to move. "I will probably know today if the enemy intends to stand behind South Anna," Grant predicted. Dana gleefully informed Stanton of developments in a companion dispatch. "The enemy have fallen back, whether to take up a position beyond the South Anna or to go to Richmond is uncertain," he wrote. "Warren, Burnside, and Hancock are pushing forward after the retreating army." [14]

Returning to Mt. Carmel Church, Meade sat in a pew, positioned a board as a desk, and wrote his wife the upbeat news. Everything appeared to be going well. The rebels had been maneuvered from Spotsylvania Court House, he crowed, "and now [we] have compelled them to fall back from the North Anna River, which they tried to hold." Warren and Hancock had won fine victories the day before, and the future looked bright. "We undoubtedly have the *morale* over them," Meade stressed, "and will eventually, I think, compel them to go into Richmond; after that, *nous verrons.*" Looking up from his paper, Meade took notice of his surroundings. The incongruity between the humble country church and its warlike occupants struck him. "I am writing this letter in the House of God, used for general headquarters," he informed his wife in closing. "What a scene and commentary on the times!" [15]

Good news, it seemed, had no end. Captain Craig "Tick" Wadsworth—son of Brigadier General James S. Wadsworth, killed in the Wilderness—rode to headquarters and reported that Sheridan was on his way. The cavalry corps had crossed the Pamunkey and expected to arrive at Chesterfield by the end of the day. Another messenger brought in a dispatch in cipher from Sherman. Dana had the note translated and read it aloud. The text, Lyman noted, was in

Sherman's "florid style" and very disparaging of Meade. "If Grant could inspire the Potomac army to do a proper degree of fighting," Sherman had written, "the final success could not be doubted." [16]

Lyman glanced over at Meade. The general's eyes had grown wide, "like a rattlesnake's," the staffer noticed. No one spoke. Then Meade cleared his throat. The sound reminded Lyman of "cutting an iron bar with a handsaw."

"Sir!" Meade roared. "I consider that dispatch an insult to the army I command, and to me personally." He took a breath and went on. "The Army of the Potomac does not require General Grant's inspiration or anybody else's inspiration to make it fight!" He grumbled about the slight the rest of the day, referring to the western army as "armed rabble." [17]

Shortly after 8:00 A.M., assured by Meade that Lee had fallen back, Hancock started his troops across the river. The 20th Indiana, under covering fire from Tidball's artillery on the north bank, ran down the steep slope and crossed Chesterfield Bridge "through a hail of bullets and bombs" from the Confederates. Sprinting over the narrow floodplain south of the bridge, the soldiers pressed against the bank, protected from Confederate pickets on the fields above them by the drop in the land. Then the 1st and 2nd United States Sharpshooters darted across. Forming a skirmish line, the three regiments overran the Confederate pickets on the crest and pushed south to the Fox house. Beyond the house, fields extended several hundred yards to woods. Still farther south ran the eastern wing of the inverted V, hidden from view in trees. At the fringe of the woods, between the Confederate line and the Federals, pickets from John Gregg's mixed Texas and Arkansas brigade and George "Tige" Anderson's Georgia brigade occupied rifle pits—"a good place to be while being shot at with any kind of gun," a Georgian observed. Birney's sharpshooters holed up in abandoned slave quarters and traded fire with the Confederate pickets three hundred yards away.[18]

Birney rushed reinforcements forward as quickly as he could bring them up. Mott's brigade, 6th New Jersey in front, sprinted over the bridge and ran the quarter-mile gauntlet across open fields under Lane's guns to the Fox house. "Though the rebels kept up a constant fire of shot and shell the crossing was effected without serious loss, which seemed miraculous, for one fair shot striking the bridge would have been sufficient to render it impassable," an officer in the 11th New Jersey reported. When Colonel Shoonover of the 11th reflexively ducked, a soldier called out, "Dodge the big ones, Colonel." Egan's brigade crossed next, followed by Pierce's. Digging with bayonets and cups, the Federals threw up two lines of earthworks, one by the Fox house and another nearer the Confederates, by the Lowry house. Birney re-

ported that he had secured the Fox property "without serious opposition."
Hancock advanced Tyler's division to Henagan's redoubt, where it could
cross quickly and support Birney if needed.[19]

Parson Fox and his family had fled, and Yankees thoroughly ransacked the
fine brick home. "Pianos were demolished, and elegant paintings and family
portraits made to do duty in the breastworks," a soldier from Maine reminisced. "A family library, containing some very rare and valuable works, was
distributed through the corps," he went on, "and the walls of the house were
ornamented with caricatures of Davis and the rebellion, and embellished with
choice and pithy advice to our 'erring sisters.'" Soldiers found relief from the
heat in a well-stocked icehouse and satisfied their hunger with twenty pounds
of smoked ham from under the kitchen floor. Hancock set up headquarters in
the yard, and staffers went to work preparing dispatches under the shade of
trees by the house. "Often a cannonball or a grenade would strike nearby," a
soldier remembered, "but unless someone had been hurt the men went right
on reading."[20]

Gibbon pushed forward along the Richmond, Fredericksburg, and
Potomac Railroad, on Birney's left. The smoldering railway bridge was impassable, but volunteers from Smyth's brigade felled trees and lashed them
together to fashion a serviceable bridge below the charred railway span.
Thomas F. Galwey led his company of the 8th Ohio across single file and deployed the troops in line along the south bank. "Forward," Galwey shouted,
and his men clambered up the steep incline by grasping tufts of grass. "With
a whoop like a band of Sioux Indians we went forward at a run," Galwey
reminisced. The whooping men from the Buckeye State dispersed a thin line
of rebel pickets on the crest. While the rest of Smyth's brigade crossed on the
makeshift bridge, Major Wesley Brainerd's 1st Battalion, 50th New York
Engineers, assembled two canvas pontoon bridges downriver from the rail
line. Soon all of Gibbon's division was over and advancing into fields east of
the railroad. Smyth, McKeen, and Owen spread into line of battle perpendicular to the tracks. The Irish Legion, now commanded by Colonel McIvor,
formed in reserve. Galwey's company deployed around a chicken coop near
the railroad. "It was diverting to see the way the Confederate bullets, which
were showering splinters amongst us, aroused excitement in the poultry,"
Galwey wrote. "The latter seemed to be greatly interested in the way the bullets whizzed through the air and struck the dust, no doubt mistaking the
leaden pellets for swarms of insects."[21]

Birney and Gibbon were south of the river by 9:30. Barlow crossed next
on Brainerd's pontoon bridges and filed into the interval between Telegraph
Road and the railway, linking the other two divisions. It seemed to Hancock

that only stray pickets and scattered artillery opposed him—horse artillery, he suspected. Lane's guns on the bluffs above Ox Ford rained shells on Chesterfield Bridge, making it a terrifying place to cross. When men from Tyler's division started across the bridge, a shell screamed into the column, killing six soldiers. Tidball tried to silence Lane by focusing fire from Ames's, Arnold's, and Roder's batteries on the Confederate guns. A shot ignited an ammunition chest in Captain John T. Wingfield's battery of Lane's battalion, but the captain and a private put out the flames before they reached the ammunition. Despite the heavy bombardment rebel artillerists kept their guns in action.[22]

Of the Union commanders, only Burnside found his way across the river blocked. The bank on the south side of Ox Ford rose sharply two hundred feet. Rebel gun pits dotted the wooded slope, and McIntosh's and Lane's artillery lined the crest. "The prospects of success are not at all flattering," Burnside unenthusiastically informed Grant, "but I think the attempt can be made without any very disastrous results, and we may possibly succeed." Studying the brush-covered bluffs across the river, Burnside's men did not see how they could get across. Willcox, whose division was posted at the ford, predicted that the place would "prove a slaughter pen to our men if we attempt to cross directly in front." Burnside, however, knew Grant was critical of his reluctance to make frontal attacks and insisted that Willcox attempt to force his way over. A resigned Willcox selected the 17th Michigan and 21st Massachusetts to lead the assault. Lieutenant Colonel George P. Hawkes of the Massachusetts regiment considered the assignment "the hardest one I ever received." A concentrated barrage by 9th Corps artillery temporarily silenced the Confederate pieces on the far side, enabling the assault force to cross to a small island in the river. Huddled in heavy undergrowth, Hawkes and his companions listened for the bugle blast that was to signal the charge.[23]

Burnside in the meantime received an urgent request from Hancock. The 2nd Corps commander had dispatched three regiments from Nelson Miles's brigade to drive the Confederates from Ox Ford and quiet Lane's guns. Miles, however, had advanced only a short distance over open ground before coming under severe musketry from Anderson's Confederates entrenched in the V's eastern leg. "Nothing but the inequalities of the surface furnished us any protection from the heavy fire we drew," a staffer recalled, "and we were compelled to lie prone and hug the ground under a hot sun and a hot musketry fire." To break the impasse, Hancock requested that Burnside send a division east to assist Miles. At about the same time, Burnside learned of the ford at Quarles's Mill. Why not flank the Confederates holding Ox Ford, Burnside reasoned, by sending a division to cooperate with Hancock and an-

other to Quarles's Mill, pinching off the Confederate force. Calling off
Willcox's assault—"Thank God General Burnside countermanded the
order," a Michigan man wrote—Burnside directed Potter to cross at Chesterfield Bridge and join Miles. Simultaneously, he instructed Crittenden to advance upriver, cross at Quarles's Mill, and double back along the south bank.
Willcox was to wait until the pincer formed by Potter and Miles on one side,
and Crittenden on the other, cleared the rebels from his front. Then he was to
cross.[24]

Grant liked Burnside's plan and decided to improve on it by strengthening
the force moving against Ox Ford from the west. At 9:30 Meade directed
Warren to send Crawford "down the river beyond Quarles' Mill till he meets
some enemy, and uncovering Ox Ford if possible." Crawford was on his way
by noon. Reaching Quarles's Mill, he found his 1st Pennsylvania still in a
heated fight with Mahone's Virginians and Alabamians. Crawford set most of
his men to constructing a horseshoe-shaped defensive line to protect the ford
for Crittenden to cross and dispatched the 12th Massachusetts and Bucktails
to drive off the Confederates. Mahone's men, however, were firmly entrenched in three-man pits protected by log and fence-rail breastworks. The
Federals tried several times to break through—a Virginian counted three
Union charges—but the rebels refused to budge. Mahone, a sharpshooter
quipped, "seemed satisfied to let us act as a 'reception committee.' "[25]

Hancock rode to the Fox home around noon to supervise his corps's advance. Birney occupied a line extending from the Lowry and Fox properties
east across Telegraph Road. Barlow picked up on Birney's left, and Gibbon
continued the formation east across the railroad. The 2nd Corps's line
crossed flat fields, and Hancock's soldiers threw up earthworks for protection
from the Confederate shells that shrieked past with disconcerting regularity.
Hancock conferred briefly with officers in Parson Fox's garden, then went
into the house. "Of magnificent physique, straight as a rail, and well groomed,
a flashing seal ring on one of his fingers, Hancock, then in the prime of his
life, was a fine looking officer," an admiring soldier reported. "I never wondered after that why they called him 'Superb.' " The general had scarcely
stepped inside when a shell exploded where he had been standing.[26]

Oblivious to his close brush with death, Hancock wrote Meade that most
of his troops were over the river, and that his artillery was starting across.
Lane's guns near Ox Ford remained troublesome, but Hancock was certain
that the Federal pincer movement—Potter and Miles on the left, Crittenden
and Crawford on the right—would soon clear them out. "We are making
everything as secure as possible," he assured headquarters.[27]

Grant and Meade felt confident that the advance was progressing smoothly.

Hancock, on the Union left, held a line south of the river controlling Telegraph Road and the Richmond, Fredericksburg, and Potomac Railroad. On the Union right Warren and Wright were both across, and Griffin had advanced to the Virginia Central Railroad with no significant opposition. Confederates had frustrated Burnside at Ox Ford, but headquarters viewed the holdup there as only an annoyance. After all, Potter was shifting to Chesterfield Bridge to join Hancock, and Crittenden was marching to Quarles's Mill, where he would cross and join Crawford. Flanked on both sides, the Confederates at Ox Ford would have to retreat, permitting Willcox to cross. Soon, reasoned headquarters, the Union army would be united south of the river.

Persuaded that the Confederates opposing Burnside were only rearguard troops and that Lee was falling back, Grant decided to continue his forward movement. His goal for the rest of the day was to finish moving his entire force south of the river. Early the next morning Hancock was to press along the Richmond, Fredericksburg, and Potomac Railroad, followed by Burnside. Warren and Wright were to form a second column west of Hancock and Burnside and also push south. Somewhere toward Richmond, Grant expected to catch up with the retreating rebel army.[28]

Lee, however, was not retreating. Grant had unwittingly marched into a trap. Hurrying over the North Anna, he had split his force and wrapped it around the inverted V formed by the Confederate army just as Lee had hoped. A single Union division—Willcox's—connected Grant's two wings across a six-mile gap. Shifting troops from one wing to the other required the Federals to cross the river twice. Lee, on the other hand, could move troops with ease between the legs of his V. Unknown to Grant, the opportunity for offensive action had passed to Lee. The Confederate general stood poised to deliver the masterstroke of the campaign.

"General Ledlie made a botch of it."

Hastening Burnside across the river was important to Grant. "You will move your entire corps, with trains, to the south side of North Anna this afternoon," he instructed the 9th Corps commander, reminding him that "Warren has sent a division [Crawford] on the south side to drive the enemy away from his position opposite you, and Hancock has sent a brigade [Miles's] for the same purpose." If the pincer movement failed, Burnside was to cross upriver at Quarles's Mill or downriver at Chesterfield Bridge. In any event, Grant stressed, Burnside "must get over and camp tonight on the south side."[29]

Potter reached Chesterfield Bridge early in the afternoon. Lane's Confederate gunners greeted the 9th Corps men as they stepped onto the timbers.

Simon Griffin's brigade, crossing first, sprinted over "as fast as men can go who know they are running for their lives," a Maine man remembered. "The roar of the guns, the crack of the musketry firing in the front, the howl of the solid shot, the explosion of the shells all around, above and below us, made a pandemonium hard to imagine," a survivor agreed. "I did not expect to reach the south bank, but the only thing to do was to keep going and keep up with the procession, which I certainly did." Miraculously, most of Lane's shells missed. "I do not to this day understand how it was possible for so much iron to be thrown at us," a Federal wondered, "with so little to show for the result." [30]

Once over the bridge, Potter's soldiers fanned southwest. Trees concealed Anderson's entrenchments, and an unexpected volley from the woods rocked Potter's troops back on their heels. "The men along the line began to drop and fall out so fast that it was evident we could not carry the position," a Federal recollected, "and the whole line fell back so that the roll of the hill protected us from the rebel fire." Potter's soldiers began digging, their right anchored on the North Anna a quarter mile upstream from Chesterfield Bridge, their left linking with Mott, near the Lowry house. A New Hampshire man reported that he and his companions "took the shot and shell with as much grace as we could, since we were not in a position to reply to our tormentors." [31]

Crittenden meanwhile advanced upriver toward Quarles's Mill. A narrow, rocky road slowed his march. At 2:00 P.M. Crittenden's lead brigade under Ledlie reached the mill, where only rotten floorboards and supports remained. Assembled in the spring of 1864, Ledlie's brigade contained an equal mix of veterans and greenhorns. The 4th and 10th United States Regular Infantry and the 35th Massachusetts were experienced regiments, wise in the ways of Virginia warfare. Not so the 56th, 57th, and 59th Massachusetts, recruited during the winter in response to Lincoln's call for troops. Their commanders were scions of prominent Boston families. Harvard-educated, twenty-two-year-old Stephen Weld, leading the 56th Massachusetts, descended from a distinguished line of shipowners and educators. Twenty-four-year-old Lieutenant Colonel Charles L. Chandler, of the 57th Massachusetts, was also a Harvard man and eldest son of an assistant treasury secretary. The brigade's commander, James Ledlie, was a political appointee whose unseemly bravado during the fighting on May 18 had made him the butt of jokes. Officers and soldiers alike regarded him with suspicion, although a few mistook his recklessness for courage. Major Mills of Crittenden's staff considered Ledlie "a little rash," but "dashing." [32]

Hailing Crawford's troops on the south bank, Ledlie's men descended to the river and picked their way across the ford, taking care not to drop into crevices in the river bottom. "The water was so deep in places that the men had to throw their cartridge boxes over their shoulders to keep their ammunition from getting wet," recalled Captain John Anderson of the 57th Massachusetts. "It was slow work floundering over the slippery rocks and through the whirling eddies." [33]

Weld and Chandler cracked jokes as they splashed across the North Anna. Chandler was amused to find a belt containing a pistol and bayonet in the stream and playfully offered it to soldiers passing by. The brigade formed on a narrow terrace on the south bank, protected by Crawford's troops, who had dug a horseshoe-shaped fortified line around the crossing. After pouring water from their shoes and wringing out their socks, Ledlie's men made ready to drive off Mahone's sharpshooters, who still blocked the route to Ox Ford. Ledlie deployed the 35th Massachusetts in front as skirmishers, the 56th, 57th, and 59th Massachusetts in a first line of battle, and the 4th and 10th United States Infantry in a second line. The day was hot and muggy. The soldiers, already tired from their march to Quarles's Mill, wanted to leave their knapsacks on the terrace. Ledlie, however, did not expect to return to Quarles's Mill and instructed them to keep their belongings. [34]

At 3:00 Ledlie's soldiers left Crawford's protective works and disappeared into thick woods along the riverbank. Five hundred yards out they encountered Mahone's skirmish line. With a flurry of musketry, they overran the Confederates and pressed on at the double-quick. Dense brush and little streams flowing into the North Anna broke their alignment. Men puffed up sharp hills and down into steep ravines. A mile east of Quarles's Mill, the 35th Massachusetts entered a clearing. A stream ran across the open ground, and on the far side, about eight hundred yards away, rose a high ridge. A chillingly familiar line of raw dirt lined the top.

Ledlie had reached the western end of the inverted V, near where the apex rested on Ox Ford. The ridge made an impressive natural fortification that Mahone's men had strengthened by employing lessons learned at Spotsylvania Court House. Earthworks topped with headlogs formed the face of the works. Traverses every fifteen feet provided shelter from the enfilading fire of Burnside's guns across the river. Ledges created elevated steps for shooting, and shallow trenches in the rear afforded safe havens for loading. Artillery, well entrenched, stood at strategic intervals, and ditches connected gun emplacements with ammunition storage depots in the rear. The earthworks varied in detail from regiment to regiment. Some officers insisted on geometrically precise lines and angles. Others favored rounded corners, and a few permitted lopsided structures that looked like the work of children.

Altogether, however, the rebel entrenchments across from Ledlie were among the most formidable constructed during the war.[35]

Three Florida regiments under Edward Perry held the right of Mahone's line. Numbering only 270 men, the brigade supported Lane's artillery and was taking considerable fire from Burnside's guns on the north bank. "Shells, shot, shrapnel, and every other blasted thing," a captain in the 5th Florida wrote, "has cut all the trees and bushes." On Perry's left, also overlooking the river, were Ambrose Wright's Georgians, supporting McIntosh's artillery. To the left of Wright, facing Ledlie, stood Nathaniel Harris's four Mississippi regiments, hardened veterans who had saved Lee's army by dogged fighting at the Bloody Angle. Occupying earthworks to Harris's left were Sanders's five Alabama regiments, also heroes of the Bloody Angle. Continuing the line south was the Virginia brigade formerly under Mahone, now commanded by Colonel David A. Weisiger. The batteries of Richardson's battalion stood interspersed along Sanders's and Weisiger's line.[36]

The 35th Massachusetts inched cautiously into the field. Mahone's sharp-shooters had climbed into rifle pits dotting the clearing and fired at the Federals as they advanced. Musketry also picked up from the main rebel fortifications along the ridge. The Massachusetts men fell back to the woods and waited for the rest of the brigade to catch up. The regiment's right protruded slightly into the field, and Mahone's sharpshooters nipped at the vulnerable flank, capturing several men and a sergeant. Soon Ledlie's remaining regiments appeared "with that swaying from side to side so noticeable in a close line of battle advancing over rough wooded ground," a soldier remembered. Ledlie deployed them to the left of the 35th Massachusetts in two lines, reaching north toward the river.[37]

Ledlie was ambitious. He realized that breaking the Confederate hold on Ox Ford would advance his career. He was also fond of whiskey, and several witnesses reported him drunk that day. His judgment clouded by ambition and alcohol, Ledlie decided to try the impossible. He would storm Mahone's works. In preparation for his forlorn assault, he advanced skirmishers to clear Mahone's sharpshooters from their rifle pits. The endeavor met with mixed results. A man from the 56th Massachusetts reportedly captured five Confederates single-handedly and brought them back despite a serious ankle wound.

Ledlie directed Captain Anderson of the 57th Massachusetts to ride back to Quarles's Mill and find Crittenden. "Tell him that there is a rebel battery in my front," Ledlie instructed the captain, who was surprised to be given an assignment more appropriately handled by a staff officer. "Ask him to please send me three regiments immediately," Ledlie went on, "one on my right, one on my left, and the other in rear for support, and I will charge and capture [the works]." [38]

Anderson returned to the ford, found Crittenden, and delivered Ledlie's message. "Go back to General Ledlie immediately," Crittenden directed. "Tell him I have not the regiments to spare. The division is not across the river yet. Tell him my orders are not to charge." Anderson turned to go, but Crittenden had more admonitions. "Tell General Ledlie not to charge unless he sees a sure thing," the Kentuckian warned. "I am afraid it will be a failure and result in bringing on a serious engagement which we are in no condition to meet now, as a large part of my division is still on the other side of the river with the rest of the corps." Again he admonished, "Tell him to use the utmost caution." [39]

Returning to the field, Anderson rode into the clearing on the right of the brigade. High ground afforded him a good view of the rebel position. Richardson's gunners stood ready at their pieces, and muskets bristled along the parapets. Distant dust indicated more Confederates were on the way to shore up the sector. Looking left, Anderson could see his own brigade poised in line of battle. Ledlie was making ready to charge. The general, Anderson thought, was either ignorant of the Confederate strength or too drunk to care.

Anderson hurried to deliver Crittenden's instructions and warn Ledlie about the artillery. Reaching the brigade, Anderson saw to his horror that soldiers had taken off their knapsacks in preparation for charging across the field. The general, on horseback, was plainly intoxicated, as were some of his aides. A staff officer stood boldly in front of the line, firing a small pistol toward the earthworks. A major in Anderson's regiment also appeared intoxicated and had to be carried from the field on a stretcher. He complained of sunstroke but waved his arms as though he wanted to fight the Confederate army single-handed. "The condition of affairs did not give promise," Anderson glumly concluded.[40]

Ledlie trotted into the field. Two lines of soldiers stepped from the woods behind him. Major Morton of Burnside's staff rode by his side, jauntily twirling a hat overhead on the point of a sword. Dark clouds, heralding rain, gathered in the west. Mississippians and Alabamians lined the works in front. "Come on, Yank!" they called, amazed that anyone would consider charging their stronghold. "Come on to Richmond!" As a playful warning, a rebel sharpshooter put a bullet through Morton's hat.[41]

In his drunken euphoria Ledlie was oblivious to the deathtrap ahead. He rode on, his men coming behind, lines straight and orderly. Musketry exploded from the earthworks, and men began falling. Soldiers sprinted ahead,

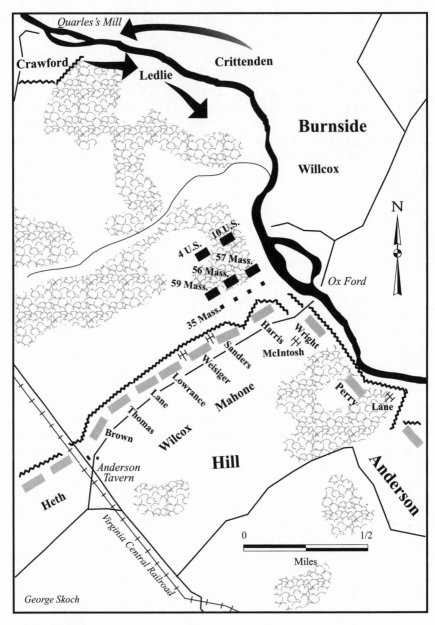

Battle of Ox Ford on May 24

and the formation lost alignment, dissolving into a blue mob. "It was just a wild tumultuous rush where the more reckless were far to the front and the cautious ones scattered along back, but still coming in," a participant recounted.

As Federals closed on the ridge, a bullet felled the 57th Massachusetts's color sergeant, Leopold Karpeles. Colonel Chandler reached for Karpeles's flag, but the sergeant regained his feet, clasped the staff tightly, and refused to relinquish the banner. He stumbled on until loss of blood forced him to hand the flag to a corporal. Now Richardson's artillery opened. "We had almost reached the silent batteries," Captain Anderson recollected, "when suddenly every gun flashed out a shower of grape and canister which shook the very ground and swept everything in front." [42]

The charge turned to carnage as musketry and artillery raked the field. Ledlie abandoned all pretense of command. "Every man," Captain Anderson reported, "became his own general." Rain fell in torrents, and lightning flashed. Colonel Weld noted the time as 6:45 P.M.

"Weld, what are you going to do?" Chandler called out.

"I don't know," Weld answered.

"I am going to rally my men and try to make a stand," Chandler announced. Weld decided to rally his troops also. Seizing the colors, he waved them overhead. In a few minutes, Chandler and Weld had assembled about 120 men. [43]

Mahone saw the soldiers forming around their banners. Hoping to scoop them up, he sent the 12th Mississippi and the 8th and 11th Alabama over the works and into the field. Halting forty yards from Chandler and Weld, the Confederates fired a volley. A bullet ripped through Weld's coat, raising a welt on his side. "The same volley seemed to me to knock over all the men I had got together," Weld recounted. It also tore off Chandler's arm below the elbow. Captain Albert Prescott and two privates tried to raise the stricken colonel. "You can do nothing for me," he protested. "Save yourselves if you can." Heeding his advice, they left him in the field. Weld hobbled to safety. [44]

The unequal fight sputtered on in the rain. The Confederates ran short of ammunition and fired anything they could cram into their guns. One Federal was shot through the leg with the point of a bayonet, and several were pierced by ramrods and iron slugs. A soldier in the 4th United States remembered Mahone's men "pouring volley after volley into us." [45]

In fading twilight, Ledlie's broken remnants beat a hasty retreat. The downpour had flooded the North Anna, ending any possibility of escaping across the river. "Looking down into the deep, black waters in rear and the charging enemy in front, presented rather a gloomy appearance to a defeated, demoralized body of men without head or guidance," recollected Captain Anderson. Ledlie's soldiers dribbled back to Quarles's Mill and joined Crittenden and Crawford behind a defensive line of logs and branches. Ledlie protested that he had become too "sleepy and tired" to command. Crittenden placed Weld temporarily in charge of the brigade while Ledlie slept off the effects of the alcohol.[46]

The ill-advised affair cost Ledlie 450 men. The Confederates, who lost about 75 soldiers, claimed to have captured 150 Federals. Three of Ledlie's staff—Lieutenants Richard H. Chute, Henry M. Cross, and George W. Crecy— were captured, as was the brigade color sergeant. Mississippians carried Chandler to their earthworks, where Colonel Merrie B. Harris of the 12th Mississippi cared for the dying officer. Harris marked Chandler's grave and saw that his possessions were returned to his family. Rumor made the rounds that Chandler had been killed taking the colors from the corporal to whom Karpeles had given the flag. Karpeles, who worshiped Chandler, was inconsolable over the thought that he might have been indirectly responsible for the colonel's death. Ledlie wrote Chandler's father that the colonel's refusal to permit his men to carry him from the field was "a fitting piece of chivalry to close such a life as his." Ledlie said nothing about his own responsibility for ordering the hopeless attack that cost Chandler his life.[47]

The officers and men knew whom to blame. "General Ledlie made a botch of it," Weld wrote home. "Had too much ——— on board, I think." Captain Anderson was livid over the affair. "Nothing whatever was accomplished, except a needless slaughter," he concluded, "the humiliation of defeat of the men, and the complete loss of all confidence in the brigade commander who was wholly responsible." Lives, Anderson insisted, had been squandered to satisfy the "blind, temporary courage of an incompetent leader." For reasons that are not clear, Ledlie escaped censure from his superiors. On June 8 Crittenden relinquished command, and Ledlie took over the division. He was to cause even greater mischief in the days ahead.[48]

At 3:00 P.M.—Ledlie was starting his fateful march from Quarles's Mill— Hancock began probing south. On Hancock's right, Miles gamely advanced the 26th Michigan and 140th Pennsylvania "to see what was in the woods." The detachment drove back a thin line of Confederate pickets, hit Anderson's strongly entrenched position, and tumbled rearward with severe loss. At the same time, Gibbon directed Colonel Thomas Smyth to advance his brigade along the Richmond, Fredericksburg, and Potomac Railroad and "ascertain the position of the enemy." Smyth deployed the 1st Delaware and 108th New York in skirmish formation and started them south through freshly plowed fields east of the rail line. Ewell's sharpshooters fired from rifle pits dotting the fields. Behind the sharpshooters, hidden in dense woods south of the field, ran a picket line manned by Ramseur's and Grimes's Tar Heels. The Delaware and New York soldiers called for reinforcements, Smyth sent in the 14th Connecticut, and the three Union regiments drove the sharpshooters into the woods.[49]

Determined to punch through the rebel picket line, Smyth brought up the 12th New Jersey. The regiment, which specialized in storming fortified positions, had been severely mauled in the Wilderness and was down to 120 men. Smyth lined the soldiers across the field two paces apart and sent them forward. Sweeping into the woods in "fine style," they overwhelmed the rebel pickets and drove them at bayonet point. Smyth had expected the New Jersey men to stop at the picket line, but Captain James McComb, commanding the regiment, kept them going until they reached Ewell's main fortifications half a mile south. Their momentum spent, the Federals returned to the captured picket line and began reversing the works to face south. "We gave the rebs a good licking," a northerner claimed. Miraculously, the 12th New Jersey sustained few casualties. The 1st Delaware, which was also heavily engaged, lost forty-one men, and horses were shot from under two of Smyth's aides. Smyth brought up the rest of his brigade—the 7th West Virginia and 10th New York Battalion—and put the regiments into the captured works.[50]

Gibbon advanced the rest of his division in support of Smyth. McKeen's and Owen's brigades entrenched behind Smyth, and McIvor's brigade moved into reserve a short distance back.

Smyth was worried about his left flank. The open fields of the Doswell plantation extended east from his line. Unless Federals occupied the clearings, Confederates could enfilade him. Gibbon directed McKeen to send his 19th Maine into the Doswell grounds and connect with Smyth's left. The aide leading the regiment got lost, however, and directed the Maine men away from Smyth and toward the Confederates. As the regiment drifted southeast, musketry became "pretty heavy," a soldier remembered, "and the shells were flying over our heads." The befuddled aide pointed south and disappeared to the rear. Charging ahead, the Maine men overran a line of rifle pits, crested a rise, and emerged in front of the eastern end of the inverted V. Ewell's rebels greeted them with a "storm of shot and shell, in the face of which no line of battle could long live," a soldier reported. The Federals tumbled behind the ridge for cover, many of them seeking shelter in the captured pits. Lieutenant O. R. Small and Corporal John D. Smith inched to the top of the rise, hoping to pull injured men to safety. Severe rebel fire frustrated their efforts. Messengers ran back to warn Smyth of the 19th Maine's predicament.[51]

While the 19th Maine clung to its isolated position in front of Ewell, Smyth waged a vicious battle in woods to the west, between the railroad and the Doswell fields. Ramseur's and Grimes's pickets returned with reinforcements, and Smyth fed troops into the woods to fight them. Dense undergrowth broke the opposing battle lines, and firefights sparked through the woods. Regiments became separated and battled invisible foes hidden in the trees. Worried that his right flank was vulnerable, Smyth directed the 4th Ohio, 8th Ohio, and 14th Indiana toward the railroad, where fighting became especially heated. "We would summon up all our courage, and occasionally without any orders would charge with a cheer, compelling the enemy to give way for a few more yards," an officer in the 8th Ohio recalled. "Then the Confederates would rally and in turn would force us back over the ground we had just won." [52]

West of the railroad, near the Lowry house, Birney found it impossible to advance. Confederate artillery shelled Telegraph Road and nearby fields with deadly accuracy. Potter's division, on Birney's right, suffered severely from Lane's guns. Men dug furiously, erecting three sets of works to protect themselves from the shelling. Prisoners confirmed that Anderson's 1st Corps was entrenched in front of Potter and Birney, and that Ewell's 2nd Corps was in front of Gibbon. Hancock informed headquarters that his skirmishers were "pretty hotly engaged." He still thought, however, that Lee had retreated. The works in his front, he surmised, were "perhaps nothing more than rifle pits," and he promised to press ahead. The Federals still did not comprehend their predicament.[53]

"We must strike them a blow."

Lee's moment had come. His plan to split the Union army had worked. The wedge formed by the Army of Northern Virginia separated Grant's two wings. Hancock, reinforced by Potter, made an inviting target. His corps was well below the river, opposed by both Ewell and Anderson. Escape lay only across Chesterfield Bridge—controlled by Lane's guns—and two pontoon bridges near the railway. Hill, holding the Confederate formation's western leg, could hold off Warren and Wright while Ewell and Anderson, reinforced by Breckinridge and Pickett, attacked Hancock. Here was the opportunity that Lee had been seeking. He had isolated Grant's best corps and was positioned to assault with superior numbers. "He now had one of those opportunities that occur but rarely in war," Grant's aide Badeau later wrote, "but which, in the grasp of a master, make or mar the fortunes of armies and decide the result of campaigns." [54]

Fate—the muse that orchestrated the wounding of Longstreet in the Wilderness, and that blinded Lee to Grant's design against the Mule Shoe on May 12—again thwarted Confederate fortunes. Lee's opportunity had ripened, but the general had become too ill to take advantage of it.

Lee had slept little in the twenty harrowing days since Grant had crossed the Rapidan. He often worked after midnight and, according to his aide Venable, was generally awake by 3:00 A.M. Dysentery was endemic in the Army of Northern Virginia, and Lee had contracted the illness by the time he reached the North Anna. Normally even-tempered and robust, he was now irritable and rode in a carriage. On the afternoon of May 24 Lee was seized with violent intestinal distress and diarrhea. Pendleton pronounced him "quite unwell," and Early termed his affliction "a most annoying and weakening disease." Taylor wrote that Lee "could attend to nothing except what was absolutely necessary for him to know or act upon." [55]

The Confederate commander lay confined to his tent, "prostrated by his sickness," Venable reported. A single thought dominated his mind. The Army of Northern Virginia must attack. "We must strike them a blow," Lee insisted. "We must never let them pass us again. We must strike them a blow." [56]

But the Army of Northern Virginia could not strike a blow. It required a firm hand to coordinate so complex an undertaking. In better times, when Jackson and Longstreet commanded the wings of the Confederate army, Lee had liberally delegated responsibility. But Jackson was dead and Longstreet disabled. Lee lacked confidence in their successors. Anderson was new to his post and had much to learn. With the exception of his march the night of May 7–8, he had never executed a complex maneuver. Ewell, senior to Anderson and in line to lead the attack against Hancock, had forfeited Lee's trust. He had lost his composure at the Mule Shoe on May 12 and had come frighteningly close to losing his corps on May 19. And now he was getting sick as well, apparently from the same intestinal ailment that had stricken Lee! Turning the army over to Ewell was unthinkable. Lee had similar reservations about Hill. He had recently returned from a lengthy illness and, by Lee's reckoning, had exercised poor judgment at Jericho Mills.

At Spotsylvania Court House, Lee took on responsibilities that he had delegated in better times. On May 12 he commanded by force of personality, ignoring his formal corps structure to draw troops from various portions of his line and direct them where needed. He had confidence that his army was still capable of performing stunning feats—witness its repulse of Grant on May 12 and 18, and its rapid march to the North Anna—but he was not sure it could do so without him. Two years of hardship had forged a close bond between Lee and his men. No one could replace him. Physically unable to com-

mand and lacking a trusted subordinate to direct the army in his stead, Lee
saw no choice but to forfeit his hard-won opportunity. "Though he still had
reports of the operations in the field constantly brought to him," wrote
Venable, "and gave orders to his officers, Lee confined to his tent was not Lee
on the battlefield." [57]

Hancock received fresh intelligence at 5:00 P.M. A Confederate captured near
the Lowry place reported Anderson's battle line 250 yards south. Hancock
was beginning to suspect that he faced something more substantial than pickets. "That the enemy are in strong force is probable," the 2nd Corps's commander advised headquarters, "as we meet them in works all along our front
some distance out." [58]

Questions about the strength of the Confederates facing Hancock were answered at 5:30, when Ramseur launched a fierce counterattack against
Smyth. Gibbon rushed the 15th and 19th Massachusetts of McKeen's brigade
to the center of Smyth's line, where ammunition was running low. The 69th
Pennsylvania of Owen's brigade and the 170th New York of McIvor's
brigade hurried to Smyth's left, on the Doswell farm. The 7th West Virginia
called for assistance, and Gibbon sent the 52nd New York of Owen's brigade.
Confederates saw the New Yorkers coming and shot at them over the heads
of the West Virginians. "We at once began to fire, without orders," a New
Yorker recollected, "and pushed on through the woods with yells and cheers,
passing over the line of pickets in our front." [59]

To relieve the pressure mounting against Gibbon, Hancock sent Brooke's
brigade of Barlow's division south along the rail line, intending it to hook onto
Smyth's right. Brooke's 148th Pennsylvania led the advance and ran headlong
into Law's Alabamians and "Tige" Anderson's Georgians, of the 1st Corps. The
64th and 66th New York, jointly commanded by Colonel Orlando H. Morris,
came up in support, drove the Confederates from their rifle pits, and advanced to
Anderson's main line. Brooke cautioned against attacking, but Barlow insisted
that he try. Brooke moved forward under scathing fire from Colonel William C.
Oates's 15th Alabama and a 12-pound napoleon posted on the tracks. Refusing
to sacrifice his men in an impossible undertaking, Brooke ordered them back.
Storm clouds billowed in the west—the same clouds were darkening the battlefield at Ox Ford—and Brooke's soldiers began entrenching. [60]

During Brooke's advance Hancock ordered Tyler's heavy artillerists
across Chesterfield Bridge. Lane's guns played on them as they crossed, killing
and wounding several. The 7th New York Heavy Artillery made it over, as
did the 2nd New York and portions of the 8th, but Lane's shelling became so

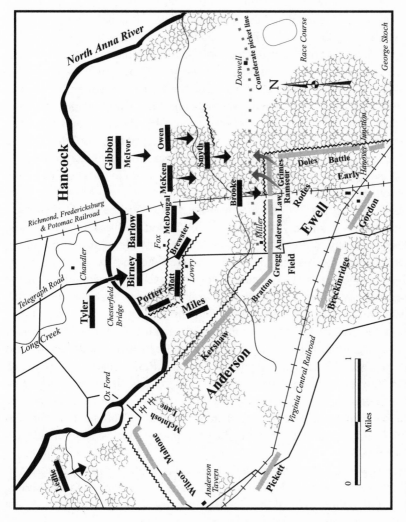

Fighting on Union and Confederate 2nd Corps fronts

severe that Tyler decided to wait until dark to bring over the remaining regiments.[61]

The 19th Maine remained isolated on the Doswell farm in its captured rifle pits. Soldiers could hear Confederates deploying behind the ridge in front and wondered why reinforcements did not come. With a rush, Grimes's Tar Heels swarmed toward the Maine soldiers. "What is it Jack?" an officer asked the man next to him. "Legs or Richmond?" Leaping up, the man answered, "Legs," and they bolted for the rear with the rest of the regiment. The Federals rallied at a stream, jumping into the water and using the bank as a breastwork. "A more angry set of men than we were never wore Union blue," Captain John Adams recounted. "We had done a brilliant thing, had captured and held a line of works for two hours against heavy odds, and could have been supported in fifteen minutes as well as not." Adding insult to injury, a staff officer rode up swinging his sword. "Go back, you cowards," he shouted, "go back." Adams and his companions "requested him to go where he would require the constant use of a fan." [62]

After driving the 19th Maine from the Doswell farm, the Confederates shifted west toward Smyth's line, held on the left by the 170th New York. Soldiers from the 43rd North Carolina thought the New Yorkers wanted to surrender and lowered their muskets. The New Yorkers assumed the rebels were surrendering, and both sides demanded their opponents throw down their weapons. When a Carolina man grabbed a New Yorker's musket, the Federal threatened to "blow his damned brains out" unless he let go. "Fire," the Confederate hollered to his companions, and the Tar Heels began shooting. Yankees fired back, and the two regiments locked in a desperate fight with clubbed muskets and bayonets. Sergeant Major Joseph Keele of the 170th New York braved a gauntlet of enemy fire to summon the 69th Pennsylvania and bring up ammunition. Grimes pushed more soldiers into the fight, but Smyth's line held. "Very hard skirmish," a Confederate in the 53rd North Carolina reported. "We killed a great many Yankees, and our side lost some killed." [63]

The sky darkened, and fighting intensified as soldiers tried to gain advantage before the storm struck. Then rain lashed the countryside in blinding sheets, and lightning laced the clouds. Musketry abruptly stopped, and men clutched their guns and sought shelter under trees to keep their powder dry. "How it did rain," a soldier recollected. "In Minnesota we should have looked to see a cyclone, but in those days we had heard of such things only in the tropics." A Federal remembered the tense scene years later. "There we stood," he reminisced, "our line and that of the enemy, poised for another deadly blow and looking at one another without firing, fearful that our am-

munition would be soaked by the rain." The downpour slackened after a few
minutes, and killing resumed. "As soon as nature's storm ceased," a Pennsylvanian put it, "man's began again." [64]

Nightfall ended active combat on Hancock's front. The Federals were
openly disappointed. They had made no appreciable progress, it was too wet
for fires, and their supply wagons were north of the river. Rebel sharpshooters gave no quarter. The only Union hero was Smyth, whom Hancock commended for "handling his troops and those sent to his support with judgment
and resolution." The Confederates considered the fight nothing more than a
heavy skirmish. Nowhere had Hancock seriously threatened their line. "In
fact," Venable observed, "one onslaught on our right was repulsed by merely
doubling the line of skirmishers." Grimes was pleased with the results, informing his wife that the Yankees "continue to rush on to their doom."
Ramseur was also satisfied with the "remarkably good execution among the
enemy." After dark Rodes adjusted his line, and Confederates from
Hoffman's brigade picketed the "miserable swamp" in front of Ewell's right,
"half a leg deep in mud and water." [65]

Crittenden and Crawford passed an anxious night at Quarles's Mill. The
North Anna, swollen from the storm, cut them off from the north bank. Not
even horses could cross. Wounded men lay in rows along the river. All were
concerned that the Confederates would discover their isolation and attack.
Soldiers tossed surplus muskets and ammunition into the water to keep them
from the rebels. Musicians from the 56th Massachusetts volunteered to swim
across carrying wounded men on their backs. When the current proved too
swift—a few men drowned trying to swim to the far bank—the musicians
built a raft out of flooring from the abandoned mill. Loading a few wounded
men at a time onto the raft, band members manhandled it to the northern
bank. They repeated the trip until they had evacuated the most serious
cases. [66]

Brainerd's engineers, already exhausted from constructing Hancock's
pontoon bridges, reached Quarles's Mill during the night and set to building
a permanent structure to unite Burnside's divided corps. "Trees were chopped
down," Brainerd wrote, "cut to the proper length and notched, some cutting,
some rolling them to the water, while others in the water placed them in position and others found stone and filled the cribs to sink and hold them in their
places." Engineers manhandled heavy logs across the cribs and covered the
resulting framework crosswise with smaller logs to make a corduroy road.
"All night long we worked thus, with the rain pouring and thunder roaring,
the gorge black with darkness," reminisced Brainerd. "Occasional flashes of
lightning revealed the men hard at work in the rolling torrent, the noise of

which drowned the voices of the officers and made altogether one of the most weird-like scenes that can be imagined."[67]

Warren's and Wright's soldiers, camped from Jericho Mills to the Virginia Central Railroad, had seen virtually no combat. They used the lull to rest, write letters, and entrench. Griffin's men entertained themselves by scooting back and forth along the tracks on handcars, whooping like children. Neighboring farms supplied fresh tobacco. Hill's sharpshooters were the only annoyance. "To raise a head above the works involved a great personal risk," a Pennsylvanian remembered, "and as nothing was to be gained by exposure, most of the men wisely took advantage of their cover." Warren's officers commandeered the home of the Matthew family, west of the Fontaine farm, and introduced a modicum of civility by ringing a bell to announce dinner. The unwilling hostess—"not very gracious," a Federal noted—was forced to furnish food from the family's larder. The body of a handsome young Confederate lay sprawled on the porch, a few steps from the diners.[68]

"I have just told the old man that he is not fit to command this army."

Late in the day, Sheridan rode up to Mt. Carmel Church. He had been away more than two weeks and now regaled Grant, Meade, and their aides with tales of his raid. "In describing a particularly hot fight, he would become highly animated in manner and dramatic in gesture," Porter related. "Then he would turn to some ludicrous incident, laugh heartily, and deem to greatly enjoy the recollection of it." Grant ribbed his fellow midwesterner about his exploits. "Now, Sheridan evidently thinks he had been clear down to the James River, and has been breaking up railroads, and even getting a peep at Richmond," Grant announced. "But probably this is all imagination, or else he has been reading something of the kind in the newspapers. I don't suppose he seriously thinks that he made such a march as that in two weeks." Sheridan reveled in Grant's attention and enjoyed Meade's discomfiture at his accomplishments. "Well, after what General Grant says," Sheridan responded, "I do begin to feel doubtful as to whether I have been absent at all from the Army of the Potomac."[69]

The last leg of Sheridan's expedition had been relatively uneventful. Fences and barns at White House supplied timber for repairing the railway span over the Pamunkey—Sheridan's men had learned all about repairing bridges on May 12 at the Chickahominy—and transports brought food from Fortress Monroe. "Hurrah for hard tack," troopers shouted as supply ships steamed up the Pamunkey. Merritt crossed on the evening of May 22, Gregg and Wilson the next morning. The bridge, an officer recalled, was "rather a pokerish looking affair," and horses had to be coaxed across single file. Artillery was disassembled and carried over piecemeal. Casualties included two mules harnessed together who fell off the bridge and drowned. Leaving the Pamunkey, the cavalry corps marched twelve miles north to King William Court House, then on to Aylett's Mills, where it camped for the night. It set out on the 24th toward the sound of battle and went into camp late in the day at Reedy Swamp, near Chesterfield Station. The troopers were relieved to be back with the Army of the Potomac. "It was like getting home again after a journey in a strange land," a cavalryman reminisced.[70]

The march had been hard on men and horses alike. Sheridan had expected to find forage and supplies between the Pamunkey and Mattaponi, but the country was desolate, and the roads were dusty. "This was one of the few instances in which we really suffered from hunger," a trooper recalled. Although Sheridan gamely professed that he was ready for action, he had only one day's rations and no forage. It would be a while before Meade could expect much from his cavalry.[71]

Near nightfall, Grant and Meade shifted headquarters to the Fontaine house. The storm broke as they crossed the North Anna. Lightning struck so near that it "really hissed," Lyman recorded, "which was disagreeable, as there was an ammunition train close by." Several miles away, at Reedy Swamp, lightning hit Sheridan's camps, melting a saber and killing two men and some horses.[72]

Troubling dispatches awaited Grant at the Fontaine house. Burnside reported that Ledlie had waged a "sharp fight" trying to drive Confederates from Ox Ford. He had been repulsed after "quite a loss" and had fallen back to Quarles's Mill, joining Crittenden and Crawford. Burnside was "quite anxious about their position," as they had no artillery and were surrounded by Confederates. He had decided to keep Willcox north of the river and planned to construct a bridge at Quarles's Mill strong enough for infantry and artillery. Hancock's news was also worrisome. "The enemy are making a strong attack down the railroad, particularly on Gibbon," the 2nd Corps commander had written at 6:30. "It looks to me as if the enemy [have] a similar line to that [at Spotsylvania Court House], with the salient resting opposite to Burnside, and their right, so far as we are concerned, thrown back toward Hanover Junction."[73]

Grant was having difficulty picturing the layout of the rebel line. He had assumed Lee was retreating, and reports all day from the front seemed to confirm his opinion. Hancock had crossed the river with token opposition, and Warren had encountered only isolated rebel skirmishers. The only exception had been at Ox Ford. "The opinion prevailed that the enemy's position was held by a rear guard only," Dana confirmed, "but the obstinacy of their skirmishers was regarded as very remarkable."[74]

Intelligence that greeted Grant at the Fontaine house suggested very different circumstances. Hancock had tried to advance, but stout Confederate opposition had brought him up short. His messages implied that Lee's 1st and 2nd Corps stood in front of him. And a substantial force was holding the south bank at Ox Ford. Taken together, Burnside's and Hancock's reports indicated that the Confederates were firmly entrenched. Part of the rebel line—the segment facing Burnside and Hancock—ran from Ox Ford southeast to Hanover Junction. But what did the rest of Lee's formation look like? Warren had advanced to the Virginia Central Railroad with little opposition, but 3rd Corps skirmishers remained active in his sector. Ledlie had encountered the 3rd Corps also when he attacked at Ox Ford. Had Hill deployed in a line running from Ox Ford to the railroad, east of Warren?

It would be morning before Warren and Wright could investigate. Only then would Grant know for certain the contours of Lee's formation. What he knew already, however, was alarming. A substantial body of Confederates—perhaps the entire Army of Northern Virginia—stood between Hancock on the Union left and Warren and Wright on the Union right. By advancing on both sides of Ox Ford, Grant had dangerously divided his army. Fresh news from Hancock heightened Grant's concern. "The latest information I have leads me to believe that a large force, if not the whole of Lee's army, is in our front," Hancock warned.

Grant had intended to advance in the morning. Now, however, he realized that his two wings would diverge as they moved forward, making them even more vulnerable. Circumstances required Grant to shift from offense to defense. He immediately instructed Hancock to entrench. Burnside was to forget about crossing the river and concentrate on connecting the divided wings of the army. "The situation of the enemy appearing so different from what I expected," Grant wrote the 9th Corps commander, "I think it important that you should hold the north side of [the river at Ox Ford]." Burnside was to build a bridge at Quarles's Mill and open a road to Chesterfield Bridge "to bring our right and left as near supporting distance as possible." At daylight Warren was to probe east and locate Hill.[75]

Grant also took a long-overdue step toward creating a unified command. "To secure the greatest attainable unanimity in cooperative movements, and greater efficiency in the administration of the army," Grant announced, "the Ninth Army Corps, Major General A. E. Burnside commanding, is assigned to the Army of the Potomac, Major General G. G. Meade commanding, and will report accordingly." Burnside seemed relieved. He was "glad to get the order assigning the corps to the Army of the Potomac," he wrote Grant, "because I think good will result from it." For the time, Crittenden, at Quarles's Mill, was placed temporarily under Warren; Potter, at Chesterfield Bridge, remained on assignment to Hancock; and Willcox, north of Ox Ford, reported to Burnside.[76]

Lee spent a frustrating evening in his tent. Each spade of dirt that Hancock's men heaped in front of their line diminished his chances of launching an offensive. During the afternoon the Union army—divided, outside its earthworks, and ignorant of Lee's proximity—had been at the mercy of the Confederates. But the situation had changed dramatically at nightfall. Grant had realized his danger and had ordered his army to entrench. Gripped by illness and embittered at the opportunity fast slipping from his grasp, Lee lashed out at his aides. An agitated Venable stalked from the general's tent "in a state of flurry and excitement, full to bursting," a witness recorded. "I have just told the old man that he is not fit to command this army," Venable announced, "and that he had better send for Beauregard."[77]

At 9:30 Lee wrote his evening dispatch to Richmond. He said nothing of his sickness or of the opportunity that had eluded him. "The enemy has been making feeble attacks upon our lines today, probably with a view of ascertaining our position," he reported. "They were easily repulsed." Mahone, he added, had driven three Federal regiments across the river, capturing a stand of colors and some prisoners, including Ledlie's aide-de-camp.[78]

Lee's inverted V had stopped Grant cold. The clever formation was an impressive demonstration of Lee's skill at defensive warfare. The southern general had shrewdly used terrain to magnify his numbers and had turned Grant's aggressiveness against him, drawing the Federals into a trap. "The game of war seldom presents a more effectual checkmate than was here given by Lee," William Swinton pronounced in his *Campaigns of the Army of the Potomac.* "The Confederate commander, thrusting his center between the two wings of the Army of the Potomac, put his antagonist at enormous disadvantage, and compelled him, for the reinforcement of the one or the other wing, to make a double passage of the river." Even Grant admitted the genius of Lee's deployment in his memoirs. "Our lines covered his front," Grant wrote, "with the six miles separating the two wings guarded by but a single division [Willcox]. To get from one wing to the other the river would have to be crossed twice. Lee could reinforce any part of his line from all points of it in a very short march; or could concentrate the whole of it wherever he might choose to assault." Conceded Grant: "We were, for the time, practically two armies besieging."[79]

Lee indeed had checked Grant's advance, but he had hoped to do much more. He had wanted to attack the Union army while it was divided and defeat it. For a few fleeting hours, Lee had the opportunity that he sought. By midafternoon, Hancock—reinforced by Potter—had advanced some 24,000 troops south of the river. Leaving Hill to hold the western leg of the inverted V, Lee could have concentrated Anderson's and Ewell's corps, Breckinridge's army, and Pickett's four brigades, approximately 30,000 soldiers, against Hancock. Lee would have held a telling advantage. Grant had no means for reinforcing Hancock. Gibbon, east of Telegraph Road, was exceedingly vulnerable, as Ramseur's and Grimes's skirmishers discovered. A strong attack would have broken Gibbon, rendering Barlow's and Birney's position at the Fox and Lowry properties untenable. Backed against a river controlled by rebel artillery, Hancock would have sustained severe casualties. Lee would have won a stunning victory.[80]

But Lee's tantalizing window of opportunity remained open for only a few hours. His advantage depended on surprise. Once Grant realized the danger and directed his troops to entrench, that advantage disappeared. By dark, Union earthworks offset the Confederate edge in numbers. Lee's chance to have "one more pull" at Grant had ended.

Historians have considered Lee's inability to attack on the afternoon of May 24 a lost opportunity of major proportions. In retrospect, it is doubtful that even a healthy Lee could have dealt a decisive blow. He would most certainly have wrecked much of Hancock's corps, but he would have lacked the strength and time to exploit the localized victory. Nightfall would likely have prevented him from crossing the North Anna. Grant could take severe casualties in stride. Terrible subtractions in the Wilderness and at Spotsylvania Court House did not deter him, nor did severe losses at Cold Harbor in the coming weeks. It is difficult to imagine Hancock's defeat inducing him to abandon his campaign. Sickness doubtless cost Lee a superb opportunity to damage an isolated portion of Grant's army at the North Anna River, but the lost opportunity should not be exaggerated. Judging from Grant's reaction to earlier and later setbacks, he likely would have treated defeat at the North Anna as a tactical reverse and gone on with his campaign.

Epilogue

"Two schoolboys trying to stare each other out of countenance."

Grant's priority on May 25 was to determine the configuration of Lee's line. Forays by Hancock and Burnside had revealed strong entrenchments running southeast from Ox Ford past Hanover Junction. What lay in front of Warren and Wright remained unknown.

At daybreak Griffin's 5th Corps division pushed east from Noel's Station along the Virginia Central Railroad and the wagon road paralleling the tracks. Colonel Tilton's 22nd Massachusetts reached south to Little River and deployed into a picket line to protect the advancing column's right flank. Wright trailed behind Griffin, extending from the railroad to Little River. "I shall keep up my connection with your right, and move with it," he assured Warren.[1]

Half a mile west of Anderson's Tavern, Griffin struck Hill's picket line. The main Confederate works were visible across a field. Griffin's troops halted and deployed in woods, stacking fence rails and railroad ties. Skirmishers advanced into the field and began burrowing with bayonets and tin plates. "It was a terribly hot skirmish line," a Federal recollected. "If anyone exposed himself to view for a moment, almost instantly the balls would be whistling around thick." Confederate sharpshooters spotted Griffin posting his line and opened fire. Bullets kicked up dirt around the general, and a ball smashed his boot heel. "Johnny, your aim was bad," Griffin shouted jauntily as he walked to a safer place. "You shot a little low this time."[2]

While Griffin developed Hill's position on the railroad, Warren moved the rest of the 5th Corps into line. Crittenden, temporarily assigned to Warren, anchored the northern flank at Quarles's Mill. Crawford formed on Crittenden's right, and Cutler filled the interval between Crawford and Griffin. At

8:00 A.M. Warren started the rest of his corps forward, driving Confederate skirmishers.[3]

Everywhere the situation was the same. Cleared fields of fire created killing zones that Warren's men dared not cross. Cutler's division, on Griffin's left, lay pinned under a "very galling fire," as Cutler described it, and the works in front of Crittenden and Crawford were as impregnable as when Ledlie had tried them the previous afternoon. "This was dangerous locality," a Bay Stater confirmed. Five minutes of skirmishing cost an Indiana regiment a captain and two privates dead and several men wounded. "Severe experience," a soldier remarked.[4]

Curious to see the state of affairs, Warren set out with Lyman. First he visited Cutler—"skirmishing very hotly in the front," Lyman noted—then rode south to the Virginia Central Railroad. Griffin and an aide were sketching a map of Hill's position as minié balls rattled through nearby bushes. Noticing Lyman's concern, Roebling assured him that the bullets were spent but "come hard enough to go through if they hit!" Griffin had requested guns to enfilade a portion of Hill's works. The 5th Massachusetts Battery rolled up, and Griffin placed the pieces near the railroad. Skirmish fire remained heavy. Stray bullets struck Captain Thomas C. Case of Griffin's staff and the artillerist Lieutenant Nathan Appleton.[5]

Warren and Lyman continued to Little River and visited the 22nd Massachusetts. Warren impressed a soldier as giving "little thought to his personal safety, and as fully grasping the details of the situation." From there they went to Wright's headquarters at Edward Anderson's house, between the railway and the river. The proprietor—"a short man," observed Lyman, who "wore the usual expression of dismal acerbity"—was at home, as were Wright and his staff. After pausing for ice water and gossip, Warren and Lyman retraced their route. They roused Crawford, who was fast asleep behind heavy breastworks, oblivious to bullets clicking through the trees. At the North Anna they visited Crittenden, who was also firmly entrenched. Crittenden was miffed at being placed under Warren, who was his junior in rank. Lyman noted, however, that he acted "very pleasant and did not visit his dissatisfaction on Warren."[6]

Midmorning saw the 5th Corps arrayed in line from Quarles's Mill to Little River, facing Hill's works. The Confederate position was manifestly impregnable. "I feel satisfied," Warren informed Meade, "that I should have great difficulty at best in whipping the enemy in my front." Warren suggested that Wright might advance a division across Little River and turn Hill's flank, but he was not sanguine about the prospects. The banks were steep, and Confederate cavalry guarded the crossings in force. Griffin whiled away the

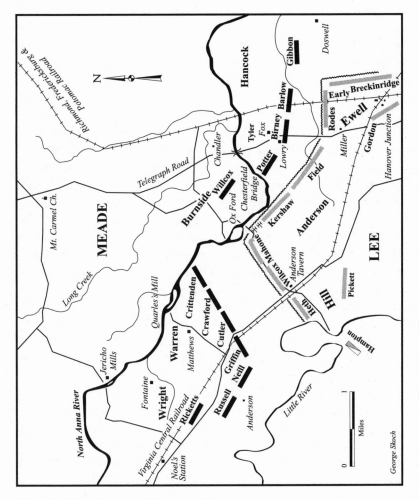

Stalemate on the North Anna River

time digging earthworks and siting guns. An old man and his womenfolk stood on their porch and watched the Yankees dig up their yard. A concerned officer urged them to go to the rear, as Hill's entrenchments were only a few hundred yards away, and firing was imminent. "No sir! Never sir!" the proprietor insisted. "I am too old to fight. I can do nothing, sir, for my invaded state but to die in my home!" The officer had a ready reply. "But my dear sir," he insisted. "If you should die in your own home it would be by bullets of your own friends, and I don't see what good that could do your state." Persuaded by irrefutable logic, the gentleman and his family abandoned their house and disappeared west along the tracks of the Virginia Central Railroad.[7]

On the other side of the inverted V, Hancock was also at a standstill. "Stronger than last night," 2nd Corps skirmishers reported of Ewell's and Anderson's earthworks. Probes persuaded Hancock that the rebels had a "very decided advantage in case we attack." Colonel Tidball made life miserable for Tige Anderson's Georgians by firing on them with Coehorn mortars. The mortars, which Tidball had first used to impressive effect at the Bloody Angle, lobbed shells high into the air and dropped them behind the rebel earthworks. The projectiles, a Georgian recollected, "seemed to be raining down from the clouds." Anderson was so concerned about the mortars that he sent sharpshooters into the no-man's land between the lines to shoot the mortar crews. His tactic ended the bombardment.[8]

By noon Grant fully understood Lee's deployment. The Confederate had entrenched in a wedge formation, apex on the river, splitting the Union army in two. "The conclusion that the enemy had abandoned the region between the North and South Anna," Dana wrote Stanton, "though shared yesterday by every prominent officer here, proves to have been a mistake." Roebling considered the situation a "deadlock." The armies, he wrote a friend, "remind me very much of two schoolboys trying to stare each other out of countenance." He predicted that "unless the rebs commit some great error they hold us in check until kingdom come." Lee, a Union newsman agreed, was "so strongly posted that an attempt to force his lines would have been little less than madness."[9]

For the third time in the campaign—at the Wilderness, at Spotsylvania Court House, and now at the North Anna River—Lee had foiled Grant. On each occasion Grant had maneuvered offensively, only to be thwarted by Lee's masterful grasp of terrain, tenacious fighting, and good luck. Lee's latest feat was impressive. "Lee's position to Grant was similar to that of Meade's to Lee's at Gettysburg, with this additional disadvantage here to Grant of a necessity of crossing the river twice to reinforce either wing," a Union man observed.[10]

What could Grant do? He realized that an immediate attack was out of the question. He could wait for reinforcements from Butler, concentrate overwhelming might against part of Lee's formation, and risk everything on a frontal assault. Or he could maneuver, using Sheridan to shield his movements. Possibilities included swinging east and south of Lee, as he had after stalemates at the Wilderness and Spotsylvania Court House. Or he could surprise Lee by swinging around the Confederate left, cross Little River, and sever the Army of Northern Virginia's escape route. "If a promising chance offers," Dana predicted, "General Grant will fight, of course: otherwise, he will maneuver without attacking." [11]

Grant was not ready to commit to a course of action. He was certain, however, about a key point. All the nation's troops must be engaged fighting rebels. Butler's troops were lying idle, as were Sigel's, now commanded by Major General David Hunter. Grant wanted them back in the war. "The enemy are evidently making a determined stand between the two Annas," he wrote Halleck, predicting that he would need "two days to get in position for a general attack or to turn their position, as may favor best." In the meantime, Halleck was to withdraw Butler from the James—leaving only sufficient men to defend the river up to City Point—and forward the troops to him. Hunter was to march on Charlottesville and Lynchburg, wreck the transportation network in the Shenandoah Valley, and then join Grant. For the time being, the Army of the Potomac would wait. "I do not think any attack should be made until preparations are made to use our whole force," Grant advised Meade. "The best Warren can do now is to cover his men well in their advanced position, and rest them all he can ready for active service." Grant saw no point in dispatching Wright across Little River as Warren had suggested. "Unless there is some reason for it that I do not know," he instructed Meade, "it would be better not to send them over until the cavalry gets around." [12]

The Army of the Potomac spent the afternoon wrecking railroads. Miles's soldiers ripped up tracks along the Richmond, Fredericksburg, and Potomac Railroad. Warren's and Wright's troops went at the Virginia Central with a vengeance. "We would form on the uphill side of the track," a Federal explained, "and taking hold and lifting turn the track completely over, and removing the ties stack and cord them, and setting fire to the piles, place the rails on top of the ties thus piled. The fire would heat a portion of the rails in the middle red hot. Then we would take the rails off the piles and wind them around trees or stumps or bend them double." Soldiers demolished the line west to Beaver Dam Station, stopping occasionally to forage. "We tore up and destroyed all we could of bridges, culverts, etc.," an orderly sergeant reported, "and got *fresh hog.*"[13]

All day, Confederate cavalry probed Grant's lines. Hampton's troopers patrolled Little River, facing the 6th Corps and Tilton's pickets. Joseph F. Waring, heading the Jeff Davis Legion, concluded that Wright's men "do not wish to bring on an attack, but are simply making a demonstration to keep us from annoying their R.R. burners." The 1st Maryland Cavalry reconnoitered east of the Union army to determine whether Grant was preparing to move. Crossing the North Anna near the Doswell farm, the Marylanders rode northeast to Penola Station, confirmed that Grant's supply line ran to Bowling Green, and attempted to retrace their route back. Sheridan barred the way, but they escaped upriver at a ford so steep that the men had to push their horses off the bank to make them cross. Along the way they captured Union couriers with dispatches detailing Grant's troop dispositions. Nothing, however, gave clues about Grant's plans.[14]

Now it was Lee's time to be thwarted. With Grant entrenched on both sides of the Confederate army, he had no choice but to wait for the Federals to move. Early in the day he renewed his plea for reinforcements. A dispatch taken from one of Ledlie's aides captured at Ox Ford confirmed that Grant had stripped the garrisons at Washington, Norfolk, and Fort Monroe and had brought every available soldier to the front. "This makes it necessary for us to do likewise," Lee insisted. "If General Beauregard is in condition to unite with me in any operation against General Grant, I should like to know it, and at what point a combination of the troops could be made most advantageously to him."[15]

In the meantime, Lee decided to hedge his bets. The twin railroads from Richmond ensured him an uninterrupted flow of supplies. Lee considered it likely that Grant would follow his invariable practice and swing east, crossing the Pamunkey, and he prepared to slide south and east as well. Engineers constructed a footbridge across the South Anna, and Rooney Lee's cavalry rode to Hanover Court House in anticipation of a rapid Confederate deployment in that direction. The engineer Smith reconnoitered the South Anna for a new defensive line in the unlikely event that Grant attacked and forced the Army of Northern Virginia to retreat.[16]

Grant and Meade crossed back over the North Anna at 2:00 P.M. and set up headquarters near Quarles's Mill, on the north bank. A lady from a neighboring house noticed the Union commander smoking a cigar in front of his tent and strolled over to chat. Her old-fashioned calico dress, sleeves rolled to the elbows, was six inches too short. "How do you do," she greeted Grant in a high-pitched voice that the aide Porter likened to a clarinet with a soft reed. "I'm powerful glad General Lee has been lickin' you all from the Rapidan clear down here, and that now he's got you just where he wants you," she began. Pulling up a campstool, she warmed to her subject. "Yes, and before long Lee will be chasing you up through Pennsylvania again," she predicted. "Were you up there in Pennsylvania when he got after you all last summer?" Grant struggled to keep a straight face. "Well, no," he replied. "I wasn't there myself." Refraining from mentioning his siege of Vicksburg, he explained: "I had some business in another direction." [17]

Grant, Meade, and their generals met that evening. All agreed that Lee's formation was too strong to assail. Meade, along with Grant's aide Comstock, urged shifting east, crossing the Pamunkey, and turning Lee's right flank. Grant could continue drawing supplies from the river network and would preserve his communication with Butler. Warren and the artillery commander Hunt favored marching west and swinging around Lee's left flank. Lee, they argued, was expecting Grant to shift east as he had done after the Wilderness and Spotsylvania Court House. Moving west, they pointed out, would catch the Confederates off guard. The tactical advantage gained by surprise would offset any supply difficulties.

Warren's and Hunt's plan intrigued Grant. At the end of the conference, he inclined toward a "bold stroke, viz: to cut clear of our communications altogether, and push to get around Lee's left, shoving right on for Richmond." But reflecting further, he changed his mind. He explained his reasoning to Halleck the next day. "To make a direct attack from either wing [of the divided Union army]," he wrote, "would cause a slaughter of our men that even success would not justify. To turn the enemy by his right, between the two Annas, is impossible on account of the swamp upon which his right rests. To turn him by his left leaves Little River, New Found River, and South Anna River, all of them streams presenting considerable obstacles to the movement of an army, to be crossed." Marching downriver and crossing the Pamunkey avoided those difficulties. "This crosses all these streams at once," Grant explained, "and leaves us still where we can draw supplies." [18]

Grant decided to evacuate the south bank in stages to guard against a Confederate attack. "Direct Generals Warren and Wright to withdraw all their teams and artillery not in position to the north side of the river to-morrow," he instructed Meade. Wright's "best division" was to accompany the teams and artillery toward Hanovertown, thirty-four miles east, taking care not to attract Lee's attention. Sheridan was to patrol the downriver fords to conceal the movement. After dark on May 26, the 5th Corps and the rest of the 6th were to cross the North Anna and start east toward Hanovertown. Hancock and Burnside were to follow.[19]

Meade was smugly satisfied. Three days earlier he had urged Grant to swing wide of Lee and cross at the Pamunkey. Grant had rejected his advice and insisted on following Lee to the North Anna. That plan had failed, costing valuable lives and giving Lee time to draw reinforcements. Now Grant saw the wisdom of Meade's proposal and was doing precisely as Meade had recommended. Vindication was sweet for Meade. Many Federals, however, considered the eastward maneuver a pointless repetition of a failed tactic. "Can it be this is the sum of our lieutenant-general's abilities?" Colonel Wainwright asked his diary. "Has he no other resource in tactics? Or is it sheer obstinacy? Three times he has tried this move, around Lee's right, and three times been foiled." Coming days would reveal whether a fourth disappointment was in the making.[20]

"The most useless sacrifice of time and men and horses made during the war."

While Lee maneuvered Grant to stalemate on the North Anna River, his nephew Fitzhugh Lee became embroiled in a pointless expedition to the James River. When Butler advanced up the James on May 5, he had established outposts to protect his supply lines. A brigade of black troops commanded by Brigadier General Edward A. Wild had secured Wilson's Wharf—also called Kennon's Landing—on the north bank of the James, some twenty miles below Richmond, and Fort Powhatan, seven miles upriver from Wilson's Wharf, on the south bank. The outpost at Wilson's Wharf immediately began constructing Fort Pocahontas to protect the landing.

Wild was a controversial figure. A thirty-eight-year-old physician from Brookline, Massachusetts, he had volunteered for combat early in the war. Rebel balls had crippled his right hand at Seven Pines and mauled his left arm at South Mountain so badly that the limb had to be amputated. He was a fervent abolitionist and, as a newspaperman put it, "an enthusiast on the subject of colored troops." After recovering from his amputation, he recruited several black regiments and formed "Wild's African Brigade." During the winter of 1863–1864, Wild led his brigade on an expedition in North Carolina. Tales of rampaging blacks incited southern newspapers to denounce the raid as contrary to "long established usages of civilization [and] the dictates of humanity."[21]

Wild's reputation preceded him to Virginia. Armed blacks sat poorly with the local white inhabitants, and stories, mostly apocryphal, abounded of atrocities perpetrated by Wild's soldiers. Wild fueled the fire by freeing slaves and recruiting them for his brigade. Things reached a head when Wild captured William H. Clopton, a planter renowned for cruelty. At Wild's direction, black soldiers tied Clopton to a tree and whipped him in front of black troops. Sergeant George W. Hatton of the 1st USCT identified one of Clopton's tormentors as a former slave who relished "bringing the blood from his loins at every stroke, and not forgetting to remind the gentleman of the days gone by." Three women previously owned by Clopton gave him twenty strokes each "to remind him that they were no longer his," Hatton noted with satisfaction. Wild justified the lashing as "the administration of Poetical justice." [22]

Richmond was up in arms. Wild's "wretches have been scouring the country committing the most atrocious and devilish excesses," the *Richmond Examiner* expostulated. "Robbing, burning, and plundering have not been enough, but these black scoundrels have literally caught white men, tied them to trees, and whipped them on their bare backs!" Rumors had it, the *Examiner* continued, that "these black demons, by violence and threats of instant death, have made some ladies, alone and unprotected, the victims of their hellish appetites." Something had to be done immediately. "Is our government to submit passively to seeing its citizens hung and shot down like dogs," editor John M. Daniel asked, "its men bayoneted and nailed to trees, its women raped and ravished by Negro troops from Boston and New York?" [23]

Public uproar demanded that President Davis act. But where could he find troops to clean out this "nest" of blacks, as the *Examiner* termed Wild's command? All the spare infantry around Richmond had left to join Lee on the North Anna. Finally the president thought of Fitzhugh Lee, whose cavalry was bivouacked at Atlee's Station. There was no military reason to send Lee to Wilson's Wharf. The enclave of black troops posed no immediate threat to Richmond, and the Army of Northern Virginia sorely needed its cavalry to fight Grant. Political considerations, however, prevailed over military ones. On the morning of May 23 General Bragg, the president's military adviser, instructed Fitzhugh Lee to ride to Wilson's Wharf and, as Lee later explained, "break up the nest and stop their uncivilized proceedings in the neighborhood." Lee detached large portions of Wickham's, Lomax's, and Gordon's brigades for the expedition, supplemented by elements from the newly arrived 5th South Carolina Cavalry. At 4:00 P.M. Lee started for Wilson's Wharf with some 2,500 men and a single piece of horse artillery. [24]

Lee's troopers marched all night, often at a gallop, trying to reach the wharf by daylight. The distance was greater than expected. Passing through Mechanicsville and Seven Pines, they reached Samaria at sunrise, a twenty-six-mile trek. Continuing another fifteen miles, Lee's advance arrived at Wilson's Wharf around 11:00 A.M. on the 24th. Pausing to reconnoiter, Lee was surprised at the strength of the position. Bragg, relying on reports from irate citizens, had led him to believe that he would meet little organized resistance. Instead, he faced a substantial body of infantry "strongly entrenched." Holding Fort Pocahontas were the 1st USCT and four companies of the 10th USCT—about 1,100 men—and a section of artillery from Battery M, 3rd New York Light Artillery, commanded by Lieutenant Nicholas Hanson. The horseshoe-shaped earthen fort covered the landing. Wild's men had cleared ground in front of the fortification and had partially completed a ditch, eight feet wide and five to six feet deep in places, along the face of the structure, stacking felled trees with interlocking branches on the outer side. In a hurry to attack, Lee evidently failed to notice that some sections of the fort's defenses were not finished. A Union gunboat, the USS *Dawn,* stood anchored in the James close by.[25]

After driving in Wild's pickets, Lee deployed to attack. Wickham's brigade formed the assault force's right wing. Colonel Dunovant of the 5th South Carolina Cavalry commanded the left wing, made up of his own regiment, Lomax's troops, and elements from Gordon's brigade under Colonel Clinton Andrews. Dismounted skirmishers advanced cautiously, spreading across the front of the fort and spilling into adjacent woods. For an hour or more, Lee's men traded shots with Wild's troops in the fort, who were backed by Hanson's two pieces and the USS *Dawn's* guns. Although the Confederates had a substantial edge in numbers, Wild's position was too strong to be taken by storm.[26]

Lee dispatched Major R. J. Mason and John Gill under a flag of truce with a note to Wild. "If the surrender of the Federal forces is made, the soldiers will be taken to Richmond and treated as prisoners of war," the note stated. "But if they do not surrender, Gen. Lee will not be answerable for the consequences." The note was silent as to the intended fate of the white officers, but Lee's meaning was clear to Wild and his men. "The interpretation of this threat was that colored soldiers taken as prisoners should be returned to their former masters," a Federal recollected, "and their officers delivered to the state authorities to be dealt with for inciting insurrection." Lieutenant Hiram W. Allen, who stood next to Wild and copied Lee's note, interpreted the communication "to mean that their success and our failure meant another Fort Pillow massacre." Wild took an envelope from his pocket, tore off a piece, and penciled in reply, "We will try it." Handing the note to Gill, Wild told him to tell Lee, "Take the fort if you can." [27]

Gill returned to Lee and handed him Wild's message. Lee asked if the fort could be captured, and Gill replied that it could not. Lee, however, saw no choice but to proceed. Retreating in the face of a black garrison must have been unthinkable.[28]

Meanwhile, the mailboat *Thomas Powell* landed some 150 unarmed soldiers at the fort. Six men from the 1st Connecticut Heavy Artillery volunteered to help man the guns, replacing some of Lieutenant Hanson's men who had fainted from heat. "We then went at it again," reported Wild.[29]

Keeping up constant skirmishing, Wickham moved his dismounted troopers along a circuitous route through woods and deployed them east of the fort, concealed in ravines of Kennon Creek. Dunovant concentrated on the other side of the fortification, intending to make a "demonstration" to attract the defenders' attention while Wickham charged. Wickham's soldiers crept close under cover of the woods and ravines. The gunboat *Dawn* kept up a demoralizing fire. The shells looked like "turkey gobblers flying over" recollected a man in the 2nd Virginia Cavalry. "We could see them plainly coming at and over us," a Tar Heel remembered, "great black masses, as big as nail kegs, hurtling in the air and making the earth tremble under us and the atmosphere jar and quake around us when they burst." A southerner called the bombardment "terrifying." The Confederates ate wild strawberries and waited for the order to attack.[30]

At a signal, Wickham's men stepped into cleared ground in front of the fort and rushed forward. "The Negroes, with uncovered heads, rose above the entrenchments and leveled their guns upon us," recorded Gill, who participated in the attack. Sun glinted off polished rifle barrels. "Then came a cloud of smoke," recollected Gill, "bullets whizzed through our ranks, and the men in our lines tumbled over each other, some forward, some backward." [31]

Wickham's soldiers pressed across the clearing, men falling along the way. "A most gallant charge under a hot fire," Lee described the attack. "The rebel fighting was very wicked," a Union correspondent observed. "It showed that Lee's heart was bent on taking the Negroes at any cost." Troopers pushed through the abatis and jumped into the ditch. Hanson's two 10-pound Parrotts spewed canister into the rebel ranks. "Again the brave and determined foe rallied under the frantic efforts of their officers," a Federal reported. "Again their ranks were scattered and torn by our deadly fire." Unable to hold the trench, Wickham ordered his men back across the field to the woods. "We retired under that awful fire from the most useless and unwise attack and the most signal failure we were ever engaged in," a North Carolinian wrote. Losses during the retreat exceeded those during the attack. Confederate casualties approximated two hundred, among them Captain P. Gilmer Breckinridge of the 6th Virginia Cavalry. Wild lost six men killed and some forty wounded.[32]

Lee reconnoitered the fort, hoping to find a weak point, but the fortification looked as imposing as ever. Around 4:00 P.M. the steamer *George Washington* brought Wild the 10th USCT's four remaining companies. Countermanding orders to renew the assault, Lee withdrew. Of the handful of blacks taken prisoner, some were shot, allegedly while attempting to escape, and one was sent to his master in Richmond. The dispirited Confederate horsemen retired at dark to Charles City Court House, then continued the next day back to Atlee's Station.[33]

The battle at Wilson's Wharf was a small affair that had no impact on the outcome of the war. It was significant, however, as the first major encounter between black troops and the Army of Northern Virginia. Rosser, it is true, had engaged elements of Ferrero's division on May 15 and 19, but only in minor skirmishes. Wilson's Wharf lasted more than five hours, and there could be no doubt about who had won. "That black men will fight is an established fact," a Union reporter asserted after the battle. The artillerist Hanson reportedly claimed that "no men in the world could do better than those who supported his gun." Captain Solon A. Carter, assistant adjutant to Brigadier General Edward W. Hincks, Wild's immediate superior, considered the battle's outcome "highly gratifying, demonstrating that the colored troops possessed nerve and courage." [34]

The Confederates admitted defeat but refused to credit Wild's soldiers with victory. Lee understated his own numbers, magnified Wild's, and claimed that several transports had brought in white troops. The *Richmond Examiner* asserted that large numbers of white marines had assisted Wild's "supposedly Negro troops," and that six gunboats had plied the river, "playing upon our men." Admitting that the black defenders had fought bravely and had held their own was something neither Lee nor the *Richmond Examiner* could bring themselves to do.[35]

Wilson's Wharf closed a dreary chapter in Fitzhugh Lee's career. His vaunted cavalry had fallen far. On May 8 Lee and his troopers were the toast of the army. They had thwarted Sheridan at Todd's Tavern and delayed Grant several critical hours, enabling Confederate infantry to win the race to Spotsylvania Court House. Their fortunes had quickly changed. On May 11 at Yellow Tavern, Sheridan had utterly routed them. Sheridan had driven them again the next day at Meadow Bridge. And now a garrison of blacks had beaten them. A trooper in the 5th North Carolina Cavalry expressed the sentiment in Lee's ranks. The expedition, he wrote, was "the most useless sacrifice of time and men and horses made during the war." [36]

"How we longed to get away from the North Anna."

Rain lashed central Virginia on May 26, providing ideal cover for Grant's withdrawal. Early in the day the cavalryman James Wilson received orders to demonstrate near Lee's left flank to create the impression that Grant meant to move in that direction. He had a "warm and cordial" reunion with Grant, Rawlins, and other friends from the west, crossed the North Anna at Jericho Mills, and continued to Little River. Rain had swollen the stream, and rebels had destroyed the bridges over Little River. Wilson's division made a strong show, firing carbines and artillery and building bonfires. "The pioneer corps cut down trees and made all the racket they could along the river," a trooper recounted, "as though we expected to cross the stream at this point." Russell's 6th Corps division meanwhile crossed to the north bank of the North Anna and headed east. Gregg's and Merritt's cavalry covered the fords downriver to hide Russell's movement from the Confederates, then rode ahead to secure the fords near Hanovertown.[37]

The withdrawal began in earnest after sunset. "Night intensely dark and roads very muddy," wrote Roebling. Engineers laid branches on the bridges over the North Anna to muffle sounds. The 6th Corps crossed at Jericho Mills, and the 5th Corps and Crittenden's division of the 9th Corps crossed at Quarles's Mill. Hancock and Potter crossed next, dismantling the pontoons and burning Chesterfield Bridge to hinder pursuit. By 3:00 A.M. on May 27 Grant's entire force was on the northern bank and threading east. The disengagement had been flawless. "How we longed to get away from the North Anna," Private Wilkeson remembered, "where we had not the slightest chance of success." At 6:45 A.M. Lee informed Richmond that Grant had withdrawn and that Union cavalry and infantry had captured the fords at Hanovertown. "I have sent the cavalry in that direction to check the movement," he wrote Secretary of War Seddon, "and will move the army to Ashland." The armies were in motion once again, with Grant attempting to turn Lee's eastern flank, and Lee shifting to keep between Grant and Richmond. The chess match would resume on a new field.[38]

Each side considered that it had won the North Anna campaign. From the Federal perspective, Grant had maneuvered Lee from Spotsylvania Court House and stood only a day's march from Richmond. One more turning movement, it seemed, and Grant could pin Lee against the Confederate capital and destroy him at leisure. Grant viewed Lee's failure to attack on May 24 as proof that the Army of Northern Virginia had lost its nerve. "Lee's army is really whipped," Grant informed Halleck. "The prisoners we now take show it, and the action of his army shows it unmistakably." The Confederates, Grant stressed, were no longer strong enough to fight outside entrenchments. "Our men feel that they have gained the morale over the enemy and attack with confidence," Grant added. "Our success over Lee's army is already assured." A New Yorker agreed. "We are still driving the enemy before us," he wrote home. "We have been successful in every fight yet and we are now within 25 miles of Richmond. If providence is in our favor we will soon have this stronghold of their Confederacy broken up." [39]

Ironically, Lee's soldiers were also confident of victory. By their estimation, they had foiled Grant at Spotsylvania Court House, beat him to the North Anna, and deadlocked him at the river. Grant's refusal to attack the inverted V persuaded the Confederates that they had broken his spirit. "The Yankees have lost all the boldness and dash which characterized their first movements," Lee's chief engineer, Smith, wrote his wife, "and are now proceeding with extreme caution." The artillerist Alexander expressed disappointment over the Federals' refusal to assail the inverted V. "They wanted to attack us," he later wrote. "And their engineers and their generals looked at our beautiful lines with longing eyes for several days. But they always shook their heads and said it would not do." The southern correspondent Peter Alexander thought the campaign had taught Grant a "wholesome lesson." Explained Alexander: "For the first ten days after crossing the Rapidan, [Grant] evinced a disposition to fight us wherever he met us. Since the 18th instant, however, the day on which he made his last effort to bring his dispirited troops up to the bloody work, he has shown quite a strong desire to avoid battle. That he had found it necessary to change his whole plan of operations, there can be but little doubt. If it has been a part of his original design to make [White House] or the Lower James his base of operations, then he has committed a great blunder in marching across the country from Culpeper at a cost of forty or fifty thousand men, when by following McClellan's route he might have reached the same destination without the loss of a single man." [40]

Traditionally, historians have contrasted Grant's and Lee's generalship, emphasizing differences in their command styles. The campaign from Spotsylvania Court House to the North Anna River suggests that the two generals had surprisingly similar military temperaments. Both were aggressive and willing to try unorthodox maneuvers. As players on the chessboard of war, they were remarkably evenly matched.

Grant's greatest strength lay in his dogged adherence to the strategic objective of destroying Lee's army. He treated stalemates in the Wilderness, at Spotsylvania Court House, and on the North Anna River as tactical reverses, not as defeats, and he persisted despite setbacks that would have discouraged most generals. The correspondent Peter Alexander's analysis missed the point of Grant's strategy. The general's goal was not to seize Richmond, as McClellan had attempted, but to defeat Lee's army. Grant was not aiming for geographic conquests, but for battlefield victories. He seized the initiative at the beginning of the campaign and held tightly to his offensive edge, keeping Lee off balance with a welter of attacks and maneuvers.

Grant also demonstrated impressive flexibility that belied his popular image as a general who eschewed maneuver in favor of pointless assaults against impregnable earthworks. Heavy casualties during the initial days at Spotsylvania Court House, culminating in the Bloody Angle on May 12, persuaded Grant that he had underestimated the strength of Lee's field fortifications. He had "looked for no such resistance" from Lee's army, he told Lyman, and he confided that Lee's tenacity had thrown "in the shade everything he ever saw." Grant responded by abandoning his hammering tactics and searching for vulnerable links in the rebel line. Four days of probing resulted in the attack of May 18. When that failed, Grant again maneuvered, first attempting to entice Lee from his entrenchments by dangling Hancock as bait, then swinging south to draw Lee out of his fortified line. Facing the Confederates at the North Anna, Grant prudently declined to assault. The attempt, he feared, would produce "slaughter of men that even success would not justify." Once again he relied on maneuver instead of force to break the impasse created by Lee's wedge-shaped formation. The Grant of May 13–25 was not the butcher of lore, but a seasoned warrior every bit as inventive as his Confederate opponent.[41]

Although Grant exhibited commendable persistence, serious tactical blunders marred his campaign. He habitually ordered major operations without allowing sufficient time for preparation and without adequate knowledge of Lee's dispositions. Releasing Sheridan was a major mistake. The absence of experienced cavalry left Grant virtually blind at several critical junctures. One can only speculate whether the presence of Sheridan's horsemen would have changed the outcome on May 14 and May 18 by affording Grant reliable information about the configuration and strength of Lee's line. It is unlikely, however, that Lee would have slipped past Grant's sleeping army on May 21–22 if Sheridan's riders had been available. Good cavalry work would also have brought order to Grant's stumbling approach to the North

Anna on May 23 and alerted him to the shape of Lee's line before his abortive—and nearly disastrous—advance on May 24. Simply put, Sheridan's absence cost Grant dearly.

Grant's freewheeling style sat poorly with the Army of the Potomac's generals, who frequently failed to act with the resolve his plans required. And Grant, as on the night of May 13–14, often made unrealistic demands. But the situation seemed to be improving. Grant corrected a major weakness by incorporating the 9th Corps into the Army of the Potomac, ending the awkward fiction that Meade and Burnside headed separate armies. He was also encouraged by what appeared to be growing signs of competence among his corps commanders. Hancock conducted his march to Milford Station with workmanlike efficiency and took Henagan's redoubt in a single bold stroke. Wright was new to his post but ably managed the rearguard action on May 21. Even Warren seemed to be doing better. He had been unaccountably lax on May 21–22, permitting Lee to pass, but demonstrated welcome initiative at Jericho Mills. And now Sheridan was back, restoring Grant's mounted arm. Meade remained the sticking point. By May 25 relations between the aggressive Grant and his cautious subordinate had reached a low point. Major Biddle of Meade's staff alluded to the bitterness in a letter home. It was "perfectly disgusting," he wrote, to see Grant "lauded to the skies as being the greatest military man of the age," when in fact Meade's generalship was as "far superior to [Grant's] as day is to night." The rift between the Union force's two top generals was to cause serious difficulty in the days ahead.[42]

Grant must bear ultimate responsibility for the Union army's poor tactical showing. Often the Federal force seemed adrift like a rudderless ship. Grant should have insisted that Meade take charge of tactical details, or should have taken charge himself. During the maneuvers from Spotsylvania Court House on May 21, both Grant and Meade settled in at Mr. Motley's house and left Warren, Burnside, and Wright to their own devices. Comparable absence of leadership slowed Federal movements on May 22. On May 23, during the approach to the North Anna, Grant and Meade remained several miles to the rear, abdicating important decisions in favor of their corps commanders. Thus, Warren's victory at Jericho Mills went unexploited, even though Wright's 6th Corps was close at hand.

Some critics had nothing good to say about Grant. The movement to the North Anna, Meade's aide Biddle asserted, had been "not only badly conceived but badly executed." Eternally pessimistic, Wainwright grumped that "officers and men are getting tired of [Grant's ways] and would like a little variety on night marches and indiscriminate attacks on earthworks in the daytime." A Vermont soldier quipped that it would "require an extraordinary military genius to comprehend the reason for all the movements that we make, and their result. We take up a position one day and fortify it, and the next day we abandon it altogether. Sometimes we think we are about to make a regular attack on the enemy, and sometimes we think they are about to make an assault upon us. We make all preparations for a fight, but no fighting is done. If we think we are going to have a day's rest, we are pretty sure to fall in immediately and commence to march, and when a day's rest does come, it comes quite unexpectedly." [43]

But dissenters were a minority. Buoyed by the mistaken belief that Lee would not fight, the Union soldiers liked and trusted their new commander. "General Grant is the boy for us," effused a Michigan man. "He understands what he is doing and makes everything sure as he goes." Grant's determination was infectious. "Hammered and pounded as this army has been," the aide Charles Francis Adams wrote his father; "worked, marched, fought, and reduced as it is, it is in better sprits and better fighting trim today than it was in the first day's fight in the Wilderness." Grant, Adams assured his father, was not McClellan. He would "not let his army be idle," Adams promised, nor would he "allow the initiative to be easily taken out of his hands." The campaign was reaching a climax, predicted Adams, "under circumstances which certainly seem to me hopeful." Writing from Quarles's Mill, Dana remarked on the "entire change which has taken place in the feelings of the armies." The Confederates had lost confidence, he reported, while the Federals were "sure of victory." Even Meade's officers had "ceased to regard Lee as an invincible military genius." [44]

Lee's performance, like Grant's, had been mixed. The Virginian displayed impressive ability as a defensive fighter. He fended off an army nearly double the size of his own, vastly superior in weaponry, supplies, and sundry accouterments of war. He defended Spotsylvania Court House against all of Grant's attacks, eluded Grant's turning movement on May 21, and beat Grant to the North Anna River, devising a defensive formation—the inverted V—that brought the Union force to a standstill. A student of the Overland campaign aptly labeled the impasse at the North Anna the "greatest unfought repulse of the war." And even though the Army of Northern Virginia was falling back, its morale remained high. Conceding that Grant had advanced uncomfortably near Richmond, a Tar Heel observed that the Federals were "no nearer having this army whipped than when the first gun was fired." A Virginian wrote simply, "Our boys are well fortified, and I think Mr. Grant with his minions will be hurled back much faster than he came." [45]

Writers later credited Lee with an extraordinary facility to divine Grant's plans. The correspondent Alexander marveled at the "way in which [Lee] un-ravels the most intricate combination of his antagonist, the instinctive knowl-edge he seems to possess of all his plans and designs." Lee's aide Taylor asserted that the "faculty of General Lee, of discovering, as if by intuition, the intention and purpose of his opponent, was a very remarkable one." The eminent biographer Douglas Southall Freeman echoed the theme. "Grant's bludgeoning tactics and flank shifts [Lee] quickly fathomed," Freeman claimed, "but he was progressively less able to combat them as his own strength declined." [46]

In truth, Lee was often unsure or plainly wrong about Grant's plans. He was unprepared for Grant's rapid march into the Wilderness at the beginning of the campaign. Grant's shift to Spotsylvania Court House caught him off guard, as did the Union attack against the Mule Shoe on May 12. On May 14 Lee failed to grasp Grant's designs against his vulnerable right flank and ne-glected to correct the oversight until evening. In an egregious lapse, Lee marched past Warren's camps on the night of May 21–22, unnecessarily ex-posing the Confederate column. And on May 23 Lee assumed that Grant was swinging east to the Pamunkey when the Federals were actually marching to confront him on the North Anna. Lee's miscalculation enabled Warren to se-cure lodgment south of the river and imperil the Confederate line.

Lee's true strength—a trait often overlooked by biographers—was his re-markable ability to rescue his army from seemingly irremediable predica-ments and to turn unfavorable situations to his advantage. He was a master at improvising, and the pressure of crisis only sharpened his wits. He took inad-equate steps to catch Grant in the Wilderness but moved boldly once he rec-ognized the opportunity offered by the Union commander's decision to overnight in the dense woodland. He left his army vulnerable at Spotsylvania Court House by withdrawing artillery from the Mule Shoe but staved off de-feat by waging a determined defense, assuming an even stronger line at the end of the battle. And at the North Anna he inadvertently permitted the Federals to cross the river but rebounded by devising the cleverest defensive formation of his career.

Lee also benefitted from his adversary's mistakes. The campaign might have taken a dramatically different course had Grant pushed through the Wilderness on his first day of march; had Sheridan cleared the way to Spotsylvania Court House; had Hancock's attack at the Mule Shoe been properly supported; had the Union 5th and 6th Corps assaulted Lee's right flank on May 14; had Warren realized that Lee was passing on Telegraph Road the night of May 21–22; or had Grant exploited his advantage on May 23 at the North Anna, before Lee reconfigured his formation. The "fog of war" operated to Lee's advantage. Hobbled by bad maps, exhaustion, and the absence of cavalry, the Union force failed to capitalize on Lee's missteps.

The Army of Northern Virginia's top command had reached a crisis. Lee's illness of May 24 conclusively demonstrated that the general was indispensable. Anderson, Hill, and Ewell were manifestly unable to substitute for him, and the debacles at Harris Farm and Jericho Mills raised serious questions about their ability to manage their own corps. However, the next level of command—that of division—was bursting with talent. Early, Gordon, and Rodes of Ewell's corps displayed commendable skill, as did Field and Kershaw of Anderson's corps, and Mahone of Hill's corps. During the coming weeks Lee would seek to advance men like Early and Gordon to positions of greater responsibility.

Lee had demonstrated considerable tactical prowess. Strategically, however, he was in trouble. Each Confederate victory ended with the Army of the Potomac closer to Richmond. Lee had warned President Davis at the beginning of the campaign that "great danger" would befall the Confederacy if Grant forced him from the Rapidan. Now Federals stood within a day's march of the Confederate capital, and Grant held the initiative. The dire consequences of Lee's prediction seemed close at hand. Lee had won most of the battles, but Grant was winning the campaign.

The mood in the North was mixed. Grant's advance to the North Anna was viewed as an encouraging development. At least Union armies were closing in on Richmond. But casualties were appalling, and the human cost of Grant's campaign was becoming starkly evident. Each day, boats from Belle Plain arrived at Washington's wharves. "There are anguished faces among the avenues of spectators who form the lanes down which the sad processions move from each boat," the correspondent Noah Brooks reported. "Some are waiting for their own loved ones; others catch a glimpse of a maimed and battle-stained form, once so proud and manly, which they recognize as of their own flesh and blood. Many women and even men weep from sympathy and cannot see the silent suffering of these wounded braves unmoved. Night before last 3,000 severely wounded men were landed at the Sixth Street Wharf, and the sight will not soon be forgotten by those who witnessed it. The long, ghastly procession of shattered wrecks; the groups of tearful, sympathetic spectators; the rigid shapes of those who are bulletined as 'since dead;' the smoothly flowing river and the solemn hush in foreground and on distant evening shores—all form a picture which must some day perpetuate for the nation the saddest sight of the war." [47]

Many wounded Federals languished in Confederate hands. Newton Kirk—the wounded Michigan soldier who had been carried to a Confederate field hospital on May 14—remained several weeks at Spotsylvania Court House. "We had no surgeon or medicines, except water and lint," he recalled, "and hardly enough of provisions to sustain life." He took special interest in a young man from Vermont. A bullet had lodged in the boy's skull. Sometimes the youth laughed and sang in delirium, and once he imagined he was driving cows in a pasture near home, calling out for his little sister. He grew progressively weaker and died after ten days. Kirk's health improved, and fellow patients engaged him writing letters. "Of all the quaint expressions I ever heard," Kirk reminisced, "some of these, from the poor whites of the south, were the quaintest." He considered that he was treated on equal terms with wounded Confederates. "All feelings of enmity between the men of the blue and the gray are forgotten and we discussed the war, and the causes which led to it, and its probable outcome, with perfect good nature," he later wrote. Doctors finally adjudged Kirk well enough to travel, and on May 26 he was on his way to prison at Andersonville. His days with the Army of the Potomac were over.[48]

During the stormy night of May 26, while Kirk traveled south with other prisoners, weary soldiers in blue marched east along the Pamunkey. "Before long," Brooks had predicted, "another vigorous campaign will be opened." Grant indeed was on the move, and he was more confident than ever. Lee had failed to attack on May 21 and had let pass his advantage on May 24. "Lee's army is really whipped," Grant had written Halleck, and he believed it. The campaign had demonstrated the futility of assailing Lee's army in an entrenched position. But if Lee were truly defeated—and Grant saw the past week's events as conclusive on that point—perhaps the way lay open for a decisive battlefield victory. Thus ran the logic at Union headquarters. And thus was planted the seed of another tragedy.

Destiny waited at an obscure Virginia crossroads named Cold Harbor.

Appendix
The Order of Battle

ARMY OF THE POTOMAC
Major General George G. Meade

PROVOST GUARD
Brigadier General Marsena R. Patrick
1st Massachusetts Cavalry, Companies C and D
80th New York
3rd Pennsylvania Cavalry
68th Pennsylvania
114th Pennsylvania

ARTILLERY
Brigadier General Henry J. Hunt
RESERVE ARTILLERY [a]
Colonel Henry S. Burton

VOLUNTEER ENGINEER BRIGADE
Brigadier General Henry W. Benham

50TH NEW YORK ENGINEERS
Lieutenant Colonel Ira Spaulding

BATTALION U.S. ENGINEERS
Captain George H. Mendell

[a] Reserve artillery distributed among infantry corps May 16 and excess guns forwarded to Belle Plain.

2ND ARMY CORPS

Major General Winfield S. Hancock
1st Vermont Cavalry, Company M

1st Division
Brigadier General Francis C. Barlow

1st Brigade
Colonel Nelson A. Miles
26th Michigan
61st New York
81st Pennsylvania
140th Pennsylvania
183rd Pennsylvania

2nd Brigade
Colonel Thomas A. Smyth [a]
28th Massachusetts
63rd New York
69th New York
88th New York
116th Pennsylvania

3rd Brigade
Colonel Clinton D. MacDougall
39th New York
52nd New York
57th New York
111th New York
125th New York
126th New York

4th Brigade
Colonel John R. Brooke
2nd Delaware
64th New York
53rd Pennsylvania
145th Pennsylvania
148th Pennsylvania

2nd Division
Brigadier General John Gibbon

1st Brigade
Colonel H. Boyd McKeen
19th Maine
1st Company Sharpshooters
15th Massachusetts
19th Massachusetts
20th Massachusetts
7th Michigan
42nd New York
59th New York
82nd New York (2nd Militia)
36th Wisconsin [b]

2nd Brigade
Brigadier General Joshua T. Owen
152nd New York
69th Pennsylvania
71st Pennsylvania
72nd Pennsylvania
106th Pennsylvania

3rd Brigade
Colonel Samuel S. Carroll [c]
14th Connecticut
1st Delaware
14th Indiana
12th New Jersey
10th New York Battalion
108th New York
4th Ohio
8th Ohio
7th West Virginia

3rd Division
Major General David B. Birney

1st Brigade
Colonel Thomas W. Egan
20th Indiana
3rd Maine
40th New York
86th New York
124th New York
99th Pennsylvania
110th Pennsylvania
141st Pennsylvania
2nd U.S. Sharpshooters

2nd Brigade
Colonel John S. Crocker [e]
4th Maine
17th Maine
3rd Michigan
5th Michigan
93rd New York
57th Pennsylvania
63rd Pennsylvania
105th Pennsylvania
1st U. S. Sharpshooters

3rd Brigade
Brigadier General Gershom Mott [f]
1st Massachusetts
16th Massachusetts
5th New Jersey
6th New Jersey
7th New Jersey
8th New Jersey

4th Division
Brigadier General Robert O. Tyler [g]

1st Maine Heavy Artillery
1st Massachusetts Heavy Artillery
2nd New York Heavy Artillery
7th New York Heavy Artillery
8th New York Heavy Artillery

Artillery Brigade
Colonel John C. Tidball
Maine Light, 6th Battery (F)
Massachusetts Light, 10th Battery
New Hampshire Light, 1st Battery
1st New Jersey Light, Battery B [h]
1st New York Light, Battery G
4th New York Heavy, 3rd Battalion
New York Light, 11th Battery [i]
New York Light, 12th Battery [j]
1st Pennsylvania Light, Battery F
1st Rhode Island Light, Battery A
1st Rhode Island Light, Battery B
4th United States, Battery K
5th United States, Batteries C and I

4th Brigade
Colonel Mathew Murphy d
155th New York
164th New York
170th New York
182nd New York

4th Brigade
11th New Jersey
26th Pennsylvania
115th Pennsylvania

4th Brigade
Colonel William R. Brewster
11th Massachusetts
70th New York
71st New York
72nd New York
73rd New York
74th New York
120th New York
84th Pennsylvania

a Assigned May 17 to command 3rd Brigade, 2nd Division, of 2nd Corps. Replaced by Colonel Richard Byrnes.

b Arrived May 19.

c Wounded May 13, replaced May 17 by Colonel Thomas A. Smyth.

d Brigade arrived May 17. Murphy wounded May 18, replaced by Colonel James P. McIvor.

e Replaced by Colonel Elijah Walker on May 18. Colonel Byron R. Pierce commanded the brigade during operations May 23.

f Mott's division assigned as 3rd and 4th brigades of Birney's division May 13.

g Brigade arrived May 18.

h Transferred from artillery reserve May 16.

i Transferred from artillery reserve May 16.

j Transferred from artillery reserve May 16.

5TH ARMY CORPS

Major General Gouverneur K. Warren

1ST DIVISION

Brigadier General Charles Griffin

1st Brigade
Brigadier General Romeyn B. Ayres
140th New York
146th New York
91st Pennsylvania
155th Pennsylvania
2nd U.S., Companies B, C, F, H, I, and K
11th U.S., Companies B, C, D, F, and G, 1st Battalion
12th U.S., Companies A, B, C, D, and G
12th U.S., A, C, D, F, and H, 2nd Battalion
14th U.S., 1st Battalion
17th U.S., Companies A, C, D, G, and H, 1st Battalion
17th U.S., Companies A, B, and C, 2nd Battalion

2nd Brigade
Colonel Jacob B. Sweitzer
9th Massachusetts
22nd Massachusetts
32nd Massachusetts
4th Michigan
62nd Pennsylvania

3rd Brigade
Brigadier General Joseph J. Bartlett
20th Maine
18th Massachusetts
1st Michigan
16th Michigan
44th New York
83rd Pennsylvania
118th Pennsylvania

3RD DIVISION

Brigadier General Samuel W. Crawford

1st Brigade
Colonel Martin D. Hardin
1st Pennsylvania Reserves
2nd Pennsylvania Reserves
6th Pennsylvania Reserves
7th Pennsylvania Reserves
11th Pennsylvania Reserves
13th Pennsylvania Reserves

2nd Brigade
Colonel Richard Coulter[a]
12th Massachusetts
83rd New York
97th New York
11th Pennsylvania
88th Pennsylvania

3rd Brigade
Colonel Joseph W. Fisher
5th Pennsylvania Reserves
8th Pennsylvania Reserves
10th Pennsylvania Reserves
12th Pennsylvania Reserves

4TH DIVISION

Brigadier General Lysander Cutler

1st Brigade
Colonel William W. Robinson
7th Indiana
19th Indiana
24th Michigan
1st Battalion, New York Sharpshooters
2nd Wisconsin
6th Wisconsin
7th Wisconsin

2nd Brigade
Colonel Edward B. Fowler[b]
76th New York
84th New York
95th New York
147th New York
56th Pennsylvania

3rd Brigade
Colonel Edward S. Bragg
121st Pennsylvania
142nd Pennsylvania
143rd Pennsylvania
149th Pennsylvania
150th Pennsylvania

4th Brigade
Colonel Peter Lyle
16th Maine
13th Massachusetts
39th Massachusetts
104th New York
90th Pennsylvania
107th Pennsylvania[c]

Maryland Brigade

Colonel Richard N. Bowerman

1st Maryland
4th Maryland
7th Maryland
8th Maryland

Heavy Artillery Brigade

6th New York Heavy Artillery
15th New York Heavy Artillery (1st and
3rd Battalions)
4th New York Heavy Artillery (2nd Battalion)

Artillery Brigade

Colonel Charles S. Wainwright

Massachusetts Light, 3rd Battery (C)
Massachusetts Light, 5th Battery (E)
Massachusetts Light, 9th Battery[d]
1st New York Light, Battery B[e]
1st New York Light, Battery C[f]
1st New York Light, Battery D
1st New York Light, Batteries E and L
1st New York Light, Battery H
New York Light, 5th Battery[g]
New York Light, 15th Battery[h]
1st Pennsylvania Light, Battery B
4th United States, Battery B
5th United States, Battery D

[a] Coulter wounded May 18 and replaced by Colonel James L. Bates.
[b] Replaced May 21 by Colonel J. William Hofmann.
[c] Joined May 16.
[d] Transferred from Artillery Reserve May 16. The 5th New York Battery was sent to Washington May 19.
[e] Transferred from Artillery Reserve May 16.
[f] Transferred from Artillery Reserve May 16.
[g] Transferred from Artillery Reserve May 16. Sent to Washington May 19.
[h] Transferred from Artillery Reserve May 16.

6TH ARMY CORPS
Brigadier General Horatio G. Wright

1st Division
Brigadier General David A. Russell

1st Brigade
Colonel Henry W. Brown
1st New Jersey
2nd New Jersey
3rd New Jersey
4th New Jersey
10th New Jersey
15th New Jersey

2nd Brigade
Colonel Emory Upton
5th Maine
121st New York
95th Pennsylvania
96th Pennsylvania
2nd Connecticut Heavy Artillery [a]

3rd Brigade
Brigadier General Henry L. Eustis
6th Maine
49th Pennsylvania
119th Pennsylvania
5th Wisconsin

4th Brigade
Colonel Nelson Cross
65th New York
67th New York
122nd New York

2nd Division
Brigadier General Thomas H. Neill

82nd Pennsylvania

1st Brigade
Brigadier General Frank Wheaton
62nd New York
93rd Pennsylvania
98th Pennsylvania
102nd Pennsylvania
139th Pennsylvania

2nd Brigade
Brigadier General Lewis A. Grant
1st Vermont Heavy Artillery [b]
2nd Vermont
3rd Vermont
4th Vermont
5th Vermont
6th Vermont

3rd Brigade
Colonel Daniel D. Bidwell
7th Maine
43rd New York
49th New York
77th New York
61st Pennsylvania

4th Brigade
Colonel Oliver Edwards
7th Massachusetts
10th Massachusetts
37th Massachusetts
2nd Rhode Island

3rd Division
Brigadier General James B. Ricketts

1st Brigade
Colonel John W. Schall [c]
14th New Jersey
106th New York
151st New York
87th Pennsylvania
10th Vermont

2nd Brigade
Colonel Benjamin F. Smith
6th Maryland
110th Ohio
122nd Ohio
126th Ohio
67th Pennsylvania
138th Pennsylvania

Artillery Brigade
Colonel Charles H. Tompkins
Maine Light, 4th Battery (D)
Maine Light, 5th Battery (E) [d]
Massachusetts Light, 1st Battery (A)
1st New Jersey Light, Battery A [e]
New York Light, 1st Battery
New York Light, 3rd Battery
4th New York Heavy (1st Battalion)
1st Ohio Light, Battery H [f]
1st Rhode Island Light, Battery C

1st Rhode Island Light, Battery E

1st Rhode Island Light, Battery G

5th United States, Battery E[g]

5th United States, Battery M

[a] Arrived May 21.

[b] Arrived May 14.

[c] Replaced May 14 by Colonel William S. Truex.

[d] Transferred from Artillery Reserve May 16.

[e] Transferred from Artillery Reserve May 16.

[f] Transferred from Artillery Reserve May 16.

[g] Transferred from Artillery Reserve May 16.

CAVALRY CORPS
Major General Philip H. Sheridan

1ST DIVISION
Brigadier General Wesley Merritt[a]

1st Brigade
Brigadier General George A. Custer
1st Michigan
5th Michigan
6th Michigan
7th Michigan

2nd Brigade
Colonel Thomas C. Devin
4th New York
6th New York
9th New York
17th Pennsylvania

Reserve Brigade
Colonel Alfred Gibbs
19th New York
6th Pennsylvania
1st U.S.
2nd U.S.
5th U.S.

2ND DIVISION
Brigadier General David McM. Gregg

1st Brigade
Brigadier General Henry E. Davies, Jr.
1st Massachusetts
1st New Jersey
6th Ohio
1st Pennsylvania

2nd Brigade
Colonel J. Irvin Gregg
1st Maine
10th New York
2nd Pennsylvania
4th Pennsylvania
8th Pennsylvania
16th Pennsylvania

3RD DIVISION
Brigadier General James H. Wilson

1st Brigade
Colonel John B. McIntosh
1st Connecticut
2nd New York
5th New York[b]
18th Pennsylvania

2nd Brigade
Colonel George H. Chapman
3rd Indiana
8th New York
1st Vermont

HORSE ARTILLERY

1st Brigade Horse Artillery
Captain James M. Robertson
6th New York Battery
2nd U.S., Batteries B and L
2nd U.S., Battery D
2nd U.S., Battery M
4th U.S., Battery A
4th U.S., Batteries C and E

2nd Brigade Horse Artillery
Captain Dunbar R. Ransom
1st U.S., Batteries E and G
1st U.S., Batteries H and I
1st U.S., Battery K
2nd U.S., Battery A

[a] Substituted for Brigadier General Alfred T. A. Torbert, who was ill. Torbert returned to active duty May 17 and temporarily commanded the Union cavalry regiments remaining at Spotsylvania Court House. He resumed command of his division May 25, and Merritt returned to command the Reserve Brigade.
[b] Detached from Cavalry Corps and left at Spotsylvania Court House during Richmond raid.

9TH ARMY CORPS [a]
Major General Ambrose E. Burnside

1ST DIVISION
Major General Thomas L. Crittenden

1st Brigade
Brigadier General James H. Ledlie
35th Massachusetts
56th Massachusetts
57th Massachusetts
59th Massachusetts
4th U.S.
10th U.S.

2nd Brigade
Colonel Joseph M. Sudsburg
3rd Maryland
21st Massachusetts
100th Pennsylvania

Artillery
2nd Maine Battery (B)
14th Massachusetts Battery

2ND DIVISION
Brigadier General Robert B. Potter

1st Brigade
Colonel John I. Curtin
36th Massachusetts
58th Massachusetts
51st New York
45th Pennsylvania
48th Pennsylvania
7th Rhode Island

2nd Brigade
Colonel Simon G. Griffin
31st Maine
32nd Maine
6th New Hampshire
9th New Hampshire
11th New Hampshire
17th Vermont

Artillery
11th Massachusetts Battery
19th New York Battery

3RD DIVISION
Brigadier General Orlando B. Willcox

1st Brigade
Colonel John F. Hartranft
2nd Michigan
8th Michigan
17th Michigan
27th Michigan
109th New York
51st Pennsylvania

2nd Brigade
Colonel William Humphrey
1st Michigan Sharpshooters
20th Michigan
79th New York
60th Ohio
50th Pennsylvania

Artillery
7th Maine, Battery G
34th New York Battery

4TH DIVISION
Brigadier General Edward Ferrero

1st Brigade
Colonel Joshua K. Sigfried
27th U.S. Colored Troops
30th U.S. Colored Troops
39th U.S. Colored Troops
43rd U.S. Colored Troops

2nd Brigade
Colonel Henry G. Thomas
30th Connecticut (Colored)
19th U.S. Colored Troops
23rd U.S. Colored Troops

Artillery
Pennsylvania Independent Battery D
3rd Vermont Battery

Cavalry
3rd New Jersey
22nd New York
2nd Ohio
13th Pennsylvania

Provisional Brigade
Colonel Elisha G. Marshall
2nd New York Mounted Rifles (Dismounted)
14th New York Heavy Artillery
24th New York Cavalry (Dismounted)
2nd Pennsylvania Provisional Heavy Artillery

---

[a] The 9th Corps operated as an independent army until May 24, when it was incorporated into the Army of the Potomac.

ARMY OF NORTHERN VIRGINIA
General Robert E. Lee

1ST ARMY CORPS
Major General Richard H. Anderson

FIELD'S DIVISION
Major General Charles W. Field

Jenkins's Brigade
Colonel John Bratton
1st South Carolina
2nd South Carolina
5th South Carolina
6th South Carolina
Palmetto Sharpshooters

Gregg's Brigade
Brigadier General John Gregg
3rd Arkansas
1st Texas
4th Texas
5th Texas

Law's Brigade
Brigadier General E. McIver Law[a]
4th Alabama
15th Alabama
44th Alabama
47th Alabama
48th Alabama

Anderson's Brigade
Brigadier General George T. Anderson
7th Georgia
8th Georgia
9th Georgia
11th Georgia
59th Georgia

PICKETT'S DIVISION[b]
Major General George E. Pickett

Kemper's Brigade
Colonel William R. Terry
1st Virginia
3rd Virginia
7th Virginia
11th Virginia
24th Virginia

Hunton's Brigade[c]
Brigadier General Eppa Hunton
8th Virginia
19th Virginia
25th Virginia Battalion (City Battalion)
32nd Virginia
56th Virginia
42nd Virginia Cavalry Battalion

Barton's Brigade
Brigadier General Seth M. Barton[d]
9th Virginia
14th Virginia
38th Virginia
53rd Virginia
57th Virginia

Corse's Brigade
Brigadier General Montgomery D. Corse
15th Virginia
17th Virginia
18th Virginia

ARTILLERY
Brigadier General E. Porter Alexander

Haskell's Battalion
Major John C. Haskell
Flanner's (North Carolina) Battery
Garden's (South Carolina) Battery
Lamkin's (Virginia) Battery
Ramsay's (North Carolina) Battery

Huger's Battalion
Lieutenant Colonel Frank Huger
Fickling's (South Carolina) Battery
Moody's (Louisiana) Battery
Parker's (Virginia) Battery
Smith's (Virginia) Battery
Taylor's (Virginia) Battery
Woolfolk's (Virginia) Battery

Cabell's Battalion
Colonel Henry C. Cabell
Callaway's (Georgia) Battery
Carlton's (Georgia) Battery
McCarthy's (Virginia) Battery
Manly's (North Carolina) Battery

KERSHAW'S DIVISION
Brigadier General Joseph B. Kershaw

Kershaw's Brigade
Colonel John W. Henagan
2nd South Carolina
3rd South Carolina
7th South Carolina
8th South Carolina
15th South Carolina
3rd South Carolina Battalion

Humphreys's Brigade
Brigadier General Benjamin G. Humphreys
13th Mississippi
17th Mississippi
18th Mississippi
21st Mississippi

Wofford's Brigade
Brigadier General William T. Wofford
16th Georgia
18th Georgia
24th Georgia
Cobb's (Georgia) Legion
Phillip's (Georgia) Legion
3rd Georgia Battalion Sharpshooters

Bryan's Brigade
Brigadier General Goode Bryan
10th Georgia
50th Georgia
51st Georgia
53rd Georgia

Benning's Brigade
Colonel Dudley M. DuBose

2nd Georgia	
15th Georgia	
17th Georgia	
20th Georgia	
29th Virginia	
30th Virginia	

[a] Colonel William F. Perry commanded Law's brigade from the opening of the campaign until approximately May 18, when Law returned.

[b] Three of Pickett's four brigades returned to the Army of Northern Virginia from May 21 through May 23.

[c] Hunton's brigade remained near Richmond.

[d] During the North Anna operations, Colonel Birkett D. Fry commanded Barton's brigade.

2ND ARMY CORPS
Lieutenant General Richard S. Ewell

RODES'S DIVISION
Major General Robert E. Rodes

Daniel's Brigade
Brigadier General Bryan Grimes
32nd North Carolina
43rd North Carolina
45th North Carolina
53rd North Carolina
2nd North Carolina battalion

Ramseur's Brigade
Brigadier General Stephen D. Ramseur
1st North Carolina[e]
2nd North Carolina
3rd North Carolina[f]
4th North Carolina
14th North Carolina
30th North Carolina

Battle's Brigade
Brigadier General Cullen A. Battle
3rd Alabama
5th Alabama
6th Alabama
12th Alabama
26th Alabama
61st Alabama

Doles's Brigade
Brigadier General George Doles
4th Georgia
12th Georgia
44th Georgia

GORDON'S DIVISION[a]
Brigadier General John B. Gordon[b]

Pegram's Brigade
Colonel John S. Hoffman
13th Virginia
31st Virginia
49th Virginia
52nd Virginia
58th Virginia

Johnston's Brigade
Colonel Thomas F. Toon
5th North Carolina
12th North Carolina
20th North Carolina
23rd North Carolina

Evans's Brigade
Colonel Clement A. Evans
13th Georgia
26th Georgia
31st Georgia
38th Georgia
60th Georgia
61st Georgia

Louisiana Brigade
Colonel Zebulon York
1st Louisiana
2nd Louisiana
5th Louisiana
6th Louisiana

ARTILLERY
Brigadier General Armistead L. Long

Braxton's Battalion
Lieutenant Colonel Carter M. Braxton
Carpenter's (Virginia) Battery
Cooper's (Virginia) Battery
Hardwicke's (Virginia) Battery

Nelson's Battalion
Lieutenant Colonel William Nelson
Kirkpatrick's (Virginia) Battery
Massie's (Virginia) Battery
Milledge's (Georgia) Battery

Page's Battalion
Major Richard C. M. Page
W. P. Carter's (Virginia) Battery
Fry's (Virginia) Battery
Page's (Virginia) Battery
Reese's (Alabama) Battery

Cutshaw's Battalion
Major Wilfred E. Cutshaw
Carrington's (Virginia) Battery
W. Garber's (Virginia) Battery
Tanner's (Virginia) Battery

Hardaway's Battalion
Lieutenant Colonel Robert A. Hardaway
Dance's (Virginia) Battery
Graham's (Virginia) Battery
B. Griffin's (Virginia) Battery
Jones's (Virginia) Battery
B. H. Smith's (Virginia) Battery

7th Louisiana
8th Louisiana
9th Louisiana
10th Louisiana
14th Louisiana
15th Louisiana

Terry's Brigade[c]
Brigadier General William Terry
2nd Virginia
4th Virginia
5th Virginia
21st Virginia
23rd Virginia
25th Virginia
27th Virginia
33rd Virginia
37th Virginia
42nd Virginia
44th Virginia
48th Virginia
50th Virginia

Hoke's Brigade[d]
Lieutenant Colonel William G. Lewis
6th North Carolina
21st North Carolina
54th North Carolina
57th North Carolina
1st North Carolina Battalion

[a] On May 21, Jubal A. Early returned to the 2nd Corps and resumed command of his division, consisting of Pegram's, Johnston's, and Evans's brigades. Gordon then assumed command of the units formerly under Major General Edward Johnson, consisting of Terry's and York's brigades.

[b] Promoted to major general on May 14.

[c] Formally constituted on May 21 to include Virginia regiments from the Stonewall Brigade, Jones's Brigade, and Steuart's Brigade, all of which took severe losses on May 12.

[d] Hoke's Brigade rejoined the Army of Northern Virginia on May 21 and was assigned to Early's division. See note a.

[e] Formerly from Steuart's Brigade.

[f] Formerly from Steuart's Brigade.

3rd ARMY CORPS
Lieutenant General Ambrose P. Hill[a]

MAHONE'S DIVISION
Brigadier General William Mahone

Sanders's Brigade
Colonel John C. C. Sanders
8th Alabama
9th Alabama
10th Alabama
11th Alabama
14th Alabama

Mahone's Brigade
Colonel David A. Weisiger
6th Virginia
12th Virginia
16th Virginia
41st Virginia
61st Virginia

Harris's Brigade
Brigadier General Nathaniel H. Harris
12th Mississippi
16th Mississippi
19th Mississippi
48th Mississippi

Perry's Brigade
Brigadier General Edward A. Perry
2nd Florida
5th Florida
8th Florida

HETH'S DIVISION
Major General Henry Heth

Davis's Brigade
Brigadier General Joseph R. Davis
2nd Mississippi
11th Mississippi
26th Mississippi
42nd Mississippi
55th North Carolina

Cooke's Brigade
Brigadier General John R. Cooke
15th North Carolina
27th North Carolina
46th North Carolina
48th North Carolina

Mayo's Brigade
Colonel Robert M. Mayo
40th Virginia
47th Virginia
55th Virginia
22nd Virginia battalion
13th Alabama
1st Tennessee (Provisional)
7th Tennessee
14th Tennessee

Kirkland's Brigade
Brigadier General William W. Kirkland
11th North Carolina
26th North Carolina

WILCOX'S DIVISION
Major General Cadmus M. Wilcox

Lane's Brigade
Brigadier General James H. Lane
7th North Carolina
18th North Carolina
28th North Carolina
33rd North Carolina
37th North Carolina

McGowan's Brigade[b]
Colonel Joseph N. Brown
1st South Carolina (Provisional)
12th South Carolina
13th South Carolina
14th South Carolina
1st South Carolina (Orr's Rifles)

Scales's Brigade
Brigadier General Alfred M. Scales[c]
13th North Carolina
16th North Carolina
22nd North Carolina
34th North Carolina
38th North Carolina

Thomas's Brigade
Brigadier General Edward L. Thomas
14th Georgia
35th Georgia
45th Georgia
49th Georgia

ARTILLERY
Colonel R. Lindsay Walker

Poague's Battalion
Lieutenant Colonel William T. Poague
Richard's (Mississippi) Battery
Utterback's (Virginia) Battery
Williams's (North Carolina) Battery
Wyatt's (Virginia) Battery

Pegram's Battalion
Lieutenant Colonel William J. Pegram
Brander's (Virginia) Battery
Cayce's (Virginia) Battery
Ellet's (Virginia) Battery
Marye's (Virginia) Battery
Zimmerman's (South Carolina) Battery

McIntosh's Battalion
Lieutenant Colonel David G. McIntosh
Clutter's (Virginia) Battery
Donald's (Virginia) Battery
Hurt's (Alabama) Battery
Price's (Virginia) Battery

Richardson's Battalion
Lieutenant Colonel Charles Richardson
Grandy's (Virginia) Battery
Landry's (Louisiana) Battery

BRECKINRIDGE'S DIVISION[d]
Major General John C. Breckinridge

Echols's Brigade
Brigadier General John Echols
22nd Virginia
23rd Virginia
26th Virginia Battalion

Wharton's Brigade
Brigadier General Gabriel C. Wharton
30th Virginia Battalion
51st Virginia
62nd Virginia (Mounted)

McLaughlin's Artillery Battalion
Major William McLaughlin
Chapman's (Virginia) Battery
Jackson's (Virginia) Battery

Maryland Line[e]
Colonel Bradley T. Johnson
2nd Maryland
1st Maryland Cavalry
1st Maryland Battery
2nd Maryland Battery
4th Maryland Battery

Wright's Brigade
Brigadier General Ambrose R. Wright
3rd Georgia
22nd Georgia
48th Georgia
2nd Georgia Battalion
10th Georgia Battalion

44th North Carolina
47th North Carolina
52nd North Carolina

Moore's (Virginia) Battery
Penick's (Virginia) Battery

Cutt's Battalion
Colonel Allen S. Cutts
Patterson's (Georgia) Battery
Ross's (Georgia) Battery
Wingfield's (Georgia) Battery

[a] On sick leave from May 8 through May 21, Major General Jubal A. Early substituting.
[b] Captured May 23.
[c] Ill during much of the campaign, brigade frequently led by Colonel William L. Lowrance.
[d] Joined Army of Northern Virginia May 22.
[e] Temporarily placed under Breckinridge May 22.

Cavalry Corps
Major General James E. B. Stuart[a]

HAMPTON'S DIVISION
Major General Wade Hampton

Young's Brigade
Brigadier General Pierce M. B. Young
7th Georgia
Cobb's (Georgia) Legion
Phillips's (Georgia) Legion
Jeff Davis (Mississippi) Legion

Rosser's Brigade
Brigadier General Thomas L. Rosser
7th Virginia
11th Virginia
12th Virginia
35th Virginia

Butler's Brigade[b]
Brigadier General Matthew C. Butler
4th South Carolina
5th South Carolina
6th South Carolina

FITZHUGH LEE'S DIVISION
Major General Fitzhugh Lee

Lomax's Brigade
Brigadier General Lunsford L. Lomax
5th Virginia
6th Virginia
15th Virginia

Wickham's Brigade
Brigadier General Williams C. Wickham
1st Virginia
2nd Virginia
3rd Virginia
4th Virginia

WILLIAM H. F. LEE'S DIVISION
Major General William H. F. Lee

Chambliss's Brigade
Brigadier General John R. Chambliss
9th Virginia
10th Virginia
13th Virginia

Gordon's Brigade
Brigadier General James B. Gordon[c]
1st North Carolina
2nd North Carolina
5th North Carolina

HORSE ARTILLERY
Major R. Preston Chew

Breathed's Battalion
Major James Breathed
Hart's (South Carolina) Battery
Johnston's (Virginia) Battery
McGregor's (Virginia) Battery
Shoemaker's (Virginia) Battery
Thomson's (Virginia) Battery

[a] Mortally wounded May 11. Not replaced during campaign.
[b] Elements from Butler's brigade began reaching the Army of Northern Virginia May 20.
[c] Mortally wounded May 13, succeeded by Colonel Clinton M. Andrews.

Notes

ACKNOWLEDGMENTS

1. Jedediah Hotchkiss to William W. Blackford, August 10, 1898, in Jedediah Hotchkiss Collection, LC.

INTRODUCTION

1. P. J. Staudenraus, ed., *Mr. Lincoln's Washington: Selections from the Writings of Noah Brooks Civil War Correspondent* (South Brunswick, N.J., 1967), 317.

2. Noah Brooks, *Washington in Lincoln's Time* (New York, 1958), 137; Ulysses S. Grant to Henry W. Halleck, May 11, 1864, in *OR*, Vol. 36, Pt. 2, p. 627.

3. *New York Tribune*, May 12, 13, 1864. The press's reaction to the Wilderness and Spotsylvania Court House battles is summarized by Brooks D. Simpson, "Great Expectations: Ulysses S. Grant, the Northern Press, and the Opening of the Wilderness Campaign," in Gary W. Gallagher, ed., *The Wilderness Campaign* (Chapel Hill, 1997), 1–35.

4. Staudenraus, *Mr. Lincoln's Washington*, 317.

5. Thomas G. Mackenzie's report, in *OR*, Vol. 36, Pt. 1, p. 273; Alfred Thompson to Emma, May 23, 1864, in Jay Luvaas Collection, USAMHI. Wagons initially crossed the Rappahannock on a dilapidated ferry that carried one vehicle at a time. Union engineers completed a four-hundred-foot pontoon bridge late on May 10; Daniel Brewster Sayre to mother, June 3, 1864, in Book 39, FSNMP.

6. W. T. G. Morton, "The First Use of Ether as an Anesthetic at the Battle of the Wilderness in the Civil War," *Journal of the American Medical Association* (April 23, 1904), 1069.

7. Ibid.; *New York Evening Post*, May 16, 1864; George T. Stevens, *Three Years in the Sixth Corps* (Albany, N.Y., 1866), 340–1; Daniel A. Hardy to wife, May 13, 1864, in Book 119, FSNMP.

8. Thomas A. McParlin's report, in *OR*, Vol. 36, Pt. 1, p. 230–1; Morton, "First Use of Ether," 1070; Nathaniel Bunker memoir, CL.

9. *New York Evening Post*, May 16, 1864; William Landon to Friend Greene, May 18, 1864,

in "Documents: Fourteenth Indiana Regiment, Letters to the Vincennes Western Sun," *Indiana Magazine of History,* 34 (1938), 91–2.

10. Morton, "First Use of Ether," 1070.

11. Ibid.

12. Newton T. Kirk reminiscences, in MSU.

13. Ibid.; J. W. Bone reminiscences, in Lowry Shuford Collection, NCDAH; George Neese, *Three Years in the Confederate Horse Artillery* (New York, 1911), 268.

14. Nick to editor, May 10, 1864, *Raleigh (N.C.) Daily Confederate,* May 25, 1864; Austin C. Dobbins, ed., *Grandfather's Journal: Company B, 16th Mississippi Infantry Volunteers, Harris' Brigade, Mahone's Division, Hill's Corps, A.N.V.* (Dayton, 1988), 196.

15. "Interesting from the 36th Regiment," *Milwaukee Daily Sentinel,* May 25, 1864.

I MAY 13 GRANT LAYS NEW PLANS

1. Theodore Lyman journal, May 12–13, 1864, in Theodore Lyman Collection, MHS; Regis De Trobriand, *Four Years with the Army of the Potomac* (Boston, 1889), 688.

2. Cyrus B. Comstock, *The Diary of Cyrus B. Comstock,* ed. Merlin E. Sumner (Dayton, 1987), 267; Lyman journal, May 12, 1864, in Lyman Collection, MHS. The Armstrong house still stands. Photographs and some of the home's history are in "And on This Farm They Had a House," *Fredericksburg (Va.) Free Lance-Star,* August 9, 1991.

3. *New York Herald,* April 1, 1864.

4. Josiah M. Favill, *The Diary of a Young Officer Serving with the Armies of the United States During the War of the Rebellion* (Chicago, 1909), 261. An engaging modern portrait of Meade appears in John J. Hennessy, "I Dread the Spring: The Army of the Potomac Prepares for the Overland Campaign," in Gallagher, ed., *Wilderness Campaign,* 67–70.

5. Allan Nevins, ed., *Diary of Battle: The Personal Journals of Colonel Charles S. Wainwright,* 1861–1865 (New York, 1962), 338; Wells B. Fox, *What I Remember of the Great Rebellion* (Lansing, Mich., 1892), 70.

6. Ulysses S. Grant's report, in *OR,* Vol. 36, Pt. 1, p. 14.

7. Ibid., 15–16. Details of Grant's plan of campaign are discussed in Gordon C. Rhea, *The Battle of the Wilderness: May 5–6, 1864* (Baton Rouge, 1994), 46–9.

8. Grant to Edwin M. Stanton, September 11, 1864, in *OR,* Vol. 42, Pt. 2, p. 783; John C. Ropes, "Grant's Campaign in Virginia in 1864," *PMHSM,* 4, 372–75; Martin T. McMahon, "From Gettysburg to the Coming of Grant," *B&L,* 4, pp. 91–92.

9. George Breck to family, May 13, 1864, *Rochester (N.Y.) Union and Advertiser,* May 18, 1864. Union casualties are reviewed in Gordon C. Rhea, *The Battles for Spotsylvania Court House and the Road to Yellow Tavern: May 7–12, 1864* (Baton Rouge, 1997), 319.

10. Grant's report, in *OR,* Vol. 36, Pt. 1, p. 18; Meade to wife, May 19, 1864, in George G. Meade Collection, HSP; Isaac R. Pennypacker, *General Meade* (New York, 1901), 296; Grant to Stanton, May 13, 1864, in *OR,* Vol. 36, Pt. 2, p. 695.

11. Horace Porter, *Campaigning with Grant* (New York, 1897), 108; Meade to John A. Rawlins, June 21, 1864, in Meade Collection, HSP; Lyman journal, May 10, 1864, in Lyman Collection, MHS; Charles A. Whittier reminiscences, in Boston Public Library. A recounting of Warren's activities through May 12, 1864, appears in Gordon C. Rhea, "The Testing of a Corps Commander: Gouverneur Kemble Warren at the Wilderness and Spotsylvania," in Gary W. Gallagher, ed., *The Spotsylvania Campaign* (Chapel Hill, N.C., 1998).

12. Morris Schaff, *The Battle of the Wilderness* (Boston, 1910), 201.

13. Grant to Henry Halleck, May 12, 1864, in *OR,* Vol. 36, Pt. 2, p. 652; Grant to wife, May 13, 1864, in John Y. Simon, ed., *The Papers of Ulysses S. Grant,* vol. 10 (Carbondale, Ill. 1967–1999), 443–4; Meade to wife, May 13, 1864, in Meade Collection, HSP; Circular, May 13, 1864, in *OR,* Vol. 36, Pt. 1, p. 197.

14. Robert E. Lee to Jefferson Davis, June 10, 1863, in Clifford Dowdey, ed., *The Wartime Papers of R. E. Lee* (New York, 1961), 508; James Longstreet to Alexander R. Lawton, March 5, 1864, in *OR,* Vol. 32, Pt. 3, p. 588.

15. *Augusta (Ga.) Constitutionalist,* January 2, 1864; John C. Waugh, *Reelecting Lincoln: The Battle for the 1864 Presidency* (New York, 1997), 149–51.

16. Francis Marion Welchel to family, April 26, 1864, in Book 81, FSNMP. Attitudes in Lee's army are deftly traced in J. Tracy Power, *Lee's Miserables: Life in the Army of Northern Virginia from the Wilderness to Appomattox* (Chapel Hill, 1998), and Gary W. Gallagher, "Our Hearts Are Full of Hope: The Army of Northern Virginia in the Spring of 1864," in Gallagher, ed., *Wilderness Campaign,* 36–65.

17. Developments on Pickett's and Beauregard's fronts are summarized in Douglas Southall Freeman, *R. E. Lee,* vol. 3 (New York, 1934–1935), 332–4, and in Clifford Dowdey, *Lee's Last Campaign: The Story of Lee and His Men Against Grant, 1864* (New York, 1960), 226–34.

18. Davis to Lee, May 13, 1864, in *OR,* Vol. 51, Pt. 2, p. 926.

19. Lee to Davis, April 15, 1864, ibid., Vol. 33, 1282–3.

20. Charles M. Blackford to wife, May 19, 1864, in Susan Leigh Blackford, comp., *Letters from Lee's Army: or, Memories of Life in and out of the Army in Virginia During the War Between the States* (New York, 1947), 246; Susan P. Lee, *Memoirs of William Nelson Pendleton, D.D.* (Philadelphia, 1893), 332. An analysis of Lee's strength on May 13 appears in Rhea, *Battles for Spotsylvania Court House,* 324.

21. The 1st Corps's third division—George Pickett's outfit—was scattered in southern Virginia and North Carolina.

22. Walter A. Montgomery, *The Days of Old and the Years That Are Past* (Raleigh, N.C., n.d.), 28; Terry L. Jones, ed., *The Civil War Memoirs of Captain William J. Seymour: Reminiscences of a Louisiana Tiger* (Baton Rouge, 1991), 125; William Allan, "Memoranda of Conversations with Lee," in SHC.

23. John O. Casler, *Four Years in the Stonewall Brigade* (Girard, Kans., 1906), 331.

24. Lee to George Washington Custis Lee, April 9, 1864, in Dowdey, ed., *Wartime Papers of R. E. Lee,* 695–6.

25. *Boston Evening Transcript,* May 12, 1864.

26. Lee to Davis, May 13, 1864, in *OR,* Vol. 51, Pt. 2, p. 925.

27. Davis to Lee, May 13, 1864, ibid., 926.

28. Lemuel A. Abbott to family, May 13, 1864, in Lemuel A. Abbott, *Personal Recollections and Civil War Diary 1864* (Burlington, Vt., 1908), 58–9; Letter from correspondent, May 16, 1864, in *Providence (R.I.) Evening Press,* May 24, 1864; Philip Cheek and Mair Pointon, *History of the Sauk County Riflemen, Known as Company A, Sixth Wisconsin Veteran Volunteer Infantry, 1861–1865* (Madison, Wisc., 1909), 98.

29. Charles Seiser, ed., "August Seiser's Civil War Diary," in *Rochester Historical Society Publication,* 22 (1844), 192; Horatio N. Warren, *Two Reunions of the 142d Regiment, Pa. Vols.* (Buffalo, 1890), 30–1; Russell C. White, ed., *The Civil War Diary of Wyman S. White, First Sergeant of Company F, 2nd United States Sharpshooter Regiment, 1861–1865* (Baltimore, Md., 1991), 242–3.

30. Abbott to family, May 13, 1864, in Abbott, *Personal Recollections,* 28.

31. David E. Holt, *A Mississippi Rebel in the Army of Northern Virginia,* ed. Thomas D. Cockrell and Michael B. Ballard (Baton Rouge, 1996), 263–4.

32. Robert T. Coles, *From Huntsville to Appomattox,* ed. Jeffrey D. Stocker (Knoxville, 1996), 170; G. Moxley Sorrel journal, May 13, 1864, in MC; Walter R. Battle to mother, May 14, 1864, in Laura Elizabeth Lee, ed., *Forget-Me-Nots of the Civil War: A Romance, Containing Reminiscences and Original Letters of Two Confederate Soldiers* (St. Louis, 1909), 116; E. A. Shiver, "Wright's Brigade at Spotsylvania Court House," *Atlanta Journal,* October 16, 1901; Eugene M. Ott Jr., "The Civil War Diary of James J. Kirkpatrick, Sixteenth Mississippi Infantry, C.S.A." (M.A. thesis, Texas A&M University, 1984), 194; Charles B. Jones, "Historical Sketch of 55th NC Inf.," *Our Living and Our Dead,* April 8, 1874, 1–2.

33. Horatio G. Wright to Andrew A. Humphreys, May 13, 1864, in *OR,* Vol. 36, Pt. 2, p. 724; Humphreys to Winfield S. Hancock, May 13, 1864, ibid., p. 702; Hancock to Humphreys, May 13, 1864, ibid.; Hancock to Humphreys, May 13, 1864, ibid., p. 703; Ulysses S. Grant, *Personal Memoirs of U. S. Grant,* vol. 2 (New York, 1885), 234.

34. R. C. White, *Civil War Diary,* 243–4.

35. Washington A. Roebling's report, 37–8, in Gouverneur K. Warren Collection, NYSLA; William H. Powell, *History of the Fifth Army Corps* (New York, 1896), 650; Arthur A. Kent, ed., *Three Years with Company K: Sergt. Austin C. Stearns, Company K, 13th Massachusetts Infantry* (Rutherford, N.J., 1976), 267; J. L. Smith, *History of the Corn Exchange Regiment: 118th Pennsylvania Volunteers, from Their First Engagement at Antietam to Appomattox* (Philadelphia, 1888), 423; George Lockley diary, May 13, 1864, in George Lockley Collection, BL.

36. Roebling's report, in Warren Collection, NYSLA; Amos M. Judson, *History of the Eighty-Third Regiment Pennsylvania Volunteers* (Erie, Pa., 1865), 205; Warren to Humphreys, in *OR,* Vol. 36, Pt. 2, p. 713; Grant's endorsement, on Samuel W. Crawford to Warren, May 13, 1864, ibid., 715–16.

37. Charles W. Cowtan, *Services of the Tenth New York Volunteers (National Zouaves) in the War of the Rebellion* (New York, 1882), 270. According to some accounts Carroll took his own brigade as well as Owen's. The reason for Owen's absence is unclear. Some sources state that he was under arrest, although they do not specify his transgression; Thomas M. Aldrich, *The History of Battery A, First Regiment Rhode Island Light Artillery in the War to Preserve the Union 1861–1865* (Providence, 1904), 327–8. He was later mustered out of service for disobeying orders on May 18 and on June 3; *OR,* Vol. 36, Pt. 1, 435–6. Another source claims that Owen's horse was shot from under him on May 12, throwing him heavily on the ground, and that he was in hospital on May 13; "Another Account," *Philadelphia Inquirer,* May 17, 1864.

38. Aldrich, *History of Battery A,* 328; William P. Shreve, "The Operations of the Army of the Potomac May 13–June 2 1864," in *PMHSM,* 4, 292; Winfield S. Hancock to Humphreys, May 13, 1864, in *OR,* Vol. 36, Pt. 2, p. 703; Hancock to Humphreys, May 13, 1864, ibid., 704.

39. Grant to Meade, May 13, 1864, in *OR,* Vol. 36, Pt. 2, p. 698; "Lee Retreating Toward Gordonsville," *New York Times,* May 14, 1864; Charles A. Dana to Stanton, May 13, 1864, in *OR,* Vol. 36, Pt. 1, p. 69; William Foster to Kate, May 13, 1864, in William Foster Papers, WRHS.

40. Grant to Meade, May 13, 1864, in *OR,* Vol. 36, Pt. 2, p. 698; Circular, May 13, 1864, ibid., 705; Warren to Seth Williams, May 13, 1864, ibid., 717; Roebling's report, in Warren Collection, NYSLA; Isaac Hall, *History of the Ninety-Seventh Regiment New York Volunteers (Conkling Rifles) in the War for the Union* (Utica, N.Y., 1890), 186; Wright to Humphreys, May 13, 1864, in *OR,* Vol. 36, Pt. 2, p. 726; Hancock to Humphreys, May 13, 1864, ibid., 706–7;

John D. Smith, *The History of the Nineteenth Regiment of Maine Volunteer Infantry, 1862–1865* (Minneapolis, Minn., 1909), 161.

41. Dana to Stanton, May 13, 1864, in *OR,* Vol. 36, Pt. 1, p. 69.

42. Charles J. Mills to mother, May 20, 1864, in Gregory A. Coco, ed., *Through Blood and Fire: The Civil War Letters of Major Charles J. Mills, 1862–1865* (Lanham, Md., 1982), 87; Committee of the Regiment, *History of the Thirty-Sixth Regiment Massachusetts Volunteers* (Boston, 1884), 172. The 6th Corps completed its deployment during the morning, Brigadier General James B. Ricketts's division forming along Brock Road, abutting Warren; Brigadier General David A. Russell's division deploying on Ricketts's left, near the Shelton house; and Brigadier General Thomas H. Neill's division bivouacking north of the Bloody Angle. In the 9th Corps, Brigadier General Robert B. Potter's division held Burnside's right, Major General Thomas L. Crittenden the center, and Brigadier General Orlando B. Willcox the left. Colonel Elisha G. Marshall's Provisional Brigade jutted forward on Fredericksburg Road to guard against a Confederate attack. Aside from Carroll's foray, the 2nd Corps's chief activity involved capturing two Confederate artillery pieces marooned between the armies. Soldiers from the 140th Pennsylvania and 20th Massachusetts viewed taking the guns as a personal challenge. A detachment crawled close to the pieces, then dragged them back while their compatriots fired to distract the Confederates. Robert L. Stewart, *History of the One Hundred and Fortieth Regiment Pennsylvania Volunteers* (Philadelphia, 1912), 199; Richard F. Miller and Robert F. Mooney, comps., *The Civil War: The Nantucket Experience, Including the Memoirs of Josiah Fitch Murphey* (Nantucket, Mass., 1994), 103.

43. Francis Cordrey manuscript, in Scott C. Patchen Private Collection; Henry Keiser diary, May 13, 1864, in Harrisburg Civil War Round Table Collection, USAMHI; Charles H. Brewster to Mary, May 13, 1864, in David W. Blight, ed., *When This Cruel War Is Over: The Civil War Letters of Charles Harvery Brewster* (Amherst, Mass., 1992), 296; William S. Tyler, ed., *Recollections of the Civil War by Mason Whiting Tyler* (New York, 1912), 196, 203; David R. Larned to sister, May 13, 1864, in David R. Larned Collection, LC; Lyman Jackman and Amos Hadley, eds., *History of the Sixth New Hampshire Regiment in the War for the Union* (Concord, N.H., 1891), 247; Committee of the Regiment, *Thirty-Sixth Regiment Massachusetts Volunteers,* 172; Allen D. Albert, *History of the Forty-Fifth Regiment Pennsylvania Veteran Volunteer Infantry, 1861–1865* (Williamsport, Pa., 1912), 129; Committee of the Regiment, *History of the Thirty-Fifth Regiment Massachusetts Volunteers* (Boston, 1884), 230.

44. John R. Brinkle to sister, May 13, 1864, in John R. Brinkle Collection, LC; Martha Derby Perry, comp., *Letters from a Surgeon of the Civil War* (Boston, 1906), 175; Samuel L. Foust diary, May 13, 1864, in FSNMP; Alfred S. Roe, *The Thirty-Ninth Regiment Massachusetts Volunteers, 1862–1865* (Worcester, Mass., 1914), 198; Rufus R. Dawes, *Service with the Sixth Wisconsin Volunteers* (Marietta, Ohio, 1890), 269; Seiser, "Civil War Diary," 192; George L. Prescott to family, May 13, 1864, in George L. Prescott Papers, MHS; Letter from correspondent, May 16, 1864, in *Providence (R.I.) Evening Press,* May 24, 1864; John D. Vautier, *History of the 88th Pennsylvania Volunteers in the War for the Union, 1861–1865* (Philadelphia, 1894), 185.

45. Kirk reminiscences, in MSU; Holt, *Mississippi Rebel,* 263–4; Willie Walker Caldwell, *Stonewall Jim: A Biography of General James A. Walker, C.S.A.* (Elliston, Va., 1990), 111–12; Margaretta Barton Colt, *Defend the Valley: A Shenandoah Family in the Civil War* (New York, 1994), 314.

46. P. T. Bennett, "General Junius Daniel," *SHSP,* 18, 346–7.

47. Warren to Meade, May 13, 1864, in *OR,* Vol. 36, Pt. 2, p. 718; Andrew A. Humphreys, *The Virginia Campaign of '64 and '65* (New York, 1883), 106.

48. Humphreys, *Virginia Campaign,* 106.

49. Special Orders, 5:45 P.M., May 13, 1864, in *OR,* Vol. 36, Pt. 2, p. 700; Grant to Burnside, 6:20 P.M., May 13, 1864, 731.

II MAY 12–13 *SHERIDAN THREATENS RICHMOND AND ESCAPES AT MEADOW BRIDGE*

1. Roy Morris Jr., *Sheridan: The Life and Wars of General Phil Sheridan* (New York, 1992), 1; Philip H. Sheridan, *Personal Memoirs of P. H. Sheridan,* vol. 1 (New York, 1888), 346–7.

2. Henry E. Davies, *General Sheridan* (New York, 1895), 93; Lyman to family, April 13, 1864, in Lyman Collection, MHS; Porter, *Campaigning with Grant,* 24.

3. The evolution of Sheridan's relationship with Meade and Sheridan's difficulties during the early days of the Overland Campaign are detailed in Gordon C. Rhea, "Union Cavalry in the Wilderness: The Education of Philip H. Sheridan and James H. Wilson," in Gallagher, ed., *Wilderness Campaign,* 106–30.

4. James H. Wilson, *Under the Old Flag,* vol. 1 (New York, 1912), 378; Humphreys, *Virginia Campaign,* 14; Philip H. Sheridan's report, in *OR,* Vol. 36, Pt. 1, p. 787.

5. Porter, *Campaigning with Grant,* 83–4.

6. Sheridan, *Personal Memoirs,* 1, pp. 368–9. Details of the campaign leading up to Yellow Tavern are described in Rhea, *Battles for Spotsylvania Courthouse,* 114–22, 189–212, and in Robert E. L. Krick, "Stuart's Last Ride: A Confederate View of Sheridan's Raid," in Gallagher, ed., *Spotsylvania Campaign,* 127–48.

7. Samuel Spencer Parmalie diary, May 11, 1864, in DU; Herman J. Viola, ed., *The Memoirs of Charles Henry Veil* (New York, 1993), 40; Michael Donlon to brother, May 21, 1864, in Civil War Miscellaneous Collection, USAMHI.

8. Sheridan, *Personal Memoirs,* 1, pp. 379–80; Sheridan to Grant, May 13, 1864, in *OR,* Vol. 36, Pt. 1, p. 777.

9. "Sheridan! The Great Cavalry Expedition Through Rebel Lines," *New York Herald,* May 17, 1864.

10. George B. Sanford, *Fighting Rebels and Redskins: Experiences in Army Life of Colonel George B. Sanford, 1861–1892,* ed. E. R. Hagemann (Norman, Okla., 1969), 234; J. B. to editor, May 15, 1864, *Rutland (Vt.) Herald,* June 1, 1864; Charles E. Phelps, "Recollections of the Wilderness Campaign," in Maryland Historical Society, Baltimore.

11. Theophilius F. Rodenbough, "Sheridan's Richmond Raid," in *B&L,* 4, 191.

12. Sheridan, *Personal Memoirs,* 1, 380; Well A. Bushnell memoirs, 269, in Palmer Regimental Papers, WRHS, Cleveland; S. H. Nowlin, "Capture and Escape," *Southern Bivouac* 2 (1883), 70; Thompson A. Snyder, *Recollections of Four Years with the Union Cavalry* (N.p., 1927), Book 42, FSNMP.

13. Isaac R. Dunkelberger memoir, in Michael Winey Collection, USAMHI; Stanton P. Allen, *Down in Dixie: Life in a Cavalry Regiment in the War Days* (Boston, 1888), 323–4; Alonzo Foster, *Reminiscences and Record of the 6th New York V. V. Cavalry* (Brooklyn, 1892), 74–5; Sanford, *Fighting Rebels and Redskins,* 234.

14. Sarah Woolfolk Wiggins, ed., *The Journals of Josiah Gorgas, 1857–1878* (Tuscaloosa, n.d.), 104; "The Enemy on the Outskirts of Richmond," *Richmond Examiner,* May 12, 1864.

15. "The Enemy on the Outskirts of Richmond," *Richmond Examiner,* May 12, 1864; "Defense of Richmond," *Richmond Enquirer,* May 13, 1864.

16. "Defense of Richmond," *Richmond Enquirer,* May 13, 1864.

17. John H. Reagan, *Memoirs, With Special Reference to Secession and the Civil War,* ed. Walter Flavius McCaleb (New York, 1906), 183–4; *Richmond Sentinel,* May 12, 1864.

18. Fitzhugh Lee's report, in MC; J. D. Ferguson, "Memoranda of the Itinerary and Operations of Major General Fitz. Lee's Cavalry Division of the Army of Northern Virginia from May 4th to October 15th 1864, Inclusive," in DU; Woodford B. Hackley, *The Little Fork Rangers: A Sketch of Company "D," Fourth Virginia Cavalry* (Richmond, 1927), 89; James M. Cadwallader diary, May 12, 1864, in Book 114, FSNMP.

19. Wilson, *Under the Old Flag,* 1, 410–11; Captain Field's account, in Rodenbough, "Sheridan's Richmond Raid," 191.

20. Wilson, *Under the Old Flag,* 1, 411–12; William L. Greenleaf, "From the Rapidan to Richmond," in *War Papers of Vermont and Miscellaneous States Papers Addresses, Military Order of the Loyal Legion,* vol.1 (Reprint, Wilmington, N.C., 1994), 18; *Annual Report of the Adjutant-General of the State of Connecticut for the Year Ending March 31, 1865* (New Haven, Conn., 1865), 412; William E. Riley to friend, May 16, 1864, *Windham County (Conn.) Transcript,* June 2, 1864; Wilson's report, *OR,* Vol. 36, Pt. 1, pp. 779–80; Rodenbough, "Sheridan's Richmond Raid," 191. One source claimed that Colonel Thomas C. Devin executed the guide; Riley to friend, May 16, 1864, *Windham County (Conn.) Transcript,* June 2, 1864.

21. Rodenbough, "Sheridan's Richmond Raid," 191; Robert G. Athearn, ed., "The Civil War Diary of John Wilson Phillips," *Virginia Magazine of History and Biography,* 62 (January 1954), 102.

22. Foster, *6th New York V.V. Cavalry,* 75; Edward P. Tobie, *History of the First Maine Cavalry* (Boston, 1887), 266.

23. Wilson's report, in *OR,* Vol. 36, Pt. 1, p. 879; Athearn, "Civil War Diary of John Wilson Philips," 102; John B. McIntosh's report, in *OR,* Vol. 36, Pt. 1, p. 887; George H. Chapman's report, ibid., 898.

24. Rodenbough, "Sheridan's Richmond Raid," 191.

25. Alexander C. M. Pennington's report, in *OR,* Vol. 36, Pt. 1, p. 903; Wilson, *Under the Old Flag,* 1, 412.

26. Wilson, *Under the Old Flag,* 1, 412–13.

27. David McM. Gregg's report, in *OR,* Vol. 36, Pt. 1, p. 854; Henry E. Davies Jr.'s report, ibid., 857.

28. "Brook Church Fight," *Charlotte (N.C.) Observer,* January 3, 1902.

29. Henry C. Dickinson, *Diary of Capt. Dickinson, C.S.A.* (Denver, n.d.), 15–16; James H. Kidd, *Personal Recollections of a Cavalryman with Custer's Michigan Cavalry Brigade in the Civil War* (Ionia, Mich., 1908), 308–9. Insufficient data exists to reconstruct the order of regiments within Lee's defensive line. According to Dickinson, the 2nd, 3rd, and 5th Virginia Cavalry, arrayed from west to east, occupied semicircular works near the terminus of the railway bridge. The 4th Virginia Cavalry was also in the works.

30. Lawrence E. Tripp, "With Custer at Yellow Tavern and in the Raid Around Richmond," *National Tribune,* July 31, 1884; Kidd, *Personal Recollections,* 310–11; Sanford, *Fighting Rebels and Redskins,* 236; Gershom Woodruff Mattson, "Sheridan's Raid," 29, in MSU.

31. Kidd, *Personal Recollections,* 310; James H. Kidd's report, NA; Rufus H. Peck, *Reminiscences of a Confederate Soldier of Co. C, 2nd Va. Cavalry* (Fincastle, Va., 1913), 47.

32. J. R. Bowen, *Regimental History of the First New York Dragoons During Three Years of Active Service in the Great Civil War* (Lyons, Mich., 1900), 163; Phelps, "Personal Recollections of the Wilderness Campaign," in Maryland Historical Society, Baltimore.

33. Phelps, "Personal Recollections of the Wilderness Campaign" in Maryland Historical Society, Baltimore.

34. Ibid.

35. Wilson, *Under the Old Flag,* 1, 414; George Perkins diary, in Michael T. Russert Private Collection, Cambridge, New York.

36. "Brook Church Fight," *Charlotte (N.C.) Observer,* January 3, 1902; E. B. Montague to editor, May 14, 1864, *Richmond Enquirer,* May 17, 1864.

37. Noble D. Preston, *History of the Tenth Regiment of Cavalry, New York State Volunteers* (New York, 1892), 182; Tobie, *First Maine Cavalry,* 266–7; Noble D. Preston, "Annals of the War: Sheridan's Ten Thousand," *Philadelphia Weekly Times,* February 10, 1883.

38. "The Raid Around Richmond," *Richmond Enquirer,* May 17, 1864 (morning edition); Montague to editor, May 14, 1864, *Richmond Enquirer,* May 17, 1864 (evening edition).

39. Montague to editor, May 14, 1864, *Richmond Enquirer,* May 17, 1864; Tobie, *First Maine Cavalry,* 267–8; "Itinerary of the First Maine Cavalry, May 1–June 24," in *OR,* Vol. 36, Pt. 1, p. 864; Henry R. Pyne, *Ride to War: The History of the First New Jersey Cavalry* (New Brunswick, N.J., 1961), 202–3; Allen Parker diary, May 12, 1864, in FSNMP.

40. Preston, *Tenth Regiment of Cavalry,* 182; Isaac H. Ressler diary, May 12, 1864, in Civil War Times Illustrated Collection, USAMHI; "Itinerary of the Eighth Pennsylvania Cavalry, May 1–June 30," *OR,* Vol. 36, Pt. 1, p. 867; "Brook Church Fight," *Charlotte (N.C.) Observer,* January 3, 1902.

41. "Brook Church Fight," *Charlotte (N.C.) Observer,* January 3, 1902; William H. H. Cowles, "The Life and Services of General James B. Gordon, Delivered in Metropolitan Hall, Raleigh, North Carolina, May 10, 1887" (N.p., n.d.); George G. Benedict, *Vermont in the Civil War: A History of the Part Taken by the Vermont Soldiers and Sailors in the War for the Union, 1861–5,* vol. 2 (Burlington, Vt., 1888), 639–40; Montague to editor, May 14, 1864, *Richmond Enquirer,* May 17, 1864.

42. Eppa Hunton, *Autobiography of Eppa Hunton* (Richmond, Va., 1933), 109.

43. Ibid.; Lewellyn A. Shaver, *History of the Sixtieth Alabama Regiment, Gracie's Alabama Brigade* (Montgomery, Ala., 1867), 48–9; "Gracie's Brigade in the Battles Around Richmond," *Mobile (Ala.) Daily Advertiser and Register,* June 3, 1864; Reagan, *Memoirs,* 184–85.

44. Reagan, *Memoirs,* 185; "Gracie's Brigade in the Battles Around Richmond," *Mobile (Ala.) Daily Advertiser and Register,* June 3, 1864; Pennington's report, in *OR,* Vol. 36, Pt. 1, p. 904; McIntosh's report, ibid., 887; Shaver, *Sixtieth Alabama Regiment,* 49; "The War News," *Richmond Daily Examiner,* May 13, 1864; Riley to friend, May 16, 1864, *Windham County (Conn.) Transcript,* June 2, 1864.

45. E. N. Maxly to George F. Savage, May 18, 1864, *Mobile (Ala.) Advertiser and Register,* May 29, 1864; Reagan, *Memoirs,* 185–6; N. Davidson, "Sketch of General Sheridan," *New York Herald,* May 22, 1864; John W. Urban, *Battle Field and Prison Pen* (Philadelphia, 1882), 278.

46. Shaver, *Sixtieth Alabama Regiment,* 49; Reagan, *Memoirs,* 185; "The War News," *Richmond Daily Examiner,* May 13, 1864.

47. Tripp, "With Custer at Yellow Tavern," *National Tribune,* July 31, 1884; Kidd, *Personal Recollections,* 311; Phelps, "Personal Recollections of the Wilderness Campaign," in Maryland

Historical Society, Baltimore; Wesley Merritt's report, in *OR,* Vol. 36, Pt. 1, p. 814; Devin's report, ibid., 835; Dunkelberger memoir, May 12, 1864.

48. Richard J. Del Vecchio, "With the First New York Dragoons: From the Letters of Jared L. Ainsworth," 91–2, in Harrisburg Civil War Roundtable Collection, USAMHI; J. R. Bowen, *First New York Dragoons,* 197; Samuel L. Gracey, *Annals of the Sixth Pennsylvania Cavalry* (Philadelphia, 1868), 145–6; Theophilius F. Rodenbough, comp., *From Everglades to Cañon with the Second Dragoons* (New York, 1875), 306; Devin's report, in *OR,* Vol. 36, Pt. 1, p. 835; Kidd, *Personal Recollections,* 312; Abraham K. Arnold, "A War Reminiscence—The Fifth United States Cavalry with General Sheridan on Raid Towards Richmond, Va., in 1864," *Journal of the United States Cavalry Association* 2 (1889), 313; Dickinson, *Diary,* 17; "4th Virginia Cavalry," *Richmond Sentinel,* May 14, 1864.

49. J. R. Bowen, *First New York Dragoons,* 163; Dickinson, *Diary,* 17; "The Second Virginia Cavalry in the Late Fights," *Richmond Sentinel,* May 21, 1864. Several Union sources claim that the Confederates abandoned two artillery pieces, but Confederate sources do not mention the loss of guns. Custer captured two Confederate pieces on May 11, which may be the same pieces referred to in accounts of May 12. See William G. Halls diary, May 12, 1864, in LC; Michael Donlon to brother, May 16, 1864, in Civil War Miscellaneous Collection, USAMHI; "The Second Virginia Cavalry in the Late Fight," *Richmond Sentinel,* May 21, 1864.

50. Alphonso D. Rockwell, "With Sheridan's Cavalry," in A. Noel Blakeman, *Personal Recollections of the War of the Rebellion* (New York, 1907), 232; Riley to friend, May 16, 1864, *Windham County (Conn.) Transcript,* June 2, 1864; "The First Connecticut Cavalry," *New Haven (Conn.) Daily Palladium,* June 1, 1864.

51. Sheridan's report, in *OR,* Vol. 36, Pt. 1, p. 791; Sheridan, *Personal Memoirs* 1, 385; S. P. Allen, *Down in Dixie,* 330.

52. Matthew W. King, *To Horse: with the Cavalry of the Army of the Potomac, 1861–65* (Cheboygan, Mich., 1926), no pagination; Phelps, "Personal Recollections of the Wilderness Campaign," in Maryland Historical Society, Baltimore; Viola, *Memoirs of Charles Henry Veil,* 41; Fitzhugh Lee's report, in MC; Ferguson, "Memoranda and Itinerary," in DU.

53. Preston, "Annals of the War: Sheridan's Ten Thousand," *Philadelphia Weekly Times,* February 10, 1883; Viola, *Memoirs of Charles Henry Veil,* 41; Bowen, *First New York Dragoons,* 164. Some of Lomax's men were involved in the attack, and a soldier in the 2nd Virginia mentioned driving the Federals one mile; John James Woodall diary, May 12, 1864, in FSNMP.

54. Phelps, "Personal Recollections of the Wilderness Campaign," in Maryland Historical Society, Baltimore; Rodenbough, *From Everglades to Cañon,* 307; Gracey, *Sixth Pennsylvania Cavalry,* 246; Charles W. Owen, *The First Michigan Infantry: Three Months and Three Years* (N.p., 1903), 17–18. The 18th Pennsylvania Cavalry of Wilson's division also had a small scrap with Fitzhugh Lee's men. When Colonel Timothy M. Bryan, commanding the regiment, failed to act swiftly enough, Wilson relieved him of command and appointed Lieutenant Colonel William P. Brinton in his stead; James H. Wilson to T. H. Rodenbough, October 14, 1908, in James H. Wilson Collection, Container 21, General Correspondence File, LC.

55. *Richmond Daily Examiner,* May 14, 1864.

56. Fitzhugh Lee's report, in MC; Ferguson, "Memoranda of the Itinerary and Operations," in DU; "Letter from Richmond, May 12, 1864," *Memphis (Tenn.) Daily Appeal,* May 24, 1864.

57. Dickinson, *Diary,* 21; "Sheridan's First Raid Around Richmond," *Olympia (Wash.) Puget Sound Weekly,* April 22, 1881.

58. Sheridan, *Personal Memoirs,* 1, 384; Phelps, "Personal Recollections of the Wilderness

Campaign," in Maryland Historical Society, Baltimore; James H. Wilson diary, May 13, 1864, in James H. Wilson Collection, LC; Mattson, "Sheridan's Raid," 31, in MSU.

59. Gracey, *Sixth Pennsylvania Cavalry,* 247; J. B. to editor, May 15, 1864, *Rutland (Vt.) Herald,* June 1, 1864; William P. Lloyd, *History of the First Regiment Pennsylvania Reserve Cavalry* (Philadelphia, 1864), 94; Thomas J. Grier, "Itinerary of the Service of the 18th Regiment of Cavalry, Pennsylvania Volunteers, September 1, 1862–October 31, 1865," in Committee of the Regiment, *History of the 18th Regiment Pennsylvania Cavalry* (New York, 1909), 52.

60. Phelps, "Personal Recollections of the Wilderness Campaign," in Maryland Historical Society, Baltimore; George Perkins diary, May 14, 1864, in Michael T. Russert Collection, Cambridge, New York; Hampton S. Thomas, *Some Personal Reminiscences of Service in the Cavalry of the Army of the Potomac* (Philadelphia, 1889), 18.

61. "Retreat and Escape of the Enemy on the Meadow Bridge Road," *Richmond Examiner,* May 14, 1864; J. B. Jones, *A Rebel War Clerk's Diary,* vol. 2 (Philadelphia, 1866), 208; Wiggins, *Journals of Josiah Gorgas,* 105–6.

62. *Richmond Daily Examiner,* May 14, 1864.

63. Special Orders No. 126, May 14, 1864, in *OR,* Vol. 36, Pt. 2, p. 1001.

64. *Richmond Enquirer,* May 17, 1864.

65. Phelps, "Personal Recollections of the Wilderness Campaign," in Maryland Historical Society, Baltimore; Fitzhugh Lee's report, May 13, 1864, in *OR,* Vol. 51, Pt. 1, p. 250; Return of Casualties, in *OR,* Vol. 36, Pt. 1, pp. 184–5. A discussion of attrition in Fitzhugh Lee's command appears in Krick, "Stuart's Last Ride," 153. I am indebted to Alfred C. Young for assistance in reconstructing Confederate losses.

66. Custer's performance at Meadow Bridge, and the criticism of Wilson, is deftly summarized in Gregory J. W. Urwin, *Custer Victorious* (Rutherford, N.J., 1983), 147.

67. Sheridan to Meade, May 13, 1864, in *OR,* Vol. 36, Pt. 1, pp. 778–9; "Two Cavalry Chieftains," *SHSP,* 16, 452; Greenleaf, "From the Rapidan to Richmond," in *War Papers of Vermont,* 21.

68. Viola, *Memoirs of Charles Henry Veil,* 41; S. J. Marks to Carrie, May 16, 1864, in Civil War Miscellaneous Collection, USAMHI; A. G. Warner to family, May 16, 1864, *Windham County (Conn.) Transcript,* May 26, 1864.

III MAY 14 *GRANT FORFEITS AN OPPORTUNITY*

1. "The Campaign in Virginia," *Philadelphia Sunday Dispatch,* May 22, 1864.

2. C. Seton Fleming diary, May 13, 1864, in Francis P. Fleming, *Memoir of Capt. C. Seton Fleming, of the Second Florida Infantry, C.S.A.* (Jacksonville, Fla., 1881), appendix; George H. Mills, *History of the 16th North Carolina Regiment (Originally 6th N.C. Regiment) in the Civil War* (Rutherfordton, N.C., 1901), 50–1.

3. Special Order, 5:45 P.M., May 13, 1864, in *OR,* Vol. 36, Pt. 2, p. 700; Grant to Ambrose E. Burnside, 9:10 P.M., May 13, 1864, ibid., p. 732; 2nd Corps Circular, 11:30 P.M., May 13, 1864, ibid., p. 709; Grant to Burnside, 9:10 P.M., May 13, 1864, ibid, p. 732.

4. Roebling's report, in Warren Collection, NYSLA; Humphreys to Wright, 8:15 P.M., May 13, 1864, in *OR,* Vol. 36, Pt. 2, pp. 728–9.

5. Circular, 9:00 P.M., May 13, 1864, in *OR,* Vol. 36, Pt. 2, p. 722; Humphreys to Warren, 8:20 P.M., May 13, 1864, ibid., p. 720; Humphreys to Warren, 9:30 P.M., May 13, 1864, ibid., p.

721. Warren estimated the marching distance as seven miles, when it fact it was four, a discrepancy that underscored the unreliability of Union maps.

6. Warren to Humphreys, 11:45 P.M., May 13, 1864, ibid., p. 721.

7. Roebling's report, in Warren Collection, NYSLA; Warren to Humphreys, 11:45 P.M., May 13, 1864, in *OR,* Vol. 36, Pt. 2, p. 721; Warren to Humphreys, 1:15 A.M., May 14, 1864, ibid., p. 755. Wright remained in the dark concerning his route and the country that he was to traverse. "I will send you my map to look at," Humphreys assured him. "Please return it." Humphreys to Wright, 8:15 P.M., May 13, 1864, ibid., pp. 728–9.

8. Royall W. Figg, *Where Men Only Dare to Go: or, The Story of a Boy Company* (Richmond, Va., 1885), 201–2; Joseph P. Fuller diary, May 14, 1864, in GDAH.

9. Wright to Humphreys, 2:55 A.M., May 14, 1864, in *OR,* Vol. 36, Pt. 2, p. 762; Francis W. Morse, *Personal Experiences in the War of the Great Rebellion, from December, 1862, to July, 1865* (Albany, N.Y., 1866), 93.

10. Roebling's report, in Warren Collection, NYSLA; Humphreys, *Virginia Campaign,* 107; Seiser, "Civil War Diary," 101; John Chester White journal, 69, in John Chester White Collection, LC; J. L. Smith, *Corn Exchange Regiment,* 424–5; George M. Barnard to father, May 14, 1864, in George M. Barnard Collection, MHS.

11. Harold A. Small, ed., *The Road to Richmond: The Civil War Memoirs of Major Abner R. Small of the 16th Maine Vols.; With His Diary as a Prisoner of War* (Berkeley, Calif., 1957), 141; Avery Harris memoir, 182, in Avery Harris Collection, USAMHI; Kent, *Three Years with Company K,* 267.

12. Roebling's report, in Warren Collection, NYSLA.

13. Ibid.; Warren to Humphreys, 4:00 A.M., May 14, 1864, in *OR,* Vol. 36, Pt. 2, p. 755; White journal, 69, in White Collection, LC; Warren to Humphreys, 6:30 A.M., May 14, 1864, in *OR,* Vol. 36, Pt. 2, p. 756; Humphreys to Warren, 7:10 A.M., May 14, 1864, ibid. Meade's visit to the Beverly house is placed at 7:00 A.M. in Fielding H. Garrison, ed., *John Shaw Billings: A Memoir* (New York, 1915), 87. A 6th Corps aide, however, claimed to have reached the Beverly house around 5:30 A.M. and found "Genl. Meade and staff on the portico" (Mark De Wolfe Howe, ed., *Touched With Fire: Civil War Letters and Diary of Oliver Wendell Holmes, Jr., 1861–1864* (New York, 1969), 118.

14. Grant to Halleck, 7:10 A.M., May 14, 1864, in *OR,* Vol. 36, Pt. 2, p. 746.

15. Roebling's report, in Warren Collection, NYSLA; Dispatch from Special Correspondent in the Field, May 14, 1864, *Boston Daily Advertiser,* May 16, 1864. According to a correspondent's account, the main set of works was sodded on the outside, indicating that it had been built earlier. A rebel officer told him that the works had been constructed after Gettysburg to bar the approaches to Richmond. "The Campaign in Virginia," *Philadelphia Sunday Dispatch,* May 22, 1864.

16. J. L. Smith, *Corn Exchange Regiment,* 425–6.

17. Nevins, *Diary of Battle,* 370–1.

18. Ibid., 369–70; Luther E. Cowles, *History of the Fifth Massachusetts Battery* (Boston, 1902), 823–4; Thomas Scott, "The Action of Battery D, 5th United States Artillery, at Spotsylvania," *National Tribune,* December 27, 1894; J. H. Moore, "Archer's Tennesseans at Spotsylvania, May 11 and 12, 1864: A Second Angle of Death," in William C. King and W. P. Derby, comps., *Camp-Fire Sketches and Battle-Field Echoes* (Springfield, Mass., 1888), 312–13. One of Rittenhouse's gunners later wrote that Confederates "crowded on their works and seemed to think we were crazy"; Scott, "Action of Battery D."

19. Morse, *Personal Experiences,* 93.

20. James L. Bowen, *History of the Thirty-Seventh Regiment Massachusetts Volunteers in the Civil War of 1861–1865* (Holyoke, Mass., 1884), 314; Humphreys to Warren, 9:00 A.M., May 14, 1864, in *OR,* Vol. 36, Pt. 2, p. 757.

21. William H. F. Lee to Robert E. Lee, 8:00 A.M., May 14, 1864, in *OR,* Vol. 51, Pt. 2, p. 930; "Copy of Diary and Leaves from Memoranda of 1st Sgt. Stephen D. Burger and Lt. George P. Bouton, Both of Co. E 6th N.Y. Artillery," 5, in FSNMP; Noel G. Harrison, *Gazetteer of Historic Sites Related to the Fredericksburg and Spotsylvania National Military Park,* vol. 2 (Fredericksburg, Va., 1986), 115; Roe, *Thirty-Ninth Regiment Massachusetts Volunteers,* 200; Vautier, *88th Pennsylvania Volunteers,* 183; "The Campaign in Virginia," *Philadelphia Sunday Dispatch,* May 22, 1864.

22. Alfred M. Apted diary, May 14, 1864, in FSNMP.

23. Winfield S. Hancock to Andrew A. Humphreys, 3:50 A.M., in *OR,* Vol. 36, pt. 2, p. 749; Second Corps Daily Memoranda, ibid., Pt. 1, p. 361.

24. Figg, *Where Men Only Dare To Go,* 202; Humphreys to Hancock, 9:30 A.M., May 14, 1864, in *OR,* Vol. 36, Pt. 2, p. 750; Hancock to Humphreys, 9:35 A.M., May 14, 1864, ibid.; Humphreys to Hancock, 10:15 A.M., May 14, 1864, ibid. ; I. B. Parker to W. G. Mitchell, 12:30 P.M., May 14, 1864, ibid.; G. Moxley Sorrel journal, May 14, 1864, in MC.

25. Hancock to Humphreys, 6:15 P.M., May 14, 1864, in *OR,* Vol. 36, Pt. 2, p. 751.

26. Gary W. Gallagher, ed., *Fighting for the Confederacy: The Personal Recollections of General Edward Porter Alexander* (Chapel Hill, N.C., 1989), 380; Joseph A. Graves, *The History of the Bedford Light Artillery* (Bedford, Va., 1903), 45.

27. Harrison, *Gazetteer of Historic Sites,* 2, 113–27; Special dispatch, May 18, 1864, *Washington, D.C. Daily Morning Chronicle,* May 20, 1864.

28. Lyman to family, May 23, 1864, in George R. Agassiz, ed., *Meade's Headquarters, 1863–1865: Letters of Colonel Theodore Lyman from the Wilderness to Appomattox* (Boston, 1922), 115–16.

29. *New York Herald,* May 27, 1864; Warren to Humphreys, 8:40 P.M., May 14, 1864, in *OR,* Vol. 36, Pt. 2, p. 760. Wartime accounts frequently confuse the Myers house and the Gayle house.

30. Samuel D. Webster diary, May 26, 1864, in Samuel D. Webster Collection, Henry E. Huntington Library, San Marino, Calif.

31. Warren to Humphreys, 7:30 A.M., May 14, 1864, in *OR,* Vol. 36, Pt. 2, p. 756. John D. Lentz's report, ibid., Pt. 1, pp. 555–6; Seiser, "Civil War Diary," 192.

32. Garrison, *Memoir,* 87; Porter, *Campaigning with Grant,* 117.

33. R. L. T. Beale, *History of the Ninth Virginia Cavalry in the War Between the States* (Richmond, 1899), 117–18; Byrd C. Willis diary, May 13, 1864, in VHS.

34. R. L. T. Beale, *Ninth Virginia Cavalry,* 118.

35. Lentz's report, in *OR,* Vol. 36, Pt. 1, p. 556; Willis diary, May 14, 1864, in VHS; R. L. T. Beale, *Ninth Virginia Cavalry,* 118. A fine recounting of the engagement is in Brian A. Bennett, *Sons of Old Monroe: A Regimental History of Patrick O'Rorke's 140th New York Volunteer Infantry* (Dayton, Ohio, 1992), 402–3.

36. Upton's report, in *OR,* Vol. 36, Pt. 1, p. 670.

37. Morse, *Personal Experiences,* 94.

38. G. W. Beale, *A Lieutenant of Cavalry in Lee's Army* (Boston, 1918), 142. The history of Zion Church, site of Lee's headquarters, is recounted in Bob Weeks, *On the Road to Traveler's Rest: The Story of Zion United Methodist Church of Spotsylvania Courthouse, Virginia, during the Nineteenth Century* (N.p., n.d.).

39. Charles S. Venable to Richard S. Ewell, 12:30 P.M., May 14, 1864, in *OR,* Vol. 51, Pt. 2, 929–30.

40. "Letter from Wright's Brigade, May 16, 1864," *Atlanta Daily Constitutionalist,* May 25, 1864; C. H. Andrews memorandum, 19–20, in C. H. Andrews Collection, SHC; Shiver, "Wright's Brigade at Spotsylvania Court House," *Atlanta Journal,* October 16, 1901; Nathaniel Harris to William Mahone, August 2, 1866, in William Mahone Collection, VSL.

41. William P. Hopkins, *The Seventh Regiment Rhode Island Volunteers in the Civil War* (Providence, R.I., 1903), 173; L. O. Merriam, "Personal Recollections of the War for the Union," 35–6, in FSNMP.

42. John H. Rhodes, *The History of Battery B, First Regiment Rhode Island Light Artillery in the War to Preserve the Union* (Providence, R.I., 1894), 287; Alexander B. Pattison diary, May 14, 1864, in Book 68, FSNMP; Jackman and Hadley, *Sixth New Hampshire Regiment,* 249; Henry C. Houston, *The Thirty-Second Maine Regiment of Infantry Volunteers* (Portland, Me., 1903), 151; Paul Wirtz, ed., *John Parker Brest, Company E, 100th Pennsylvania Volunteer Regiment, Journal 1861–1865* (Baltimore, Md., 1991), 27; Charles D. Todd diary, May 14, 1864, in Coco Collection, USAMHI.

43. Upton's report, in *OR,* Vol. 36, Pt. 1, p. 670; Isaac O. Best, *History of the 121st New York State Infantry* (Chicago, 1921), 149–50.

44. Upton's report, in *OR,* Vol. 36, Pt. 1, p. 670; Henry Keiser diary, May 14, 1864, in Harrisburg Civil War Round Table Collection, USAMHI.

45. George W. Bicknell, *History of the Fifth Regiment Maine Volunteers* (Portland, Me., 1871), 323–4.

46. Upton's report, in *OR,* Vol. 36, Pt. 1, p. 670; Andrews memorandum, 19–20, in Andrews Collection, SHC; Shiver, "Wright's Brigade at Spotsylvania Courthouse," *Atlanta Journal,* October 16, 1901.

47. Andrews memorandum, 19–20, in Andrews Collection, SCH; *Macon (Ga.) Daily Telegraph,* May 31, 1864; "A Gallant Lieutenant," *Macon (Ga.) Daily Telegraph,* June 4, 1864; G. W. Beale, *Lieutenant of Cavalry,* 143; Ott, "Diary of James J. Kirkpatrick," 195; Maurus Oestreich diary, May 14, 1864, in Harrisburg Civil War Round Table Collection, USAMHI.

48. John F. L. Hartwell, *To My Beloved Wife and Boy at Home,* ed. Ann Hartwell Britton and Thomas J. Reed (Madison, N.J., 1997), 228; Bicknell, *Fifth Regiment Maine Volunteers,* 324; Keiser diary, May 14, 1864, in Harrisburg Civil War Round Table Collection, USAMHI; James M. Greiner et al., eds., *A Surgeon's Civil War: The Letters and Diary of Daniel M. Holt, M.D.* (Kent, Ohio, 1994), 189.

49. Thomas W. Hyde, *Following the Greek Cross, or, Memories of the Sixth Army Corps* (Boston, 1894), 203–4.

50. Morse, *Personal Experiences,* 94; James C. Biddle to wife, May 16, 1864, in George G. Meade Collection, HSP; William Brooke Rawle diary, May 15, 1864, in Civil War Library and Museum, Philadelphia; "Narrow Escape of General Meade," *New York Herald,* May 18, 1864; R. Roy's dispatch of May 15, 1864, *New York Daily News,* May 19, 1864. The Confederate who almost caught Meade was probably Major Thomas E. Upshaw.

51. Jubal A. Early, *Autobiographical Sketch and Narrative of the War Between the States* (Bloomington, Ind., 1960), 357; Alanson A. Haines, *History of the Fifteenth Regiment New Jersey Volunteers* (New York, 1883), 183; George Weiser, *Nine Months in Rebel Prisons* (Philadelphia, 1890), 9; W. D. Mountcastle diary, May 14, 1864, in UDC Collection, Rome/Floyd County Library, Rome, Georgia; J. Henry Read to unknown, May 15, 1864, *Macon (Ga.) Daily Telegraph,* May 26, 1864; Upton's report, in *OR,* Vol. 36, Pt. 1, p. 670; Morse, *Personal Experiences,* 96.

52. G. W. Beale, *Lieutenant of Cavalry,* 144.

53. Richard H. Anderson to Lee, 3:30 P.M., May 14, 1864, in *OR,* Vol. 51, Pt. 2, p. 929.

54. Lee to Ewell, 4:00 P.M., May 14, 1864, ibid.

55. Sorrel's journal, May 14, 1864, in MC; Richard H. Anderson's report, 5, in DU.

56. W. H. Arehart diary, *Harrisonburg (Va.) Rockingham Recorder,* 2 (1959), 154; Thomas A. McParlin's report, in *OR,* Vol. 36, Pt. 1, p. 231; Katherine Couse to friend, May 4–22, 1864, in UV; E. W. Brown, "Reminiscences," in South Carolina Division, United Daughters of the Confederacy, *Recollections and Reminiscences,* vol. 1 (N.p., 1990), 28–9; Harrison, *Gazetteer of Historic Sites,* 2, 81–4.

57. Couse to friend, May 14–21, 1864, in UV; Hancock to Meade, 6:45 P.M., May 14, 1864, in *OR,* Vol. 36, Pt. 2, p. 752; Hancock to Warren and Meade, 9:50 P.M., May 14, 1864, ibid., 753; McParlin's report, ibid., Pt. 1, p. 232; James F. Wood diary, May 14, 1864, in VSL; George A. Bowen diary, May 14, 1864, in FSNMP; William P. Haines, *History of the Men of Company F, with Description of the Marches and Battles of the 12th New Jersey Volunteers* (Mickleton, N.J., 1897), 63; J. R. Sypher, *History of the Pennsylvania Reserve Corps* (Lancaster, Pa., 1865), 534.

58. Meade to Warren, 5:15 P.M., May 14, 1864, in *OR,* Vol. 36, Pt. 2, p. 758; Wright to Warren, May 14, 1864, ibid.; James M. Read diary, May 14, 1864, in James B. Ricketts Papers, Manassas Battlefield Park Library, Manassas; Charles Harvey Brewster to mother, May 15, 1864, in Blight, *When This Cruel War Is Over,* 297. Sources disagree over whether Ricketts formed on Neill's right or rear.

59. Charles Thomas Bowen diary, May 14, 1864, in FSNMP.

60. Ibid.; A. A. Haines, *Fifteenth Regiment New Jersey Volunteers,* 183.

61. "Notes from the Battle-Field," *Xenia (Ohio) Torch-Light,* June 1, 1864; "From the Sixth Corps," *Providence (R.I.) Daily Journal,* June 1, 1864; Edwin M. Haynes, *A History of the Tenth Regiment, Vermont Volunteers, with Biographical Sketches of the Officers Who Fell in Battle* (Lewiston, Me., 1870), 128.

62. Warren to Meade, 7:50 P.M., May 14, 1864, in *OR,* Vol. 36, Pt. 2, p. 760; Meade to Warren, May 14, 1864, ibid.; Porter, *Campaigning with Grant,* 118.

63. Milton Myers diary, May 14, 1864, p. 23, in Richmond National Battlefield Park, Richmond; Bowen, *Thirty-Seventh Regiment Massachusetts Volunteers,* 315; Abbott, *Personal Recollections,* 60; Brewster to mother, May 15, 1864, in Blight, *When This Cruel War Is Over,* 297. During the evening Colonel William S. Truex of the 14th New Jersey replaced the 87th Pennsylvania's Colonel John W. Schall as commander of Ricketts's 1st Brigade, formerly under Brigadier General William H. Morris, who had been shot on May 9; George R. Prowell, *History of the Eighty-Seventh Regiment, Pennsylvania Volunteers* (York, Pa., 1901), 138.

64. Porter, *Campaigning with Grant,* 118–19. According to Porter, the injured man survived the war.

65. Meade to Grant, 9:00 P.M., May 14, 1864, in *OR,* Vol. 36, Pt. 2, p. 747; Grant to Meade, 9:30 P.M., May 14, 1864, ibid.; Humphreys to Hancock, 10 :00 P.M., May 14, 1864, ibid., 753.

66. Hancock to Humphreys, 6:15 P.M., May 14, 1864, ibid., 751; Warren to Humphreys, 8:40 P.M., May 14, 1864, ibid., 760; Wright to Humphreys, May 14, 1864, ibid., 763; Meade to Wright, 8:40 P.M., May 14, 1864, ibid.

67. Rawle diary, May 14, 1864, in Civil War Library and Museum, Philadelphia; Porter, *Campaigning with Grant,* 119–20.

68. Lockley diary, May 21, 1864, in Lockley Collection, BL; Augustus C. Brown, *The Diary of a Line Officer* (New York, 1906), 47; Tyler, *Recollections of the Civil War,* 204; Nevins, *Diary of Battle,* 372; Howe, *Touched With Fire,* 118–19.

69. Annette Tapert, ed., *The Brother's War: Civil War Letters to Their Loved Ones from the Blue and Gray* (New York, 1988), 198; William H. Stewart, *A Pair of Blankets: War-Time History in Letters to the Young People of the South* (New York, 1914), 134–5.

70. Tapert, *Brother's War*, 198; Marion Hill Fitzpatrick to Amanda Fitzpatrick, May 19, 1864, in Henry M. Hammock, ed., *Letters to Amanda from Sergeant Marion Hill Fitzpatrick, 45th Georgia Regiment, Thomas' Brigade, Wilcox' Division, Hill's Corps CSA to His Wife Amanda Olive Elizabeth Fitzpatrick, 1862–1865* (Culloden, Ga., n.d.), 128; G. W. Grimes to father, May 21, 1864, in Book 113, FSNMP.

71. Lee to Davis, May 14, 1864, in Dowdey, *Wartime Papers of R. E. Lee*, 730; Lee to John C. Breckinridge, May 14, 1864, ibid., 729.

72. Gallagher, ed., *Fighting for the Confederacy*, 380.

73. George Breck to family, May 17, 1864, *Rochester (N.Y.) Union and Advertiser*, May 27, 1864; Thomas F. Galwey, *The Valiant Hours: An Irishman in the Civil War* (Harrisburg, Pa., 1961), 215; Ruth L. Silliker, ed., *The Rebel Yell and the Yankee Hurrah: The Civil War Journal of a Maine Volunteer, Private John W. Haley, 17th Maine Regiment* (Camden, Me., 1985), 158.

74. "Letter from Wright's Brigade, May 16, 1864," *Atlanta Daily Constitutionalist*, May 25, 1864; Nathaniel Harris to William Mahone, August 20, 1866, in William Mahone Collection, VSL; William Judkins memoir, 81–2, in Book 189, FSNMP.

IV MAY 15–16 *GRANT SETTLES ON A NEW OFFENSIVE*

1. Diary of Unknown Rebel, May 16, 1864, in BU; Nevins, *Diary of Battle*, 372; Imri A. Spencer to Cris, May 20, 1864, in Book 76, FSNMP; Francis Solomon Johnson Jr. to Emily Hutchings, May 17, 1864, in Special Collections, University of Georgia; Isaac C. Hadden to Kate, May 15, 1864, in New York Historical Society.

2. Grant to Halleck, 7:00 A.M., May 15, 1864, in *OR*, Vol. 36, Pt. 2, p. 781.

3. Grant to Halleck, May 10, 1864, ibid., p. 595–6; Grant to Halleck, May 11, 1864, ibid, p. 627–8; Grant to Halleck, May 12, 1864, ibid., p. 652.

4. Halleck to Grant, May 13, 1864, ibid., 695–6; Halleck to Grant, May 13, 1864, ibid., 696–7. In his second letter Halleck listed the regiments that were underway and those under orders to go.

5. Grant to Halleck, ibid., 781; Wilbur Fisk diary, May 15, 1864, in LC; Lewis A. Grant's report, in *OR*, Vol. 36, Pt. 1, p. 704; Benedict, *Vermont in the Civil War*, 1, p. 451.

6. Grant to Meade, endorsed on F. Van Vliet to Rawlins, 11:36 A.M., May 15, 1864, in *OR*, Vol. 36, Pt. 2, p. 794; Charles H. Banes, *History of the Philadelphia Brigade* (Philadelphia, 1876), 251.

7. Robert McAllister to Gershom Mott, May 15, 1864, in *OR*, Vol. 36, Pt. 2, p. 784; Birney to Hancock, May 15, 1864, ibid., 786; 2nd Corps Daily Memorandum, ibid., Pt. 1, p. 361.

8. John S. Crocker diary, May 15, 1864, in Cornell University, John Olin Library; Gilbert Adams Hays, comp., *Under the Red Patch: Story of the Sixty Third Regiment Pennsylvania Volunteers, 1861–1864* (Pittsburgh, 1908), 242; Silliker, *Rebel Yell*, 158; Birney to Morgan, 12:45 P.M., May 15, 1864, in *OR*, Vol. 36, Pt. 2, p. 787.

9. F. Van Fleet to Rawlins, 11:36 A.M., May 15, 1864, in *OR*, Vol. 36, Pt. 2, p. 794.

10. Ibid.

11. Thomas D. Marbaker, *History of the Eleventh New Jersey Volunteers* (Trenton, N.J., 1898), 177–9; Robert McAllister to Ellen and family, May 16, 1864, in James I. Robertson Jr.,

ed., *The Civil War Letters of General Robert McAllister* (New Brunswick, N.J., 1965), 421–2; Gershom Mott's report of May 17, 1864, in *OR,* Vol. 36, Pt. 1, p. 486.

12. Benjamin Y. Draper diary, May 15, 1864, in Book 47, FSNMP; Lyman journal, May 15, 1864, in Lyman Collection, MHS.

13. Birney to Morgan, 12:45 P.M., May 15, 1864, in *OR,* Vol. 36, Pt. 2, p. 787; Sorrel journal, May 15, 1864, in MC; William Rhadamanthus Montgomery diary, May 15, 1864, in Atlanta Historical Society.

14. "Letter from Virginia from Our Special Correspondent, May 16, 1864," *Mobile (Ala.) Daily Advertiser and Register,* May 28, 1864.

15. Davis to Lee, May 15, 1864, in *OR,* Vol. 51, Pt. 2, p. 933.

16. Lyman journal, May 7, 1864, in Lyman Collection, MHS; Free S. Bowley, "A Boy Lieutenant in a Black Regiment," *National Tribune,* May 11, 1899.

17. During the evening of May 14, units from the 2nd Ohio that had escorted ambulances to Belle Plain rejoined the regiment. See Rogers Hanneford Memoir, May 13–15, 1864, in Cincinnati Historical Society.

18. Katherine Couse to unknown, May 15, 1864, in UV.

19. Hanneford memoir, May 13–15, 1864, in Cincinnati Historical Society.

20. Ibid.

21. George A. Purington's report, in *OR,* Vol. 36, Pt. 1, p. 894; Robert W. Hatton, ed., "Just a Little Bit of the Civil War, as Seen by W[illiam] J. Smith, Company M, 2nd O. V. Cavalry," *Ohio History,* 84 (1975), 114; Frank M. Myers, *The Comanches: A History of White's Battalion, Virginia Cavalry, Laurel Brigade, Hampton Division, A.N.V., C.S.A.* (Baltimore, 1871), 281; William N. McDonald, *A History of the Laurel Brigade, Originally the Ashby Cavalry of the Army of Northern Virginia and Chew's Battery* (Baltimore, 1907), 239; Wood diary, May 15, 1864, in VSL.

22. Edward Ferrero to Rawlins, May 15, 1864, in *OR,* Vol. 36, Pt. 1, p. 986.

23. Bowley, "Boy Lieutenant."

24. Ibid.; Hanneford Memoir, May 15, 1864, in Cincinnati Historical Society.

25. Ferrero to Rawlins, May 15, 1864, in *OR,* Vol. 36, Pt. 1, p. 986; Noel G. Harrison, "A Moment in Black History: May 15, 1865," *Fredericksburg (Va.) Town Hall Crier,* 6 (1991), 6–7; Hanneford memoir, May 15, 1864; Luman Harris Tenny, *War Diary, 1861–1865* (Cleveland, Ohio, 1914), 116. Although Rosser denied any losses, a soldier from the 2nd Ohio later claimed that twenty dead Confederates and as many wounded lay in the roadway; Hatton, "Just a Little Bit of the Civil War," 114.

26. Thomas L. Rosser, "Annals of the War: Operations with Lee's Army During the Battle of Spotsylvania," *Philadelphia Weekly Tribune,* April 19, 1884.

27. Meade to Wright, 1 P.M., May 15, 1864, in *OR,* Vol. 36, Pt. 2, p. 790; Jacob H. Dewees to Burnside, May 15, 1864, ibid., 797.

28. Richard E. Beaudry, ed., *War Journal of Louis N. Beaudry, Fifth New York Cavalry* (Jefferson, N.C., 1996), 118; Donald Chipman, "An Essex County Soldier in the Civil War: The Diary of Cyril Fountain," *New York History,* 64 (1985), 292.

29. Beaudry, *War Journal,* 118–19; Dewees to Burnside, May 15, 1864, in *OR,* Vol. 36, Pt. 2, p. 797. Elder F. L. Kreger was pastor during the war; Thomas Sanford Dunaway, *An Historical Sketch of Massaponax Baptist Church of Spotsylvania County Virginia* (N.p., 1938).

30. Thomas L. Rosser's report, in *OR,* Vol. 36, Pt.1, p. 1098; Wood diary, May 15, 1864, in VSL.

31. Garrison, *Memoir,* 90.

32. Burnside to Grant, 2:40 P.M., May 15, 1864, in *OR,* Vol. 36, Pt. 2, p. 795; Grant to Burnside, 3:05 P.M., May 15, 1864, ibid.; Burnside to Grant, 3:20 P.M., May 15, 1864, ibid., 796.

33. Dispatch of May 17, 1864, *New York Daily Tribune,* May 18, 1864.

34. Burnside to Grant, 3:30 P.M., May 15, 1864, in *OR,* Vol. 36, Pt. 2, p. 796; Grant to Meade, May 15, 1864, ibid., 782; Meade to Grant, 3:30 P.M., May 15, 1864, ibid.

35. Grant to Meade, May 15, 1864, ibid.

36. Meade to Burnside, 4:40 P.M., May 15, 1864, ibid., 796; David B. Birney to Burnside, May 15, 1864, ibid., 797.

37. Meade to Warren, 3:30 P.M., May 15, 1864, ibid., 788–9; Meade to Burnside, 4:40 P.M., May 15, 1864, ibid., 796; Warren to Meade, 4:50 P.M., ibid., 789; Meade to Warren, 5:00 P.M., May 15, 1864, ibid.

38. Rosser's report, in *OR,* Vol. 36, Pt. 1, p. 1098; Katherine Couse to unknown, May 15, 1864, in UV; Dispatch, May 18, 1864, *Philadelphia Inquirer,* May 20, 1864.

39. Lyman journal, May 15, 1864, in Lyman Collection, MHS; Roebling's report, in Warren Collection, NYSLA; 6th Corps Orders, May 15, 1864, in *OR,* Vol. 36, Pt. 2, p. 791; Keiser diary, May 15, 1864, in Harrisburg Civil War Roundtable Collection, USAMHI; Wright to Humphreys, undated, in Army of the Potomac Correspondence, Box 70, NA; Fisk diary, May 15, 1864, in LC; Benedict, *Vermont in the Civil War,* I, 451. At 4:40 P.M., Warren received orders to prepare to attack; Warren to Meade, May 15, 1864, in *OR,* Vol. 36, Pt. 2, pp. 788–9. The rescinding order was issued at 7:45 P.M.; Humphreys to Warren, *OR,* Vol. 36, Pt. 2, p. 789.

40. Lyman journal, May 15, 1864, in Lyman Collection, MHS.

41. A. T. Brewer, *History of the Sixty-First Regiment Pennsylvania Volunteers, 1861–1865* (Pittsburgh, 1911), 97.

42. Thomas H. Parker, *History of the 51st Regiment of Pennsylvania Volunteers and Veteran Volunteers* (Philadelphia, 1869), 551; A. A. Haines, *Fifteenth Regiment New Jersey Volunteers,* 183; Greiner, *Surgeon's Civil War,* 189; F. Larue to editor, May 16, 1864, *Xenia (Ohio) Torch-Light,* June 1, 1864; Haynes, *Tenth Regiment, Vermont Volunteers,* 128; Ellis Spear, *Civil War Recollections,* ed. Abbott Spear et al. (Orono, Me., 1997), 109.

43. Brewer, *Sixty-First Regiment Pennsylvania Volunteers,* 96–7.

44. Charles S. Venable to Richard S. Ewell, May 15, 1864, in *OR,* Vol. LI, P.2, p. 933; Ott, "Diary of James J. Kirkpatrick," 195–96.

45. Clement A. Evans to wife, May 15, 1864, in Robert Grier Stephens Jr., *Intrepid Warrior: Clement Anselm Evans* (Dayton, Ohio, 1992), 397; Walter H. Taylor to Bettie, May 15, 1864, in R. Lockwood Tower, ed., *Lee's Adjutant: The Wartime Letters of Colonel Walter Herron Taylor, 1862–1865* (Columbia, S.C., 1995), 161. Evans was promoted to brigadier general on May 19.

46. Breckinridge Message, 7:00 P.M., May 15, 1864, in *OR,* Vol. 36, Pt. 1, p. 87.

47. Susan W. Benson, ed., *Berry Benson's Civil War Book: Memoirs of a Confederate Scout and Sharpshooter* (Athens, Ga., 1991), 77.

48. Charles A. Dana, *Recollections of the Civil War* (New York, 1899), 199.

49. Wainwright, *Diary of Battle,* ed. Nevins, 373–4; Grant to Halleck, May 16, 1864, in *OR,* Vol. 36, Pt. 2, pp. 809–10.

50. Lyman, *Meade's Headquarters,* ed. Agassiz, 115; Lyman journal, May 16, 1864, in Lyman Collection, MHS.

51. Ibid.; George Meade, ed., *Life and Letters of George Gordon Meade,* vol. 2 (New York, 1913), 197–8.

52. Dana to Stanton, 9:00 A.M., May 16, 1864, in *OR,* Vol. 36, Pt. 1, p. 71; Dana, *Recollections,* 199.

53. Seth Williams to Warren, May 16, 1864, in *OR,* Vol. 36, Pt. 2, pp. 818–19; Warren to Williams, May 16, 1864, ibid., 819; Williams to Warren, ibid., 819.

54. Grant to John J. Abercrombie, May 16, 1864, ibid., 828; Abercrombie to Williams, May 16, 1864, ibid., 828–9; Grant to Robert O. Tyler, May 16, 1864, ibid., 829.

55. Dana to Stanton, 8:00 A.M., May 7, 1864, ibid., Pt. 1, p. 72; Halleck to Grant, 9:30 P.M., May 16, 1864, ibid., Pt. 2, p. 810.

56. Grant to Meade, May 11, 1864, ibid., 628; Rawlins to Meade, 4:45 P.M., May 16, 1864, ibid., 811; Rawlins to Burnside, 3:00 P.M., May 16, 1864, ibid., 826; Grant, *Personal Memoirs,* 2, p. 241.

57. Henry J. Hunt's report, in *OR,* Vol. 36, Pt. 1, pp. 287–8; Henry J. Hunt journal, 21–27, in LC; Rawlins to Burnside, 6:00 P.M., May 17, 1864, in *OR,* Vol. 36, Pt. 2, p. 849; Burnside to Rawlins, 6:20 P.M., May 17, 1864, ibid.; Special Orders No. 136, May 16, 1864, ibid., 813; Nevins, *Diary of Battle,* 374–5.

58. Halleck to Grant, 1:00 P.M., May 16, 1864, in *OR,* Vol. 36, Pt. 2, p. 810; Simon, *Papers of Ulysses S. Grant,* 10, pp. 453–4, n.1.

59. Grant to Burnside, May 16, 1864, in *OR,* Vol. 36, Pt. 2, p. 825.

60. Dana to Stanton, 7:00 A.M., May 16, 1864, ibid., Pt. 1, pp. 70–1.

61. L. A. Hendrick's dispatch, May 16, 1864, *New York Herald,* May 19, 1864; Meade to Warren, in *OR,* Vol. 36, Pt. 2, p. 816.

62. Warren to Meade, 12:35 P.M. May 16, 1864, ibid., 816; Charles Thomas Bowen diary, May 16, 1864, in FSNMP; Roebling's report, in Warren Collection, NYSLA.

63. "General Burnside's Corps," *New York Times,* May 24, 1864; Burnside to Grant, May 16, 1864, in *OR,* Vol. 36, Pt. 2, p. 825; Burnside's report, ibid., Pt. 1, p. 910; John W. Roder's report, ibid., 535; J. C. Fitzpatrick's dispatch, May 17, 1864, in *New York Tribune,* May 20, 1864; Cadmus M. Wilcox's report, in VSL; Charles E. Wood diary, May 16, 1864, in Civil War Miscellaneous Collection, USAMHI; Hopkins, *Seventh Regiment Rhode Island Volunteers,* 173.

64. Meade to Warren, 1:45 P.M., May 16, 1864, in *OR,* Vol. 36, Pt. 2, p. 817; Meade to Burnside, 1:45 P.M., May 16, 1864, ibid., 826; 2nd Corps Daily Memoranda, ibid., Pt. 1, p. 361.

65. Couse to unknown, May 16, 1864, in UV; Dispatch, May 18, in *Philadelphia Inquirer,* May 20, 1864.

66. Couse to unknown, May 16, 1864, in UV; E. W. B., "Reminiscences," in *Recollections and Reminiscences,* I, 29.

67. Porter, *Campaigning with Grant,* 121.

68. Abbott, *Personal Recollections,* 61; Nevins, *Diary of Battle,* 374.

69. Francis Cordrey manuscript, in Scott C. Patchen Private Collection.

70. Cockrell and Ballard, *Mississippi Rebel,* 265; J. F. J. Caldwell, *The History of a Brigade of South Carolinians, First Known as Gregg's, and Subsequently as McGowan's Brigade* (Philadelphia, 1866), 151; Shiver, "Wright's Brigade at Spotsylvania Courthouse," *Atlanta Journal,* October 16, 1901; John H. Worsham, *One of Jackson's Foot Cavalry* (Jackson, Tenn., 1964), 138.

71. Anderson's report, in DU; Sorrel Journal, May 15–16, 1864, in MC; John Bratton's report, in *SHSP,* 8, p. 549; Ott, "Diary of James J. Kirkpatrick," 196; Robert K. Krick, *Parker's Virginia Battery C.S.A.* (Berryville, Va., 1975), 250–1; Jennings C. Wise, *The Long Arm of Lee; or, The History of the Artillery of the Army of Northern Virginia,* vol. 2 (Lynchburg, Va., 1915), 799. The brigades of Brigadier Generals Edward L. Thomas and Alfred M. Scales held the northern end of Hill's division, where Samuel McGowan's brigade—now under Colonel Joseph N. Brown—was stationed in reserve. Farther south, Hill's line bulged toward the Federals to form

Heth's Salient, occupied by Brigadier General Joseph R. Davis's Mississippians and a mixed Virginia, Tennessee, and Alabama outfit under Colonel Robert M. Mayo. Below them stood the brigades of Brigadier Generals James Lane, John R. Cooke, William W. Kirkland, and Colonel David A. Weisiger. Wright's, Harris's, and Perry's men deployed toward Massaponax Church Road to form the junction with Anderson's corps. Colonel R. Lindsay Walker's five artillery batteries commanded the approaches to Hill's position. See Wilcox's report, in VSL, and Lee to Ewell, May 16, 1864, in *OR*, Vol. 36, Pt. 2, p. 1012.

72. Coles, *From Huntsville to Appomattox,* 171; Gallagher, ed., *Fighting for the Confederacy,* 381.

73. Seddon to Lee, May 16, 1864, in *OR,* Vol. 61, Pt. 2, pp. 936–7; Lee to Breckinridge, May 16, 1864, in Dowdey, *Wartime Papers of R. E. Lee,* 731–2.

74. Henry Herbert Harris diary, May 16, 1864, in FSNMP; Louis N. Beaudry, *Historic Records of the Fifth New York Cavalry, First Ira Harris Guard* (Albany, N.Y., 1874), 129; Hammond to Wright, May 16, 1864, in *OR,* Vol. 36, Pt. 2, pp. 824–5; W. H. F. Lee to R. E. Lee, May 16, 1864, ibid., Vol. 61, Pt. 2, p. 937; W. H. F. Lee to R. E. Lee, 7:30 P.M., May 16, 1864, ibid. Harry L. Jackson, *First Regiment Engineer Troops P.A.C.S.: Robert E. Lee's Combat Engineers* (Louisa, Va., 1998), 37–39, details the work of the Confederate engineers at Stanard's Mill.

75. Lee to Davis, May 16, 1864, ibid., Vol. 36, Pt. 2, p. 1011; Lee to Seddon, May 16, 1864, ibid.; Lee to Ewell, May 16, 1864, ibid., 1012.

76. Henry B. McClellan manuscript, quoted in Freeman, *R. E. Lee,* 3, p. 334.

V MAY 17–18 *GRANT LAUNCHES HIS GRAND ASSAULT*

1. George Breck to family, May 17, 1864, *Rochester (N.Y.) Union and Advertiser,* May 27, 1864.

2. Dana to Stanton, 4:00 P.M., May 17, 1864, in *OR,* Vol. 36, Pt. 1, p. 72.

3. Grant's report, ibid., 20; Lee to Seddon, May 17, 1864, ibid., Pt. 2, p. 1015.

4. Dowdey, *Wartime Papers of R. E. Lee,* 732–3.

5. Grant to Burnside, May 17, 1864, in *OR,* Vol. 36, Pt. 2, p. 850; Dana to Stanton, 4 P.M., May 17, 1864, ibid., Pt. 1, p. 72.

6. Lyman journal, May 17, 1864, in Lyman Collection, MHS. "Mr. Anderson's house was surrounded by a fine garden, in which bloomed many varieties of fragrant roses and honeysuckles," a Federal with an eye to horticulture noted. "An extensive young orchard in a very flourishing condition formed one of the many attractions of this snug little homestead." S. F. P., "The Scenery on the Path of Our Army," *Providence (R.I.) Daily Journal,* June 11, 1864. Today the Anderson property is the site of a quarry.

7. Luther Rose memorandum, May 16, 1864, in LC; Meade to Hancock, May 17, 1864, in *OR,* Vol. 36, Pt. 2, p. 844; 2nd Corps circular, May 17, 1864, ibid., 845; Roebling's report, in Warren Collection, NYSLA.

8. Shreve, "Operations of the Army of the Potomac May 13–June 2,1864," *PMHSM,* 4, pp. 294–5; Morse, *Personal Experiences,* 98.

9. Joseph K. Newell, *Ours: Annals of 10th Regiment, Massachusetts Volunteers in the Rebellion* (Springfield, Mass., 1875), 271; Benedict, *Vermont in the Civil War,* 1, p. 451 (mistakenly places 3rd Vermont's reconnaissance on May 16).

10. Humphreys, *Virginia Campaign,* 110.

11. Ibid.; Grant to Burnside, May 17, 1864, in *OR,* Vol. 36, Pt. 2, p. 850.

12. Porter, *Campaigning with Grant,* 122; Meade to Hancock, 7:00 P.M., May 17, 1864, in *OR,* Vol. 36, Pt. 2, p. 844; Grant to Burnside, ibid., 850.

13. John C. Tidball's report, in *OR,* Vol. 36, Pt. 1, p. 510; Abbott, *Personal Recollections,* 61; Nevins, *Diary of Battle,* 375; L. A. Hendrick's dispatch, May 17, 1864, *New York Tribune,* May 20, 1864; Meade to wife, May 17, 1864, in Meade, *Life and Letters,* 2, pp. 196–7.

14. Lee to Seddon, May 17, 1864, in *OR,* Vol. 36, Pt. 2, p. 1015; "The Battles in Northern Virginia," *Richmond Enquirer,* May 24, 1864.

15. Theodore Lyman, "Extract from Diary," *PMHSM,* 4, p. 237.

16. Long's report, in *OR,* Vol. 36, Pt. 1, p. 1046; William S. White, "A Diary of the War, or What I Saw of It," in *Contributions to a History of the Richmond Howitzer Battalion,* vol. 2 (Richmond, 1883), 253.

17. William H. Palmer to Douglas Southall Freeman, June 25, 1920, in Freeman, *R. E. Lee,* 3, pp. 330–1. Wright's unsuccessful action that provoked Hill's rebuke is described in *Richmond Daily Dispatch,* May 23, 1864. Palmer thought the incident occurred on May 18. Freeman presumed that it occurred on May 15, assuming that it corresponded with the operation against Myers Hill (which in fact occurred on May 14). Wright, however, was not with his brigade at Myers Hill, and the brigade's performance there was so successful that Early commended it. The engagement on the evening of May 17, however, was conducted by Wright and was bungled. As Wright undertook no reported operations on May 18, the action of May 17 is the most probable occasion for Lee's comments.

18. William T. Poague to father, June 1, 1864, in Monroe F. Cockrell, ed., *Gunner with Stonewall: Reminiscences of William Thomas Poague* (Jackson, Tenn., 1957), 93.

19. "Diary of a Confederate Officer," *Our Living and Our Dead,* February 11, 1874, p 3; Orders, Third Division, in *OR,* Vol. 36, Pt. 2, p. 815; Itinerary of Third Division, Second Army Corps, ibid., Pt. 1, p. 467; P. Regis de Trobriand's report, ibid., 471; William B. Neeper's report, ibid., 484; David Craft, *History of the One Hundred Forty-First Regiment Pennsylvania Volunteers, 1862–1865* (Towanda, Pa., 1885), 200.

20. "Diary of a Confederate Officer," *Our Living and Our Dead,* February 11, 1874.

21. Tidball's report, in *OR,* Vol. 36, Pt. 1, p. 510.

22. John Gibbon's report, ibid., 431; John R. Brooke's report, ibid., 411; Thomas A. Smyth's report, ibid., 449.

23. Hancock to Williams, 3:00 A.M., May 18, 1864, ibid., Pt. 2, p. 866; Walter S. Gilman, "Life in Virginia or Thirty-Four Days in Grant's Army in the Field," 5–7, in Lewis Leigh Collection, USAMHI.

24. Delavan S. Miller, *Drum Taps in Dixie: Memories of a Drummer Boy, 1861–1865* (Watertown, N.Y., 1905), 86; William H. Morgan, comp., *A Narrative of the Service of Company D, First Massachusetts Heavy Artillery, in the War of the Rebellion, 1861–1865* (Boston, 1907), 17; Alfred S. Roe and Charles Nutt, *History of the First Regiment of Heavy Artillery Massachusetts Volunteers* (Worcester, Mass., 1917), 33–4.

25. Robert G. Carter, comp., *Four Brothers in Blue; or, Sunshine and Shadows of the War of the Rebellion* (Austin, Tex., 1978), 399; D. S. Miller, *Drum Taps in Dixie,* 82.

26. Wilbur Fisk to family, May 25, 1864, in Emil Rosenblatt and Ruth Rosenblatt, eds., *Hard Marching Every Day: The Civil War Letters of Wilbur Fisk, 1861–1865* (Lawrence, Kans., 1992), 224; Charles H. Tompkins's report, in *OR,* Vol. 36, Pt. 1, pp. 756–7; Charles W. White's report, ibid., 759.

27. A. M. Stewart, *Camp, March and Battlefield; or, Three Years and a Half with the Army of the Potomac* (Philadelphia, 1865), 384–5.

28. George W. Getty's report, in *OR,* Vol. 36, Pt. 1, p. 679; Lewis Grant's report, ibid., 705. Wheaton's regiments, from left to right, were the 102nd Pennsylvania, the 93rd Pennsylvania, the 98th Pennsylvania, the 62nd New York, and the 139th Pennsylvania; Wheaton's report, ibid., 685. The regimental alignment of Neill's other brigades is not known.

29. Agassiz, *Meade's Headquarters,* 166–7.

30. Lyman to family, May 23, 1864, ibid., 116; Massachusetts Historical Society, *War Diary and Letters of Stephen Minot Weld, 1861–1865* (Boston, 1979), 291; Joseph H. Barnes's report, in *OR,* Vol. 36, Pt. 1, pp. 920; Warren Wilkinson, *Mother, May You Never See the Sights I Have Seen: The Fifty-Seventh Massachusetts Veteran Volunteers in the Last Year of the Civil War* (New York, 1990), 116.

31. Weld, *War Diary and Letters,* 293–4; Committee of the Regiment, *Thirty-Fifth Regiment Massachusetts Volunteers,* 231.

32. Nevins, *Diary of Battle,* 376–7; Powell, *History of the Fifth Army Corps,* 652. Major Robert H. Fitzhugh commanded Sheldon's battery.

33. Committee of the Regiment, *Thirty-Fifth Regiment Massachusetts Volunteers,* 232; Jackman and Hadley, *History of the Sixth New Hampshire Regiment,* 250.

34. Wainwright's report, in *OR,* Vol. 36, Pt.1, p. 644; Nevins, *Diary of Battle,* 376–7; William N. Pendleton's report, in *OR,* Vol. 36, Pt. 1, p. 1046; Peter S. Carmichael, *Lee's Young Artillerist: William R. J. Pegram* (Charlottesville, Va., 1995), 120. Warren reported that the Confederate guns fired back "but little"; Warren to Humphreys, 7:20 A.M., May 18, 1864, in *OR,* Vol. 36, Pt. 2, p. 873.

35. Marion H. Fitzpatrick to Amanda Fitzpatrick, May 20, 1864, in Hammock, *Letters to Amanda,* 128.

36. Jackman and Hadley, *Sixth New Hampshire Regiment,* 251.

37. Ibid., 251–2; Howard M. Hanson diary, May 18, 1864, University of New Hampshire Library; Houston, *Thirty Second Maine Regiment,* 156–7.

38. J. N. Jones diary, May 18, 1864, in Civil War Times Illustrated Collection, USAMHI; Wood diary, May 18, 1864, in Civil War Miscellaneous Collection, USAMHI.

39. James H. Ledlie's report, in *OR,* Vol. 36, Pt. 1, p. 917; Weld, *War Diary and Letters,* 294.

40. Weld, *War Diary and Letters,* 294; John Anderson, *The Fifty-Seventh Regiment of Massachusetts Volunteers in the War of the Rebellion* (Boston, 1896), 89.

41. Weld, *War Diary and Letters,* 294; Committee of the Regiment, *Thirty-Fifth Regiment Massachusetts Volunteers,* 232.

42. Committee of the Regiment, *Thirty-Fifth Regiment Massachusetts Volunteers,* 232–3.

43. "From the Seventh Rhode Island," *Providence (R.I.) Evening Press,* June 13, 1864; Hopkins, *Seventh Regiment Rhode Island Volunteers,* 174–5.

44. J. C. Fitzpatrick's dispatch, May 18, 1864, *New York Herald,* May 21, 1864.

45. Hancock to Humphreys, 4:05 A.M., May 18, 1864, in *OR,* Vol. 36, Pt. 2, p. 866; Lyman journal, May 18, 1864, in Lyman Collection, MHS.

46. Howe, *Touched with Fire,* 125; J. L. Bowen, *Thirty-Seventh Regiment Massachusetts Volunteers,* 317; Unsigned letter "From the Rifle Pits," May 19, 1864, in *Providence (R.I.) Daily Journal,* June 1, 1864.

47. Thomas Benton Reed, *A Private in Gray* (Camden, Ark., 1905), 78; "Army of Northern Virginia," *Richmond Examiner,* May 23, 1864; White, "A Diary of the War," II, 254.

48. W. E. Cutshaw, "An Address Before R. E. Lee Camp, No. 1, C. V., on the Night of January 20, 1905," *SHSP,* 33, pp. 332–3.

49. William G. Mitchell, 2nd Corps Daily Memoranda, in *OR,* Vol. 36, Pt. 1, p. 361.

50. Wesley Brainerd, *Bridge Building in Wartime,* ed. Ed Malles (Knoxville, Tenn., 1997), 221.

51. Unsigned letter "From the Rifle Pits," May 19, 1864, *Providence (R.I.) Daily Journal,* June 1, 1864; Cutshaw, "Address Before R. E. Lee Camp," 333; "H. W. Wingfield Diary," May 18, 1864, *Bulletin of the Virginia State Library,* 16 (1927), 39.

52. J. D. Smith, *Nineteenth Regiment of Maine Volunteer Infantry,* 162–3; George A. Bruce, *The Twentieth Regiment of Massachusetts Volunteer Infantry, 1861–1865* (Boston, 1906), 384–5; Henry Roback, *The Veteran Volunteers of Herkimer and Otsego Counties in the War of the Rebellion, Being a History of the 152nd New York* (Little Falls, N.Y., 1888), 83–4; "Charges and Specifications Preferred Against Brigadier General J. T. Owen, U. S. Volunteers," in *OR,* Vol. 36, Pt. 1, pp. 435–6. Additional charges were preferred against Owen for dereliction on June 3, 1864, and he was mustered out of service.

53. D. P. Conyngham, *The Irish Brigade and Its Campaigns* (New York, 1867), 450–3; Mathew Murphy's report, in *OR,* Vol. 36, Pt. 1, p. 459; Galwey, *Valiant Hours,* 217–18.

54. St. Claire A. Mulholland, *The Story of the 116th Regiment Pennsylvania Volunteers in the War of the Rebellion: The Record of a Gallant Command* (Philadelphia, 1899), 222–3; Kenneth H. Power memoir, May 18, 1864, in Book 45, FSNMP. The 125th New York's historian contended that his regiment occupied the Confederate works. He probably confused the abandoned rebel reserve line, which the Federals did occupy, with the actual Confederate line. Ezra D. Simons, *A Regimental History of the One Hundred and Twenty-Fifth New York State Volunteers* (New York, 1888), 211.

55. Tyler, *Recollections of the Civil War,* 206.

56. Penrose G. Mark, *Red, White, and Blue Badge: Pennsylvania Veteran Volunteers, A History of the 93rd Regiment, Known as the "Lebanon Infantry" and "One of the 300 Fighting Regiments" from September 12th, 1861 to June 27th, 1865* (Harrisburg, Pa., 1911), 269.

57. Ibid.; Wheaton's report, in *OR,* Vol. 36, Pt. 1, pp. 685–6.

58. Oliver Edwards memorandum, 158–9, in ISHL; Newell, *Annals of 10th Regiment, Massachusetts Volunteers,* 272; J. L. Bowen, *Thirty-Seventh Regiment Massachusetts Volunteers,* 317.

59. Frederick D. Bidwell, comp., *History of the Forty-Ninth New York Volunteers* (Albany, N.Y., 1916), 57; Edgar O. Burts diary, May 18, 1864, in Michael T. Russert Collection, Cambridge, New York; Newell, *Annals of 10th Regiment, Massachusetts Volunteers,* 272; Edwards memorandum, 159, in ISHL.

60. Henry Houghton, "The Ordeal of Civil War: A Recollection," *Vermont History,* 61 (1973), 37; Benedict, *Vermont in the Civil War,* 1, p. 452; Wilbur Fisk to family, May 25, 1864, in Rosenblatt, *Hard Marching Every Day,* 224.

61. Robert Hunt Rhodes, ed., *All for the Union: The Civil War Diary and Letters of Elisha Hunt Rhodes* (New York, 1991), 154; Harrison B. George diary, May 18, 1864, in Minnesota Historical Society.

62. Newell, *Annals of 10th Regiment, Massachusetts Volunteers,* 272–3; J. L. Bowen, *Thirty-Seventh Regiment Massachusetts Volunteers,* 317.

63. F. Larue, "Notes from the Battlefield," *Xenia (Ohio) Torch-Light,* June 1, 1864; Prowell, *Eighty-Seventh Regiment, Pennsylvania Volunteers,* 140–1.

64. Read diary, May 18, 1864, in Ricketts Collection, Manassas National Battlefield Park Library; Howe, *Touched with Fire,* 125; Wheaton's report, in *OR,* Vol. 36, Pt. 1, p. 686.

65. Weld, *War Diary and Letters,* 294; Committee of the Regiment, *Thirty-Fifth Regiment Massachusetts Volunteers,* 233; Wilkinson, *Mother, May You Never See,* 120.

66. Committee of the Regiment, *Thirty-Fifth Regiment Massachusetts Volunteers,* 233–4.

67. Potter to Burnside, 6:10 A.M., May 18, 1864, in *OR,* Vol. 36, Pt. 2, pp. 880–1.

68. Jackman and Hadley, *Sixth New Hampshire Regiment,* 254.

69. Mills to mother, May 20, 1864, in Coco, *Through Blood and Fire,* 87; Jackman and Hadley, *Sixth New Hampshire Regiment,* 255.

70. Hancock to Humphreys, 5:40 A.M., May 18, 1864, in *OR,* Vol. 36, Pt. 2, p. 867.

71. Humphreys to Hancock, 6:15 A.M., May 18, 1864, ibid., 867; Hancock to Seth Williams, 6:50 A.M., May 18, 1864, ibid., 867–8; Wright to Humphreys, May 18, 1864, ibid., 878.

72. Porter, *Campaigning with Grant,* 123–24; Garrison, *Memoir,* 91.

73. Frank Wilkeson, *Recollections of a Private Soldier in the Army of the Potomac* (New York, 1887), 91–3.

74. Hancock to Humphreys, 8:30 A.M., May 18, 1864, in *OR,* Vol. 36, Pt. 2, p. 868; Unsigned letter "From the Rifle Pits," May 19, 1864, *Providence (R.I.) Daily Journal,* June 1, 1864.

75. John W. Kimball to wife, May 19, 1864, in Roe and Nutt, *First Regiment of Heavy Artillery,* 49; D. S. Miller, *Drum Taps in Dixie,* 84–5.

76. Humphreys to Hancock, 8:45 A.M., May 18, 1864, in *OR,* Vol. 36, Pt. 2, p. 869; Grant to Burnside, 9:00 A.M., May 18, 1864, ibid., 880; Cutshaw, "Address Before R. E. Lee Camp," *SHSP,* 33, p. 333; George Q. Peyton, *A Civil War Record for 1865–1865,* ed. by Robert A. Hodge (Fredericksburg, Va., 1981), 31; T. L. Jones, *Memoirs of Captain William J. Seymour,* 128; White, "A Diary of the War," 256; Henry J. Egan to brother, June 21, 1864, in L. S. Egan Collection, LSU.

77. Mulholland, *116th Regiment, Pennsylvania Volunteers,* 223–5; Howe, *Touched With Fire,* 126. Dana reported that Grant ordered the assault to cease at 9:00 A.M.; Dana to Stanton, May 18, 1864, in *OR,* Vol. 36, Pt. 1, p. 73.

78. "Army of Northern Virginia," *Richmond Examiner,* May 23, 1864; Robert J. Driver, *52nd Virginia Infantry* (Lynchburg, Va., 1986), 57; Long's report, in *OR,* Vol. 36, Pt. 1, pp. 1087–8.

79. White, "A Diary of the War," 256.

80. Lyman journal, May 18, 1864, in Lyman Collection, MHS.

81. Ibid.; Porter, *Campaigning with Grant,* 125–6; Halleck to Grant, 11:30 P.M., May 17, 1864, in *OR,* Vol. 36, Pt. 2, p. 840.

82. Grant, *Personal Memoirs,* 2, p. 238; Porter, *Campaigning with Grant,* 126.

83. Lyman journal, May 18, 1864, in Lyman Collection, MHS; McParlin's report, in *OR,* Vol. 36, Pt. 1, p. 232.

84. McParlin's report, in *OR,* Vol. 36, Pt. 1, p. 254; Francis A. Walker, *General Hancock* (New York, 1895), 206; Francis A. Walker, *History of the Second Army Corps in the Army of the Potomac* (New York, 1887), 486; Joseph R. C. Ward, *History of the One Hundred and Sixth Regiment Pennsylvania Volunteers* (Philadelphia, 1883), 254; Norman M. Covert, ed., *Two Civil War Diaries: Sgt. John L. Ryno and Bandmaster John Chadwick, Company C, 126th New York Regiment, 3rd Brigade, 2nd Division, II U.S. Corps* (N.p., n.d.), 21; Unsigned letter "From the Rifle Pits," May 19, 1864, *Providence (R.I.) Daily Journal,* June 1, 1864.

85. Walker, *General Hancock,* 206–7; Francis C. Barlow to mother, May 18, 1864, in Francis C. Barlow Collection, MHS; Lyman journal, May 18, 1864, in Lyman Collection, MHS.

86. J. L. Bowen, *Thirty Seventh Regiment Massachusetts Volunteers,* 318; Rawle to mother, May 29, 1864, in Civil War Library and Museum, Philadelphia; Meade to wife, May 19, 1864, in Meade, *Life and Letters,* 2, p. 197.

87. Grant's Report, in *OR,* Vol. 36, Pt. 1, p. 19. At noon on May 18, Dana wrote War Secretary Stanton: "General Grant had issued his orders for another movement which he has for several days had in contemplation, but which he did not wish to try till after this last attempt to get the enemy out of his stronghold by attacking it on one of its flanks"; Dana to Stanton, 12:00 M., May 18, 1864, ibid., Pt. 1, p. 73.

88. Grant, *Memoirs,* 2, p. 239; William Swinton's dispatch, May 25, 1864, *New York Times,* May 28, 1864.

89. William Swinton's dispatch, May 25, 1864, *New York Times,* May 28, 1864. A British student of the campaign aptly noted, "Meade's famous instructions, 'Wherever Lee goes, there will you go too,' are now modified, and the Army of the Potomac is to act so that wherever it goes, Lee is compelled to follow"; C. F. Atkinson, *Grant's Campaigns of 1864 and 1865: The Wilderness and Cold Harbor* (London, 1908), 328.

90. Grant to Meade, May 18, 1864, in *OR,* Vol. 36, Pt. 2, pp. 864–5.

91. Warren to Humphreys, 6:00 P.M., May 18, 1864, ibid., 875; Wright to Warren, May 18, 1864, ibid., 874; Wheaton's report, ibid., Pt. 1, p. 686; Howe, *Touched With Fire,* 126; Read diary, May 18, 1864, in Ricketts Collection, Manassas National Battlefield Park; Nelson V. Hutchinson, *History of the Seventh Massachusetts Volunteer Infantry in the War of the Rebellion* (Taunton, Mass., 1890), 187.

92. Roebling's report, in Warren Collection, NYSLA; John Chester White journal, 70–1, in LC; O. R. Howard Thomson and William H. Rauch, *History of the Bucktails: Kane Rifle Regiment of the Pennsylvania Reserve Corps* (Philadelphia, 1906), 307–8; Sypher, *Pennsylvania Reserve Corps,* 536.

93. John W. Jaques, *Three Years' Campaign of the Ninth N.Y.S.M. During the Southern Rebellion* (New York, 1865), 191–2; Hall, *Ninety-Seventh Regiment New York Volunteers,* 186–87; Crawford to A. S. Marvin. Jr., May 18, 1864, in *OR,* Vol. 36, Pt. 2, p. 877.

94. Humphreys to Hancock, 8:45 A.M., May 18, 1864, in *OR,* Vol. 36, Pt. 2, p. 869; Humphreys to Hancock, received 5:45 P.M., May 18, 1864, ibid.; Charles H. Morgan to Birney, May 18, 1864, ibid., 872; William R. Driver Circular, May 18, 1864, ibid., 871; Burnside circular, 10:00 P.M., May 18, 1864, ibid., 881; Burnside to Grant, 5:45 A.M., May 19, 1864, ibid., 927; Burnside to Grant, 1:45 P.M., May 19, 1864, ibid., 927–8; Grant to Burnside, May 19, 1864, ibid., 928; Wright to Humphreys, 7:15 A.M., May 19, 1864, ibid., 924; Frank Wheaton's report, ibid., Pt. 1, p. 686; Willcox's report, ibid., 945; John F. Hartranft's report, ibid., 951. From left to right, the 5th Corps's divisions were those of Cutler, Crawford, and Griffin; the 6th Corps's divisions, those of Russell, Neill, and Ricketts; and the 9th Corps's divisions, those of Willcox, Crittenden, and Potter.

95. Fitzpatrick to wife, May 19, 1864, in Hammock, *Letters to Amanda,* 128.

96. Joseph B. Parsons, *The 10th Regiment: Salient Points in Its History* (N.p., n.d.), 12–13.

97. Perry, *Letters from a Surgeon,* 181–3.

98. G. W. Grimes to father, May 21, 1864, in Book 113, FSNMP; Lewis Warlick to Corrie, May 19, 1864, in McGimsey Collection, SHC.

99. William N. Pendleton to Edward P. Alexander, 9:00 P.M., May 18, 1864, in *OR,* Vol. 36, Pt. 2, pp. 1019–20.

100. William H. F. Lee to Charles S. Venable, 6:00 A.M., May 18, 1864, ibid., Vol. 51, Pt. 2, p. 942; Breckinridge to Lee, May 18, 1864, ibid., 943.

101. Davis to Lee, May 17, 1864, ibid., Vol. 51, Pt. 2, p. 939; Lee to Davis, May 18, 1864, ibid., 942; Lee to Fitzhugh Lee, May 18, 1864, ibid., 943.

102. Lee to Seddon, 7:00 P.M., May 18, 1864, ibid., Pt. 2, p. 1019; Lee to Davis, May 18,

1864, in Douglas Southall Freeman, ed., *Lee's Dispatches to Jefferson Davis* (New York, 1957), 183–4.

103. Freeman, *Lee's Dispatches*, 184–5.

104. Lee to Davis, May 18, 1864, ibid., 187.

VI MAY 19–20 *EWELL STRIKES AT HARRIS FARM*

1. Aldrich, *History of Battery A*, 333; Luther A. Rose memorandum, May 19, 1864, in Rose Collection, LC; L. A. Hendrick's dispatch, May 19, 1864, *New York Herald*, May 21, 1864.

2. Hyland C. Kirk, *Heavy Guns and Light: A History of the 4th New York Heavy Artillery* (New York, 1890), 137–8, 177; Joel Brown, "The Charge of the Heavy Artillery," *Rockland (Me.) Bugle*, 1 (1894), 4. Company E of the 2nd Battalion was assigned to the ordnance train and did not join Kitching; Howard L. Kelly to father, May 20, 1864, *Rochester (N.Y.) Union and Advertiser*, May 27, 1864.

3. Warren to J. Howard Kitching, May 18, 1864, in *OR*, Vol. 36, Pt. 2, p. 878; Kelly to father, May 20, 1864, *Rochester (N.Y.) Union and Advertiser*, May 27, 1864; Harrison, *Gazetteer of Historic Sites*, 2, pp. 128, 302.

4. A. C. Brown, *Diary of a Line Officer*, 48; Kirk, *Heavy Guns and Light*, 218–19; Kelly to father, May 20, 1864, *Rochester (N.Y.) Union and Advertiser*, May 27, 1864.

5. Kirk, *Heavy Guns and Light*, 219–20; Meade to Warren, 9:30 A.M., May 19, 1864, in *OR*, Vol. 36, Pt. 2, p. 913; Humphreys to Warren, 9:00 A.M., May 19, 1864, ibid., 913; Warren to Humphreys, 10:15 A.M., May 19, 1864, ibid., 914; Warren to Humphreys, 11:30 A.M., May 19, 1864, ibid.

6. Walter H. Taylor, *General Lee: His Campaigns in Virginia, 1861–1865, with Personal Reminiscences* (Norfolk, Va. 1906), 243; Charles S. Venable, "General Lee in the Wilderness Campaign," *B&L*, 4, p. 243; Lee to Seddon, May 19, 1864, in *OR*, Vol. 36, Pt. 2, p. 1022; Ewell's report, ibid., Pt. 1, p. 1073.

7. Ewell's report, in *OR*, Vol. 36, Pt. 1, p. 1073. William N. Pendleton's report, ibid., 1046; Wade Hampton, "Connected Narrative," 37, in University of South Carolina, South Caroliniana Room; Myers, *Comanches*, 284; Diary of the First Army Corps, May 19, 1864, in *OR*, Vol. 36, Pt. 1, p. 1058.

8. Peyton, *Civil War Record*, 32; Pulaski Cowper, comp., *Extracts of Letters of Major General Bryan Grimes to His Wife* (Raleigh, N.C., 1884), 53.

9. Joseph T. Durkin, ed., *Confederate Chaplin: A War Journal of Rev. James B. Sheeran, c.ss.r., 14th Louisiana, C.S.A.* (Milwaukee, 1960), 88–9.

10. Peyton, *Civil War Record*, 32; Pendleton's report, in *OR*, Vol. 36, Pt. 1, p. 1046; T. M. Gorman memoir, May 19, 1864, in NCDAH.

11. Grant to Halleck, 1 P.M., May 19, 1864, in *OR*, Vol. 36, Pt. 2, p. 906; Halleck to Grant, 10:00 P.M., May 19, 1864, ibid., 907.

12. Humphreys to Hancock, 1:30 P.M., May 18, 1864, in *OR*, Vol. 36, Pt. 2, p. 910; Hancock to Humphreys, May 18, 1864, ibid.; Humphreys to Hancock, 1:50 P.M., May 18, 1864, ibid.; Aldrich, *History of Battery A*, 334.

13. Kelly to father, May 20, 1864, *Rochester (N.Y.) Union and Advertiser*, May 27, 1864.

14. D. S. Miller, *Drum Taps in Dixie*, 86; William H. Morgan, *Narrative of the Service of Company D*, 17; Roe and Nutt, *First Regiment of Heavy Artillery*, 33–4. The sequence and times that Tyler's regiments became engaged is subject to interpretation. Discrepancies among

accounts are numerous and frequently irreconcilable. Two superb historians have tried to make sense of the battle in recent years. See William D. Matter, *If It Takes All Summer: The Battle of Spotsylvania* (Chapel Hill, N.C., 1988), 320–5; and Noah Andre Trudeau, *Bloody Roads South: The Wilderness to Cold Harbor, May–June 1864* (Boston, 1989), 198–207. My rendition posits yet another version. Perhaps Civil War engagements are destined to remain as controversial to historians as they were to the men who fought in them.

15. N. P. Cutler diary, May 19, 1864, in Roe and Nutt, *First Regiment of Heavy Artillery,* 156; Charles A. Lewis account, ibid., 156–57; A. C. Brown, *Diary of a Line Officer,* 48; George H. Coffin, *Three Years in the Army* (N.p., 1925), 11.

16. N. P. Cutler diary, May 19, 1864, in Roe and Nutt, *First Regiment of Heavy Artillery,* 156.

17. Kirk, *Heavy Guns and Light,* 220.

18. A. C. Brown, *Diary of a Line Officer,* 48–9.

19. Kirk, *Heavy Guns and Light,* 220–1.

20. Kelly to father, May 20, 1864, *Rochester (N.Y.) Daily Union and Advertiser,* May 27, 1864; Kirk, *Heavy Guns and Light,* 221–2.

21. Kirk, *Heavy Guns and Light,* 222; James B. Lockwood, *Life and Adventures of a Drummer Boy; or, Seven Years a Soldier* (Albany, N.Y., 1893), 68.

22. Theodore Irving, *More Than Conqueror, or Memorials of Col. J. Howard Kitching* (New York, 1873), 129.

23. A. C. Brown, *Diary of a Line Officer,* 49–50; Kirk, *Heavy Guns and Light,* 223.

24. J. Payson Bradley, "Historical Address, May 19, 1901," in Joseph W. Gardner, *Souvenir: First Regiment of Heavy Artillery Massachusetts Volunteers, Dedication of Monument* (N.p., n.d.), 24; Roe and Nutt, *First Regiment of Heavy Artillery,* 153.

25. Bradley, "Historical Address," 24–5; Roe and Nutt, *First Regiment of Heavy Artillery,* 153, 156.

26. Bradley, "Historical Address," 25; Roe and Nutt, *First Regiment of Heavy Artillery,* 35.

27. D. S. Miller, *Drum Taps in Dixie,* 87–90; Roe and Nutt, *First Regiment of Heavy Artillery,* 154.

28. Ramseur's report, in *OR,* Vol. 36, Pt. 1, pp. 1032–3; F. C. Cox to editor, May 25, 1864, *Richmond Sentinel,* June 3, 1864. According to Cox, who led the foray to the wagons, the Confederates were from the former Stonewall Brigade and from the Louisiana brigade formerly commanded by Leroy Stafford.

29. A. C. Brown, *Diary of a Line Officer,* 50.

30. Porter, *Campaigning with Grant,* 126–7; Garrison, *Memoir,* 91–2.

31. Gilman, "Life in Virginia," 9, in Lewis Leigh Collection, USAMHI; Coffin, *Three Years in the Army,* 11; T. O. Talbot, "The Heavy Artillery," *National Tribune,* January 23, 1890.

32. Coffin, *Three Years in the Army,* 11.

33. Ibid.; Charles J. House, *The First Maine Heavy Artillery* (Portland, Me., 1903), 109–10; Rufus W. Clark, *The Heroes of Albany: A Memorial of the Patriot- Martyrs of the City and County of Albany* (Albany, N.Y., 1866), 340; Charles J. House, "How the First Maine Heavy Artillery Lost 1179 Men in 30 Days," *Rockland (Me.) Bugle,* 2 (1895), 89–90; A. C. Brown, *Diary of a Line Officer,* 50–1.

34. House, "How the First Maine Heavy Artillery Lost 1179 Men in 30 Days," 90–1.

35. Major Springfield to editor, May 20, 1864, *Albany (N.Y.) Evening Journal,* May 24, 1864; Fred Mather, "A 7th N.Y.H.A. Man Gives Some Experiences," *National Tribune,* January 30, 1896; Robert Keating, *Carnival of Blood: The Civil War Ordeal of the Seventh New York Heavy Artillery* (Baltimore, 1998), 45–7.

36. Cyrus B. Watson, "Remarks, May 19, 1901," in Gardner, *Souvenir,* 30.

37. Ibid., 30–1; Cyrus B. Watson, "Forty-Fifth Regiment," in Walter Clark, comp., *Histories of the Several Regiments and Battalions from North Carolina in the Great War,* vol. 3 (Goldsboro, N.C., 1901), 54; Risden T. Bennett, "Fourteenth Regiment," ibid., I, 726; J. A. Stikeleather reminiscences, in NCDAH.

38. Bradley, "Historical Address," 26; Cadwallader's dispatch, May 21, 1864, *New York Tribune,* May 23, 1864; Roe and Nutt, *First Regiment of Heavy Artillery,* 154; Harrison, *Gazetteer of Historic Sites,* 1, p. 303.

39. Roe and Nutt, *First Regiment of Heavy Artillery,* 158.

40. Porter, *Campaigning with Grant,* 127.

41. Prowell, *Eighty-Seventh Regiment, Pennsylvania Volunteers* 139; Charles Camper and J. W. Kirkley, *Historical Record of the First Regiment Maryland Infantry* (Washington, D.C., 1871), 143–4; "The Maryland Brigade," *Baltimore American and Commercial Advertiser,* May 26, 1864; Erastus M. Spaulding's report, in *OR,* Vol. 36, Pt. 1, p. 462. It cannot be said with certainty which of Tyler's regiments advanced with Dushane's battalion, although the 8th New York is the best candidate. Precise times are also difficult to gauge. The 8th New York reached the battlefield at approximately 6:00 P.M. (Arthur L. Chase diary, May 19, 1864, in Niagara County Historical Society, Lockport, N.Y.) See also Wilbur R. Dunn, *Full Measure of Devotion: The Eighth New York Volunteer Heavy Artillery,* vol. 1 (Kearney, Nebr., 1997), 285–90.

42. Roebling's report, in Warren Collection, NYSLA; Humphreys to Hancock, May 19, 1864, in *OR,* Vol. 36, Pt. 2, p. 911; Francis A. Walker circular, 5:30 P.M., May 19, 1864, ibid., 912; Hays, *Under the Red Patch,* 243; Craft, *One Hundred Forty-First Regiment,* 201; Charles H. Weygant, *History of the One Hundred and Twenty-Fourth Regiment New York State Volunteers* (Newburgh, N.Y., 1877), 341.

43. Richard N. Bowerman's report, in *OR,* Vol. 36, Pt. 1, p. 600; Samuel A. Graham's report, ibid., 602; Roebling's report, in Warren Collection, NYSLA; 2nd Corp addenda, ibid., 362; Edwin B. Houghton, *The Campaigns of the Seventeenth Maine* (Portland, Me., 1866), 184–85; Wainwright's report, in *OR,* Vol. 36, Pt. 1, p. 644. For communications describing the Maryland Brigade's outrage at its humiliating treatment by Warren, see E. F. M. Faehtz to Warren, May 16, 1864, ibid., Pt. 2, pp. 819–20, and Warren to Commanding Officer Maryland Brigade, May 16, 1864, ibid., 820–21.

44. Silliker, *Rebel Yell,* 160; Nevins, *Diary of Battle,* 379.

45. F. C. Cox to editor, May 25, 1864, *Richmond Sentinel,* June 3, 1864; Crocker diary, May 19, 1864, in Cornell University, John M. Olin Library; *Richmond Enquirer,* May 20, 1864; James N. Bosang, *Memoirs of a Pulaski Veteran of the Stonewall Brigade* (Pulaski, Va., 1912), 7; Peyton, *Civil War Record,* 32–3.

46. *South Danvers (Mass.) Wizard,* June 8, 1864; J. T. Watkins memoir, in Book 85, FSNMP. A Federal reported that Confederate sharpshooters concealed in treetops "came tumbling down like squirrels when our men discovered their leafy haunts"; *South Danvers (Mass.) Wizard,* June 8, 1864.

47. Early, *Autobiographical Sketch,* 357; Wiley J. Smith to Nannie, May 21, 1864, in Wiley J. Smith Collection, GDAH; Wilcox's report, in VSL; J. F. J. Caldwell, *Brigade of South Carolinians,* 151.

48. George A. Purington's report, in *OR,* Vol. 36, Pt. 1, p. 894; Hampton, "Connected Narrative," 27; Peyton, *Civil War Record,* 33; Neese, *Three Years in the Confederate Horse Artillery,* 272. Some Union reports asserted that Ferrero's division of black troops helped repel Rosser. Andrew Humphreys contended that Ferrero's men supported the union cavalry but "had

not a casualty of any kind whatever, handled nobody, . . . [and] were not engaged"; Humphreys, *Virginia Campaign,* 114–15n1. See also Edward Ferrero to Lewis Richmond, May 26, 1864, in *OR,* Vol. 36, Pt. 1, p. 987.

49. Casler, *Four Years in the Stonewall Brigade,* 217–18; "Army Correspondence, May 23, 1864," *Richmond Sentinel,* May 25, 1864; D. S. Miller, *Drum Taps in Dixie,* 90.

50. Walter Raleigh Battle to mother, May 25, 1864, in L. E. Lee, *Forget-Me-Nots,* 119.

51. Meade to Warren, 8:00 P.M., May 19, 1864, in *OR,* Vol. 36, Pt. 2, p. 918; Warren to Meade, 9:15 P.M., May 19, 1864, ibid., 919–20; Warren to Humphreys, 9:15 P.M., May 19, 1864, ibid., 921.

52. Grant to Halleck, 10:00 P.M., May 19, 1864, ibid., 906.

53. Sypher, *Pennsylvania Reserve Corps,* 536.

54. Peyton, *Civil War Record,* 33; Battle to mother, May 25, 1864, in L. E. Lee, *Forget-Me-Nots,* 119–20; Thomas F. Toon, "Twentieth Regiment," in W. Clark, *Histories of the Several Regiments,* 2, p. 122; J. F. J. Caldwell, *Brigade of South Carolinians,* 152; "Experiences with Army in Virginia," *Our Living and Our Dead* (New Bern, N.C.), February 11, 1864.

55. Kirk, *Heavy Guns and Light,* 231; Coffin, *Three Years in the Army,* 11; Porter, *Campaigning with Grant,* 128–9; House, "How the First Maine Heavy Artillery Lost 1179 Men in 30 Days," *Rockland (Me.) Bugle,* 2 (1895), 91.

56. E. B. Houghton, *Campaigns of the Seventeenth Maine,* 185; Hays, *Under the Red Patch,* 244; Stephen P. Chase diary and memoirs, Civil War Times Illustrated Collection, USAMHI, 111.

57. Ewell's Report, in *OR,* Vol. 36, Pt. 1, p. 1073; Richard L. Apple to wife, May 20, 1864, *Kennesaw (Ga.) Cadence,* October 28, 1987; Peter W. Alexander dispatch, May 20, 1864, *Columbia (S.C.) Daily South Carolinian,* May 29, 1864.

58. Apple to wife, May 20, 1864, *Kennesaw (Ga.) Cadence,* October 28, 1987; J. F. J. Caldwell, *Brigade of South Carolinians,* 152. After the war William Allen represented Lee as stating that he found Ewell on May 19 "prostrate on the ground, and declaring he cd not get Rodes div. out." Lee allegedly told Ewell "to order Rodes back, and that if he could not get him out, [Lee] could." Allen must have confused events on May 12 with those of May 19, as Lee did not go near the battle on May 19. The tenor of Lee's remarks to Allen, however, reflected Ewell's decreasing stature in Lee's eyes. William Allen, "Conversations with General Lee," in SHC.

59. Charles A. Page, *Letters of a War Correspondent* (Boston, 1899), 73–4; Kirk, *Heavy Guns and Light,* 232–3; Roe and Nutt, *First Regiment Heavy Artillery,* 155; House, "How the First Maine Heavy Artillery Lost 1,179 Men in 30 Days," 90; Tabular List of Casualties in the 2nd Corps from May 4 to November 1, 1864, Record Group 94, Entry 729, Box 98, NA; Samuel A. Graham's report, in *OR,* Vol. 36, Pt. 1, p. 602; Garrison, *Memoir,* 92; Roebling's report, in Warren Collection, NYSLA; Keating, *Carnival of Blood,* 53–4; Humphreys, *Virginia Campaign,* 115. Grant reported his losses for May 19 at 1,535; Grant to Halleck, May 20, 1864, in *OR,* Vol. 36, Pt. 3, p. 1.

60. Watson, "Remarks, May 19, 1901," 30; Brown, "Charge of the Heavy Artillery," *Rockland (Me.) Bugle,* 1 (1894), 5; Page, *Letters of a War Correspondent,* 72; Roebling's report, in Warren Collection, NYSLA; Wilkeson, *Recollections of a Private Soldier,* 86.

61. Hays, *Under the Red Patch,* 244; Meade to Grant, 5:30 A.M., May 20, 1864, in *OR,* Vol. 36, Pt. 3, p. 4; Hancock to Williams, May 20, 1864, ibid., 9.

62. Katherine Couse to friend, May 20, 1864, in UV.

63. Chase diary and memoirs, May 20, 1864, in Civil War Times Illustrated Collection,

USAMHI; Roe and Nutt, *First Regiment of Heavy Artillery*, 158; A. C. Brown, *Diary of a Line Officer*, 52–3; House, *First Maine Heavy Artillery*, 111–12.

64. Special Orders No. 137, May 17, 1864, in *OR*, Vol. 36, Pt. 2, p. 843; Jacob L. Bechtel to Miss Carrie, May 1, 1864, in Gettysburg National Military Park Library; John Gibbon, *Personal Recollections of the Civil War* (New York, 1928), 223; Banes, *Philadelphia Brigade*, 256–7.

65. J. D. Smith, *Nineteenth Regiment of Maine Volunteer Infantry*, 172–3; Banes, *Philadelphia Brigade*, 257–8; Gibbon, *Personal Recollections*, 224. Eric J. Mink of the Richmond National Military Park generously shared with me his research into Starbird, whom Mr. Mink discovered also went by the name of Lawrence J. Hoyt.

66. John G. B. Adams, *Reminiscences of the Nineteenth Massachusetts Regiment* (Boston, 1899), 94; Banes, *Philadelphia Brigade*, 259; Galwey, *Valiant Hours*, 219; John C. Anderson to Sister, May 20, 1864, in David G. Townshend, *The Seventh Michigan Volunteer Infantry* (Fort Lauderdale, Fl., 1993), 178–79; Imri A. Spencer to Cris, May 20, 1864, in Book 76, FSNMP.

67. Porter, *Campaigning with Grant*, 129–30; Aldrich, *History of Battery A*, 336.

68. Roebling's report, in Warren Collection, NYSLA; Silliker, *Rebel Yell*, 160; Cowtan, *Tenth New York Volunteers*, 274.

69. Paul E. Wilson and Harriett S. Wilson, eds., *The Civil War Diary of Thomas White Stephens, Sergeant, Company K, 20th Indiana Regiment of Volunteers* (Lawrence, Kans., 1985), 182; Roe, *Thirty-Ninth Regiment Massachusetts Volunteers*, 204; John Chester White journal, May 19, 1864, in LC; George Breck to wife, May 30, 1864, *Rochester (N.Y.) Union and Advertiser*, June 21, 1864; Addison S. Boyce to Mary, May 20, 1864, in Addison S. Boyce Collection, BL; McAllister to Ellen, May 20, 1864, in Robertson Jr., *Letters of General Robert McAllister*, 424.

70. Halleck to Grant, 2:00 P.M., May 20, 1864, in *OR*, Vol. 36, Pt. 3, p. 4; Meade to Grant, 5:30 P.M., May 20, 1864, ibid., 5; Rawlins to Abercrombie, 8:00 P.M., May 20, 1864, ibid., 26.

71. Hancock to Humphreys, 8:52 P.M., May 20, 1864, ibid., 8; Meade to Hancock, 9:00 P.M., May 20, 1864, ibid.; Hancock to Meade, 9:40 P.M., ibid., 9; Alfred T. A. Torbert's report, May 18, 1864, ibid., Pt. 1, p. 803; Humphreys to Torbert, 1:30 P.M., May 19, 1864, ibid., Pt. 2, p. 931; Beaudry, *War Journal*, 120; F. F. Robbins diary, May 20, 1864, in FSNMP; Lestor Hildreth diary, May 20, 1864, in Book 153, FSNMP; 2nd Corps circular, 5:00 P.M., May 20, 1864, in *OR*, Vol. 36, Pt. 3, p. 10.

72. The composition of Torbert's command is described in "Preliminary Movements of the Army, May 21, 1864," *Philadelphia Inquirer*, May 25, 1864.

73. Humphreys to Wright, 9:30 A.M., May 20, 1864, in *OR*, Vol. 36, Pt. 3, p. 16; Humphreys to Wright, 5:20 P.M., May 20, 1864, ibid., 17; Burnside to Grant, 7:30 P.M., May 20, 1864, ibid., 19; Horace Porter to Burnside, 9:00 P.M., May 20, 1864, ibid., 19.

74. Wilkeson, *Recollections of a Private Soldier*, 99–100.

75. Jedediah Hotchkiss diary, May 20, 1864, in Jedediah Hotchkiss Collection, LC.

76. G. T. Beauregard memorandum, May 18, 1864, in *OR*, Vol. 36, Pt. 2, pp. 1021–2.

77. Braxton Bragg enclosure, May 19, 1864, ibid., 1024–5.

78. Lee to Seddon, May 20, 1864, ibid., Pt. 3, p. 800; Charles Field to G. Moxley Sorrel, May 20, 1864, ibid., 800–1; Charles Marshall to Ewell, May 20, 1864, ibid., 801.

79. Venable to Ewell, 8:30 P.M., May 20, 1864, ibid., 801; Martin L. Smith diary, May 20, 1864, in Charles E. Phelps Collection, Maryland Historical Society. To accommodate Ewell's deployment, Anderson was to pull Gregg's mixed Texas and Arkansas brigade from the north-

ern portion of his line and shift it below the Po. In turn, Early was to send a regiment from Kirkland's brigade and a regiment from Harris's brigade into the works vacated by Gregg. Charles W. Field to G. Moxley Sorrel, May 20, 1864, in *OR,* Vol. 36, Pt. 3, pp. 800–1; Jubal A. Early to Walter H. Taylor, 10:15 P.M., May 20,1864, ibid., 801.

80. Grant to Halleck, 8:45 A.M., May 17, 1864, ibid., Pt. 2, p. 840; Sheridan to Halleck, 3:00 P.M., May 17, 1864, ibid., p. 851; Fitzhugh Lee to G. W. C. Lee, May 17, 1864, ibid., Vol. 51, Pt. 2, pp. 944–5.

81. Samuel H. Merrill, *The Campaigns of the 1st Maine and 1st District of Columbia Cavalry* (Portland, Me., 1866), 199–200; James H. Wilson diary, May 18–19, 1864, in Wilson Collection, LC; Fitzhugh Lee's report, in MC; J. D. Ferguson memorandum, in DU; Fitzhugh Lee to Bragg, 4:00 P.M., May 19, 1864, in *OR,* Vol. 51, Pt. 2, p. 949.

82. Sheridan to Meade, May 19, 1864, ibid., Vol. 36, Pt. 2, pp. 930–1; James W. Forsyth to David McM. Gregg, ibid., 932; Sheridan, *Personal Memoirs,* 1, pp. 388–9.

83. Gregg's report, in *OR,* Vol. 36, Pt. 1., p. 854; Itinerary of the Eighth Pennsylvania Cavalry, ibid., 867; Chapman's report, ibid., 899; Merrill, *Campaigns of the 1st Maine,* 201; Wilson's diary, May 20, 1864, in Wilson Collection, LC.

84. Fitzhugh Lee's report, in MC; Ferguson memorandum, in DU.

85. William W. Goldsborough, *The Maryland Line in the Confederate States Army* (Baltimore, Md., 1900), 124–5; Louis H. Manarin, ed., "The Civil War Diary of Rufus J. Woolwine," *Virginia Magazine of History and Biography,* 62 (October, 1963), 436; Michael West, *30th Battalion Virginia Sharpshooters* (Lynchburg, Va., 1995), 89–90.

86. Davis to Lee, May 20, 1864, in *OR,* Vol. 51, Pt. 2, p. 951. Davis also reviewed Beauregard's request that the Army of Northern Virginia fall back to the Chickahominy for co-operative attacks against Grant and Butler, reiterating the deleterious impact that Lee's withdrawal would have on Confederate morale and the disadvantage of abandoning the Virginia Central Railroad. He was willing, however, to leave the final decision to Lee. "You are better informed than any other can be of the necessities of your position—at least as well informed as any other of the wants and dangers of the country in your rear, including the railroad and other lines of communication," Davis wrote. "I cannot do better than to leave your judgment to reach its own conclusions." Lee's thinking coincided with Davis's. He would shift to meet Grant's new movement, dropping south only as far as necessary to block the Federals. If possible, he would impede Grant's advance at Mud Tavern. That failing, he would retire to the river system around Hanover Junction to protect the railroad. Withdrawing to the Chickahominy was out of the question. Lee remained determined to bring Grant to battle as far from Richmond as circumstances permitted.

87. Billie B. Elliott diary, May 20, 1864, Roanoke City Library ; W. H. Morgan, *Personal Reminiscences of the War of 1861–5* (Lynchburg, Va., 1911), 206; Charles T. Loehr, "The Battle of Milford Station," *SHSP,* 26, p. 110; W. Marion Seay, "Forty Men Fought Grant's Army," *Confederate Veteran,* 17 (1909), 319. In their raid on Guinea Station late on May 18, Torbert's men had burned the depot and a quantity of supplies, captured the telegraph operator, and seized considerable Confederate mail; "Another Account," in *Washington Daily Morning Chronicle,* May 20, 1864.

88. J. O. Thurmond Jr. to John G. Scurry, May 25, 1864, in Gilder-Lehrman Collection, Pierpont Morgan Library, New York; W. H. Morgan, *Personal Reminiscences,* 208; Loehr, "Battle of Milford Station," 111; Seay, "Forty Men Fought Grant's Army," 319.

VII MAY 21 *GRANT SWINGS SOUTH AND LEE COUNTERS*

1. Rank A. Burr, *Life and Achievements of James Addams Beaver* (Philadelphia, 1882), 133; Simons, *Regimental History,* 212; J. D. Smith, *Nineteenth Regiment of Maine Volunteer Infantry,* 174; Wilkeson, *Recollections of a Private Soldier,* 101; John D. Billings, *The History of the Tenth Massachusetts Battery of Light Artillery in the War of the Rebellion* (Boston, 1881), 243; "Movements of the Second Corps," *Philadelphia Inquirer,* May 25, 1864.

2. Hancock to Williams, 1:30 A.M., May 21, 1864, in *OR,* Vol. 36, Pt. 3, p. 46.

3. Robert S. Robertson, *Personal Recollections of the War* (Milwaukee, 1895), 112; D. S. Miller, *Drum Taps in Dixie,* 96–7; Wilkeson, *Recollections of a Private Soldier,* 101–2.

4. Hancock to Williams, 4:30 A.M., May 21, 1864, in *OR,* Vol. 36, Pt. 3, p. 46.

5. R. L. T. Beale, *Ninth Virginia Cavalry,* 119; E. C. Moncure, "Reminiscences of the Civil War," *Bulletin of the Virginia State Library,* 26 (1927), 49; G. W. Beale, *Lieutenant of Cavalry,* 146.

6. G. W. Beale, *Lieutenant of Cavalry,* 146–7.

7. F. S. Dickinson, "Death of Sergeant Sortore," *National Tribune,* January 14, 1892; Beaudry, *War Journal,* 120.

8. Hancock to Williams, 5:30 A.M., May 21, 1864, in *OR,* Vol. 36, Pt. 3, p. 47; J. D. Smith, *Nineteenth Regiment of Maine Volunteer Infantry,* 174.

9. G. W. Beale, *Lieutenant of Cavalry,* 147; Beaudry, *War Journal,* 120; Francis U. Long's dispatch, May 21, 1864, *New York Herald,* May 25, 1864.

10. "Preliminary Movements of the Army, May 21, 1864," *Philadelphia Inquirer,* May 25, 1864.

11. For the time of Ewell's departure, see "Army Correspondence, May 23, 1864," *Richmond Sentinel,* May 25, 1864. *Atlas to Accompany the OR,* Plate 81, Map No. 5, indicates that Ewell's corps took cross-country shortcuts.

12. P. T. Hanley dispatch, in Warren to Humphreys, 3:30 A.M., May 21, 1864, in *OR,* Vol. 36, Pt. 3, p. 52; Wright to Humphreys, 5:30 A.M., May 21, 1864, ibid., 60; Lyman journal, May 21, 1864, in Lyman Collection, MHS; Humphreys to Warren, 5:15 A.M., May 21, 1864, in *OR,* Vol. 36, Pt. 3, p, 52; George J. Clarke to Humphreys, 6:00 A.M., ibid.; Griffin to Warren, 6:30 A.M., ibid., 53; Meade to Warren, 6:30 A.M., May 21, 1864, ibid.; A. S. Marvin Jr. to Charles Griffin, May 21, 1864, ibid.

13. Hancock to Williams, 4:30 A.M., May 21, 1864, ibid., 46.

14. Humphreys to Warren, 7:30 A.M., May 21, 1864, ibid., 53; Williams to Hancock, 7:30 A.M., May 21, 1864, ibid., 47; Humphreys, *Virginia Campaign,* 120.

15. Hancock to Williams, 5:30 A.M., May 21, 1864, in *OR,* Vol. 36, Pt. 3, p. 47.

16. Humphreys to Warren, 9:30 A.M., May 21, 1864, and Warren to Humphreys, indorsement, ibid., 55; Humphreys to Wright, 8:25 A.M., May 21, 1864, ibid., 62; Grant to Burnside, 8:25 A.M., May 21, 1864, ibid., 64.

17. Henry H. Sturgis to Thomas L. Owen, October 4, 1912, in Alabama Department of Archives and History, Montgomery; R. L. T. Beale, *Ninth Virginia Cavalry,* 120; J. Willard Brown, *The Signal Corps, U.S.A., in the War of the Rebellion* (Boston, 1896), 384–5. Grant's aide Adam Badeau noted that "the same code of signals was in use in both armies, having been devised by a West Point graduate before the war. Although the key was frequently changed, Grant's officers were skilful enough to decipher many of the enemy's despatches, when they could perceive the motions of the signal flag by which field messages were communicated."

Adam Badeau, *Military History of General Ulysses S. Grant, from April, 1861, to April, 1865,* vol. 2 (New York, 1881), 222*n.*

18. Lee to Seddon, 8:40 A.M., May 21, 1864, in *OR,* Vol. 36, Pt. 3, p. 812.

19. George Clark, *A Glance Backward; or, Some Events in the Past History of My Life* (Houston, 1914), 53–4.

20. For the locations of Ewell's various headquarters during the morning of May 21, see Donald C. Pfanz, *Richard S. Ewell: A Soldier's Life* (Chapel Hill, 1998), 395. A tavern had occupied the road junction at modern Thornburg for several years. Richard Pound, a miller employed at nearby Jerrell's Mill, purchased the tavern in 1860 and apparently gave it the name Mud Tavern. Numerous stories abound concerning the origin of the tavern's name, but the area's persistent mud is the chief candidate. Virginia Wright Durrett, *Mud Tavern* (Spotsylvania, Va., 1988).

21. Humphreys to Warren, 9:45 A.M., May 21 1864, in *OR,* Vol. 36, Pt. 3, p. 55; Humphreys to Hancock, 9:45 A.M., May 21, 1864, ibid., 48.

22. Shreve, "Operations of the Army of the Potomac May 13–June 2 1864," *PMHSM,* 4, p. 301; Covert, *Two Civil War Diaries,* 21; Marbaker, *Eleventh New Jersey Volunteers,* 183; R. L. Stewart, *One Hundred and Fortieth Regiment Pennsylvania Volunteers,* 200–1.

23. Carleton to Editor, May 21, 1864, in *Boston Evening Transcript,* May 25, 1864; Warren L. Goss, *Recollections of a Private: A Story of the Army of the Potomac* (New York, 1890), 301–2; Wilkeson, *Recollections of a Private Soldier,* 103–4. Some houses along the Union army's path escaped looting. Carroll Hayden, present owner of Stirling Plantation on Guinea Station Road, relates that elderly John Halladay and his ailing wife lived in the house in 1864. Family tradition holds that the Federals took pity on the couple and never entered the house.

24. "Movements of the Second Corps," *Philadelphia Inquirer,* May 25, 1864.

25. "Preliminary Movements of the Army, May 21, 1864," *Philadelphia Inquirer,* May 25, 1864; Beaudry, *War Journal,* 120.

26. Marbaker, *Eleventh New Jersey Volunteers,* 183; Aldrich, *History of Battery A,* 338; "From the 50th Regiment, May 24, 1864," *Corning (N.Y.) Journal,* June 2, 1864.

27. Aldrich, *History of Battery A,* 338; Roe and Nutt, *First Regiment of Heavy Artillery,* 37; G. W. W. dispatch, *Detroit Advertiser and Tribune,* June 2, 1864; "Movements of the Second Corps," *Philadelphia Inquirer,* May 25, 1864; Billings, *Tenth Massachusetts Battery,* 245; Hays, *Under the Red Patch,* 245.

28. J. D. Smith, *Nineteenth Regiment of Maine Volunteer Infantry,* 174; Silliker, *Rebel Yell,* 161; Wilson and Wilson, *Civil War Diary of Thomas White Stephens,* 182; Hays, *Under the Red Patch,* 245; William Y. W. Ripley, *Vermont Riflemen in the War for the Union, 1861–1865: A History of Company F, First United States Sharpshooters* (Rutland, Vt., 1883), 166–7.

29. Wilkeson, *Recollections of a Private Soldier,* 104.

30. Loehr, "Battle of Milford Station," *SHSP,* 26, p. 111.

31. Ibid.; "Correspondence from the Field," New York *Daily News,* May 30, 1864.

32. Seay, "Forty Men Fought Grant's Army," *Confederate Veteran,* 17, p. 319.

33. Ibid.; "The Exploit of Captain Hess," *Forney's War Press* (Philadelphia), June 18, 1864.

34. "The First Virginia Regiment," *Richmond Examiner,* May 28, 1864; David E. Johnston, *The Story of a Confederate Boy in the Civil War* (Portland, Ore., 1914), 261; Loehr, "Battle of Milford Station," 113.

35. Seay, "Forty Men Fought Grant's Army," 319.

36. W. H. Morgan, *Personal Reminiscences,* 211; Seay, "Forty Men Fought Grant's Army," 320.

37. Seay, "Forty Men Fought Grant's Army," 320.

38. W. H. Morgan, *Personal Reminiscences,* 212–13; Torbert to Hancock, May 21, 1864, in *OR,* Vol. 36, Pt. 3, p. 48. One account reported that Hess lost six men killed and eight wounded; *Forney's War Press* (Philadelphia), June 18, 1864.

39. Humphreys to Wright, 8:10 A.M., May 21, 1864, in *OR,* Vol. 36, Pt. 3, p. 61; R. E. McBride, *In the Ranks: from the Wilderness to Appomattox Court House* (Cincinnati, 1881), 60.

40. Alexander B. Pattison diary, May 21, 1864, in Book 68, FSNMP; Roebling's report, in Warren Collection, NYSLA; George Lockley diary, May 21, 1864, in George Lockley Collection, BL; Benedict, *Vermont in the Civil War,* 1, p. 454.

41. Lyman journal, May 21, 1864, in Lyman Collection, MHS; William Frassanito, *Grant and Lee: The Virginia Campaigns* (New York, 1983), 116–19; Edward J. Hagerty, *Collis' Zouaves: The 114th Pennsylvania Volunteers in the Civil War* (Baton Rouge, 1997), 287–8.

42. Lee to Seddon, May 21, 1864, in *OR,* Vol. 36, Pt. 3, p. 812; Walter Taylor to Bettie, May 23, 1864, in Tower, ed., *Lee's Adjutant,* 161–2.

43. William N. Pendleton to wife, May 22, 1864, in S. P. Lee, *Memoirs of William Nelson Pendleton,* 335.

44. Lee to Commanding Officer, Hanover Junction, 11:40 A.M., May 21, 1864, in *OR,* Vol. 36, Pt. 3, p. 815; Lee to Breckinridge, May 21, 1864, ibid.

45. Manarin, ed., "Civil War Diary of Rufus J. Woolwine," 436; West, *30th Battalion Virginia Sharpshooters,* 89–90; Mattson, "Sheridan's Raid," 34–5, in MSU; J. D. Ferguson memorandum, DU; Custer's report, in *OR,* Vol. 36, Pt. 1, pp. 819–20; Russell A. Alger's report, ibid., 829; Merritt's report, ibid., 814–15 "Custer's Cavalry Brigade," *Detroit Advertiser and Tribune,* June 16, 1864; Greenleaf, "From the Rapidan to Richmond," 23; Sheridan, *Personal Memoirs,* 1, p. 389.

46. "Diary of Creed T. Davis," *Contributions to a History of the Richmond Howitzer Battalion,* 2, p. 11; Buckner McGill Randolph diary, May 21, 1864, in VHS.

47. Archie P. McDonald, ed., *Make Me a Map of the Valley: The Civil War Journal of Stonewall Jackson's Topographer* (Dallas, 1973), 206.

48. Special Orders No. 128, May 21, 1864, in *OR,* Vol. 36, Pt. 3, pp. 813–14. A Confederate in Terry's brigade recollected that "while our brigade was known officially as Terry's, its members continued to designate the different bodies as the Stonewall, Second, and Third Brigades.... Thus, the Stonewall Brigade consisted in our view of its old members who were present, however few. We spoke of other brigades in the same way. We did this instead of using regiments to designate portions of this multiform brigade." Worsham, *One of Jackson's Foot Cavalry,* 142. Lee had been forced to substantially reorganize his army on May 7, following Longstreet's wounding, and on May 8, in the wake of Hill's disability.

49. John Esten Cooke, *A Life of Gen. Robert E. Lee* (New York, 1871), 400.

50. Lyman's journal, May 21, 1864, in Lyman Collection, MHS; R. E. McBride, *In the Ranks,* 62; Roe, *Thirty-Ninth Regiment Massachusetts Volunteers,* 204–5. The 5th Corps's order of march was Crawford, Cutler, and Griffin; "Correspondence from the Field," *New York Daily News,* May 22, 1864.

51. George Breck to wife, May 30, 1864, *Rochester (N.Y.) Union and Advertiser,* June 21, 1864; David S. Sparks, ed., *Inside Lincoln's Army: The Diary of Marsena Rudolph Patrick, Provost Marshal General, Army of the Potomac* (New York, 1964), 375; Lyman journal, May 22, 1864, in Lyman Collection, MHS.

52. Ibid.; Garrison, *Memoir,* 93. Mr. Motley's crabby ways were well known to his neighbors. See Mary Evans to Clement A. Evans, May 30, 1863, in Stephens Jr., *Intrepid Warrior,* 171.

53. Porter, *Campaigning with Grant,* 132.

54. William B. Rawle, *History of the Third Pennsylvania Cavalry, Sixtieth Regiment Pennsylvania Volunteers, in the American Civil War* (Philadelphia, 1905), 428.

55. Ibid.; R. L. T. Beale, *Ninth Virginia Cavalry,* 120–1.

56. Sparks, *Inside Lincoln's Army,* 375; Lyman journal, May 21, 1864, in Lyman Collection, MHS; William Brooke Rawle to mother, May 29, 1864, in Civil War Library and Museum, Philadelphia; Gilbert Thompson, *The Engineer Battalion in the Civil War* (Washington, D.C., 1910), 62; Carleton to editor, May 21, 1864, *Boston Evening Transcript,* May 25, 1864. A recent account of the fight at Guinea Bridge appears in Hagerty, *Collis' Zouaves,* 288.

57. Rawle, *Third Pennsylvania Cavalry,* 429; R. L. T. Beale, *Ninth Virginia Cavalry,* 120–21; Collis's report, in *OR,* Vol. 51, Pt. 1, p. 243; "Movements of the Second Corps," *Philadelphia Inquirer,* May 25, 1864.

58. Sypher, *Pennsylvania Reserves,* 538.

59. Kent, *Three Years with Company K,* 270.

60. Thomson and Rauch, *History of the Bucktails,* 312–13; JCB to Myrtle, private manuscript of Raymond and Virginia Bruce, present owners of Laurel Springs.

61. Porter, *Campaigning with Grant,* 133–4; "National Park Service, Historic Structures Report for Jackson Shrine," 1, pp. 62–4, in FSNMP. Mrs. Vernon Lucy, present owner of the Motley house, provided family lore about Grant's encounter with Mr. Motley.

62. Grant to Halleck, 7:00 A.M., May 21, 1864, in *OR,* Vol. 36, Pt. 3, p. 43.

63. Williams to Hancock, 8:00 P.M., May 21, 1864, ibid., 50.

64. Silliker, *Rebel Yell,* 61; E. B. Houghton, *Campaigns of the Seventeenth Maine,* 187–8.

65. Nelson Armstrong, *Nuggets of Experience* (San Bernardino, Calif., 1904), 46.

66. Galwey, *Valiant Hours,* 220; J. D. Smith, *Nineteenth Regiment of Maine Volunteer Infantry,* 174; Heinz K. Meier, ed., *Memoirs of a Swiss Officer in the American Civil War* (Bern, 1972), 161; Luther A. Rose diary, May 21, 1864, in LC; "From the 50th Regiment, May 24, 1864," *Corning (N.Y.) Journal,* June 2, 1864; Long's dispatch, *New York Herald,* May 25, 1864.

67. J. W. Muffly, ed., *The Story of Our Regiment: A History of the 148th Pennsylvania Volunteers* (Des Moines, 1904), 126; Burr, *James Addams Beaver,* 134.

68. R. L. Stewart, *One Hundred and Fortieth Regiment Pennsylvania Volunteers,* 201; Francis Yeager diary, May 21, 1864, in FSNMP; Lestor Hildreth diary, May 21, 1864, in Book 153, FSNMP; J. D. Smith, *Nineteenth Regiment of Maine Volunteer Infantry,* 175; William H. Morgan, *Narrative of the Service of Company D,* 21; Kenneth H. Power memoir, May 21 entry, in Book 45, FSNMP; Brainerd, *Bridge Building in Wartime,* 223. I am deeply indebted to Ray Campbell, Clerk of Caroline County, for helping identify local landmarks. Wright's Tavern, also referred to as Campbell's Tavern and Dickinson's Tavern, is the present Poplar Inn, at the junction of modern routes 722 and 638. In 1864 it was owned by William H. Wright, who had purchased it from the estate of Ira E. Dickinson, who married Jane Campbell, daughter of Matthew Campbell. The poorhouse was less than a mile south on present day Route 676; Ray Campbell to author, June 26, 1997.

69. John R. Zimmerman diary, May 21, 1864, in Lloyd House, Alexandria, Virginia; George Wise, *History of the Seventeenth Virginia Infantry* (Baltimore, Md., 1870), 182–3; Arthur Herbert, *Sketches and Incidents of Movements of the Seventeenth Virginia Infantry* (Alexandria, Va., N.d.), 31; Loehr, "Battle of Milford Station," 114. According to a soldier in the 11th Virginia, the train carrying Corse's brigade left Richmond around 5:00 P.M. on May 20. The trip took nearly twenty hours because the train "was stopped every few minutes and skirmishers sent forward." John O. Thurmond Jr. to John G. Scurry, May 25, 1864, in Gilder-Lehrman Collection, Pierpont Morgan Library, New York.

70. Hampton to Breckinridge, 9:30 P.M., May 21, 1864, in *OR,* Vol. 36, Pt. 3, p. 816; D. B. Bridgford to Breckinridge, May 21, 1864, ibid.; John R. Zimmerman diary, May 21, 1864, in Lloyd House, Alexandria, Virginia; Thurmond Jr. to Scurry, May 25, 1864, in Pierpont Morgan Library. "A party of rebel cavalry made a dash on our picket line before we had fairly got established," a Federal in the 26th Michigan of Barlow's brigade wrote, "but they were so warmly welcomed they were glad to turn their horses tails to us"; William Bradford Irwin journal, May 21, 1864, in BL. Rosser, who was with Hampton, noted only that "I found a small force of the enemy's cavalry which had crossed the Mattaponi river, but retired, after firing a few shots, on my approach in the direction of Milford, and in pursuing this force I ran into a large force of infantry and artillery, which convinced us that the whole of Grant's army was in motion toward Hanover Junction"; Rosser, "Annals of the War: Operations with Lee's Army During Battles of Spotsylvania," *Philadelphia Weekly Tribune,* April 19, 1884.

71. Hampton to Breckinridge, 9:30 P.M., May 21, 1864, in *OR,* Vol. 36, pt. 3, p. 816.

72. Johnston, *Story of a Confederate Boy,* 262.

73. 2nd Corps Daily Memoranda, May 21, 1864, in *OR,* Vol. 36, Pt. 1, pp. 362–3; Simons, *Regimental History,* 212; Galwey, *Valiant Hours,* 221.

74. Simons, *Regimental History,* 212; Goss, *Recollections of a Private,* 303–4; Kirk, *Heavy Guns and Light,* 242–4.

75. Lee to Anderson, 4:15 P.M., May 21, 1864, in *OR,* Vol. 36, Pt. 3, p. 815.

76. Grant, *Personal Memoirs,* 2, p. 244.

77. Humphreys to Warren, 4:00 P.M., May 21, 1864, in *OR,* Vol. 36, Pt. 3, p. 56; Warren to Humphreys, 6:00 P.M., May 21, 1864, ibid., pp. 56–7; Grant to Burnside, May 21, 1864, ibid., 64–5.

78. Edmund M. Pope to Roebling, 9:00 P.M., May 21, 1864, ibid., 57–8; Roebling's report, in Warren Collection, NYSLA. The Schooler property had a grand view of the Matta. Samuel Schooler had been teaching at Edgehill Academy—a plain building containing eight classrooms 150 yards west of his house—but had closed the school and volunteered for Confederate service in 1862. Ralph Emmett Fall, *People, Post Offices, and Communities in Caroline County, Virginia, 1727–1969* (McDonough, Ga., 1989), 140–1; Samuel Schooler to George W. Randolph, April 2, 1862, in Samuel Schooler Compiled Service Record, M331, Role 220, NA.

79. Burnside's report, in *OR,* Vol. 36, Pt. 1, p. 911; Potter's report, ibid., 929; "The Campaign in Virginia," *Philadelphia Sunday Dispatch,* May 22, 1864; Houston, *Thirty-Second Maine Regiment,* 165; Hopkins, *Seventh Regiment Rhode Island Volunteers,* 177.

80. Potter's report, in *OR,* Vol. 36, Pt. 1, p. 929.

81. R. S. Williams, "Thirteenth Regiment," in W. Clark, *Histories of the Several Regiments,* 1, p. 677; James H. Lane's report, in James H. Lane Collection, AU; E. J. Hale Jr.'s report, in Lane Collection, AU; James S. Harris, *Historical Sketches of the Seventh Regiment North Carolina Troops* (Mooresville, N.C., 1893), 49; Abbott, *Personal Recollections,* 63; George H. Mills, "Supplemental Sketch Sixteenth Regiment," in W. Clark, *Histories of the Several Regiments,* IV, 195; Samuel Walkup diary, May 21, 1864, SHC.

82. Reuben C. Benton's report, in *OR,* Vol. 36, Pt. 1, p. 717; Greenleaf T. Stevens's report, ibid., 761; William A. Harn's report, ibid., 767; Lane's report, in Lane Collection, AU; Oestreich diary, May 21, 1864, in Harrisburg Civil War Roundtable Collection, USAMHI.

83. Wilcox's report, in VSL; Greiner, *Surgeon's Civil War,* 192; Oestreich diary, May 21, 1864, in Harrisburg Civil War Roundtable Collection, USAMHI.

84. Burnside's report, in *OR,* Vol. 36, Pt.1, p 911. The earthworks on the bluffs at Stanard's Mill (present-day Roxbury Mill) are very well preserved.

85. Potter's report, ibid., 929; Edward O. Lord, *History of the Ninth Regiment New Hampshire Volunteers in the War of the Rebellion* (Concord, N.H., 1895), 393.

86. Lord, *Ninth Regiment New Hampshire Volunteers, 393.*

87. Wheaton's report, in *OR,* Vol. 36, Pt. 1, p. 687; Burnside's report, ibid., 912; Read diary, May 21, 1864, in Ricketts Collection, Manassas National Battlefield Park; Albert, *Forty-Fifth Regiment,* 130.

88. Roebling's report, in Warren Collection, NYSLA; A. C. Brown, *Diary of a Line Officer,* 54.

89. Roebling's report, in Warren Collection, NYSLA; J. Howard Kitching to Warren, 9:00 P.M., May 21, 1864, in *OR,* Vol. 36, Pt. 3, p. 60, also containing a drawing by Kitching showing his brigade deployed across the road to Nancy Wright's Corner in a horseshoe-shaped formation, the 15th New York on the left, the 6th New York across the road, and the 4th New York on the right.

90. Roebling's report, in Warren Collection, NYSLA.

91. Warren to Humphreys, 9:30 P.M., May 21, 1864, in *OR,* Vol. 36, Pt. 3, p. 58; Humphreys to Warren, 10:30 P.M., with 11:15 P.M. Addendum, May 21, 1864, ibid., 58–9.

92. Fifth Corps Orders, May 21, 1864, ibid., 59.

93. Harris diary, May 21, 1864, in FSNMP; Cary Whitaker diary, May 21, 1864, in SHC; A. P. McDonald, *Make Me a Map of the Valley,* 206.

94. St. George Tucker Bryan Memoir, VHS.

95. Moncure, "Reminiscences of the Civil War," 50.

96. Ibid.

97. Unknown Rebel Diary, Boston University, Muger Memorial Library, Boston; Gallagher, ed., *Fighting for the Confederacy,* 387; Bratton's report, in *OR,* Vol. 36, Pt. 1, p. 1067.

98. Moncure, "Reminiscences of the Civil War," 50.

99. Ibid.

100. Peyton, *Civil War Record,* 34; Wingfield diary, May 21, 1864, *Bulletin of the Virginia State Library,* 16 (1927), 39.

101. George S. Bernard diary, May 23, 1864, in UVL; Ott, "Diary of James J. Kirkpatrick," 198; Shiver, "Wright's Brigade at Spotsylvania Court House," *Atlanta Journal,* October 16, 1901.

102. Moncure, "Reminiscences of the Civil War," 50.

103. Gallagher, ed., *Fighting for the Confederacy,* 387; Humphreys, *Virginia Campaign,* 126–7.

104. Badeau, *Military History of Ulysses S. Grant,* 2, p. 220; Joseph F. Waring diary, May 21, 1864, in SHC.

105. Myers, *Comanches,* 287–8.

VIII MAY 22 *LEE WINS THE RACE TO THE RIVER*

1. John W. F. Hatton memoir, May 22, 1864, in LC; John A. Sloan, *Reminiscences of the Guilford Grays, Co. B, 27th N.C. Regiment* (Washington, D.C., 1883), 92–3.

2. Charles B. Jones, "Historical Sketch of 55th N.C. Infantry," *New Bern (N.C.) Our Living and Our Dead,* April 15, 1874.

3. Read diary, May 21, 1864, in Ricketts Collection, Manassas National Battlefield Park Library; Howe, ed., *Touched with Fire,* 129; Abbott, *Personal Recollections,* 63; Diary of unidentified 6th Corps soldier, May 21, 1864, in Book 32, FSNMP.

4. Hyde, *Following the Greek Cross,* 205; Wilbur Fisk to family, May 25, 1864, in Rosenblatt and Rosenblatt, *Hard Marching Every Day,* 225; Wright to Humphreys, 12:10 A.M., May 22, 1864, in *OR,* Vol. 36, Pt. 3, pp. 94–5.

5. Humphreys to Warren, May 22, 1864, in *OR,* Vol. 36, Pt. 3, p. 91; Warren to Humphreys, 3:00 A.M., May 22, 1864, ibid., 87–8; Warren's journal, ibid., Pt. 1, p. 542. Humphreys' dispatch is entered as "2 P.M." in the official reports, but this must have been in error, as the context of the dispatch refers to events that happened shortly after midnight.

6. Sypher, *Pennsylvania Reserve Corps,* 538; Joseph B. Pattee's report, in *OR,* Vol. 36, Pt. 1, p. 607; Warren to Meade, 8:30 A.M., May 22, 1864, ibid., Pt. 3, p. 90; Hall, *Ninety-Seventh Regiment New York Volunteers,* 189; William H. Locke, *The Story of the Regiment* (Philadelphia, 1868), 341–2; Benjamin F. Cook, *History of the Twelfth Massachusetts Volunteers (Webster Regiment)* (Boston, 1882), 132.

7. Roebling's report, in Warren Collection, NYSLA.

8. Ibid.; Warren to Lysander Cutler, May 22, 1864, in *OR,* Vol. 36, Pt. 3, p. 94; Dawes, *Service with the Sixth Wisconsin Volunteers,* 274; Rufus R. Dawes's report, in *OR,* Vol. 36, Pt. 1, p. 620. In his report Dawes mistakenly calls the Matta the Po.

9. Roebling's report, in Warren Collection, NYSLA; Roebling to Humphreys, 6:00 A.M., May 22, 1864, in *OR,* Vol. 36, Pt. 3, p. 88.

10. Lyman journal, May 22, 1864, in Lyman Collection, MHS.

11. James C. Biddle to wife, June 4, 1864, in Meade Collection, HSP; Meade to wife, May 23, 1864, in Meade, *Life and Letters,* 2, p. 198.

12. Meade to wife, May 19, 1864, in Meade Collection, HSP; Biddle to wife, June 5, 1864, ibid.

13. Sparks, ed., *Inside Lincoln's Army,* 377; Grant to Meade, April 9, 1864, in *OR,* Vol. 33, 828.

14. Tyler Dennett, ed., *Lincoln and the Civil War in the Diaries and Letters of John Hay* (New York, 1939), 180; John W. Forney, quoted in Carl Sandburg, *Abraham Lincoln: The War Years,* vol. 4 (New York, 1943), 47.

15. Gideon Welles, *The Diary of Gideon Welles,* vol. 2 (Boston, 1911), 33; J. Cutler Andrews, *The North Reports the Civil War* (Pittsburgh, 1955), 541; Noah Brooks, *Lincoln Observed: Civil War Dispatches of Noah Brooks,* ed. Michael Burlingame (Baltimore, 1998), 109; George Templeton Strong, *Diary of the Civil War, 1860–1865,* ed. Allan Nevins (New York, 1962), 448. An excellent discussion of the North's expectations and its reaction to the stalemate at Spotsylvania Court House is Simpson, "Great Expectations: Ulysses S. Grant, the Northern Press, and the Opening of the Wilderness Campaign," in Gallagher, ed., *Wilderness Campaign,* 1–35.

16. Grant, *Personal Memoirs,* 2, pp. 245–6; Orders, May 22, 1864, in *OR,* Vol. 36, Pt. 3, p. 80; Lyman journal, May 22, 1864, in Lyman Collection, MHS.

17. Ott, "Diary of James J. Kilpatrick," 198.

18. Lee to Davis, 5:00 A.M., May 22, 1864, in Dowdey, *Wartime Papers of R. E. Lee,* 746.

19. Ibid.

20. Hatton memoir, May 22, 1864, in LC.

21. George W. Booth, *Personal Reminiscences of a Maryland Soldier in the War Between the States, 1861–1865* (Baltimore, Md., 1898), 109–10; Goldsborough, *Maryland Line,* 125.

22. Goldsborough, *Maryland Line,* 125.

23. Hatton memoir, May 22, 1864, in LC; B. Welch Owens to editor, September 12, 1895, *Richmond Dispatch,* March 9, 1902; Booth, *Personal Reminiscences,* 110–11.

24. Lee to Davis, 9:30 A.M., May 22, 1864, in Dowdey, *Wartime Papers of R. E. Lee,* 746–7; J. William Thomas diary, May 22, 1864, in FSNMP, Book 79.

25. Tower, ed., *Lee's Adjutant,* 162.

26. Jedediah Hotchkiss to William W. Blackford, August 10, 1898, in Hotchkiss Collection, LC; Hotchkiss, "Comments on Chapter XVII of Col. Henderson's *Life of Stonewall Jackson,*" in Hotchkiss Collection, LC.

27. James H. Lane, "Battle of Jericho Ford—Report of General Lane," *SHSP,* 9, p. 241; Blackford, comp., *Letters from Lee's Army,* 247; Wilcox's report, in VSL; James L. Coker, *History of Company G, Ninth S. C. Regiment, Infantry, S. C. Army and of Company E, Sixth South Carolina Regiment, Infantry, S. C. Army* (Charleston, S. C., 1899), 147; S. P. Lee, *Memoirs of William Nelson Pendleton,* 335; Tower, ed., *Lee's Adjutant,* 161; Harris diary, May 22, 1864, in FSNMP; Marshall Wingfield, *A History of Caroline County Virginia from Its Formation in 1727 to 1924* (Richmond, 1924), 261–2.

28. Moncure, "Reminiscences of the Civil War," *Bulletin of the Virginia State Library,* 26 (1927), 51–2.

29. Potter's report, in *OR,* Vol. 36, Pt. 1, p. 929; Burnside to Crittenden, May 22, 1864, ibid., Pt. 3, p, 97; Burnside to Potter, May 22, 1864, ibid., 98; Burnside to Willcox, May 22, 1864, ibid., 98; Byron M. Cutcheon, comp., *The Story of the Twentieth Michigan Infantry* (Lansing, Mich., 1904), 126; J. N. Jones diary, May 22, 1864, in Civil War Times Illustrated Collection, USAMHI; Committee of the Regiment, *Thirty-Fifth Regiment Massachusetts Volunteers,* 236.

30. Chipman, "Diary of Cyril Fountain," 293; Humphreys to Warren, 6:45 A.M., May 22, 1864, in *OR,* Vol. 36, Pt. 3, p. 88; Humphreys to Warren, 9:30 A.M., May 22, 1864, ibid., 90; Warren to Meade, 9:45 A.M., May 22, 1864, ibid., 90.

31. Roebling's report, in Warren Collection, NYSLA.

32. Roebling's report, in Warren Collection, NYSLA; John L. Parker, *History of the Twenty-Second Massachusetts Infantry, the Second Company Sharpshooters, and the Third Light Battery, in the War of the Rebellion* (Boston, 1887), 445; Nevins, *Diary of Battle,* 383; D. P. Marshall, *Company K, 155th Pa. Volunteer Zouaves* (N.p., 1888), 161.

33. Robert S. Westbrook, *History of the 49th Pennsylvania Volunteers* (Altoona, Pa., 1898), 202; Edmund D. Halsey diary, May 22, 1864, in USAMHI; A. A. Haines, *Fifteenth Regiment New Jersey Volunteers,* 193; William McVey diary, May 22, 1864, in Ohio Historical Society; John E. Irwin diary, May 22, 1864, in MSU.

34. Meier, *Memoirs of a Swiss Officer,* 161; Lyman journal, May 22, 1864, in Lyman Collection, MHS; William S. Pike diary, May 22, 1864, in Niagara County Historical Society, Lockport, New York; J. D. Smith, *Nineteenth Regiment of Maine Volunteer Infantry,* 175.

35. Francis A. Walker to David B. Birney, 7:00 A.M., May 22, 1864, in *OR,* Vol. 36, Pt. 3, p. 86; Ripley, *Vermont Riflemen,* 167–8.

36. Hancock to Williams, 10:45 A.M., May 22, 1864, in *OR,* Vol. 36, Pt. 3, p. 83; Gibbon to Hancock, 12:30 P.M., May 22, 1864, ibid., 85; Hancock to Williams, 12:45 P.M., May 22, 1864, ibid., 84; Smyth's report, ibid., Pt. 1, p. 449–50; Beaver to family, May 26, 1864, in Muffly, *Story of Our Regiment,* 126; Lyman journal, May 22, 1864, in Lyman Collection, MHS.

37. P. Regis de Trobriand's report, in *OR,* Vol. 36, Pt. 1, pp. 471–2; Weygant, *One Hundred and Twenty-Fourth Regiment,* 342–3.

38. Roebling's report, in Warren Collection, NYSLA; Warren to Meade, 1:00 P.M., May 22, 1864, in *OR,* Vol. 36, Pt. 3, p. 91; J. L. Smith, *Corn Exchange Regiment,* 435–6; John J. Pullen, *The Twentieth Maine: A Volunteer Regiment in the Civil War* (Philadelphia, 1957), 203; Spear,

Civil War Recollections, 111. Federals reported prisoners from the 42nd North Carolina and 38th Virginia; E. M. Pope to Adjutant General, 5th Army Corps, 4:30 P.M., May 22, 1864, in *OR,* Vol. 36, Pt. 3, p. 92.

39. Eugene A. Nash, *A History of the Forty-Fourth Regiment New York Volunteer Infantry in the Civil War, 1861–1865* (Chicago, 1911), 193; J. L. Smith, *Corn Exchange Regiment,* 436.

40. G. W. Beale, *Lieutenant of Cavalry,* 149–50; R. L. T. Beale, *Ninth Virginia Cavalry,* 121.

41. G. W. Beale, *Lieutenant of Cavalry,* 150. Beale thought the officer commanding the guns was James Breathed, head of Lee's horse artillery. He was in error, because Breathed was with Fitzhugh Lee. I am indebted to Robert Trout for helping me confirm Breathed's whereabouts and identifying McGregor's pieces as the guns at Littleton Flippo's farm.

42. Nash, *Forty-Fourth Volunteer New York Infantry,* 194; J. L. Smith, *Corn Exchange Regiment,* 436.

43. J. L. Smith, *Corn Exchange Regiment,* 437; Judson, *Eighty-Third Regiment Pennsylvania Volunteers,* 206.

44. J. L. Smith, *Corn Exchange Regiment,* 436–7.

45. Judson, *Eighty-Third Regiment Pennsylvania Volunteers,* 206–7; J. L. Smith, *Corn Exchange Regiment,* 437; G. W. Beale, *Lieutenant of Cavalry,* 150; R. L. T. Beale, *Ninth Virginia Cavalry,* 122–3.

46. Spear, *Civil War Recollections,* 111; Roebling's report, in Warren Collection, NYSLA; John W. Chowning diary, May 22, 1864, in Mary Ball Washington Library, Fredericksburg.

47. J. L. Parker, *Twenty-Second Massachusetts Regiment,* 446; J. L. Smith, *Corn Exchange Regiment,* 439.

48. Small, *Road to Richmond,* 144.

49. Roebling's report, in Warren Collection, NYSLA; Warren to Humphreys, 5:00 P.M., May 22, 1864, in *OR,* Vol. 36, Pt. 3, p. 92; J. L. Smith, *Corn Exchange Regiment,* 439; Robert Tilney, *My Life in the Army: Three Years and a Half with the Fifth Army Corps, Army of the Potomac, 1862–1865* (Philadelphia, 1912), 74–5; Nash, *Forty-Fourth Regiment New York Volunteer Infantry,* 193; Roe, *Thirty-Ninth Regiment Massachusetts Volunteers,* 204; Samuel L. Foust diary, May 22, 1864, in FSNMP; Kent, *Three Years With Company K,* 271.

50. Humphreys to Hancock, 3:30 P.M., May 2, 1864, in *OR,* Vol. 36, Pt. 3, p. 85; Meade to Hancock, 4:00 P.M., May 22, 1864, ibid.; Warren to Hancock, 5:30 P.M., May 22, 1864, ibid.; Walker to Birney, 9:30 P.M., May 22, 1864, ibid., 87; William R. Driver to Birney, 7:00 P.M., May 22, 1864, ibid., 87.

51. Craft, *One Hundred Forty-First Regiment,* 203; Seiser, "Civil War Diary," 193–4; Halsey diary, May 22, 1864, in USAMHI; Cheek and Pointon, *Sauk County Riflemen,* 101; Greiner, *Surgeon's Civil War,* 193.

52. Theodore Gerrish, *Army Life: A Private's Reminiscences of the Civil War* (Portland, Me., 1882), 189–90.

53. Rufus Ingalls's report, in *OR,* Vol. 26, Pt. 1, pp. 278–9; Bowley, "A Boy Lieutenant in a Black Regiment," *National Tribune,* May 1, 1899. A northern newspaperman reported that Ferrero's men insulted "all the women they met in the grossest manner, taking their last mouthful of food, while they threw their rations away; and finally, burning down three houses, one of which belonged to a poor woman with several children, the entire contents being consumed at the same time." He also claimed that black troops committed "no less than three gross outrages on females," and that "in one case the victim committed suicide after the act was perpetrated." R. Roy Dispatch, May 30, 1864, *New York Daily News,* June 7, 1864. I have found no contem-

poraneous reports that shed light on the accuracy of Roy's allegation. One would expect arrests and courts-martial for rapes, but none are on record, raising questions about the accuracy of Roy's stronger charges.

54. Grant to Halleck, 8:30 A.M., May 22, 1864, in *OR,* Vol. 36, Pt. 3, p. 77; Circular, May 22, 1864, ibid., 77–8; Rawlins to Abercrombie, 9:00 A.M., May 22, 1864, ibid., 100; Meade to Williams, 7:00 A.M., May 22, 1864, ibid., 78.

55. Abercrombie to Grant, May 22, 1864, ibid., 101; H. W. Benham to Abercrombie, May 22, 1864, ibid., p, 101.

56. McParlin's report, ibid., Pt. 1, p. 232, 235–6; Edward B. Dalton's report, ibid., 271.

57. Spear, *Civil War Recollections,* 111; Lyman journal, May 22, 1864, in Lyman Collection, MHS; Grant to Halleck, 8:00 P.M., May 22, 1864, in *OR,* Vol. 36, Pt. 3, p. 77.

58. Lyman journal, May 22, 1864, in Lyman Collection, MHS.

59. Ibid.

60. William Brooke Rawle to mother, May 29, 1864, in Civil War Library and Museum, Philadelphia, Pa.; Lyman journal, May 22, 1864, in Lyman Collection, MHS; Lyman to family, May 22, 1864, in Agassiz, *Meade's Headquarters,* 118–19.

61. Porter, *Campaigning with Grant,* 136–7.

62. Ibid., 137–9.

63. Ibid., 139.

64. Ibid., 137; Lyman journal, May 22, 1864, in Lyman Collection, MHS; Dana, *Recollections,* 202–3; Coco, *Through Blood and Fire,* 88.

65. Hamilton Dunlap diary, May 22, 1864, in M. Gayla McDowell Collection, Pennsylvania State University Libraries; Rawle diary, May 22, 1864, in Civil War Library and Museum, Philadelphia, Pa.; Wilbur Fisk to family, May 25, 1864, in Rosenblatt and Rosenblatt, *Hard Marching Every Day,* 225; Nevins, *Diary of Battle,* 383.

66. Grant to Meade, 10:00 P.M., May 22, 1864, in *OR,* Vol. 36, Pt. 3, pp. 81–2.

IX May 23 *Grant Attacks at the North Anna*

1. Edwin C. Bennett, *Musket and Sword, or, The Camp, March, and Firing Line in the Army of the Potomac* (Boston, 1900), 236–7; Kent, *Three Year with Company K,* 272.

2. Orders, May 23, 1864, in *OR,* Vol. 36, Pt. 3, p. 130; Roebling's report, in Warren Collection, NYSLA.

3. 2nd Corps Daily Memoranda, in *OR,* Vol. 36, Pt. 1, p. 363; Orders, 2:30 A.M., May 23, 1864, ibid., Pt. 3, 123; Francis Yeager diary, May 23, 1864, in FSNMP; Silliker, *Rebel Yell,* 161; Galwey, *Valiant Hours,* 223.

4. Spear, *Civil War Recollections,* 112; Roebling's report, in Warren Collection, NYSLA.

5. Hancock to Warren, 11:00 A.M., May 23, 1864, in *OR,* Vol. 36, Pt. 3, p. 116.

6. Roebling's report, in Warren Collection, NYSLA; Warren to Hancock, 11:30 A.M., May 23, 1864, in *OR,* Vol. 36, Pt. 3, p. 117; William D. W. Miller to Francis Walker, 11:40 A.M., May 23, 1864, ibid. Chesterfield Bridge was also called Taylor's Bridge and Fox's Bridge. The original bridge was destroyed in 1862 and rebuilt by Confederate artillery commander Lieutenant J. Thompson Brown; Freeman, *R. E. Lee,* 3, p. 350n4.

7. Warren to Hancock, 11:30 A.M., May 23, 1864, in *OR,* Vol. 36, Pt. 3, p. 117; Small, *Road to Richmond,* 144; David R. P. Neely diary, May 23, 1864, in Pennsylvania State Archives, Harrisburg.

8. Orders, May 23, 1864, in *OR,* Vol. 36, Pt. 3, p. 133; Wright to Humphreys, 7:30 A.M., and Wright to Humphreys, 11:45 A.M., May 23, 1864, ibid., 132; Howe, *Touched With Fire,* 130; Blight, *When This Cruel War Is Over,* 302–3.

9. Circular, May 23, 1864, in *OR,* Vol. 36, Pt. 3, p. 135; Sparks, *Inside Lincoln's Army,* 376; Lyman journal, May 23, 1864, in Lyman Collection, MHS.

10. Lyman journal, May 23, 1864, in Lyman Collection, MHS; Agassiz, *Meade's Headquarters,* 122.

11. Lyman journal, May 23, 1864, in Lyman Collection, MHS. Several sources state that Grant rode on May 23 with Hancock. Most likely he accompanied the 2nd Corps from where Meade turned off on the side road until he rejoined Meade at the Moncure house. Badeau, *Military History of U. S. Grant,* 2, p. 227; Porter, *Campaigning with Grant,* 142.

12. Lyman journal, May 23, 1864, in Lyman Collection, MHS; Agassiz, *Meade's Headquarters,* 122; Wingfield, *History of Caroline County,* 428–30.

13. Taylor to Bettie, May 23, 1864, in Tower, *Lee's Adjutant,* 162.

14. Lee to Davis, May 23, 1864, in Dowdey, *Wartime Papers of R. E. Lee,* 747–8; Lee to wife, May 23, 1864, ibid., 748.

15. Francis Solomon Johnson Jr. to Emily Hutchings, May 23, 1864, in University of Georgia Libraries; Joseph D. Joyner to mother, May 23, 1864, in SHC.

16. Lee to Davis, May 23, 1864, in Dowdey, *Wartime Papers of R. E. Lee,* 747; Wilcox's report, in VSL; John W. Chowning diary, May 23, 1864, in Mary Ball Washington Library, Fredericksburg, Va.; R. L. T. Beale, *Ninth Virginia Cavalry,* 123.

17. William H. McLaurin, "Eighteenth Regiment," in W. Clark, *Histories of the Several Regiments,* 2, pp. 54–5.

18. "Further Details of the Gallant Charge by Birney's Division," *Philadelphia Inquirer,* May 27, 1864; "Our Army Correspondence," *Boston Evening Transcript,* May 28, 1864; James A. Milling, "Recollections," *Confederate Veteran,* 6 (1997), 9; Mac Wyckoff, *A History of the 2nd South Carolina Infantry: 1861–65* (Fredericksburg, Va., 1994), 122–5. Sources vary widely concerning the position of the South Carolina regiments, although all agree that the 7th South Carolina was on the left.

19. James W. Reagan, "More About Fight at Brooks Crossroads," *Confederate Veteran,* 28 (1910), 229.

20. Francis C. Long's dispatch, *New York Herald,* May 30, 1864; Beaudry, *War Journal,* 121; Wood diary, May 23, 1864, in VSL; Fred Mather, "Under Old Glory," *National Tribune,* January 30, 1896.

21. Neese, *Three Years in the Confederate Horse Artillery,* 274–5; Report of Special Correspondent, May 26, 1864, *Richmond Enquirer,* May 27, 1864.

22. Roebling's report, in Warren Collection, NYSLA; James S. Thorpe, *Reminiscences of the Army Life During the Civil War* (N.p., n.d.), 45; Warren to Hancock, 1:30 P.M., May 23, 1864, in *OR,* Vol. 36, Pt. 3, p. 118; Warren to Meade, 1:30 P.M., May 23, 1864, ibid., 125.

23. Hancock to Williams, 1:00 P.M., May 23, 1864, in *OR,* Vol. 36, Pt. 3, p. 118.

24. Meade's endorsement, May 23, 1864, ibid., 125; Grant to Meade, 2:00 P.M., May 23, 1864, ibid., 115.

25. Humphreys to Warren, 3:20 P.M., May 23, 1864, ibid., 127.

26. Thorpe, *Reminiscences of the Army Life,* 45; J. L. Parker, *Twenty-Second Massachusetts Infantry,* 446; Warren to wife, May 23, 1864, in Warren Collection, NYSLA; R. G. Carter, *Four Brothers in Blue,* 406; Wainwright's report, in *OR,* Vol. 36, Pt. 1, p. 645; Nevins, *Diary of Battle,* 384.

27. J. F. J. Caldwell, *Brigade of South Carolinians,* 153.

28. E. C. Bennett, *Musket and Sword,* 237–8.

29. Tilton's report, in *OR,* Vol. 36, Pt. 1, p. 563; J. L. Parker, *Twenty-Second Massachusetts Infantry,* 446–7.

30. Daniel G. McNamara, *The History of the Ninth Regiment Massachusetts Volunteer Infantry, Second Brigade, First Division, Fifth Army Corps, Army of the Potomac, June 1861–June 1864* (Boston, 1899), 397.

31. E. C. Bennett, *Musket and Sword,* 239–40.

32. Francis J. Parker, *The Story of the Thirty-Second Regiment Massachusetts Infantry* (Boston, 1880), 216–7; Tilton's report, in *OR,* Vol. 36, Pt.1, p. 563; Mason W. Burt's report, ibid., 568; E.C. Bennett, *Musket and Sword,* 239.

33. Wilcox's report, in VSL.

34. Walter H. Parcels, "Laying a Bridge," *National Tribune,* March 10, 1887; Mary G. Brainard, *Campaigns of the One Hundred and Forty-Sixth Regiment New York State Volunteers* (New York, 1915), 210; Judson, *Eighty-Third Regiment Pennsylvania Volunteers,* 207; Warren to wife, May 24, 1864, in Warren Collection, NYSLA.

35. R. E. McBride, *In the Ranks,* 63–4; Locke, *Story of the Regiment,* 342–3.

36. Warren to Humphreys, 3:20 P.M., May 23, 1864, in *OR,* Vol. 36, Pt. 3, pp. 125–6; Warren to Humphreys, 4:15 P.M., May 23, 1864, ibid., 127; Humphreys to Warren, 4:45 P.M., May 23, 1864, ibid., 128.

37. Ira Spaulding's report, ibid., Pt.1, p. 310; Cheek and Pointon, *Sauk County Riflemen,* 102; Nevins, *Diary of Battle,* 384–5; Thomas Chamberlin, *History of the One Hundred and Fiftieth Regiment Pennsylvania Volunteers, Second Regiment, Bucktail Brigade* (Philadelphia, 1905), 244–5; Wainwright's report, in *OR,* Vol. 36, Pt. 1, p. 645.

38. Marshall, *History of Company K,* 161; Brainard, *Campaigns,* 210.

39. J. D. Smith, *Nineteenth Regiment of Maine Volunteer Infantry,* 176.

40. Hancock to Williams, 2:35 P.M., May 23, 1864, in *OR,* Vol. 36, Pt. 3, p. 119.

41. Second endorsement, Grant to Meade, 3:00 P.M., May 23, 1864, ibid.

42. Hancock to Williams, 3:15 P.M., and endorsement, Grant to Meade, 4:15 P.M., May 23, 1864, ibid., 120.

43. Hancock to Williams, 3:30 P.M., and Hancock to Williams, 4:00 P.M., May 23, 1864, ibid., 120–1; Birney to Hancock, 3:33 P.M., May 23, 1864, ibid., 124.

44. Hancock to Williams, 4:20 P.M., and Hancock to Meade, 4:35 P.M., May 23, 1864, ibid., 121.

45. 2nd Corps Daily Memorandum, ibid., Pt. 1, p. 363; "The Campaign," *Springfield (Mass.) Daily Republican,* May 27, 1864; John C. Tidball's report, in *OR,* Vol 36, Pt. 1, pp. 510–11; A. Judson Clark's report, ibid., 522; John E. Burton's report, ibid., 529; George F. McKnight's report, ibid., 530; Ricketts's report, ibid., 532; T. Fred Brown's report, ibid, 533.

46. Pendleton's report, ibid., 1047; Krick, *Parker's Virginia Battery,* 252; Gallagher, ed., *Fighting for the Confederacy,* 388.

47. Gallagher, ed., *Fighting for the Confederacy,* 388; Sorrel journal, May 23, 1864, in MC; Richard Anderson's report, in DU. According to the 1860 census, John W. Lowry lived in the house with his wife and seven children.

48. J. Henry Sleeper's report, in *OR,* Vol. 36, Pt. 1, p. 517; Billings, *Tenth Massachusetts Battery of Light Artillery,* 245–6; J. H. Rhodes, *History of Battery B,* 291; Davis G. McIntosh, "Sketch of the Military Career of David G. McIntosh," in United Daughters of the Confederacy,

Treasured Reminiscences (Columbia, S.C., 1911), 50; Special Correspondent's Report, May 26, 1864, *Richmond Enquirer,* May 27, 1864.

49. Coles, *From Huntsville to Appomattox,* 171; John Bratton's report, *SHSP,* 8, p. 550; Coker, *History of Company G,* 147; Wilkeson, *Recollections of a Private,* 111–14.

50. Freeman, *R. E. Lee,* 3, pp. 352–3; Edward P. Alexander to father, May 29, 1864, in SHC; Gallagher, ed., *Fighting for the Confederacy,* 388–9.

51. D. Augustus Dickert, *History of Kershaw's Brigade* (Newberry, S.C., 1899), 359; Milling, "Recollections," 9.

52. Casper W. Tyler's report, in *OR,* Vol. 36, Pt. 1, p. 478; Craft, *One Hundred Forty-First Regiment,* 204. Egan's brigade started the campaign under Brigadier General J. H. Hobart Ward, whom Meade removed for drunkenness on May 12.

53. "Further Details of the Gallant Charge by Birney's Division," *Philadelphia Inquirer,* May 27, 1864. Pierce's brigade began the campaign under fiery Brigadier General Alexander Hays, mortally wounded in the Wilderness.

54. "The Campaign," *Springfield (Mass.) Daily Republican,* May 27, 1864; Weygant, *One Hundred and Twenty-Fourth Regiment,* 343–4; Stephen P. Chase, "Battle of North Anna, Leads Charge on Enemy," in Civil War Times Illustrated Collection, USAMHI; Frederick C. Floyd, *History of the Fortieth (Mozart) Regiment, New York Volunteers* (Boston, 1909), 221; Wilkeson, *Recollections of a Private,* 114; Kate M. Scott, *History of the One Hundred and Fifth Regiment of Pennsylvania Volunteers* (Philadelphia, 1877), 106; Crocker diary, May 23, 1864, in Cornell University, John M. Olin Library. After the attack, the 86th New York's colonel complimented Chase before both regiments. "I never had so much praise said over me in all my life put together, and I had not the true courage to tell them why I went forward; that it was because I was afraid to go to the rear," Chase was to write. "I went where I thought there was the least danger and consequently cannot see any great amount of heroism in the act." Chase, "Battle of North Anna, Leads Charge on Enemy," in Civil War Times Illustrated Collection, USAMHI.

55. D. G. Crotty, *Four Years Campaigning in the Army of the Potomac* (Grand Rapids, Mich., 1874), 136; Milling, "Recollections," 9; Dickert, *Kershaw's Brigade,* 360.

56. Craft, *One Hundred Forty-First Regiment,* 204–5; Henri LeFevre Brown, *History of the Third Regiment, Excelsior Brigade, 72nd New York Volunteer Infantry, 1861–1865* (Jamestown, N.Y., 1902), 132; Chase, "Battle of North Anna, Leads Charge on Enemy," in Civil War Times Illustrated Collection, USAMHI.

57. Gibson Clark, "Reminiscences of Civil War Days," in *Annals of Wyoming,* 15 (1943), 380.

58. Silliker, *Rebel Yell,* 161–2; "A Dashing and Splendid Charge," *Springfield (Mass.) Daily Republican,* May 26, 1864; John W. Wofford, "A Gallant Company," in Jane Wofford Wait, et al., *History of the Wofford Family* (Spartanburg, S.C., 1928), 208–9; J. W. Reagan, "More About Fight at Brooks Crossroads," 229; Robertson, *Personal Recollections of the War,* 114; Dickert, *Kershaw's Brigade,* 360.

59. "Further Details of the Gallant Charge by Birney's Division," *Philadelphia Inquirer,* May 27, 1864; Mather, "Under Old Glory," *National Tribune,* January 30, 1896.

60. Galwey, *Valiant Hours,* 223; J. D. Smith, *Nineteenth Regiment of Maine Volunteer Infantry,* 176; Bratton's report, *SHSP,* 8, 550; Diary of Unknown Rebel, May 23, 1864, in Boston University, Muger Memorial Library.

61. "Gallantry of Birney's Division," *Philadelphia Inquirer,* May 27, 1864; "Further Details of the Gallant Charge by Birney's Division," ibid.

62. J. F. J. Caldwell, *Brigade of South Carolinians,* 153; Wilcox's report, in VSL.

63. Tilton's report, in *OR,* Vol. 36, Pt. 1, p. 563.

64. Wilcox's report, in VSL; William S. Dunlop, *Lee's Sharpshooters; or, The Forefront of Battle: A Story of Southern Valor That Has Never Been Told* (Little Rock, Ark., 1899), 79–80.

65. Tilton's report, in *OR,* Vol. 36, Pt. 1, p. 563; R. G. Carter, *Four Brothers in Blue,* 407; J. L. Parker, *Twenty-Second Massachusetts Infantry,* 447–8.

66. Kent, *Three Years with Company K,* 272.

67. Hall, *Ninety-Seventh Regiment New York Volunteers,* 189; R. E. McBride, *In the Ranks,* 64–5; Sypher, *Pennsylvania Reserve Corps,* 541.

68. R. E. McBride, *In the Ranks,* 65; Vautier, *88th Pennsylvania Volunteers,* 184–5; "Annual Reunion of Pegram Battalion Association in the Hall of House of Delegates, Richmond, Va., May 21st, 1886," *SHSP,* 14, 7; Charles P. Young, "The Crenshaw Battery," *Richmond Star,* January 15, 1894.

69. Dunlop, *Lee's Sharpshooters,* 80; E. C. Bennett, *Musket and Sword,* 241–2; J. L. Parker, *Twenty-Second Massachusetts Infantry,* 447. During the afternoon the 22nd Massachusetts's picket line had been extended on its left by the 91st Pennsylvania and 14th United States Regulars of Ayres's brigade, and on its right by the 95th New York of Hofmann's brigade.

70. Brainard, *Campaigns,* 211; William Fowler to family, May 31, 1864, in *Memorials of William Fowler* (New York, 1875), 83; One Hundred and Forty-Fifth Pennsylvania Association, *Under the Maltese Cross: Antietam to Appomattox, the Loyal Uprising in Western Pennsylvania, 1861–1865, Campaigns 155th Pennsylvania Regiment* (Pittsburgh, 1910), 276–7.

71. Marshall, *Company K,* 161–2; Augustus C. Golding diary, May 23, 1864, in FSNMP.

72. Charles Thomas Bowen diary, May 23, 1864, in FSNMP; McLaurin, "Eighteenth Regiment," in W. Clark, *Histories of the Several Regiments,* 2, p. 55; Lane's report, in Lane Collection, AU. Lane's alignment, from right to left, was the 18th, 37th, 33rd, and 28th North Carolina. The 7th North Carolina had been detached to guard a ford upriver.

73. Bowen diary, May 23, 1864, in FSNMP; Lane's report, in Lane Collection, AU.

74. John D. Lentz's report, in *OR,* Vol. 36, Pt. 1, p. 556; Bowen diary, May 23, 1864, in FSNMP.

75. Cutler's report, in *OR,* Vol. 36, Pt. 1, p. 612; Dawes's report, ibid., 621; O. B. Curtis, *History of the Twenty-Fourth Michigan of the Iron Brigade* (Detroit, Mich., 1891), 250.

76. Cheek and Pointon, *Sauk County Riflemen,* 102; Dawes's report, in *OR,* Vol. 36, Pt. 1, p. 621.

77. Dawes's report, in *OR,* Vol. 36, Pt. 1, p. 621; McNamara, *Ninth Regiment Massachusetts Volunteer Infantry,* 397.

78. Wilcox's report, in VSL.

79. Cutler's report, in *OR,* Vol. 36, Pt. 1, p. 612; Nevins, *Diary of Battle,* 385.

80. Chamberlin, *Bucktail Brigade,* 245–6; Warren, *Two Reunions of the 142d Regiment,* 32; John W. Nesbitt, *History of Company D, 149th Pennsylvania Volunteer Infantry* (Oakdale, Calif., 1908), 31; Edward S. Bragg's report, in *OR,* Vol. 36, Pt.1, p. 636; Dawes's report, ibid., 622; Samuel D. Webster diary, May 23, 1864, in Samuel D. Webster Collection, Henry E. Huntington Library, San Marino. The misadventures of Bragg's brigade on May 23 are recounted in Richard E. Matthews, *The 149th Pennsylvania Volunteer Infantry Unit in the Civil War* (Jefferson, N.C., 1994), 163–4. Chamberlin's claims for the 150th Pennsylvania are derided in Avery Harris memoir, USAMHI.

81. J. William Hoffman's report, in *OR,* Vol. 36, Pt. 1, p. 626; David F. Ritchie, *Four Years in the First New York Light Artillery,* ed. Norman L. Ritchie (New York, 1997), 162.

82. Nevins, *Diary of Battle,* 385; Thomas W. Osborn, "Battery D—Winslow's First New York Light Artillery," in *New York Monuments Commission, Final Report of the Battle of Gettysburg,* vol. 3 (Albany, 1902), 1211; Levi W. Baker, *History of the Ninth Massachusetts Battery* (South Framingham, Mass., 1888), 113.

83. J. F. J. Caldwell, *Brigade of South Carolinians,* 153–4; Wilcox's report, in VSL; George Breck to Editor, May 30, 1864, *Rochester (N.Y.) Union and Advertiser,* June 21, 1864; Wainwright's report, in *OR,* Vol. 36, Pt. 1, p. 645; L. I. Richardson's report, ibid., 652; Ritchie, *First New York Light Artillery,* 162–3.

84. E. S. Coan, "At the North Anna," *National Tribune,* August 11, 1887.

85. Breck to Editor, May 30, 1864, Rochester (N.Y.) *Union and Advertiser,* June 21, 1864; Osborn, "Battery D—Winslow's First New York Light Artillery," in *New York Monuments Commission, Final Report of the Battlefield of Gettysburg,* 3, p. 1211.

86. DeWitt C. McCoy's report, in *OR,* Vol. 36, Pt. 1, p. 589; Spear, *Civil War Recollections,* 114.

87. Judson, *Eighty-Third Regiment Pennsylvania Volunteers,* 208; William A. Throop's report, in *OR,* Vol. 36, Pt. 1, p. 582; Guy W. Fuller's report, ibid., 585; DeWitt C. McCoy's report, ibid., 589; George G. Hooper memoir, in Military Order of the Loyal Legion of the United States Collection, BL.

88. Judson, *Eighty-Third Regiment Pennsylvania Volunteers,* 208; Gerrish, *Army Life,* 192; J. F. J. Caldwell, *Brigade of South Carolinians,* 154. Rival claims for capturing Brown were made by Corporal Corbin, of Company B, 83rd Pennsylvania, and by Jean Brown, of the regiment's Company C. Judson, *Eighty-Third Regiment Pennsylvania Volunteers,* 208n2; Carleton to Editor, May 26, 1864, *Boston Evening Transcript,* May 31, 1864. See also Argus, "The Fight on the North Anna," *New York Daily News,* May 30, 1864, which describes Warren as catching the Confederates in artillery crossfire.

89. Marion Hill Fitzpatrick to wife, May 24, 1864, in Hammock, *Letters to Amanda,* 129–30; W. T. Irvine, "Old 35th Georgia," *Atlanta Sunny South,* May 2, 1891; Francis Solomon Johnson Jr. to Emily Hutchings, May 23, 1864, in University of Georgia Libraries; Mills, "Supplemental Sketch Sixteenth Regiment," in W. Clark, *Histories of the Several Regiments,* 4, pp. 196–7; Wilcox's report, in VSL.

90. Tom to brother, June 10, 1864, *New York Irish American,* July 2, 1864; Cook, *Twelfth Massachusetts Volunteers,* 133; Samuel D. Webster diary, May 23, 1864, in Samuel D. Webster Collection, Henry E. Huntington Library, San Marino.

91. Wilcox's report, in VSL; J. F. J. Caldwell, *Brigade of South Carolinians,* 154–5; Lane's report, in AU. The *Richmond Examiner* described the collapse of the Confederate line as follows: "During the engagement, the enemy were pressed back as far as the river, and would doubtless have been driven across, when, for some unexplained reason, Thomas' brigade gave back, and then McGowan's and Lane's, thus destroying the certain prospect of a very brilliant success; for at the time these brigades gave back, Scales' North Carolina brigade had most opportunely thrown itself around on the enemy's flank, and were firing into them with considerable success, and doubtless but for this inexcusable giving way in front, we should have realized a splendid success." Correspondent Report, May 25, 1864, *Richmond Examiner,* May 27, 1864.

92. Henry Heth's report, in MC; Wilcox's report, in VSL; Charles B. Jones, "Historical Sketch of 55th North Carolina," *New Bern (N.C.) Our Living and Our Dead,* April 15, 1874; Joseph Mullen Jr. diary, May 23, 1864, in MC.

93. Cockrell, *Gunner with Stonewall,* 94–5.

94. Francis Gardner Walter diary, May 23, 1864, in FSNMP.

95. J. L. Parker, *Twenty-Second Massachusetts Infantry,* 449; E. C. Bennett, *Musket and Sword,* 243–5.

96. George C. Hooper memoir, in BL; John P. Arthur, *Western North Carolina: A History* (Raleigh, N.C., 1914), 624.

97. Nathan Appleton diary, May 23, 1864, in Cowles, *Fifth Massachusetts Battery,* 835; Seiser, "Civil War Diary," 94.

98. "Further Details of the Gallant Charge by Birney's Division," *Philadelphia Inquirer,* May 27, 1864.

99. Fifth Corps casualties, May 4–November 1, 1864, in Record Group 94, Entry 729, Box 69, NA; Meade to Warren, 10:30 P.M., May 23, 1864, in *OR,* Vol. 36, Pt. 1, pp. 129–30; Warren to wife, May 24, 1864, in Warren Collection, NYSLA; Emerson Taylor, *Gouverneur Kemble Warren: Life and Letters of an American Soldier* (New York, 1932), 114.

100. Judson, *Eighty-Third Regiment Pennsylvania Volunteers,* 208–9; Breck to Editor, May 30, 1864, *Rochester (N.Y.) Union and Advertiser,* June 21, 1864.

101. Carleton to Editor, May 26, 1864, *Boston Evening Journal,* May 31, 1864; Nevins, *Diary of Battle,* 386.

102. Correspondent's report, May 25, 1864, *Richmond Examiner,* May 27, 1864; Nevins, *Day of Battle,* 386–7.

103. J. F. J. Caldwell, *Brigade of South Carolinians,* 155; Wilcox's report, in VSL; Lane's report, in AU; Irvine, "Old 35th Georgia." Following Colonel Brown's capture, Colonel J. F. Hunt of the 13th South Carolina assumed command of McGowan's brigade. I am grateful to Alfred Young for sharing with me his tabulation of Confederate losses.

104. Burnside to Grant, 9:00 P.M., May 23, 1864, in *OR,* Vol. 36, Pt. 3, p. 134; Hancock to Williams, ibid., 122; *New York Daily News,* May 28, 1864.

105. Grant to Halleck, 11:00 P.M., May 23, 1864, in *OR,* Vol. 36, Pt. 3, pp. 113–14.

106. Hancock to Williams, 7:50 P.M., May 23, 1864, in *OR,* Vol. 36, Pt. 3, p. 122; Hancock to Williams, 9:20 P.M., May 23, 1864, ibid.; Meade to Hancock, 11:00 P.M., May 23, 1864, ibid., 122–3.

107. Grant to Burnside, 10:30 P.M., May 23, 1864, ibid., 134; "Lee Retreats During the Night," *Philadelphia Inquirer,* May 25, 1864; "Movements to the North Anna," *Springfield (Mass.) Daily Republican,* May 27, 1864.

108. Jedediah Hotchkiss journal, May 23, 1864, in LC; Gallagher, ed., *Fighting for the Confederacy,* 389.

109. Jedediah Hotchkiss, *Confederate Military History, Vol. 3, Virginia* (Atlanta, 1899), 210–11; Martin L. Smith to Sarah, May 29, 1864, in James S. Schoff Collection, CL.

110. Francis Walter diary, May 23, 1864, in FSNMP; Martin L. Smith diary, May 23, 1864, in Maryland Historical Society, Baltimore.

111. Hotchkiss diary, May 23, 1864, in Hotchkiss Collection, LC.

112. Gallagher, ed., *Fighting for the Confederacy,* 390.

113. Ibid.

114. *Atlas to Accompany the OR,* Plate 81 (7).

115. Cockrell, *Gunner with Stonewall,* 94; Fitzpatrick to wife, May 24, 1864, in Hammock, *Letters to Amanda,* 130.

116. A. J. McBride, "Tenth Georgia at Spotsylvania," *Atlanta Journal,* July 20, 1901; "Gallantry of Birney's Division," *Philadelphia Inquirer,* May 27, 1864; Keating, *Carnival of Blood,* 73–5.

117. Pendleton to wife, May 25, 1864, in S. P. Lee, *Memoirs of William Nelson Pendleton,* 336–7.

X MAY 24 *GRANT MARCHES INTO LEE'S TRAP*

1. Robert S. Robertson, "From Spotsylvania Onward," in *War Papers Read Before the Indiana Commandery Military Order of the Loyal Legion of the United States* (Indianapolis, 1898), 347; Henry Herbert Harris diary, May 14, 1864, in FSNMP; B. L. Wynn diary, May 24, 1864, in Mississippi Department of Archives and History; J. O. Thurmond Jr. to John G. Scurry, May 25, 1864, in Gilder-Lehrman Collection, Pierpont Morgan Library, NYC; T. L. Jones, *Memoirs of Captain William J. Seymour,* 129–30; Cooke, *Life of Gen. Robert E. Lee,* 404.

2. A. P. McDonald, ed., *Make Me a Map of the Valley,* 207.

3. Jedediah Hotchkiss to Henry Alexander White, January 12, 1897, in Hotchkiss Collection, LC; William McWillie notebook, Mississippi Department of Archives and History, Montgomery.

4. H. R. McIlwaine, ed., "Diary of Captain H. W. Wingfield," *Bulletin of the Virginia State Library,* 16 (July 1927), 39; Thurmond Jr. to Scurry, May 25, 1864, in Gilder-Lehrman Collection, Pierpont Morgan Library; Early, *Autobiographical Sketch,* 259–60; Pendleton's report, in *OR,* Vol. 36, Pt. 1, p. 1047.

5. Dana, *Recollections,* 203.

6. Roebling's report, in Warren Collection, NYSLA; Wright to Humphreys, 6:15 A.M., May 24, 1864, in *OR,* Vol. 36, Pt. 3, p. 165; Warren to Meade, 6:00 A.M., May 24, 1864, ibid., 157; Apted diary, May 24, 1864, in FSNMP; Joshua L. Chamberlain, "The Fifth Battery Men as Barn Movers," in Cowles, *Fifth Massachusetts Battery,* 836–7.

7. Civil War letters of Sergeant Charles Thomas Bowen, May 24, 1864, in FSNMP; Seiser, "Civil War Diary," 194; Roe, *Thirty-Ninth Regiment Massachusetts Volunteers,* 206; Cheek and Pointon, *Sauk County Riflemen,* 103; Dawes, *Service with the Sixth Wisconsin Volunteers,* 275.

8. Sypher, *Pennsylvania Reserve,* 542; John E. Laughton Jr., "The Sharpshooters of Mahone's Brigade, " *SHSP,* 22, pp. 102–3. Mahone commanded the Virginia brigade when he organized the sharpshooters. On May 7, Mahone was promoted to head a division, and Colonel David Weisiger assumed commanded of Mahone's brigade. Afterwards, the sharpshooters were sometimes referred to as "Weisiger's Sharpshooters."

9. Sypher, *Pennsylvania Reserve Corps,* 542; Laughton Jr., "Sharpshooters of Mahone's Brigade," 102–3.

10. Helena A. Howell, comp., *Chronicles of the One Hundred Fifty-First Regiment New York State Volunteer Infantry* (Albion, N.Y., 1911), 67; Abbott, *Personal Recollections,* 65; Ann A. Britton and Thomas J. Reed, *To My Beloved Wife and Boy at Home: The Letters and Diaries of Orderly Sergeant John F. L. Hartwell* (Madison, N.J., 1997), 232.

11. Hancock to Williams, 5:00 A.M., May 24, 1864, in *OR,* Vol. 36, Pt. 3, p. 148; Hancock to Williams, 6:30 A.M., May 24, 1864, ibid.

12. Lyman journal, May 24, 1864, in Lyman Collection, MHS; Agassiz, *Meade's Headquarters,* 122–3.

13. Warren to Meade, 7:30 A.M., May 24, 1864, in *OR,* Vol. 36, Pt. 3, pp. 157–8; Hancock to Williams, and Meade's endorsement, May 24, 1864, ibid., 148–9.

14. Grant to Halleck, 8:00 A.M., May 24, 1864, ibid., 145; Dana to Stanton, May 24, 1864, ibid., Pt. 1, p. 77.

15. Meade to wife, 9:00 A.M., May 24, 1864, in Meade, *Life and Letters,* 198.

16. Lyman journal, May 24, 1864, in Lyman Collection, MHS; Meade endorsement, in *OR,* Vol. 36, Pt. 3, p. 149.

17. Lyman journal, May 24, 1864, in Lyman Collection, MHS; Agassiz, *Meade's Headquarters,* 126.

18. Meier, *Memoirs of a Swiss Officer,* 162–3; John W. Hamil, *The Story of a Confederate Soldier* (N.p., n.d.), 20–1; C. A. Stevens, *Berdan's United States Sharpshooters in the Army of the Potomac, 1861–1865* (St. Paul, Minn., 1892), 434–5; Craft, *One Hundred Forty-First Regiment,* 205.

19. Marbaker, *Eleventh New Jersey Volunteers,* 184–5; E. B. Houghton, *Campaigns of the Seventeenth Maine,* 190–1; 2nd Corps addenda, in *OR,* Vol. 36, Pt. 1, p. 363.

20. Hays, *Under the Red Patch,* 217; E. B. Houghton, *Campaigns of the Seventeenth Maine,* 191; Meier, *Memoirs of a Swiss Officer,* 163.

21. Galwey, *Valiant Hours,* 224–5; Cowtan, *Tenth New York Volunteers,* 227; J. D. Smith, *Nineteenth Regiment of Maine Volunteer Infantry,* 177; Ira Spaulding's report, in *OR,* Vol. 36, Pt. 1, p. 311; Gibbon's report, ibid., 432. A third pontoon bridge, also below the railway bridge, was built later in the day; Brainerd, *Bridge Building in Wartime,* 225.

22. R. L. Stewart, *One Hundred and Fortieth Regiment Pennsylvania Volunteers,* 201; Armstrong, *Nuggets of Experience,* 15; Hancock to Williams, 10:40 A.M., in *OR,* Vol. 36, Pt. 3, p. 151; Pendleton's report, ibid., Pt. 1, pp. 1047–8.

23. Burnside to Grant, 6:30 A.M., May 24, 1864, in *OR,* Vol. 36, Pt. 3, p. 166; H. B., "Crossing the North Anna River," *New York Times,* May 29, 1864; George P. Hawkes diary, May 24, 1864, in Gregory A. Coco Collection, USAMHI; Charles F. Walcott, *History of the Twenty-First Massachusetts Volunteers in the War for the Preservation of the Union* (Boston, 1882), 327.

24. Hancock to Miles, May 24, 1864, in *OR,* Vol. 36, Pt. 3, p. 151; Burnside to Grant, 6:30 A.M., May 24, 1864, ibid., 166; Burnside's report, ibid., Pt. 1, p. 912; Willcox's report, ibid., 945; Raymond J. Herek, *These Men Have Seen Hard Service: The First Michigan Sharpshooters in the Civil War* (Detroit, 1998), 165–6; Robertson, *Personal Recollections,* 114.

25. Meade to Grant, 9:30 A.M., May 24, 1864, in *OR,* Vol. 36, Pt. 3, p. 146; Sypher, *Pennsylvania Reserve Corps,* 542; Locke, *Story of the Regiment,* 343–4; Cook, *Twelfth Massachusetts Volunteers,* 133; Laughton Jr., "Sharpshooters of Mahone's Brigade," 103.

26. Albert, *Forty-Fifth Regiment,* 130; C.A. Stevens, *Berdan's United States Sharpshooters,* 436–7. Stevens, who reported Hancock's brush with death, placed Burnside and Crittenden at the conference. He must have been mistaken, as Burnside and Crittenden were at Ox Ford preparing the operation toward Quarles's Mill.

27. Hancock to Williams, 11:05 A.M., May 24, 1864, in *OR,* Vol. 36, Pt. 3, p. 151.

28. Humphreys to Hancock, 1:30 P.M., May 24, 1864, ibid., 152; Humphreys to Warren, 1:00 P.M., May 24, 1864, ibid., 159; Humphreys to Wright, 1:00 P.M., May 24, 1864, ibid., 165–6.

29. Rawlins to Burnside, 1:00 P.M., May 24, 1864, ibid., 167.

30. L. O. Merriam recollections, 37, in FSNMP; Houston, *Thirty-Second Maine Regiment,* 169.

31. Merriam recollections, 37, in FSNMP; Jackman and Hadley, *Sixth New Hampshire Regiment,* 268.

32. Wilkinson, *Mother, May You Never See,* 116; Coco, *Through Blood and Fire,* 93.

33. Anderson, *Fifty-Seventh Regiment of Massachusetts Volunteers,* 98.

34. H. B., "Crossing the North Anna River," *New York Times,* May 29, 1864; Edward P. Roche,

"Rescue of Union Wounded of North Anna is Recalled," *Boston Journal,* March 20, 1886; Charles M. Weld to Miss Andrew, June 28, 1864, in *Lt. Col. Charles Lyon Chandler* (Cambridge, Mass., 1864), 5–16; Anderson, *Fifty-Seventh Regiment of Massachusetts Volunteers,* 98; Committee of the Regiment, *Thirty-Fifth Regiment Massachusetts Volunteers,* 238.

35. George S. Bernard diary, May 24, 1864, in UV. Mahone's segment of the inverted V lies within the North Anna Battlefield Park. The earthworks are among the best preserved remaining from the campaign. It is still possible to walk along Mahone's entrenchments and see the variation in construction from regiment to regiment.

36. C. Seton Fleming diary, May 23–24, 1864, in Fleming, *Memoir of Capt. C. Seton Fleming,* appendix; Council Bryan to wife, May 25, 1864, in Florida Department of Archives and History, Tallahassee.

37. "Special Despatch," *Boston Daily Advertiser,* May 30, 1864; H. B., "Crossing the North Anna River," *New York Times,* May 29, 1864; Committee of the Regiment, *Thirty-Fifth Regiment Massachusetts Volunteers,* 238–9.

38. Anderson, *Fifty-Seventh Regiment of Massachusetts Volunteers,* 99.

39. Ibid.

40. Ibid., 100–1. The officer on the stretcher was Major James W. Cushing of the 57th Massachusetts. Whether he was intoxicated, as Anderson believed, or simply overcome by heat, as others claimed, was the subject of controversy. Captain John W. Hudson, who saw Cushing being borne away, insisted that the major was prostrate from heat; John W. Hudson to Editor, June 6, 1864, *Boston Evening Journal,* June 21, 1864.

41. J. S. C. Morton to brother, May 26, 1864, in Huntington Library, San Marino; Anderson, *Fifty-Seventh Regiment of Massachusetts Volunteers,* 101.

42. Anderson, *Fifty-Seventh Regiment of Massachusetts Volunteers,* 101. On May 6 Karpeles had rallied the retreating regiment in the Wilderness and inspired the soldiers to check a Confederate advance. He was to receive the Medal of Honor for his exploit of May 6.

43. Massachusetts Historical Society, *Letters of Stephen Minot Weld,* 296–7; Anderson, *Fifty-Seventh Regiment of Massachusetts Volunteers,* 102.

44. Maurice S. Fortin, ed., "Colonel Hilary A. Herbert's 'History of the Eighth Alabama Volunteer Regiment,'" *Alabama Historical Quarterly,* 39 (1977), 141; Nathaniel Harris to William Mahone, August 2, 1866, in William Mahone Collection, VSL; Massachusetts Historical Society, *Letters of Stephen Minot Weld,* 296–7; Anderson, *Fifty-Seventh Regiment of Massachusetts Volunteers,* 102.

45. *Boston Journal* excerpt, in *Lt. Col. Charles Lyon Chandler,* 13; Gerhard Luhn diary, May 25, 1864, quoted in J. Michael Miller, *The North Anna Campaign: "Even to Hell Itself,"* *May 21–26, 1864* (Lynchburg, Va., 1989), 105.

46. Anderson, *Fifty-Seventh Regiment of Massachusetts Volunteers,* 103; Massachusetts Historical Society, *Letters of Stephen Minot Weld,* 297.

47. *New York Times,* May 25, 1864; W. R. Knox to M. J. Williams, May 27, 1864, *Selma (Ala.) Morning Reporter,* June 7, 1864; A. Manning Wright to T. P. Chandler, June 8, 1864, and James H. Ledlie to T. P. Chandler, July 3, 1864, in *Lt. Col. Charles Lyon Chandler,* 8–9. Several sources mentioned the capture of colors, but Colonel Weld denounced the reports as false, claiming: "We have never lost our colors, and I hope never shall" (Weld to Hannah, May 25, 1864, in Massachusetts Historical Society, *Letters of Stephen Minot Weld,* 298. Alfred Young places Harris's losses at 17 and Sanders's at 58.

48. Massachusetts Historical Society, *Letters of Stephen Minot Weld,* 296–7; Anderson, *Fifty-Seventh Regiment of Massachusetts Volunteers,* 104.

49. Francis Yeager diary, May 24, 1864, in FSNMP; Nelson Miles' report, in *OR*, Vol. 36, Pt. 1, p. 371; Smyth's report, ibid., 450; Thomas S. Kenan, comp., *Sketch of the Forty-Third Regiment North Carolina Troops* (Raleigh, 1895), 16.

50. George A. Bowen diary, May 24, 1864, in FSNMP; W. P. Haines, *Men of Company F,* 64; Edward G. Longacre, *To Gettysburg and Beyond: The Twelfth New Jersey Volunteer Infantry, II Corps, Army of the Potomac, 1862–1865* (Heightstown, N.J., 1988), 210; Benjamin Y. Draper diary, May 24, 1864, in FSNMP.

51. J. D. Smith, *Nineteenth Regiment of Maine Volunteer Infantry,* 177–9; Ernest L. Waitt, *History of the Nineteenth Regiment Massachusetts Volunteer Infantry* (Salem, Mass., 1906), 316.

52. Smyth's report, in *OR*, Vol. 36, Pt. 1, p. 450; Galwey, *Valiant Hours,* 225.

53. Houston, *Thirty-Second Maine Regiment of Infantry Volunteers,* 170; Gibbon to Hancock, 3:15 P.M., May 24, 1864, in *OR*, Vol. 36, Pt. 3, p. 153; Hancock to Williams, 4:00 P.M., May 24, 1864, ibid., 152.

54. Badeau, *General Ulysses S. Grant,* 2, p. 235.

55. Taylor to Bettie, May 30, 1864, in Tower, *Lee's Adjutant,* 164; Pendleton to wife, May 25, 1864, in S. P. Lee, *Memoirs of William Nelson Pendleton,* 336; Robert Stiles, *Four Years Under Marse Robert* (New York, 1903), 266–7. "Much dysentery prevails in our army," the head of the Confederate War Bureau wrote on May 30. "General Lee has been quite sick with it for some days"; Edward Younger, ed., *Inside the Confederate Government: The Diary of Robert Garlick Hill Kean* (New York, 1957), 153. Lee's medical history is discussed in Jack D. Welsh, *Medical Histories of Confederate Generals* (Kent, Ohio, 1995), 134–6; John C. Krantz Jr., "The Implications of the Medical History of General Lee," *Virginia Medical Monthly,* 86 (June, 1959), 308; and Freeman, *R. E. Lee,* 4, pp. 521–5. Krantz diagnoses Lee's ailment as "bacillary dysentery or amebiasis, " Freeman characterizes it as "a ten-day debilitating diarrhea," and Walsh describes "violent intestinal complaints," noting that one observer termed the disease "bilious dysentery."

56. Venable, "General Lee in the Wilderness Campaign," 244; Charles S. Venable, "The Campaign from the Wilderness to Petersburg," *SHSP,* 14, p. 535.

57. Venable, "Campaign from the Wilderness to Petersburg," 535.

58. Hancock to Williams, 5:10 P.M., May 24, 1864, in *OR*, Vol. 36, Pt. 3, p. 153.

59. Smyth's report, ibid., Pt. 1, p. 451; Roback, *Veteran Volunteers,* 87.

60. Brooke's report, in *OR*, Vol. 36, Pt. 1, p. 412; William Glenny's report, ibid., 417; William C. Oates, *The War Between the Union and the Confederacy and Its Lost Opportunities* (New York, 1905), 363; "64th New York Memoir," in Indiana University, Lilly Library. While examining his lines near the railroad, General Law became embroiled in a duel with a Union sharpshooter, whom he wounded; Evander McI. Law, "From the Wilderness to Cold Harbor," *B&L,* 4, pp. 136–7.

61. Arthur L. Chase diary, May 25, 1864, in Niagara County Historical Society, Lockport, N.Y.; Keating, *Carnival of Blood,* 80.

62. Adams, *Reminiscences,* 95–6.

63. Smyth's report, in *OR*, Vol. 36, Pt. 1, p. 451; Cary Whitaker diary, May 24, 1864, in SHC; Kenan, *Forty-Third Regiment North Carolina,* 16; Benjamin F. Hall autobiographical sketch, in NCDAH; St. Claire A. Mulholland, *Military Order Congressional Medal of Honor Legion of the United States* (Philadelphia, 1905), 413–14; John E. Green Diary, May 24, 1864, in NCDAH. Keele was awarded the Congressional Medal of Honor.

64. Merriam recollections, FSNMP; Galwey, *Valiant Hours,* 225; Ward, *One Hundred and Sixth Regiment Pennsylvania Volunteers,* 259.

65. Gibbon, *Personal Recollections,* 224; F. A. Walker, *Second Army Corps,* 496; Charles D. Walker, *Biographical Sketches of the Graduates and Eleves of the Virginia Military Institute Who Fell during the War between the States* (Philadelphia, 1875), 453; Ewell's report, in *OR,* Vol. 36, Pt. 1, p. 1074; Ramseur's report, ibid., 1083; Venable, "Campaign from the Wilderness to Petersburg," 534; McIlwaine, "Diary of Captain H. W. Wingfield," 39; Buckner McGill Randolph diary, May 24, 1864, in VHS; Peyton, *Civil War Record,* May 24, 1864; Bryan Grimes to wife, May 25, 1864, in Cowper, *Extracts of Letters,* 54; "Diary of a Confederate Officer," *New Bern (N.C.) Our Living and Our Dead,* February 11, 1874. According to Alfred Young's calculations, Grimes lost about 150 men, Ramseur about 20.

66. Roche, "Rescue of Union Wounded." The 56th Massachusetts's bands' exploits are detailed in W. J. Martland, "Band of the Fifty-Sixth at the North Anna," *Boston Journal,* March 20, 1886.

67. Brainerd, *Bridge Building in Wartime,* 226.

68. R. G. Carter, *Four Brothers in Blue,* 407; E. C. Bennett, *Musket and Sword,* 246; J. L. Smith, *Corn Exchange Regiment,* 444–5; Chipman, "Diary of Cyril Fountain," 293.

69. Porter, *Campaigning with Grant,* 143–4.

70. Greenleaf, "From the Rapidan to Richmond," 23–4; "Supplying Sheridan's Army," undated clipping from *Cincinnati Commercial,* in Daniel O. Drennan papers, LC; Rodenbough, *From Everglades to Cañon,* 308.

71. Sheridan to Humphreys, 5:00 P.M., May 24, 1864, in *OR,* Vol. 36, Pt. 3, p. 171; J. R. Bowen, *First New York Dragoons,* 167.

72. Agassiz, *Meade's Headquarters,* 126; Pyne, *Ride to War,* 206.

73. Burnside to Grant, May 24, 1864, in *OR,* Vol. 36, Pt. 3, p. 168; Hancock to Williams, 6:30 P.M., May 24, 1864, ibid., 153.

74. Dana, *Recollections,* 203.

75. Hancock to Humphreys, May 24, 1864, ibid., 155; Humphreys to Hancock, 11:15 P.M., May 24, 1864, ibid., 155–6; Grant to Burnside, 8:20 P.M., May 24, 1864, ibid., 168–9. Crawford was to move south from Quarles's Mill, forming on Crittenden's right; Cutler and the Maryland Brigade were to push downriver along the southern bank, retracing Ledlie's route; and Griffin was to advance along the Virginia Central Railroad toward Hanover Junction. Warren to Crawford, 11:00 P.M., May 24, 1864, and Warren to Cutler, 11:30 P.M., May 24, 1864, both ibid., 164.

76. Special Orders 25, May 24, 1864, in *OR,* Vol. 36, Pt. 3, p. 169; Burnside to Grant, May 24, 1864, ibid., 169; Humphreys to Burnside, 11:15 P.M., May 24, 1864, ibid., 170; Porter, *Campaigning with Grant,* 144–5.

77. H. B. McClellan manuscript, quoted in Freeman, *R. E. Lee,* 3, p. 359.

78. Lee to Seddon, 9:30 P.M., May 24, 1864, in *OR,* Vol. 36, Pt. 3, p. 827.

79. William Swinton, *Campaigns of the Army of the Potomac* (New York, 1866), 477; Grant, *Personal Memoirs,* 2, pp. 249–50.

80. Humphreys, *Virginia Campaign,* 132.

EPILOGUE

1. Roebling's report, in Warren Collection, NYSLA; Tilton's report, in *OR,* Vol. 36, Pt. 1, p. 564; Wright to Warren, ibid., Pt. 3, p. 191.

2. Marshall, *Company K,* 164; One Hundred and Fifty-fifth Pennsylvania Association, *Under the Maltese Cross,* 279.

3. Warren to Meade, 8:00 A.M., May 25, 1864, in *OR,* Vol. 36, Pt. 3, p. 190.

4. Tom to brother, June 10, 1864, *New York Irish American,* July 2, 1864; Roe, *Thirty-Ninth Regiment Massachusetts Volunteers,* 206; Kent, *Three Years with Company K,* 273–4.

5. Lyman journal, May 25, 1864, in Lyman Collection, MHS; "Lieut. Appleton's Notes," in Cowles, *Fifth Massachusetts Battery,* 839–41.

6. Lyman journal, May 25, 1864, in Lyman Collection, MHS; Bennett, *Musket and Sword,* 247. Crittenden protested to Burnside about having to report to Warren. "I fully appreciate your feelings in the matter to which you refer," Burnside replied, "but under all the circumstances I would as a friend advise you to remain where you are" (Thomas L. Crittenden to Burnside, May 25, 1864, and Burnside to Crittenden, May 25, 1864, in *OR,* Vol. 36, Pt. 3, pp. 198–9.

7. Roebling's report, in Warren Collection, NYSLA; Warren to Meade, 10:00 A.M., May 25, 1864, in *OR,* Vol. 36, Pt. 3, p. 191; Warren to Meade, 12:00, May 25, 1864, ibid., 192–3; Augustus Buell, *The Cannoneer: Recollections of Service in the Army of the Potomac* (Washington, D.C., 1890), 204. The 15th New Jersey tried to cross Little River but was driven back by Confederate cavalry; A. A. Haines, *Fifteenth Regiment New Jersey Volunteers,* 194–5.

8. Crocker diary, May 25, 1864, in Cornell University, John M. Olin Library; Charles H. Morgan to Hancock, 5:00 A.M., May 25, 1864, in *OR,* Vol. 36, Pt., 3, p. 185; A. J. McBride, "Tenth Georgia at Spotsylvania."

9. Dana to Stanton, noon, May 25, 1864, in *OR,* Vol. 36, Pt. 1, pp. 78–9; Roebling to Emily Warren, May 24, 1864, in Washington A. Roebling Papers, Rutgers University Libraries; Argus, "From the Army of the Potomac, May 28, 1864," *New York Daily News,* June 2, 1864.

10. Hall, *Ninety-Seventh Regimental New York Volunteers,* 190.

11. Dana to Stanton, noon, May 25, 1864, in *OR,* Vol. 36, Pt. 1, pp. 78–9.

12. Grant to Halleck, noon, May 25, 1864, ibid., Pt. 3, p. 183; Meade and Grant endorsements, Warren to Meade, 12:00, May 25, 1864, ibid.

13. Robertson, *Personal Recollections,* 115; John N. Terrill, *Campaign of the Fourteenth Regiment New Jersey Volunteers* (New Brunswick, N.J., 1866), 62; Best, *121st New York State Infantry,* 153; Hartwell, *To My Beloved Wife,* 232.

14. Hampton, "Connected Narrative," in University of South Carolina, South Caroliniana Library; Joseph F. Waring diary, May 25, 1864, in SHC; W. E. Arehart, "Diary," *Rockingham (Va.) Historical Society Recorder,* 2 (Oct. 1959), 156; Goldsborough, *Maryland Line,* 198; Booth, *Personal Reminiscences,* 111.

15. Lee to Davis, 4:45 A.M., May 25, 1864, in Dowdey, *Wartime Papers of R. E. Lee,* 750.

16. Henry Herbert Harris diary, May 25, 1864, in FSNMP; Martin L. Smith diary, May 25, 1864, in Maryland Historical Society, Baltimore.

17. Porter, *Campaigning with Grant,* 147–8.

18. Grant to Halleck, May 26, 1864, in *OR,* Vol. 36, Pt. 3, pp. 206–7. The council of war is described in Nevins, *Diary of Battle,* 388, and in Comstock, *Diary,* 269–70.

19. Grant to Meade, May 25, 1864, in *OR,* Vol. 36, Pt. 3, p. 183.

20. Nevins, *Diary of Battle,* 388.

21. "The Wilson's Wharf Fight," *New York Tribune,* May 30, 1864. Wild's background is colorfully described in Noah Andrew Trudeau, *Like Men of War: Black Troops in the Civil War, 1862–1865* (Boston, 1998), 113–18, and in Leonne Hudson, "Valor at Wilson's Wharf," *Civil War Times Illustrated* (March, 1998), 48.

22. George W. Hatton, *Philadelphia Christian Recorder,* May 10, 1864; Edwin S. Redkey, ed., *A Grand Army of Black Men: Letters from African American Soldiers in the Union Army,*

1861–1865 (New York, 1992), 95–6; Edwin W. Besch, "Action at Wilson's Wharf, 24 May 1864," 22, in Richmond National Battlefield Park, Richmond, Va.

23. Besch, "Action at Wilson's Wharf, 24 May 1864," 22.

24. Fitzhugh Lee's report, in DU; J. D. Ferguson memorandum, in MC. Ferguson reported 800 men from Wickham, 750 from Lomax, and 420 from Gordon accompanied Lee on the expedition. "Barringer's North Carolina Brigade of Cavalry," *Raleigh (N.C.) Daily Confederate,* February 22, 1865, states that Gordon's brigade contributed 225 men. No precise figures exist for the portion of the 5th South Carolina Cavalry that went along, although one correspondent placed it at 400; Orlando dispatch, *Charleston (S.C.) Daily Courier,* August 24, 1864. Edwin W. Besch, who is writing the definitive work on Wilson's Wharf, estimates South Carolina numbers at 500 to 600. I am indebted to Mr. Besch for sharing his thoughts and material. Fitzhugh Lee placed the total size of his force at 1,600 men.

25. Fitzhugh Lee's report, in MC; Paul B. Means, "Additional Sketch, Sixty-Third Regiment," in Clark, *Histories of the Several Battalions,* 3, p. 604; Edwin Simonton, "The Campaign up the James to Petersburg," in *Glimpses of the Nation's Struggle: A Series of Papers Read Before the Minnesota Commandery of the Military Order of the Loyal Legion of the United States* (St. Paul, Minn., 1903), 483.

26. Fitzhugh Lee's report, in DU; Ferguson memorandum, in MC; Edward A. Wild's report, in *OR,* Vol. 36, Pt. 2, p. 270.

27. Simonton, "Campaign up the James to Petersburg," 483–4; Solon A. Carter, "Fourteen Months Service with Colored Troops," in *Civil War Papers Read Before the Commandery of the State of Massachusetts, Military Order of the Loyal Legion of the United States* (Wilmington, N.C, 1993), 161; John Gill, *Reminiscences of Four Years as a Private Soldier in the Confederate Army, 1861–1865* (Baltimore, Md., 1905), 98.

28. Gill, *Reminiscences,* 98.

29. Wild's report, in *OR,* Vol. 36, Pt. 2, p. 271; Besch, "Action at Wilson's Wharf," 33–9.

30. Fitzhugh Lee's report, in DU; Gill, *Reminiscences,* 98; Means, "Additional Sketch, Sixty-Third Regiment," 605.

31. Fitzhugh Lee's report, in DU; Simonton, "Campaign up the James to Petersburg," 484; Gill, *Reminiscences,* 98.

32. Simonton, "Campaign up the James to Petersburg," 485; Fitzhugh Lee's report, in DU; "Damaging Repulse of Rebel Cavalry," *New York Times,* May 30, 1864; Charles T. Price to Editor, February 6, 1902, *Richmond Dispatch,* February 16, 1902; Means, "Additional Sketch, Sixty-Third Regiment," 606. Casualties reported by Confederate and Union sources varied widely. The estimates are analyzed in Besch, "Action at Wilson's Wharf," 39–48. Apparently, Captain Breckinridge was carrying his brother Cary Breckinridge's memorandum book, which led Wild to misidentify the corpse in his report.

33. Fitzhugh Lee's report, DU; Ferguson memorandum, MC.

34. M. W. S., "The Rebel Attack on Wilson's Wharf," *Newark (N.J.) Advertiser,* May 28, 1864; Carter, "Fourteen Months Service," 161.

35. Fitzhugh Lee's report, DU; *Richmond Examiner,* May 26, 28, 1864.

36. Means, "Additional Sketch, Sixty-Third Regiment," 604.

37. Wilson's diary, May 26, 1864, in LC; Wilson's report, in *OR,* Vol. 36, Pt. 1, p. 880; Beaudry, *War Journal,* 123; Sheridan's report, in *OR,* Vol. 36, Pt. 1, pp. 792–3.

38. Roebling's report, in Warren Collection, NYSLA; Wilkeson, *Recollections,* 122–3; Lee to Seddon, 6:45 A.M., May 27, 1864, in *OR,* Vol. 36, Pt. 3, p. 836.

39. Grant to Halleck, May 26, 1864, in *OR,* Vol. 36, Pt. 3, p. 206; Dana to Stanton, 8:00 A.M., May 26, 1864, ibid., Pt. 1, p. 79; Robert S. Robertson to parents, May 25, 1864, in FSNMP.

40. Martin L. Smith to wife, May 29, 1864, in James S. Scoff Collection, William L. Clements Library, University of Michigan; Gallagher, ed., *Fighting for the Confederacy,* 390; P. W. Alexander, dispatch of May 27, 1864, *Columbia (S.C.) Daily South Carolinian,* June 3, 1864.

41. Lyman to family, May 24, 1864, in Agassiz, *Meade's Headquarters,* 126.

42. James C. Biddle to wife, June 5, 1864, in Meade Collection, HSP.

43. James Biddle to wife, June 3, 1864, in Meade Collection, HSP; Nevins, *Diary of Battle,* 388; Simon B. Cummins to family, May 25, 1864, in Melvin Jones, ed., *Give God the Glory: Memoirs of a Civil War Soldier* (N.p., n.d.), 59–60.

44. Charles S. Fall to parents, May 24, 1864, in BL; Charles Francis Adams Jr. to father, May 29, 1864, in Worthington Chauncey Ford, ed., *A Cycle of Adams Letters* (Cambridge, Mass., 1920), 131; Dana to Stanton, May 26, 1864, in *OR,* Vol. 36, Pt. 1, p. 79.

45. Dowdey, *Lee's Last Campaign,* 267; John H. Chamberlayne to mother, May 24, 1864, in C. G. Chamberlayne, ed., *Ham Chamberlayne—Virginian: Letters and Papers of an Artillery Officer in the War for Southern Independence, 1861–1865* (Richmond, 1932), 222; J. A. Lineback diary, May 26, 1864, in *Winston-Salem (N.C.) Daily Sentinel,* January 9, 1915; William A. Miller to sister, May 26, 1864, in FSNMP.

46. Peter W. Alexander dispatch, May 18, 1864, *Columbia (S.C.) Daily South Carolinian,* May 29, 1864; W. H. Taylor, *General Lee,* 238; Freeman, *R. E. Lee,* 4, p. 172.

47. Staudenraus, *Mr. Lincoln's Washington,* 323.

48. Newton T. Kirk reminiscences, MSU; *In Memoriam: Newton Thorne Kirk* (San Francisco, 1909). Kirk spent six months in Andersonville, was transferred to Savannah, and was paroled November 20, 1864. He joined the 127th USCT in the Army of the James as a captain, served with the Army of the Gulf in Louisiana, and went on to a long and prosperous life as a businessman in Los Angeles. He died in 1909.

Bibliography

MANUSCRIPTS

Alabama Department of Archives and History, Montgomery

Henry H. Sturgis Letter

Atlanta Historical Society

William Rhadamanthus Montgomery Diary

Auburn University Libraries, Special Collections

James H. Lane Collection
   E. J. Hale Jr.'s Report
   James H. Lane's Report

Boston Public Library

Charles A. Whittier Reminiscences

Boston University, Muger Memorial Library

Military Historical Society of Massachusetts Collection
   Unknown Rebel Diary

Cincinnati Historical Society

Rogers Hanneford Memoir

Civil War Library and Museum, Philadelphia

William Brooke Rawle Diary and Letters

Cornell University, John M. Olin Library

John S. Crocker Diary

Duke University, William R. Perkins Library

Richard H. Anderson's Report
J. D. Ferguson Memoranda
Samuel Spencer Parmalie Diary

Florida Department of Archives and History, Tallahassee

Council Bryan Letter

Fredericksburg and Spotsylvania National Military Park Library

Alfred M. Apted Diary
Charles T. Bowen Diary
George A. Bowen Diary
Daniel Sayre Brewster Letter
Stephen D. Burger and George P. Bouton Memoir
James M. Cadwallader Diary
Benjamin Y. Draper Diary
Samuel L. Foust Diary
Augustus C. Golding Diary
G. W. Grimes Letter
Daniel A. Hardy Letter
Henry Herbert Harris Diary
Lestor Hildreth Diary
Historic Structures Report for Jackson Shrine
William Judkins Memoir
L. O. Merriam Recollections
William A. Miller Letter
Allen Parker Diary
Alexander B. Pattison Diary
Kenneth H. Power Memoir
F. F. Robbins Diary
Robert S. Robertson Letter
Thompson A. Snyder Recollections
Imri A. Spencer Letter
J. William Thomas Diary
Francis Gardner Walter Diary
J. T. Watkins Memoir
Francis Marion Welchel Letter

John James Woodall Diary
Francis Yeager Diary

Georgia Department of Archives and History, Atlanta

Joseph P. Fuller Diary
Wiley J. Smith Letter

Gettysburg National Military Park Library

Jacob L. Bechtel Letter

Historical Society of Pennsylvania, Philadelphia

George G. Meade Collection
    James C. Biddle Letters
    George G. Meade Letters

Henry E. Huntington Library, San Marino, California

Samuel D. Webster Diary

Illinois State Historical Library, Springfield

Oliver Edwards Memorandum

Indiana University, Lilly Library

64th New York Memoir

Library of Congress, Manuscript Division

John R. Brinkle Letter
Daniel O. Drennan Letter
Wilbur Fisk Diary
William G. Halls Diary
John W. F. Hatton Memoir
Jedediah Hotchkiss Diary and Letters
Henry J. Hunt Journal
David R. Larned Letter
Luther A. Rose Memorandum
John Chester White Journal
James H. Wilson Diary and Memorandum

Lloyd House, Alexandria, Virginia

John R. Zimmerman Diary

Louisiana State University Libraries

Henry J. Egan Letter

Manassas National Battlefield Park Library

James M. Read Diary
James B. Ricketts Papers

Mary Ball Washington Library, Fredericksburg, Virginia

John W. Chowning Diary

Maryland Historical Society, Baltimore

Charles E. Phelps Collection
    Charles E. Phelps Recollections
    Martin L. Smith Diary

Massachusetts Historical Society, Boston

Francis C. Barlow Letter
George M. Barnard Letter
Theodore Lyman Journal
George L. Prescott Letter

Michigan State University Libraries

John E. Irwin Diary
Newton T. Kirk Reminiscences
Gershom Woodruff Mattson, "Sheridan's Raid"

Minnesota Historical Society, Minneapolis

Harrison B. George Diary

Mississippi Department of Archives and History, Jackson

William McWillie Notebook
B. L. Wynn Diary

Museum of the Confederacy, Eleanor S. Brockenbrough Library, Richmond, Virginia

Fitzhugh Lee's Report
Joseph Mullen Jr. Diary
G. Moxley Sorrel Journal

National Archives, Washington, D.C.

James H. Kidd's Report
Samuel Schooler Compiled Service Record, M331, Role 220
Tabular List of Casualties, 2nd Corps
Tabular List of Casualties, 5th Corps

New York Historical Society, New York

Isaac C. Hadden Letter

New York State Library and Archives, Albany

Gouverneur K. Warren Collection
   Washington A. Roebling's Report
   Gouverneur K. Warren Letters

Niagara County Historical Society, Lockport, New York

Arthur L. Chase Diary
William S. Pike Diary

North Carolina Department of Archives and History, Raleigh

T. M. Gorman Memoir
John E. Green Diary
Benjamin F. Hall Autobiographical Sketch

Lowry Shuford Collection
   J. W. Bone Reminiscences
   J. A. Stikeleather Reminiscences

Ohio Historical Society

William McVey Diary

Scott C. Patchen Private Collection

Francis Cordrey Manuscript

Pennsylvania State University Library

M. Gayla McDowell Collection
  Hamilton Dunlap Diary

Pennsylvania State Archives, Harrisburg

David R. P. Neely Diary

Pierpont Morgan Library, New York

Gilder-Lehrman Collection
  J. O. Thurmond Jr. Letter

Richmond National Battlefield Park

Edwin W. Besch, "Action at Wilson's Wharf, 24 May 1864"
Milton Myers Diary

Roanoke City Library, Virginia

Billie B. Elliott Diary

Michael T. Russert Private Collection, Cambridge, New York

Edgar O. Burts Diary
George Perkins Diary

Rome/Floyd County Library, Rome, Georgia

United Daughters of the Confederacy Collection
  W. D. Mountcastle Diary

Rutgers University Library

Washington A. Roebling Letter

United States Army Military History Institute, Carlisle, Pennsylvania

Civil War Miscellaneous Collection
  Michael Donlon Letter
  S. J. Marks Letter
  Charles E. Wood Diary

Civil War Times Illustrated Collection
  Stephen P. Chase Diary and Memoirs
  Isaac H. Ressler Diary
  J. N. Jones Diary

Gregory Coco Collection
    George P. Hawkes Diary
    Charles D. Todd Diary
    Edmund D. Halsey Diary
    Avery Harris Memoir

Harrisburg Civil War Round Table Collection
    Henry Keiser Diary
    Richard J. Del Vecchio, "With First New York Dragoons"
    Maurus Oestreich Diary
Lewis Leigh Collection
    Walter S. Gilman Memoir

Jay Luvaas Collection
    Alfred Thompson Letter

Michael Winey Collection
    Isaac R. Dunkelberger Memoir

University of Georgia Libraries

Francis Solomon Johnson Jr. Letter

University of Michigan, Bentley Historical Library

Addison S. Boyce Letter
Charles S. Fall Letter
William Bradford Irwin Journal
George Lockley Diary

Military Order of the Loyal Legion of the United States Collection
    George G. Hooper Memoir

University of Michigan, William L. Clements Library

James S. Schoff Collection
    Nathaniel W. Bunker, "War Record"
    Martin L. Smith Letter

University of New Hampshire Libraries

Howard M. Hanson Diary

University of North Carolina, Southern Historical Collection

Edward P. Alexander Letter
William Allen Memorandum
C. H. Andrews Memorandum

Joseph D. Joyner Letter

Cornelia McGimsey Collection
    Samuel Walkup Diary
    Joseph F. Waring Diary
    Lewis Warlick Letter
    Cary Whitaker Diary

University of South Carolina, South Caroliniana Library

Wade Hampton Connected Narrative

University of Virginia, Alderman Library

George S. Bernard Diary
Katherine Couse Letter

Virginia Historical Society, Richmond

St. George Tucker Bryan Memoir
Buckner McGill Randolph Diary
Byrd C. Willis Diary

Virginia State Library, Richmond

Edwin B. Loving Manuscript

William Mahone Collection
    Nathaniel Harris Letter
    Cadmus M. Wilcox Report
    James F. Wood Diary

Western Reserve Historical Society, Cleveland, Ohio

Palmer Regimental Papers
    Well A. Bushnell Memoirs
    William Foster Letter

NEWSPAPERS

Albany Evening Journal, May 24, 1864.
Atlanta Daily Constitutionalist, May 25, 1864.
Atlanta Journal, July 20, October 16, 1901.
Atlanta Sunny South, May 2, 1891.
Augusta (Ga.) Constitutionalist, January 2, 1864.
Baltimore American and Commercial Advertiser, May 26, 1864.

Boston Daily Advertiser, May 16, 30, 1864.

Boston Evening Journal, June 21, 1864.

Boston Evening Transcript, May 12, 25, 26, 28, 31, 1864.

Boston Journal, March 20, 1886.

Charleston (S.C.) Daily Courier, August 24, 1864.

Charlotte (N.C.) Observer, January 3, 1902.

Columbia (S.C.) Daily South Carolinian, May 29, June 3, 1864.

Corning (N.Y.) Journal, June 2, 1864.

Detroit Advertiser and Tribune, June 2, 16, 1864.

Forney's War Press (Philadelphia), June 18, 1864.

Fredericksburg (Va.) Free Lance-Star, August 9, 1991.

Kennesaw (Ga.) Cadence, October 28, 1987.

Macon (Ga.) Daily Telegraph, May 26, 31, June 4,1864.

Memphis (Tenn.) Daily Appeal, May 24, 1864.

Milwaukee Daily Sentinel, May 25, 1864.

Mobile (Ala.) Daily Advertiser and Register, May 28, 29, June 3, 1864.

Montgomery (Ala.) Daily Advertiser, June 3, 1864.

Newark (N.J.) Advertiser, May 28, 1864.

New Bern (N.C.) Our Living and Our Dead, February 11, April 8, 15, 18, 1874.

New Haven (Conn.) Daily Palladium, June 1, 1864.

New York Daily News, May 19, 22, 28, 30, June 2, 7, 1864.

New York Evening Post, May 16, 1864.

New York Herald, April 1, May 17, 18, 19, 21, 22, 25, 27, 30, 1864.

New York Irish American, July 2, 1864.

New York Times, May 14, 24, 25, 28, 29, 30, 1864.

New York Tribune, May 12, 13, 18, 20, 23, 30, 1864.

Olympia (Wash.) Puget Sound Weekly, April 22, 1881.

Philadelphia Christian Recorder, May 10, 1864.

Philadelphia Inquirer, May 17, 20, 25, 27,1864.

Philadelphia Sunday Dispatch, May 22, 1864.

Philadelphia Weekly Times, February 10, 1883.

Philadelphia Weekly Tribune, April 19, 1884.

Providence (R.I.) Daily Journal, June 1, 11, 1864.

Providence (R.I.) Evening Press, May 24, June 13, 1864.

Raleigh (N.C.) Daily Confederate, May 25, 1864, February 22, 1865.

Richmond Daily Dispatch, May 23, 1864, February 16, March 9, 1902.

Richmond Enquirer, May 13, 17, 20, 24, 27, 1864.

Richmond Examiner, May 12, 13, 14, 23, 25, 26, 27, 28, 1864.

Richmond Sentinel, May 12, 14, 21, 25, June 3, 1864.

Richmond Star, January 15, 1894.

Rochester (N.Y.) Union and Advertiser, May 18, 27, June 21, 1864.

Rutland (Vt.) Herald, May 15, June 1, 1864.

Selma (Ala.) Morning Reporter, June 7, 1864.

South Danvers (Mass.) Wizard, June 8, 1864.
Springfield (Mass.) Daily Republican, May 26, 27, 1864.
Washington, D.C., Daily Morning Chronicle, May 20, 1864.
Windham County (Conn.) Transcript, May 26, June 2, 1864.
Winston-Salem (N.C.) Daily Sentinel, January 9, 1915.
Xenia (Ohio) Torch-Light, June 1, 1864.

Official Compilations

Annual Report of the Adjutant-General of the State of Connecticut for the Year Ending March 31, 1865. New Haven, 1865.
Harrison, Noel G. *Gazetteer of Historic Sites Related to the Fredericksburg and Spotsylvania National Military Park.* 2 vols. Fredericksburg, Va., 1986.
The War of the Rebellion: A Compilation of the Official Records of the Union and Confederate Armies. 130 vols. Washington, D.C., 1880–1901.

Biographies, Memoirs, and Narratives

Abbott, Lemuel A. *Personal Recollections and Civil War Diary 1864.* Burlington, Vt., 1908.
Agassiz, George R., ed. *Meade's Headquarters, 1863–1865: Letters of Colonel Theodore Lyman from the Wilderness to Appomattox.* Boston, 1922.
Allen, Stanton P. *Down in Dixie: Life in a Cavalry Regiment in the War Days.* Boston, 1888.
Andrews, J. Cutler. *The North Reports the Civil War.* Pittsburgh, 1955.
"Annual Reunion of Pegram Battalion Association in the Hall of House of Delegates, Richmond, Va., May 21st, 1886." In *SHSP* 14, pp. 5–34.
Arehart, W. E. "Diary." *Rockingham (Va.) Historical Society Recorder,* 2 (1959), 147–228.
Armstrong, Nelson. *Nuggets of Experience.* San Bernardino, Calif., 1904.
Arnold, Abraham K. "A War Reminiscence—The Fifth United States Cavalry with General Sheridan on Raid Towards Richmond, Va., in 1864." *Journal of the United States Cavalry Association,* 2 (1889), 28–33.
Arthur, John P. *Western North Carolina: A History.* Raleigh, 1914.
Athearn, Robert G., ed. "The Civil War Diary of John Wilson Phillips." *Virginia Magazine of History and Biography,* 62 (January 1954), 98–104.
Badeau, Adam. *Military History of General Ulysses S. Grant, from April, 1861, to April, 1865.* 3 vols. New York, 1881.
Beale, G. W. *A Lieutenant of Cavalry in Lee's Army.* Boston, 1918.
Beaudry, Richard E., ed. *War Journal of Louis N. Beaudry, Fifth New York Cavalry.* Jefferson, N.C., 1996.

Bennett, Edwin C. *Musket and Sword; or, The Camp, March, and Firing Line in the Army of the Potomac.* Boston, 1900.

Bennett, P. T. "General Junius Daniel." In *SHSP* 18, pp. 346–7.

Benson, Susan W., ed. *Berry Benson's Civil War Book: Memoirs of a Confederate Scout and Sharpshooter.* Athens, Ga., 1991.

Blackford, Susan Leigh, comp. *Letters from Lee's Army: or, Memories of Life In and Out of the Army in Virginia During the War Between the States.* New York, 1947.

Blakeman, A. Noel. *Personal Recollections of the War of the Rebellion.* New York, 1907.

Blight, David W., ed. *When This Cruel War Is Over: The Civil War Letters of Charles Harvery Brewster.* Amherst, Mass., 1992.

Booth, George W. *Personal Reminiscences of a Maryland Soldier in the War Between the States, 1861–1865.* Baltimore, 1898.

Bosang, James N. *Memoirs of a Pulaski Veteran of the Stonewall Brigade.* Pulaski, Va., 1912.

Bowley, Free S. "A Boy Lieutenant in a Black Regiment." *National Tribune,* May 11, 1899.

Bradley, J. Payson. "Historical Address, May 19, 1901." In *Souvenir: First Regiment of Heavy Artillery Massachusetts Volunteers, Dedication of Monument,* edited by Joseph W. Gardner. N.p., n.d.

Britton, Ann A., and Thomas J. Reed. *To My Beloved Wife and Boy at Home: The Letters and Diaries of Orderly Sergeant John F. L. Hartwell.* Madison, N.J., 1997.

Brooks, Noah. *Lincoln Observed: Civil War Dispatches of Noah Brooks.* Edited by Michael Burlingame. Baltimore, 1998.

————. *Washington in Lincoln's Time.* New York, 1958.

Brown, Augustus C. *The Diary of a Line Officer.* New York, 1906.

Brown, Joel. "The Charge of the Heavy Artillery." *Rockland (Me.) Bugle,* 1 (1894), 4–19.

Buell, Augustus. *The Cannoneer: Recollections of Service in the Army of the Potomac.* Washington, D.C., 1890.

Burr, Rank A. *Life and Achievements of James Addams Beaver.* Philadelphia, 1882.

Caldwell, Willie Walker. *Stonewall Jim: A Biography of General James A. Walker, C.S.A.* Elliston, Va., 1990.

Carmichael, Peter S. *Lee's Young Artillerist: William R. J. Pegram.* Charlottesville, Va., 1995.

Carter, Robert G., comp. *Four Brothers in Blue; or, Sunshine and Shadows of the War of the Rebellion.* Austin, Tex., 1978.

Carter, Solon A. "Fourteen Months Service with Colored Troops." In *Civil War Papers Read Before the Commandery of the State of Massachusetts, Military Order of the Loyal Legion of the United States,* 155–82. Wilmington, N.C., 1993.

Casler, John O. *Four Years in the Stonewall Brigade.* Girard, Kans., 1906.

Chamberlayne, C. G., ed. *Ham Chamberlayne—Virginian: Letters and Papers of an Artillery Officer in the War for Southern Independence, 1861–1865.* Richmond, 1932.

Chipman, Donald. "An Essex County Soldier in the Civil War: The Diary of Cyril Fountain." *New York History,* 66 (July 1985), 281–98.

Clark, George. *A Glance Backward; or, Some Events in the Past History of My Life.* Houston, Tex., 1914.

Clark, Gibson. "Reminiscences of Civil War Days." *Annals of Wyoming,* 15 (1943), 377–86.

Clark, Rufus W. *The Heroes of Albany: A Memorial of the Patriot-Martyrs of the City and County of Albany.* Albany, N.Y., 1866.

Coan, E. S. "At the North Anna." *National Tribune,* August 11, 1887.

Cockrell, Monroe F., ed. *Gunner with Stonewall: Reminiscences of William Thomas Poague.* Jackson, Tenn., 1957.

Coco, Gregory A., ed. *Through Blood and Fire: The Civil War Letters of Major Charles J. Mills, 1862–1865.* Lanham, Md., 1982.

Coffin, George H. *Three Years in the Army.* N.p., 1925.

Colt, Margaretta Barton. *Defend the Valley: A Shenandoah Family in the Civil War.* New York, 1994.

Comstock, Cyrus B. *The Diary of Cyrus B. Comstock.* Edited by Merlin E. Sumner. Dayton, Ohio, 1987.

Cooke, John Esten. *A Life of Gen. Robert E. Lee.* New York, 1871.

Covert, Norman M., ed. *Two Civil War Diaries: Sgt. John L. Ryno and Bandmaster John Chadwick, Company C, 126th New York Regiment, 3rd Brigade, 2nd Division, II U. S. Corps.* N.p., n.d.

Cowles, William H. H. "The Life and Services of General James B. Gordon." N.p., n.d.

Cowper, Pulaski, comp. *Extracts of Letters of Major General Bryan Grimes to His Wife.* Raleigh, 1884.

Crotty, D. G. *Four Years Campaigning in the Army of the Potomac.* Grand Rapids, Mich., 1874.

Cutshaw, W. E. "An Address Before R. E. Lee Camp, No. 1, C. V., on the Night of January 20, 1905." In *SHSP* 33, pp. 320–34.

Dana, Charles A. *Recollections of the Civil War.* New York, 1899.

Davies, Henry E. *General Sheridan.* New York, 1895.

Davis, Creed T. "Diary." In *Contributions to a History of the Richmond Howitzer Battalion,* vol. 2, pp. 3–28. Richmond, 1883–1886.

Dennett, Tyler, ed. *Lincoln and the Civil War in the Diaries and Letters of John Hay.* New York, 1939.

De Trobriand, Regis. *Four Years with the Army of the Potomac.* Boston, 1889.

Dickinson, F. S. "Death of Sergeant Sortore." *National Tribune,* January 14, 1892.

Dickinson, Henry C. *Diary of Capt. Dickinson, C.S.A.* Denver, Colo., n.d.

Dobbins, Austin C., ed. *Grandfather's Journal: Company B, 16th Mississippi Infantry Volunteers, Harris' Brigade, Mahone's Division, Hill's Corps, A.N.V.* Dayton, Ohio, 1988.

"Documents: Fourteenth Indiana Regiment, Letters to the *Vincennes Western Sun.*" *Indiana Magazine of History,* 34 (March 1938), 71–98.

Douglas, Henry Kyd. *I Rode with Stonewall.* Chapel Hill, N.C., 1968.

Dowdey, Clifford, ed. *The Wartime Papers of R. E. Lee.* New York, 1961.

Dunaway, Thomas Sanford. *An Historical Sketch of Massaponax Baptist Church of Spotsylvania County Virginia.* N.p., 1938.

Durkin, Joseph T., ed. *Confederate Chaplain: A War Journal of Rev. James B. Sheeran, c.ss.r., 14th Louisiana, C.S.A.* Milwaukee, 1960.

Durrett, Virginia Wright. *Mud Tavern.* Spotsylvania, Va., 1988.

Early, Jubal A. *Autobiographical Sketch and Narrative of the War Between the States.* Bloomington, Ind., 1960.

Fall, Ralph Emmett. *People, Post Offices, and Communities in Caroline County, Virginia, 1727–1969.* McDonough, Ga., 1989.

Favill, Josiah M. *The Diary of a Young Officer Serving with the Armies of the United States During the War of the Rebellion.* Chicago, 1909.

Field, Charles W. "Campaign of 1864 and 1865." In *SHSP* 14, pp. 542–63.

Fleming, Francis P. *Memoir of Capt. C. Seton Fleming, of the Second Florida Infantry, C.S.A.* Jacksonville, Fla., 1881.

Ford, Worthington Chauncey, ed. *A Cycle of Adams Letters.* Cambridge, Mass., 1920.

Foster, Alonzo. *Reminiscences and Record of the 6th New York V. V. Cavalry.* Brooklyn, 1892.

Fox, Wells B. *What I Remember of the Great Rebellion.* Lansing, Mich., 1892.

Freeman, Douglas Southall. *R. E. Lee.* 4 vols. New York, 1934–1935.

———, ed. *Lee's Dispatches to Jefferson Davis.* New York, 1957.

Gallagher, Gary W. "Our Hearts Are Full of Hope: The Army of Northern Virginia in the Spring of 1864." In *The Wilderness Campaign,* edited by Gary W. Gallagher, 36–65. Chapel Hill, N.C., 1997.

Gallagher, Gary W., ed. *Fighting for the Confederacy: The Personal Recollections of General Edward Porter Alexander.* Chapel Hill, N.C., 1989.

———. *The Spotsylvania Campaign.* Chapel Hill, N.C., 1998.

———. *The Wilderness Campaign.* Chapel Hill, N.C., 1997.

Galwey, Thomas F. *The Valiant Hours: An Irishman in the Civil War.* Harrisburg, Pa., 1961.

Gardner, Joseph W. *Souvenir: First Regiment of Heavy Artillery Massachusetts Volunteers, Dedication of Monument.* N.p., n.d.

Garrison, Fielding H., ed. *John Shaw Billings: A Memoir.* New York, 1915.

Gerrish, Theodore. *Army Life: A Private's Reminiscences of the Civil War.* Portland, Me., 1882.

Gibbon, John. *Personal Recollections of the Civil War.* New York, 1928.

Gill, John. *Reminiscences of Four Years as a Private Soldier in the Confederate Army, 1861–1865.* Baltimore, 1905.

Goss, Warren L. *Recollections of a Private: A Story of the Army of the Potomac.* New York, 1890.

Grant, Ulysses S. *Personal Memoirs of U. S. Grant.* 2 vols. New York, 1885.

Greenleaf, William L. "From the Rapidan to Richmond." In *War Papers of Vermont and Miscellaneous States Papers and Addresses, Military Order of the Loyal Legion,* pp. 1–24. Wilmington, N.C., 1994.

Greiner, James M., et al., eds. *A Surgeon's Civil War: The Letters and Diary of Daniel M. Holt, M.D.* Kent, Ohio, 1994.

Hamil, John W. *The Story of a Confederate Soldier.* N.p., n.d.

Hammock, Henry M., ed. *Letters to Amanda from Sergeant Marion Hill Fitzpatrick, 45th Georgia Regiment, Thomas' Brigade, Wilcox' Division, Hill's Corps CSA to His Wife Amanda Olive Elizabeth Fitzpatrick, 1862–1865.* Culloden, Ga., N.d.

Harrison, Noel G. "A Moment in Black History: May 15, 1865." *Fredericksburg Town Hall Crier,* 6 (1991), 6–7.

Hartwell, John F. L. *To My Beloved Wife and Boy at Home.* Edited by Ann Hartwell Britton and Thomas J. Reed. Madison, N.J., 1997.

Hatton, Robert W., ed. "Just a Little Bit of the Civil War, as Seen by W[illiam] J. Smith, Company M, 2nd O. V. Cavalry." *Ohio History,* 84 (1975), 113–4.

Hennessy, John J. "I Dread the Spring: The Army of the Potomac Prepares for the Overland Campaign." In *The Wilderness Campaign,* edited by Gary W. Gallagher, 66–105. Chapel Hill, N.C., 1997.

Holt, David E. *A Mississippi Rebel in the Army of Northern Virginia.* Edited by Thomas D. Cockrell and Michael B. Ballard. Baton Rouge, 1996.

Houghton, Henry. "The Ordeal of Civil War: A Recollection." *Vermont History* 41 (1973).

House, Charles J. "How the First Maine Heavy Artillery Lost 1179 Men in 30 Days." *Rockland (Me.) Bugle,* 2 (1895), 87–95.

Howe, Mark De Wolfe, ed. *Touched With Fire: Civil War Letters and Diary of Oliver Wendell Holmes, Jr., 1861–1864.* New York, 1969.

Hudson, Leonne. "Valor at Wilson's Wharf." *Civil War Times Illustrated,* March 1998, 46–52.

Hunton, Eppa. *Autobiography of Eppa Hunton.* Richmond, 1933.

Hyde, Thomas W. *Following the Greek Cross; or, Memories of the Sixth Army Corps.* Boston, 1894.

In Memoriam: Newton Thorne Kirk. San Francisco, 1909.

Irving, Theodore. *More Than Conqueror; or, Memorials of Col. J. Howard Kitching.* New York, 1873.

Johnston, David E. *The Story of a Confederate Boy in the Civil War.* Portland, Ore., 1914.

Jones, J. B. *A Rebel War Clerk's Diary.* 2 vols. Philadelphia, 1866.

Jones, Melvin, ed. *Give God the Glory: Memoirs of a Civil War Soldier.* N.p., n.d.

Jones, Terry L., ed. *The Civil War Memoirs of Captain William J. Seymour: Reminiscences of a Louisiana Tiger.* Baton Rouge, 1991.

Kent, Arthur A., ed. *Three Years With Company K: Sergt. Austin C. Stearns, Company K, 13th Massachusetts Infantry.* Rutherford, N.J., 1976.

Kidd, James H. *Personal Recollections of a Cavalryman with Custer's Michigan Cavalry Brigade in the Civil War.* Ionia, Mich., 1908.

King, Matthew W. *To Horse: With the Cavalry of the Army of the Potomac, 1861–65.* Cheboygan, Mich., 1926.

Krantz, John C. Jr. "The Implications of the Medical History of General Lee." *Virginia Medical Monthly,* 86 (June 1959), 306–10.

Krick, Robert E. L. "Stuart's Last Ride: A Confederate View of Sheridan's Raid." In *The Spotsylvania Campaign,* edited by Gary W. Gallagher, 127–48. Chapel Hill, N.C., 1998.

Krick, Robert K. *Lee's Colonels: A Biographical Register of the Field Officers of the Army of Northern Virginia.* Dayton, Ohio, 1992.

Law, Evander McI. "From the Wilderness to Cold Harbor." In *B&L* 4, pp. 118–44.

Lee, Fitzhugh. *General Lee: A Biography of Robert E. Lee.* New York, 1894.

Lee, Laura Elizabeth, ed. *Forget-Me-Nots of the Civil War: A Romance, Containing Reminiscences and Original Letters of Two Confederate Soldiers.* St. Louis, Mo., 1909.

Lee, Susan P. *Memoirs of William Nelson Pendleton, D.D.* Philadelphia, 1893.

Letters of Major Peter Vredenburgh. Privately printed, N.p. n.d.

Lockwood, James B. *Life and Adventures of a Drummer Boy; or, Seven Years a Soldier.* Albany, N.Y., 1893.

Loehr, Charles T. "The Battle of Milford Station." In *SHSP* 26, pp. 110–5.

Lt. Col. Charles Lyon Chandler. Cambridge, Mass., 1864.

Lyman, Theodore. "Extract from Diary." In *PMHSM* 4, pp. 234–41.

McBride, R. E. *In the Ranks: From the Wilderness to Appomattox Court House.* Cincinnati, Ohio, 1881.

McDonald, Archie P., ed. *Make Me a Map of the Valley: The Civil War Journal of Stonewall Jackson's Topographer.* Dallas, Tex., 1973.

McIlwaine, H. R., ed. "Diary of Captain H. W. Wingfield." *Bulletin of the Virginia State Library,* 16 (July 1927), 9–47.

McIntosh, David G. "Sketch of the Military Career of David G. McIntosh." In United Daughters of the Confederacy, *Treasured Reminiscences,* 47–52. Columbia, S.C., 1911.

McMahon, Martin T. "From Gettysburg to the Coming of Grant." In *B&L* 4, pp. 81–94.

Manarin, Louis H., ed. "The Civil War Diary of Rufus J. Woolwine." *Virginia Magazine of History and Biography,* 71 (October 1963), 432–8.

Marvel, William. *Burnside.* Chapel Hill, N.C., 1991.

Massachusetts Historical Society. *War Diary and Letters of Stephen Minot Weld, 1861–1865.* Boston, 1979.

Mather, Fred. "A 7th N.Y.H.A. Man Gives Some Experiences." *National Tribune,* January 30, 1896.

———. "Under Old Glory." *National Tribune,* January 30, 1896.

Meade, George, ed. *Life and Letters of George Gordon Meade.* 2 vols. New York, 1913.

Meier, Heinz K., ed. *Memoirs of a Swiss Officer in the American Civil War.* Bern, Switzerland, 1972.

Memorials of William Fowler. New York, 1875.

Miller, Delavan S. *Drum Taps in Dixie: Memories of a Drummer Boy, 1861–1865.* Watertown, N.Y., 1905.

Miller, Richard F., and Robert F. Mooney, comps. *The Civil War: The Nantucket Experience, Including the Memoirs of Josiah Fitch Murphey.* Nantucket, Mass., 1994.

Milling, James A. "Recollections." *Confederate Veteran,* 6 (1997), 6–18.

Moncure, E. C. "Reminiscences of the Civil War." *Bulletin of the Virginia State Library,* 26 (1927), 49–64.

Montgomery, Walter A. *The Days of Old and the Years That Are Past.* Raleigh, n.d.

Morgan, W. H. *Personal Reminiscences of the War of 1861–5.* Lynchburg, Va., 1911.

Morris, Roy Jr. *Sheridan: The Life and Wars of General Phil Sheridan.* New York, 1992.

Morse, Francis W. *Personal Experiences in the War of the Great Rebellion, from December, 1862, to July, 1865.* Albany, N.Y., 1866.

Morton, W. T. G. "The First Use of Ether as an Anesthetic at the Battle of the Wilderness in the Civil War." *Journal of the American Medical Association* (April 1904), 1068–73.

Mulholland, St. Claire A. *Military Order Congressional Medal of Honor Legion of the United States.* Philadelphia, 1905.

Neese, George. *Three Years in the Confederate Horse Artillery.* New York, 1911.

Nevins, Allan, ed. *Diary of Battle: The Personal Journals of Colonel Charles S. Wainwright, 1861–1865.* New York, 1962.

Nowlin, S. H. "Capture and Escape." *Southern Bivouac* 2 (October 1883).

Oates, William C. *The War Between the Union and the Confederacy and Its Lost Opportunities.* New York, 1905.

Page, Charles A. *Letters of a War Correspondent.* Boston, 1899.

Parcels, Walter H. "Laying a Bridge." *National Tribune,* March 10, 1887.

Peck, Rufus H. *Reminiscences of a Confederate Soldier of Co. C, 2nd Va. Cavalry.* Fincastle, Va., 1913.

Pennypacker, Isaac R. *General Meade.* New York, 1901.

Perry, Martha Derby, comp. *Letters from a Surgeon of the Civil War.* Boston, 1906.

Peyton, George Q. *A Civil War Record for 1865–1865.* Edited by Robert A. Hodge. Fredericksburg, Va., 1981.

Pfanz, Donald C. *Richard S. Ewell: A Soldier's Life.* Chapel Hill, N.C., 1998.

Porter, Horace. *Campaigning with Grant.* New York, 1897.

Power, J. Tracy. *Lee's Miserables: Life in the Army of Northern Virginia from the Wilderness to Appomattox.* Chapel Hill, N.C., 1998.

Reagan, James W. "More About Fight at Brooks Crossroads." *Confederate Veteran,* 28 (1910), 228–30.

Reagan, John H. *Memoirs, With Special Reference to Secession and the Civil War.* Edited by Walter Flavius McCaleb. New York, 1906.

Redkey, Edwin S., ed. *A Grand Army of Black Men: Letters from African American Soldiers in the Union Army, 1861–1865.* New York, 1992.

Reed, Thomas Benton. *A Private in Gray.* Camden, Ark., 1905.

Rhea, Gordon C. "The Testing of a Corps Commander: Gouverneur Kemble Warren at the Wilderness and Spotsylvania." In *The Spotsylvania Campaign,* edited by Gary W. Gallagher, 61–79. Chapel Hill, N.C., 1998.

———. "Union Cavalry in the Wilderness: The Education of Philip H. Sheridan and James H. Wilson." In *The Wilderness Campaign,* edited by Gary W. Gallagher, 106–35. Chapel Hill, N.C., 1997.

Rhodes, Robert Hunt, ed. *All for the Union: The Civil War Diary and Letters of Elisha Hunt Rhodes.* New York, 1991.

Ritchie, David F. *Four Years in the First New York Light Artillery.* Edited by Norman L. Ritchie. New York, 1997.

Robertson, James I. Jr., ed. *The Civil War Letters of General Robert McAllister.* New Brunswick, N.J., 1965.

Robertson, Robert S. "From Spotsylvania Onward." In *War Papers Read Before the Indiana Commandery Military Order of the Loyal Legion of the United States,* 344–58. Indianapolis, 1898.

———. *Personal Recollections of the War.* Milwaukee, 1895.

Roche, Edward P. "Rescue of Union Wounded on North Anna is Recalled." In *National Tribune,* November 17, 1938.

Rodenbough, Theophilius F., comp. *From Everglades to Cañon with the Second Dragoons.* New York, 1875.

———. "Sheridan's Richmond Raid." In *B&L* 4, pp. 188–94.

Ropes, John C. "Grant's Campaign in Virginia in 1864." In *PMHSM* 4, pp. 363–405.

Rosenblatt, Emil, and Ruth Rosenblatt, eds. *Hard Marching Every Day: The Civil War Letters of Wilbur Fisk, 1861–1865.* Lawrence, Kans., 1992.

Runge, William H., ed. *Four Years in the Confederate Artillery: The Diary of Private Henry Robinson Berkeley.* Chapel Hill, N.C., 1961.

Sandburg, Carl. *Abraham Lincoln: The War Years.* 4 vols. New York, 1943.

Sanford, George B. *Fighting Rebels and Redskins: Experiences in Army Life of Colonel George B. Sanford, 1861–1892.* Edited by E. R. Hagemann. Norman, Okla., 1969.

Scott, Thomas. "The Action of Battery D, 5th United States Artillery, at Spotsylvania." *National Tribune,* December 27, 1894.

Seay, W. Marion. "Forty Men Fought Grant's Army." *Confederate Veteran,* 17 (1909), 319–20.

Seiser, Charles, ed. "August Seiser's Civil War Diary." *Rochester Historical Society Publication,* 22 (1944), 174–98.

Sheridan, Philip H. *Personal Memoirs of P. H. Sheridan.* 2 vols. New York, 1888.

Silliker, Ruth L., ed. *The Rebel Yell and the Yankee Hurrah: The Civil War Journal of a Maine Volunteer, Private John W. Haley, 17th Maine Regiment.* Camden, Me., 1985.

Simon, John Y., ed. *The Papers of Ulysses S. Grant.* 20 vols. Carbondale, Ill., 1967–1999.

Simonton, Edwin. "The Campaign up the James to Petersburg." In *Glimpses of the Nation's Struggle: A Series of Papers Read Before the Minnesota Commandery of the Military Order of the Loyal Legion of the United States,* 481–94. St. Paul, Minn., 1903.

Simpson, Brooks D. "Great Expectations: Ulysses S. Grant, the Northern Press, and the Opening of the Wilderness Campaign." In *The Wilderness Campaign,* edited by Gary W. Gallagher, 1–35. Chapel Hill, N.C., 1997.

Small, Harold A., ed. *The Road to Richmond: The Civil War Memoirs of Major Abner R. Small of the 16th Maine Vols.; With His Diary as a Prisoner of War.* Berkeley, Calif., 1957.

South Carolina Division, United Daughters of the Confederacy. *Recollections and Reminiscences.* 3 vols. N.p., 1990.

Sparks, David S., ed. *Inside Lincoln's Army: The Diary of Marsena Rudolph Patrick, Provost Marshal General, Army of the Potomac.* New York, 1964.

Spear, Ellis. *Civil War Recollections.* Edited by Abbott Spear. Orono, Me., 1997.

Staudenraus, P. J., ed. *Mr. Lincoln's Washington: Selections from the Writings of Noah Brooks, Civil War Correspondent.* South Brunswick, N.J., 1967.

Stephens, Robert Grier Jr. *Intrepid Warrior: Clement Anselm Evans.* Dayton, Ohio, 1992.

Stevens, George T. *Three Years in the Sixth Corps.* Albany, N.Y., 1866.

Stewart, A. M. *Camp, March, and Battlefield; or, Three Years and a Half with the Army of the Potomac.* Philadelphia, 1865.

Stewart, William H. *A Pair of Blankets: War-Time History in Letters to the Young People of the South.* New York, 1914.

Stiles, Robert. *Four Years Under Marse Robert.* New York, 1903.

Strong, George Templeton. *Diary of the Civil War, 1860–1865.* Edited by Allan Nevins. New York, 1962.

Talbot, T. O. "The Heavy Artillery." *National Tribune,* January 23, 1890.

Tapert, Annette, ed. *The Brothers' War: Civil War Letters to Their Loved Ones from the Blue and Gray.* New York, 1988.

Taylor, Emerson. *Gouverneur Kemble Warren: Life and Letters of an American Soldier.* New York, 1932.

Taylor, Walter H. *General Lee: His Campaigns in Virginia, 1861–1865, with Personal Reminiscences.* Norfolk, Va., 1906.

Tenny, Luman Harris. *War Diary, 1861–1865.* Cleveland, Ohio, 1914.

Thomas, Hampton S. *Some Personal Reminiscences of Service in the Cavalry of the Army of the Potomac.* Philadelphia, 1889.

Thorpe, James S. *Reminiscences of the Army Life During the Civil War.* N.p., n.d.

Tilney, Robert. *My Life in the Army: Three Years and a Half with the Fifth Army Corps, Army of the Potomac, 1862–1865.* Philadelphia, 1912.

Tower, R. Lockwood, ed. *Lee's Adjutant: The Wartime Letters of Colonel Walter Herron Taylor, 1862–1865.* Columbia, S.C., 1995.

Tripp, Lawrence E. "With Custer at Yellow Tavern and in the Raid Around Richmond." *National Tribune,* July 31, 1884.

Trudeau, Noah Andre. *Like Men of War: Black Troops in the Civil War, 1862–1865.* Boston, 1998.

"Two Cavalry Chieftains." In *SHSP* 16, p. 452.

Tyler, William S., ed. *Recollections of the Civil War by Mason Whiting Tyler.* New York, 1912.

Urban, John W. *Battle Field and Prison Pen.* Philadelphia, 1882.

Urwin, Gregory J. W. *Custer Victorious.* Rutherford, N.J., 1983.

Venable, Charles S. "The Campaign from the Wilderness to Petersburg." In *SHSP* 14, pp. 522–42.

———. "General Lee in the Wilderness Campaign." In *B&L* 4, pp. 240–6.

Viola, Herman J., ed. *The Memoirs of Charles Henry Veil.* New York, 1993.

Wait, Jane Wofford, et al. *History of the Wofford Family.* Spartanburg, S.C., 1928.

Walker, Charles D. *Biographical Sketches of the Graduates and Eleves of the Virginia Military Institute Who Fell during the War between the States.* Philadelphia, 1875.

Walker, Francis A. *General Hancock.* New York, 1895.

Warner, Ezra J. *Generals in Blue: Lives of the Union Commanders.* Baton Rouge, 1964.

———. *Generals in Gray: Lives of the Confederate Commanders.* Baton Rouge, 1964.

Waugh, John C. *Reelecting Lincoln: The Battle for the 1864 Presidency.* New York, 1997.

Weeks, Bob. *On the Road to Traveler's Rest: The Story of Zion United Methodist Church of Spotsylvania Courthouse, Virginia, during the Nineteenth Century.* N.p., n.d.

Weiser, George. *Nine Months in Rebel Prisons.* Philadelphia, 1890.

Welles, Gideon. *The Diary of Gideon Welles.* 2 vols. Boston, 1911.

Welsh, Jack D. *Medical Histories of Confederate Generals.* Kent, Ohio, 1995.

White, Russell C., ed. *The Civil War Diary of Wyman S. White, First Sergeant of Company F, 2nd United States Sharpshooter Regiment, 1861–1865.* Baltimore, 1991.

White, William S. "A Diary of the War, or What I Saw of It." In *Contributions to a History of the Richmond Howitzer Battalion* 2, pp. 89–286.

Wiggins, Sarah Woolfolk, ed. *The Journals of Josiah Gorgas, 1857–1878.* Tuscaloosa, n.d.

Wilkeson, Frank. *Recollections of a Private Soldier in the Army of the Potomac.* New York, 1887.

Wilson, James H. *Under the Old Flag.* 2 vols. New York, 1912.

Wilson, Paul E., and Harriett S. Wilson, eds. *The Civil War Diary of Thomas White Stephens, Sergeant, Company K, 20th Indiana Regiment of Volunteers.* Lawrence, Kans., 1985.

"H. W. Wingfield Diary." *Bulletin of the Virginia State Library,* 16 (July 1927), 27–48.

Wingfield, Marshall. *A History of Caroline County Virginia from Its Formation in 1727 to 1924*. Richmond, 1924.

Wirtz, Paul, ed. *John Parker Brest, Company E, 100th Pennsylvania Volunteer Regiment, Journal 1861–1865*. Baltimore, 1991.

Worsham, John H. *One of Jackson's Foot Cavalry*. Jackson, Tenn., 1964.

Younger, Edward, ed. *Inside the Confederate Government: The Diary of Robert Garlick Hill Kean*. New York, 1957.

Unit Histories

Adams, John G. B. *Reminiscences of the Nineteenth Massachusetts Regiment*. Boston, 1899.

Albert, Allen D. *History of the Forty-Fifth Regiment Pennsylvania Veteran Volunteer Infantry, 1861–1865*. Williamsport, Pa., 1912.

Aldrich, Thomas M. *The History of Battery A, First Regiment Rhode Island Light Artillery in the War to Preserve the Union, 1861–1865*. Providence, R.I., 1904.

Anderson, John. *The Fifty-Seventh Regiment of Massachusetts Volunteers in the War of the Rebellion*. Boston, 1896.

Baker, Levi W. *History of the Ninth Massachusetts Battery*. South Framingham, Mass., 1888.

Banes, Charles H. *History of the Philadelphia Brigade*. Philadelphia, 1876.

Beale, R. L. T. *History of the Ninth Virginia Cavalry in the War Between the States*. Richmond, 1899.

Beaudry, Louis N. *Historic Records of the Fifth New York Cavalry, First Ira Harris Guard*. Albany, N.Y., 1874.

Benedict, George G. *Vermont in the Civil War: A History of the Part Taken by the Vermont Soldiers and Sailors in the War for the Union, 1861–5*. 2 vols. Burlington, Vt., 1888.

Bennett, Brian A. *Sons of Old Monroe: A Regimental History of Patrick O'Rorke's 140th New York Volunteer Infantry*. Dayton, Ohio, 1992.

Bennett, Risden T. "Fourteenth Regiment." In *Histories of the Several Regiments and Battalions from North Carolina in the Great War*, edited by Walter Clark, vol. 1, pp. 705–32. Goldsboro, N.C., 1901.

Best, Isaac O. *History of the 121st New York State Infantry*. Chicago, 1921.

Bicknell, George W. *History of the Fifth Regiment Maine Volunteers*. Portland, Me., 1871.

Bidwell, Frederick D., comp. *History of the Forty-Ninth New York Volunteers*. Albany, N.Y., 1916.

Billings, John D. *The History of the Tenth Massachusetts Battery of Light Artillery in the War of the Rebellion*. Boston, 1881.

Blackford, Charles M. Jr. *Annals of the Lynchburg Home Guard*. Lynchburg, Va., 1891.

Bowen, James L. *History of the Thirty-Seventh Regiment Massachusetts Volunteers in the Civil War of 1861–1865.* Holyoke, Mass., 1884.

Bowen, James R. *Regimental History of the First New York Dragoons During Three Years of Active Service in the Great Civil War.* Lyons, Mich., 1900.

Brainard, Mary G. *Campaigns of the One Hundred and Forty-Sixth Regiment New York State Volunteers.* New York, 1915.

Brainerd, Wesley. *Bridge Building in Wartime.* Edited by Ed Malles. Knoxville, Tenn., 1997.

Brewer, A. T. *History of the Sixty-First Regiment Pennsylvania Volunteers, 1861–1865.* Pittsburgh, 1911.

Brown, Henri LeFevre. *History of the Third Regiment, Excelsior Brigade, 72nd New York Volunteer Infantry, 1861–1865.* Jamestown, N.Y., 1902.

Brown, J. Willard. *The Signal Corps, U.S.A., in the War of the Rebellion.* Boston, 1896.

Bruce, George A. *The Twentieth Regiment of Massachusetts Volunteer Infantry, 1861–1865.* Boston, 1906.

Caldwell, J. F. J. *The History of a Brigade of South Carolinians, First Known as Gregg's, and Subsequently as McGowan's Brigade.* Philadelphia, 1866.

Camper, Charles, and J. W. Kirkley. *Historical Record of the First Regiment Maryland Infantry.* Washington, D.C., 1871.

Chamberlin, Thomas. *History of the One Hundred and Fiftieth Regiment Pennsylvania Volunteers, Second Regiment, Bucktail Brigade.* Philadelphia, 1905.

Cheek, Philip, and Mair Pointon. *History of the Sauk County Riflemen, Known as Company A, Sixth Wisconsin Veteran Volunteer Infantry, 1861–1865.* Madison, Wisc., 1909.

Clark, Walter, ed. *Histories of the Several Regiments and Battalions from North Carolina in the Great War, 1861–65.* 5 vols. Goldsboro, N.C., 1901.

Coker, James L. *History of Company G, Ninth S. C. Regiment, Infantry, S. C. Army and of Company E, Sixth South Carolina Regiment, Infantry, S. C. Army.* Charleston, S.C., 1899.

Coles, Robert T. *From Huntsville to Appomattox.* Edited by Jeffrey D. Stocker. Knoxville, Tenn., 1996.

Committee of the Regiment. *History of the Thirty-Fifth Regiment Massachusetts Volunteers.* Boston, 1884.

Committee of the Regiment. *History of the Thirty-Sixth Regiment Massachusetts Volunteers.* Boston, 1884.

Contributions to a History of the Richmond Howitzer Battalion. 3 vols. Richmond, 1883–1886.

Conyngham, D. P. *The Irish Brigade and Its Campaigns,* New York, 1867.

Cook, Benjamin F. *History of the Twelfth Massachusetts Volunteers (Webster Regiment).* Boston, 1882.Cowles, Luther E. *History of the Fifth Massachusetts Battery.* Boston, 1902.

Cowtan, Charles W. *Services of the Tenth New York Volunteers (National Zouaves) in the War of the Rebellion.* New York, 1882.

Craft, David. *History of the One Hundred Forty-First Regiment Pennsylvania Volunteers, 1862–1865.* Towanda, Pa., 1885.

Curtis, O. B. *History of the Twenty-Fourth Michigan of the Iron Brigade.* Detroit, Mich., 1891.

Cutcheon, Byron M., comp. *The Story of the Twentieth Michigan Infantry.* Lansing, Mich., 1904.

Dawes, Rufus R. *Service with the Sixth Wisconsin Volunteers.* Marietta, Ohio, 1890.

Dickert, D. Augustus. *History of Kershaw's Brigade.* Newberry, S.C., 1899.

Driver, Robert J. *52nd Virginia Infantry.* Lynchburg, Va., 1986.

Dunlop, William S. *Lee's Sharpshooters; or, The Forefront of Battle: A Story of Southern Valor That Has Never Been Told.* Little Rock, Ark., 1899.

Dunn, Wilbur R. *Full Measure of Devotion: The Eighth New York Volunteer Heavy Artillery.* 2 vols. Kearney, Nebr., 1997.

Figg, Royall W. *Where Men Only Dare Go: or, The Story of a Boy Company.* Richmond, 1885.

Floyd, Frederick C. *History of the Fortieth (Mozart) Regiment, New York Volunteers.* Boston, 1909.

Folsom, James M. *Heroes and Martyrs of Georgia: Georgia's Record in the Revolution of 1861.* Macon, Ga., 1864.

Fortin, Maurice S., ed. "Colonel Hilary A. Herbert's 'History of the Eighth Alabama Volunteer Regiment.'" *Alabama Historical Quarterly,* 39 (1977), 5–160.

Gavin, William G. *Campaigning with the Roundheads: The History of the Hundredth Pennsylvania Veteran Volunteer Infantry Regiment in the American Civil War, 1861–1865.* Dayton, Ohio, 1989.

Goldsborough, William W. *The Maryland Line in the Confederate States Army.* Baltimore, 1900.

Gracey, Samuel L. *Annals of the Sixth Pennsylvania Cavalry.* Philadelphia, 1868.

Graves, Joseph A. *The History of the Bedford Light Artillery.* Bedford, Va., 1903.

Hackley, Woodford B. *The Little Fork Rangers: A Sketch of Company D, Fourth Virginia Cavalry.* Richmond, 1927.

Hagerty, Edward J. *Collis' Zouaves: The 114th Pennsylvania Volunteers in the Civil War.* Baton Rouge, 1997.

Haines, Alanson A. *History of the Fifteenth Regiment New Jersey Volunteers.* New York, 1883.

Haines, William P. *History of the Men of Company F, with Description of the Marches and Battles of the 12th New Jersey Volunteers.* Mickleton, N.J., 1897.

Hall, Isaac. *History of the Ninety-Seventh Regiment New York Volunteers (Conkling Rifles) in the War for the Union.* Utica, N.Y., 1890.

Harris, James S. *Historical Sketches of the Seventh Regiment North Carolina Troops.* Mooresville, N.C., 1893.

Haynes, Edwin M. *A History of the Tenth Regiment, Vermont Volunteers, with Biographical Sketches of the Officers Who Fell in Battle.* Lewiston, Me., 1870.

Hays, Gilbert Adams, comp. *Under the Red Patch: Story of the Sixty Third Regiment Pennsylvania Volunteers, 1861–1864.* Pittsburgh, Pa., 1908.

Herbert, Arthur. *Sketches and Incidents of Movements of the Seventeenth Virginia Infantry.* Alexandria, Va., N.d.

Herek, Raymond J. *These Men Have Seen Hard Service: The First Michigan Sharpshooters in the Civil War.* Detroit, Mich., 1998.

Hopkins, William P. *The Seventh Regiment Rhode Island Volunteers in the Civil War.* Providence, R.I., 1903.

Houghton, Edwin B. *The Campaigns of the Seventeenth Maine.* Portland, Me., 1866.

House, Charles J. *The First Maine Heavy Artillery.* Portland, Me., 1903.

Houston, Henry C. *The Thirty-Second Maine Regiment of Infantry Volunteers.* Portland, Me., 1903.

Howell, Helena A., comp. *Chronicles of the One Hundred Fifty-First Regiment New York State Volunteer Infantry.* Albion, N.Y., 1911.

Hutchinson, Nelson V. *History of the Seventh Massachusetts Volunteer Infantry in the War of the Rebellion.* Taunton, Mass., 1890.

Jackman, Lyman, and Amos Hadley, eds. *History of the Sixth New Hampshire Regiment in the War for the Union.* Concord, N.H., 1891.

Jackson, Harry L. *First Regiment Engineer Troops P.A.C.S.: Robert E. Lee's Combat Engineers.* Louisa, Va., 1998.

Jaques, John W. *Three Years' Campaign of the Ninth N.Y.S.M. During the Southern Rebellion.* New York, 1865.

Judson, Amos M. *History of the Eighty-Third Regiment Pennsylvania Volunteers.* Erie, Pa., 1865.

Keating, Robert. *Carnival of Blood: The Civil War Ordeal of the Seventh New York Heavy Artillery.* Baltimore, 1998.

Kenan, Thomas S., comp. *Sketch of the Forty-Third Regiment North Carolina Troops.* Raleigh, 1895.

Kirk, Hyland C. *Heavy Guns and Light: A History of the 4th New York Heavy Artillery.* New York, 1890.

Krick, Robert K. *Parker's Virginia Battery C.S.A.* Berryville, Va., 1975.

Lane, James H. "Battle of Jericho Ford—Report of General Lane." In *SHSP* 9, pp. 241–45.

Laughton, John E. Jr. "The Sharpshooters of Mahone's Brigade." In *SHSP* 22, pp. 98–105.

Lloyd, William P. *History of the First Regiment Pennsylvania Reserve Cavalry.* Philadelphia, 1864.

Locke, William H. *The Story of the Regiment.* Philadelphia, 1868.

Loehr, Charles T. *War History of the Old First Virginia Infantry Regiment, Army of Northern Virginia.* Richmond, 1884.

Longacre, Edward G. *To Gettysburg and Beyond: The Twelfth New Jersey Volunteer Infantry, II Corps, Army of the Potomac, 1862–1865.* Heightstown, N.J., 1988.

Lord, Edward O. *History of the Ninth Regiment New Hampshire Volunteers in the War of the Rebellion.* Concord, N.H., 1895.

McDonald, William N. *A History of the Laurel Brigade, Originally the Ashby Cavalry of the Army of Northern Virginia and Chew's Battery.* Baltimore, 1907.

McLaurin, William H. "Eighteenth Regiment." In *Histories of the Several Regiments and Battalions from North Carolina in the Great War,* edited by Walter Clark, vol. 2, pp. 15–64. Goldsboro, N.C., 1901.

McNamara, Daniel G. *The History of the Ninth Regiment Massachusetts Volunteer Infantry, Second Brigade, First Division, Fifth Army Corps, Army of the Potomac, June 1861–June 1864.* Boston, 1899.

Marbaker, Thomas D. *History of the Eleventh New Jersey Volunteers.* Trenton, N.J., 1898.

Mark, Penrose G. *Red, White, and Blue Badge: Pennsylvania Veteran Volunteers, A History of the 93rd Regiment, Known as the "Lebanon Infantry" and "One of the 300 Fighting Regiments" from September 12th, 1861 to June 27th, 1865.* Harrisburg, Pa., 1911.

Marshall, D. P. *Company K, 155th Pa. Volunteer Zouaves.* N.p., 1888.

Matthews, Richard E. *The 149th Pennsylvania Volunteer Infantry Unit in the Civil War.* Jefferson, N.C., 1994.

Means, Paul B. "Additional Sketch, Sixty-Third Regiment." In *Histories of the Several Battalions and Regiments from North Carolina,* edited by Walter Clark, vol. 3, pp. 545–657. Goldsboro, N.C., 1901.

Merrill, Samuel H. *The Campaigns of the 1st Maine and 1st District of Columbia Cavalry.* Portland, Me., 1866.

Mills, George H. *History of the 16th North Carolina Regiment (Originally 6th N.C. Regiment) in the Civil War.* Rutherfordton, N.C., 1901.

———. "Supplemental Sketch Sixteenth Regiment." In *Histories of the Several Regiments and Battalions from North Carolina in the Great War,* edited by Walter Clark, vol. 4, pp. 137–219. Goldsboro, N.C., 1901.

Moore, J. H. "Archer's Tennesseans at Spotsylvania, May 11 and 12, 1864: A Second Angle of Death." In *Camp-Fire Sketches and Battle-Field Echoes,* compiled by William C. King and W. P. Derby, 311–13. Springfield, Mass., 1888.

Morgan, William H., comp. *A Narrative of the Service of Company D, First Massachusetts Heavy Artillery, in the War of the Rebellion, 1861–1865.* Boston, 1907.

Muffly, J. W., ed. *The Story of Our Regiment: A History of the 148th Pennsylvania Volunteers.* Des Moines, Iowa, 1904.

Mulholland, St. Claire A. *The Story of the 116th Regiment Pennsylvania Volunteers in the War of the Rebellion: The Record of a Gallant Command.* Philadelphia, 1899.

Myers, Frank M. *The Comanches: A History of White's Battalion, Virginia Cavalry, Laurel Brigade, Hampton Division, A.N.V., C.S.A.* Baltimore, 1871.

Nash, Eugene A. *A History of the Forty-Fourth Regiment New York Volunteer Infantry in the Civil War, 1861–1865.* Chicago, 1911.

Nesbitt, John W. *History of Company D, 149th Pennsylvania Volunteer Infantry.* Oakdale, Calif., 1908.

Newell, Joseph K. *Ours: Annals of 10th Regiment, Massachusetts Volunteers in the Rebellion.* Springfield, Mass., 1875.

One Hundred and Fifty-fifth Pennsylvania Association. *Under the Maltese Cross: Antietam to Appomattox, the Loyal Uprising in Western Pennsylvania, 1861–1865, Campaigns 155th Pennsylvania Regiment.* Pittsburgh, Pa., 1910.

Osborn, Thomas W. "Battery D—Winslow's First New York Light Artillery." In *Final Report of the Battle of Gettysburg,* by the New York Monuments Commission, vol. 3, pp. 1210–13. New York, 1902.

Owen, Charles W. *The First Michigan Infantry: Three Months and Three Years.* N.p., 1903.

Parker, Francis J. *The Story of the Thirty-Second Regiment Massachusetts Infantry.* Boston, 1880.

Parker, John L. *History of the Twenty-Second Massachusetts Infantry, the Second Company Sharpshooters, and the Third Light Battery, in the War of the Rebellion.* Boston, 1887.

Parker, Thomas H. *History of the 51st Regiment of Pennsylvania Volunteers and Veteran Volunteers.* Philadelphia, 1869.

Parsons, Joseph B. *The 10th Regiment: Salient Points in Its History.* N.p., n.d.

Powell, William H. *History of the Fifth Army Corps.* New York, 1896.

Preston, Noble D. *History of the Tenth Regiment of Cavalry, New York State Volunteers.* New York, 1892.

Prowell, George R. *History of the Eighty-Seventh Regiment, Pennsylvania Volunteers.* York, Pa., 1901.

Pullen, John J. *The Twentieth Maine: A Volunteer Regiment in the Civil War.* Philadelphia, 1957.

Pyne, Henry R. *Ride to War: The History of the First New Jersey Cavalry.* New Brunswick, N.J., 1961.

Rawle, William B. *History of the Third Pennsylvania Cavalry, Sixtieth Regiment Pennsylvania Volunteers, in the American Civil War.* Philadelphia, 1905.

Rhodes, John H. *The History of Battery B, First Regiment Rhode Island Light Artillery in the War to Preserve the Union.* Providence, R.I., 1894.

Ripley, William Y. W. *Vermont Riflemen in the War for the Union, 1861–1865: A History of Company F, First United States Sharpshooters.* Rutland, Vt., 1883.

Roback, Henry. *The Veteran Volunteers of Herkimer and Otsego Counties in the War of the Rebellion, Being a History of the 152nd New York.* Little Falls, N.Y., 1888.

Roe, Alfred S. *The Thirty-Ninth Regiment Massachusetts Volunteers, 1862–1865.* Worcester, Mass., 1914.

Roe, Alfred S., and Charles Nutt. *History of the First Regiment of Heavy Artillery Massachusetts Volunteers.* Worcester, Mass., 1917.

Scott, Kate M. "The Action of Battery D." *National Tribune,* December 27, 1894.

———. *History of the One Hundred and Fifth Regiment of Pennsylvania Volunteers.* Philadelphia, 1877.

———. "The Action of Battery D." *National Tribune,* December 27, 1894.

Shaver, Lewellyn A. *History of the Sixtieth Alabama Regiment, Gracie's Alabama Brigade.* Montgomery, 1867.

Simons, Ezra D. *A Regimental History of the One Hundred and Twenty-Fifth New York State Volunteers.* New York, 1888.

Sloan, John A. *Reminiscences of the Guilford Grays, Co. B, 27th N.C. Regiment.* Washington, D.C., 1883.

Smith, J. L. *History of the Corn Exchange Regiment: 118th Pennsylvania Volunteers, from Their First Engagement at Antietam to Appomattox.* Philadelphia, 1888.

Smith, John D. *The History of the Nineteenth Regiment of Maine Volunteer Infantry, 1862–1865.* Minneapolis, Minn., 1909.

Stevens, C. A. *Berdan's United States Sharpshooters in the Army of the Potomac, 1861–1865.* St. Paul, Minn., 1892.

Stewart, Robert L. *History of the One Hundred and Fortieth Regiment Pennsylvania Volunteers.* Philadelphia, 1912.

Sypher, J. R. *History of the Pennsylvania Reserve Corps.* Lancaster, Pa., 1865.

Terrill, John N. *Campaign of the Fourteenth Regiment New Jersey Volunteers.* New Brunswick, N.J., 1866.

Thompson, Gilbert. *The Engineer Battalion in the Civil War.* Washington, D.C., 1910.

Thomson, O. R. Howard, and William H. Rauch. *History of the Bucktails: Kane Rifle Regiment of the Pennsylvania Reserve Corps.* Philadelphia, 1906.

Tobie, Edward P. *History of the First Maine Cavalry.* Boston, 1887.

Toon, Thomas F. "Twentieth Regiment." In *Histories of the Several Regiments and Battalions from North Carolina in the Great War,* edited by Walter Clark, vol. 2, pp. 111–27. Goldsboro, N.C., 1901.

Townshend, David G. *The Seventh Michigan Volunteer Infantry.* Fort Lauderdale, 1993.

Vautier, John D. *History of the 88th Pennsylvania Volunteers in the War for the Union, 1861–1865.* Philadelphia, 1894.

Waitt, Ernest L. *History of the Nineteenth Regiment Massachusetts Volunteer Infantry.* Salem, Mass., 1906.

Walcott, Charles F. *History of the Twenty-First Massachusetts Volunteers in the War for the Preservation of the Union.* Boston, 1882.

Walker, Francis A. *History of the Second Army Corps in the Army of the Potomac.* New York, 1887.

Ward, Joseph R. C. *History of the One Hundred and Sixth Regiment Pennsylvania Volunteers.* Philadelphia, 1883.

Warren, Horatio N. *Two Reunions of the 142d Regiment, Pa. Vols.* Buffalo, N.Y., 1890.

Watson, Cyrus B. "Forty-Fifth Regiment." In *Histories of the Several Regiments and Battalions from North Carolina in the Great War,* edited by Walter Clark, vol. 3, pp. 35–61. Goldsboro, N.C., 1901.

West, Michael. *30th Battalion Virginia Sharpshooters.* Lynchburg, Va., 1995.

Westbrook, Robert S. *History of the 49th Pennsylvania Volunteers.* Altoona, Pa., 1898.

Weygant, Charles H. *History of the One Hundred and Twenty-Fourth Regiment New York State Volunteers.* Newburgh, N.Y., 1877.

Wilkinson, Warren. *Mother, May You Never See the Sights I Have Seen: The Fifty-Seventh Massachusetts Veteran Volunteers in the Last Year of the Civil War.* New York, 1990.

Williams, R. S. "Thirteenth Regiment." In *Histories of the Several Regiments and Battalions from North Carolina in the Great War,* edited by Walter Clark, vol. 1, pp. 653–87. Goldsboro, N.C., 1901.

Wise, George. *History of the Seventeenth Virginia Infantry.* Baltimore, 1870.

Wise, Jennings C. *The Long Arm of Lee; or, The History of the Artillery of the Army of Northern Virginia.* 2 vols. Lynchburg, Va., 1915.

Wyckoff, Mac. *A History of the 2nd South Carolina Infantry: 1861–65.* Fredericksburg, Va., 1994

Campaign Studies

Atkinson, C.F. *Grant's Campaigns of 1864 and 1865: The Wilderness and Cold Harbor.* London, 1908.

Dowdy, Clifford. *Lee's Last Campaign: The Story of Lee and His Men Against Grant, 1864.* New York, 1960

Frassanito, William. *Grant and Lee: The Virginia Campaigns.* New York, 1983.

Hotchkiss, Jedediah. *Confederate Military History.* Vol. 3, *Virginia.* Atlanta, 1899.

Humphreys, Andrew A. *The Virginia Campaign of '64 and '65.* New York, 1883.

Matter, William D. *If It Takes All Summer: The Battle of Spotsylvania.* Chapel Hill, N.C., 1988.

Miller, J. Michael. *The North Anna Campaign: "Even to Hell Itself," May 21–26, 1864.* Lynchburg, Va., 1989.

Rhea, Gordon C. *The Battle of the Wilderness: May 5–6, 1864.* Baton Rouge, 1994.

———. *The Battles for Spotsylvania Court House and the Road to Yellow Tavern: May 7–12, 1864.* Baton Rouge, 1997.

Schaff, Morris. *The Battle of the Wilderness.* Boston, 1910.

Shreve, William P. "The Operations of the Army of the Potomac May 13–June 2, 1864." In *PMHSM* 4, pp. 289–318.

Swinton, William. *Campaigns of the Army of the Potomac.* New York, 1866.

Trudeau, Noah Andre. *Bloody Roads South: The Wilderness to Cold Harbor, May–June 1864.* Boston, 1989.

Thesis

Ott, Eugene M. Jr. "The Civil War Diary of James J. Kirkpatrick, Sixteenth Mississippi Infantry, C.S.A." Master's thesis, Texas A&M University, 1984.

Index

May 23 success of, 316–7; May 23 night position of, 319, 320; and Lee's May 24 plans, 323; May 24 position, movements and fighting of, 326, 327, 329–35, 342–4, 346–52; crossing of North Anna by, 331–3; May 25 plans for and movements of, 335, 352, 355, 358; May 26 plan for, and withdrawal from North Anna, 362, 367; order of battle of, 378–9. *See also* Barlow, Brig. Gen. Francis C.; Birney, Maj. Gen. David B.; Gibbon, Brig. Gen. John; Hancock, Maj. Gen. Winfield S.; Tyler, Brig. Gen. Robert O.

Union 5th Corps: leadership of, 15, 253, 370; May 5 position of, 22, 26–7; May 13–14 plans for, and movements of, 33, 67–75, 80; headquarters of, at Beverly house, 75, 77, 199; at Myer's Hill, 78–80, 89–90; May 14 position of, 84, 88, 91, 92, 93; May 15–16 plans for and position of, 97–8, 113, 120, 121; casualties of, 118, 188; May 17–18 plans for and position of, 128, 129, 130, 133, 138; in May 18 attack, 139; May 18–19 plans for and position of, 157–60, 164–7, 169, 184; New York Heavy Artillerymen assigned to, 165; at Spotsylvania Court House battle, 165; and Harris Farm battle, 181–5, 188; May 20–21 plans for and movements of, 191–3, 212; May 21 plans for and movements of, 217, 219–23, 227–8, 230–5, 240–2, 247–8, 251, 253, 370; May 22 plans for and movements of, 248, 252, 256–8, 261, 262, 268–9, 271–4; May 21–22 night position of, 255–6; May 23 plans for and daytime movements of, 279–84, 289–94; May 23 crossing of North Anna by, 290–4, 303–4, 372; at Jericho Mills battle, 306–17, 321, 330, 370, 437n88; May 23 night position of, 319, 320, 322; and Lee's May 24 plans, 323; May 24 position and movements of, 326–9, 334, 335, 344, 350, 352; May 25 plans for, and movements and skirmishes by, 335, 352, 355–60; May 26 plan for, and withdrawal from North Anna, 361–2, 367; order of battle of, 380–1. *See also* Crawford, Brig. Gen. Samuel W.; Cutler,

Brig. Gen. Lysander; Griffin, Brig. Gen. Charles; Warren, Maj. Gen. Gouverneur K.

Union 6th Corps: leadership of, 15, 253, 370; May 13 position of, 27–9, 397n42; May 13–14 plan for, 33, 67–9; at Bloody Angle, 67; May 13–14 night and morning movements of, 69–71, 74–5, 80; May 14 position of, 84, 86, 88, 91–3; at Myer's Hill, 89–90; May 15–16 position of, 97–8, 113–4, 120, 121, 125; casualties of, 118, 203; May 17–18 plans for and position of, 127, 128, 130, 133, 135–6; in May 18 attack, 142–52; May 18–19 plans for and position of, 157–60, 164, 167, 169; May 20 plans for and movements of, 191–3; May 21 position and movements of, 217, 220, 221, 228, 229, 240–2, 244–7, 251, 253, 370; confusion due to improper use of rapid-firing arms, 256; May 21–22 night movements of, 256; May 22 plans for and movements of, 261–2, 268–70, 274; May 23 plans for and daytime movements of, 279–81, 284; May 23 night position of, 319, 320; and Lee's May 24 plans, 323; May 24 position and movements of, 326, 327, 329, 335, 344, 350, 352; May 25 plans for and movements of, 335, 355, 359–60; May 26 plan for, and withdrawal from North Anna, 361–2, 367. *See also* Neill, Brig. Gen. Thomas H.; Ricketts, Brig. Gen. James B.; Russell, Brig. Gen. David A.; Wright, Brig. Gen. Horatio G.

Union 9th Corps: Grant's plans for, 12; leadership of, 15, 67, 253, 370; May 13 position of, 22, 26, 29, 72, 397n42; May 13–14 plan for, 33, 67; on Fredericksburg Road, 66; May 14 position of, 72, 77, 82, 84, 91; May 15–16 plans for and position of, 97–9, 105–7, 120–2; casualties of, 118, 154; May 17–18 plans for and position of, 127, 129, 130, 133, 136, 138–9; in May 18 attack, 139–42, 149–51; May 18–19 plans for and position of, 157–60, 165; May 20 plans for and position of, 191–3; May 21 plans for and position of, 219–21, 228, 229, 240–2, 244–8, 251, 253, 370; May 22 plans for and movements of, 261, 262,